Lecture Notes in Computer S

Commenced Publication in 1973
Founding and Former Series Editors:
Gerhard Goos, Juris Hartmanis, and Jan van Leeuwen

Andrea Fusiello   Vittorio Murino
Rita Cucchiara (Eds.)

Computer Vision – ECCV 2012

Workshops and Demonstrations

Florence, Italy, October 7-13, 2012
Proceedings, Part II

 Springer

Volume Editors

Andrea Fusiello
Università degli Studi di Udine
Dipartimento di Ingegneria Elettrica,
Gestionale e Meccanica (DIEGM)
Via delle Scienze, 208, 33100 Udine, Italy
E-mail: andrea.fusiello@uniud.it

Vittorio Murino
IIT Istituto Italiano di Tecnologia
Via Morego 30, 16163 Genoa, Italy
E-mail: vittorio.murino@iit.it

Rita Cucchiara
Università degli Studi di Modena e Reggio Emilia
Strada Vignolege, 905, 41125 Modena, Italy
E-mail: rita.cucchiara@unimore.it

ISSN 0302-9743   e-ISSN 1611-3349
ISBN 978-3-642-33867-0   e-ISBN 978-3-642-33868-7
DOI 10.1007/978-3-642-33868-7
Springer Heidelberg Dordrecht London New York

Library of Congress Control Number: 2012948004

CR Subject Classification (1998): I.4, I.5, I.2.10, I.2, H.5, H.3

LNCS Sublibrary: SL 6 – Image Processing, Computer Vision, Pattern Recognition,
and Graphics

Typesetting: Camera-ready by author, data conversion by Scientific Publishing Services, Chennai, India

Printed on acid-free paper

Springer is part of Springer Science+Business Media (www.springer.com)

Foreword

The European Conference on Computer Vision is one of the top conferences for researchers in this field and is held biennially in alternation with the International Conference on Computer Vision. It was first held in 1990 in Antibes (France) with subsequent conferences in Santa Margherita Ligure (Italy) in 1992, Stockholm (Sweden) in 1994, Cambridge (UK) in 1996, Freiburg (Germany) in 1998, Dublin (Ireland) in 2000, Copenhagen (Denmark) in 2002, Prague (Czech Republic) in 2004, Graz (Austria) in 2006, Marseille (France) in 2008, and Heraklion (Greece) in 2010. To our great delight, the 12th conference was held in Florence, Italy.

ECCV has an established tradition of very high scientific quality and an overall duration of one week. ECCV 2012 began with a keynote lecture from the honorary chair, Tomaso Poggio. The main conference followed over four days with 40 orals, 368 posters, 22 demos, and 12 industrial exhibits. There were also 9 tutorials and 21 workshops held before and after the main event. For this event we introduced some novelties. These included innovations in the review policy, the publication of a conference booklet with all paper abstracts and the full video recording of oral presentations.

This conference is the result of a great deal of hard work by many people, who have been working enthusiastically since our first meetings in 2008. We are particularly grateful to the Program Chairs, who handled the review of about 1500 submissions and co-ordinated the efforts of over 50 area chairs and about 1000 reviewers (see details of the process in their preface to the proceedings). We are also indebted to all the other chairs who, with the support of our research teams (names listed below), diligently helped us manage all aspects of the main conference, tutorials, workshops, exhibits, demos, proceedings, and web presence. Finally we thank our generous sponsors and Consulta Umbria for handling the registration of delegates and all financial aspects associated with the conference.

We hope you enjoyed ECCV 2012. Benvenuti a Firenze!

October 2012

Roberto Cipolla
Carlo Colombo
Alberto Del Bimbo

Preface

Welcome to the Workshops and Demonstrations proceedings of the 12th European Conference on Computer Vision, held during October 7–13, 2012 in Florence, Italy. We are delighted that the main ECCV 2012 was accompanied by 21 workshops and 22 demonstrations.

We received 38 workshop proposals on diverse computer vision topics. The evaluation process was not easy because of the high quality of the submissions, and the final 21 selected workshops complemented the main conference program. They were mostly one-day workshops, with a few limited to half day, and one workshop lasting one day and a half. In the end, the addressed workshop topics constituted a good mix between novel current trends and traditional issues, without forgetting to address the fundamentals of the computational vision area.

On Sunday, October 7, three workshops took place: the 5th Workshop on Non-Rigid Shape Analysis and Deformable Image Alignment (NORDIA), the First Workshop on Visual Analysis and Geo-Localization of Large-Scale Imagery, and the Workshop on Web-scale Vision and Social Media.

The majority of the workshops were held on Friday 12 and Saturday 13. On October 12 we had nine workshops: WebVision, the Workshop on Computer Vision for the Web, with only invited speakers, the traditional PASCAL Visual Object Classes Challenge 2012 (VOC2012) Workshop, the 4th International Workshop on Video Event Categorization, Tagging and Retrieval (VECTaR 2012), the First International Workshop on Re-Identification (Re-Id 2012), the Workshop on Biological and Computer Vision Interfaces, also with only invited speakers, VISART, "Where Computer Vision Meets Art" Workshop, the Second Workshop on Consumer Depth Cameras for Computer Vision (CDC4CV), the Workshop on Unsolved Problems in Optical Flow and Stereo Estimation, and the "What's in a Face?" Workshop.

On October 13, ten workshops were held: The remaining half day of the Web-Vision Workshop, the 4th Color and Photometry in Computer Vision Workshop, the Third Workshop on Computer Vision in Vehicle Technology: From Earth to Mars, the Second Workshop on Parts and Attributes, the Third IEEE International Workshop on Analysis and Retrieval of Tracked Events and Motion in Imagery Streams (ARTEMIS 2012), the First Workshop on Action Recognition and Pose Estimation in Still Images, the Workshop on Higher-Order Models and Global Constraints in Computer Vision, the Workshop on Information Fusion in Computer Vision for Concept Recognition, the QU3ST Workshop "2.5D Sensing Technologies in Motion: The Quest for 3D", and the Second International Workshop on Benchmarking Facial Image Analysis Technologies (BeFIT 2012).

We hope that participants enjoyed the workshops, together with the associated 179 papers included in these volumes.

Following the tradition of the major conferences in the field, ECCV 2012 was also proud to host live demonstrations given by companies and academic research groups. These were presented during the days of the main conference and are described in detail in the papers of the last volume.

Presenting a demo is one of the most concrete and exciting ways of demon-strating results of research and providing strong interaction between researchers, practitioners, and scholars in many topics, both theoretical and practical, of com-puter vision.

Among the proposed demos, submitted with a four-page summary together with slides, videos and rich supplementary material, after peer-review, we selected 22 demos on different subjects spanning topics such as biometry, content-based retrieval, classification and categorization, vision for computer graphics, 3D vision for interfaces, tracking and pose estimation, gesture analysis for human–computer interaction, text recognition, augmented reality, surveillance, and assisted driving.

Demos were presented by authors coming from different nations of Europe (Czech Republic, France, Germany, Italy, The Netherlands, Spain, Switzerland, and UK) and of the rest of the world (Australia, China, Japan, Taiwan, and USA).

The best demo was selected based on the scientific value and the technical presentation as well as the success in researcher interaction during the Demo Sessions.

We believe the scientific prototypes and the technical demonstrations presented at ECCV 2012 will contribute to strengthen the great success of computer vision technologies in industrial, entertainment, social, and everyday applications.

Finally, we would like to thank the individual chairs of each workshop (listed in the respective workshop programs) for soliciting and reviewing submissions, and the demo proposers, who made it possible to build such a rich supplementary program beside the main ECCV 2012 scientific plan.

October 2012

Andrea Fusiello
Vittorio Murino
Rita Cucchiara

Organization

General Chairs

Roberto Cipolla   University of Cambridge, UK
Carlo Colombo   University of Florence, Italy
Alberto Del Bimbo   University of Florence, Italy

Program Coordinator

Pietro Perona   California Institute of Technology, USA

Program Chairs

Andrew Fitzgibbon   Microsoft Research, Cambridge, UK
Svetlana Lazebnik   University of Illinois at Urbana-Champaign, USA
Yoichi Sato   The University of Tokyo, Japan
Cordelia Schmid   INRIA, Grenoble, France

Honorary Chair

Tomaso Poggio   Massachusetts Institute of Technology, USA

Tutorial Chairs

Emanuele Trucco   University of Dundee, UK
Alessandro Verri   University of Genoa, Italy

Workshop Chairs

Andrea Fusiello   University of Udine, Italy
Vittorio Murino   Istituto Italiano di Tecnologia, Genoa, Italy

Demonstration Chair

Rita Cucchiara   University of Modena and Reggio Emilia, Italy

Industrial Liaison Chair

Björn Stenger   Toshiba Research Europe, Cambridge, UK

Web Chair

Marco Bertini   University of Florence, Italy

Publicity Chairs

Terrance E. Boult   University of Colorado at Colorado Springs, USA
Tat Jen Cham   Nanyang Technological University, Singapore
Marcello Pelillo   University Ca' Foscari of Venice, Italy

Publication Chair

Massimo Tistarelli   University of Sassari, Italy

Video Processing Chairs

Sebastiano Battiato   University of Catania, Italy
Giovanni M. Farinella   University of Catania, Italy

Travel Grants Chair

Luigi Di Stefano   University of Bologna, Italy

Travel Visa Chair

Stefano Berretti   University of Florence, Italy

Local Committee Chair

Andrew Bagdanov   MICC, Florence, Italy

Local Committee

Lamberto Ballan   Giuseppe Lisanti
Laura Benassi   Iacopo Masi
Marco Fanfani   Fabio Pazzaglia
Andrea Ferracani   Federico Pernici
Claudio Guida   Lorenzo Seidenari
Lea Landucci   Giuseppe Serra

Workshops Organizers

5th Workshop on Non-Rigid Shape Analysis and Deformable Image Alignment (NORDIA)

Stefano Berretti	University of Florence, Italy
Alexander Bronstein	Tel Aviv University, Israel
Michael Bronstein	University of Lugano, Switzerland
Umberto Castellani	University of Verona, Italy

First Workshop on Visual Analysis and Geo-Localization of Large-Scale Imagery

Mubarak Shah	University of Central Florida, USA
Luc Van Gool	ETH Zurich, Switzerland
Asaad Hakeem	ObjectVideo, USA
Alexei Efros	Carnegie Mellon University, USA
Niels Haering	ObjectVideo, USA
James Hays	Brown University, USA
Hui Cheng	SRI International Sarnoff, USA

Workshop on Web-Scale Vision and Social Media

Lamberto Ballan	University of Florence, Italy
Alex C. Berg	Stony Brook University, USA
Marco Bertini	University of Florence, Italy
Cees G.M. Snoek	University of Amsterdam, The Netherlands

WebVision: The Workshop on Computer Vision for the Web

Manik Varma	Microsoft Research India
Samy Bengio	Google, USA

The PASCAL Visual Object Classes Challenge 2012 (VOC2012) Workshop

Chris Williams	University of Edinburgh, UK
John Winn	MSR Cambridge, UK
Luc Van Gool	ETH Zurich, Switzerland
Andrew Zisserman	University of Oxford, UK
Alex Berg	Stony Brook University, USA
Fei-Fei Li	University of Stanford, USA

4th International Workshop on Video Event Categorization, Tagging and Retrieval (VECTaR 2012)

Tieniu Tan	Chinese Academy of Sciences, China
Thomas S. Huang	University of Illinois at Urbana-Champaign, USA
Ling Shao	University of Sheffield, UK
Jianguo Zhang	University of Dundee, UK
Liang Wang	Chinese Academy of Sciences, China

First International Workshop on Re-Identification (Re-Id 2012)

Marco Cristani	University of Verona, Italy
Shaogang Gong	Queen Mary University London, UK
Yan Shuicheng	NUS, Singapore

Workshop on Biological and Computer Vision Interfaces

Olivier Faugeras	INRIA, France
Pierre Kornprobst	INRIA, France

VISART: "Where Computer Vision Meets Art" Workshop

João Paulo Costeira	IST Lisbon, Portugal
Gustavo Carneiro	University of Adelaide, Australia
Nuno Pinho da Silva	IST Lisbon, Portugal
Alessio Del Bue	Istituto Italiano di Tecnologia, Italy

Second Workshop on Consumer Depth Cameras for Computer Vision (CDC4CV)

Andrea Fossati	ETH Zurich, Switzerland
Jürgen Gall	Max-Planck-Institut für Informatik, Germany
Helmut Grabner	ETH Zurich, Switzerland
Xiaofeng Ren	Intel Labs, USA
Kurt Konolige	Industrial Perception, USA
Seungkyu Lee	Samsung, South Korea
Miles Hansard	Queen Mary University London, UK

Workshop on Unsolved Problems in Optical Flow and Stereo Estimation

Daniel Kondermann	University of Heidelberg, Germany
Bernd Jähne	University of Heidelberg, Germany
Daniel Scharstein	Middlebury College, USA

"What's in a Face?" Workshop

Arun Ross	West Virginia University, USA
Alice O'Toole	University of Texas, USA
Maja Pantic	Imperial College London, UK
Antitza Dantcheva	West Virginia University, USA
Stefanos Zafeiriou	Imperial College London, UK

4th Color and Photometry in Computer Vision Workshop

Theo Gevers	University of Amsterdam, The Netherlands
Raimondo Schettini	University of Milano Bicocca, Italy
Joost van de Weijer	Universitat Autònoma de Barcelona, Spain
Todd Zickler	Harvard University, USA
Javier Vazquez-Corral	Universitat Autònoma de Barcelona, Spain

Third Workshop on Computer Vision in Vehicle Technology: From Earth to Mars

Atsushi Imiya   IMIT, Japan
Antonio M. López   UAB/CVC, Spain

Second Workshop on Parts and Attributes

Christoph H. Lampert   IST, Austria
Rogerio S. Feris   IBM Research, USA

Third IEEE International Workshop on Analysis and Retrieval of Tracked Events and Motion in Imagery Streams (ARTEMIS 2012)

Anastasios Doulamis   TUC, Greece
Nikolaos D. Doulamis   NTUA, Greece
Jordi Gonzàlez   UAB/CVC, Spain
Thomas B. Moeslund   University of Aalborg, Denmark
Marco Bertini   University of Florence, Italy

First Workshop on Action Recognition and Pose Estimation in Still Images

Vittorio Ferrari   University of Edinburgh, UK
Ivan Laptev   INRIA/Ecole Normale Superieure, France
Josef Sivic   INRIA/Ecole Normale Superieure, France
Bangpeng Yao   Stanford University, USA

Workshop on Higher-Order Models and Global Constraints in Computer Vision

Karteek Alahari   INRIA-WILLOW/Ecole Normale Superieure, France
Dhruv Batra   TTI-Chicago, USA
Srikumar Ramalingam   MERL, USA
Nikos Paragios   Paristech, France
Rich Zemel   University of Toronto, Canada

Workshop on Information Fusion in Computer Vision for Concept Recognition

Jenny Benois-Pineau   LABRI, University of Bordeaux, France
Georges Quenot   LIG INPG, Grenoble, France
Tomas Piatrik   Queen Mary University London, UK
Bogdan Ionescu   LAPI, University Politehnica of Bucharest, Romania

QU3ST Workshop - 2.5D Sensing Technologies in Motion: The Quest for 3D

David Fofi   Université de Bourgogne, France
Adrien Bartoli   Université d'Auvergne, France

Second International Workshop on Benchmarking Facial Image Analysis Technologies (BeFIT 2012)

Hazim Kemal Ekenel   KIT, Germany/Istanbul Technical University, Turkey
Gang Hua   Stevens Institute of Technology/IBM Research, USA
Shiguang Shan   Chinese Academy of Sciences, China

Sponsoring Companies and Institutions

Gold Sponsors

Silver Sponsors

Bronze Sponsors

Institutional Sponsors

Table of Contents

Unsolved Problems in Optical Flow and Stereo Estimation

What's in a Face?

4th Color and Photometry in Computer Vision Workshop 2012

Third Workshop on Computer Vision in Vehicle Technology: From Earth to Mars

High Accuracy TOF and Stereo Sensor Fusion at Interactive Rates

Rahul Nair[1,2], Frank Lenzen[1,2], Stephan Meister[1,2], Henrik Schäfer[1,2],
Christoph Garbe[1,2], and Daniel Kondermann[1,2]

[1] Heidelberg Collaboratory for Image Processing, Heidelberg University
[2] Intel Visual Computing Institute, Saarland University
{rahul.nair,frank.lenzen}@iwr.uni-heidelberg.de

Abstract. We propose two new GPU-based sensor fusion approaches for
time of flight (TOF) and stereo depth data. Data fidelity measures are defined to deal with the fundamental limitations of both techniques alone.
Our algorithms combine TOF and stereo, yielding megapixel depth maps,
enabling our approach to be used in a movie production scenario. Our
local model works at interactive rates but yields noisier results, whereas
our variational technique is more robust at a higher computational cost.
The results show an improvement over each individual method with TOF
interreflection remaining an open challenge. To encourage quantitative
evaluations, a ground truth dataset is made publicly available.

1 Introduction

Knowledge of scene geometry is required in many areas such as visual effects,
human computer interfaces or augmented reality systems. While Lidar scanners
are accurate, they usually are expensive, slow and require extensive postprocessing. Stereo matching works well on textured scenes, but has difficulties at depth
boundaries, in homogeneous regions and when repetitive patterns introduce am-
biguities. TOF cameras recently have become an interesting alternative source of
3D data. They deliver consistent results even on textureless surfaces at the cost
of a lower resolution, systematic errors such as flyig pixels, interreflections as well
as high noise - especially in regions with low infrared reflectance. By harnessing
the advantages of both methods we are able to improve the reconstructed depth.

1.1 Contributions

1. We define fidelity measures to identify those regions were either TOF, stereo
   or both approaches are likely to fail.
2. We locally fuse both sensors by appropriately dealing with problems such as
   missing textures in the stereo and low IR reflectance in TOF data.
3. We transfer this model to a slower but accurate variational approach using a
   new higher order TV regularization with a joint stereo and TOF data term.
4. The methods upsamples the 200 x 200px TOF depth to 1082x1082px.

A. Fusiello et al. (Eds.): ECCV 2012 Ws/Demos, Part II, LNCS 7584, pp. 1–11, 2012.

5. Both local and global approaches are implemented on GPU.
6. Finally, we have created a publicly available ground truth dataset to which we compare the results of our approach.

2 Related Work

3D reconstruction is a broad field of research in measurement sciences, photogrammetry and computer vision. TOF imaging is an active illumination system where infrared light is emitted by a source and reflected by the target. In each pixel the phase shift between emitted and reflected waveform is then calculated[1, 2]. TOF imaging suffers from several systematic errors such as an offset between actual depth and measured data as well wiggling errors due to deviations of the modulation from a pure sine function. A detailed description of the TOF noise sources and model is given in [3]. An interesting approach to estimating TOF noise has recently given in [4]. Here a regression forest is used to learn the noise model given lidar data as ground truth. Depth from stereo on the other hand has a long-standing history in computer vision. An overview of the methods and their shortcomings have been discussed in [5]

TOF based sensor fusion methods can be differentiated by the camera setup employed: *a)* With a single additional camera typically edge information from the high resolution intensity image is used to guide the upsampling of the depth image [6, 7]. *b)* Methods combining TOF and stereo not only filter the data to gain a higher lateral resolution; they also refine the actual depth information in textured regions. TOF imaging is a comparatively young field with a limited number of methods that have been proposed. As in pure stereo methods [5], these can be broadly grouped into local and global methods.

Local methods [8–13] tend to be faster and parallelizable but cannot cope with locally erroneous data. [9] applies a hierarchical stereo matching algorithm directly on the remapped TOF depth data without considering uncertainties. [8, 11] compute confidences in the TOF image and let stereo refine the result in regions with low confidence. The latter are similar to our method but only use binary confidence maps based on the TOF anmplitude image and therefore only sparsely use stereo information. Instead, we use the rich information of both data sources in the form of data fidelity measures to guide the fusion process.

Global methods apply spatial regularization techniques to propagate more information to regions with low confidence. Among the global methods, [14] applied an extension of semiglobal matching [15] to additionally handle TOF data. [16] applied a graph cut approach with a discrete number of disparities to sensor fusion. The methods closest to ours were proposed in [17] and [18] who employ an MAP-MRF framework and and a energy minimization scheme with quadratic regularization terms respectively. We employ adaptive first and second order total variation (TV) with L1 regularization. Such approaches already have been used for optical flow estimation [19–21]. For denoising TOF data, adaptive TV methods have been introduced in [22]. Our proposed approach differs to existing methods in the way adaptivity is defined: we include adaptivity in the differential operators, not in the TV norm.

3   Experimental Setup

The experimental setup (Fig. 1) consists of two high-resolution cameras (L, R)[1] and a low-res TOF camera[2] (T). To enable depth estimation in all areas of the primary (L) camera, the TOF camera is positioned such that the regions of occlusion between L-T and L-R are on opposite sides. Both our algorithms use the TOF intensity (TOFI) and depth (TOFD), as well as left and right images (Fig. 2). The setup is calibrated such that TOF and the right camera are registered to the left stereo image.

Fig. 1. Camera setup

Fig. 2. Input data: TOFD, TOFI (200x200), L and R (1312x1082, cropped for vis.)

4   Data Fidelity Measures

Various fidelity measures are then computed based on the input data.

1. TOF depth estimates are corrupted either when the reflectance of the illuminated surface is low or when the active light is not strong enough. A map C^{TOFI} is obtained by normalizing the inverse TOF intensity.
2. Due to flying pixels, the measurements at depth boundaries are error prone. The gradient of the TOF depth image $C^{\nabla TOFD}$ is used to account for this.
3. In stereo matching, disparities can only be estimated when the texture within a region is sufficiently unambiguous. Regions with high horizontal gradients

---

[1] Photon Focus MV1-D1312-160-CL-12 with Linos Mevis-C lenses at 25mm/1.6, 1312x1082px.
[2] PMDTech Camcube, 200x200px.

can be used as indicator: the third fidelity map is the horizontal gradient of L, denoted by $C^{\nabla_x L}$.

4. Finally, occluded areas can partly be detected using a regular photo-consistency check [15] on the TOF depth information projected on L. We denote this binary map as C^{LOcc}, where occluded pixels are marked with 0.

All fidelity measures are normalized to the range $[0 \ldots 1]$ (Fig. 3). These measures enable to find regions with noisy depths, systematically inaccurate or simply missing. However, regions with corrupted data not covered by our measures (e.g. interreflection) may remain. Therefore, the next steps have to be robust.

Fig. 3. Fidelity of scene in Fig. 2. Left to right: C^{TOFI}, $C^{\nabla TOFD}$, $C^{\nabla_x L}$ and C^{LOcc}.

5   Local Fusion of TOF and Stereo

Once calibrated, each TOF depth pixel j can be projected into the L frame. Since $TOFD$ is at a lower resolution and itself has an error, each $TOFD_j$ maps to multiple pixel locations i in L, with a certainty $\alpha_1 C_j^{TOFI}$ in each pixel. Conversely, for each pixel i in L the viewing ray intersects with the TOF depth map at multiple locations. Thus there may be multiple possible depths and probabilities $(TOFD_j, p_j)$, $j = 1, \ldots, N$. With L and R rectified, these depth measurements can be converted into disparities. Using stereo block matching we can then probe the matching score of the candidate disparities and choose the best candidate. This is only feasible if the pixel at i can be used for matching at all. This depends on C_i^{LOcc} and $C_i^{\nabla_x L}$. We make two simplifications at this point to speed up the method:

1. We are using C_i^{TOFI} as an uncertainty along rays from L even though it is defined along rays from T. Since we are observing objects at a long distance this simplification is justified.
2. Instead of keeping a list of all candidate disparities in L we keep the **most probable disparity (disp^{TOF}) and a range**.

Putting all together, we compute a **joint per pixel search range map** $[\text{disp}_i^{TOF} - C_i, \text{disp}_i^{TOF} + C_i]$ by combing the measures as follows:

$$C_i = (\alpha_1 C_i^{TOFI} + \alpha_2 C_i^{\nabla TOFD} + \beta_1 C_i^{\nabla_x L}) C_i^{LOcc}. \tag{1}$$

The parameters $\{\alpha_1, \alpha_2, \beta_1\}$ can be easily fixed for a given camera setup and lighting conditions. With the most probable depth and range standard block-matching is applied using a SSD cost on a square support window. This search space reduction not only speeds up the process: Also, repetitive pattern regions (multiple likely matches) are biased towards the TOF depth.

6 Variational Fusion of TOF and Stereo

In the following we describe a variational approach for the estimation of a smooth disparity map from both stereo and TOF data. A regularization term based on total variation (TV) of first and second order guarantees that the solution has the required smoothness.

Our approach considers two fidelity terms: the first one incorporates the stereo data and is based on a linearized 1D optical flow constraint (BCCE) [23], the second one incorporates the upsampled TOF data. Since the linearization of the BCCE assumes small displacements, we perform an incremental update (cf. [24]) of the targeted disparity map, i.e. $d^{k+1} := d^k + \delta^k$, starting with the TOF disparity $d^0 := \mathrm{disp}^{TOF}$. δ^k is found by solving the variational problem

$$\delta^k := \underset{\delta}{\mathrm{argmin}}\ \mathcal{S}_1(\delta) + \mathcal{S}_2(\delta, d^k) + \mathcal{R}(\delta, d^k) \tag{2}$$

with the two fidelity terms $\mathcal{S}_1, \mathcal{S}_2$ and a regularization term $\mathcal{R}$. We describe the terms $\mathcal{S}_1, \mathcal{S}_2$ and $\mathcal{R}$ in detail below.

The first fidelity term $\mathcal{S}_1$ is to penalize derivations from the linearized BCCE. To be robust against outliers, we use the L^1-norm. Since we already know from the map $C^{\nabla_x L}$ where to expect matchable structures, we only apply $\mathcal{S}_1$ in regions where $C^{\nabla_x L}$ is large. To this end we define $g_i := C_i^{\nabla_x L} \cdot C_i^{LOcc}$ and set

$$\mathcal{S}_1(\delta) := \sum_i g_i\,|(D_x R^{\mathrm{wrp}})_i \cdot \delta_i + R_i^{\mathrm{wrp}} - L_i)|, \tag{3}$$

where the summation is performed over all pixel indices i and D_x denotes a discrete differential operator for the horizontal derivative. R^{wrp} is the right stereo image warped according to the current disparity map d^k using bi-cubic interpolation (cf. [24]). When no matchable structures are present, we rely on the disparity map disp^{TOF} given by the TOF camera and make use of the uncertainty map C^{TOFI} and occlusion map C^{LOcc}. The second fidelity term $\mathcal{S}_2$ penalizes the deviation from the data disp^{TOF} with weights $w_i := (1/C_i^{TOFI} - 1) \cdot C_i^{LOcc}$. Again, to be robust against possible outliers, we use the L^1-norm:

$$\mathcal{S}_2(\delta, d^k) = \sum_i (1 - g_i)\,w_i\,|\delta_i + d_i^k - \mathrm{disp}_i^{TOF}|. \tag{4}$$

We now specify the regularization term $\mathcal{R}$. We use first and second order TV, which is adapted to local edges obtained as follows: Edges are defined as the maximum of the eigenvalue differences of a local structure tensor of an upsampled gradient image (see [25]) above a certain threshold. Inspired by Canny[26] edges below a certain length are rejected. Unlike Canny's double thresholding, we check for an angular alignment of the normal vectors of neighboring pixels. The orientation of the edge can be determined since the upsampling gradient filters yield edge locations with subpixel accuracy. We denote the location of such edges by binary data terms c_x and c_y, which are zero if an horizontal/vertical edge is present. For TV regularization we consider finite difference operators D_x and D_y for calculating horizontal and vertical derivatives. We adapt the finite differences to the edge information described above and use $\overline{D}_x := c_x D_x$ instead of D_x, and $\overline{D}_y := c_y D_y$ instead of D_y, respectively. Second order finite differences $\overline{D}_{xx}$ and $\overline{D}_{yy}$ then can be defined based on $\overline{D}_x$ and $\overline{D}_y$ (see [27]). In the regularization term $\mathcal{R}(\delta, d^k)$ we then penalize the norms of the first and second order derivatives of the targeted disparity map $d^k + \delta$. Thus, we set $\mathcal{R}(\delta, d^k) := \mathcal{R}(d^k + \delta)$, where

$$\mathcal{R}(v) := \sum_i \left(\gamma_1 \sqrt{(\overline{D}_x(v))_i^2 + (\overline{D}_y(v))_i^2} + \gamma_2 \sqrt{(\overline{D}_{xx}(v))_i^2 + (\overline{D}_{yy}(v))_i^2} \right). \quad (5)$$

Mixed derivatives of second order were omitted as no significant changes could be observed in experiments by [27]. Parameters $\gamma_1 \geq 0$ and $\gamma_2 \geq 0$ can be chosen pixel-wise in order to locally switch between the two orders. However, our experiments indicate that fixed positive values for the whole data set suffice. The mixture of first and second order TV in particular avoids stair-casing and provides piecewise affine reconstructions (cf. Section 7).

The numerical solution of (2) is obtained by a reformulation using variable splitting [20, 28]: after introducing auxiliary variables $\tilde{\delta}$ and $\overline{\delta}$ and penalizing their difference to δ with additional cost terms, problem (2) can be approximated by

$$\min_{\delta, \tilde{\delta}, \overline{\delta}} \mathcal{S}_1(\tilde{\delta}) + \mathcal{S}_2(\overline{\delta}, d^k) + \mathcal{R}(\delta, d^k) + \frac{1}{2\lambda_1} \|\tilde{\delta} - \delta\|_2^2 + \frac{1}{2\lambda_2} \|\overline{\delta} - \delta\|_2^2, \quad (6)$$

with $\lambda_1, \lambda_2 > 0$ tending to zero. In practice, however, we use fixed small values $\lambda_1 = \lambda_2 = 0.01$. Problem (6) then is solved by alternating minimization w.r.t. $\delta, \tilde{\delta}, \overline{\delta}$, where for the minimization w.r.t. $\tilde{\delta}, \overline{\delta}$ closed forms can be provided using the pseudo-inverse of $(D_x R^{\text{wrp}})_i$ and thresholding. For minimizing (6) w.r.t. δ we apply the primal-dual algorithm proposed by Chambolle & Pock [29].

7   Experiments and Results

7.1   TOF Only versus Stereo Only versus Our Approaches

Both proposed methods were implemented in C++ and make use of the CUDA framework. Fig. 4 shows a comparison of depth maps obtained from Fig.2 : using TOF only, SGM [15] stereo with rank filtering [30], and our local/TV fusion. The local method was parametrized with $(\alpha_1, \alpha_2, \beta_1) = (0.7, 1.5, 0.1)$, the global method with $(\gamma_1, \gamma_2) = (5, 1)$.

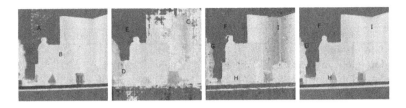

Fig. 4. Comparison of our approach. TOF only, SGM stereo, local and global fusion.

Besides the low resolution a considerable amount of noise can be observed in the TOF image, esp. in the dark regions of the poster (a) and the foam plate (b). Stereo matching fails on the wooden plates (c) due to lack of texture. Bleeding of disparities between the two statues (d) is also observable. Due to the fine texture on the poster (e) the SGM estimates the right disparity in that region.

Both our methods eliminate most of the noise around the poster (f) by using the available texture from stereo. The silhouettes (g) are reconstructed more precisely than in either TOF or stereo alone and fine details retained (e.g. pyramid (h)). Also the corner between the plates (i) that was corrupted due to interreflections is reconstructed properly as stereo cues are present there. The TV approach furthermore eliminates artifacts that could not be removed by the local method.

7.2   Ground Truth Evaluation

In the style of the Cornell Box [31], we have created a target box containing objects of different complexity (Fig. 5). The box has a size of (1 x 1 x 0.5)m. A synthetic model was then created with an accuracy within 1mm. For the shown scene we estimated the extrinsic camera parameters using manually selected 2D-to-3D correspondences. A ground truth (GT) depth map was then rendered with values that are an order of magnitude more precise than the TOF/stereo values. With few exceptions the reprojection error is lower than one pixel [31].

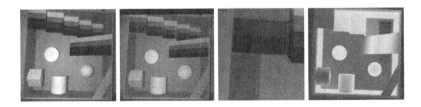

Fig. 5. *Left to right:* Box, Overlay of the GT mesh, largest alignment error, GT

To evaluate our measurements in a quantitative fashion, depth maps of the box were computed using the both approaches (Fig. 6). The variational approach was parameterized with $(\gamma_1, \gamma_2) = (5, 1)$ and the local method method with $(\alpha_1, \alpha_2, \beta_1) = (0.05, 0.05, 1.6)$. The difference between the GT image and

Table 1. Summary of GT evaluation on regions without interreflections

Data	Method	Mean	Std. dev.	1st Quart.	Median	3rd Quart.
TOF-data	upsampling	2.75	3.76	0.81	1.69	2.95
TOF-data	glob. meth./std. TV	2.92	3.85	0.81	1.72	3.14
TOF-data	glob. meth./adapt. TV	2.73	3.85	0.80	1.63	2.86
Stereo	SGM	2.92	3.89	0.84	1.78	3.24
Fusion	local method	2.78	3.81	0.81	1.70	2.98
Fusion	glob. meth./adapt. TV	2.57	3.53	0.75	1.58	2.78

Fig. 6. *Top:* local method. *Bottom:* variational method. *From left to right:* disparities, 3D reconstruction and difference between reconstruction and GT in cm.

Fig. 7. Reliefs of row 50, 280 and 500. Regions of importance (a-f) are discussed in 7.2.

the obtained depth maps were then calculated. Both methods show similar results with differences to GT on the box sides due to interreflection. Interreflection is not accounted for by our confidence measures, thus the confidence is overestimated. The results without interreflecting regions are shown in Table 1. Our fusion methods are compared with pure TOF upsampling, SGM stereo as well standard and adaptive TV regularized smoothing applied to the TOF data only. The fusion methods improve on the results of TOF or stereo alone and also of to global methods using TOF data alone. The best method having a median error of 1.58 cm compared to 1.78 cm using stereo alone and 1.69 cm using TOF alone. This justifies the combination of stereo with TOF data. Among the fusion methods the local one produces results very close to pure TOF. The first two quartiles of the local method error are almost equal to pure TOF and the third quartile slightly higher. From this (and from visual inspection) we can assume that the slight increase in error here is introduced by a few localized outliers. In retrospect this is quite clear as this scene contains too few stereo cues to use in a purely local ansatz. On such data regularization is required to propagate good stereo cues to the other regions. When stereo cues are present the local method also improves on each individual method (cf. Fig. 4).

To give some further insight, relief plots (Fig. 7) along rows of the depth images were made. Our method produces results that are less corrupted and resemble the GT relief more closely than SGM. This can be seen on *a)* the stairs where the stereo results could be interpreted as a slope, *b)* the sphere and *c)* the slope. The effects of interreflection can be observed in *d)* and *e)* .

8 Conclusion and Future Work

We have combined stereo and TOF depth data to overcome their respective limitations. Our method is based on fidelity measures derived from TOF intensities and depth gradients as well as horizontal image gradients and stereo photo consistency. This information was fed into a local and a variational framework. Both approaches yield semantically similar results, while the local approach is faster but noisier and the TV approach is less noisy but slower. We also created a publicly available millimeter-accurate ground truth dataset for the evaluation of sensor fusion systems. With this we could show that our method improves on the results of individual methods. Yet, further investigation is needed on how to handle interreflection.

Acknowledgements. This work has been co-financed by the Intel Visual Computing Institute and the MFG Baden-Württemberg. The content is under sole responsibility of the authors.

References

1. Xu, Z., Schwarte, R., Heinol, H., Buxbaum, B., Ringbeck, T.: Smart pixel–photonic mixer device (pmd). In: Proc. Int. Conf. on Mechatron. & Machine Vision (1998)
2. Lange, R., Seitz, P.: Solid-state time-of-flight range camera. JQE 37 (2001)
3. Schmidt, M.: Dissertation, IWR, Faculty of Physics, Univ. Heidelberg (2011)
4. Reynolds, M., Dobos, J., Peel, L., Weyrich, T., Brostow, G.: Capturing time-of-flight data with confidence. In: 2011 IEEE Conference on Computer Vision and Pattern Recognition (CVPR), pp. 945–952. IEEE (2011)
5. Scharstein, D., Szeliski, R.: A taxonomy and evaluation of dense two-frame stereo correspondence algorithms. IJCV 47, 7–42 (2002)
6. Huhle, B., Fleck, S., Schilling, A.: Integrating 3d time-of-flight camera data and high resolution images for 3dtv applications. In: Proc. 3DTV Conf. IEEE (2007)
7. Park, J., Kim, H., Tai, Y., Brown, M., Kweon, I.: High quality depth map upsampling for 3d-tof cameras. In: IEEE Proc. ICCV (2011)

8. Kuhnert, K., Stommel, M.: Fusion of stereo-camera and pmd-camera data for real-time suited precise 3d environment reconstruction. In: Int. Conf. on Intelligent Robots and Systems, pp. 4780–4785. IEEE (2006)
9. Gudmundsson, S., Aanaes, H., Larsen, R.: Fusion of stereo vision and time-of-flight imaging for improved 3d estimation. IJISTA 5, 425–433 (2008)
10. Bartczak, B., Koch, R.: Dense Depth Maps from Low Resolution Time-of-Flight Depth and High Resolution Color Views. In: Bebis, G., Boyle, R., Parvin, B., Koracin, D., Kuno, Y., Wang, J., Pajarola, R., Lindstrom, P., Hinkenjann, A., Encarnação, M.L., Silva, C.T., Coming, D. (eds.) ISVC 2009, Part II. LNCS, vol. 5876, pp. 228–239. Springer, Heidelberg (2009)
11. Hahne, U., Alexa, M.: Depth imaging by combining time-of-flight and on-demand stereo. In: Dynamic 3D Imaging, pp. 70–83 (2009)
12. Dal Mutto, C., Zanuttigh, P., Cortelazzo, G.M.: A probabilistic approach to tof and stereo data fusion. In: 3DPVT, Paris, France (2010)
13. Yang, Q., Tan, K.H., Culbertson, B., Apostolopoulos, J.: Fusion of active and passive sensors for fast 3d capture. In: MMSP (2010)
14. Fischer, J., Arbeiter, G., Verl, A.: Combination of time-of-flight depth and stereo using semiglobal optimization. In: Int. Conf. on Robotics and Automation (ICRA), pp. 3548–3553. IEEE (2011)
15. Hirschmuller, H.: Stereo processing by semiglobal matching and mutual information. TPAMI 30, 328–341 (2008)
16. Hahne, U., Alexa, M.: Combining time-of-flight depth and stereo images without accurate extrinsic calibration. IJISTA 5, 325–333 (2008)
17. Zhu, J., Wang, L., Yang, R., Davis, J., et al.: Reliability fusion of time-of-flight depth and stereo for high quality depth maps. TPAMI, 1 (2011)
18. Kim, Y., Theobalt, C., Diebel, J., Kosecka, J., Miscusik, B., Thrun, S.: Multi-view image and tof sensor fusion for dense 3d reconstruction. In: ICCV Workshops, pp. 1542–1549. IEEE (2009)
19. Trobin, W., Pock, T., Cremers, D., Bischof, H.: An Unbiased Second-Order Prior for High-Accuracy Motion Estimation. In: Rigoll, G. (ed.) DAGM 2008. LNCS, vol. 5096, pp. 396–405. Springer, Heidelberg (2008)
20. Wedel, A., Pock, T., Zach, C., Bischof, H., Cremers, D.: An Improved Algorithm for TV-L^1 Optical Flow. In: Cremers, D., Rosenhahn, B., Yuille, A.L., Schmidt, F.R. (eds.) Visual Motion Analysis. LNCS, vol. 5604, pp. 23–45. Springer, Heidelberg (2009)
21. Werlberger, M., Unger, M., Pock, T., Bischof, H.: Efficient Minimization of the Non-local Potts Model. In: Bruckstein, A.M., ter Haar Romeny, B.M., Bronstein, A.M., Bronstein, M.M. (eds.) SSVM 2011. LNCS, vol. 6667, pp. 314–325. Springer, Heidelberg (2012)
22. Lenzen, F., Schäfer, H., Garbe, C.: Denoising Time-Of-Flight Data with Adaptive Total Variation. In: Bebis, G., Boyle, R., Parvin, B., Koracin, D., Wang, S., Kyungnam, K., Benes, B., Moreland, K., Borst, C., DiVerdi, S. (eds.) ISVC 2011, Part I. LNCS, vol. 6938, pp. 337–346. Springer, Heidelberg (2011)
23. Horn, B., Schunck, B.: Determining optical flow. AI 17, 185–204 (1981)
24. Papenberg, N., Bruhn, A., Brox, T., Didas, S., Weickert, J.: Highly accurate optic flow computation with theoretically justified warping. IJCV 67, 141–158 (2006)
25. Köthe, U.: Edge and Junction Detection with an Improved Structure Tensor. In: Michaelis, B., Krell, G. (eds.) DAGM 2003. LNCS, vol. 2781, pp. 25–32. Springer, Heidelberg (2003)
26. Canny, J.F.: A Computational Approach to Edge Detection. TPAMI 8 (1986)

27. Setzer, S., Steidl, G., Teuber, T.: Infimal convolution regularizations with discrete l1-type functionals. Comm. Math. Sci. 9, 797–872 (2011)
28. Clason, C., Jin, B., Kunisch, K.: A duality-based splitting method for l1-tv image restoration with automatic regularization parameter choice. SIAM J. Sci. Comp., 1484–1505 (2010)
29. Chambolle, A., Pock, T.: A first-order primal-dual algorithm for convex problems with applications to imaging. JMIV 40, 120–145 (2011)
30. Hirschmüller, H., Scharstein, D.: Evaluation of cost functions for stereo matching. In: Proc. CVPR, pp. 1–8. IEEE (2007)
31. Goral, C., Torrance, K., Greenberg, D., Battaile, B.: Modeling the interaction of light between diffuse surfaces. In: ACM SIGGRAPH Computer Graphics, vol. 18, pp. 213–222. ACM (1984)

A Modular Framework for 2D/3D and Multi-modal Segmentation with Joint Super-Resolution

Benjamin Langmann, Klaus Hartmann, and Otmar Loffeld

ZESS - Center for Sensor Systems, University of Siegen,
Paul-Bonatz-Str. 9-11, 57068 Siegen, Germany
{langmann,hartmann,loffeld}@zess.uni-siegen.de
http://www.zess.uni-siegen.de

Abstract. A versatile multi-image segmentation framework for 2D/3D or multi-modal segmentation is introduced in this paper with possible application in a wide range of machine vision problems. The framework performs a joint segmentation and super-resolution to account for images of unequal resolutions gained from different imaging sensors. This allows to combine high resolution details of one modality with the distinctiveness of another modality. A set of measures is introduced to weight measurements according to their expected reliability and it is utilized in the segmentation as well as the super-resolution. The approach is demonstrated with different experimental setups and the effect of additional modalities as well as of the parameters of the framework are shown.

Keywords: Segmentation, Image Processing, Range Imaging, Time-of-Flight (ToF), Photonic Mixer Device (PMD).

1 Introduction

Segmentation is a well known and widely studied topic in the area of image processing, computer and machine vision with many applications in associated subjects. The main sources of information are color images and several approaches have been proposed like pixel based methods, edge oriented methods, region and texture based approaches. Another research topic is how to apply these methods to other information sources, e.g. radar data, MRI scans or depth measurements.

The capability of a single modality to distinct objects is for some applications not sufficient or robust enough. The obvious approach is to utilize an additional modality acquired with another imaging sensor. But the measurements of the imaging sensors need to be registered, which is often non-trivial and sometimes needs certain assumptions. Additionally, one cannot assume that the resolutions of the imaging devices match. In the case that the lowest resolution is not sufficient for the task at hand a super-resolution method is required, since normal scaling methods are often not appropriate. In this paper we introduce a segmentation and joint super-resolution framework, which utilizes a standard

A. Fusiello et al. (Eds.): ECCV 2012 Ws/Demos, Part II, LNCS 7584, pp. 12–21, 2012.

segmentation method (Mean-Shift) and estimates super-resolved input images in an iterative process. The proposed method incorporates validity measures to judge the measurement quality of input data in order to account for noise and disturbances. The method is widely applicable and we demonstrate its capabilities in given test setups.

This paper is structured as follows: In section 2 the related work is discussed and in section 3 modalities used in the experiments and their acquisition are detailed. Afterwards, the segmentation and super-resolution framework is introduced in section 4. In section 5 experimental results of this framework are reviewed and this paper ends with a conclusion in section 6.

2   Related Work

In this section research dealing with multi-image and depth image segmentation will be reviewed. In [1] the Mean-Shift algorithm is applied to color and depth images acquired with two cameras (binocular setup). The depth images are firstly resized with a bilateral filter and then segmented. Different super-resolution methods for depth imaging including several variants of bilateral filtering are compared in [2]. Color and depth are used for the task of alpha matting in [3]. Furthermore, several approaches have been studied for plain background subtraction, e.g. in [4] an approach utilizing Gaussian Mixture Models is demonstrated.

The segmentation of depth maps is performed in [5] for compression purposes and in [6] intensity and depth information of the same size is segmented with the graph-cut method and aimed at the detection of planar surfaces. In [7] a watershed based segmentation is utilized to analyze biological samples with 2D or 3D data and it combines intensity, edge and shape information. Lastly, the segmentation of ultrasound images in 2D or 3D in studied in [8].

3   Multi-modal Sensor Data

In the area of machine vision standard color or grayscale images are the predominant source of information, but nevertheless, supplemental modalities play a growing role. In addition to a color chip we utilize in this paper a continuous wave (CW) Time-of-Flight imaging chip in which is able to provide depth and near infrared reflectivity measurements. But the lateral resolution of such imaging chips is significantly lower than those of standard color or grayscale chips and also to low to capture fine details which are searched for in many applications. On the other hand these additional modalities may be able to provide valuable clues depending on the application.

The measurements often do not provide the information we want to utilize in the segmentation directly. For color chips shadows or varying lighting is not what we want to distinguish. Usually, the same is true for depth measurements. Even planes parallel to the imaging plane do not have similar depth values. Therefore, the first step is to derive the information of the images to be used in

MultiCam characteristics	
Interface	Gigabit Ethernet
Lens adapter	C-mount
Frame rate	12 fps (up to 80 fps with reduced 2D resolution)
Color chip	Aptina MT9T031
- Resolution	2048x1536
- Chip size	6.55mm x 4.92mm
PMD chip	PMDTec 19k
- Resolution	160x120
- Chip size	7.2mm x 5.4mm

Fig. 1. The MultiCam, a 2D/3D monocular camera and its specifications

the segmentation. Color images are often transformed to L*u*v* color space to make differences perceptually uniform and to be able to eliminate the influence of lighting conditions. Concerning depth images we can derive normal vectors of the depth image and use them in the segmentation if we have mostly planar objects in the scene. In the following these transformed information will be referred to as features.

We estimate normal vectors by firstly calculating 3D points of the depth values using a range camera model. Afterwards, the surface normal $\underline{n} = (n_x, n_y, n_z)$ at each 3D point $\underline{p} = (p_x, p_y, p_z)$ can be estimated by averaging over the 8 normal vectors of triangles spanned by $\underline{p}$ and combinations of its neighbor points. This will lead to interpolation errors at the borders of objects and may need additional handling.

The measurements performed have usually varying reliability. In some cases it is useful to utilize validity measures to judge the usefulness of a measurement. The quality of lighting greatly influences color information and it can be estimated based on the Luminance. For CW ToF imaging the modulation amplitude is a measure describing the amount of active lighting at given point and serves as a valuable descriptor. The variance over time is for all measurements a reliable validity measure as long as it is available, see section 4.2 for more details.

Additionally, we need to register the different images or multi-modal information. With our monocular camera shown in figure 1 this simply consists in applying a scale factor and an offset. When using multiple cameras this is more complicated in general, but for some machine vision applications an affine transformation may suffice.

4 Multi-image Segmentation Framework

Many traditional segmentation methods perform a clustering of points in the so-called feature space consisting of coordinates and measurements. The main advantage is that these methods are typically fast. On the down side these methods require input images of the same size. In section 4.1 a well known feature space segmentation method, the Mean-Shift algorithm, is detailed.

Furthermore, a given segmentation can be utilized to generate high resolution images of the input images of lower resolution. In section 4.3 such a super-resolution method is discussed. This leads to an estimation problem, which can be formulated in the Expectation Maximization (EM) framework as follows: all labels of feature points make up the parameter set Ω and the missing measurements due to lower resolutions are unobserved latent variables Z. This is based on the assumption that the segmentation algorithm maximizes the likelihood given Z.

1. **Initialization**: Generate uniform segmentation $\Omega^{(0)}$.
2. **Estimation**: Perform a super-resolution to estimate Z.
3. **Maximization**: Perform a multi-image segmentation to retrieve $\Omega^{(t+1)}$.

The E- and M-steps are iterated until a convergence is reached or a maximum number of iterations were performed. In the following sections the segmentation and super-resolution methods are detailed.

4.1   Mean-Shift Segmentation

The Mean-Shift algorithm [9] is a feature space approach and consists of two steps. In the first one (filtering) the mean-shift vectors are calculated iteratively and the feature points are moved accordingly until a convergence is reached. These vectors are determined by calculating the weighted average of neighboring feature points. In the second step the filtered feature points are merged to form regions or segments.

Let $P_i = \left(\underline{p}_i, \underline{f}_i \right)$ and $P_j = \left(\underline{p}_j, \underline{f}_j \right)$ be points of the feature space with lattices $\underline{p} \in \mathbb{R}^2 = \Psi$ and features $\underline{f} = \Phi$. For the weight $g(P_i, P_j)$ between two points we use the product of two separate Gaussian kernels but simpler and faster kernels are of course possible

$$g(P_i, P_j) = \exp\left\{ -\frac{\left\| \underline{p}_i - \underline{p}_j \right\|_2^2}{h_{space}} \right\} \cdot \exp\left\{ -\frac{\left\| \underline{f}_i - \underline{f}_j \right\|_r^2}{h_{range}} \right\}. \tag{1}$$

The first term is based on the squared Euclidean distance between the two points and the second uses a (pseudo-)norm to measure differences between features. h_{space} and h_{range} are bandwidth parameters to control the influence of the kernels.

Given a point $P_i^{(t)}$ in the feature space in iteration t the next point can be computed with

$$P_i^{(t+1)} = \frac{\sum_{P \in N\left(P_i^{(t)}\right)} P \cdot g\left(P_i^{(t)}, P\right)}{\sum_{P \in N\left(P_i^{(t)}\right)} g\left(P_i^{(t)}, P\right)}, \tag{2}$$

where the set $N(\cdot)$ denotes a spatial neighborhood. The Mean-Shift vector is the difference $P_i^{(t+1)} - P_i^{(t)}$ and for each point these iterative calculations are

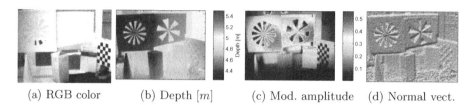

(a) RGB color	(b) Depth $[m]$	(c) Mod. amplitude	(d) Normal vect.

Fig. 2. Different modalities (colorization) acquired with the MultiCam

performed independently. Once the Mean-Shift filtering is finished, the feature points are merged using a distance threshold in the spatial domain as well as in the range domain.

4.2 Weighted Multi-modal Mean-Shift

The update formula of the Mean-Shift section can be easily extended with additional weights $\omega(P)$ leading to

$$P_i^{(t+1)} = \frac{\sum_{P \in N\left(P_i^{(t)}\right)} P \cdot \omega(P) \cdot g\left(P_i^{(t)}, P\right)}{\sum_{P \in N\left(P_i^{(t)}\right)} \omega(P) \cdot g\left(P_i^{(t)}, P\right)}. \tag{3}$$

The weights are specific to a feature Point P and not separate for subspaces of the feature space, since we perform a joint segmentation over all modalities. In figure 2 different modalities acquired with the MultiCam are shown. Let $P = (\underline{p}, \underline{f})$ be a feature point and $\underline{f} = (f_L, f_u, f_v, f_d, f_{mod}, n_x, n_y, n_z, f_\sigma) \in \Phi$ with a color value (f_L, f_u, f_v) in the L*u*v* color space, a depth value f_d, a modulation amplitude f_{mod}, a normal vector $\underline{n} = (n_x, n_y, n_z)$ and a variance f_σ of the depth measurements. We can the define validity measures as follows. $\gamma_{lum}(P)$ gives penalties for low and high luminance levels with an appropriate parameter, e.g. $\alpha_{lum} = 70$, and a bandwidth $h_{lum} = 2$

$$\gamma_{lum}(P) = \exp\left\{-\frac{(f_L - \alpha_{lum})^2}{h_{lum}}\right\}. \tag{4}$$

Similarly, the modulation amplitude of CW ToF imaging describes reliably the noise level of the depth measurements and its influence in the validity measure $\gamma_{mod}(P) = 1 - \exp\left\{-\frac{f_{mod}^2}{h_{mod}}\right\}$ is controlled with a bandwidth parameter h_{mod}. Another indicator of the quality of the depth measurement is the variance over time, which is exploited in $\gamma_{var}(P) = \exp\left\{-\frac{f_\sigma^2}{h_\sigma}\right\}$. The complete additional weight is given by $\omega(P) = \gamma_{lum}(P) \cdot \gamma_{mod}(P) \cdot \gamma_{var}(P)$.

In the weight $g(P_i, P_j)$ between two feature points each subspace is typically treated independently, i.e. the range (pseudo)-norm $\|\cdot\|_r$ consists of separate norms for each subspace. Euclidean norms are commonly used, but this is not appropriate for some modalities, especially for comparison of two normal vectors. Here the squared sine of the enclosed angle is much more suitable. Nevertheless, for simplicity it is also possible to use the distance measure $\delta_n\left(\underline{n}_i, \underline{n}_j\right)$ between normal vectors $\underline{n}_i$ and $\underline{n}_j$ of unit length, which embeds a Euclidean distance in a Gaussian kernel

$$\delta_n(\underline{n}_i, \underline{n}_j) = \exp\left\{-\frac{\left(\left\|\underline{n}_i - \underline{n}_j\right\|_2^2 - 2\right)^2}{h_{normal}}\right\}. \tag{5}$$

In the experiments we use the following weighting kernel to measure differences between the feature points $P_i = (\underline{p}_i, \underline{c}_i, d_i, \underline{n}_i)$ and $P_j = (\underline{p}_j, \underline{c}_j, d_j, \underline{n}_j)$ with lattices $\underline{p}$, color values $\underline{c}$, depth values d. and normal vectors $\underline{n}$. with associated bandwidths

$$g\left(P_i, P_j\right) = \exp\left\{-\frac{\left\|\underline{p}_i - \underline{p}_j\right\|_2^2}{h_{space}} - \frac{\left\|\underline{c}_i - \underline{c}_j\right\|_2^2}{h_{col}} - \frac{(d_i - d_j)^2}{h_{depth}}\right\}\delta_n(\underline{n}_i, \underline{n}_j). \tag{6}$$

4.3   Joint Super-Resolution

A given segmentation can be used to estimate high resolution images of multi-modal images of lower resolution. Super-resolution for multiple images is often performed under the assumption that data of the different images coincides, e.g. color and depth. In the area of depth imaging cross bilateral filtering working on this assumption is commonly used. The same notion is true for segments found in multi-modal data.

Let $S_1, S_2, \ldots, S_m \subset \Psi \times \Phi$ be segments with $S_i \cap S_j = \emptyset$ for $i \neq j$ with a subspace $\underline{\Phi}$ of Φ, for which a super-resolution should be performed. Let $q^{(t)} = (p, \underline{f}^{(t)}) \in S_i$ be a point at iteration t of the EM algorithm with arbitrary lattice p and feature $\underline{f}^{(t)}$. Let further $g(\cdot, \cdot)$ be a (Gaussian) kernel and $N(\cdot)$ a spatial neighborhood. In the subsequent iteration $q^{(t+1)}$ is computed with

$$\underline{q}^{(t+1)} = \frac{\sum_{\underline{u} \in S_i \cap N(\underline{q}^{(t)})} \underline{u} \cdot \omega\left(\underline{u}\right) \cdot g\left(\underline{q}^{(t)}, \underline{u}\right)}{\sum_{\underline{u} \in S_i \cap N(\underline{q}^{(t)})} \omega\left(\underline{u}\right) \cdot g\left(\underline{q}^{(t)}, \underline{u}\right)}. \tag{7}$$

There are different possibilities to calculate this formula, e.g. the spatial neighborhood can include only the direct measurements or every feature point on a finer lattice and there are many ways to choose the kernel. In the experiments with the MultiCam we firstly create feature points on the lattice of the color image, since it has the highest resolution. To this end the other images are transformed, which includes here only a nearest neighbor scaling and a translation. Then the formula is applied with a spatial kernel for each feature point yielding a new set of points.

5   Experimental Evaluation

In order to evaluate the proposed segmentation and super-resolution framework
we start with the well known high quality Middlebury benchmark dataset [10],
which consists of sets of color images taken from different views and associated
disparity maps. A view of one setup was chosen and is shown in figure 3, where
the disparity map was converted to a depth map and the normal vectors were
computed. The depth map was downsampled with a factor of 5 to simulate
measurements of different lateral resolutions. One exemplary segmentation is
shown and the super-resolution results are displayed also, which show weaknesses
for thin objects but work in general as expected. Furthermore, the iterative
estimates of the high resolution depth maps are shown in figure 4. One can
observe a very smooth initial estimate and a sharpening in following iterations.

In figure 5 a similar setup, in which a variety of mostly white objects are
arranged, is shown. The setup was acquired with the MultiCam and depth as
well as normal maps were calculated. It shall be noted that it is usually possible to

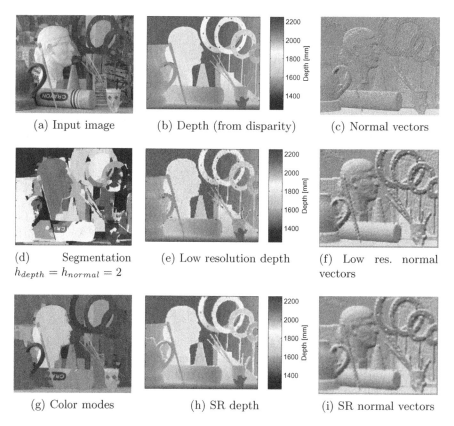

(a) Input image   (b) Depth (from disparity)   (c) Normal vectors

(d)   Segmentation
$h_{depth} = h_{normal} = 2$ (e) Low resolution depth   (f) Low   res. normal
vectors

(g) Color modes   (h) SR depth   (i) SR normal vectors

Fig. 3. Multi-modal segmentation results for a benchmark image of the Middlebury
dataset and super-resolution images

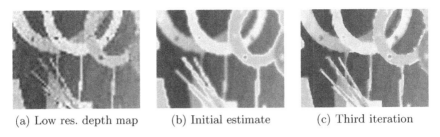

(a) Low res. depth map   (b) Initial estimate   (c) Third iteration

Fig. 4. Incremental estimation of the super-resolved depth map

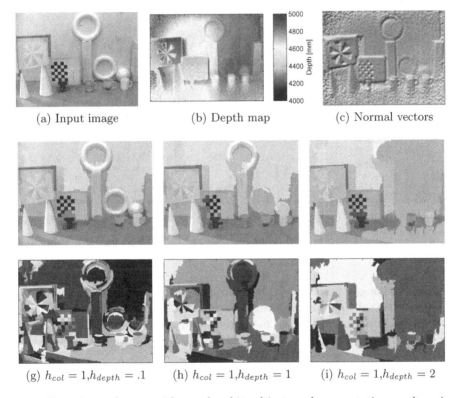

(a) Input image   (b) Depth map   (c) Normal vectors

(g) $h_{col} = 1, h_{depth} = .1$ (h) $h_{col} = 1, h_{depth} = 1$ (i) $h_{col} = 1, h_{depth} = 2$

Fig. 5. Experimental setup with mostly white objects and segmentation results using depth map and estimated normal vectors

find parameters for the Mean-Shift algorithm to perform a valuable segmentation of such uniform scenes. Nevertheless, this segmentation is not robust and thus not reliable. The normal vectors do not provide valuable segmentation hints for this scene due to the parallel planes and curvatures. Segmentation results based on color and depth for three different parameter settings are shown with colored labels and average color of the segments. The depth bandwidth h_{depth} was changed to demonstrate the influence of the depth measurements and its

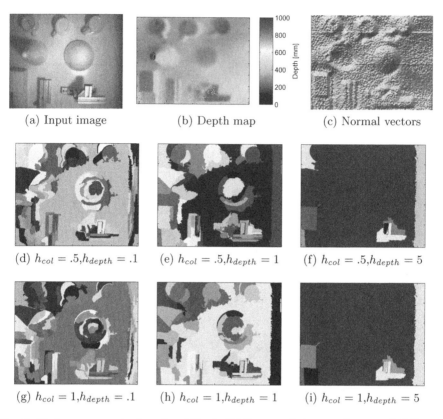

(a) Input image   (b) Depth map   (c) Normal vectors

(d) $h_{col} = .5, h_{depth} = .1$ (e) $h_{col} = .5, h_{depth} = 1$ (f) $h_{col} = .5, h_{depth} = 5$

(g) $h_{col} = 1, h_{depth} = .1$ (h) $h_{col} = 1, h_{depth} = 1$ (i) $h_{col} = 1, h_{depth} = 5$

Fig. 6. Test scene acquired under difficult lighting conditions and a set of different segmentations

significant value can be observed. In figure 6 a similar setup was acquired and it is demonstrated that color information provides in this case only small hints for the segmentation. The depth measurements can be utilized in conjunction with normal vectors to perform the segmentation and the color information is exploited mainly in the super-resolution task.

6   Conclusion

In this paper a modular multi-image segmentation framework for multi-modal data is introduced. Since the acquisition of multi-modal data is usually performed with different imaging chips, the segmentation approach needs to account for different resolutions and necessary transformations to align the different modalities. The proposed framework uses an estimation approach to jointly perform a segmentation and super-resolution, in which results of the segmentation influence the super-resolution and vice versa. The generated high resolution images are not only needed to accomplish the segmentation at borders of objects but can also be utilized in subsequent processing steps. A set of validity measures is defined to give measurements of expected lower quality lower weights in the segmentation and super-resolution. The proposed multi-modal segmentation framework is demonstrated by applying it to 2D/3D segmentation and different experimental setups are utilized to evaluate the validity measures as well as the influence of the parameters of the approach. This should give valuable hints in which area of application the method can be applied successfully.

Acknowledgments. This work was funded by the German Research Foundation (DFG) as part of the research training group GRK 1564 'Imaging New Modalities'.

References

1. Bleiweiss, A., Werman, M.: Fusing Time-of-Flight Depth and Color for Real-Time Segmentation and Tracking. In: Kolb, A., Koch, R. (eds.) Dyn3D 2009. LNCS, vol. 5742, pp. 58–69. Springer, Heidelberg (2009)
2. Langmann, B., Hartmann, K., Loffeld, O.: Comparison of depth super-resolution methods for 2d/3d images. International Journal of Computer Information Systems and Industrial Management Applications 3, 635–645 (2011)
3. Wang, O., Finger, J., Yang, Q., Davis, J., Yang, R.: Automatic natural video matting with depth. In: Proceedings of the 15th Pacific Conference on Computer Graphics and Applications, Maui, Hawaii, pp. 469–472 (2007)
4. Langmann, B., Ghobadi, S.E., Hartmann, K., Loffeld, O.: Multi-modal background subtraction using gaussian mixture models. In: ISPRS Technical Commission III Symposium on Photogrammetry Computer Vision and Image Analysis (PCV 2010), pp. 61–66 (2010)
5. Jager, F.: Contour-based segmentation and coding for depth map compression. In: IEEE Visual Communications and Image Processing (VCIP), pp. 1–4 (November 2011)
6. Kahler, O., Rodner, E., Denzler, J.: On fusion of range and intensity information using graph-cut for planar patch segmentation. International Journal of Intelligent Systems Technologies and Applications 5(3), 365–373 (2008)
7. Wählby, C., Sintorn, I.M., Erlandsson, F., Borgefors, G., Bengtsson, E.: Combining intensity, edge and shape information for 2d and 3d segmentation of cell nuclei in tissue sections. Journal of Microscopy 215(Pt 1), 67–76 (2004)
8. Boukerroui, D.: Segmentation of ultrasound images: multiresolution 2d and 3d algorithm based on global and local statistics. Pattern Recognition Letters 24(4-5), 779–790 (2003)
9. Comaniciu, D., Meer, P.: Mean shift: A robust approach toward feature space analysis. IEEE Transactions on Pattern Analysis and Machine Intelligence 24(5), 603–619 (2002)
10. Scharstein, D., Pal, C.: Learning conditional random fields for stereo. In: IEEE Conference on Computer Vision and Pattern Recognition, pp. 1–8 (June 2007)

Real-Time Plane Segmentation and Obstacle Detection of 3D Point Clouds for Indoor Scenes

Zhe Wang, Hong Liu, Yueliang Qian, and Tao Xu

Key Laboratory of Intelligent Information Processing &&
Beijing Key Laboratory of Mobile Computing and Pervasive Device
Institute of Computing Technology, Chinese Academy of Sciences
Beijing 100190, China
{wangzhe01,hliu,ylqian,xutao}@ict.ac.cn

Abstract. Scene analysis is an important issue in computer vision and extracting structural information is one of the fundamental techniques. Taking advantage of depth camera, we propose a novel fast plane segmentation algorithm and use it to detect obstacles in indoor environment. The proposed algorithm has two steps: the initial segmentation and the refined segmentation. Firstly, depth image is converted into 3D point cloud and divided into voxels, which are less sensitive to noises compared with pixels. Then area-growing algorithm is used to extract the candidate planes according to the normal of each voxel. Secondly, each point that hasn't been classified to any plane is examined whether it actually belongs to a plane. The two-step strategy has been proven to be a fast segmentation method with high accuracy. The experimental results demonstrate that our method can segment planes and detect obstacles in real-time with high accuracy for indoor scenes.

Keywords: plane segmentation, point cloud, obstacle detection.

1 Introduction

Understanding the structural information of the surrounding environment is a principal issue for indoor service robots and wearable obstacle avoidance devices. There are many man-made planes in indoor scene. Plane detection and segmentation is the fundamental technique for understanding the structure and can be used in many important applications, such as robot navigation, object detection, scene labeling and so on. The accuracy of plane segmentation is highly related to the performance of the whole scene understanding system. Furthermore, as the basic step of scene understanding systems, plane segmentation should be processed in real-time.

Recently, depth cameras, such as the Microsoft Kinect, generate a booming effect in the computer vision filed. Kinect acquires depth information at high frame rates (30Hz) and the accuracy is roughly equal to 3D laser scanners in low ranges. With depth data, the shape, size, geometric information and several other properties of the objects can be more precisely determined. As a result,

A. Fusiello et al. (Eds.): ECCV 2012 Ws/Demos, Part II, LNCS 7584, pp. 22–31, 2012.

depth cameras greatly stimulate researchers' enthusiasm and have been widely used in plenty of computer vision systems, such as mobile robot navigation[1], 3D reconstruction[2] and indoor navigation systems[3].

Based on single depth camera from one view, we focus on fast plane segmentation method and use it to detect obstacles in indoor scenes. Depth image grabbed by single depth camera has some noises. Furthermore, the resolution of depth image by Kinect is 640×480 pixels, which has excessive amount of data for real-time processing.

In this paper we present an algorithm to accurately segment all planes using depth image, and then detect the obstacles in indoor scenes. A novel two-step strategy PVP for fast **P**lane segmentation mainly consists of **V**oxel-wise initial segmentation and **P**ixel-wise accurate segmentation is proposed. Firstly, we convert the depth image into 3D point cloud and divide the point cloud into voxels. Then the normal of each voxel is calculated and an area-growing based algorithm is used to extract the candidate planes according to the normal of each voxel. Secondly, each point in point cloud that hasn't been classified to any plane is examined whether it actually belongs to a plane or not. Then the fragments of the same plane are merged together. The experimental results show the proposed two-step strategy PVP is a fast segmentation method with high accuracy.

2   Related Work

Many plane segmentation algorithms for 3D data have been proposed in recent years. Some researchers treat depth images as 2D images and apply 2D segmentation methods on depth images directly. The only difference is that the value of each pixel in depth images is not in the range of 0 to 255. When adopting advanced segmentation algorithms like mean-shift clustering[4] or graph-based segmentation[5], this approach gives good results in some scenes. However, in other situations such as the case of close or touching objects, these methods perform badly. Some algorithms, like[6] or[7], use RANSAC or J-linkage[8] to robustly estimate the parameters of all planes in a depth image. But this kind of algorithms is usually slow and can hardly be adopted in real-time systems. Furthermore, these methods are unsuitable for large and complex scenes such as office rooms. So some researchers begin to find other more efficient methods. Holz et al.[9] use integral images to compute local surface normals of point clouds. Then the points are clustered, segmented, and classified in both normal space and spherical coordinates. The experiments show the algorithm could achieve a frame rate at 30Hz at the resolution of 160×120 pixels. However other advanced tasks like object classification may need a higher resolution. Dube et al.[10] extract planes from depth images based on the Randomized Hough Transformation. They use a noise model for the sensor to solve the task of finding proper parameter metrics for the Randomized Hough Transform. This algorithm is real-time capable on the platform of a mobile robot. However it can only detect planes, and cannot accurately segments the planes.

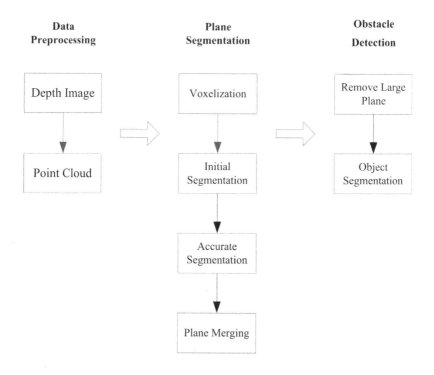

Fig. 1. System architecture

3   Overview of Our Approach

Fig. 1 gives the architecture of our system. Basically, our system contains three stages: data preprocessing, plane segmentation and obstacle detection. First of all, in the data preprocessing stage, the depth image obtained from the Kinect is converted to the corresponding 3D point cloud. Then a voxel grid is created on the point cloud. For each voxel, a plane equation is estimated using least square estimation technique and the normal of the plane can be obtained from the coefficient of the equation. Next, in the plane segmentation stage, an area-growing based algorithm is firstly adopted to extract candidate planes at the initial segmentation step. Then the remaining points are examined one by one to achieve accurate segmentation. For each point, we search in the 3D space within a certain radius to determine whether it belongs to a plane or not. Plane fragments are merged together at the last step of plane segmentation. In the obstacle detection stage, all the planes are removed from the point cloud. Then we use an area-growing based algorithm to extract point clusters and each point cluster is considered to be an obstacle.

4   Real-Time Plane Segmentation Algorithm PVP

3D point cloud contains much structural information that can be used for plane segmentation. However, the point cloud obtained from the Kinect has a large amount of data. So algorithms for point cloud are often time consuming. In this paper, we propose a novel two-step plane segmentation algorithm PVP that firstly applies a voxel-wise initial segmentation and then a pixel-wise refinement. The voxel-wise segmentation gives a rough but extremely fast result and then the pixel-wise refinement greatly enhance the accuracy. The combination of the two steps is a great balance between speed and accuracy.

4.1   Initial Plane Segmentation

Normally, plane segmentation algorithms would check each pixel of the image to determine whether this pixel can be classified to a certain plane. However, we find that in 3D point cloud, planes always consist of many flat pieces of points. These pieces have the same normal and are next to each other. Inspired by this idea, we construct voxel grid on the point cloud and let each voxel be the smallest unit to do initial plane segmentation. A voxel is a small 3D box containing several points as Fig. 2 shows. The side-length of the voxel used in our experiments is 20 cm. For each voxel, we use the least square estimation technique to estimate a plane equation that fits all the points in the voxel. Assume that the plane equation is $Ax + By + Cz + 1 = 0$, the least square estimation for A, B, C is

$$\begin{bmatrix} A \\ B \\ C \end{bmatrix} = \begin{bmatrix} \sum x_i^2 & \sum x_i y_i & \sum x_i z_i \\ \sum x_i y_i & \sum y_i^2 & \sum y_i z_i \\ \sum x_i z_i & \sum y_i z_i & \sum z_i^2 \end{bmatrix}^{-1} \begin{bmatrix} \sum x_i \\ \sum y_i \\ \sum z_i \end{bmatrix} \qquad (1)$$

where $(x_i, y_i, z_i), i = 1, 2, 3, ..., N$ represents a point in the voxel. It is an obvious result in analytic geometry that vector $[A\ B\ C]^T$ is exactly the normal of this plane. After calculating the plane equations for all the voxels, we use the normals to extract initial planes.

Plane segmentation can be treated as a clustering problem. However, if we directly cluster points in the 3D point cloud, the efficiency of the algorithm would not meet the demand of a real-time system. We notice that planes in point cloud consist of small flat pieces, and the pieces of the same plane have the same normal direction. After constructing voxel grid on 3D point cloud, each voxel actually is a piece of points. If the adjacent voxels have the same normal direction, they can be considered in the same plane. So we obtain all the clusters of voxels and in each cluster the normal direction of the voxels are the same. Finally if a voxel cluster is larger than a threshold, it is determined to be a plane. The detailed algorithm is described in Algorithm 1. The number of adjacent voxels is a parameter whose value is 26 in our experiments.

After these steps, we can get many voxel clusters. The cluster contains more than a certain number of voxels is considered as a candidate plane. The voxels

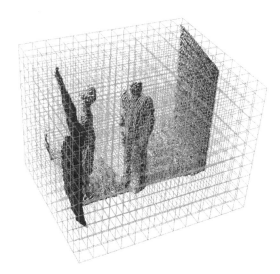

Fig. 2. Construct voxel grid on 3D point cloud

belong to a plane are called planar-voxel, and the remaining voxels are called non-planar-voxel. Points in all the non-planar-voxels should be accurately examined pixel by pixel in the refined segmentation. Furthermore, the voxel-wise plane segmentation is less sensitive to noise because several noise points would not influence the normal of a voxel.

4.2   Refined Plane Segmentation

After initial plane segmentation, we get several roughly segmented candidate plans. In order to obtain an accurate segmentation result, we check each point in the non-planar point cloud to determine whether it belongs to a certain existed plane. We know that if a point is on a plane, then the distance from the point to that plane is near zero. For each point, the distance between it and a candidate plane is calculated. If the distance is small, the point is considered belongs to that plane. However, comparing with every candidate plane is too global, neglecting the local structural restrictions. So we search the neighborhood of a point for candidate planes. And if there are planes near this point, then we just calculate the distance between the point and these neighbor planes to determine which plane the point belongs to.

More specifically, we traverse the voxels grid and find the voxels that haven't been clustered to a plane. Then we take one of these voxels as the center and search the space surrounding the center with radius r. In order to speed up the algorithm, we just search in a cube of side r cm and r is an integral multiple of the length of the voxel's side. If there are no planar-voxels near the center, then all the points in the central voxel are considered as non-planar points. Otherwise, if there are planar-voxels near the center, then for each point in the central voxel,

---

Algorithm 1. Initial Plane Segmentation

1: Traverse the voxel grid and find a voxel V_0 that hasn't been processed before. Calculate the average distance d of the points in V_0 to the estimated plane of V_0. If d is smaller than a threshold then create a queue Q and add V_0 to Q. Otherwise, find another V_0;

2: Examine each of the 26 adjacent voxels $V_i(i = 1, 2, ..., 26)$ surrounding V_0. If V_i hasn't been processed, then go on with the calculation. Let $n_i = (x_i, y_i, z_i)$ denote the normal of V_i and $n_0 = (x_0, y_0, z_0)$ denote the normal of V_i. Calculate the cosine of the angle of n_i and n_0 :

$$\cos\theta = \frac{x_i \cdot x_0 + y_i \cdot y_0 + z_i \cdot z_0}{|n_i| \cdot |n_0|} \tag{2}$$

If $|\cos\theta|$ is larger than a threshold, record V_i and V_0 belongs to the same plane and then insert V_i into Q;

3: Pick up an element from Q and regard it as V_0. Then return to step 2;

4: If Q is empty, return to step 1;

5: Repeat step 1 to step 4 until all the voxels are examined;

---

we calculate the distances between the point and every neighbor planar-voxel. The plane equation of each voxel has been calculated when we create the voxel grid, so we can directly use the result to calculate the distance. Let p denotes the coordinate of one point in the central voxel, V_{ij} denotes the ith planar-voxel in the neighborhood that belongs to plane P_j and the plane equation of V_{ij} is $Ax + By + Cz + 1 = 0$. Then the distance from p to V_{ij} is:

$$d_{ij} = \frac{|Ax' + By' + Cz' + 1|}{\sqrt{A^2 + B^2 + C^2}} \tag{3}$$

For each planar-voxel we recorded, the distance is calculated. Then we choose $d = \min d_{ij}$. If d is smaller than a threshold, then point p is considered a point in the corresponding plane P_j. Otherwise point p is a not a point in a plane. All the points in the central voxel are determined like this. After applying this process for all the non-planar-voxels, we can get a refined plane segmentation result.

After the fine segmentation, all the planes are segmented. However, some planes may be divided into several parts. So the planes actually belong to one big plane should be merged together. For each segmented plane, we estimate the plane normal based all the points that belong to the plane. If the angle of two normal directions of two planes is smaller than a threshold and the two planes are adjacent with each other, then they are merged as one plane and the new plane would replace these two planes. Repeat these steps until no plane can be merged with another. Fig. 3 presents an example of the result after accurate segmentation and plane merge.

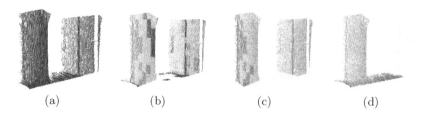

(a)   (b)   (c)   (d)

Fig. 3. An example of plane segmentation. (a) is the original point cloud. (b) shows the result of initial segmentation. Gray points represent the points that haven't been divided to a plane. And points are painted with color if they belong to a plane. (c) is the result of accurate segmentation. (d) is the result after plane merging.

5 Obstacle Detection

Plane segmentation is a fundamental technic and can be used in obstacle detection, scene segmentation, environment understanding and so on. We apply our plane segmentation algorithm PVP in an indoor obstacle detection system and it performs very well. The idea of our obstacle detection algorithm is that ground and walls are planes in indoor environment. Obstacles often lie on the ground or beside the walls. If the ground and walls can be removed, the remaining objects are all obstacles.

Following this idea, we propose an algorithm to detect obstacles in the point cloud. At first, all the planes are extracted using our plane segmentation algorithm PVP. Then we set a threshold to filter out large planes because they may be ground or walls in the scene, while the small planes could be the surfaces of desks or boxes. Next, the large planes are removed from the point cloud, so the remaining points are potential obstacles. To segment all the obstacles, we adopt an area-growing based algorithm. We do not directly cluster the points in the point cloud because it's too slow. Here we use the same idea as the initial segmentation of our plane segmentation algorithm. A voxel grid is created at first, and then we use the area-growing method to extract every voxel cluster. In area-growing, voxels are clustered if they are adjacent and both contain more than a certain number of points. The area-growing algorithm used for obstacle detection is different with that of the plane segmentation as the growing strategy is different. This technique can correctly handle weakly connected obstacles, preventing them to be clustered together. After area-growing, we can get several voxel clusters. All the points in voxels of the same cluster form an obstacle.

The method is simple and fast, which makes it very suitable for indoor navigation system or guiding system. Furthermore, as we detect obstacles in 3D environment, the size, direction and distance of each obstacle can be easily calculated. The above information can be used for automatic navigation of indoor robots or wearable guidance devices.

Fig. 4. Plane segmentation and obstacle detection results of three scenes. The first row is a sample of the corridor. The second is the classroom and the third is the office room. In each row, the first column is the original point cloud generated from depth images. The second column is the result of plane segmentation. Different planes are painted with different colors. The third column is the result of obstacle detection. Different obstacles are painted with different colors.

6   Experimental Results

We test the proposed algorithm on the dataset from[11]. The dataset is acquired from a Kinect mounted on a remotely controlled robot. The results have been measured over 30 depth images taken in 3 different scenes: classroom, office room and corridor. Each scene contains 10 images and totally 30 images. Firstly we use our algorithm to segment large planes like ground and walls. Then use the result to detect obstacles in the scene. Fig. 4 shows the results of plane segmentation and obstacle detection of each scene.

Our system is deployed on an Intel Core i7 2.0 GHz CPU laptop computer. The algorithms run sequentially on a single thread within a single core. As the detection rates would not be affected by the input image and the CPU we used is the bottom model of i7 series, which means our CPU would be no powerful than the CPU used in[9], we just take the result from[9] to make a comparison. The results are recorded in Table 1. Clearly our method achieves real-time processing at VGA resolution while Holz's method only runs at 7Hz under this resolution. When the image resolution reduced, our method also performs much better than Holz's method. Data shows that our algorithm is truly capable of real-time processing. And if we take advantage of multi-thread technique on multi-core CPU, the frame rate would be improved significantly.

A subjective evaluation is also conducted to quantitatively analyze the proposed algorithm. For each depth image, we label all the planes and obstacles in the image and then manually analyze the performance of our system according to the ground truth labels. In order to quantitatively measure the accuracy of our system, we calculate two commonly used benchmark recall and precision in our dataset. The results are presented in Table 2. The performance is related to the complexity of the scene. In complex scenes, there are less planar areas so that the plane segmentation results are bad and thus influence the performance of obstacle detection. It is clear that the scenes of the classroom and the corridor are simple and the scenes of the office room are complex. So it is natural that both the recall and precision are high in classroom and corridor. And for a more complex environment, like office room in our experiment, the performance is degraded.

Table 1. Frame rate of different resolution. The processing time of our method is measured and compared with Holz's method.

Image resolution	Holz's method	Our method
VGA(640 × 480 pixels)	7Hz	25Hz
QVGA(320 × 240 pixels)	27Hz	67Hz
QQVGA(160 × 120 pixels)	30Hz	130Hz

Table 2. Recall and precision of the system. For each scene, the recall and precision is calculated. And then the total results are given.

Scene	Plane segmentation		Obstacle detection	
	recall	precision	recall	precision
Classroom	100%	100%	100%	85%
Office room	90.91%	96.30%	97.83%	91.30%
Corridor	100%	100%	100%	92%
Total	97.18%	98.70%	98.94%	89.19%

7   Conclusion

In this paper, we propose a two-step plane segmentation method which is capable of real-time segmenting VGA resolution depth images. The depth image is converted into 3D point cloud and a voxel grid is created on it. Then we apply the voxel-wise initial segmentation on the voxel grid. Next, the pixel-wise accurate segmentation is used to refine the result. After plane segmentation, we use the result to implement obstacle detection in indoor environment. We implement the system on a laptop computer and conduct several experiments to evaluate the algorithms. The frame rate is measured and compared with another algorithm and the accuracy is quantitatively analyzed. The experimental result shows our method is fast and accurate. Thus, our system proves to be very suitable for indoor robots navigation or object avoidance systems, which require high efficiency. As an extension of this work, we are going to combine gray or color information acquired simultaneously from the Kinect to recognize detected objects.

Acknowledgments. The research work is supported by the National Nature Science Foundation of China No.60802067 and the Nature Science Foundation of Ningbo No.2012A610046.

References

1. Benavidez, P., Jamshidi, M.: Mobile robot navigation and target tracking system. In: International Conference on System of Systems Engineering (SoSE), pp. 299–304 (June 2011)
2. Izadi, S., Kim, D., Hilliges, O., Molyneaux, D., Newcombe, R., Kohli, P., Shotton, J., Hodges, S., Freeman, D., Davison, A., Fitzgibbon, A.: Kinectfusion: real-time 3d reconstruction and interaction using a moving depth camera. In: Proceedings of the 24th Annual ACM Symposium on User Interface Software and Technology, pp. 559–568 (2011)
3. Mann, S., Huang, J., Janzen, R., Lo, R., Rampersad, V., Chen, A., Doha, T.: Blind navigation with a wearable range camera and vibrotactile helmet. In: Proceedings of the 19th ACM International Conference on Multimedia, pp. 1325–1328 (2011)
4. Comaniciu, D., Meer, P.: Mean shift: a robust approach toward feature space analysis. IEEE Transactions on Pattern Analysis and Machine Intelligence, 603–619 (May 2002)
5. Felzenszwalb, P.F., Huttenlocher, D.P.: Efficient graph-based image segmentation. International Journal of Computer Vision, 167–181 (September 2004)
6. Zuliani, M., Kenney, C.S., Manjunath, B.S.: The multiransac algorithm and its application to detect planar homographies. In: International Conference on Image Processing, pp. 153–156 (2005)
7. Schwarz, L.A., Mateus, D., Lallemand, J., Navab, N.: Tracking planes with time of flight cameras and j-linkage. In: 2011 IEEE Workshop on Applications of Computer Vision (WACV), pp. 664–671 (2011)
8. Toldo, R., Fusiello, A.: Robust Multiple Structures Estimation with J-Linkage. In: Forsyth, D., Torr, P., Zisserman, A. (eds.) ECCV 2008, Part I. LNCS, vol. 5302, pp. 537–547. Springer, Heidelberg (2008)
9. Holz, D., Holzer, S., Rusu, R.B., Behnke, S.: Real-time plane segmentation using rgb-d cameras. In: RoboCup Symposium (2011)
10. Dub, D., Zell, A.: Real-time plane extraction from depth images with the randomized hough transform. In: IEEE International Conference on Computer Vision Workshops (ICCV Workshops), pp. 1084–1091 (2011)
11. Wolf, C., Mille, J., Lombardi, L., Celiktutan, O., Jiu, M., Baccouche, M., Dellandra, E., Bichot, C.E., Garcia, C., Sankur, B.: The liris human activities dataset and the icpr human activities recognition and localization competition. Technical report, LIRIS Laboratory (March 28, 2012)

Combining Textural and Geometrical Descriptors for Scene Recognition

Neslihan Bayramoğlu, Janne Heikkilä, and Matti Pietikäinen

Center for Machine Vision Research, University of Oulu, Finland
{nyalcinb,janne.heikkila,matti.pietikainen}@ee.oulu.fi

Abstract. Local description of images is a common technique in many computer vision related research. Due to recent improvements in RGB-D cameras, local description of 3D data also becomes practical. The number of studies that make use of this extra information is increasing. However, their applicabilities are limited due to the need for generic combination methods. In this paper, we propose combining textural and geometrical descriptors for scene recognition of RGB-D data. The methods together with the normalization stages proposed in this paper can be applied to combine any descriptors obtained from 2D and 3D domains. This study represents and evaluates different ways of combining multi-modal descriptors within the BoW approach in the context of indoor scene localization. Query's rough location is determined from the pre-recorded images and depth maps in an unsupervised image matching manner.

Keywords: 2D/3D description, feature fusion, localization.

1 Introduction

The scene recognition problem is widely studied in many research areas such as robot localization, path planning, similarity retrieval, matching and classification. In this study we focus on the indoor image matching problem in which the scene information is gathered from multi-modal (2D/3D) sensors. Today, extracting such information from real environments is rather effortless with the help of the new generation depth cameras and range scanners such as Kinect [1].

These RGB-D cameras, can acquire both color data (RGB) and the depth data in real dimensions. They have significant advantages compared to laser scanning devices: *i)* they can operate in real time (up to 30 Hz), *ii)* they are affordable, and *iii)* depth data is synchronized with the color information.

Unlike the Simultaneous Localization and Mapping (SLAM) [2] methods where the exact pose of the robot (position and orientation) is required and unlike the scene classification problems [3] in which semantics and categories are extracted, in this paper, scene recognition is regarded as determining a rough location (topological place) from the pre-recorded images and depth-maps associated with labels in an unsupervised image matching manner (Fig. 1). In this context, our main aim is to investigate the effects of local geometrical properties in scene recognition research. This study also represents different ways of combining textural and geometrical descriptors within the Bag-of-words approach.

A. Fusiello et al. (Eds.): ECCV 2012 Ws/Demos, Part II, LNCS 7584, pp. 32–41, 2012.

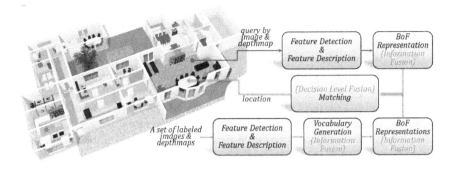

Fig. 1. Flowchart of the proposed method. Information fusion can be performed in different stages depending on the combination method.

1.1   Related Work

In literature, indoor scene matching is considered to be more challenging than the outdoor scene matching problem [4, 5] because outdoor scenes contain more discriminative and unique features leading to comparatively easy recognition. Besides, indoor scenes comprise many similar structures such as doors, windows, chairs, etc. Consequently, such images resemble each other in the global sense but can still contain local distinguishing patterns. The accuracy of this inspiration is testified by the state-of-the-art scene matching methods. Sivic and Zisserman [6] demonstrated efficiency of the region based descriptors within the Bag-of-words (BoW), or Bag-of-Features (BoF), approach for scene retrieval by making analogy between the text retrieval. After that, substantial amount of work adopted this BoF model for scene matching [2, 4, 5].

Until recently, vision based scene recognition methods were utilizing texture based features (2D) [4–7]. After the release of RGB-D cameras, 3D features have also started to be used for scene recognition purposes [8–11]. Ren et al. [8] utilized local 3D features together with texture based descriptors for supervised object classification. Similarly, Janoch et al. [9] applied histogram of oriented gradients (HOG) on depth maps for supervised object classification. However, they did not integrate depth features with the texture based ones. Browatzki et al. [11] also combined 2D features with 3D ones for supervised object categorization in which the objects are isolated and viewed from several angles.

The closest work to our study is described in [10]. While the main emphasis in their work is on the scene classification and segmentation with object labelling, they applied texture based descriptors onto the depth maps for scene classification. However, in this study, we are extracting several 3D features from the 3D point cloud representations instead of mapped 3D information (depth maps). We also demonstrate three different ways of combining 2D and 3D information for scene matching.

2 Theoretical Background

2.1 Bag-of-Words/Features

In the BoF approach there are three main steps: *i)* feature detection and description, *ii)* construction of visual vocabulary(dictionary), *iii)* matching. The main goal in the feature detection is to find keypoints holding significant information that are also robust across transformed versions of the image. A comparison of some of the interest point detection algorithms can be found in [12]. Feature descriptors which are usually represented as vectors carry local information in the neighbourhood of each keypoint. Scale Invariant Feature Transform (SIFT)[13] and Speeded Up Robust Feature (SURF) [14] are popular descriptors because of their accomplished performances. Visual vocabulary is built by clustering all the extracted features from a dataset of images. The selection of the number of clusters (k) is empirical, although it is critical. Obtaining BoF representation of database images is the next stage. First, features are extracted from an image. After that features are assigned to the closest cluster (word) in the vocabulary. Then, the count of each word that appears in the image is used to form the BoF representation of the image. When a query is placed, firstly the BoF representation is constructed. After that, the BoF representation of query image and the BoF representation of the database images are compared and matched.

2.2 Local 3D Features

Since the 3D object description has become popular during the last decade the number of research efforts is less than the 2D counterparts. In the shape analysis research, global description of 3D mesh models is popular. Still there exist local 3D feature detectors and descriptors. We refer the reader to Tangelder and Veltkamp [15] for a detailed survey.

Methods that rely on the global descriptors are usually utilized in similarity retrieval of 3D mesh models among the database of the same type, whereas local ones are employed in partial matching and point correspondences. There are two challenges regarding the 3D local descriptors. First one is the time complexity. Most of the 3D (or point cloud) descriptors rely on the normal vector information. The normal vector estimation step usually requires analysis of a covariance matrix. Besides, the nearest neighbourhood search or a similar strategy is utilized in finding the local neighbourhood of a keypoint which, if repeated many times, lead to high computation cost. The second and the critical challenge is the following: 3D local descriptors are considered to be less discriminative and far from being robust, since 3D shapes (surfaces) have insufficient features and keypoint repeatability is usually not satisfied [16].

In this study, we employed *spin images* descriptor which is one of the well-known local surface descriptors [17]. It is a two-dimensional histogram of the spatial distribution of neighbouring points around a keypoint (Fig. 2). Utilizing the keypoint's normal vector makes the descriptor rotation and translation invariant. However, *spin images* descriptor does not ensure the scale invariance.

We also utilized *D2 distributions* descriptor which is a simple yet an efficient descriptor. It is originally proposed as a global descriptor for 3D mesh model retrieval [18] and corresponds to the distribution of the Euclidean distances between object points that are selected randomly. The *D2 distributions*, which is also rotation and translation invariant, does not rely on the normal vector information, it is faster than the *spin images* descriptor. In addition to these descriptors, one could also use more sophisticated methods such as *Fast Point Feature Histograms* [19] for describing local geometry.

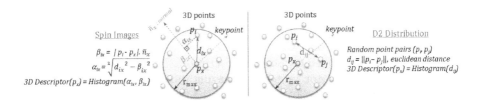

Fig. 2. Local 3D descriptors, *left*: spin images, *right*: D2 Distributions.

3   Combining 2D and 3D Features

Since RGB-D data is composed of two different modalities (texture and 3D geometry), there are several ways for extracting and also for combining this information. Table 1 shows straightforward ways of feature detection and feature description for RGB-D data. Feature detectors in 3D domain generally depend on the curvature information. Mapped data can be considered as 2D image in which the pixels represent a function value at the corresponding 3D location for the given geometry such as depth maps, shape index mapped images, etc.

Table 1. Feature Detection and Description for RGB-D Data

Feature Detection	Feature Description
2D Detector	2D Descriptor
3D Detector	3D Descriptor
Detection on mapped data	

The most critical point of feature detection is keypoint repeatability. We believe that keypoint repeatability is higher in 2D images than in the 3D domain. Therefore, in our tests feature detection is performed only on 2D images. We employed SURF as a feature detector. Also, in this study, we utilized only SURF features as the texture based descriptor, since the objective is not to optimize the performance of the 2D descriptors but to find the best way to combine the two types of descriptors.

After extracting information from the 2D and 3D representations, gathering them to obtain a single descriptor is the next stage. We employed following strategies to combine these descriptors: *i)* Point Description Fusion, *ii)* Scene Description Fusion, and *iii)* Decision Level Fusion.

3.1   Point Description Fusion

A keypoint can be described locally by its textural and geometrical properties if both the 2D image and the 3D information are available. These descriptors can be concatenated to form a single vector as is done in [10] and in [20]. In this type of fusion, keypoints should be selected from the single modality. Dense feature detectors can also be utilized; however, both (2D and 3D) descriptors should exist for each keypoint. Contrary to the previous studies, we carried out a normalization step before concatenating descriptors. Normalization is necessary if the 2D and 3D descriptor vectors are having different lengths and/or their order-of-magnitudes differs a lot. We propose the following normalization on the descriptor vectors f_k:

$$\mu[i] = \frac{1}{N} \sum_{k=1}^{N} f_k[i], \ \tilde{f}_k[i] = \frac{f_k[i]}{\sqrt{\frac{1}{N} \sum_{j=1}^{N} \sum_{l=1}^{n} \left(f_j[l] - \mu[l]\right)^2}}, \ i \in (1, 2, \ldots, n) \ (1)$$

where N is the total number of descriptors (2D/3D) obtained from the training set, n is the size of the descriptor vectors and $\tilde{f}_k$ is the normalized descriptor of point k. The final descriptor is then formed by scaling these normalized descriptor vectors by some constants φ and γ as in Fig. 3. These constants can be selected as $\varphi = 1$ and $\gamma = 1$ for equal contribution and also be adjusted if one of the modalities (2D/3D) is desired to have more influence on the description than the other. This normalization enables to concatenate point descriptors which are extracted from any means of modality.

Fig. 3. Final descriptor is a concatenation of normalized and scaled feature vectors which are obtained from texture and shape

3.2   Scene Description Fusion

Information fusion can also be done in the stage of scene representation (Fig 4). In this case, BoF descriptors that are separately obtained from textures and point clouds are concatenated. This configuration introduces the flexibility of choosing different number of clusters for 2D and 3D descriptors. Also keypoint detection can be performed in different modalities.

The algorithm makes two passes over the scenes: one-pass to construct the dictionary of 2D descriptors and second to obtain the dictionary of 3D descriptors. After that, each scene is described by two histograms obtained from the

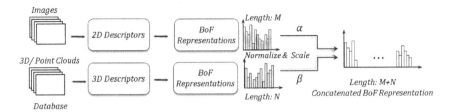

Fig. 4. Scene representations are combined after Bof Representations are extracted from 2D and 3D features seperately

BoF representations. We propose normalizing and scaling these individual BoF representations before concatenating. Histograms are normalized such that their sums are equal to one. Scaling histograms with some constants α and β is again necessary to compensate the effects of different vocabulary sizes and also for assigning weights to the description type (2D/3D) because individual description performances of 2D and 3D descriptors are different.

3.3   Decision Level Fusion

Decision level fusion is a common approach for combining classifiers [21]. A similar strategy can be employed in image matching methods. For combining the 2D and 3D information, we propose evaluating the BoF based indexing approach separately for 2D images and 3D point clouds. After the query is presented, images in the database are indexed (rank list) according to their similarity measures for both 2D and 3D. Then, using the ranked results of each modality re-indexing is utilized. The new criterion puts emphasis on the joint position on the ranked lists. That is, if the similarity score of an image (location) is higher in both the 2D similarity list and the 3D similarity list, then the probability of being the true location increases. We propose the new score of an image as a weighted combination of the individual scores:

$$score(image_k)_{2D/3D} = 1 - \frac{index_{k(2D/3D)}}{\#of images} \qquad (2)$$

$$score(image_k)_{combined} = w_1 \times score(image_k)_{2D} + w_2 \times score(image_k)_{3D}$$

where $index_k$ denotes the position of the $image_k$ in the similarity list and w_1 and w_2 are the weights. The ratio of the weights w_1 and w_2 can be tuned such that it can reflect the ratio of the matching performances of 2D and 3D descriptors. The highest scored image's label is returned as the location of the query.

4   Dataset and Experimental Results

Our dataset sampled from the publicly available dataset [10] consists of 1626 unique Kinect frames, spread over 64 different indoor environments. In the original dataset, *"Bookstore"* scenes have higher number of samples. We reduced this number since this may affect the fair evaluation of the methods. Fig. 5 represents a sample image from the dataset, corresponding raw depth map and the registered point cloud respectively. Table 2 gives a list of location types and the number of scenes belonging to that type. In our experiments, instead of using raw depths we utilized processed depth maps provided by [10].

Fig. 5. Sample image from the dataset, associated raw depth map and the registered point cloud respectively

Given a query we search for the closest image from the dataset depending on the distance measure. To evaluate the accuracy of descriptors all images are included in both test and training sets. Therefore the top match is always the query itself, we report recognition rates for the second match. *OpenCV*'s SURF implementation is employed in our experiments. The implementation of BoF stage is standard, built dictionaries using k-means clustering and hard assignment is utilized in feature mapping. We use the Fast Library for Approximate Nearest Neighbors *(FLANN)* also from the *OpenCV* library for ranking the image similarities. BoF representations are compared using L_2 norm. SURF generates feature descriptors of size 64, and in our implementation sizes for *D2 Distribution* and *spin images* are 16 and 100 ($\alpha \times \beta$) respectively. Originally *spin images* are 2D histograms, but we vectorized them for combination purposes.

Firstly, individual recognition rates are evaluated for 2D and 3D descriptors. The optimal cluster number k is decided by evaluating the recognition rates for different k values. Fig. 6 represents the recognition rate as a function of dictionary size. The SURF descriptor achieves the highest recognition rate at 87.57%, whereas *D2 Distribution* has a 72.44% and *spin images* has a 68.17% recognition rate at best. The highest recognition rate is achieved with 2D descriptor at dictionary size of 100, whereas it is 50 with the 3D descriptors. However, k is not the the only parameter which needs to be tuned. The local region size is another important parameter which affects the discriminative power of the 3D descriptors. For very small regions, 3D descriptors cannot convey significant information, since surfaces tend to change smoothly. On the other hand, if evaluation is performed on bigger regions, due to clutter and occlusion, descriptor may contain unrepeatable representation of a combination of different objects. Fig. 7 shows the relation between the recognition rate and the local region size. Both of the 3D descriptors achieved highest rates at 0.7 m with recognition rates of 72.44% with *D2 Distribution* and 75.46% with *spin images* descriptor.

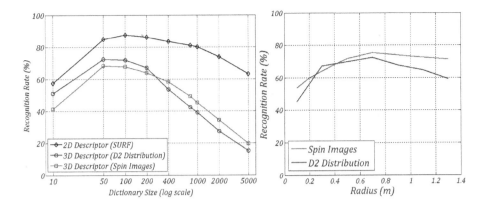

Fig. 6. Individual performances

Fig. 7. Effet of local region size

Table 2. Dataset Statistics

Place Type	Scenes
Living Room	13
Office	14
Kitchen	10
Bedroom	17
Bathroom	6
Book store	3
Cafe	1
Total	64

Table 3. Scene Description Fusion

	Recognition Rate (%)	
Parameters	SURF-D2	SURF-Spin
$(\alpha = 1, \beta = 1)$	85.17	87.27
$(\alpha = 1, \beta = 2)$	86.41	88.49
$(\alpha = 1, \beta = 4)$	**89.85**	**89.98**
$(\alpha = 1, \beta = 8)$	88.42	88.93

Table 4 gives the overall evaluation of the methods presented here. In combining the point descriptors, normalization constants are tuned as $\varphi = 2, \gamma = 1$ for *D2 Distribution* and $\varphi = 4, \gamma = 1$ for *spin images* descriptor with the dictionary size of 100. Dictionary sizes *(M/N)* for scene description fusion are 100 and 50 for 2D and 3D respectively. The normalization constants are tuned as $\alpha = 1, \beta = 4$ for both *D2 Distribution* and *spin images* descriptor (Table 3). In decision-level fusion, highest recognition rate is achieved with parameters $w_1 = 20$ and $w_2 = 1$.

Individual performances of 3D descriptors are lower than that of the 2D descriptor, since local 3D features are not as rich as 2D ones. After combining 2D and 3D features we obtained about a 6% improvement with the decision-level method. Other combination methods did not improve the recognition rates significantly. At first glance, one can expect that concatenated feature vector should describe a keypoint more precisely. However, some keypoints which own different texture descriptors may have same 3D descriptors (similar surface properties) and some other keypoints having similar textures may reside on different surfaces. Therefore, introducing 3D features decreases the discriminative power of the texture based descriptors for the former case, similarly 3D features will

Table 4. Overall Evaluation

Method	Recognition rates
2D only Description (SURF)	**87.57%**
3D only Description (D2-Distributions)	72.44%
3D only Description (Spin Images)	75.46%
Point Fusion, SURF/D2-Distributions	87.69%
Point Fusion, SURF/Spin-Images	86.28%
Scene Fusion, SURF/D2-Distributions	89.85%
Scene Fusion, SURF/Spin-Images	89.98%
Decision-Level, SURF/D2-Distributions	**93.54%**
Decision-Level, SURF/Spin-Images	93.41%

become less effective in the latter case. Besides, using single dictionary size also decreases the performance. Therefore, fusing scene descriptions that enables utilizing individual dictionaries in different sizes performs better.

5   Discussions and Conclusions

In this study, we proposed and evaluated integrating local descriptors of images and 3D data in the context of indoor scene localization. We proposed normalization methods which are necessary and critical in information fusion. Since the RGB-D data contains complementary information with depth maps and RGB, their combination always introduces improvements in recognition. In our dataset, images belonging to same location is captured at the same time with similar illumination conditions. As a result, 2D descriptors achieved a considerably high recognition rate by themselves. We believe that 3D information will be more effective for datasets containing high illumination variations among images. In that case, 2D descriptors will not be as successful as in our case. Since 3D descriptors are not affected from the illumination they would have better impact on the combined result. We can conclude that local 3D features enhance the performances of local 2D descriptors with proper combinations. However, depending on the application, the increased complexity introduced by 3D descriptor extraction and also by file I/O operations of 3D point clouds should be considered.

Acknowledgments. This work is supported by Infotech Oulu.

References

1. Microsoft: Introducing kinect for xbox 360, http://www.xbox.com/en-US/Kinect/
2. Cummins, M., Newman, P.: Fab-map: Probabilistic localization and mapping in the space of appearance. Int. J. Rob. Res. 27, 647–665 (2008)

3. Lazebnik, S., Schmid, C., Ponce, J.: Beyond bags of features: Spatial pyramid matching for recognizing natural scene categories. In: IEEE CVPR, pp. 2169–2178 (2006)
4. Kang, H., Efros, A.A., Hebert, M., Kanade, T.: Image matching in large scale indoor environment. In: IEEE CVPR Workshop on Egocentric Vision (2009)
5. Quattoni, A., Torralba, A.: Recognizing indoor scenes. In: IEEE CVPR, pp. 413–420 (2009)
6. Sivic, J., Zisserman, A.: Video google: a text retrieval approach to object matching in videos. In: IEEE ICCV, pp. 1470–1477 (2003)
7. Grauman, K., Darrell, T.: Efficient image matching with distributions of local invariant features. In: IEEE CVPR, pp. 627–634 (2005)
8. Ren, X., Bo, L., Fox, D.: Rgb-(d) scene labeling: Features and algorithms. In: IEEE CVPR (2012)
9. Janoch, A., Karayev, S., Jia, Y., Barron, J., Fritz, M., Saenko, K., Darrell, T.: A category-level 3-D object dataset: Putting the kinect to work. In: IEEE ICCV Workshops, pp. 1168–1174 (2011)
10. Silberman, N., Fergus, R.: Indoor scene segmentation using a structured light sensor. In: IEEE ICCV Workshop on 3DRR (2011)
11. Browatzki, B., Fischer, J., Graf, B., Bulthoff, H., Wallraven, C.: Going into depth: Evaluating 2D and 3D cues for object classification on a new, large-scale object dataset. In: IEEE ICCV Workshops, pp. 1189–1195 (2011)
12. Mikolajczyk, K., Tuytelaars, T., Schmid, C., Zisserman, A., Matas, J., Schaffalitzky, F., Kadir, T., Van Gool, L.: A comparison of affine region detectors. Int. J. Computer Vision 65, 43–72 (2005)
13. Lowe, D.G.: Distinctive image features from scale-invariant keypoints. Int. J. Computer Vision 60, 91–110 (2004)
14. Bay, H., Ess, A., Tuytelaars, T., Van Gool, L.: Speeded-up robust features (surf). Computer Vision Image Underst. 110, 346–359 (2008)
15. Tangelder, J.W.H., Veltkamp, R.C.: A survey of content based 3D shape retrieval methods. Multimedia Tools Appl. 39, 441–471 (2008)
16. Bronstein, A.M., Bronstein, M.M., Guibas, L.J., Ovsjanikov, M.: Shape google: Geometric words and expressions for invariant shape retrieval. ACM Trans. Graph. 30, 1–20 (2011)
17. Johnson, A.E., Hebert, M.: Using spin images for efficient object recognition in cluttered 3D scenes. IEEE Transactions on PAMI 21, 433–449 (1999)
18. Osada, R., Funkhouser, T., Chazelle, B., Dobkin, D.: Matching 3D models with shape distributions. In: IEEE Int. Conf. on Shape Mod. & App. (2001)
19. Rusu, R.B., Blodow, N., Beetz, M.: Fast Point Feature Histograms (FPFH) for 3D Registration. In: IEEE ICRA, pp. 3212–3217 (2009)
20. Tombari, F., Salti, S., Di Stefano, L.: A combined texture-shape descriptor for enhanced 3D feature matching. In: IEEE ICIP, pp. 809–812 (2011)
21. Kittler, J., Hatef, M., Duin, R., Matas, J.: On combining classifiers. IEEE Transactions on PAMI 20, 226–239 (1998)

Human-Centric Indoor Environment Modeling from Depth Videos

Jiwen Lu[1] and Gang Wang[1,2]

[1] Advanced Digital Sciences Center, Singapore
[2] Nanyang Technological University, Singapore

Abstract. We propose an approach to model indoor environments from depth videos (the camera is stationary when recording the videos), which includes extracting the 3-D spatial layout of the rooms and modeling objects as 3-D cuboids. Different from previous work which purely relies on image appearance, we argue that indoor environment modeling should be human-centric: not only because humans are an important part of the indoor environments, but also because the interaction between humans and environments can convey much useful information about the environments. In this paper, we develop an approach to extract physical constraints from human poses and motion to better recover the spatial layout and model objects inside. We observe that the cues provided by human-environment intersection are very powerful: we don't have a lot of training data but our method can still achieve promising performance. Our approach is built on depth videos, which makes it more user friendly.

Keywords: Scene understanding, environment modeling, human-centric, depth videos.

1   Introduction

In recent years, astonishing progress has been made in modeling indoor environments [1], [2], [3], [4], [5], [6], [7], [8], [9], [10], [11]. However, none of these work considers humans living in the room. They estimate spatial layout of rooms purely from image appearance, which turns out to be a challenging task. Indoor environments are essentially built for humans, to afford humans' daily activities. The interaction between humans and environments can help tell us the essential information of the environments. As shown in Fig. 1, from a person who is standing, we can roughly know where the floor plane is; from a person who is sitting, we can roughly know where the chair is. Based on these observations, we argue in this paper that modeling indoor environments should fully exploit the cues provided by human-environment interaction. And human-environment interaction is a long-term process because people interact with the rooms all the time. Suppose we have a sensor installed in the room, then the life-long process of human-environment interaction can provide us a huge amount of information to help accurately model the environments. Our current experimental results are based on videos which only last for several minutes. We believe the results will

A. Fusiello et al. (Eds.): ECCV 2012 Ws/Demos, Part II, LNCS 7584, pp. 42–51, 2012.

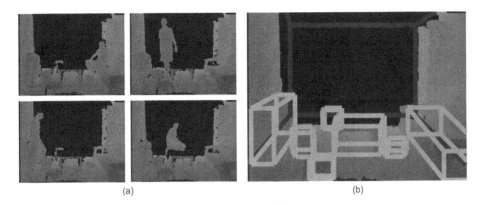

(a)   (b)

Fig. 1. Our approach extracts the spatial layout of a cluttered room and represents objects as 3-D cuboids in the environment from a depth video by exploiting information from human-environment interaction. (a) Four frames of an indoor environment depth video (the camera is stationary). (b) The modeling results.

be much more impressive if we record videos for several days or weeks, though which is beyond the scope of a "proof of concept" research paper.

Our work is based on depth videos recorded by the Microsoft Kinect sensor, different from previous work which is based on RGB images [1], [2], [3], [4], [5], [6], [7], [8]. There are two advantages of using the Kinect: 1) depth videos can better preserve the privacy information than RGB images/videos, which makes this technique easier to be accepted by the public; 2) depth images record the depth information, from which we can create a real 3-D model with more physical meanings. In this 3-D model, we can know how big an object is, how far between two objects, etc.

In this paper, we develop several methods to extract physical constraints from human poses and motion. For example, from a sitting pose, we estimate the support surface and know it must be from a sittable object. These constraints are effectively used in a statistical framework to help estimate the spatial layout of the environment and prune object hypotheses. We collect a number of depth videos with different types of human-environment interaction. The experimental results show that our method is very promising to solve this problem.

2 Overview of Approach

Given an indoor depth video (Fig. 2(a)), we estimate the spatial layout of the room and model objects insides as 3-D cuboids simultaneously. Our approach is illustrated in Fig. 2. Since the camera is stationary, the spatial layout of the room in each frame of the video is the same. Hence, we adopt the median filter [12] to recover the indoor scene background image (without humans inside) from the video (Fig. 2(b)). There are some missing values in the original depth images, we fill up each image by using a recursive median filter [13], [14]. We perform

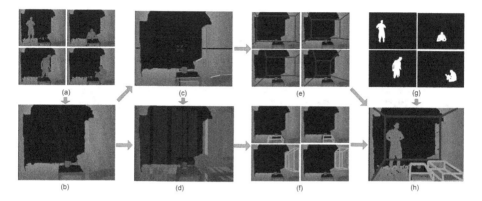

Fig. 2. Overview of our approach for indoor environment modeling. (a) Several frames in the depth video. (b) Indoor scene background image. (c) The detected long line segments and vanishing points of the scene background image. (d) Orientation map of the scene background image. (e) Room hypotheses generated from the vanishing points. (f) Object hypotheses generated from the orientation map. (g) Extracted human silhouettes for each frame of the depth video. (h) Spatial layout and objects modeled using the 3-D interactions between the room, objects, and humans.

line detection and vanishing points estimation on the scene background image (Fig. 2(c)). The vanishing points define the orientations of the major surfaces of the scene and provide constraints on its layout. Using these line segments and the vanishing points, we generate multiple room hypotheses (Fig. 2(e)) [15]. Moreover, we obtain the orientation map (Fig. 2(d)) from these line segments and vanishing points, and generate a number of object hypotheses (Fig. 2(f)). On the other hand, we subtract the scene background image from each frame of the depth video to obtain human silhouette (Fig. 2(g)). Then, we obtain human pose information in each frame and motion information over the whole video. Pose information is used to discover support surfaces, and motion information is used to discover objects. Finally, we test human-room-object compatibility and pick up the best compatible scene configuration over the whole video (Fig. 2(h)).

3   Generating Room and Object Hypotheses

A room hypothesis reflects the positions and orientations of walls, floor and ceiling. In this paper, we adopt the idea of [4] to represent the spatial layout of a room by a parametric model. Given a depth video, we first extract a scene background image by removing humans to generate room and object hypotheses. Fig. 2(b) shows the extracted indoor scene background image of the depth video. Following [4], we detect long line segments in the scene background image and find three dominant groups of lines corresponding to three vanishing points. By sampling pairs of rays from two of these vanishing points, we generate room hypotheses, and several of them are shown in Fig. 2(e).

One advantage of using depth images is that these room hypotheses can represent the 3-D geometry information, and each surface can be characterized by a plane in the 3-D coordinate system. Similar to [3], we represent objects as 3-D cuboids. We adopt the object hypothesis generation method in [3] by testing each pair of regions in the orientation map to check whether they can form convex edges. Fig. 2(f) shows four object hypotheses generated from the orientation map. Since there are a big number of hypotheses, we resort to human-environment interaction to select the best compatible scene configuration.

4 Human-Environment Interaction for Environment Modeling

We analyze human poses and motion to extract physical constraints to model the environment. While joint points of humans can be obtained by the SDK of Kinect, we find that the generated skeletons are still not stable to describe human poses for our environment modeling task because of mis-matching, scale change, and erroneous joint estimation. Hence, we adopt human silhouettes to extract human poses and motion information for indoor environment modeling.

4.1 Support Surface Estimation from Poses

Human poses are constrained by the environment. Humans have to be supported by stable surfaces. Hence, we can estimate support surfaces from human silhouettes. Having obtained the scene background image, we subtract it from each frame of the depth video to obtain human silhouette [12]. We apply two erosion and one dilation operations with a 3×3 template for each segmented human silhouette to remove noises and obtain one connected region [12]. Fig. 2(g) shows four segmented human silhouettes.

For each binary human silhouette image, we detect horizontal lines in the silhouette image and compute the length of each horizontal line. If the length is larger than a threshold L, we assume there is a support surface. In our experiment, L is set as 10. Given a horizontal edge line extracted from the silhouette image, suppose there are N_l pixels in the line and the 3-D coordinate of the ith point is $(X(u_i, v_i), Y(u_i, v_i), Z(u_i, v_i))$, where $1 \leq i \leq N_l$. We assume that the support surface P is parallel to the floor plane, then the plane equation of the support surface P can be written as $X = c$, where c is the parameter. We obtain c by solving the following optimization problem:

$$\min_c \sum_{i=1}^{N_l} \|X(u_i, v_i) - c\|_2^2 \tag{1}$$

Since there are some erroneous human silhouettes due to imperfect image segmentation, which may produce false positive surfaces, we only consider surfaces which are consistent in a sequence with at least N_T frames. In our experiments, N_T is set to 50.

Having estimated the support surfaces, we use them to generate constraints for indoor environment modeling. There are two types of surfaces that can be estimated: floor surfaces and object surfaces. For example, if the person stands or walks on the floor without occlusions, the estimated support surface should be the floor plane; if the person sits on a chair, the estimated surface should be the top surface of the chair cuboid. We differentiate different types of surfaces according to the aspect ration of the the human silhouette. Assume P_d be the floor surface and P_e be the eth object surfaces discovered from human-environment interaction. We exploit human-object and human-room interaction for environment modeling, as the constraints used in Eqs (8) and (9) in Section 5.

4.2   Object Discovery from Motion

Human motion also provides useful information for indoor environment modeling. For example, if human silhouettes are occluded by objects, we can localize these objects from the occluded silhouettes. Hence, we analyze human motion for object discovery.

We calculate the integral projections [16] of human binary silhouettes. For the tth human silhouette $I_t(u, v)$, we compute the horizontal integral projection (HIP_t) as follows:

$$HIP_t(u) = \sum_{v=1}^{wid} I_t(u, v)$$
(2)

Having calculated the HIP_t for the tth human silhouette $I_t(u, v)$, we detect the lowest row position u_t^{low} where $HIP_t(u_t) \geq 1$. The position u_t^{low} reflects the lowest position of the tth human silhouette $I_t(u, v)$. Now, we compute the absolute difference $D_t = |u_t - u_{t+1}|$ of u_t and u_{t+1} for two sequential frames, and determine the occlusion condition as follows:

1. If $D_t < \tau$, there is no occlusion change in the tth and $(t + 1)$th frames. In our experiments, τ is set to 10.
2. If $D_t \geq \tau$, there is an occlusion change in the tth and $(t + 1)$th frames. Specifically, if $u_t < u_{t+1}$, the person is occluded by some objects in the $(t + 1)$th frame and not occluded by the tth frame; otherwise, he/she is occluded by some objects in the tth frame and not occluded by the $(t+1)$th frame.

Having determined the image frames with occlusions, we detect an object surface in the environment. Assume the object rests on the floor, we can estimate the top surface of the object. This cue is used as a constraint in Eq. (9) in Section 5.

4.3   Human-Object and Human-Room Volumetric Reasoning

Humans must be compatible with objects and environment in terms of volume. Similar to [3], we perform human-object and human-room volumetric reasoning.

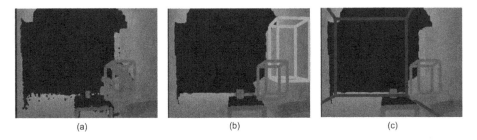

(a)   (b)   (c)

Fig. 3. An example to show how human-object and human-room volumetric reasoning can remove the incompatible object and room hypotheses. (a) The human cuboid obtained from human silhouette. (b) An incompatible object hypothesis that intersects with the human cuboid. (c) An incompatible room hypothesis which doesn't fully contain the human cuboid.

After obtaining the 3-D coordinate for each pixel of a human silhouette, we model the human as a 3-D cuboid. Ideally, the volumetric intersection between any object and the human cuboid should be empty. And the human cuboid should be fully contained in the free space defined by the walls of the room. With these two constraints, we can remove objects and room hypotheses which are incompatible with humans, as shown in Fig. 3.

5   Evaluating Environment Configurations

Given a depth video, we generate a set of room hypotheses $\{R_1, R_2, \cdots, R_N\}$, a set of 3-D object cuboid hypotheses $\{O_1, O_2, \cdots, O_K\}$, $R_n = \{F_1^n, F_2^n, \cdots, F_5^n\}$ defines the five faces [4], corresponding to the ceiling, left wall, middle wall, right wall, and floor of the nth room hypothesis, respectively. We also obtain the human silhouette for each frame. Our objective now is to find the best environment configuration, under which the spatial layout, objects, and humans are most compatible with each other. We find the best room hypothesis and object configurations which are most compatible with humans in the environment based on the following objective function:

$$\min_{R_n, Y} \sum_{i=1}^{5} \sum_{j=1}^{N_i} d(Q_{ij}^n, F_i^n) + \alpha \sum_{i=1}^{5} S(F_i^n, M) - \beta \sum_{k=1}^{K} Y_{O_k} \qquad (3)$$

$$s.t. \ C_1(O_k, O_l) \leq \delta_1, \forall k, l, \, and \, k \neq l \qquad (4)$$

$$C_2(O_k, F_i^n) \leq \delta_2, \forall k, i \qquad (5)$$

$$C_3(H_s, O_k) \leq \delta_3, \forall s, k \qquad (6)$$

$$C_4(H_s, F_i^n) \leq \delta_4, \forall s, i \qquad (7)$$

$$C_5(P_d, F_5^n) \leq \delta_5, \forall d \qquad (8)$$

$$Y_{O_k} = 1, if \ C_6(P_e, O_k^T) \leq \delta_6, \forall e, k \qquad (9)$$

where N_i denotes the number of pixels in the ith plane and it is zero if the ith face is missing in the the spatial layout of the room, $d(Q_{ij}^n, F_i^n)$ is the distance between the jth pixel and the ith plane of the nth room hypothesis, $S(F_i^n, M)$ denotes the inconsistency between the ith plane of the nth room hypothesis and the orientation map, α and β are two parameters to balance the scales of these two terms, and they were empirically set to 1000 and 1000 in our experiments. $C_1(O_k, O_l)$ denotes the volumetric intersection between the kth and the lth objects, $C_1(O_k, O_l)$ must be small (ideally, 0) if they are both present in the scene configuration. $C_2(O_k, F_i^n)$ denotes the volume of O_k (or a part of O_k) which is not contained by the plane F_i^n. Again, $C_2(O_k, F_i^n)$ must be small as an object should be contained by the room. We keep all the object hypotheses which don't violate volumetric constraints by maximizing $\beta \sum_{k=1}^{K} Y_{O_k}$. $C_3(H_s, O_k)$ denotes the volumetric intersection between the human cuboid estimated from the sth frame and the kth object hypothesis, $C_3(H_s, O_k)$ must be small if O_k is present. $C_4(H_s, F_i^n)$ denotes the volume of the human cuboid (or a part of the cuboid) which is not contained by the plane F_i^n. Similarly, $C_4(H_s, F_i^n)$ must be small for a valid room hypothesis R_n. $C_5(P_d, F_5^n)$ denotes the distance between the floor discovered from humans and the floor plane of the nth room hypothesis. This distance must be small for a good room hypothesis. $C_6(P_e, O_k^T)$ denotes the distance between the eth object surface discovered from humans and the top surface of the kth object hypothesis, and O_k should be present in the scene configuration if $C_6(P_e, O_k^T)$ is small enough. δ_1, δ_2, δ_3, δ_4, δ_5 and δ_6 are six parameters and empirically set to 300, 1000, 300, 1000, 5, and 2, respectively.

We first obtain the 3-D coordinate for each pixel and obtain the plane equations of F_i^n. Then, the distance $d(Q_{ij}^n, F_{ti})$ can be computed. On the other hand, we penalize inconsistency between the orientation map and room surfaces. A good room hypothesis's floor and ceiling should be parallel to the YOZ plane of the orientation map, left and right walls should be parallel to the XOZ plane of the orientation map, and the middle wall should be parallel to the XOY plane of the orientation map, respectively. We find our approach is insensitive to these parameters because there is usually a big difference between instances which obey these constraints and instances which violate these constraints. These parameters are not tuned on our test videos.

It is intractable to obtain a closed-form solution to the constrained optimization problem in Eqs. (3)-(9). To address this, we resort to using a fast greedy search method to obtain an approximate solution. Specifically, we first select the top C room hypotheses $R_{top} = \{R_1, R_2, \cdots, R_C\}$ with the smallest objective function values in the first two terms of Eq. (3). In our experiments, the parameter C is empirically set as 10. Then, we remove the false object hypotheses according to the constraints in Eqs. (4) and (5), and keep the positive object hypotheses according to the constraint in Eq. (9), respectively. For the remaining room and object hypotheses, we compute the number of frames which satisfy the constraints in Eqs. (6-(8) over the whole video and select the one which has the largest number of frames satisfying these constraints as the final room hypothesis. For a depth video with 300 frames, our algorithm can find the best

Table 1. Statistics of our dataset. NF: number of frames; RH: number of room hypotheses; OH: number of object hypotheses; NO: number of objects interacted with humans in the room. Note that only the objects with human-object interactions in the environments were considered in our experiments.

Dataset	NF	RH	OH	NO	Dataset	NF	RH	OH	NO	Dataset	NF	RH	OH	NO
Video 1	348	324	10	2	Video 2	423	324	10	2	Video 3	294	360	12	2
Video 4	331	360	66	2	Video 5	345	144	17	1	Video 6	344	144	17	1
Video 7	306	196	5	1	Video 8	264	324	32	1	Video 9	305	324	32	2
Video 10	344	252	19	2	Video 11	370	324	48	2	Video 12	511	324	16	2
Video 13	371	324	4	2	Video 14	277	252	28	1	Video 15	297	252	24	1

scene configuration in less than 3 minutes with unoptimized matlab code using an Intel Core 2.80GHz CPU.

6 Experimental Results

6.1 Dataset

We collect a new dataset for our experiments. We cannot collect a large-scale dataset because it is very hard to get permissions from many room owners. In our study, we test on 15 depth videos with resolution of 320×240. These videos are collected in 5 different rooms, and the camera is stationary. In each room, we capture 2-6 video clips by changing the viewpoint of the depth camera. In each video, there is one person moving (e.g., standing, sitting, walking) freely in the room. We have two different persons for these 15 videos. Table 1 tabulates some statistics of our dataset including the number of frames for each video, the number of room hypotheses, the number of object hypotheses generated in Section 2, and the number of objects. Some example frames are shown in Fig. 2(a).

6.2 Results

To show the advantage of using human-environment interaction, we consider two baselines: 1) Baseline 1: Environment modeling without human and object information, and 2) Baseline 2: Environment modeling using objects but without human information.

Qualitative Evaluation: Fig. 4 illustrates some qualitative results of Baseline 1, Baseline 2 and our approach of three rooms, which clearly shows the benefits of human-environment interaction: our approach can better extract the spatial layout of the rooms and model objects than the other two baselines.

Quantitative Evaluation: We also quantitatively evaluate the performance of our approach in estimating the spatial layout. For each depth video, we manually labeled the ground truth of the five planes (i.e., three walls, ceiling plane and

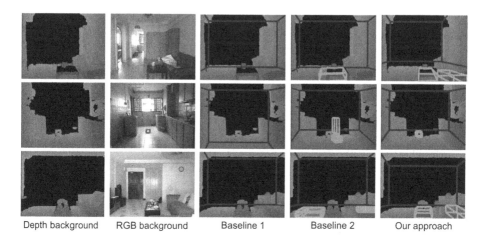

Depth background   RGB background   Baseline 1   Baseline 2   Our approach

Fig. 4. Qualitative results for our indoor environment modeling (best viewed in color). From top to down are the 1st, 5th, and 10th videos in our dataset, respectively. Our approach can better find the floors of the rooms (rows 1-2) and model objects in the environments (rows 1-3) than the other two baselines.

Table 2. Spatial layout estimation error (%) of different methods

Dataset	Video 1	Video 2	Video 3	Video 4	Video 5	Video 6	Video 7	Video 8
Baseline 1	37.14	37.14	29.93	36.06	39.39	39.01	38.18	34.27
Baseline 2	37.14	37.14	29.93	34.24	24.33	28.42	38.18	24.26
Our method	18.96	22.11	16.91	19.36	24.33	27.34	15.26	22.12

Dataset	Video 9	Video 10	Video 11	Video 12	Video 13	Video 14	Video 15	Average
Baseline 1	36.32	31.21	37.30	22.42	31.38	29.66	29.57	33.93
Baseline 2	25.65	31.21	28.46	22.42	24.56	29.66	29.57	29.68
Our method	22.12	21.44	22.64	19.15	22.32	21.61	24.36	21.34

floor plane) in the scene background image. We use the pixel-based measure introduced in [4] which counts the percentage of pixels on the room surfaces that disagree with the ground truth. Table 2 records the quantitative results on all these depth videos when different methods were applied. Our approach achieves an average error rate of 21.34%, while the performance number of Baseline 1 and Baseline 2 are 33.94% and 29.68%, respectively. The methods in [4] and [3] cannot be directly applied to our data because it is very hard for us to collect enough data to learn a structural model for scene configuration evaluations.

7   Conclusion and Future Work

In this paper, we have demonstrated the promise of exploiting human-environment interaction to model indoor environments. As a proof of concept research paper, our experiments are performed on short video clips. However, we believe much better results will be observed if we have videos for days or weeks, as more human-environment interaction information will be provided. In the near future, we are interested in applying this technique in realistic scenarios, such as hospital wards, nuring homes, etc.

Acknowledgment. This study is supported by the research grant for the Human Sixth Sense Program at the Advanced Digital Sciences Center from the Agency for Science, Technology and Research (A*STAR) of Singapore.

References

1. Hoiem, D., Efros, A., Hebert, M.: Recovering surface layout from an image. IJCV 75, 151–172 (2007)
2. Lee, D.C., Hebert, M., Kanade, T.: Geometric reasoning for single image structure recovery. In: CVPR, pp. 2136–2143 (2009)
3. Lee, D.C., Gupta, A., Hebert, M., Kanade, T.: Estimating spatial layout of rooms using volumetric reasoning about objects and surfaces. In: NIPS, pp. 1288–1296 (2010)
4. Hedau, V., Hoiem, D., Forsyth, D.: Recovering the spatial layout of cluttered rooms. In: ICCV, pp. 1849–1856 (2009)
5. Wang, H., Gould, S., Koller, D.: Discriminative Learning with Latent Variables for Cluttered Indoor Scene Understanding. In: Daniilidis, K., Maragos, P., Paragios, N. (eds.) ECCV 2010, Part IV. LNCS, vol. 6314, pp. 497–510. Springer, Heidelberg (2010)
6. Li, L., Socher, R., Fei-Fei, L.: Towards total scene understanding: classification, annotation and segmentation in an automatic framework. In: CVPR, pp. 2036–2043 (2009)
7. Gupta, A., Satkin, S., Efros, A., Hebert, M.: From 3d scene geometry to human workspace. In: CVPR, pp. 1961–1968 (2011)
8. Hedau, V., Hoiem, D., Forsyth, D.: Thinking Inside the Box: Using Appearance Models and Context Based on Room Geometry. In: Daniilidis, K., Maragos, P., Paragios, N. (eds.) ECCV 2010, Part VI. LNCS, vol. 6316, pp. 224–237. Springer, Heidelberg (2010)
9. Tsai, G., Xu, C., Liu, J., Kuipers, B.: Real-time indoor scene understanding using bayesian filtering with motion cues. In: ICCV (2011)
10. Delage, E., Lee, H., Ng, A.: A dynamic bayesian network model for autonomous 3d reconstruction from a single indoor image. In: CVPR, pp. 2418–2428 (2006)
11. Yu, S.X., Zhang, H., Malik, J.: Inferring spatial layout from a single image via depth-ordered grouping. In: CVPRW, pp. 1–7 (2008)
12. Lu, J., Zhang, E.: Gait recognition for human identification based on ica and fuzzy svm through multiple views fusion. Pattern Recognition Letters 28, 2401–2411 (2007)
13. Herbst, E., Ren, X., Fox, D.: Rgb-d object discovery via multi-scene analysis. In: IROS, pp. 4850–4856 (2011)
14. Lai, K., Bo, L., Ren, X., Fox, D.: A large-scale hierarchical multi-view rgb-d object dataset. In: ICRA, pp. 1817–1824 (2011)
15. Rother, C.: A new approach to vanishing point detection in architectural environments. Image and Vision Computing 20, 647–655 (2002)
16. Zhou, Z., Geng, X.: Projection functions for eye detection. Pattern Recognition 37, 1049–1056 (2004)

Human Daily Action Analysis
with Multi-view and Color-Depth Data

Zhongwei Cheng[1], Lei Qin[2], Yituo Ye[1], Qingming Huang[1,2], and Qi Tian[3]

[1] Graduate University of Chinese Academy of Sciences, Beijing 100190, China
[2] Key Lab of Intelli. Info. Process., ICT CAS, Beijing 100190, China
[3] University of Texas at San Antonio, TX 78249, U.S.A.
{zwcheng,lqin,ytye,qmhuang}@jdl.ac.cn, qitian@cs.utsa.edu

Abstract. Improving human action recognition in videos is restricted by the inherent limitations of the visual data. In this paper, we take the depth information into consideration and construct a novel dataset of human daily actions. The proposed ACT4^2 dataset provides synchronized data from 4 views and 2 sources, aiming to facilitate the research of action analysis across multiple views and multiple sources. We also propose a new descriptor of depth information for action representation, which depicts the structural relations of spatiotemporal points within action volume using the distance information in depth data. In experimental validation, our descriptor obtains superior performance to the state-of-the-art action descriptors designed for color information, and more robust to viewpoint variations. The fusion of features from different sources is also discussed, and a simple but efficient method is presented to provide a baseline performance on the proposed dataset.

Keywords: Daily action, Multi-View, RGB-D, Depth descriptor.

1 Introduction

Human action analysis has attracted sustaining attentions in computer vision community. Along with the huge demands in intelligent surveillance, advanced human-computer interaction and smart-house/e-monitoring, it inspires more and more interests to tackle practical problems by adopting action analysis techniques these years. Recognizing daily activities may have comparatively greater potential in real applications. To imagine if computers could promptly detect people's fall or correctly perceive the behavior of taking medicine, it would have significant merits for the digitized guardianship of the kids and olds. However, existing methods of modeling and understanding human daily activities are far from satisfactory in practical applications. The main challenges come from two aspects: 1) Traditional vision based approaches [1–4] depend on single data source of color cameras, which has inherent limitations and insuperable defects, such as illumination changes, looks and clothing variations, and cluttered background patterns. 2) Due to the viewpoint variations, which are common in real conditions, the observed actions have conspicuous intra-class diversities.

A. Fusiello et al. (Eds.): ECCV 2012 Ws/Demos, Part II, LNCS 7584, pp. 52–61, 2012.
© Springer-Verlag Berlin Heidelberg 2012

Introducing depth modality is likely helpful for action analysis, as motion characteristics are critical to represent actions and temporal depth data reflect the motion properties directly. Additionally, depth information has an advantage in privacy preserving, for that only distances between targets and sensors are captured (as visualized in Fig. 2). Therefore in this paper, we construct a multi-view action dataset with both color and depth sources. It focuses on human daily activities to innovate technology facilitating real applications. We also propose a novel method to represent actions utilizing depth information, and investigate the fusion of heterogeneous features from color and depth sources to present a baseline performance on the proposed dataset. Our contributions are two-fold:

1) We build a large dataset of human daily actions, which is well organized with multi-view and color-depth information.

2) We propose a new descriptor to represent depth information for action recognition, which is efficient and relatively robust to viewpoint changes.

The remainder of the paper is organized as follows. We introduce related work in Section 2. The construction of the $ACT4^2$ dataset is detailed in Section 3, and the new depth descriptor is proposed in Section 4. We present the experimental results and discussions in Section 5, and finally conclude the paper in Section 6.

2   Related Work

Some benchmark datasets have been published in the last decade, and they promote the development of human action analysis. In Table 1, we summarize some action datasets related to our work. The KTH [2] dataset is extensively used in action recognition domain, while it only contains simple and basic actions such as "running" and "waving". The IXMAS dataset [5] takes viewpoint changes into consideration and provides action frames observed from 5 views, but the action content is still about basic movements. Some relatively complex actions are presented in the Activities of Daily Living dataset (UR ADL) [6], which are semantic actions like "dialing a phone". The MuHAVi [7] is a large multi-view dataset for the evaluation of action recognition methods. All of above databases adopt only the conventional color cameras as data source. With the emergence of Microsoft Kinect, human action datasets employing depth information sprout in past two years. The dataset in [8] supplies the sequences of depth maps for actions focused on human-computer interaction in games. Furthermore, Sung et al. [9] construct a RGBD dataset for human activity detection and recognition in the living environment, and the RGBD-HuDaAct [10] is aiming to encourage application of assisted living in health-care. The last two are most related to our dataset, but there are clearly different emphases on activity categories and specific targets. More importantly, as shown in Table 1, the proposed $ACT4^2$ is the first multi-view RGBD human action dataset.

Action representations with traditional color information often exploit global features such as silhouettes or shapes [1], and local features like space-time interest points [3]. For the newly introduced depth information, there are also some similar methods proposed. Li et al. [8] sample 3D points from the depth maps

Table 1. Benchmark databases for human action recognition

Database	Data Source	Multi-View	Action Classes	Samples
KTH [2]	Color	No	6	2391
IXMAS [5]	Color	Yes	13	2340
UR ADL [6]	Color	No	10	150
MuHAVi [7]	Color	Yes	17	1904
MSR ADS[8]	Depth	No	20	4020
CU HAD [9]	Color+Depth	No	12	N/A
HuDaAct [10]	Color+Depth	No	12	1189
ACT4^2	Color+Depth	Yes	14	6844

within human contours, and propose a bag of 3D points representation to characterize the key postures in actions. Shotton et al. [11] present a human pose recognition method based on body part expressions, with predicting the body joints from single depth images. However, these pose-level representations may encounter problems of occlusions. When part of human body is shaded by background objects or occluded by other body parts, the observed representations become unstable and noisy. On the other hand, Zhang et al. [12] consider the actions of color and depth information as 4D hyper cuboids to extract local feature points. Ni et al. [10] employ local features from color space and utilize the depth as a reference channel in feature pooling. These two methods are straightforward extensions of local representations for color data, and therefore they are not very appropriate to capture the characteristics of depth information. In this paper, we design a novel comparative coding descriptor, aiming to extract inherent properties from the depth data.

3   The ACT4^2 Dataset

To break the bottleneck of existing action recognition approaches, we construct a new dataset. We aim to provide an infrastructure for investigating both color and depth information in human action analysis and handling action variations over viewpoints. Furthermore, we expect it to facilitate practical applications in real life, like smart house or e-healthcare. Consequently, the action categories in ACT4^2 mainly focus on the activities of daily living. Other than simple atomic movements as 'wave' or 'clap', these actions are complete activities with clear semantics in real life. For additional consideration of multiple views and indoor settings, we finally choose 14 actions: *Collapse, Drink, MakePhonecall, MopFloor, PickUp, PutOn, ReadBook, SitDown, SitUp, Stumble, TakeOff, ThrowAway, TwistOpen* and *WipeClean*. Intuitive samples of these daily activities are illustrated in the PNG figure in supplementary material. *Collapse* and *Stumble*, which are seldom introduced in previous datasets, are interesting activities especially for Homecare applications. *Collapse* stands for people falling by inner factors, such as hurt or giddiness, while *Stumble* means body dropping caused by outside effects such as tripped by an obstacle.

3.1 Data Acquisition

To simultaneously capture color and depth data from different views, we install four Microsoft Kinects which are connected to four computers respectively. These devices are placed in a common living room with different heights and diverse angles to the action area, as illustrated in Fig. 1. Totally 24 people are invited to perform each of the selected 14 activities several times. The recorded data are synchronized in the capturing procedure. For individual views, the frames from color and depth cameras are spatio-temporally aligned in pixel level by the Kinect drivers. Cross-view synchronization is achieved by the time stamps of frames. Although it would not assure precise frame-to-frame alignment, it can provide satisfying quality for cross-view action analysis. Finally, about 34 hours data are recorded with the resolution of 640 × 480 at 30 FPS, in the form of 8-bit 3-channel color images and 16-bit 1-channel depth images.

3.2 Data Preprocessing

Due to the mechanism of depth camera in Kinect, it will obtain zero value which may generate "black holes" in depth images, when the measure procedure fails. Especially, when four Kinects work simultaneously within the same area, the "black hole" effect is magnified as shown in Fig. 2(a), because of the interference of each other. To reduce its impact, we produce clean background depth images from the four viewpoints individually. Then all of the raw depth frames are refined by filling "black holes" with respect to the depth values at the same coordinates in adjacent frames and those background depth images. As shown in Fig. 2(b), the quality of processed depth data is improved obviously. Notice that the refinement is not to enhance but to restore depth data to the original quality which should be obtained by depth sensor individually.

Sequential data are segmented manually by labeling the start/stop points of single actions. With dropping the irrelevant interlude frames, complete action instances are extracted. The durations of action samples vary from seconds to tens of seconds. Finally, ACT4^2 contains 6844 action clips with both color and depth information, which are collected from 4 viewpoints. To the best of our knowledge, the proposed dataset is the largest multi-view color-depth human action dataset to date.

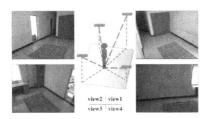

Fig. 1. The environment setting

Fig. 2. Depth data preprocessing. (a) is the raw frame; (b) is the refined frame

4   Depth Information Representation

Data captured by depth camera are spatial distances between targets and camera. Therefore, the spatial structure of targets is inherently embedded in depth information. We believe it provides complementary information to visual color data. Depth can be straightforwardly used as auxiliaries to improve foreground segmentation in color images, or quantization weights of ordinary color features. But focused on the characteristics of depth information itself, we propose a new descriptor to explore the embedded structural relations for action analysis.

4.1   Comparative Coding Descriptor

The new depth descriptor is designed to capture the spatial geometrical relations and related variations over time. For differences of values in depth images can properly reflect the relative distances between positions, and also inspired by the idea of comparative description in LBP [13], we propose Comparative Coding Descriptor (CCD) to represent the depth information for action analysis.

Depth data of an action instance is regarded as a spatiotemporal volume of depth values. Small cuboids can be extracted from the volume with selected reference points as centers. For action representation, the reference points can be chosen as salient points or spatiotemporal corners. Cuboid with size of $3 \times 3 \times 3$ is treated as atomic cuboid, based on which CCD feature is extracted. The value on the reference point is compared with that of the other 26 points respectively, and the differences are coded. The coding scheme is noted in Eq. 1,

$$\Psi(p_i) = \begin{cases} 1, & D(p_i) - D(p_r) \geq \gamma \\ -1, & D(p_i) - D(p_r) \leq -\gamma \\ 0, & else \end{cases} \tag{1}$$

where p_r denotes the reference point, and p_i is other point in cuboid, $i = 1, ..., 26$. $D(p)$ indicates the depth value of p, and γ is a comparison threshold. Then the 26 codes are sequentially composed to form the CCD feature vector, according to the order of a spiral line over the atomic cuboid.

Via describing the structure of the depth cuboid by sequential codes, CCD properly presents the spatiotemporal constraints within actions. Benefitting from coding with qualitative comparisons and preserving the neighborhoods, CCD could have some degree of robustness to perspective variation. Furthermore, it can be easily expanded by introducing a spatial scalar s and a temporal scalar t. To express every $s \times s \times t$ sub-cuboid with a single value, for example the mean value, the expanded $(3 \times s) \times (3 \times s) \times (3 \times t)$ cuboid can be converted to an atomic cuboid. Fig. 3 illustrates the generation of CCD features. Colored slices present depth frames over time, and the red dot presents the reference point. The coding scheme is demonstrated in the rightmost chart.

4.2   Distance Metric

CCD is in the form of sequential codes with values restricted to [-1, 0, 1]. To measure the similarity between CCD features, we design a corresponding

Fig. 3. Comparative Coding Descriptor. Blue cuboid on the left denotes the depth volume. The middle cuboid with green vertexes is the atomic cuboid for CCD extraction. The numbers in the right chart indicate the coding order. (best viewed in color).

distance metric. As defined in Eq. 2, this metric consists of two parts, considering both code pattern and sequential structure.

$$M(f_i, f_j) = \alpha_1 M_p(f_i, f_j) + \alpha_2 M_s(f_i, f_j) \qquad (2)$$

$f_i = (c_{i1}, ..., c_{in})$ is a CCD feature for the i-th reference point, c_{in} denotes the code at position n and α_1, α_2 are the weights of the metrics for code pattern (M_p) and sequential structure (M_s). The code pattern is measured by the consistency of the codes in different CCD features, which is defined as Eq. 3,

$$M_p(f_i, f_j) = \sum_{k=1}^{k=n} \|c_{ik} - c_{jk}\|_2 \qquad (3)$$

The sequential structure of CCD holds the spatiotemporal relations within action volumes. To consider this specialty in distance metric, the discrimination power can be well retained. We employ the first-order derivatives of the features to present the characters of their sequential structures, as formalized in Eq. 4, 5.

$$M_s(f_i, f_j) = M_p(\nabla f_i, \nabla f_j) = \sum_{k=1}^{k=n-1} \|d(c_{ik}, c_{i(k+1)}) - d(c_{jk}, c_{j(k+1)})\|_2 \qquad (4)$$

$$d(c_{ik}, c_{i(k+1)}) = \begin{cases} 1, & c_{ik} < c_{i(k+1)} \\ 0, & c_{ik} = c_{i(k+1)} \\ -1, & c_{ik} > c_{i(k+1)} \end{cases} \qquad (5)$$

5   Experiments

We evaluate the performance on ACT4^2 by considering color and depth modalities independently and jointly. All experiments are performed on a subset of the database for efficiency. With randomly choosing 2 samples per person per action from all 4 views, the subset consists of 2648 instances in total. 8 out of 24 persons' data are used for training, and the rest are for testing. Every experiment is performed 10 times by random sampling training set, and the average performance is reported. We adopt a popular, local feature based action recognition approach as the baseline method. It extracts action features based on the space-time interest points (STIP) [3], and then represent actions as histograms with the Bag of Visual Words (BoVW) method [4]. Finally, one-against-all Support Vector Machine is introduced for classification. With this broadly employed approach, we expect to present a baseline performance on ACT4^2 and demonstrate the characteristics of this dataset.

5.1   Color Information versus Depth Information

Color data provide visual appearance clues of actions, on the other hand, depth data supply the structural information. In this experiment, we extract local features from both modalities respectively, and evaluate their discrimination capabilities. The image sequences of actions are encoded into video clips. For depth data, the 16-bit images are firstly converted to 8-bit intensity images with min-max normalization. The detector in [3] is applied on the videos to generate STIPs. Then features of the Histograms of Oriented Gradients (HOG) and Histograms of Optical Flow (HOF) are extracted according to color and depth STIPs respectively. Codebooks are generated by k-means with varied size from 200 to 2000. As illustrated in Fig. 4, the recognition precision of features in depth is consistently superior to features from color data. It is interesting that with exactly the same recognition approach, the performance gap between depth and color features is beyond 10%. This reveals depth information is more effective than color data for presenting actions on ACT4^2 dataset. There might be two reasons: 1) It is more "direct" to get motion clues from depth data, so depth features are more accurate. Foreground location variations can be obtained immediately from the distance changes in depth maps. But for color data, motions are estimated implicitly with visual appearance matching. 2) Depth features are comparatively less noisy. The distance information in depth data is robust to environment variations. However, visual information in color data suffers from the appearance diversity. And inevitable consideration of unrelated visual clues also impacts the quality of color features.

5.2   Evaluation of Depth Descriptor

Depth information has shown inherent advantages for action recognition in the previous experiment. It motivates us to design a new depth descriptor to explore its distinct characters. And we evaluate the proposed CCD descriptor here. The STIPs extracted from depth videos are considered as the reference points. And we generate CCD features with s and t varying from 3 to 11. The used depth values are from original 16-bit depth images. To maintain the properties of CCD features, k-medoids clustering with the distance metric in Section 4.2 is adopted in codebook generation. The metric weights α_1 and α_2 are equally set to 0.5. Related experimental results are shown in Fig. 5.

The recognition precision is increasing with the spatiotemporal scales of CCD expanding, while the rate of increase is declining. This may be related to how the cuboid scale matches the movement range. Therefore, CCD provides a flexibility

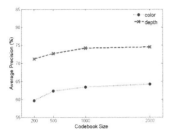

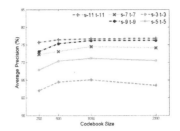

Fig. 4. Performance comparison of color and depth information

Fig. 5. Recognition performance of CCD features in various scales

to represent depth characteristics for different scales. The validity of CCD can be proved by comparing recognition performance with HOGHOF, which is a state-of-the-art descriptor for action recognition[14]. On depth data, HOGHOF achieves its best performance of 74.5% at k=2000, while CCD obtains superior performance of 76.2% at k=1000. It should be noted that dimension of CCD is only 26 and it requires simple calculation. In contrast, dimension of HOGHOF is 144 and it requires complex computing for gradients and optical flows. That is, CCD gains better performance with fewer dimensions and lower computation cost. This advantage may be attributed to the effective description of the motion structure in actions with depth information.

5.3   Action Recognition Fusing Two Modalities

Though the previous results suggest depth information is superior to color information in representing human actions, it should be beneficial to jointly use the features from the heterogeneous modalities. Color and depth actually present actions from different perspectives in essence. Thus a united representation can be enhanced with introducing broader characteristics. It is not trivial to fuse color and depth information in action recognition tasks. We have attempted a Cascade BoVW method with hierarchically clustering color and depth features in different levels, but its performance is disappointing.

Combining different feature vectors into a united vector is proved to be a valid method in existing works. For example, Spatial Pyramid Matching [15] concatenates features vectors from different pyramid levels. Thus in this paper, we adopt such idea and utilize a Super Feature Representation (SFR) to fuse features from the heterogeneous sources. For each action instance, the BoVW histogram vectors of different features are concatenated together and normalized. Additionally, we implement another fusion method, the DLMC-STIPs, with applying the same setting in [10]. The recognition performances of different approaches are shown in Table 2.

Comparing with HOGHOF features on color data, the performance gain of 16.3% is achieved by our SFR, whereas only 2.1% by DLMC-STIPs. This is probably because DLMC-STIPs just applies primitive combination by treating depth as a reference channel in color feature pooling, while we describe the characteris-

Table 2. Comparison of different features

Feature	Avg. Precision
Color-HOGHOF	64.2%
Depth-HOGHOF	74.5%
Depth-CCD	76.2%
DLMC-STIPs (SPM) [10]	66.3%
SFR	**80.5%**

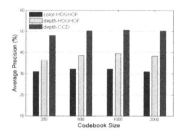

Fig. 6. Cross-view performances

tics of depth directly and fuse the discriminative features. Notice that although our fusion method is algorithmically simple, its efficiency and effectiveness are satisfactory. In addition, the performance of our fusion representation is superior to that of any single feature. This may indicate color and depth are complementary information for modeling human actions. To further investigate joint models over the heterogeneous feature spaces is promising for improving action analysis.

5.4   Cross-View Performance on ACT4^2

All previous experiments do not distinguish action samples from different views. In this section, we investigate the cross-view action recognition by choosing 2 views for training and the other 2 views for testing. The codebook generation and classifier construction are restricted to the training views. All 6 cases of train/test views combinations are evaluated, and the average of recognition precisions is reported. Fig. 6 shows the cross-view performances of different features.

Compare to previous results, the cross-view performance decreases by 25.4% for CCD, 31.9% and 35% for HOGHOF in color and depth data. The performance drop is reasonable, as the model trained on selected views is hard to handle the missing variations in other views. It should be pointed out that HOGHOF loses its half precision in cross-view evaluation, while CCD loses only one third. And CCD achieves its best performance of 50.8%, which is more than 11% superior to HOGHOF. These results show that CCD has a better robustness to the view variations. This advantage may be benefited from preserving the relative sequential restrictions in both feature description and distance metric.

6   Conclusion

In this paper, we construct a large multi-view and multi-source benchmark dataset of human actions. Both color and depth information is provided to innovate better action representations. We also propose a novel descriptor to depict the characteristics of depth information. The experimental results prove the effectiveness and efficiency of the proposed feature. With fusion of color and depth features, a baseline performance on the proposed dataset is demonstrated. In the future work, we plan to investigate representations for the joint space of color and depth information and action models adapting to viewpoint variations.

Acknowledgments. This work was supported in part by National Basic Research Program of China (973 Program): 2009CB320906, in part by National Natural Science Foundation of China: 61025011, 61035001, 61003165 and 61133003, and in part by Beijing Natural Science Foundation: 4111003.

References

1. Blank, M., Gorelick, L., Shechtman, E., Irani, M., Basri, R.: Actions as space-time shapes. In: ICCV 2005, vol. 2, pp. 1395–1402. IEEE (2005)
2. Schuldt, C., Laptev, I., Caputo, B.: Recognizing human actions: A local svm approach. In: ICPR 2004, vol. 3, pp. 32–36. IEEE (2004)
3. Laptev, I.: On space-time interest points. IJCV 64(2), 107–123 (2005)
4. Niebles, J., Wang, H., Fei-Fei, L.: Unsupervised learning of human action categories using spatial-temporal words. IJCV 79(3), 299–318 (2008)
5. Weinland, D., Boyer, E., Ronfard, R.: Action recognition from arbitrary views using 3d exemplars. In: ICCV 2007, pp. 1–7. IEEE (2007)
6. Messing, R., Pal, C., Kautz, H.: Activity recognition using the velocity histories of tracked keypoints. In: ICCV 2009, pp. 104–111. IEEE (2009)
7. Singh, S., Velastin, S., Ragheb, H.: Muhavi: A multicamera human action video dataset for the evaluation of action recognition methods. In: International Conference on Advanced Video and Signal Based Surveillance, pp. 48–55. IEEE (2010)
8. Li, W., Zhang, Z., Liu, Z.: Action recognition based on a bag of 3d points. In: CVPRW, pp. 9–14. IEEE (2010)
9. Sung, J., Ponce, C., Selman, B., Saxena, A.: Human activity detection from rgbd images. In: AAAI Workshop on PAIR (2011)
10. Ni, B., Wang, G., Moulin, P.: Rgbd-hudaact: A color-depth video database for human daily activity recognition. In: IEEE Workshop on Consumer Depth Cameras for Computer Vision in conjunction with ICCV (2011)
11. Shotton, J., Fitzgibbon, A., Cook, M., Sharp, T., Finocchio, M., Moore, R., Kipman, A., Blake, A.: Real-time human pose recognition in parts from single depth images. In: CVPR, vol. 2, p. 3 (2011)
12. Zhang, H., Parker, L.: 4-dimensional local spatio-temporal features for human activity recognition. In: IROS, pp. 2044–2049. IEEE (2011)
13. Ahonen, T., Hadid, A., Pietikäinen, M.: Face Recognition with Local Binary Patterns. In: Pajdla, T., Matas, J. (eds.) ECCV 2004. LNCS, vol. 3021, pp. 469–481. Springer, Heidelberg (2004)
14. Wang, H., Ullah, M.M., Klaser, A., Laptev, I., Schmid, C.: Evaluation of local spatio-temporal features for action recognition. In: BMVC 2009 (2009)
15. Lazebnik, S., Schmid, C., Ponce, J.: Beyond bags of features: Spatial pyramid matching for recognizing natural scene categories. In: CVPR 2006, vol. 2, pp. 2169–2178. IEEE (2006)

Viewpoint Invariant Matching
via Developable Surfaces

Bernhard Zeisl, Kevin Köser, and Marc Pollefeys

Computer Vision and Geometry Group
ETH Zurich, Switzerland
{zeislb,kkoeser,pomarc}@inf.ethz.ch

Abstract. Stereo systems, time-of-flight cameras, laser range sensors and consumer depth cameras nowadays produce a wealth of image data with depth information (RGBD), yet the number of approaches that can take advantage of color and geometry data at the same time is quite limited. We address the topic of wide baseline matching between two RGBD images, i.e. finding correspondences from largely different viewpoints for recognition, model fusion or loop detection. Here we normalize local image features with respect to the underlying geometry and show a significantly increased number of correspondences. Rather than moving a virtual camera to some position in front of a dominant scene plane, we propose to unroll developable scene surfaces and detect features directly in the "wall paper" of the scene. This allows viewpoint invariant matching also in scenes with curved architectural elements or with objects like bottles, cans or (partial) cones and others. We prove the usefulness of our approach using several real world scenes with different objects.

1 Introduction and Previous Work

Utilizing image based features to compactly describe image content or to identify corresponding points in images has become a de facto standard in computer vision over recent years. Applications where a feature based approach proved particularly successful are for example structure-from-motion, image registration, visual SLAM systems or object detection and recognition. However, a major problem when trying to find correspondences between widely separated views is that the appearance of objects can change drastically with viewpoint. To remedy this problem techniques have been developed which normalize images or image regions such that they become (at least approximately) invariant to viewpoint changes. In case one matches two images (without depth information) against each other the most popular method is to use local image features that compensate for the first order effects of viewpoint change by normalization, i.e. affine transformations (cf. to [1,2]) or slightly weaker models (e.g. [3]). Since scale, orientation and (anisotropic) stretch are all effects that could have been caused by a viewpoint change they need to be factorized out and therefore it is not possible to distinguish, e.g. real-world circles from ellipses or a small round dot from a huge sphere any more. This is a general dilemma of discriminative power

A. Fusiello et al. (Eds.): ECCV 2012 Ws/Demos, Part II, LNCS 7584, pp. 62–71, 2012.

Fig. 1. Examplary objects and their developed surfaces. To normalize wrt. viewpoint changes we propose to detect and describe features in the unrolled surface textures rather than in the original images.

vs. invariance. For an in depth discussion of invariant feature constructions we refer the reader to [4].

When depth information is available one can normalize wrt. the given 3D structure. In [5,6] the authors have shown that it is possible to virtually move a camera to a frontal view and then render a canonical representation of a local image feature. Similarly, normalization can also be obtained by extracting vanishing points in Manhattan scenarios [7,8] and virtually rotating the camera. However, all these approaches have strong limitations: While [5] still requires an affine detector and thus the number of features obtained is limited, other approaches [6,7,8] rely on the existence of dominant scene planes. In contrast to this assumption we observe that many structures in our environment are also curved, e.g. like cylinders, cones or consist of free-form shapes. Many man-made objects are made by bending sheets or plates and thus - by construction - form *developable surfaces* that can virtually be "unrolled" when their geometric structure (depth) is known (see Fig. 1). For the particular application of pose-robust face recognition, Liu and Chen [9] coarsely approximate a human head via a 3D ellipsoid and back-project images onto its surface. Recognition is then conducted in the flat, but stretched and distorted texture maps. In comparison, we are interested in objects possessing developable surfaces and by this allow to create an undistorted texture map.

Further, in this work we follow the idea to develop such observed scene surfaces and to extract image features in the flat 2D wall-paper version of that very same surface, allowing for less invariant (and more discriminative) detectors/descriptors. In case scale is known (e.g. from a Kinect camera) the affine or perspective invariance requirement of the original problem is reduced to rotation in the image plane and can be reduced even further for surfaces such as cones or cylinders. We strongly believe that this technique is useful in several applications such as robotic scenarios, where a robot has to identify and manipulate an object, for automatically registering overlapping 2.5D or 3D models or loop detection in large structure-from-motion or SLAM systems.

The paper is organized as follows: Developable surfaces are discussed in Sec. 2, while Sec. 3 presents our algorithmic approach and Sec. 4 states implementation details. In Sec. 5 we illustrate experiments and results on both, data from active and passive consumer depth sensors, followed by concluding remarks.

Fig. 2. Developable surfaces present in our environment. Note, that in the left image only cones are highlighted although planes and cylinders exist as well.

2 Developable Surfaces

As our approach builds on the notion of developable surfaces, we start by briefly introducing the underlying concept. In general a surface with *zero* Gaussian curvature at every surface point is developable [10] and can be flattened onto a plane without distortion (such as stretching or shortening).

To determine the Gaussian curvature of a surface, suppose we are given a smooth function s that maps 2D parameters u, v to points in 3D space, i.e. $s : \mathbb{R}^2 \to \mathbb{R}^3$ such that $s(u, v) = (x, y, z)^T$. The graph S of this function is a two-dimensional manifold and our surface of interest in 3D space. The derivatives $s_u = \frac{\partial s}{\partial u}$ and $s_v = \frac{\partial s}{\partial v}$ of s with respect to the parameters u and v define tangent vectors to the surface at each point. Their cross product yields the normal vector $n = s_u \times s_v$ to the surface. The second partial derivatives of s with respect to u, v are now used for constructing the shape operator

$$II = \begin{pmatrix} L & M \\ M & N \end{pmatrix} = \begin{pmatrix} n^T s_{uu} & n^T s_{uv} \\ n^T s_{uv} & n^T s_{vv} \end{pmatrix}, \tag{1}$$

which is also called the second fundamental form of s. The principal curvatures κ_1, κ_2 of the surface at a given position are defined as the eigenvalues of II. They measure how the surface bends by different amounts in different directions at a particular point. Finally, the determinant $\det(II) = \kappa_1 \kappa_2$ denotes the Gaussian curvature; in case it vanishes everywhere on the surface (at least one of the eigenvalues is zero) the surface is developable. The intuition is that in direction of zero curvature the surface can be described as a line. Hence, the surface development is just an unrolling of all corresponding lines into one plane. We refer the interested reader to [10] for more details.

For example a cylinder is developable, meaning that at every point the curvature in one direction vanishes. Its mean curvature is not zero, though; hence it is different from a plane. Contrary, a sphere is not developable, since its surface has constant positive Gaussian curvature at every point. Other basic developable shapes are planes, cylinders, cones and oloids[1] and variants thereof, such as cylindroids, or oblique cones. Intuitively, they are flattened by rolling the object on a flat surface, where it will develop its entire surface. In fact, all surfaces which

---

[1] An oloid is defined as the convex hull of two equal disks placed at right angles to each other, so that the distance between their centers is equal to their radius.

are composed of the aforementioned objects are developable as well. In practice, many objects in our environment are made by bending sheets or plates and thus form developable surfaces. Fig. 2 illustrates several real-world developable surfaces; note that even such complex structures as the church roof top (Fig. 2 very right) are (piece-wise) developable.

3 Exploiting Developable Surfaces for Viewpoint Invariant Matching

In the following we present our approach of matching two views of a rigid scene, separated by a wide-baseline, by means of developable surfaces. However, we point out that the same techniques are applicable for identifying and recognizing a single object in a database, for loop detection or for automatically registering multiple overlapping textured 3D models. As input to our algorithm we assume two RGBD images with sufficient overlap. Given pixel-wise depth measurements $d_{u,v}$ and camera intrinsics K a 2.5D point cloud is obtained per view via

$$(x, y, z)_{u,v}^{\mathrm{T}} = K^{-1}(u, v, 1)^{\mathrm{T}} d_{u,v} \quad \forall u, v \in I, \tag{2}$$

with image coordinates u, v. Then our method progresses in four steps, which are (a) detection and parameter estimation of certain developable surfaces in the depth data, (b) generating flat object textures by means of developing the detected surfaces, (c) detecting/describing features in the unrolled images (i.e. in the surface) and matching against the other views, and (d) verification of found correspondences. We will explain them in more detail in following Sec. 3.1 to 3.4.

3.1 Multi-model Estimation

As described in the previous Sec. 2, many different developable surfaces exist. In this paper we focus on three basic shapes, the plane, the cylinder and the cone, because these shapes possess a low parametric representation and thus are detected reliably in depth data. Identifying these surfaces falls into the category of multi-model estimation and several techniques have been suggested to cope with it, including randomized hough transform, sequential RANSAC or more recently J-Linkage [11], multi-structure segmentation [12] or more problem-specific machine-learning inspired geometric classification approaches in the spirit of [13].

3.2 Developing Surfaces

Subsequent to the initial model estimation and parameterization is the generation of a flat texture per detected model. We describe obtained mappings for principal geometric shapes in the following.

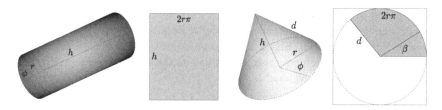

Fig. 3. (left) Cylinder with height h and radius r and its developed texture of dimensions $h \times 2\pi r$. (right) Cone with height h and radius r and its developed texture with radius d. Note that angles ϕ around cone axis and β in developed texture differ by $\frac{r}{d}$ and thus a 360 turn of the cone does not describe a full circle.

Planes. From the previous model estimation (Sec. 3.1) we know a four parameter description $\pi_S = (\mathbf{n}^T, d)$ with normal vector $\mathbf{n}$ and distance to the origin d, as well as a bounding box (or mask) for the region of interest on the 3D plane. Two orthogonal vectors $\mathbf{u}, \mathbf{v}$ in the plane are chosen as a basis $\mathcal{B}_S$ and we sample the plane in equidistant steps, i.e. we define a grid in the plane. Original image plane π_I and surface plane π_S together with the origin of $\mathcal{B}_S$ define a unique mapping $\mathbf{P}$. It is used to project each of the grid vertices (u_i, v_j) into the original image to obtain the appropriate color. The resolution is chosen such that we do not lose any image details; this means we project the four bounding box corners into the original image and evaluate the Jacobian matrix of the texture warp for some arbitrary grid resolution. Afterwards we increase or decrease the grid resolution such that the smallest minification between the developed surface and the original image is 1 (for details on texture mapping see [14]). In practice the transformation $\mathbf{P}$ will be a homography and the result is equivalent to [6]. Here, the frontal view of the plane coincides with the developed plane, however we will now generalize this to other developable surfaces.

Cylinders. After model detection a cylinder is parameterized as $(\mathbf{c}, \mathbf{a}, r)$ with cylinder base center $\mathbf{c}$, axis vector $\mathbf{a}$ of length h and radius r. In order to unroll the cylinder we represent 3D points on the surface in their cylinder coordinates (r, ϕ, z) (with $\mathbf{c}$ as the origin). By removing the radius coordinate we obtain a 2D parameterization (ϕ, z) of the surface. The projection of surface points into the image plane π_I is thus defined by a unique mapping $\mathbf{P}$. The angular resolution in ϕ is determined to match the resolution along the cylinder axis and to obtain an image of aspect ratio $h \times 2\pi r$ for a full 3D development of the cylinder (see Fig. 3). In case scale is known (e.g. when a Kinect camera is used) and when it is desirable not to normalize over scale (e.g. because of similar features at different scales) we choose a metric surface resolution. Otherwise, we evaluate the local magnification/minification between the original image and the surface texture and ensure that no resolution is lost during unrolling. Given 2D coordinates (ϕ_i, z_j) in the unrolled surface texture, each corresponding 3D surface point (r, ϕ_i, z_j) is identified and projected into the original image via $\mathbf{P}$

to obtain the color. This mapping is very efficiently implemented on the GPU or using standard backward mapping on the CPU.

Cones. A cone is parameterized and developed very similarly to the cylinder, taking into account that the surface tappers smoothly towards the apex. To obtain a flat surface texture, it is positioned with a line from the apex to the base circle of length $d = \sqrt{r^2 + h^2}$ (see Fig. 3) in the plane for development (imagine laying it on a piece of paper). Afterwards the apex is fixed and the cone rolled around it, resulting in a circle segment. The created circular texture contains the apex in the center, where the radial lines connect the apex with the cone's base circle (consequently of radius d, up to resolution). Thus 2D texture coordinates (β_i, d_j) are directly related to points on the cone surface. Similar to the cylinder, we backward map texture coordinates across the 3D surface into the original image to obtain the colors for the surface texture, maximizing its resolution.

3.3 Feature Detection and Matching

Feature detection is performed directly in the unrolled textures. This is conceptually different to [1,5] which first detect features and then try to normalize these wrt. to viewpoint variations. It is related to [6,7,8], however these approaches only consider planes for normalization. The unrolled textures allow to reach perspective invariance with only normalizing in-plane rotation in the image (or similarity normalization in case absolute scale is unknown). Even better, since cylinder[2] and cone define an inherent reference direction with their axis, all features can be expressed with respect to this orientation rather than computing an orientation from the local region as for example in SIFT [3]. Consequently it is possible to extract very basic features on the surface, which is very fast on the one hand and on the other hand allows to distinguish local regions that differ only by scale, orientation or linear shape. All detected features on the different developed textures are combined to form the set of features for a RGBD image and are subsequently used for wide-baseline matching.

3.4 Correspondence Verification

Naturally the set of estimated matches contains numerous outliers, which do not satisfy the underlying camera pose change. Therefore, correspondences are checked using geometric verification (e.g. using RANSAC). As observed in [6], each feature does not only include information about the 3D position, but also the local normal. Additionally, when orientation is known from the cylinder or cone geometry or when local orientations are estimated from gradients [3], three characteristic directions are known at each 3D feature point. This allows for a stratified verification as in [6] or for a minimal solution in RANSAC that requires only a single correspondence.

---

[2] For the cylinder there is still a $180°$ ambiguity for the direction of the axis.

4   Implementation Details

We employ RANSAC to obtain model parameters for planes, cylinders and cones in the captured RGBD data. Since surfaces are mostly local and continuous we utilize a local sampling strategy, where consecutive samples are drawn within a 0.5m radius. Surface models are searched for in order of increasing complexity, i.e. initially planes are detected, followed by cylinders and cones. We limit the size of models to physically plausible extents for the expected outdoor or indoor environments. In addition, found models need to guarantee that they show sufficient support over their surface to avoid algorithmic plausible, but incorrect estimations. Consequently, we reject models whose support is only defined at isolated points or clusters. Once detected, we robustly determine the model size in the image and estimate the spatial extent (e.g. height of cylinder). Subsequently, initial model parameters are updated via a non-linear optimization on the evaluated inlier set. After each iteration 3D points supporting the estimated model are removed from the search space, which prohibits assignment to multiple models. This iterative procedure terminates as soon as no model with sufficiently large support is found any more.

As mentioned in Sec. 3.3, image feature estimation in the developed surfaces can be accomplished with a basic detector such as a Harris corner detector. However, since we aim to compare obtained matches from developed surfaces with matches in the original RGBD data, we chose standard SIFT as our detector and descriptor to guarantee comparability. (Note, that employing upright-SIFT would also treat our approach with favor due to its greater discriminative power.) Detected image features are matched against each other in their descriptor space. To eliminate ambiguous matches (e.g. between repetitive structures) all best matches are kept for which the distance ratio to the second best match falls below 0.6 (known as the ratio test in [3]). Then, each feature is additionally augmented by its position in 3D space, which is determined by the corresponding 3D surface model (according to the derived mappings in Sec. 3.2). For features in the original RGBD images we consider present pixel-wise depth measurements and neglect them in case no depth is available, e.g. due to occlusions.

To obtain a robust estimate of correct matches, we employ a correspondence rejection method via RANSAC, which samples from the feature correspondence set and estimates a 6 DoF transformation between the two views. Since correspondences between 3D points are explicitly defined, we utilize Procrustes analysis [15] (and do not need an iterative non-linear optimization scheme) for the estimation of rotation and translation. Finally, the estimated transformation is validated on all potential correspondences, which gives a final set of correct and consistent matches. These consistent matches are visualized in the different experiments presented in the following.

5   Results for Active and Passive Stereo Devices

In this section we demonstrate our novel technique for different scenes and cameras. Fig. 4, Fig. 5 and Fig. 6 illustrate obtained results for a synthetic setup,

Fig. 4. Wide baseline matching for a synthetic setup. (top row) Outer left and right image illustrate the found models in the 2.5D point cloud; images in-between show developed textures. (bottom row) SIFT matches consistent wrt. the underlying 6DoF transformation between the initial RGBD images and between developed surfaces.

Table 1. Quantitative comparison of SIFT descriptor matches between original RGBD images and developed surfaces for different scenes

Scene type	Synthetic setup	Floor (Kinect)	Table (Kinect)	Trees (stereo)	Pylon (stereo)
Matches orig. RGBD images	37	9	27	3	56
Matches developed surfaces	255	79	195	22	227
Enhancement ratio	6.89	8.78	7.22	7.33	4.05

indoors scenes captured with a Kinect camera and outdoor scenes taken with a Fuji3D stereo camera, respectively. Rectified textures of detected planes are not illustrated due to space limitations; though, they are included in the evaluation.

Comparing feature detection and matching in the original images and in the images of developed surfaces (see Tab. 1) we can record the following: While approximately the same number of features are detected and an equal amount of potential matches is obtained, evaluation shows that for the latter the amount of finally remaining *correct* matches is significantly larger. Between the original RGBD images many potential matches are wrong due to viewpoint distortions in the descriptor space and thus need to be rejected. This validates that our approach of viewpoint invariant description of developable surfaces is able to extract features, which are stable over a variety of largely different viewpoints and improves wide-baseline matching considerable. In addition, rather than interpreting our approach as a competitor to standard feature matching, one should see it as an additional cue for obtaining more stable features.

6   Conclusion and Future Work

We have presented a novel technique to exploit depth information for viewpoint invariant matching between RGBD images. It develops the surface and detects features in the surface's wall paper which removes perspective effects. While

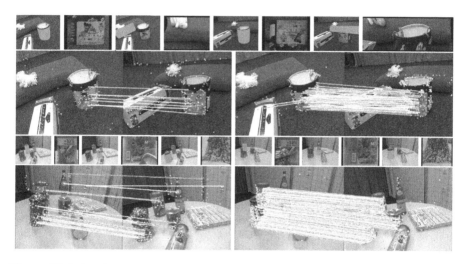

Fig. 5. Wide baseline matching for RGBD data captured with a Kinect sensor (Floor and Table scene). (1st and 3d row) Detected objects (green) and their respective developed surface for the two views. (2nd and 4th row) Consistent SIFT matches between original images and developed surfaces, respectively.

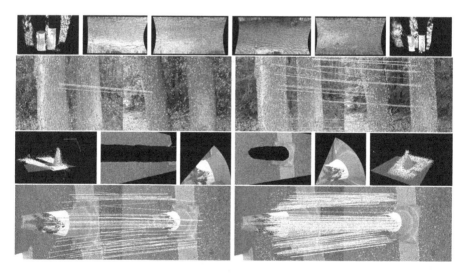

Fig. 6. Wide baseline matching between images taken by a Fuji3D consumer stereo camera (Trees and Pylon scene). (1st and 3rd row) Detected models in the 2.5 point cloud and their respective developed surfaces. (2nd and 4th row) SIFT feature matches between original scenes and developed surfaces, respectively. Note, that for the bottom experiment depth estimates are noisy and contain a considerable amount of errors, leading to degraded parameter estimation for the detected cone.

we have shown drastically increased number of matches as compared to classical SIFT, the feature detector can actually be chosen freely for the given application. Scale can easily be integrated (when known from the range sensor) to allow for using simple and more discriminative features such as Harris corners and in the special case of cylinders and cones even in-plane rotation is known. In any case, while we have demonstrated the approach as a competitor that outperforms standard SIFT by far, it should be clear that both can easily be combined for a real system. Compared to earlier viewpoint normalization approaches that relied on global scene planes we have shown that many other geometric shapes are feasible and demonstrated this using cones and cylinders. Possible further work will include the extension from detectable parametric surfaces to flattening of general (approximately developable) surfaces.

References

1. Mikolajczyk, K., Tuytelaars, T., Schmid, C., Zisserman, A., Matas, J., Schaffalitzky, F., Kadir, T., Van Gool, L.: A Comparison of Affine Region Detectors. IJVC 65(1-2), 43–72 (2005)
2. Mikolajczyk, K., Schmid, C.: A Performance Evaluation of local Descriptors. IEEE Trans. Pattern Anal. Mach. Intell. 27(10), 1615–1630 (2005)
3. Lowe, D.G.: Distinctive Image Features from Scale-Invariant Keypoints. IJVC 60(2), 91–110 (2004)
4. Van Gool, L., Moons, T., Pauwels, E., Oosterlinck, A.: Vision and Lie's Approach to Invariance. Image and Vision Computing 13(4), 259–277 (1995)
5. Köser, K., Koch, R.: Perspectively Invariant Normal Features. In: ICCV, Workshop on 3D Representation and Recognition (2007)
6. Wu, C., Clipp, B., Li, X., Frahm, J.M., Pollefeys, M.: 3D Model Matching with Viewpoint-Invariant Patches (VIP). In: Proc. CVPR, pp. 1–8 (2008)
7. Robertson, D., Cipolla, R.: An Image-Based System for Urban Navigation. In: Proc. BMVC, pp. 819–828 (2004)
8. Cao, Y., McDonald, J.: Viewpoint Invariant Features from Single Images using 3D Geometry. In: Workshop on App. of Comp. Vision, pp. 1–6 (2009)
9. Liu, X., Chen, T.: Pose-robust Face Recognition using Geometry Assisted Probabilistic Modeling. In: Proc. CVPR, vol. 1, pp. 502–509. IEEE (2005)
10. Kuehnel, W.: Differential Geometry: Curves - Surfaces - Manifolds. American Mathematical Society, Providence (2006)
11. Toldo, R., Fusiello, A.: Robust Multiple Structures Estimation with J-Linkage. In: Forsyth, D., Torr, P., Zisserman, A. (eds.) ECCV 2008, Part I. LNCS, vol. 5302, pp. 537–547. Springer, Heidelberg (2008)
12. Wang, H., Chin, T.J., Suter, D.: Simultaneously Fitting and Segmenting Multiple-Structure Data with Outliers. IEEE Trans. Pattern Anal. Mach. Intell. 34(6), 1177–1192 (2012)
13. Rusu, R., Holzbach, A., Blodow, N., Beetz, M.: Fast Geometric Point Labeling using Conditional Random Fields. In: Proc. IROS, pp. 7–12. IEEE (2009)
14. Heckbert, P.S.: Fundamentals of Texture Mapping and Image Warping. Technical report, U.C Berkeley (1989)
15. Eggert, D., Lorusso, A., Fisher, R.: Estimating 3-D Rigid Body Transformations: A Comparison of Four Major Algorithms. Machine Vision and Applications 9(5), 272–290 (1997)

A Unified Energy Minimization Framework for Model Fitting in Depth⋆

Carl Yuheng Ren and Ian Reid

Oxford University, Dept. Engineering Science, Parks Road, Oxford, OX1 3PJ, UK
{carl,ian}@robots.ox.ac.uk

Abstract. In this paper we present a unified energy minimization framework for model fitting and pose recovery problems in depth cameras. 3D level-set embedding functions are used to represent object models implicitly and a novel 3D chamfer matching based energy function is minimized by adjusting the generic projection matrix, which could be parameterized differently according to specific applications. Our proposed energy function takes the advantage of the gradient of 3D level-set embedding function and can be efficiently solved by gradients-based optimization methods. We show various real-world applications, including real-time 3D tracking in depth, simultaneous calibration and tracking, and 3D point cloud modeling. We perform experiments on both real data and synthetic data to show the superior performance of our method for all the applications above.

1 Introduction

Since the recent release of consumer-priced video-rate depth sensors, there has been an explosion in the field of tracking[1], 3D reconstruction [2] and object recognition [3], etc. using depth data. A large proportion of these works use a model-based paradigm; i.e. given an object model, try to align a known object model with the observed depth map.

Model-based approaches generate model hypotheses and evaluate them on the available visual observations, defining an objective function that measures the discrepancy between the visual cues that are expected from a model hypothesis and the observed ones. Based on how the optimization of this objective is performed, we can define two categories of methods: sampling based solvers and gradient-based solvers.

Sampling based solvers [1,4] rely on many evaluations of energy function at arbitrary points in the multidimensional model hypothesis space. The authors of [1] solve the energy minimization problem using a variant of Particle Swarm Optimization (PSO). The GPU implementation of the their method yields near real-time performance (15Hz). Another recent work in this category is by Ryohei Ueda [4], which formulates a very similar energy function to [1]. The energy functions in both works [1,4] above measure the discrepancy between the expected depth generated by pose hypothesis and the real depth. In Ryohei Ueda's work

---

⋆ This work is funded by REWIRE project under the 7-Framework Programme.

A. Fusiello et al. (Eds.): ECCV 2012 Ws/Demos, Part II, LNCS 7584, pp. 72–82, 2012.

[4], a particle filter is used for for solving the optimization. Methods in this category usually require extensive computational power, because evaluation of the energy function online is usually computationally expensive.

Gradient-based solvers try to use the depth image gradient to guide the search for the best hypothesis in the high dimensional hypothesis space. Iterative Closest Point (ICP) [5] framework is the most commonly used method in this category. Temporary point correspondences between an observed point cloud and the known model are established by finding the nearest neighbor for each vertex on the object model, and the resulting sum of pair-wise square-distance based energy function is differentiated with respect to model hypothesis parameters. Using the depth image gradient in this way can yield much more efficient optimization with many fewer energy function evaluations. However, establishing point correspondences can be as computational expensive as energy function evaluation. Furthemore, the depth image gradients are often very noisy, thus they can not be used without smoothing or resolution hierarchy.

This paper presents a unified energy minimization framework for model fitting problems in depth. Instead of projecting the model down to the image plane and measuring the discrepancy between expected image cues and the observed ones, the depth images permit us to back project all observed pixels into the object coordinate, where a level-set embedding function is defined to encode the object model implicitly. Our formulation of energy function is a natural extension to the chamfer-matching based tracking method [6] in 2D. This proposed method has the following advantages over existing model based approaches:

1. The search can be solved efficiently using a gradient-based solver, but instead of relying on the noisy gradient of the depth image, our method takes advantage of the smooth gradient of level-set embedding function to guide the search. Furthermore, for a given level-set embedding, the per-voxel gradients are independent of the pose parameters, and can therefore be computed in advance for computational efficiency (for objects with constant shape).

2. Instead of "rendering" the model into each image, which would require z-buffering or other means to determine depth order, our method back projects the depth pixels into the object coordinate frame, aiming for alignment with the zero-level of the level-set embedding function. Thus no z-buffer is required and the method is inherently more suitable for the parallelization on a GPU.

3. Our framework is a region-based method, so no point correspondences are required. As we show in subsection 3.2, our framework can, for example, be used for calibrating the intrinsic parameters of a depth camera without the need to establish any point correspondences (manually or automatically).

2   Notation

Let I_d be a depth image obtained from the depth camera, and the depth image domain denoted by Ω. Without lose of generality, a pixel at (u, v) in the depth image is has homogeneous coordinates $\mathbf{x} = [ud, vd, d]^T \in \Omega$ with explicit depth d. A depth point $\mathbf{x}$ in the projected image region of the object is projected from a 3D object surface point $\mathbf{X} = [x, y, z, 1]^T$ in the object frame as:

$$\mathbf{x} = P\mathbf{X} \tag{1}$$

where P is a 3×4 projection.

An object model is implicitly represented by a 3D level-set embedding function Ψ defined in the object coordinate frame. The surface of an object can be recovered from the zero-level of the level-set embedding function i.e. $\Psi(\mathbf{X}) = 0$. The value of Ψ increases monotonically in space as a point moves further from the nearest surface of the object model. The most convenient form of Ψ is thus the 3D distance transform Φ, which we use to formulate variants of Ψ for different applications.

3   Energy Function

Given that a pixel in the projected object region of the depth image is projected from a 3D point on the object model surface, its value in object coordinates $\mathbf{X}$ can be obtained exactly via back-projection from $\mathbf{x}$.

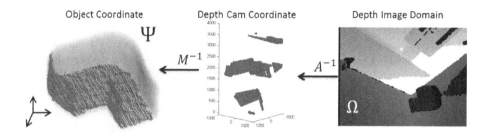

Fig. 1. Example of our back-projection formulation, from left to right: all pixels on the depth image are first unprojected into depth camera coordinate by intrinsic matrix A, then inverse transformed by extrinsic matrix M into the object coordinate, where the level-set embedding function is defined.

If the projection matrix P is correctly recovered, all depth pixels $\mathbf{x}$ in the object region should be back-projected onto the model surface $\Psi(\mathbf{X}) = 0$. Fig. 1 showcases an example of formulating such projection by the simplest pinhole model, which decomposes P into an intrinsic (calibartion) matrix A and extrinsic (pose) matrix M. Our base energy function is defined as:

$$E = \sum_{\mathbf{x} \in \Omega} \Psi(\mathbf{X}) \tag{2}$$

Thus an evaluation of the energy function comprises back projecting all the pixels in the depth image into the local coordinate of the object and summing the corresponding values in the level-set embedding function. As discussed above, a convenient form of embedding function is a distance transform, though more specifically we use a truncated distance transform since points that back-project outside the local volume of the object are assigned a nominal "large" distance value. In this way, the pixels in the object region are automatically segmented from the background and the whole energy function will take minimum value when the model is aligned with the depth point cloud.

3.1 Tracking Rigid 3D Objects

The first and simplest application of this energy function is to track rigid 3D objects in depth. Assuming known object model (encoded in 3D distance transform Φ), we formulate the level-set embedding function Ψ using German-McClure object function, which is robust to outlier pixels in the object region:

$$\Psi = \frac{\Phi^2}{\Phi^2 + \sigma} \tag{3}$$

where σ is a constant parameter to determine the width of the energy function. The projection matrix P can be decomposed into intrinsic matrix A and 3×4 extrinsic matrix M: $P = AM$. Assuming calibrated camera (i.e. A known), P is parameterized only by the pose of the object p, we differentiate the energy function w.r.t. p

$$\frac{\partial E}{\partial p} = \sum_{x \in \Omega} \frac{2\sigma\Phi}{(\sigma + \Phi^2)^2} \frac{\partial \Phi}{\partial \mathbf{X}} \frac{\partial \mathbf{X}}{\partial p} \tag{4}$$

Where $\frac{2\sigma\Phi}{(\sigma+\Phi^2)^2} \frac{\partial \Phi}{\partial \mathbf{X}}$ is the gradient of the level-set embedding function, which could be computed in advance. We use Levenberg-Marquardt method to compute the step at each iteration then use local frame to update the pose:

$$\tilde{p} = -\left(J_E^T J_E + \alpha \mathbf{diag}\left[J_E^T J_E\right]\right)^{-1} \frac{\partial E}{\partial p} \tag{5}$$

$$M_n \leftarrow \tilde{M}(\tilde{p}) M_{n-1} \tag{6}$$

where J_E is the Jacobian matrix of the energy function. The automatic step-size controlling parameter α decreases when a step causes the energy function to decrease and increases when energy function increases.

3.2 Simultaneous Tracking and Calibration

When the intrinsic matrix A and the extrinsic matrix M are both unknown, the projection matrix P is parameterized by both the intrinsic parameters $k = [fx, fy, cx, cy, kc]$ and pose p. We formulate the level-set embedding function using square energy function, and then we differentiate the energy function w.r.t the joint intrinsic-pose parameter $\lambda = [k, p]$:

$$\Psi = \Phi^2, \quad \frac{\partial E}{\partial \lambda} = \sum_{x \in \Omega} 2\Phi \frac{\partial \Phi}{\partial \mathbf{X}} \frac{\partial \mathbf{X}}{\partial \lambda} \tag{7}$$

Note that the reason that we use the square energy function instead of German-McClure robust object function for simultaneous calibration and tracking is that square energy function provides better convergence around the true value of intrinsics and fewer local minima when optimizing in the joint intrinsic-pose parameter space. Also, we assume that when users try to calibrate a camera using our method, the frames that are captured have few outliers in the object region. Again, we use Levenberg-Marquardt method to obtain the optimal intrinsic parameter k and pose p at each frame and form an estimate via weighted least squares using all values up to frame t:

$$\hat{k} = arg_k \max \left\{ \sum_{i=1}^{t} (k - k_i)^T \Sigma_i^{-1} (k - k_i) \right\} \tag{8}$$

where Σ_i is the covariance of intrinsic parameter k at frame i, and is approximated by the inverse of the Hessian.

3.3 Point Cloud Modeling with Adaptive Primitive Models

In this application, we use our energy function to model a point cloud with adaptive primitive object models (spheres, cylinders and cones, etc.) with unknown size. Given the intrinsic parameters and each object class, our energy function can fit shape primitives into a point cloud with correct scale. Assuming the scale of object model is along x, y, z axis in object frame, P is decomposed:

$$P = AMS, \quad S = \begin{bmatrix} s_x & 0 & 0 & 0 \\ 0 & s_y & 0 & 0 \\ 0 & 0 & s_z & 0 \\ 0 & 0 & 0 & 1 \end{bmatrix} \tag{9}$$

where S is the scaling matrix. Now the 3D point $\mathbf{X}$ is a function of both the 3D pose p and the scaling parameters $[s_x, s_y, s_z]$, We optimize the energy function w.r.t. the joint parameter $\lambda = [s_x, s_y, s_z, p]$. We follow the same optimization method in 3.2 to jointly recover the pose of the object and its size. For multiple frames, we use weighted least squares as in Section 3.2 to estimate the scale.

4   Experiment and Evaluation

We tested our energy function on the three applications we introduced above. The performance of our energy function is evaluated both quantitatively and qualitatively for the application of tracking rigid 3D object and stimulations calibration and tracking. We also showcase the real world result of our energy function for the application of point cloud modeling. The initial poses of the objects are manually initialized in the following experiments, but motion detection and object recognition algorithms can also be used for automatic initialization.

Fig. 2. Film strips showing our algorithm successfully tracking a real rigid object through heavy occlusion. The upper row shows the observed depth sequence, while we show the tracking result on the lower row.

4.1   Tracking Rigid 3D Object

We have tested our energy function for tracking rigid 3D object on various real-world sequences, Fig 2 shows an example of using our energy function to track an real object with heavy occlusion. As is shown, even when more than half of the object is occluded by hand, the tracker still did not lose track. This is because our method back projects the depth point on the image into object coordinate and use the gradient of the level-set embedding function to guide the search for the best pose. In this way, our energy function is naturally robust to occlusion and missing data: as long as the back-projected points encodes sufficient information of the location of the object, our method can converge correctly.

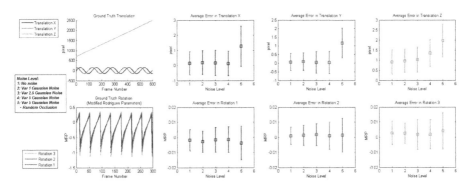

Fig. 3. Quantitative evaluation of the precision and robustness of our method for tracking 3D rigid object on synthetic data, with respect to different level of noise and occlusion. The error in translation is measured in pixel while rotation is measured in modified rodrigues parameters.

Because it is very difficult to evaluate the performance of 3D rigid object tracker without ground truth data, we use known model to generate synthetic depth sequences and run our tracker on such sequences to evaluate the precision and robustness of our energy function for tracking 3D rigid objects. As is shown in Fig. 3, we generated synthetic depth sequences with 5 levels of noise and occlusion, ranging from no noise to variance 5 gaussian noise plus random occlusion. The ground truth translation (in pixel) and rotation (in modified rodrigues parameters, MRP) for 600 frames are shown in the first chart on the first and second row.The rest of the charts shows the mean and 2-times standard deviation of the error in translation and rotation through all 600 frames on different noise level. We can see that even with the highest noise and occlusion, the tracking errors of our method can still remains very low (< 2.5 pixels in all translation and < 0.01 MRP in all rotation).

4.2   Simultaneous Tracking and Calibration

The second set of experiments is to test the performance of our method for simultaneous calibration and tracking. We first evaluate calibration result using synthetic data. With known intrinsic camera model, we generated depth sequences using the same method in subsection 3.1 with 3 different noise levels, then we use our energy function to run simultaneous calibration and tracking algorithm on these sequences. Fig. 4 shows the values of intrinsic parameters estimated from 300 synthetic frames. With low noise, our method can recover the intrinsic parameter accurately from less than 200 tracking frames, even with variance 5 gaussian distributed noise on the observed depth sequence, our method can still recover some reasonable intrinsic parameters.

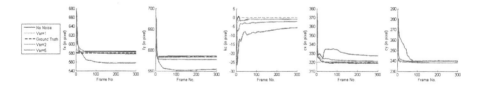

Fig. 4. Quantitative evaluation of our method for calibration on synthetic data, with respect to different level of noise, all intrinsic parameters are in pixels

We have also tested our method on real data. Note that, in order to get precise calibration result, a simple object (such as a box) is not sufficient since it has ambiguity. A slightly more complex calibration object (see Fig. 5) is used for the experiment. We initialize the tracking with an initial guess of the intrinsics ($fx = 600, fy = 600, cx = 300, cy = 200, kx = 0$), then track the object for 500 frames to estimate the intrinsic matrix. Fig. 5 shows some example frames.

Reprojection error is the most commonly used criteria to evaluate intrinsic calibration, however, without point correspondences in depth, we can not use this criteria. Thus we use similar criteria as in D. Herrera et al. [7], which is based on orthogonal planes, to evaluate the quality of our intrinsic estimation. As is illustrated in 6, we use the depth camera which we try to calibrate to capture a depth frame of three known orthogonal planes, then we un-project all depth pixels into the camera coordinate and compute the angle between the

Fig. 5. The leftmost images shows our calibration object, Film strips to the right shows an example sequence that we used for simultaneous calibration and tracking

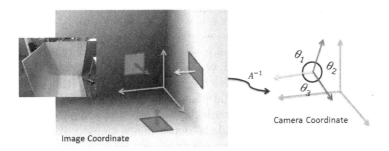

Fig. 6. Illustration of the criteria for the evaluation of intrinsic parameters: given a depth image of three orthogonal planes, we unproject all depth pixels from image coordinate to camera coordinate, then we compute the angle between the norms of the three orthogonal planes as criteria. If the intrinsic matrix is correctly recovered, the angle between the tree norm should all be 90°.

Table 1. Quantitative evaluation of the performance of our method for calibration on real data: criteria are based on the angle between the norms of up-projected orthogonal planes, all angles are in degree

Method	θ_1	θ_2	θ_3	Overall Err
Ours	**90.1849**	91.6065	**89.6874**	**2.1040**
Checker Board [8]	90.8706	92.1943	87.9618	5.1031
D. Herrera et al. [7]	91.6082	**89.2167**	90.3549	2.7464
Initial guess	88.4047	87.9643	94.1769	7.8079

normals of the three planes. If the intrinsic matrix is correct, the angle between the three norms should all be 90°.

With this criteria, we compare our calibration result with the standard checkerboard calibration method with non-linear refinement [8] and the the state-of-the-art Kinect calibration toolbox by D. Herrera et al. [7]. Note that, for the standard checker board method, we attached checker board patter on a piece of glass then cut off the white area, so that we can do automatic corner detection in depth image. In Table 1 we shows the experiment result, the three norm angles computed from our initial guess are also listed in the table for comparison. As is shown, our method shows the best result for recovering orthogonal plane normals. The disadvantage of our method compared to D. Herrera et al. [7] is that, our method can not calibrate the relative pose between the depth camera and the color camera. [7] requires the user to define the boundary of the calibration plane at all frames, however, given a known object model, our method can calibrate the depth sensor with one-click initialization on the first frame. No point correspondences, either by manual clicking or automatic corner detection is required.

4.3   Point Cloud Modeling with Adaptable Primitive Models

Due to the lack of ground truth data, we only qualitatively showcase the application of our energy function for point cloud modeling with adaptable primitive models. Fig. 7 illustrates the method we use to remove ground plane. Given the depth map of a scene, we first remove the ground plane. We do this by fitting a plane patch to any part of the ground plane using our 3D rigid object tracker. Then we extend the plane to cover whole depth image,and compute the discrepancy between the extended plane and the depth image on each pixel. All pixels that has small discrepancies are removed as ground plane.

Fig. 7. Illustration of the ground plane removal step: a) fitting a plane patch to any part of the ground plane. b) Extend the plane patch. c) Ground plane is segmented out by removing all depth pixels that are close to the extended plane patch.

After removing the ground plane, we initialize primitive models with arbitrary size, then run the rigid 3D object tracker to align the primitives to the point cloud. The primitive models will not fit the point cloud perfectly since the size is not correct, but the tracking result will be used as initialization for the shape adaptation step. In the final shape adaptation step we used the energy function parameterized by extrinsic and scaling matrix to simultaneously workout the size and position of the primitive models. Results are shown in Fig. 8.

Finally, we also tested the speed of the GPU implementation of the above 3 experiments on a Core-i7 870 (2.93GHz) machine with GTX680 graphic card: rigid tracking (6 pose parameters) runs at 10ms/frame@640×480; simultaneous calibration & tracking (11 parameters) and point cloud modeling (9 parameters) runs at around 20ms~30ms/frame@640×480. This shows that our method yields real-time performance in all above applications.

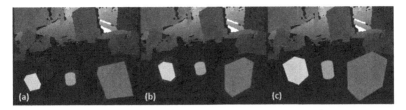

Fig. 8. Illustration of the model adaptation step: a) primitive models are initialized with arbitrary size; b) using our rigid 3D object tracking energy function, models are fitted into point cloud as rigid objects; c) shape adaptations energy function is used to simultaneously deform and track the primitives towards final fitting.

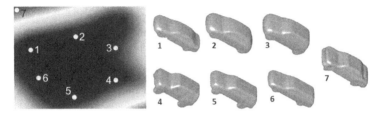

Fig. 9. Illustration of a 3D latent space of 3D car shapes: valid 3D car models (1~6) can be generated from the high-probability (blue) area in the latent space [9]

5   Conclusion and Future Work

In this paper we have presented a novel generic framework for model fitting problems in depth, which could be used for tracking 3D rigid objects, simultaneous calibration and tracking, point cloud modeling, shape adaptation and etc. Our framework formulates the model fitting problem as an optimization problem for the best projection matrix that back projects depth points onto the zero-level of a level-set embedding function, which encodes the 3D shape of the object. The framework is generic in that various energy functions can be formulated for different purposes. By leveraging the gradient of the level-set embedding function, the formulated object functions can be solved efficiently with gradient-based optimization methods. The per-pixel back projection mechanism is perfectly parallelizable thus real-time GPU-based applications can be implemented using our framework. We have demonstrated the performance of our framework in various applications with extensive experiment on both real and synthetic data.

One possible extension to the current framework is to apply it to track deformable or articulated object classes. In subsection 3.1, 3.2 and 3.3, Φ is fully defined and constant for a given object model, however, we note that Φ could also be generated from a point in latent object shape space as well. For example, the authors in [9] capture 3D shape variance in Gaussian Process Latent Variable Models (GPLVM) [10] (Fig. 9 shows an example of such latent space).

Our optimization would then proceed as a minimization simultaneously over the latent space parameters governing the shape and the pose parameters, retaining all of the advantages of our method.

References

1. Oikonomidis, I., Kyriazis, N., Argyros, A.: Efficient model-based 3D tracking of hand articulations using kinect. In: Proceedings of the British Machine Vision Conference, pp. 101.1–101.11. BMVA Press (2011)
2. Newcombe, R.A., Izadi, S., Hilliges, O., Molyneaux, D., Kim, D., Davison, A.J., Kohli, P., Shotton, J., Hodges, S., Fitzgibbon, A.W.: Kinectfusion: Real-time dense surface mapping and tracking. In: ISMAR, pp. 127–136. IEEE (2011)
3. Koppula, H.S., Anand, A., Joachims, T., Saxena, A.: Semantic labeling of 3D point clouds for indoor scenes. In: NIPS, pp. 244–252 (2011)
4. Ueda, R.: Tracking 3D objects with point cloud library (2012), pointclouds.org
5. Besl, P.J., McKay, N.D.: A method for registration of 3-D shapes. IEEE Trans. Pattern Anal. Mach. Intell. 14, 239–256 (1992)
6. Thayananthan, A., Stenger, B., Torr, P.H.S., Cipolla, R.: Shape context and chamfer matching in cluttered scenes. In: 2012 IEEE Conference on Computer Vision and Pattern Recognition, vol. 1, p. 127 (2003)
7. Daniel Herrera, C., Kannala, J., Heikkila, J.: Joint depth and color camera calibration with distortion correction. IEEE Transactions on Pattern Analysis and Machine Intelligence 99 (2012)
8. Zhang, Z.: A flexible new technique for camera calibration. IEEE Transactions on Pattern Analysis and Machine Intelligence 22, 1330–1334 (2000)
9. Prisacariu, V., Reid, I.: Simultaneous monocular 2D segmentation, 3D pose recovery and 3D reconstruction. Technical report, University of Oxford (2012)
10. Lawrence, N.D.: Probabilistic non-linear principal component analysis with gaussian process latent variable models. Journal of Machine Learning Research 6, 1783–1816 (2005)

Object Recognition Robust to Imperfect Depth Data

David F. Fouhey, Alvaro Collet, Martial Hebert, and Siddhartha Srinivasa

Robotics Institute, Carnegie Mellon University, USA
{dfouhey,acollet,hebert,siddh}@cs.cmu.edu

Abstract. In this paper, we present an adaptive data fusion model that robustly integrates depth and image only perception. Combining dense depth measurements with images can greatly enhance the performance of many computer vision algorithms, yet degraded depth measurements (e.g., missing data) can also cause dramatic performance losses to levels below image-only algorithms. We propose a generic fusion model based on maximum likelihood estimates of fused image-depth functions for both available and missing depth data. We demonstrate its application to each step of a state-of-the-art image-only object instance recognition pipeline. The resulting approach shows increased recognition performance over alternative data fusion approaches.

Despite its tremendous potential, dense depth estimation has fundamental limitations that must be addressed for robust performance. In many realistic scenes, depth sensors fail to compute depth measurements on portions of the associated color data (as shown in Fig. 1). We refer to this phenomenon of missing depth data as *depth fading*. Objects close to the camera, reflective or specular surfaces, poor lighting conditions, and surfaces seen at oblique angles often suffer from depth fading. These issues arise from fundamental physical limitations in depth perception, and affect all depth estimation approaches to varying degrees.

Although some problems are naturally robust to depth fading (e.g., by easily factoring into subproblems with and without depth [1]), many authors [2–4] resort to interpolating depth data and then propagating the interpolated values. Common interpolation methods include the recursive median filter [2], inpainting [3], or optimization techniques that minimize curvature [4]. These methods are effective when used for interpolation (the small holes in Fig. 1(top)), but produce severely inaccurate results when used for extrapolation (the moderate fading in Fig. 1(bottom). This inaccuracy has consequences for end-to-end performance: our results demonstrate that not distinguishing between interpolated and measured depth can lead to worse performance than not using depth at all.

In contrast to propagating interpolated data, this paper proposes to address the limitations of depth sensors at an algorithmic level by making the perception system aware of interpolated data. We propose a general model to adaptively combine depth and image measurements. We derive joint image-depth measurements as the maximum likelihood estimate given the independent image and

A. Fusiello et al. (Eds.): ECCV 2012 Ws/Demos, Part II, LNCS 7584, pp. 83–92, 2012.

RGB	Depth	RMF Interp.	NN Interp.	Confid.	Non-Adaptive	Adaptive

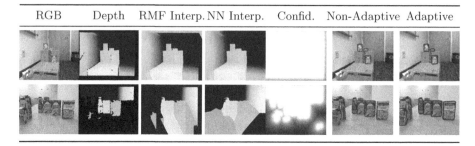

Fig. 1. Recursive median filter and nearest neighbor succeed at removing small depth fading (top row), but fail in scenes with stronger depth fading (bottom row). Our adaptive model yields robust performance under both conditions.

depth measurements. We combine a depth-filling technique with per-pixel confidences to extend depth measurements to areas with depth fading. In this way, we adaptively combine image and depth measurements for every pixel. To demonstrate the flexibility and effectiveness of our model, we integrate it into each of the components of a state-of-the-art image-only object instance recognition system, MOPED [5]. We use it to derive an adaptive distance metric for feature-based pose estimation; a prior generation technique based on adaptive 2D/3D similarity; and a depth-adaptive feature matching scheme.

We evaluate all contributions on a set of realistic scenes with up to 10 objects per scene, with depth fading ranging from 15% to 85% of the image. Each proposed algorithm is validated independently, and the adaptive model is evaluated in comparison to non-adaptive approaches via an integrated system that uses all algorithms. Our adaptive model demonstrates substantial gains over the image-only system with little depth fading present and a seamless transition to image-only performance with severe depth fading. In contrast, we demonstrate that under less favorable conditions, non-adaptive approaches (such as simply propagating interpolated data) can perform substantially worse than not using depth altogether (a decrease of 15% recall) while not performing any better than an adaptive approach under favorable conditions.

1   Adaptive 2D/3D Measurement Model

We propose a general model to adaptively combine image and depth measurements into a joint image-depth function. Given partial observations $x_{2D} \in \mathcal{X}_{2D}$ (image only) and $x_{3D} \in \mathcal{X}_{3D}$ (depth only), let $\phi_{2D} : \mathcal{X}_{2D} \to \mathbb{R}$ be an image-only function, and $\phi_{3D} : \mathcal{X}_{3D} \to \mathbb{R}$ a depth-only function. Defining the full observation $x = \{x_{2D}, x_{3D}\} \in \mathcal{X} = \mathcal{X}_{2D} \times \mathcal{X}_{3D}$, the joint image-depth function $\phi : \mathcal{X} \to \mathbb{R}$ is a combination of the partial functions ϕ_{2D}, ϕ_{3D}.

The functions ϕ, ϕ_{2D} and ϕ_{3D} are general functions which can model a wide array of processes, as we show in Sections 4, 5, and 6. For the remainder of this paper, we assume that $\phi_{2D}(x_{2D})$ and $\phi_{3D}(x_{3D})$ are measured in the same units. We also assume that $\phi_{2D}(x_{2D})$ and $\phi_{3D}(x_{3D})$ are noisy observations, conditioned

Fig. 2. The role of confidence values. (a) $c(x)$ vs $d(x, N(x))$ for $\psi = 1$ and varying b; (b) $c(x)$ plotted for Fig. 1(bottom) with $\psi = 0$ and $b = 1, 10, 32$ (l. to r.).

on $\phi(x)$, of the true values $\bar{\phi}_{2D}(x_{2D})$, $\bar{\phi}_{3D}(x_{3D})$, corrupted with i.i.d. noise with distributions $\mathcal{N}(0, \sigma_{2D}(x_{2D}))$ and $\mathcal{N}(0, \sigma_{3D}(x_{3D}))$ respectively.

Our goal is to find $\phi(x)$ that maximizes $P(\phi(x)|\phi_{2D}(x_{2D}), \phi_{3D}(x_{3D}))$. Using Bayes' Rule and assuming no prior on the function distributions, the optimal fused function $\phi^*(x)$ corresponds to the Maximum Likelihood Estimate (MLE)

$$\phi^*(x) = \arg\max_{\phi(x)} \; P(\phi_{2D}(x_{2D}), \phi_{3D}(x_{3D})|\phi(x)). \tag{1}$$

Following [6], the MLE $\phi^*(x)$ is computed as

$$\phi^*(x) = \frac{\sigma_{2D}^2(x_{2D})}{\sigma_{2D}^2(x_{2D}) + \sigma_{3D}^2(x_{3D})} \phi_{3D}(x_{3D}) + \frac{\sigma_{3D}^2(x_{3D})}{\sigma_{2D}^2(x_{2D}) + \sigma_{3D}^2(x_{3D})} \phi_{2D}(x_{2D}). \tag{2}$$

Parameterizing Eq. 2 in terms of a depth confidence function $c(x)$, and defining the ratio of variances $\gamma^2(x) = \frac{\sigma_{3D}^2(x_{3D})}{\sigma_{2D}^2(x_{2D})}$, then

$$c(x) = \frac{1}{1 + \gamma^2(x)}, \qquad \phi^*(x) = c(x)\phi_{3D}(x_{3D}) + [1 - c(x)]\phi_{2D}(x_{2D}). \tag{3}$$

In this formulation, $c(x)$ reflects the confidence of the depth function relative to the image function. The value of $c(x)$, and thus $\phi^*(x)$, depends only on the ratio of variances γ^2 of the noise distributions of $\phi_{2D}(x_{2D})$, $\phi_{3D}(x_{3D})$.

We now extend the model in Eq. 3 to depth-filling methods (e.g., nearest neighbor, recursive median filter) by estimating the ratio of variances $\gamma^2(x)$ in areas with depth fading. Let INT be an interpolation method which computes depth z_x for a point x with missing depth from a set of support datapoints $N(x)$ with depth measurements, such that $z_x = \text{INT}(N(x))$. We assume that the variance $\sigma_{3D}^2(x)$ for an interpolated datapoint x is higher than for support datapoints $N(x)$, i.e., $\sigma_{3D}^2(x) > \sigma_{3D}^2(N(x))$. Then, given that the variance $\sigma_{2D}^2(x)$ remains constant, the ratio of variances $\gamma^2(x) > \gamma^2(N(x))$, and thus $c(x) < c(N(x))$. The resulting dense depth map contains depth values and confidences for every datapoint, with decreasing confidences $c(x)$ for areas with depth fading.

We estimate the ratio of variances γ^2 of interpolated datapoints from ones with measured depth. For a known datapoint: $\gamma^2(x) = \psi^2(x)$ where $\psi^2(x)$ is from a sensor model or is a fixed value (effectively a prior). For an interpolated datapoint x,

$$\gamma^2(x) \approx \psi^2(N(x)) + d(x, N(x))^2/b^2, \tag{4}$$

where $d(x, N(x))$ is a distance function between the interpolated datapoint x and its support datapoints $N(x)$ in the image plane. The scalar parameter b encodes the trust in interpolated values with respect to measured values.

The confidence model $c(x)$ for dense depth depends exclusively on the interpolator INT, the scalar b, and $\psi^2(x)$ for known datapoints. For the remainder of this paper, we use simple Nearest Neighbor as our interpolator, but other alternatives (e.g., recursive median filter) are also possible.

The ratio of variances for known datapoints ψ^2 depends on the particular task and sensor. ψ^2 can be estimated empirically in some cases, but it is hard in the general case. The alternative is to set ψ^2 to a fixed value: $c(x)$ is constant for known datapoints, but $c(x)$ adapts for datapoints with unknown depth. If both noise distributions are believed to have equal variances, $\psi^2 = 1$; then $c(x) = 0.5$ for all datapoints with *known* depth, weighing both functions equally. An alternative, useful when the depth function is more informative than the image function, is $\psi^2 = 0$; then $c(x) = 1$ for all datapoints with known depth, thus exclusively using the depth function when depth is known, and adaptively reverting to the image function when depth is not available.

We illustrate common values of parameters ψ^2 and b in Fig. 2. In Fig. 2(a), we show $c(x)$ for a variety of values of b as the interpolation distance increases. The scalar b parameterizes the confidence decrease rate as a function of interpolation distance; analytically, for a fixed ψ^2, a point b pixels away from the known value has confidence $(\psi^2 + 1)/(\psi^2 + 2)$. Fig. 2(b) shows maps of $c(x)$ plotted for Fig. 1 (bottom) for b ranging from 1 to 32 pixels.

Setting ψ and b for a new algorithm is straightforward. Sensible values of ψ are $\psi = 1$ (for balanced image and depth measurements), $\psi = 0$ (for no information in the image), or values from a depth sensor model. To find a suitable b, we perform a logarithmic grid search over the validation set for a fixed ψ. We establish the stability of b in extensive experiments detailed in Section 7.

2   Problem Formulation

We demonstrate the application of our model to each step of a feature-based object instance recognition system [5]. In this section, we briefly introduce the structure of its pipeline. The input to the system is a calibrated RGBD image $I = \{Rgb, \mathbf{z}\}$ such that each color pixel value has a corresponding depth z_i. The output of the system is a set of object hypotheses $\mathbf{H}$ represented by an object identity and the pose of the object in the camera's reference frame. Each object model to be recognized is represented as a set of features $\mathbf{F}_o$; each feature is represented by a 3D point location $P = [X, Y, Z]^T$ in the object's reference frame and a feature descriptor D, (e.g., SIFT [7]).

The general approach is to find object poses by solving the Perspective-N-Point (PnP) problem on a set of image-model matches. The system first detects features and matches them to the stored database of model. Nearby matches are grouped together to generate priors for object poses in order to efficiently handle multiple object instances and reject outliers. Given that objects are mostly continuous in image space, clustering feature locations in image space produces good object priors. Using these priors as an initialization, the resulting PnP problems given the image-model matches are solved using RANSAC and non-linear minimization of the reprojection error.

In the image-only system [5], matching is done with the standard 2-nearest neighbors ratio test [7], clustering with mean-shift in the image plane, and pose estimation optimizes the reprojection error [8] with Levenberg-Marquardt minimization. In Sections 4-6, we add depth data to each approach with our adaptive model: we adapt the match acceptance threshold, integrate depth features into prior generation, and derive an adaptive pose estimation error function.

3   Data Sets

Scenes in common RGBD datasets [3, 4] are captured by a human operator in the sensor's recommended operating range, but still miss up to 85% [3] and 83% [4] of their depth data in some cases. In fact, $2.5 - 3.8\%$ of the scenes in [3, 4] are missing over half of their depth data. In applications where sensor position and scene composition cannot be controlled (e.g., in mobile robotics), depth fading becomes a critical factor to address for robust perception [9].

We replicate this spectrum with two datasets with varying depth quality. We captured all scenes using a Microsoft Kinect RGBD sensor with registered RGB and depth data. Additionally, we gathered a smaller training set that contains the same objects in 79 scenes of various environments.

Offices Dataset: In this first set, we aim to represent optimal operating conditions for RGBD sensors; most scenes show little or no depth fading. These scenes only depict small gaps due to partial occlusion or shadowing, with an average depth coverage of 66% of the image; most fading is due to registering the depth and color images and does not fall on the objects. We captured 350 scenes with an average of 4.4 objects per scene.

Tables Dataset: In the second set, we captured 200 scenes with large sections of depth fading. These scenes show, among other anomalies, missing surfaces due to steep viewing angles and objects at short distances away from the sensor which cause heavy depth fading. These 200 scenes contain an average of 5.2 objects and have 35% average depth coverage.

4   Depth-Adaptive Pose Estimation

In the first demonstration of the model, we derive an adaptive algorithm for feature-alignment-based pose estimation. In general, the estimation of an object pose given a set of 2D/3D correspondences between image features and a known model is the well-known PnP problem. The most accurate solutions are usually found by non-linear least squares minimization of pose parameters using the reprojection or backprojection errors [5]. To adaptively use depth information, we introduce a 2D/3D distance metric, or ϕ.

Given a set of features F with 2D positions p_i and 3D positions P_i, we parameterize P_i as a line L_i through p_i and the camera center, as well as a depth z_i. Given a pose hypothesis with transformation T, we define $P_{T;i}$ as the position of the corresponding feature of the hypothesis that matches P_i. Let $\hat{P}_{T;i}$ be the projection of $P_{T;i}$ onto L. Using $\hat{P}_{T;i}$ we derive two common image-only errors: the backprojection error is the 3D distance $||\hat{P}_{T;i} - P_{T;i}||^2$ and the reprojection error is the distance when projected on the image plane.

To formulate our adaptive model ϕ, we select the backprojection error as ϕ_{2D}, and introduce an orthogonal penalty in depth $||P_i - \hat{P}_{T;i}||^2$ to serve as ϕ_{3D}. Our objective function is the sum of $\phi^*(i) = c(i)\phi_{3D}(i) + [1 - c(i)]\phi_{2D}(i)$, $\forall$ i. We set $\psi(i) = 1$ and use our validation set to determine $b = 0.1$, which is held constant throughout the experiments.

Validation: On the Offices data set, optimizing the adaptive error results in lower average relative translation error (1.5% vs. 3.7%) and rotation error ($5.6°$ vs. $7.6°$) with respect to the ground-truth when compared to optimizing the standard reprojection error.

5   Depth-Adaptive Priors for Object Recognition

Model-based object recognition and pose estimation from local features requires solving two sub-problems: data association and pose optimization. In simple scenes, RANSAC and a PnP solver are sufficient. However, realistic scenarios may contain large numbers of outliers and multiple instances of the same object. In this case, it is vital to compute object priors to limit the otherwise overwhelming search space of potential hypotheses. A number of approaches have been used to generate priors, both from depth and image data. Collet *et al.* use estimate spatial feature density with Mean Shift to find plausible regions for objects in [10]. Other approaches [11, 12] use an horizontal plane detector to generate priors.

In this work, we use clustering for prior generation akin to [5]. We partition the set of matches for a object into clusters and search only within the poses supported by these clusters. An ideal cluster contains only matches supporting one object instance and no outliers.

To provide a prior generation algorithm that is robust to depth fading, we propose an agglomerative clustering scheme based on 2D/3D feature similarity. Here, we extend our model to pairs of measurements and fuse a 2D-similarity function $\phi_{2D} : \mathcal{X} \times \mathcal{X} \to \mathbb{R}$ with a 3D-similarity function $\phi_{3D} : \mathcal{X} \times \mathcal{X} \to \mathbb{R}$. To model the confidence of a pair of points, we assume their independence and set $c(\{i, j\}) = c(i)c(j)$. Our similarity function is then:

$$\phi^*(i, j) = c(i)c(j)\phi_{3D}(i, j) + [1 - c(i)c(j)]\phi_{2D}(i, j) \qquad (5)$$

We build each term of our similarity function using simple features. We denote p_i and P_i as the 2D and 3D positions of image feature F_i, respectively; $\hat{P}_i$ is the 3D position of the corresponding feature in the model; and $d(\cdot, \cdot)$ is the Euclidean distance between two vectors.

Spatial Proximity: Objects are generally continuous; we thus use the feature $S_{2E}(i, j) = \exp(-d(p_i, p_j)^2/\sigma_{2D})$, and equivalently S_{3E} in 3D using P_i, P_j.

Depth Discontinuity: Two matches are unlikely to belong to the same object if there is a significant depth discontinuity between them. We formalize this intuition by sampling N points along the line through p_i and p_j in the image plane, and measuring the change in depth as an angle over each segment compared to the global change in depth θ of line $\overline{p_i p_j}$. This yields a penalty on strong changes in depth: $S_D(i, j) = \exp(-\max_{1 \leq k \leq N}\{(\theta_k - \theta)\}/\sigma_{\text{disc}})$.

Distance Consistency: The availability of depth measurements enables us to check the consistency of the distance between points in the world and their locations in the model coordinate frame: we can prevent the clustering of two matches if they are at inconsistent distances and thus cannot support the same pose. The consistency similarity function is defined as:

$$S_C(i, j) = \exp\left(-\left(|d(P_i, P_j) - d(\hat{P}_i, \hat{P}_j)|/d(\hat{P}_i, \hat{P}_j)\right)/\sigma_{\text{cons}}\right). \tag{6}$$

To combine these features into similarity functions, we choose $\phi_{2D}(i, j) = S_{2E}(i, j)$ and $\phi_{3D}(i, j) = \frac{1}{2}S_C(i, j)(S_D(i, j) + S_{3E}(i, j))$. We enforce the S_C feature more strongly as it is a hard requirement for clustering, rather than a preference (such as spatial proximity). We set $\psi(i) = 1$ and use our validation set to determine $b = 25$, which is held constant throughout for all experiments. We use Agglomerative Clustering with group-average linkage to cluster.

Validation: We define a match as an inlier if the match has reprojection error 2 pixels or less with regards to a correctly detected object. We define *cluster precision* as the fraction of matches in any clusters that are inliers and *cluster recall* is the fraction of inlier matches appearing in any cluster. On the Offices data set, while obtaining similar cluster recall, the proposed adaptive clustering approach obtains 82% cluster precision, in comparison to 28% with Mean Shift in the image plane; further, since it can reject mismatches on objects, it even achieves 2% higher precision than using the ground-truth outlines of objects.

6   Adaptive Feature Matching

We demonstrate the application of our method to situations in which the function depends only on 3D. For instance, depth can constrain the scale at which one searches for objects (e.g., [13]). However, such techniques are problematic when depth data is largely absent. Our model transitions between aggressive scale constraining during optimal conditions and cautious behavior when depth data is unavailable. To achieve this, we let ϕ_{2D} be a constant function and set $\psi(i) = 0$.

One way to constrain the search scale for objects is to adjust the number of feature matches that are accepted by adjusting the threshold used in the ratio

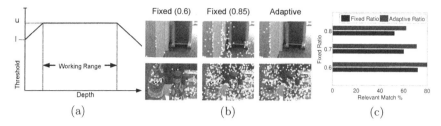

Fig. 3. (a) The threshold $\theta(z)$ as a function of depth. (b) A qualitative illustration: our adaptive approach provides more matches in relevant regions while not increasing the number of matches in the background. (c) Quantitative results on the Offices data set; when one replaces each fixed threshold with an adaptive one that retains the same number of relevant matches, one achieves a higher fraction of relevant matches.

test. The ratio test [7] is a common criterion to evaluate whether a pair of local features are sufficiently similar to be considered a match. A match between a local feature F_i and its nearest neighbor $N(F_i)$ in a database is only made if the ratio between that distance and the distance to the second nearest neighbor $d(F_i, N_2(F_i))$ is less than a threshold τ. The only parameter in the ratio test is the threshold τ. In the absence of *a priori* information, an educated guess is used. With RGBD sensors, however, we have depth measurements for each local feature, and we know the scale of the objects in the database. Thus, we can use the working ranges at which we expect to detect our objects based on the object's size and density of features.

To maximize recognition and speed performance, our goal is to find just enough matches for an object to be detected throughout the object's entire working range (determined by physical size), and no matches outside this range. We approximate this behavior by replacing the fixed τ with a function ϕ^* that depends on the depth measurement z_i and the confidence score $c(i)$. When depth information is present, a function $\theta(z)$ maps depth z to a threshold. The form of $\theta(z)$ is illustrated in Fig. 3(a). To make this approach robust to imperfect depth data, we set $\phi_{3D}(i)$ to $\theta(z_i)$ and $\phi_{2D}(i)$ to a default ratio $\theta(z_0)$, where z_0 is a default depth. In our experiments, z_0 is fixed at $1m$. Since ϕ_{3D} completely determines ϕ with known depth, we set $\psi(i) = 0$; we use our validation set to determine $b = 75$, which is held constant throughout the experiments. Parameters l, u are fixed using grid search to maximize recall on a validation set; they are not sensitive to particular values, and are in the vicinity of usually used values.

Validation: We evaluate the matching performance by counting the fraction of relevant matches; we define a feature as *relevant* if it falls on any ground-truth object. Higher thresholds yield more relevant features at the cost of more irrelevant ones. Since our approach reverts to a per-object fixed threshold in the absence of depth data, we only consider matches with sufficiently high confidence (above 0.5) to focus the evaluation on the depth-dependent scheme. Fig. 3(b,c) demonstrates that one can replace a fixed ratio with an adaptive ratio that yields the same number of relevant matches, but fewer irrelevant matches.

7   Integrated Testing

We evaluate our adaptive model applied to an integrated system using all proposed algorithms, which we refer to as **MOPED-RGBD**. To evaluate the adaptive model, we compare to using two non-adaptive models on the integrated system: **3D Only**, which uses only data points for which there is depth data, and **Non-Adaptive**, which just propagates interpolated values, thus trusting all depth values (interpolated and measured) equally. All results are reported relative to the image-only system, **MOPED** [5].

We process each image 5 times to account for the non-determinism of RANSAC. A detection is correct if translation and rotation to the ground truth is less than 10 cm and 20°. *Precision* is the fraction of correct objects in the hypotheses, and *recall* is the fraction of ground-truth objects with a correct hypothesis.

Our results demonstrate the importance of an adaptive approach to depth fading. These results are summarized in Fig. 4(a,b) via area under the precision-recall curve (AUPRC) relative to the image-only system MOPED, as well as true and false positive rates; detailed graphs and qualitative examples apppear in the supplementary materials. Under optimal conditions (Fig. 4(a) Offices Full), all approaches to depth fading perform similarly, outperforming the image-only system. With moderate to severe depth fading (Tables Full), **the non-adaptive approaches (including propagating interpolated values) perform substantially worse than the image-only baseline.** In contrast, our adaptive model performs comparably.

To distinguish performance changes due to depth fading from those due to scene composition, we perform experiments, shown in Fig. 4(a), with synthetically degraded data. We remove data within circles with varying radii (5-30 pixels) to produce scenes with 35% depth coverage (average coverage of Tables) and 15% depth coverage (the lowest coverage in our data and in [3]) for each RGBD image in each dataset, yielding Offices 15%, etc. Again, only the adaptive approach consistently performs comparably to the image-only baseline.

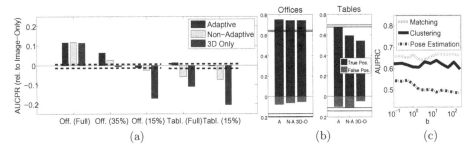

Fig. 4. (a) Average area under the precision-recall curve (AUPRC) for adaptive vs. non-adaptive approaches, relative to image-only. The range of the image-only system on 10 runs is plotted with black lines. (b) True and false positive rate at maximum F1 score for Adaptive (A), Non-Adaptive (NA), and 3D-Only (3DO). (c) Average AUPRC for individual algorithms for fixed ψ^2 and varying b (log scale) on the validation set.

Finally, we show the stability of b for each algorithm by showing the AUPRC of a system using only each algorithm for varying b and fixed $\psi(i)$ in Fig. 4(c). Performance is not sensitive to specific values, and only the order of magnitude is relevant. The best-performing b are small ($b < 1$) for tasks needing precise values (pose estimation), and larger for those needing rough values (e.g., clustering).

8   Conclusions

We have introduced an adaptive model to robustly integrate depth data into image-only perception and have applied it to object recognition. The adaptive model outperforms the image-only baseline under optimal conditions and transitions to image-only performance under severe depth fading; in contrast, non-adaptive approaches lead to worse performance than not using depth altogether.

Acknowledgments. This work was supported in part by the NSF under ERC Grant No. EEEC-0540865, by a NSF Graduate Research Fellowship to DF, and the Caja Madrid Fellowship to AC.

References

1. Cadena, C., McDonald, J., Leonard, J.J., Neira, J.: Place recognition using near and far visual information. In: IFAC World Congress (2011)
2. Lai, K., Bo, L., Ren, X., Fox, D.: A Large-Scale Hierarchical Multi-View RGB-D Object Dataset. In: ICRA (2011)
3. Silberman, N., Hoiem, D., Kohli, P., Fergus, R.: Indoor Segmentation and Support Inference from RGBD Images. In: Fitzgibbon, A., Lazebnik, S., Perona, P., Sato, Y., Schmid, C. (eds.) ECCV 2012, Part V. LNCS, vol. 7576, pp. 746–760. Springer, Heidelberg (2012)
4. Janoch, A., Karayev, S., Jia, Y., Barron, J., Fritz, M., Saenko, K., Darrell, T.: A category-level 3-D object dataset: Putting the kinect to work. In: Workshop on Consumer Depth Cameras in Computer Vision (in conjunction with ICCV) (2011)
5. Collet, A., Martinez, M., Srinivasa, S.S.: The MOPED framework: Object Recognition and Pose Estimation for Manipulation. International Journal of Robotics Research 30, 1284–1306 (2011)
6. Hackett, J., Shah, M.: Multi-sensor fusion: a perspective. In: ICRA (1990)
7. Lowe, D.: Distinctive Image Features from Scale-Invariant Keypoints. International Journal of Computer Vision 60, 91–110 (2004)
8. Szeliski, R.: Computer Vision: Algorithms and Applications. Springer (2011)
9. Chiu, W.C., Blanke, U., Fritz, M.: Improving the kinect by cross-modal stereo. In: BMVC (2011)
10. Collet, A., Berenson, D., Srinivasa, S.S., Ferguson, D.: Object recognition and full pose registration from a single image for robotic manipulation. In: ICRA (2009)
11. Lai, K., Fox, D.: A Scalable Tree-based Approach for Joint Object and Pose Recognition. In: Conference on Artificial Intelligence (2011)
12. Kootstra, G., Kragic, D.: Fast and Bottom-Up Object Detection, Segmentation, and Evaluation using Gestalt Principles. In: ICRA (2011)
13. Helmer, S., Lowe, D.: Using stereo for object recognition. In: ICRA (2010)

3D Object Detection with Multiple Kinects

Wandi Susanto, Marcus Rohrbach, and Bernt Schiele

Max Planck Institute for Informatics, Saarbrücken, Germany

Abstract. Categorizing and localizing multiple objects in 3D space is
a challenging but essential task for many robotics and assisted living
applications. While RGB cameras as well as depth information have been
widely explored in computer vision there is surprisingly little recent work
combining multiple cameras and depth information. Given the recent
emergence of consumer depth cameras such as Kinect we explore how
multiple cameras and active depth sensors can be used to tackle the
challenge of 3D object detection. More specifically we generate point
clouds from the depth information of multiple registered cameras and use
the VFH descriptor [20] to describe them. For color images we employ
the DPM [3] and combine both approaches with a simple voting approach
across multiple cameras.

On the large RGB-D dataset [12] we show improved performance for
object classification on multi-camera point clouds and object detection
on color images, respectively. To evaluate the benefit of joining color and
depth information of multiple cameras, we recorded a novel dataset with
four Kinects showing significant improvements over a DPM baseline for
9 object classes aggregated in challenging scenes. In contrast to related
datasets our dataset provides color and depth information recorded with
multiple Kinects and requires localizing and categorizing multiple objects
in 3D space. In order to foster research in this field, the dataset, including
annotations, is available on our web page.

1 Introduction

Accurate 3D localization and categorization of objects is an important ingredi-
ent for many robotic, assisted living, surveillance, and industrial applications.
Consumer depth cameras, such as Microsoft's Kinect, provide depth information based on an active structured light sensor combined with color images. The
additional depth information simplifies estimating the position in 3D real world
coordinates; however, a single (color and depth) camera is still limited especially
in highly cluttered scenes, with object occlusion and objects which are difficult
to distinguish from a single view. While a plate and bowl might not be distinguishable from above in a color image (see e.g. Fig. 1, 1st column), additional
cameras (2nd column) and depth information (3rd and 4th column) can help to
resolve these problems. Given the low price (and likely increasing accuracy in
near future), multiple devices observing the same area are a viable and likely
setting for smart homes or surveillance. While the benefit has been argued before

A. Fusiello et al. (Eds.): ECCV 2012 Ws/Demos, Part II, LNCS 7584, pp. 93–102, 2012.

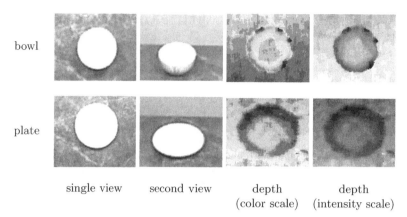

bowl

plate

single view   second view   depth   depth
                                  (color scale)   (intensity scale)

Fig. 1. Objects (here bowl and plate) are sometimes difficult to distinguishable from a certain single view (1st column). Having additional views (2nd column) or depth (3rd and 4th column) can frequently resolve the problem.

we find this scenario of combining multiple views and active depth sensors underrepresented in related work. Multiple works have shown that object recognition can be improved using stereo/depth information [17,1,12,8] or by using multiple (color) images [7,19]. However, fusing information from multiple *depth* cameras for object detection has hardly been addressed. An exception is [14], which however uses the depth information only to estimate if an object is occluded but does not combine depth from multiple views and does not use depth for representing objects. Given the emergence of low-cost depth sensors we would like to intensify research in this area and thus propose a dataset for multi-camera object recognition to explore how to use color and depth information from multiple views.

Our dataset is recorded in a kitchen scenario which we found to be typical to contain large amounts of similar objects, frequently occluding each other. We have four Kinects attached to the ceiling as can be seen in Fig. 3. The idea of our approach is to combine strong visual cues from color images by using the deformable part model (DPM) [3] together with the viewpoint feature histogram (VFH) [20] extracted from depth based point clouds. We first detect the object in all views with DPM and vote for the location of objects in 3D space, using the depth information. Additionally we validate the 3D location with the VFH, extracted on the registered point clouds from all cameras.

Our contributions are as follows: First, we show the benefits of multiple depth cameras for multi-class object detection. To our knowledge we are the first to show the benefit of multiple cameras for point cloud-based object recognition. As the second main contribution we recorded a novel, challenging dataset of 9 object classes with four Kinects to evaluate our approach. As we discuss in our related work section, this setting and kind of dataset has hardly been explored previously. Additionally we show improved performance for classification on multi-camera view point clouds and improvements over related work for object detection on the Multi-View RGB-D Object dataset [12].

The remaining paper is structured as follows: We first discuss related approaches, scenarios, and datasets in Section 2. Next we introduce our approach (Section 3) and our newly recorded dataset (Section 4). For evaluation we first report the performance of our chosen feature on the RGB-D dataset (Section 5.1) and then examine the detection performance of our proposed approach on the multiple depth camera setting (Section 5.2). We conclude with a summary and ideas for future work in Section 6.

2 Related Work

We organize this section into related feature representations for depth information, multi-camera approaches, and available datasets recorded with (consumer) depth cameras.

Several ways to represent depth information and to extract feature representations have been proposed. The most common or basic way is to represent depth information as an image of depth values. On such depth images one can extract features, such as HOG [2], which have shown good performance on color images. Depending on the application HOG on depth images was found to perform worse [17] (for pedestrian recognition) or better [12] (for object recognition) than on 2D intensity images but in all cases a combination of both yielded significantly better results indicating the obvious complementary information contained in depth and color/intensity images. Combination of depth and intensity has also shown to be beneficial for template based method allowing real time object detection [8]. Another direction is to compute features on 3D point clouds. Spin image [11], VFH [20], or 3D shape context [5] are prominent examples. An alternative to represent 3D objects are 3D meshes: The 3D surf descriptor in combination with spatial pyramids in 3D achieves significant performance improvements for 3D object classification [16]. Depth has also been used to constraint the size of objects for improved detection [22]. Laser range scanners provide more accurate but less dense information and can be used to define multi-modal 3D features [6]. In our work we similarly want to benefit from the complimentary information contained in color and depth images. We choose point clouds for representing depth, as point clouds allow to easily integrate depth information from multiple views. We extract the VFH descriptor from the point clouds which has shown good performance [20].

With respect to related approaches, we first would like to note that this work focuses on a multi-camera setup, which is sometimes denoted as multi-view [4]. In most cases however, *multi-view* refers to multiple views of an object category. Although our work looks at multi-view categorization we additionally want to explore how beneficial multiple depth cameras are for object detection in 3D space. There exists several prior works which use registered color/intensity images to improve 3D object detection: E.g. [1] shows that using two cameras can improve performance. [19] detects cars, buses, and people on street scenes with six cameras, while [4] localizes objects in 3D from four X-Ray cameras. [4] uses, similar to us, a voting based approach to combine multiple views. Multiple camera views have also been used for marker-less motion capture, e.g. [13] is able to distinguish two interacting people in a studio (green box) scenario. 3D object detection can be achieved from a single monocular camera using video and structure from motion [14,25].

Our work is most similar to [7], that detects and classifies objects in an indoor environment using multiple camera views. In a follow up work the authors use depth information to estimate which object is an occluder of another object [14]. In contrast to this we build a feature representation on the depth information and use not only depth from each view individually but use registered 3D point cloud data from multiple cameras in addition to color images. Furthermore we distinguish 9 object categories while [7,14] only distinguish 4 and 2, respectively.

Fusing point cloud videos from a single moving Kinect has previously been used to build high-resolution 3D representations [9] but without the direction of object detection but rather interaction and rendering. With a similar use case, [24] uses multiple Kinects to increase the interaction space.

Finally we will discuss the most relevant and related datasets: The Multi-View RGB-D Object dataset provides object classification and object detection task [12]. The dataset includes 51 classes with color image, depth image, and 3D point cloud data. While for the classification challenge there exist multiple views per object, the detection scenes are only recorded from a single camera/view. Another dataset of 75 scenes with over 50 classes was recently proposed [10]. In contrast to these datasets our dataset contains test scenes recorded by multiple depth (and RGB) cameras.

The UBC VRS dataset [7] is most similar to ours. In an indoor detection setting, recordings from multiple view-points of four object categories in 26 scenes have to be distinguished. In [14] a few scenes with Kinect recordings of mugs and bowls have been added. In contrast to our dataset the recordings are performed from a mobile robot platform exploring the room, while our cameras are installed statically. Our dataset contains more object categories (9) but a similar number of scenes (33).

3   Approaches for Recognition with Multiple Kinects

In this section we first introduce how we perform object classification on point clouds from a single and multiple cameras, and then we discuss several approaches to perform 3D object detection.

3.1   Object Classification on 3D Data

We represent depth information as point clouds, i.e. as a set of points with 3D coordinates. This allows easy aggregation if depth information is available from multiple registered cameras views.

For a given bounding box we extract the 3D point cloud descriptor viewpoint feature histogram (VFH) [20]. We do this for the single-camera and multi-camera setting. For the multi-camera setting we first register multiple object point clouds of different cameras into a single point cloud (see Section 4.2). Only for experiments on the RGB-D dataset we combine multiple views by averaging classifiers scores due to the unavailability of registration information.

3.2 3D Object Detection

We use the deformable part model (DPM) [3] to detect objects in 2D color images. To detect objects in 3D we distinguish three approaches. The first is a baseline based on DPM, in the second we verify single camera DPM detections with the 3D VFH object classifier, while the third combines DPM detections from multiple RGB cameras and depth-based VFH verification.

sDPM (single-camera DPM): As a baseline we evaluate the detection score from a single camera and compute the 3D bounding box by using the 3D information from the depth image of the same camera.

sDPM+mVFH (single-camera DPM + multi-camera VFH): In this approach we first detect the object in the 2D color image with DPM and back-project the detected bounding box into 3D space as described above. We then verify the detection bounding box by using the 3D VFH object classifier computed on the registered point cloud from multiple cameras. For a given hypothesis h we combine the DPM scores $s_{sDPM}(h)$ and the nearest neighbor distance of the 3D VFH classifier $d_{mVFH}(h)$ with the following function, setting $\alpha = 2$ and $\beta = 100$ to provide a similar score range.

$$s_{sDPM+mVFH}(h) = s_{sDPM}(h) + \alpha \exp\left(-\frac{d_{mVFH}(h)}{\beta}\right) \qquad (1)$$

mDPM+mVFH (multi-camera DPM + multi-camera VFH): Finally we want to benefit from both, multi-camera color and multi-camera depth information. We combine the sDPM+mVFH hypotheses from multiple cameras by voting for a 3D location.

The single-camera hypotheses are given in 2D bounding boxes. Fusing these 2D bounding boxes in 3D space forms polyhedrons, which are not simple to work with. Therefore, we use the center point of each object, which is defined by the center pixel of the 2D bounding box and the depth value at the corresponding pixel in the depth image. We transform all hypotheses from different cameras into a single 3D coordinate system. Each hypothesis votes for all its neighbors $\mathcal{N}$, which are closer than a threshold t with 50% of its own score. Thus the accumulated score of a hypothesis is given by:

$$s_{mDPM+mVFH}(h) = s_{sDPM+mVFH}(h) + 0.5 \sum_{i \in \{j \in \mathcal{N}(h) \mid \|h-j\| \leq t\}} s_{sDPM+mVFH}(i) \quad (2)$$

We then perform 3D non-maximum suppression with the distance threshold t in 3D space to yield the final set of hypotheses. We set $t = 10cm$ in all experiments.

| avocado | bowl | coffee box | container | cup |

| nutella can | plate | soup powder can | sponge |

Fig. 2. Sample object images for each class in the MPII Multi-Kinect dataset

4   MPII Multi-Kinect Dataset

Our *MPII Multi-Kinect* dataset is collected with four Kinect cameras at training and test time in the same kitchen as [18]. We recorded RGB color and depth images as well as 3D point clouds per camera and registered multi-view point clouds computed from the depth images. The dataset consists of 9 classes of kitchen objects shown in Fig. 2. Class *bowl* and *cup* have two instances, all others only one. Each class in the dataset is captured in different locations and poses. The dataset consists of two parts. In the first part (classification challenge) only one object is present at a time. There are 560 shots taken from 4 cameras giving a total of 2240 pairs of color and depth images (Note we have a 10th class, namely orange, is this first part of the dataset). The second part (detection challenge) is again recorded from 4 camera views. Here we recorded six to ten objects in each of a total of 33 scenes, which partially/fully occlude each other, see Fig. 3 for an example scene. We annotate each object with a bounding-polygon, providing a segmentation of the object in all RGB camera views. The dataset is publicly available on our web page including the annotations. In our detection experiments we use the camera installed on top of the scene only for ground truth as it contains no occlusions. We evaluate the multi-camera detections with a distance-based criterion with a threshold of 20 cm between the detection center and the ground truth center in 3D space (the largest extension of objects in the dataset range from 10-25 cm).

4.1   Data Preprocessing

We found the depth data provided by Kinect to be very noisy and incomplete. Noisy refers to variations between 2 to 4 different discrete depth levels. We smooth the depth data by taking the mean over 9 depth frames. For incomplete regions we median-filter with a 5x5 pixel window.

| Groundtruth camera | Camera A | Camera B | Camera C |

Fig. 3. Example scene from four different views in our MPII Multi-Kinect dataset

4.2 Calibration

We calibrate the extrinsic matrix between different Kinect cameras using ICP from the PCL [21]. We choose one camera as reference to which we calibrate the other cameras. Since the cameras look at the scene from very different viewpoints, we initialize the transformation matrix between two cameras by manually rotating the point clouds before running ICP. Due to the noisy, inaccurate depth data, and position of our Kinect cameras, we found the different calibrated views can still disagree by up to about 13 cm in 3D space. The active light patterns of multiple Kinects might potentially interfere with each other. However, during our experiments we could not observe any disturbance between different Kinects, most likely due to the large angle between the different Kinects.

5 Evaluation

First, in Section 5.1, we present four initial experiments: (1) we extract the VFH descriptor from point clouds and compare it to related work on the RGB-D dataset [12]; (2) we repeat this for the DPM detector on color image scenes; (3) we show the benefit of multi-camera information for classification on the RGB-D dataset; and (4) on our dataset using registered point clouds.

In Section 5.2, after having shown the effectiveness of our individual components, we test our detection approaches (detailed in Section 3) using multi-view, depth, and color information on our multi-camera color and depth dataset.

5.1 Initial Experiments

We first evaluate object classification performance using VFH as a descriptor for point clouds on the RGB-D dataset [12]. We achieve a classification accuracy of 57.8% with nearest-neighbors [15] and 59.4% with χ^2 kernel SVM [23], while [12] reports 64.7% using Spin Image [11] with a Gaussian kernel SVM. We note that there is a drop in performance from Spin Image to VFH, but we found VFH faster to compute and to work very well on registered point clouds from multiple camera views as we will see below.

Second, we evaluate the DPM [3] detector on the RGB-D dataset. Not surprisingly DPM outperforms HOG (with sliding window) used in [12] on the depth (see blue vs. green in Fig. 4(a) for class *mug*) and on the color/intensity (violet vs. red) channel. In the following we use DPM as detector on the color image.

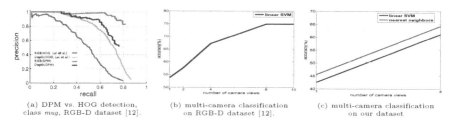

(a) DPM vs. HOG detection, class *mug*, RGB-D dataset [12].

(b) multi-camera classification on RGB-D dataset [12].

(c) multi-camera classification on our dataset

Fig. 4. Initial experiments, evaluating features and multiple cameras

In a third experiment we use multi-view object information in the classification RGB-D dataset by taking the mean of the scores from different views. There is a significant improvement from 53.7% (1 view) to 74.9% (8 views) accuracy (Fig. 4(b)) and hardly any improvement for more than 8 views.

The second object classification evaluation is performed on our MPII Multi-Kinect dataset, classification challenge. Here we register the point clouds from different views into a single point cloud. We improve the classification accuracy from 42.6% (1 view) to 61.0% (4 views) with linear SVM and from 45.5% (1 view) to 64.2 (4 views) with a nearest neighbors classifier, as can be seen in Fig. 4(c). In the following we will use the nearest neighbors classifier for VFH.

5.2   Detection with Multiple Kinects

For the 3D object detection challenge in our MPII Multi-Kinect dataset, we use three cameras for detection and one as ground truth as shown in Fig. 3.

In Table 1 we compare a DPM-baseline to our approaches introduced in Sec. 3 for all classes. We first examine the DPM-baseline present in the first three columns, comparing the mean performance in the last row. Evaluated on the color image of a single camera DPM achieves a detection mean average precision (AP) of 49.1%, 74.2%, and 61.8% for cameras A, B, and C, respectively. The benefit of camera B (see Fig. 3) is of being the one with steepest angle witnessing the least occlusion of all cameras.

Our first multi-camera approach, sDPM+mVFH, uses still single camera DPM, but verifies hypotheses with the multi-camera 3D object classifier. This significantly improves the performance of each camera to 54.9%, 85.0%, and 68.4% by 5.8%, 10.8%, and 6.6%, respectively. This consistent improvement shows the strength of adding depth information aggregated from multiple cameras.

In our second multi-camera approach we combine all cameras from the previous approach by voting for a 3D location and achieve 92.4% which is an increase by 7.4% compared to the best sDPM+mVFH (85.0% AP) and an increasy by 18.2% compared to the best DPM-baseline (74.2% AP). This shows again the benefit of multiple cameras.

In Fig. 5 we show the detection of a highly occluded *sponge* fails for the single-camera DPM (a), while we can detected it using multi-camera and depth information (b). However, the multi-view approach sometimes does not provide very accurate detections (c).

| (a) Single-camera DPM fails to detect an occluded sponge. | (b) Multi-camera voting approach successfully detects the occluded sponge. | (c) Multi-camera voting locates the sponge inaccurately. |

Fig. 5. Multi-camera voting approach successfully detects an occluded object

Table 1. 3D detection using multiple cameras, color, and depth (AP in %). Single-camera DPM, single-camera DPM + multi-camera VFH, multi-camera DPM+VFH.

Class	sDPM (baseline)			sDPM+mVFH			mDPM+mVFH
	cam A	cam B	cam C	cam A	cam B	cam C	multi-cam voting
avocado	50.7	85.0	56.9	54.6	100.0	81.4	100.0
bowl	3.0	75.1	48.5	2.1	76.1	51.2	87.0
coffee box	68.7	69.1	63.0	76.7	78.5	67.2	80.0
container	85.7	76.5	48.0	89.3	89.8	42.1	89.6
cup	35.7	77.3	72.6	33.2	83.6	73.5	100.0
nutella can	80.9	83.4	83.6	82.0	83.8	84.1	89.2
plate	15.4	78.1	80.2	14.6	80.2	82.5	90.2
soup powder can	70.2	65.4	62.7	69.7	75.3	70.5	98.5
sponge	31.3	58.1	40.9	71.7	97.5	63.2	97.0
mean	49.1	**74.2**	61.8	54.9	**85.0**	68.4	**92.4**

6 Conclusion

In this work we explored the benefit of using multiple Kinects providing color and depth information, compared to just single color cameras. In comparison to the DPM baseline we found adding point clouds from multiple depth cameras we achieve a performance increase from 74.2% AP to 85.0% for the best camera view. Adding additionally all RGB cameras further increases the performance to 92.4% improving by 18.2% AP over the best single RGB camera view. This shows that multi-view and depth information can be very beneficial for 3D object detection.

As part of future work we plan to add the recently proposed and improved point cloud descriptors [16]. We are also interested in the important direction of human-object interactions which will further increase occlusion and thus require multiple cameras.

References

1. Coates, A., Ng, A.Y.: Multi-camera object detection for robotics. In: ICRA (2010)
2. Dalal, N., Triggs, B.: Histogram of oriented gradients for human detection. In: CVPR (2005)
3. Felzenszwalb, P.F., Girshick, R.B., McAllester, D., Ramanan, D.: Object detection with discriminatively trained part based models. PAMI (2010)
4. Franzel, T., Schmidt, U., Roth, S.: Object Detection in Multi-view X-Ray Images. In: Pinz, A., Pock, T., Bischof, H., Leberl, F. (eds.) DAGM/OAGM 2012. LNCS, vol. 7476, pp. 144–154. Springer, Heidelberg (2012)
5. Frome, A., Huber, D., Kolluri, R., Bülow, T., Malik, J.: Recognizing Objects in Range Data Using Regional Point Descriptors. In: Pajdla, T., Matas, J. (eds.) ECCV 2004. LNCS, vol. 3023, pp. 224–237. Springer, Heidelberg (2004)

6. Gould, S., Baumstarck, P., Quigley, M., Ng, A.Y., Koller, D.: Integrating visual and range data for robotic object detection. In: M2SFA2 (2008)
7. Helmer, S., Meger, D., Muja, M., Little, J.J., Lowe, D.G.: Multiple Viewpoint Recognition and Localization. In: Kimmel, R., Klette, R., Sugimoto, A. (eds.) ACCV 2010, Part I. LNCS, vol. 6492, pp. 464–477. Springer, Heidelberg (2011)
8. Hinterstoisser, S.H.S., Cagniart, C., Ilic, S., Konolige, K., Navab, N., Lepetit, V.: Multimodal templates for real-time detection of texture-less objects in heavily cluttered scenes. In: ICCV (2011)
9. Izadi, S., Kim, D., Hilliges, O., Molyneaux, D., Newcombe, R., Kohli, P., Shotton, J., Hodges, S., Freeman, D., Davison, A., Fitzgibbon, A.: Kinectfusion: real-time 3D reconstruction and interaction using a moving depth camera. In: UIST (2011)
10. Janoch, A., Karayev, S., Jia, Y., Barron, J.T., Fritz, M., Saenko, K., Darrell, T.: A category-level 3-D object dataset: Putting the kinect to work. In: ICCV (2011)
11. Johnson, A., Hebert, M.: Using spin images for efficient object recognition in cluttered 3D scenes. PAMI (1999)
12. Lai, K., Bo, L., Ren, X., Fox, D.: A large-scale hierarchical multi-view rgb-d object dataset. In: ICRA (2011)
13. Liu, J., Shah, M., Kuipers, B., Savarese, S.: Cross-view action recognition via view knowledge transfer. In: CVPR (2011)
14. Meger, D., Wojek, C., Little, J.J., Schiele, B.: Explicit occlusion reasoning for 3D object detection. In: BMVC (2011)
15. Muja, M., Lowe, D.: Fast approximate nearest-neighbors with automatic algorithm configuration. In: VISAPP (2009)
16. Redondo-Cabrera, C., López-Sastre, R.J., Acevedo-Rodríguez, J., Maldonado-Bascón, S.: Surfing the point clouds: Selective 3D spatial pyramids for category-level object recognition. In: CVPR (2012)
17. Rohrbach, M., Enzweiler, M., Gavrila, D.M.: High-Level Fusion of Depth and Intensity for Pedestrian Classification. In: Denzler, J., Notni, G., Süße, H. (eds.) DAGM 2009. LNCS, vol. 5748, pp. 101–110. Springer, Heidelberg (2009)
18. Rohrbach, M., Regneri, M., Andriluka, M., Amin, S., Pinkal, M., Schiele, B.: Script Data for Attribute-Based Recognition of Composite Activities. In: Fitzgibbon, A., Lazebnik, S., Perona, P., Sato, Y., Schmid, C. (eds.) ECCV 2012, Part I. LNCS, vol. 7572, pp. 144–157. Springer, Heidelberg (2012)
19. Roig, G., Boix, X., Shitrit, H.B., Fua, P.: Conditional random fields for multi-camera object detection. In: ICCV (2011)
20. Rusu, R.B., Bradski, G., Thibaux, R., Hsu, J.: Fast 3D Recognition and Pose Using the Viewpoint Feature Histogram. In: IROS (2010)
21. Rusu, R.B., Cousins, S.: 3D is here: Point Cloud Library (PCL). In: ICRA (2011)
22. Saenko, K., Karayev, S., Yia, Y., Shyr, A., Janoch, A., Long, J., Fritz, M., Darrell, T.: Practical 3-D object detection using category and instance-level appearance models. In: IROS (2011)
23. Vedaldi, A., Zisserman, A.: Efficient additive kernels via explicit feature maps. In: CVPR (2010)
24. Wilson, A.D., Benko, H.: Combining multiple depth cameras and projectors for interactions on, above and between surfaces. In: UIST (2010)
25. Wojek, C., Roth, S., Schindler, K., Schiele, B.: Monocular 3D Scene Modeling and Inference: Understanding Multi-Object Traffic Scenes. In: Daniilidis, K., Maragos, P., Paragios, N. (eds.) ECCV 2010, Part IV. LNCS, vol. 6314, pp. 467–481. Springer, Heidelberg (2010)

Combining Monocular Geometric Cues with Traditional Stereo Cues for Consumer Camera Stereo

Adarsh Kowdle, Andrew Gallagher, and Tsuhan Chen

Cornell University, Ithaca, NY, USA

Abstract. This paper presents an algorithm for considering both stereo cues and structural priors to obtain a geometrically representative depth map from a narrow baseline stereo pair. We use stereo pairs captured with a consumer stereo camera and observe that traditional depth estimation using stereo matching techniques encounters difficulties related to the narrow baseline relative to the depth of the scene. However, monocular geometric cues based on attributes such as lines and the horizon provide additional hints about the global structure that stereo matching misses. We merge both monocular and stereo matching features in a piecewise planar reconstruction framework that is initialized with a discrete inference step, and refined with a continuous optimization to encourage the intersections of hypothesized planes to coincide with observed image lines. We show through our results on stereo pairs of manmade structures captured outside of the lab that our algorithm exploits the advantages of both approaches to infer a better depth map of the scene.

Keywords: narrow baseline stereo, consumer stereo camera.

1 Introduction

Recent developments in consumer electronics have paved the way for handheld stereo cameras such as Fujifilm FinePix 3D® and Sony Bloggie 3D®, which allow users to capture stereo pairs in the wild (i.e. outside the lab). Using a *single* stereo pair captured with such a camera, we observe that while standard depth-from-stereo allows us to observe the ordering of various objects in the scene, even the state-of-art algorithms fail to give a good depth map that captures the geometry of the scene such as, the 3D structure of the facades of distant buildings and the depth of homogeneous surfaces (Fig. 3). The problems with stereo matching include: narrow baseline (typically 77 mm, similar to our eyes) that limits the depth from parallax [9], camera properties such as image resolution, and mismatches between sensors in terms of contrast, exposure, and focus, that lead to heavy distortion. In addition, problems due to scene irregularities such as ill-effects of lighting, specularities and homogeneous surfaces make the stereo matching task challenging.

However, humans (with eyes arranged similar to the cameras of a stereo camera), effectively use monocular cues from the scene to infer the 3D structure of the scene as illustrated in Fig. 1a. While the depth perception from stereo of the human visual system is also restricted to only a few meters, we have enough cues from monocular geometric cues and prior learning to obtain the global geometric structure of say, a building beyond the maximum depth from stereo. A number of recent works on depth from a single image have shown that one can obtain a fairly detailed depth map using trained models

A. Fusiello et al. (Eds.): ECCV 2012 Ws/Demos, Part II, LNCS 7584, pp. 103–113, 2012.

(a)   (b)

Fig. 1. (a) Monocular geometric cues: (Left) Müller-Lyer illusion: Equal line segments appear different since we tend to interpret them from a 3D geometry point of view; (Right) Prominent monocular geometric cues like vanishing points not captured in generic stereo matching reveal the structure of a scene even in the absence of texture cues; (b) Stereo cues: Ames room, a famous illusion gives you the above illusion when you look though a peephole (or a monocular image). Viewing it as a stereo pair, would rid of the illusion revealing that the girl on the left is far away compared to the girl on the right.

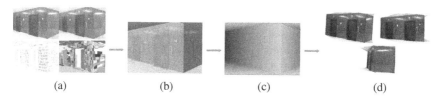

(a)   (b)   (c)   (d)

Fig. 2. Overview: (a) Input stereo pair with the lines detected and superpixel map which help capture some of the monocular cues; (b) Resulting labeling using proposed algorithm; (c) Synthesized depth map (white is close, black is far); (d) 3D reconstruction from novel viewpoints.

[8,16,17,25]. Prior work on single-view 3D reasoning [7,22] and cognitive science have shown monocular *geometric* cues like lines and edges to be a critical aspect of human vision [3, 15]. While these help obtain a globally consistent structure, stereo cues can further disambiguate details or the depth ordering of objects in the scene as illustrated in Fig. 1b.

An overview of our approach and sample results are shown in Fig. 2 and Fig. 3. The main contributions of this paper are:

- We propose an algorithm to combine stereo cues with monocular structural priors (e.g. lines, horizon and plane intersections) that are not considered in generic stereo matching and prior works that combine monocular and stereo cues [24].
- We introduce monocular cues in two ways:
  1) By proposing possible parameterized planes. Stereo matching is used to then find the cost of assigning each plane to each superpixel. This is the discrete step.
  2) By continuous optimization that performs fine adjustment to encourage planes to meet at observed lines in the scene.
- We propose a novel use of distance transforms to encode monocular information from image lines within the discrete and continuous optimization steps.
- We show the effectiveness of the algorithm via a thorough comparison of the 3D reconstruction using a user study allowing users to fly-through the 3D rendering.

2   Related Work

3D reconstruction of a scene is an active field in the community. Given a a single stereo pair of images, we give an overview of prior work to reconstruct the scene.

Depth from a Single Image. On one end of the spectrum is single-view modeling, which exploits solely monocular image cues [7, 8, 16, 17, 22, 25]. Some of these use trained models based on image features [16, 17, 25], under weak assumptions such as colinearity or coplanarity. A key idea that pervades single image reconstruction work is that some scene compositions (e.g. ground plane with perpendicular vertical planes) are more likely than others. We build on these by adding stereo analysis to our algorithm.

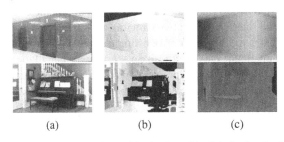

(a)   (b)   (c)

Fig. 3. Comparison with stereo matching (white is close, black is far for the depth maps): (a) Left image of stereo pair; (b) Depth map from stereo matching [29] shows errors such as the depth of the ceiling, and the depth of the piano; (c) Our result is geometrically representative of the scene.

Multiview Stereo. On the other end of the spectrum for 3D reconstruction is multiview stereo. A number of these approaches work with many images to obtain a fairly dense reconstruction [13, 27]. Recent works propose piecewise planar multiview stereo by using a discrete labeling over a set of hypothesized planes [11, 12, 14, 23, 28]. However, with a consumer stereo camera we face two problems: hypothesizing planes using a depth map is unreliable, and using multi-view stereo approaches using only photoconsistency across views does not perform well.

Depth from Stereo. A natural approach to obtain depth from a stereo pair is to use dense stereo matching [1, 26]. While the stereo matching algorithms have been extensively evaluated on benchmarking datasets, we find that these algorithms are very sensitive to the data. Saxena et. al. [24] proposed making a depth map from traditional stereo matching. Holes in this map were filled using his learned single-view depth estimate. In practice, this tends to prefer a smooth reconstruction and given the poor performance of stereo matching on the consumer stereo pairs it would not recover geometric structures (intersecting planar surfaces).

In this work, we show that irrespective of inaccurate depth from stereo obtained due to scene irregularities, we can leverage the monocular geometric cues with the stereo cues to obtain a better, geometrically representative depth map.

3 Algorithm

In this section, we describe our algorithm in detail. We obtain the depth map of the scene in a two-step process. The first step is a discrete optimization that estimates a coarse structure of the scene, followed by a continuous optimization that refines the structure to render a geometrically representative depth map.

3.1 Discrete Optimization

Motivated by recent works in piecewise planar stereo [12,14,23,28] we try to achieve a globally consistent depth map of the scene by formulating depth estimation as a discrete optimization problem, where each pixel belongs to one of many hypothesized planes.

Plane Hypothesis. We first calibrate the stereo camera to obtain the camera parameters (relative translation and rotation) of the two cameras. Given the camera parameters and matched SIFT features on the stereo pair, we estimate the 3D positions of the points resulting in a sparse point cloud. We hypothesize a set of dominant planes (L) by analyzing the distribution of depths of the 3D points along each hypothesized normals ([28]). Note that other plane hypotheses approaches can be used for this initial step [4, 14].

Energy Minimization Formulation. Let $i \in S$ denote superpixels in an image computed using color features from [10]. We describe an energy minimization formulation to estimate a labeling l, where each superpixel i is given a label $l_i \in L$. We define an MRF with the set of superpixels S as nodes, and all adjacent superpixels denoted as $\mathcal{N}$ as edges. We compute the labeling l that minimizes the following energy:

$$E(l) = \sum_{i \in S} E_i(l_i) + \sum_{(i,j) \in \mathcal{N}} E_{i,j}(l_i, l_j), \qquad (1)$$

where $E_i(l_i)$ is the unary term indicating the cost of assigning a superpixel i to a label l_i, and $E_{i,j}(l_i, l_j)$ is the pairwise term for penalizing label disagreement when neighboring superpixels i and j take the labels l_i and l_j, respectively.

Unary Term. Piecewise planar stereo algorithms typically capture this using a photoconsistency term measured over the multiple views. However, in case of a single narrow baseline stereo pair, a unary cost alone does not suffice. We model the term using monocular geometric cues in addition to the stereo photoconsistency term:

$$E_i(l_i) = \Psi(i, l_i) * \left(E_i^P(l_i) + E_i^N(l_i) \right), \qquad (2)$$

where $E_i^P(l_i)$ is the photoconsistency term, $E_i^N(l_i)$ is a surface normal term and $\Psi(i, l_i)$ are additional monocular hard constraints we add to the unary term. We now explain these terms in detail.

Photoconsistency Term (E^P). The photoconsistency term is similar to that used in recent multiview stereo algorithms. For each superpixel on the left image (say), for every plane hypothesis we estimate the warp error (via homography) from the right to the left view, quantified using normalized cross correlation (NCC). We refer the reader to [28] for more details. We compute the NCC using the superpixel as support at each pixel as opposed to a constant window.

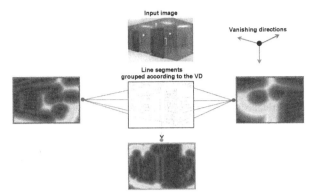

Fig. 4. Illustration of the surface normal term. Given the lines in the image, they are first grouped according to the vanishing directions (three in this case). The distance map for each vanishing direction is an ensemble of distance transforms with respect to the lines grouped to that direction. For example, the figure in the bottom shows the distance map for the green vanishing direction where, blue is a small distance transform value and red is large. Details in Section 3.1.

Surface Normal Term (E^N). With a narrow baseline stereo pair, the two cameras lack enough parallax to differentiate planes beyond a certain depth. Monocular cues such as the lines and vanishing directions provide support to penalize the planes that would result in a globally inconsistent reconstruction.

We estimate the likelihood of each pixel belonging to a particular surface normal direction by developing a novel approach to exploit this information using the lines detected in the image. These lines were used to estimate the vanishing directions and hence hypothesize plane normals spanning the scene[1]. The lines are first assigned to one of the vanishing directions {VD} as shown in Fig. 4. For each vanishing direction $v_p \in \{VD\}$, we compute a distance map (δ_{v_p}) using all the lines assigned to v_p.

$$\delta_{v_p} = \min_{line \in v_p} DT(line), \tag{3}$$

where, $DT(line)$ is the normalized distance transform, i.e., the distance of a pixel to the nearest point on the *line*. Now, considering the normal n_{l_i} of a plane l_i obtained using the cross product of two vanishing directions v_p and v_q. The per-pixel distance likelihood map for the surface normal n_{l_i} is estimated as:

$$D^{n_{l_i}} = \frac{(\delta_{v_p} + \delta_{v_q})}{2}, \tag{4}$$

The surface normal term represents the cost of superpixel i taking plane label l_i and is:

$$E_i^N(l_i) = median\left(D^{n_{l_i}}(p_i)\right), \tag{5}$$

where p_i represents all pixels within superpixel i.

---

[1] Vanishing points and horizon were computed using the algorithm by Kosecka et. al. [20]

Fig. 5. Result of the discrete optimization. The discrete optimization stage assigns the correct normal, but it fails to distinguish between two parallel planes at different depths splitting the left wall into two regions (as shown by the two different shades of green) at different depths.

Monocular Constraints (Ψ). The monocular constraints for each superpixel i, $\Psi(i, l_i)$ gives the cost of choosing a plane that leads to an improbable scene. This depends on the normal of the hypothesized plane. We estimate the position of the horizon [17]. We add a large penalty for a superpixel above the horizon from choosing a plane with normal pointing upwards and for a superpixel below the horizon choosing a plane with normal downwards. For the space below the horizon, the penalty linearly decreases from 1.0 at the horizon to 0.0 at the bottom of the image. In case we fail to detect the horizon then this penalty is always 1.

Pairwise Term. We model the pairwise term using the well-known contrast-sensitive Potts model.

$$E_{i,j}(l_i, l_j) = I(l_i \neq l_j) \exp(-\beta d_{ij}), \qquad (6)$$

where $I(\cdot)$ is an indicator function that is $1(0)$ if the input argument is true(false), d_{ij} is the contrast between superpixels i and j and β is a scale parameter.

Modeling the Contrast Term. (d_{ij}) The contrast is modeled as,

$$d_{ij} = O_{ij} * \left(\lambda_S \, d_{ij}^S + \lambda_C \, d_{ij}^C \right), \qquad (7)$$

The first term (d_{ij}^S) is the stereo matching term. While the depth from stereo is not accurate, the precision is good to capture depth discontinuities. We model d_{ij}^S as $\frac{|d_i - d_j|}{d_j}$ where d_i and d_j are the mean disparities of the pixels within superpixel i and j respectively. The neighboring superpixels with disparity discontinuity are penalized if they take the same plane (and vice-versa). The second term (d_{ij}^C) is the normalized score from a coplanar classifier that captures the contrast between the features of adjacent superpixels [21]. If the coplanar classifier gives a high score for neighboring superpixels, it is penalized for not taking the same plane (and vice-versa). In order to handle inaccuracies in the contrast terms we obtain a soft normalized occlusion map [18]. We weight the pairwise term by the occlusion map, which intuitively captures the ambiguity of stereo matching algorithms in case of occlusions and allows label discontinuity across occlusions. The occlusion weight O_{ij} between superpixels i and j is given by the maximum occlusion confidence along the boundary between the two superpixels. λ_S and λ_C are regularization parameters that are manually tuned by observing the result on one stereo pair but are constant across all the datasets. In practice, equal weights gave good results on all stereo pairs.

Given the unary term and the pairwise term, we use graph-cuts with α-expansion to compute the MAP labels, using the implementation provided by Bagon [2] and Boykov et. al. [5, 6, 19]. The result on our sample stereo pair is shown in Fig. 5.

3.2 Continuous Optimization

The discrete optimization quantizes the 3D space into meaningful planes that allow us to obtain a geometrically pleasing reconstruction. With a single stereo pair, the lack of parallax at large depths results in errors in the reconstruction; for example, it does not help distinguish between parallel planes at different depths (Fig. 5). We counter this problem by again using monocular cues, via a continuous optimization. This refinement stage will try to enforce the monocular constraint that we observe strong edges (or lines) when two non-coplanar surfaces meet.

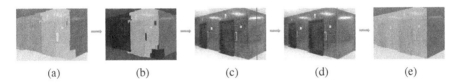

| (a) | (b) | (c) | (d) | (e) |

Fig. 6. Continuous optimization: (a) shows the result from discrete optimization; (b) highlights two regions that after the discrete step are labeled with the correct normals, but incorrect depths such that they are not connected (at the apparent intersection in the image); (c) shows the 2D projection of the line of intersection of planes represented by the highlighted regions (in red); (d) shows the target line of intersection which obeys image cues (in blue); (e) shows the final result, after the continuous optimization and refining the segmentation

---

Algorithm 1. Continuous optimization algorithm

---

1) Consider each region r_m where, $m \in \{1, 2, \ldots, N\}$ with plane parameters, $\pi_m = (\hat{n}_m, p_{(0,m)})$
2) Fix the normal $\hat{n}_m$ and optimize for $p_{(0,m)}$
3) Start from region r_i with highest number of non-parallel neighbors say $nei(r_i) = nei_1, nei_2, \ldots$

Do for each region r_i: {

Optimize for the vector of parameters,

$$p_0 = \left[p_{(0,i)}, p_{(0,nei_1)}, p_{(0,nei_2)}, \ldots \right]'$$

Constrained continuous optimization - bound the deviation of neighboring planes

$$\underset{p_0^*}{\operatorname{argmin}} \sum_{j \in nei(r_i)} err(\pi_i, \pi_j)$$

$$s.t : \forall j \neq i, \ p_{0,j} - \gamma < p_{0,j} < p_{0,j} + \gamma$$

where, γ decides the amount of deviation allowed for the neighboring planes.

}

Consider the erroneous region shown in Fig. 6b. We observe that the two adjacent planar regions say, π_m and π_n are segmented in the 2D fairly accurately. However, on projecting the 3D line of intersection onto the image, we observe that the plane estimate is inaccurate, Fig. 6c. We denote the projected line of intersection by the two points where the line meets the image *boundary* $(x_{mn,1}, y_{mn,1})$ and $(x_{mn,2}, y_{mn,2})$. We fix the plane normals, and using the 2D edge between the two segments we search the space of possible lines of intersection using the lines detected in the image. Once we obtain a target line of intersection defined by $(x'_{mn,1}, y'_{mn,1})$ and $(x'_{mn,2}, y'_{mn,2})$, (Fig. 6d) we optimize the plane parameters by minimizing the error function,

$$err(\pi_m, \pi_n) = |x_{mn,1} - x'_{mn,1}| \tag{8}$$
$$+ |y_{mn,1} - y'_{mn,1}| + |x_{mn,2} - x'_{mn,2}| + |y_{mn,2} - y'_{mn,2}|$$

The continuous optimization algorithm summarized in Algorithm 1. Fig. 6e shows the final result obtained by refining the segmentation using the new plane parameters.

4   Results and Discussions

We perform our experiments on stereo pairs[2] captured using a recent consumer stereo camera, Fujifilm FinePix 3D W1®, which has a narrow baseline of 77mm. Given a stereo pair, we apply our algorithm to obtain plane parameters for each pixel. Given the 2D labeling and the plane parameters, we back-project to estimate the 3D position of each pixel. This allows us to synthesize the depth map, as well as render fly-throughs of the scene. We show the results of the algorithm in Fig. 7.

The importance of the continuous optimization stage can be shown with statistics. On an average, the algorithm resulted in eight unique plane labels for each scene in our dataset of ten stereo pairs. Each of these regions share support from an average of three non-parallel regions that contributes to refining the structure in the continuous optimization stage. The average error per region being optimized, computed using (8) decreased 72% from 87.1 to 24.0 pixels as a result of our continuous optimization stage.

4.1   Comparisons

We compare our work with other possible approaches to obtain the depth map of the scene with a single stereo pair.

We first compare the depth from stereo matching using [29] against our result in Fig. 3 and note that we perform better. Recent works have shown that we can obtain a reasonable depth map from a single image with prior trained models [8, 16, 17, 25]. We show some results in columns 1 and 2 of Fig. 8, and compare with our result. While Saxena et. al. enforce a smooth reconstruction without respecting the monocular geometry, Hoiem et. al. tend to rely on the ground segmentation, which results in inaccurate cutting and folding; we perform better than depth from a single image, which serves as a sanity check. While we do not re-implement work by Saxena et. al. [24], we note that

---

[2] http://chenlab.ece.cornell.edu/projects/ConsumerCamStereo

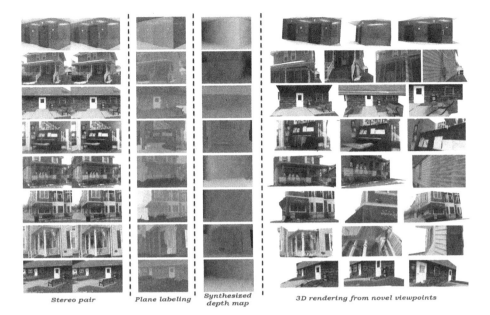

Stereo pair   Plane labeling   Synthesized   3D rendering from novel viewpoints
                                     depth map

Fig. 7. Results (white=close and black=far for depth maps). Note that while the depth of the scene is more than 3 - 4 meters, given a *single* stereo pair of each scene we obtain depth maps that are geometrically representative. Row 2: while the stereo cues helped infer the porch being in front of the main facade, it is not strong enough (due to the depth of the scene) to infer the details of the porch. Row 4: the bench is correctly inferred as a horizontal region above the ground.

due to the inaccurate depth map we would obtain a smooth reconstruction similar to column 1 in Fig. 8. Multi-view stereo approaches strongly rely on the photo-consistency constraint, and fails to differentiate between differently oriented planes as as shown in column 3 in Fig. 8. Micusik et. al. [23] encode some normal information using the spatial structure of the superpixels but without the continuous optimization. Their results are less accurate, as shown in Fig. 5.

Qualitative Comparison: User Study We perform a qualitative comparison of our result, with single view modeling and multiview stereo via a psycho-visual study using 7 subjects. Each subject was presented results on ten stereo pairs without giving any indication about which of the three results they were looking at. They were given complete control to fly through the reconstructed scene and instructed to rank the three results from 1 (best) to 3 (worst) based on the geometric accuracy of the reconstruction. We expect the responses to be more consistent with relative ranking because absolute scores are hard to give, and need calibration across subjects. The average rank for single view modeling[3], multiview stereo and the proposed approach were obtained. The proposed approach was ranked as the best 69% of the time, more than triple the next best. This provides strong evidence that indicates the effectiveness of our approach.

---

[3] The subject used the better result between [17] and [25] for ranking.

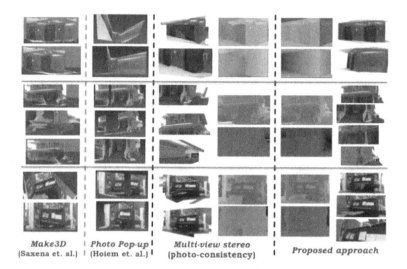

| Make3D (Saxena et. al.) | Photo Pop-up (Hoiem et. al.) | Multi-view stereo (photo-consistency) | Proposed approach |

Fig. 8. Comparison with other approaches

5   Conclusions

We propose an algorithm to combine stereo cues with monocular structural priors to obtain geometrically accurate depth maps using stereo pairs captured in the wild using consumer stereo cameras. We introduce the idea of using both discrete and continuous optimization for 3D reasoning. Our approach leverages the use of monocular cues and exploits the benefits of discrete optimization to obtain a superpixel-to-plane labeling, followed by continuous optimization for refinement. We show through our results and comparisons that the proposed approach works well even in presence of homogeneous surfaces and specularities. The algorithm we propose can be used with any existing stereo matching algorithm, and additional monocular cues can easily be added to the same algorithm. For example, we can incorporate monocular cues such as depth from focus as a prior over the depth of different regions of the scene.

References

1. Middlebury stereo vision, vision.middlebury.edu/stereo/
2. Bagon, S.: Matlab wrapper for graph cut (December 2006)
3. Barrow, H.G., Tenenbaum, J.: Interpreting line drawings as three-dimensional surfaces. Artificial Intelligence 17(1-3), 75–116 (1981)
4. Bleyer, M., Rhemann, C., Rother, C.: Patchmatch stereo - stereo matching with slanted support windows. In: BMVC (2011)
5. Boykov, Y., Kolmogorov, V.: An experimental comparison of min-cut/max-flow algorithms for energy minimization in vision. PAMI 26(9), 1124–1137 (2004)
6. Boykov, Y., Veksler, O., Zabih, R.: Efficient approximate energy minimization via graph cuts. PAMI 20(12), 1222–1239 (2001)
7. Criminisi, A., Reid, I.D., Zisserman, A.: Single view metrology. In: ICCV (1999)

8. Delage, E., Lee, H., Ng, A.Y.: Automatic single-image 3D reconstructions of indoor manhattan world scenes. In: ISRR (2005)
9. Delon, J., Rougé, B.: Small baseline stereovision. Journal of Mathematical Imaging and Vision 28(3), 209–223 (2007)
10. Felzenszwalb, P.F., Huttenlocher, D.P.: Efficient graph-based image segmentation. IJCV 59(2), 167–181 (2004)
11. Furukawa, Y., Curless, B., Seitz, S.M., Szeliski, R.: Reconstructing building interiors from images. In: ICCV (2009)
12. Furukawa, Y., Curless, B., Seitz, S.M., Szeliski, R.: Manhattan-world stereo. In: CVPR (2009)
13. Furukawa, Y., Ponce, J.: Accurate, dense, and robust multi-view stereopsis. PAMI (2009)
14. Gallup, D., Frahm, J.-M., Pollefeys, M.: Piecewise planar and non-planar stereo for urban scene reconstruction. In: CVPR (2010)
15. Gibson, J.J.: Perception of the visual world. Houghton Mifflin (1950)
16. Gupta, A., Efros, A.A., Hebert, M.: Blocks World Revisited: Image Understanding Using Qualitative Geometry and Mechanics. In: Daniilidis, K., Maragos, P., Paragios, N. (eds.) ECCV 2010, Part IV. LNCS, vol. 6314, pp. 482–496. Springer, Heidelberg (2010)
17. Hoiem, D., Efros, A., Hebert, M.: Automatic photo pop-up. In: ACM SIGGRAPH (2005)
18. Hoiem, D., Efros, A., Hebert, M.: Putting objects in perspective. IJCV (2008)
19. Kolmogorov, V., Zabih, R.: What energy functions can be minimized via graph cuts? PAMI 26(2), 147–159 (2004)
20. Kŏsecká, J., Zhang, W.: Video Compass. In: Heyden, A., Sparr, G., Nielsen, M., Johansen, P. (eds.) ECCV 2002, Part IV. LNCS, vol. 2353, pp. 476–490. Springer, Heidelberg (2002)
21. Kowdle, A., Chang, Y., Gallagher, A., Chen, T.: Active learning for piecewise planar multi-view stereo. In: CVPR (2011)
22. Lee, D.C., Hebert, M., Kanade, T.: Geometric reasoning for single image structure recovery. In: CVPR (2009)
23. Micusík, B., Kosecká, J.: Multi-view superpixel stereo in urban environments. IJCV 89(1), 106–119 (2010)
24. Saxena, A., Schulte, J., Ng, A.Y.: Depth estimation using monocular and stereo cues. In: IJCAI (2007)
25. Saxena, A., Sun, M., Ng, A.Y.: Make3D: Learning 3D scene structure from a single still image. PAMI 31(5), 824–840 (2009)
26. Scharstein, D., Szeliski, R., Zabih, R.: A taxonomy and evaluation of dense two-frame stereo correspondence algorithms. In: SMBV (2001)
27. Seitz, S., Curless, B., Diebel, J., Scharstein, D., Szeliski, R.: A comparison and evaluation of multi-view stereo reconstruction algorithms. In: CVPR (2006)
28. Sinha, S., Steedly, D., Szeliski, R.: Piecewise planar stereo for image-based rendering. In: ICCV (2009)
29. Yang, Q., Wang, L., Yang, R., Stewenius, H., Nister, D.: Stereo matching with color-weighted correlation, hierachical belief propagation and occlusion handling. PAMI 31(3), 492–504 (2009)

Quality Assessment of Non-dense Image Correspondences

Anita Sellent and Jochen Wingbermühle

Robert Bosch GmbH, CV Research Lab, Hildesheim, Germany
sellent@iam.unibe.ch, jochen.wingbermuehle@de.bosch.com

Abstract. Non-dense image correspondence estimation algorithms are known for their speed, robustness and accuracy. However, current evaluation methods evaluate correspondences point-wise and consider only correspondences that are actually estimated. They cannot evaluate the fact that some algorithms might leave important scene correspondences undetected - correspondences which might be vital for succeeding applications. Additionally, often the reference correspondences for real world scenes are also sparse. Outliers that do not hit a reference measurement can remain undetected with the current, point-wise evaluation methods. To assess the quality of correspondence fields we propose a histogram based evaluation metric that does not rely on point-wise comparison and is therefore robust to sparsity in estimate as well as reference.

1 Introduction

Image correspondence algorithms such as optical flow and stereo disparity estimation do not always return dense correspondences [4], especially if confidence measures [5] or consistency checks [4] are applied, Fig. 1. The results of both dense and non-dense algorithms are usually evaluated by point-wise comparison to dense ground truth fields [3, 6]. This evaluation, however, does not take into account the danger of sparse image correspondences to entirely miss complete objects. For correct evaluation and comparison of non-dense image correspondences, the evaluation measure should take into account the sparseness of a correspondence field as well as the distribution of correspondences over the objects in the scene. Many applications in computer vision and image processing are designed to deal also with sparse image correspondences, for example ego-motion estimation [7]. Therefore, direct evaluation of non-dense image correspondences is desirable.

A general problem in full-reference quality assessment is the availability of ground truth data. Dense ground truth correspondences are available only for a very small set of test sequences that are either synthetic, cf. Ref. [8,9] or acquired in a controlled environment, cf. Ref. [1,10]. For real world scenarios, laser scanners are often used to generate ground truth data, since they provide the easiest way to obtain reference measurements in realistic environments and to evaluate the performance of correspondence algorithms also outside of laboratories [11,12]. Even carefully calibrated reference devices always contain a residual

A. Fusiello et al. (Eds.): ECCV 2012 Ws/Demos, Part II, LNCS 7584, pp. 114–123, 2012.
© Springer-Verlag Berlin Heidelberg 2012

(a) First input frame   (b) Dense flow estimation (c) Reliable flow estimates

Fig. 1. (a) Input image from scene taken from [1]. (b) Dense flow estimation with [2]. (c) Confidence measures [3] can eliminate spurious correspondences, yielding a non-dense but more accurate flow field.

calibration error [13], so that in these set-ups point-wise evaluation might not be a fair measurement.

We propose a histogram based error metric that compares dense as well as non-dense correspondences to given ground truth and does not depend on any additional algorithms such as interpolation or warping [14]. By design, our histogram based evaluation method can deal competently with alignment errors and is robust to reference measurements with a coarse sampling grid. In the evaluation of our error measure we focus on two aspects: **Distribution** (i.e. evaluate, how well correspondence are distributed between all different scene entities) and **Outliers** (i.e. indicate the presence and frequency of outliers).

1.1   Related Work

Due to its importance, a variety of optical flow and disparity estimation methods exist, c.f. Ref. [1, 6, 8, 9]. Some of these algorithms estimate correspondences for every pixel in the image [2, 15], while others focus on salient points [16] or apply confidence measures [3] and consistency checks [4] resulting in non-dense correspondence fields. In spite of the estimated correspondence fields being dense or non-dense, comparison is usually performed by using a point-wise error measure [9]. Point-wise error measures can also be evaluated for different image regions, e.g., highly textured or occluded regions [1,6] and so indicate where the results can be improved.

A further common measure is the ratio of wrong correspondences [6, 13, 17]. On the basis of the point-wise differences between test and reference fields, the correspondence is labeled wrong if a fixed threshold is exceeded. This approach takes the sparseness of the algorithm into account by normalizing with the total number of valid correspondences but evaluates accuracy only where both estimate and reference are defined. To obtain independence from reference measurements, Steingrube et al. [18] consider the free space in front of an object that moves without collisions and count the ratio of correspondence predicting spurious collisions. However, wrong pixel ratios cannot evaluate whether some objects remain completely undetected in non-dense correspondence estimation.

Szeliski [14] introduces a different metric in form of the prediction error for additional frames. Assuming that correspondences can be used to extrapolate or interpolate an additional frame, the prediction error towards this additional frame gives rise to an error measure that does not require known ground truth correspondences. Given these additional frames [1,6], this metric depends heavily on the warping scheme, is sensitive to locally cast shadows and most of all, it requires dense correspondences to warp the images.

While for synthetic scenes, e.g. in Ref. [1,9], ground truth is known exactly, this assumption does not hold for all references. Correspondence established with fluorescent color [1] or structured light [10] are restricted to controlled indoor scenarios. In outdoor or real world dynamic scenarios, the need to approximate reference correspondences e.g. on known planar surfaces [17] arises. Relying on estimated correspondences, the approximated surface is not sure to either reflect the actual location of the surface, nor does it give any indication of the accuracy. Or, reference devices such as laser scanners are used to establish at least sparse measurements [12, 13]. This requires careful registration of the reference measurements to the images. Additionally, the resolution of laser-scanners is considerably lower than of images, so that references are given only for a sparse set of pixels which, however, is usually reasonabley distributed between the objects in the scene.

2   Evaluation Measures

We will use the same notational framework for stereo imagery and video imagery here. For a pair of rectified images from a stereo camera and for two temporally adjacent images from a monocular camera we use the notations of mappings from the image plane to gray- or color-values $I_1 : \Omega_1 \to \mathbb{R}^3$ and $I_2 : \Omega_2 \to \mathbb{R}^3$ with $\Omega_1, \Omega_2 \subset \mathbb{R}^2$. Likewise, image correspondence $w : \Omega \to \Omega_2$ with $\Omega \subset \Omega_1$ designates optical flow with its two independent components as well as stereo disparity with only one independent component.

We distinguish between two types of correspondences: the output of a correspondence algorithm is designated with $w_{est} : \Omega_{est} \to \Omega_2$ while the reference correspondence is designated with $w_{ref} : \Omega_{ref} \to \Omega_2$ where $\Omega_{est}, \Omega_{ref} \subset \Omega_1$ are the subsets for which correspondence are estimated or given, respectively. Note that the set $\Omega_0 = \Omega_{est} \cap \Omega_{ref}$ on which both estimate and reference are defined might be the empty set.

2.1   Point-Wise Evaluation Measures

For $\Omega_0 \neq \emptyset$ the usual error measure to compare correspondences is the point-wise difference, also known as the point-wise endpoint error [6]

$$EE(z) = \|w_{est}(z) - w_{ref}(z)\|_2 \quad \forall z \in \Omega_0 \tag{1}$$

together with the ratio of pixels that exceed a fixed threshold on the EE

$$R_\tau = \frac{1}{|\Omega_0|} |\{z \in \Omega_0 | EE(z) > \tau\}| \tag{2}$$

where $|\cdot|$ returns the number of elements in a set. For optical flow evaluation, also the point-wise angular error

$$AE(z) = \frac{(w_{est}(z) - z; 1)^{\top} (w_{ref}(z) - z; 1)}{\|(w_{est}(z) - z; 1)\|_2 \; \|(w_{ref}(z) - z; 1)\|_2} \tag{3}$$

and the ratio of wrong pixels in reference to this error, A_τ, are considered.

Usually the spatial means of the errors over all valid pixels are reported [3], i.e. $MEE = \frac{1}{|\Omega_0|} \sum_{z \in \Omega_0} EE(z)$ and $MAE = \frac{1}{|\Omega_0|} \sum_{z \in \Omega_0} AE(z)$ or - for stereo disparities [6] - the root-mean-squared-error

$$RMSE = \sqrt{\frac{1}{|\Omega_0|} \sum_{z \in \Omega_0} \|w_{est}(z) - w_{ref}(z)\|_2^2} \; .$$

Given exactly aligned ground truth correspondence fields, point-wise measures are highly suited to find where estimated correspondences are accurate and where they are inaccurate. While outliers are clearly distinguishable in the differences between estimate and reference, Eqs. (1), (3), averaging over all valid pixels for $RMSE$, MEE and MAE mixes outliers with the accuracy of correct estimates and therefore these values are found to be of limited significance [1]. Considering the percentage of pixels with an error larger than a threshold τ, outliers can be identified more clearly, requiring however to set this threshold appropriately.

These measures are not sufficient for non-dense image correspondences: A scene can contain objects with properties that inhibit confident estimation of image correspondences on this object, e.g. low texture or changing illumination. However, the undetected object might be of significant importance in the scene. Additionally, if reference correspondences are sparse, the set of joint correspondences Ω_0 might contain only few, possibly non-representative correspondences.

2.2 Histogram-Based Evaluation Measures

We propose to consider the normalized distribution of flow vectors, i.e. the normalized histogram $h_w(u)$. For stereo disparity, the histogram is one dimensional (u denotes the disparity value), while for optical flow fields the histogram has two dimensions (u denotes the vertical and horizontal flow component), Figs. 2b, 2c. If the correspondences for every object in the scene are detected reliably, the normalized histograms h_{ref} and h_{est} are similar in shape and amplitude. If, in contrast, an entire object with independent correspondences remains undetected, the corresponding bins have smaller amplitude or might even remain empty, Fig. 2. In the definition of the histograms the set Ω_0 of jointly defined correspondences is not relevant. Thus, the comparison of normalized histograms is independent towards sparseness as long as the correspondences are evenly distributed over all objects.

Histograms are expressed in a discretized form by choosing a suitable bin size b. Discretized histograms can be compared bin-wise [19]. Here, however, the choice of the bin size b as well as slight inaccuracies of the image correspondences

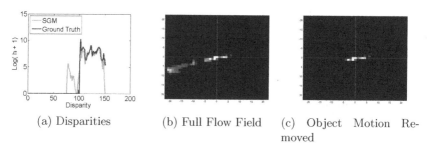

(a) Disparities   (b) Full Flow Field   (c) Object Motion Re-
                                                 moved

Fig. 2. Histograms of disparity fields (a) are 1-dimensional. Histograms of flow fields are 2-dimensional. The difference between the full field (b) and flow fields with object-wise removed correspondences (c) is clearly visible.

have a high influence on the result of the comparison. A more robust method to compare normalized histograms has been proposed by Rubner et al. [20], known as the *Earth Mover's Distance* (EMD). The metric $EMD(h_1, h_2)$ between two histograms h_1 and h_2 gives the minimal cost required to match both histograms. With the choice of the EMD for histogram comparison, dependency on bin size can be reduced.

The advantage of histogram based evaluation is that it is robust towards different densities of reference and estimated correspondences, and considers distribution of the correspondences over different scene entities. Building histograms over the entire image, however, looses the property to distinguish between different regions of error. Thus, noise in one part of the image can compensate for erroneous correspondences in other parts of the image. In addition to the histogram over the entire image, we therefore consider histograms $h_w^{A_i}$ on subregions A_i of the image domain. As the location of objects is in general unknown, we simply partition the image domain in 2^n equally sized tiles and average the histogram distances

$$H^n = \frac{1}{2^n} \sum_{i=1}^{2^n} EMD(h_{est}^{A_i}, h_{ref}^{A_i}) \ . \tag{4}$$

Note that for $|A_i| = 1$ this corresponds to a version of the mean endpoint error where the error is discretized by the bin size. If a correspondence field contains numerous motions and a high degree of noise, we expect H^n to increase with increasing n, as on small regions noise can no longer be balanced. We noticed however, that usually consideration up to $n = 2$, i.e. on four tiles, suffices.

3   Implementation Details

We have chosen a bin size $b = 1$ for the discretized histograms in all our experiments. In the EMD calculation, the Euclidean l^2 norm between the two histograms has been chosen as the *ground distance*. For simplicity and reproducibility, we use the MATLAB implementation of [21] for the calculation of the

| (a) | (b) | (c) | (d) |

Fig. 3. (a) From the synthetic scene *Urban2* [1] with known ground-truth correspondences, (b), we remove 50% of the correspondences either (c) randomly or (d) contiguously, simulating flow estimates that are rejected by a confidence measure.

EMD. The number of non-empty bins influences the size of the problem and on the speed with which a solution can be found. For example, the determination of H^1 and H^2 for the *Urban 2* scene with 64 non-empty ground-truth bins and 193 non-empty bins in the estimated flow field requires $0.58s$ using a MATLAB implementation on a $3.40GHz$ CPU while the scenes *Venus* with 18 and 48 non-empty bins requires only $0.11s$.

4   Experiments

We evaluate the proposed histogram measure to show its sensitivity to missed objects, its robustness to misalignments and its sensitivity to outliers. For comparable visualizations we use the color encoding as proposed in Ref. [22].

4.1   Non-densely Estimated Correspondences

One motivation for our metric is the desire to evaluate whether a sparse algorithm misses a complete object. Figure 3 shows an exemplary scene, from which we successively remove the motion of the back-ground objects. As reference and test field differ only in missed correspondences, point-wise error metrics report zero differences. The value of the histogram distances between the fields, however, differs from zero, Fig. 4a. Considering correspondences estimated with the algorithm by Chambolle and Pock with default parameters [2] a similar behavior can be observed, Fig. 4. Histogram based measures detect the removal of objects while MEE and $R_{1.0}$ do not show a significant response. As the removed pixels have small motions, the MAE shows a tendency to decrease. However, if the fast moving objects in the foreground are removed, the MAE increases, Fig. 4c. Fig. 4d shows that the actual density does not have a significant effect on any error measure, as long as the distribution is approximately uniform.

As neither point-wise nor histogram-based evaluation distinguishes between reference and estimated correspondences, the considerations from above also hold for sparse reference measurements. We note that a disadvantage of the histogram based evaluation is that reference correspondences need to be evenly distributed over the objects in the scene.

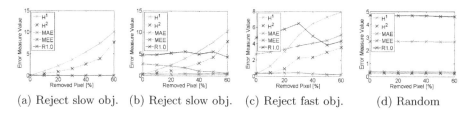

(a) Reject slow obj.   (b) Reject slow obj.   (c) Reject fast obj.   (d) Random

Fig. 4. Error metric response to missing pixel correspondences. Contiguous removal of correspondences from ground truth (a) and from estimation results using [2] (b), (c), as well as random removal from estimation results (d).

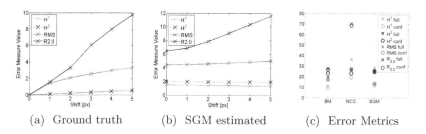

(a) Ground truth   (b) SGM estimated   (c) Error Metrics

Fig. 5. (a) Shifting ground truth correspondences [10] or (b) correspondences estimated with SGM [4] relative to dense ground truth. (c) Influence of rejection of disparities by confidence measure on error metric response.

4.2   Measured Reference Correspondences

Reference fields are usually acquired with a different device that needs to be calibrated to the input images. We compare the reference fields to a shifted version of themselves using the data from Ref. [10]. Also, we estimate disparities with an implementation of the semi-global matching (SGM) algorithm [4] and compare to shifted references. We note, Fig. 5, that in both cases the histogram-based error measure does not show any significant changes while the point-wise RMS error and the ratio of wrong correspondences shows larger deviation.

We simulate the influence of confidence measures on stereo correspondences by removing disparities for overexposed pixels which have an overexposed 4-neighborhood. Due to the - correct - absence of reference measurements in the overexposed sky, the RMS and ratio of wrong pixels only react to the rejection of overexposed regions in the cars. They are approximately indifferent to the impact of the confidence measure, utilizing block matching (BM), cross correlation (NCC), and SGM estimation, Fig. 5c. In contrast, the histogram-based error measure H^1 clearly indicates the improvement in the correspondence fields. The sub-region measure H^2 is of limited significance in this example as half the sub-regions contain less than 50 pixels of the reference field.

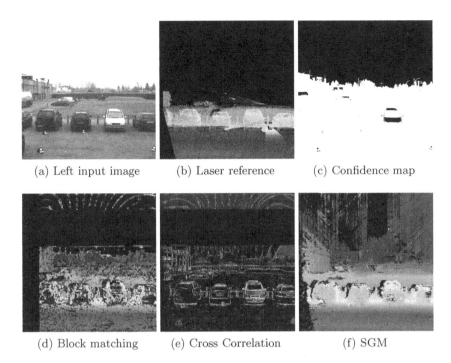

(a) Left input image   (b) Laser reference   (c) Confidence map

(d) Block matching   (e) Cross Correlation   (f) SGM

Fig. 6. For the scene *parking lot 3* [12] we compare estimated disparities to laser scanned reference data and evaluate the impact of a confidence map that eliminates correspondences with overexposed pixels

4.3 The Influence of Noise

Due to the loss of locality, the histogram-based metric cannot distinguish between noise and reliable estimates. Considering e.g. a purely diverging flow field and a flow field with random values in the same range, Fig. 7, only the point-based error measure can identify the poor quality of the noise field with $MEE = 10.44$ and $R_{1.0} = 99.79\%$ while the overall histogram distance $H^1 = 0.03$ is small. Here only the consideration of sub-level histogram distances H^n with $n > 1$, e.g. $H^2 = 7.65$ and $H^3 = 9.07$ that are considerably larger than H^1 hints at a noisy quality of the flow.

However, purely random correspondence fields can generally already be dismissed by visual inspection [22]. More important is the detection of small regions which are assigned a random correspondence field, Fig. 7c. To the purely diverging flow field we therefore add regions of random correspondences: randomly chosen image regions with a diameter of 10 pixels are replaced with an arbitrary correspondence somewhere in the image. As show in Fig. 7d, both point-wise and histogram based measures are able to detect the disturbance as both errors increase in a strictly monotone way with the number of outlier regions.

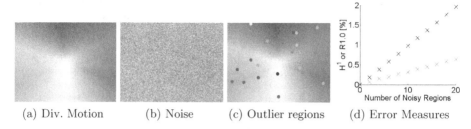

(a) Div. Motion	(b) Noise	(c) Outlier regions	(d) Error Measures

Fig. 7. Histogram-based error measures cannot distinguish the diverging motion in (a) from random values in the same range (b). However, if an increasing number of regions is substituted with arbitrary matches within the image (c), point-based and histogram-based measures increase in a monotone fashion (d).

5   Conclusion and Future Work

Usual point-wise error measures can evaluate accuracy of a correspondence field only at those points where estimated and reference correspondence are defined. We have shown that this can be misleading in the evaluation of non-dense correspondences where entire objects can be undetected. Our histogram based measure can reliably detect missed objects in correspondence fields. Additionally, it is robust to misalignments between reference and estimates that occur due to reference sensor calibration errors. We have shown in our experiments that our histogram based measure is also suitable to evaluate the frequency of random outliers in correspondence fields. However, we believe no single metric should be used to evaluate correspondence algorithms. We strongly encourage authors of algorithms also to evaluate the accuracy of their correspondences, e.g. via point-wise error measures on suitable data set, the robustness of their algorithm to noise in the input images or the drift of their results when concatenated over long sequences.

References

1. Baker, S., Scharstein, D., Lewis, J., Roth, S., Black, M., Szeliski, R.: A database and evaluation methodology for optical flow. IJCV 92, 1–31 (2011)
2. Chambolle, A., Pock, T.: A first-order primal-dual algorithm for convex problems with applications to imaging. JMIV 40, 120–145 (2011)
3. Bruhn, A., Weickert, J.: A confidence measure for variational optic flow methods. In: Geometric Properties for Incomplete Data, pp. 283–298 (2006)
4. Hirschmuller, H.: Accurate and efficient stereo processing by semi-global matching and mutual information. In: CVPR, vol. 2, pp. 807–814 (2005)
5. Kondermann, C., Kondermann, D., Jähne, B., Garbe, C.: An Adaptive Confidence Measure for Optical Flows Based on Linear Subspace Projections. In: Hamprecht, F.A., Schnörr, C., Jähne, B. (eds.) DAGM 2007. LNCS, vol. 4713, pp. 132–141. Springer, Heidelberg (2007)

6. Scharstein, D., Szeliski, R.: A taxonomy and evaluation of dense two-frame stereo correspondence algorithms. IJCV 47, 7–42 (2002)
7. Schill, F., Mahony, R., Corke, P.: Estimating Ego-Motion in Panoramic Image Sequences with Inertial Measurements. In: Pradalier, C., Siegwart, R., Hirzinger, G. (eds.) Robotics Research. STAR, vol. 70, pp. 87–101. Springer, Heidelberg (2011)
8. Barron, J., Fleet, D., Beauchemin, S.: Performance of optical flow techniques. IJCV 12, 43–77 (1994)
9. Klette, R., Kruger, N., Vaudrey, T., Pauwels, K., Van Hulle, M., Morales, S., Kandil, F., Haeusler, R., Pugeault, N., Rabe, C.: Performance of correspondence algorithms in vision-based driver assistance using an online image sequence database. IEEE T-VT, 1 (2011)
10. Scharstein, D., Szeliski, R.: High-accuracy stereo depth maps using structured light. In: CVPR, vol. 1, p. I–195. IEEE (2003)
11. Morales, S., Klette, R.: Ground Truth Evaluation of Stereo Algorithms for Real World Applications. In: Koch, R., Huang, F. (eds.) ACCV 2010 Workshops, Part II. LNCS, vol. 6469, pp. 152–162. Springer, Heidelberg (2011)
12. Reulke, R., Luber, A., Haberjahn, M., Piltz, B.: Validierung von mobilen Stereokamerasystemen in einem 3D-Testfeld. In: 3D-NordOst, vol. 12 (2009)
13. Geiger, A., Lenz, P., Urtasun, R.: Are we ready for autonomous driving? In: CVPR, Providence, USA (2012)
14. Szeliski, R.: Prediction error as a quality metric for motion and stereo. In: ICCV, vol. 2, pp. 781–788. IEEE (1999)
15. Stein, F.J.: Efficient Computation of Optical Flow Using the Census Transform. In: Rasmussen, C.E., Bülthoff, H.H., Schölkopf, B., Giese, M.A. (eds.) DAGM 2004. LNCS, vol. 3175, pp. 79–86. Springer, Heidelberg (2004)
16. Lucas, B., Kanade, T.: An iterative image registration technique with an application to stereo vision. In: Proc. of the Conf. on Art. Intelligence (1981)
17. Liu, Z., Klette, R.: Approximated Ground Truth for Stereo and Motion Analysis on Real-world Sequences. In: Wada, T., Huang, F., Lin, S. (eds.) PSIVT 2009. LNCS, vol. 5414, pp. 874–885. Springer, Heidelberg (2009)
18. Steingrube, P., Gehrig, S.K., Franke, U.: Performance Evaluation of Stereo Algorithms for Automotive Applications. In: Fritz, M., Schiele, B., Piater, J.H. (eds.) ICVS 2009. LNCS, vol. 5815, pp. 285–294. Springer, Heidelberg (2009)
19. Stricker, M., Orengo, M.: Similarity of color images. In: Proc. SPIE Storage and Retrieval for Image and Video Databases, vol. 2420, pp. 381–392 (1995)
20. Rubner, Y., Tomasi, C., Guibas, L.: A metric for distributions with applications to image databases. In: ICCV, pp. 59–66. IEEE (1998)
21. Zhang, Y.: Solving large-scale linear programs by interior-point methods under the matlab environment. Technical Report TR96-01, Department of Mathematics and Statistics, University of Maryland (1995)
22. Sellent, A., Lauer, P.S., Kondermann, D., Wingbermühle, J.: A toolbox to visualize dense image correspondences. Technical report, Heidelberg Collaboratory for Image Processing, HCI (2012)

A Complete Confidence Framework for Optical Flow*

Patricia Márqucz-Valle, Debora Gil, and Aura Hernàndez-Sabaté

Computer Vision Center
Edifici O, Campus UAB, 08193 Bellaterra, Barcelona, Spain
{pmarquez,debora,aura}@cvc.uab.cat

Abstract. Assessing the performance of optical flow in the absence of ground truth is of prime importance for a correct interpretation and application. Thus, in recent years, the interest in developing confidence measures has increased. However, by its complexity, assessing the capability of such measures for detecting areas of poor performance of optical flow is still unsolved.

We define a confidence measure in the context of numerical stability of the optical flow scheme and also a protocol for assessing its capability to discard areas of non-reliable flows. Results on the Middlebury database validate our framework and show that, unlike existing measures, our measure is not biased towards any particular image feature.

Keywords: Optical flow, confidence measures, sparsification plots, error prediction plots.

1 Introduction

Analysis and interpretation of optical flow, plays a central role in several safety-critical applications as diverse as decision making in car driver assistance and pathology discrimination for medical diagnosis support. A good interpretation and application of flow fields requires a measure of the confidence on the accuracy of the computed flow field.

Two main approaches compute dense flow fields: local and global. Local approaches go back to the early 80's [1] and compute optical flow from the Brightness Constancy Constraint (BCC) in a neighborhood of each pixel. They produce sparse vector fields that are further interpolated to obtain dense flows [2]. In order to minimize the impact of erroneous vectors in the interpolation stage, plenty of confidence measures for local methods have been developed [2]. Global techniques produce dense flow fields by combining into a variational framework a data-term and a smoothness-term. The data-term puts into correspondence one frame with the following one using either the BCC [3–5] or local techniques [6–8]. The smoothness-term determines the global properties of the vector field across the image [9]. Given that current variational schemes are more stable under a local drop of the data-term performance, the use of confidence measures has decreased. However, in dense flow fields we still need a measure to determine in which points the estimation is reliable or not.

Current confidence measures are based on either local image structure, the energy of the computed flow or statistical patterns [10]. Given that data-terms depend on sequence

---

* This work was supported by the Spanish projects TIN2009-13618, TRA2011-29454-C03-01, CSD2007-00018 and the 2nd author by The Ramon y Cajal Program.

A. Fusiello et al. (Eds.): ECCV 2012 Ws/Demos, Part II, LNCS 7584, pp. 124–133, 2012.

derivatives, measures based on local image structures take into account either the image gradient or its structure tensor [2]. The local energy of computed flows introduced in [11] can be computed for any scheme, but its value is strongly linked to the assumptions made by the variational model. Finally, statistical confidence measures [10] are based on the estimation of the flow distribution from a training data-set. They are independent of the particular variational formulation, but require a database including any unusual motion pattern. The bootstrap method proposed in [12] computes the variability of the computed flow with respect to a perturbation of the variational model. Pixels with high variability are associated to model inconsistencies and, thus, discarded. A main concern is that none of the above measures have been defined taking into account the error sources of the numerical schemes.

Assessing the capability of a confidence measure for discarding areas of poor performance is as important as the definition of the measure itself. A reliable confidence measure should present a decreasing dependency on optical flow error in order to guarantee that a bound on its values also bounds the error. As far as we know, the only way of assessing the performance of confidence measures are the Sparsification Plots (SP) reported in [11]. These plots represent the average error for those points with a measure above a value against the measure sorted values. It follows that the more decreasing SP are, the better the confidence measure should be. Although they successfully reflect the overall performance of a given measure, they are unable to assess any dependency between confidence measures and flow errors. As a consequence, they can not be used to determine confidence measure ranges ensuring a bound on flow error.

We introduce a complete confidence framework to define and assess confidence measures. First, we propose defining a confidence measure using error analysis techniques [13]. In particular, we give a measure for Lucas-Kanade-based approaches: the classic local [1] and the Combined-Local-Global (CLG) method described in [11]. Second, we assess the performance of confidence measures by computing the probability density function of having a decreasing dependency between flow errors and confidence measures. The plot of this probability for confidence measure values is called Error Prediction Plot, EPP. Our framework is validated in the benchmark Middlebury database [14] and compared to state-of-art measures and SP. Results show the discriminative power of EPP for detecting bias in existing measures. Both, SP and EPP plots show the higher stability of our measure based on numerical errors compared to existing measures. Consequently it is better suited for defining ranges ensuring a bound on optical flow errors with a given confidence.

2 State of the Art

Most local approaches are based on the method of Lucas-Kanade (LK) [1]. This approach is based on the assumption that optical flow keeps constant in a neighborhood of each pixel. Under this assumption the flow (u, v) solves:

$$\underbrace{\begin{pmatrix} K_\sigma * (I_x^2) & K_\sigma * (I_x I_y) \\ K_\sigma * (I_x I_y) & K_\sigma * (I_y^2) \end{pmatrix}}_{A_{LK}} \begin{pmatrix} u \\ v \end{pmatrix} = \underbrace{\begin{pmatrix} -K_\sigma * (I_x I_t) \\ -K_\sigma * (I_y I_t) \end{pmatrix}}_{b_{LK}} \tag{1}$$

for $I(x, y, t)$ denoting the image sequence, the subscripts the partial derivatives (x and y for spatial derivatives and t for temporal ones), $*$ the convolution operator and K_σ a Gaussian kernel of standard deviation σ.

Variational approaches compute the flow field by minimizing an energy functional that combines a data and a smoothness term:

$$E(u, v) = \int \underbrace{D(u, v, \nabla I)}_{\text{Data Term}} + \alpha \underbrace{S(\nabla u, \nabla v)}_{\text{Smoothness Term}} \, dx \, dy \qquad (2)$$

where the data-term is usually based on the Optical Flow Constraint (OFC) ($I_x u + I_y v + I_t = 0$) and the smoothness-term models the general properties of the flow field.

Confidence measures can be split in three main groups:

Local Structure-Based: Since the data-term is formulated using the image partial derivatives, several measures are defined in terms of the image local structure, either gradient or structure tensor. Gradient-based measures [2] is defined as the magnitude of the gradient. Note that for large values of the magnitude of the gradient we expect reliable motion vectors. However, large gradients usually denote occlusions or noise [11], and in those pixels the optical flow computation is not reliable. In order to minimize the impact of noise, structure tensor based measures use information about the local structure of the image. These measures are especially well suited for LK-based schemes.

A main concern about local structure based measures is that they only take into account the data-term, so that, the impact of the filling-in effect of the smoothness-term is not considered. This limits their applicability to variational approaches, which are based on an energy functional that includes assumptions about the computed flow. In order to account for all assumptions of the underlying energy functional, a confidence measure based on the flow model was introduced by [11].

Energy-Based: This measure takes into account that variational techniques compute optical flow by minimizing an energy functional (2), and thus, the confidence measure is computed evaluating the flow field over the functional. We will refer to it as c_e. A main advantage of c_e is that it can be computed for any variational scheme.

We note that c_e only measures that (u, v) minimizes the energy functional and, thus, that it fulfils the assumptions made in the model. However, this does not guarantee that (u, v) corresponds to the true flow field, since defining a model for variational flow is still an open problem. Measures based on pattern analysis of computed flows are an alternative for defining confidence measures regardless of the model assumptions [10].

Bootstrap-Based: The measure defined by [12] quantifies the uncertainty of the flow method, that is, in those points where the flow field varies, the computation is not reliable. They compute such measure using bootstrap resampling. We refer to this measure as c_b, and we will consider the inverse of ψ_{bootg} defined in [12] eq.(15). Like the energy-based measure, this measure assesses the consistency of the model assumptions.

Observe that none of the above measures take into account the numerical stability of the method itself and, thus, it is not straightforward to derive their link to flow error.

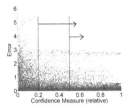 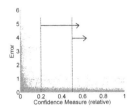 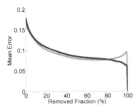

Fig. 1. Sparsification plots. On the left and on the middle the scatter plot of a confidence measure and the error. On the left a poor cm, on the middle a good one. The SP of both measures on the right.

2.1 Sparsification Plots

The most extended way to represent the performance of confidence measures is by means of the Sparsification Plots (SP) [11]. Such plots are given by the remaining mean error for fractions of removed flow vectors having increasing confidence measure values (cm). The scatter plots in fig. 1 illustrate the computation of SP for two representative cases selected from the Middlebury database. For a given removed percentage (vertical line in scatter plots and x-axis in SP below), arrows indicate the points that are considered for the computation of average errors (y-axis in SP).

Under the assumption that higher values of cm are associated to lower flow errors, SP should have decreasing profiles. An increase in their values for the higher removed fractions indicates artifacts in the decreasing dependency possibly due to a high error despite a high cm. However, the inverse does not always hold and random uniform dependencies could produce sensible plots. This is the case of the second representative sequence shown in fig. 1. Even if the dependency shown in the scatter plot is worse in the first sequence, its SP (blue line) indicates a better performance for high fractions.

Besides a poor power for assessing decreasing dependencies between confidence measures and flow error, SP are unable to properly detect if a measure is appropriate for giving a bound on flow accuracy. This is mainly due to the fact that its computation only considers confidence measure values for removing pixels regardless of optical flow error. Therefore, if the distribution of errors for high cm values concentrates around zero, the SP will be low even if we have some outliers with high errors.

3   A Complete Confidence Framework

From confidence measures we should expect a decreasing dependency between the measure and the accuracy, i.e., higher values of the measure are, higher accuracy we expect and viceversa. Thus, we state the dependency between confidence measure cm and error e using the following inequalities:

$$cm > \tau_c \Rightarrow e < \tau_e$$

for τ_c and τ_e chosen thresholds. That is, for a given probability, the ideal confidence measure should be able to guarantee that for a threshold τ_c on cm, the error, e, is bounded. We call the above requirement the Condition of the Quality Threshold (CQT). We note that under CQT, the values of confidence measures would determine the accuracy of the flow field in the absence of ground-truth. Bearing the above requirements in mind, we propose the following confidence framework on the grounds of numerical stability analysis:

A Confidence Measure Based on OF Numerical Stability. There are two main sources of error: a deficient design of the algorithm (ill-conditioned) and round-off numerical propagation errors. The former can not be predicted from optical flow equations and requires a thorough analysis of the algorithm properties. The latter, can be analyzed using numerical stability concepts [13].

In regard to LK approaches [1, 7], the solution follows from a linear system. On the one hand, for local approaches [1] the system is given by (1). On the other hand, for the variational CLG method, the system (1) is the data-term of a variational framework:

$$E(u,v) = \int \underbrace{\psi_1\left(K_\sigma * (I_x u + I_y v + I_t)^2\right)}_{E_{LK}} + \alpha\,\psi_2\left(|\nabla w|^2\right) \mathrm{d}x\,\mathrm{d}y \qquad (3)$$

for $\psi_i(s^2) = \sqrt{\beta_i^2 + s^2}$ a penalizing function, β_i a scaling parameter and $|\nabla w|^2 = |\nabla u|^2 + |\nabla v|^2$. The Euler-Lagrange equations of (3) are given in terms of the local LK system:

$$\frac{1}{\alpha}\psi_1'(E_{LK})\left[A_{LK}\begin{pmatrix}u\\v\end{pmatrix} - b_{LK}\right] = \begin{pmatrix}\mathrm{div}\left(\psi_2'(|\nabla w|^2)\nabla u\right)\\\mathrm{div}\left(\psi_2'(|\nabla w|^2)\nabla v\right)\end{pmatrix} \qquad (4)$$

for $\psi_i'(s^2) = 1/(\sqrt{1 + \frac{s^2}{\beta_i^2}})\ i = 1, 2.$

Therefore, we can determine the sources of errors of LK schemes by studying the properties and numerical stability of the system given by (1). Errors in the output data that come from errors in the input of the algorithm are called propagation errors. In our case, the error given by the input data is produced by the acquisition of the sequences.

The condition number [13] associated to a system of equations $Ax = b$, gives an upper bound of the error of the solution in relation with the error given in b. Given a square matrix A, if e is the error in b, then the error in the solution $x = A^{-1}b$ is $A^{-1}e$. The relative error in the solution to the relative error in b is the mentioned condition number and determines the error propagation. It is defined as follows:

$$K(A) = \frac{\|A^{-1}e\|/\|A^{-1}b\|}{\|e\|/\|b\|} = \|A\|\|A^{-1}\| \qquad (5)$$

for $\|\cdot\|$ a matrix norm. If we consider the L^2 norm and the matrix A is symmetric, the condition number simplifies to: $\kappa(A) = \lambda_{max}/\lambda_{min}$, where λ_{max} and λ_{min} are the maximum and minimum eigenvalues of A, respectively.

The condition number range is $[1, \infty)$. For large values the propagation of input errors is bad (ill-conditioned problem), whereas for low values (near to one) errors in the output compare to input errors and the problem is well-conditioned. In other words, if the condition number is large, then, the output error may not be bounded, that is, it can take any value (errors comparable with the input data errors or higher errors in the output data). Meanwhile, if the condition number is close to one, the error of the output data is comparable to the error of the input data, and thus, the output data is reliable. It follows that low values of the confidence measure are associated with stability of the numeric solution, and, thus it can been used as a measure of the confidence of the computed OF.

Since the condition number is not bounded, we propose the following equivalent measure:

$$c_k = \frac{\lambda_{min}}{\lambda_{max}} \qquad (6)$$

Notice that now, the range is $(0, 1]$. And thus, for small values the error propagation might be large, whereas for values near to 1 the error propagation will be small. We note that with this formulation, singularity of the system (1) cancels c_k, so that, one of the design errors of LK is also under control. In order to avoid indeterminate values such as $0/0$, formula (6) is computed setting to zero such cases. Since the LK matrix is symmetric, we propose c_k given by (6) as a measure that correlates with the accuracy.

The Capability of Confidence Measures for Predicting Errors. The CQT is fulfilled only if the scatter plots between a confidence measure cm and an error e show a decreasing pattern. Such pattern is difficult to measure using mathematical analysis tools because they are unable to properly handle point distributions. The best way to explore point distribution is by means of probability density functions. In probabilistic terms CQT can be stated as a conditional probability:

$$P_C(\tau_e, \tau_c) := P(e \geq \tau_e | cm \geq \tau_c) < \varepsilon \qquad (7)$$

for $\varepsilon < 1$ the probability of having an error above τ_e provided that cm is above τ_c. The conditional probability can be computed by scanning the scatter plots given by cm-e. Taking into account that the condition $cm \geq \tau_c$ corresponds to a vertical line and $e \geq \tau_e$ to an horizontal one, the conditional probability is given by the fraction of points lying on the superior quadrant defined by the former lines. The scatter plots in fig.2 illustrate the computation of (7) for two representative cases selected from the Middlebury database. Arrows indicate the points that are considered for the computation of conditional probabilities.

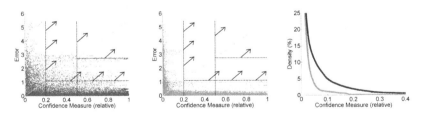

Fig. 2. Error Prediction plots. On the left and on the middle the scatter plot of a confidence measure and the error. On the left a poor measure, on the middle a good one. The EPP plot of both measures on the right.

The conditional probability (7) is a bi-dimensional graph, not easy to interpret. In order to get a simpler representation able to assess the capability of the measure for predicting the error, it suffices to consider the values for the diagonal of the square support of the variables e, cm. In this way, we ensure that unusual non-decreasing patterns (as the one shown in the green scatter point cloud in fig.2) are detected. We define our Error Prediction Plots, EPP, as the plot given by $(cm, P_C(e_{max} \cdot cm/cm_{max}, cm))$, for e_{max} and cm_{max} the maximum values of e and cm. Figure 2 shows scatter plots and their corresponding EPP. Unlike the SP shown in 1, we observe that EPP is worse for the non-decreasing case.

Besides their better potential for detecting poor confidence measures, EPP also serve to determine a threshold τ_c ensuring a bounded error, $e \leq \tau_e$. Given that points having $cm < \tau_c$ should be discarded, we will determine τ_c in terms of the percentage, $100 * \varepsilon$, of discarded points. In this context, τ_c is given by the intersection of the horizontal line $y = 100 * \varepsilon$ with EPP. That is, τ_c is given by the value of the confidence measure that satisfies:

$$P_C(e_{max}cm/cm_{max}, cm) = 100 * \varepsilon \qquad (8)$$

The procedure described so far can only be computed for a representative sample of sequences with a ground truth. For the generalization to any sequence, statistical inference should be applied. In this framework, we should determine a confidence interval for τ_c ranges. In order to do so, the variability of EPP across the representative sequences should be as low as possible [17]. In this context, *the most relevant feature of confidence measures is not a highly decreasing pattern but a stable behavior across different sequences*. An homogeneous profile of EPP plots ensure small ranges for τ_c and, thus, reflect a higher capability for bounding e in terms of cm.

4   Experiments

Our framework has been validated on the well-known Middlebury database [14]. Motion has been computed using the CLG scheme implemented by [18]. In addition to c_k, the measures c_e, c_d and c_b have also been computed. The End-Point Error (EE) [14] is our accuracy score.

Two experiments have been carried out, one to validate the confidence framework, and a second one to test the error prediction capabilities of measures.

Validation of the Confidence Framework. In order to validate the presented framework, we firstly test the overall performance of c_k as well as the capability of EPP for assessing the decreasing dependency between confidence measures and errors. We assess c_k overall performance compared to other cm's by means of the gold-standard SP. Our EPP is validated by comparing their profiles to scatter plots.

We compare the different confidence measures in fig.3, which shows SP (left) and EPP (right) plots for two representative sequences of the Middlebury database. Below each quality plot we show the error scatter plots for each measure.

According to SP, none of the measures can be chosen as the best performer in global terms. We observe that c_k presents a more stable profile without any sudden increase for higher removed fractions, as Urban3 shows. This is consistent with the distribution

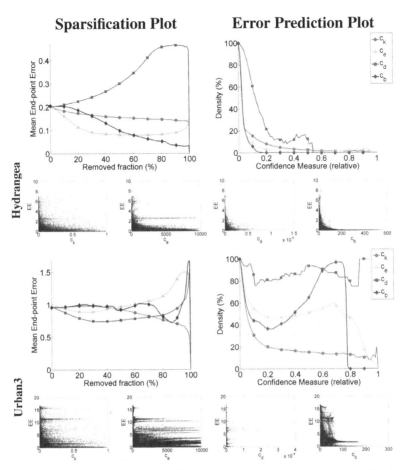

Fig. 3. On the left, the SP, on the right the EPP for the sequences Hydrangea and Urban3. Below the SP and EPP the scatter plots for the measures: c_k, c_e, c_d and c_b (from left to right).

of scatter plots for Urban3 shown below. However, in the case of Hydrangea, SP profile for c_d does not reflect the tendency observed in the scatter plots, which presents a clear decreasing dependency. This discrepancy between sparsification and scatter plots follow from few pixels having non-zero error (below 1 pixel) at the highest removed fractions. In comparison, SP for c_e has a lower profile, despite having pixels with an error above 2 for any removed fraction. Therefore, we must conclude that SP do not reflect dependencies between the confidence measure and error for all cases.

The ranking given by EPP plots agrees with SP for the Urban3 sequence, but clearly indicates a specific poor performance for the measures based on the model, c_e and c_b. Concerning Hydrangea, EPP profiles better reflect the dependency observed in scatter plots and indicate a slightly poorer performance for c_e. Another worthy point is the stability across the two sequences of the non-model based measures, c_k and c_d.

Error Prediction Capabilities of Confidence Measures. The goal of this experiment is two-fold. Firstly, detecting any grouping in cm behavior arising from a biased

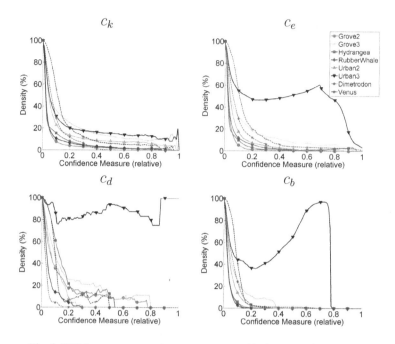

Fig. 4. EPP for c_k, c_e, c_d and c_b measures considering several sequences

definition. Secondly, assessing the variability across sequences and thus the accuracy of a confidence measure for controlling flow errors. For each cm we will consider the EPP for all sequences for the joint comparison of their profiles.

In order to assess the variability across sequences and detect any bias in confidence measures definition, for each measure we show its EPP for several sequences in fig.4. Observe that the measure that has stable behavior across different sequences is c_k. On the contrary, c_d, c_e and c_b are biased by the sequence. Firstly, the measure c_d has a different behavior for each sequence. Secondly, since the measures c_e and c_b are biased towards the assumptions of the flow model, both have similar profiles for the same sequences. Therefore, the measures c_d, c_e and c_b are less accurate for assessing bounds on optical flow error.

5   Conclusions and Future Work

We presented a confidence framework for assessing the performance of flow techniques by means of a numerical stability-based confidence measure and EPP.

As far as we know, none of the existing measures take into account the numerical stability of the method itself.

The SP can not give faithful comparisons across sequences because, the score they plot (mean EE) is not normalized across cases. On the contrary, the proposed EPP take into account both, the measure and the accuracy. That is, they provide a global vision of the capability of a measure to discard high errors. And thus, the problems that we were facing with the SP are now solved and we can also determine a threshold for the confidence measure that gives a bound for the flow error.

Finally, in order to assess the flow field accuracy by means of a measure we need a stable behavior of the measure across different sequences.

In the near future we plan to generalize the proposed confidence measure based on the condition number for any kind of variational framework. In addition, we plan to explore the results considering different choices of evaluating EPP; that is, not only on the diagonal of the graph. And also, it would be interesting to do the same experiments considering different flow algorithms.

References

1. Lucas, B., Kanade, T.: An iterative image registration technique with an application to stereo vision. In: DARPA IU Workshop, pp. 121–130 (1981)
2. Barron, J.L., Fleet, D.J., Beauchemin, S.S.: Performance of optical flow techniques. IJCV 12(1), 43–77 (1994)
3. Horn, B., Schunck, B.: Determining optical flow. AI 17, 185–203 (1981)
4. Nagel, H.H., Enkelmann, W.: An investigation of smoothness constraints for the estimation of displacement vector fields from image sequences. PAMI 8, 565–593 (1986)
5. Sun, D., Roth, S., Black, M.J.: Secrets of optical flow estimation and their principles. In: CVPR, pp. 2432–2439 (2010)
6. Bigün, J., Granlund, G.H., Wiklund, J.: Multidimensional orientation estimation with applications to texture analysis and optical flow. PAMI 13(8), 775–790 (1991)
7. Bruhn, A., Weickert, J., Schnörr, C.: Lucas/Kanade meets Horn/Schunck: Combining local and global optic flow methods. IJCV 61(2), 221–231 (2005)
8. García-Barnés, J.: Variational framework for assessment of the left ventricle motion. Math. Mod. of Nat. Phen. 3(6), 76 (2008)
9. Weickert, J., Schnörr, C.: A theoretical framework for convex regularizers in pde-based computation of image motion. IJCV 45, 245–264 (2001)
10. Kondermann, C., Mester, R., Garbe, C.: A Statistical Confidence Measure for Optical Flows. In: Forsyth, D., Torr, P., Zisserman, A. (eds.) ECCV 2008, Part III. LNCS, vol. 5304, pp. 290–301. Springer, Heidelberg (2008)
11. Bruhn, A., Weickert, J.: A confidence measure for variational optic flow methods. In: Geometric Properties for Incomplete Data, pp. 283–298 (2006)
12. Kybic, J., Nieuwenhuis, C.: Bootstrap optical flow confidence and uncertainty measure. Computer Vision and Image Understanding, 1449–1462 (2011)
13. Cheney, W., Kincaid, D.: Numerical Mathematics and Computing, 6th edn. Bob Pirtle, USA (2008)
14. Baker, S., Scharstein, D., Lewis, J., Roth, S., Black, M.J., Szeliski, R.: A database and evaluation methodology for optical flow. IJCV 92(1), 1–31 (2011)
15. Haussecker, H., Spies, H.: Handbook of Computer Vision and Applications, vol. 2. Academic Press (1999)
16. Shi, J., Tomasi, C.: Good features to track, pp. 593–600 (1994)
17. Newbold, P., Carlson, W., Thorne, B.: Statistics for Business and Economics. Pearson Education (2007)
18. Liu, C.: Beyond pixels: exploring new representations and applications for motion analysis. Ph.D. dissertation, Cambridge, MA, USA (2009)

An Improved Stereo Matching Algorithm with Ground Plane and Temporal Smoothness Constraints

Cevahir Çığla[1,2] and A. Aydın Alatan [2]

[1] ASELSAN Inc.
Ankara, Turkey
[2] Middle East Technical University
Ankara, Turkey
{cevahir,alatan}@eee.metu.edu.tr

Abstract. In this study, novel techniques are presented addressing the challenges of stereo matching algorithms for surveillance and vehicle control. For this purpose, one of the most efficient local stereo matching techniques, namely permeability filter, is modified in terms of road plane geometry and temporal consistency in order to take the major challenges of such a scenario into account. Relaxing smoothness assumption of the permeability filter along vertical axis enables extraction of road geometry with high accuracy, even for the cases where ground plane does not contain sufficient textural information. On the other hand, temporal smoothness is enforced by transferring reliable depth assignments against illumination changes, reflections and instant occlusions. According to the extensive experiments on a recent challenging stereo video dataset, the proposed modifications provide reliable disparity maps under severe challenges and low texture distribution, improving scene analyses for surveillance related applications. Although improvements are illustrated for a specific local stereo matching algorithm, the presented specifications and modifications can be applied for the other similar stereo algorithms as well.

1 Introduction

The advances in robotics and automation introduce new application areas for stereo matching that provide 3D data from two cameras. In this manner, the passive technology behind such a scheme enables stereo matching [1] to be the most common way of depth extraction, especially for outdoor scenes through simple data acquisition capability. Moreover, current benchmarks [2] enabled stereo matching algorithms to improve rapidly by providing objective comparison with the available ground truth depth maps. On the other hand, these datasets have limited realism and may not model the characteristics of the real world data that involve various imperfections. Hence, new challenges are introduced in [3] for stereo matching to provide robust solutions against non-Lambertian surfaces, different lightening conditions, and complex scenes. These challenges require modifications over the well-known stereo matching algorithms.

A. Fusiello et al. (Eds.): ECCV 2012 Ws/Demos, Part II, LNCS 7584, pp. 134–147, 2012.
© Springer-Verlag Berlin Heidelberg 2012

Among many alternatives [1], local stereo matching techniques [4]-[10] have been popular recently due to low memory requirement, non-iterative computation and moderate quality. As pioneered by the well-known bilateral filter (BF) [4], edge-aware filters are excessively utilized to aggregate cost functions of disparity candidates to enforce smoothness among color-wise similar regions for disparity maps. However, it is expensive to provide content adaptability, since filter coefficients alternate according to image statistics, which requires special attention for each pixel individually.

Several approximations over bilateral filter are proposed in order to increase their efficiency. In [5], constant time computation of BF has been demonstrated yielding window size independency. One of the most efficient implementation is introduced in [6], in which piecewise linear approximation is provided through discritization of image intensities into a number of intensity levels. Content adaptive filtering is conducted for these levels which are defined as Principle Bilateral Filtered Image Component (PBFIC). Filtered values of the remaining levels are calculated by the linear interpolation of the two closest quantization levels to the pixel intensity.

In [7], an alternative edge-preserving filtering technique is presented, denoted as *image guided filtering*, in which adaptive weights are provided by a local linear model between the guidance image and the filtered data. In another approach [8], guided image filtering is applied for stereo matching where the computational complexity of adaptive weights is reduced drastically by use of box filters over mean and variance of the cost volume. As a different technique, orthogonal cross aggregation is exploited by considering connected pixel groups having similar intensity characteristics [9]. The aggregation is performed by two passes in vertical and horizontal direction over integral images, which approximates BF by constant weights along arbitrary regions. This approach is recently extended to soft weights by [10] through recursive horizontal and then vertical weighted summation. In [10], for each pixel aggregation is effectively provided among connected support regions with soft weights. The recursive structure in [10] enables complete content adaptability yielding competitive performance based on Middlebury stereo benchmark.

In this study, permeability filter (PF) introduced in [10] is modified for stereo matching among challenging videos that involve various imperfections. Giving a brief summary for permeability filter and its implementation for stereo, details of the modifications for real world data are given in the following section. In Section 4, experimental results are presented for challenging stereo videos, and Section 5 is devoted to the concluding remarks.

2   Permeability Filter

In [10], an efficient approximate edge-aware filter is introduced engaging computationally efficient two pass integration approach by weighted and connected support regions. The main motivation behind PF is to calculate the output as a result of infinite impulse response (IIR) type filter in a recursive manner. For this purpose, successive weighted summations are conducted among horizontal and vertical axes that yield adaptive 2D aggregation. The weights (μ) correspond to pixel similarities, i.e. data transfer rates among four neighboring pixels ($N^4(x)$) given as

$$\mu_{x \to z} = e^{-|I(x)-I(z)|/\sigma} \qquad z \in N^4(x) \tag{1}$$

where $I(x)$ indicates the intensity value of the pixel with index of x and σ corresponds to the smoothing factor.

Successive weighted summation (SWS) rules for horizontal filter are given as,

$$C^{LtoR}(x) = C(x) + \mu^R(x-1)\, C^{LtoR}(x-1)$$
$$C^{RtoL}(x) = C(x) + \mu^L(x+1)\, C^{RtoL}(x+1) \tag{2}$$
$$C^H(x) = C^{LtoR}(x) + C^{RtoL}(x)$$

where $C(x)$ corresponds to the data to be filtered (vertical index, y, is dropped for simplicity), C^{LtoR} and C^{RtoL} are the left-to-right and right-to-left aggregations; when the scans are completed, the input is updated by the unification of these values that provides horizontal accumulation, $C^H(x)$. The same update and progress rule is utilized along vertical axis to extend supporting regions to 2D as follows:

$$C^{TtoB}(y) = C^H(y) + \mu^B(y-1)\, C^{TtoB}(y-1)$$
$$C^{BtoT}(y) = C^H(y) + \mu^U(y+1)\, C^{BtoT}(y+1) \tag{3}$$
$$C^F(y) = C^{TtoB}(y) + C^{BtoT}(y)$$

Top-to-bottom (C^{TtoB}) and bottom-to-top (C^{BtoT}) aggregations are conducted on the horizontally filtered data and the final aggregated cost, C^F, is obtained by summing both as given in (3). This approach has some similarities with separable linear-time-invariant (LTI) filters based on the orthogonal decomposition. The characteristics of the permeability filter depend on the transfer rate distribution of pixels, in which data penetration is prevented along low weights (edges) and permitted along smooth color variation that provide high transition rates.

The effective filter coefficients for two pixels are illustrated in Figure 1 after horizontal and vertical SWS. It is important to note that the support regions are not restricted by any pre-defined window sizes which provides complete content adaptability. In Figure 1.a, the effective horizontal weight distribution of each pixel on the same column is given, where lighter regions correspond to higher weights. It is clear that color-wise smooth regions provide   high correlative supports within, and the data transfer is prevented along edge regions. In Figure 1.b, vertical effective weights of the corresponding pixels are illustrated which are the result of two pass vertical transfer. The final 2D effective support weights in Figure 1.c are constructed by further weighting horizontal support region with vertical weights.

The effect of PF can be simulated by direct calculation of weighted summation through the supporting weights in Figure 1.c which correspond to contribution of neighboring pixels. However, compared to direct implementation, a permeability filter requires only six additions and four multiplications per pixel.

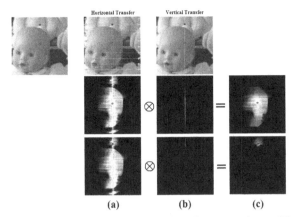

Fig. 1. (a) Horizontal effective weights of the pixels on the same column, (b) vertical effective weights for squared pixel, (c) 2D effective weights after horizontal and vertical SWS

2.1   Stereo Matching via PF

Application of an edge-aware filter to local stereo matching is provided by conducting aggregation on disparity dependent cost functions. For this purpose, pixel-wise cost values of each disparity candidate are calculated as follows:

$$C_d^{SAD}(x) = \left| I_{left}(x) - I_{Right}(x+d) \right|$$

$$C_d^{CENSUS}(x) = Ham(CT_{left}(x), CT_{Right}(x+d)) \tag{4}$$

$$C_d(x) = \alpha . C_d^{SAD}(x) + (1-\alpha) C_d^{CENSUS}(x)$$

where $C_d^{SAD}(x)$ corresponds to the *SAD* cost value of the pixel (x) in the left image for disparity d, I_{left} and I_{right} are left and right images. For the *census* measure $C_d^{CENSUS}(x,y)$, Hamming distance $(Ham(.))$ between the bit streams of the correspondences in the *Census* Transformed images (CT) is calculated. This step involves noisy measures that yield insufficient correlation between candidate pixel matches in left and right images. Hence, these cost values are filtered, especially through edge-aware filters, to provide crisp and reliable correlation measures. Then, for each pixel the disparity candidate with minimum filtered cost is determined which finalizes the initial disparity estimation. These operations are conducted for left and right pairs independently resulting in two disparity maps. The consistency between stereo pairs is enforced by cross check and occlusion handling steps.

As analyzed in [11], each step has an influence on the quality of the estimated disparity maps. Among all, the most crucial step is the filtering of cost values that determines the computational complexity and accuracy of the algorithms. In [10], it has been shown through experiments on well known Middlebury stereo pairs that permeability filter is one of the most efficient techniques providing comparable even better performance against various edge-aware filters. Besides, an extensive discussion is given in [12] for the utilization of various cost functions. According to [12], unification of sum of absolute difference (SAD) and Census transform (CT) yield robust measures providing high quality estimates compared to the remaining cost functions. Tough, in this study, permeability filter and SAD+CT measure are considered as the fundamental tools for cost calculation and aggregation steps.

It is agreed that the real world data have several imperfections that affect the performance of stereo matching algorithms. In this manner, direct application of state-of-the-art techniques for challenging data might not provide reliable estimates, since they are developed on well-defined static stereo pairs with reduced imperfections, such as Middlebury stereo benchmark [2]. Typical results for direct application of SAD+CT based cost calculation and PF [10] are illustrated in Figure 2 and Figure 3 addressing lack of texture, high occlusion and temporal inconsistencies. It is obvious that the performance of stereo matching is not sufficient to determine scene geometry. Though, several modifications are required over traditional local approaches to obtain robust stereo matching for real world data having imbalances between left-right pairs.

Fig. 2. (a), (c) two frames with lack of texture, (b), (d) estimated disparity maps involve resolution and quantization loss

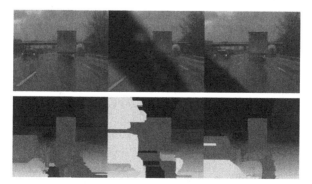

Fig. 3. First row: Three consecutive frames involving large occluded regions and texture inconsistencies, second row: erroneous disparity maps due to imperfections

3   Proposed Stereo Matching Algorithm

In this study, a stereo matching algorithm dedicated to surveillance and automatic vehicle control applications is introduced. The real world data for these types of applications involve various inconsistencies between stereo pairs and along consecutive frames corresponding to spatial and temporal imbalances. In order to develop reliable stereo matching techniques for these types of data, specific scene structure and requirements should be analyzed that determine fundamental road maps for algorithm development. Thus, an analysis is given in the following section addressing the specific problems and characteristics of the input stereo data. Then, several modifications are proposed to boost up stereo matching performance.

3.1   Constraints on Surveillance and Vehicle Control Application

For the problem of surveillance and vehicle control, stereo camera is ported in front of a car and the road is observed by this camera setup. Two fundamental aims in such a scenario are estimation of 3D structure of the road terrain and distances of the vehicles in the field of view at a time instant. These aims yield two implications; high disparity differences are observed among pixels on the same column with different vertical coordinates due to the orientation of road ground plane (as illustrated in Figure 4) and scene change is not severe among consecutive frames due to physical limitations on the vehicle speed.

The first implication contradicts with the smoothness assumption of the stereo matching algorithms, enforcing the same disparity levels among color-wise similar neighbor pixels. The disparity variation might be lost during local stereo matching due to uniform texture variation on the road. The similarities between pixels yield same disparity levels introducing compaction as illustrated in Figure 2.b-d. This case is also valid under extreme lightening conditions such as night views and flare situations. Therefore, a relaxation is required to allow disparity changes.

The second implication enforces temporal smoothness between consecutive frames by cumulating temporal data, which increases robustness and accuracy of the estimation. Though, each frame should be related to the previous frames instead of independent operations.

Fig. 4. Marked pixels with almost same intensity values on the same column have 21 disparity level differences in the disparity map

3.2   Proposed Improvements

In order to address aforementioned spatial and temporal specifications, two improvements are introduced for permeability based stereo matching.

3.2.1   Spatial Improvements

In order to relax smoothness of pixels only in vertical direction, a *vertical damping factor* is included during SWS along vertical axis. This goal is achieved by updating the formula in (3) as follows:

$$C^{TtoB}(y) = C^{H}(y) + \lambda.\mu^{B}(y-1).C^{TtoB}(y-1)$$

$$C^{BtoT}(y) = C^{H}(y) + \lambda.\mu^{U}(y+1).C^{BtoT}(y+1) \tag{5}$$

$$C^{F}(y) = C^{TtoB}(y) + C^{BtoT}(y)$$

where constant λ scaling is applied to the update term involving previously aggregated values in vertical direction. The effect of this parameter depends on the vertical distance between two pixels which is observed as a power term. Actually, this term can be considered as a spatial range function in vertical axis which damps the accumulation of cost values independent of color-wise similarity. In this way, vertical aggregation is softened enabling disparity variation between vertical neighboring pixels with same texture characteristics. The relaxation of disparity values eliminates compaction of disparity levels providing smoothly varying road terrain. It is important to note that scaling factor affects the degree of relaxation which should be limited to preserve smoothness of the disparity map.

In Figure 5, the effect of scaling factor on the distribution of effective aggregation weights is illustrated for three pixels on different types of scenes from the challenge database [3]. The support regions for the corresponding pixels extend to distant pixels in vertical direction due to lack of texture, in which pixels are forced to be located on the same disparity levels. On the other hand, utilization of a damping factor limits the support regions along vertical axis, yielding relaxation. It is clear that as λ decreases, support regions tend to shrink and after a certain level vertical aggregation is not observed. The effect of vertical damping on disparity estimation is illustrated in Figure 6 in which disparity resolution is preserved with the introduction of vertical scale. As expected, noise artifacts are observable when the scale factor is decreased below a certain level. According to parametric analyses, setting λ to the value 0.9 is optimal to provide a balance between disparity resolution and smoothness.

3.2.2   Temporal Improvements

Treating each frame in a stereo video independently is a sub-optimal solution to provide disparity. In such a case, flickers and inconsistencies within disparity maps of consecutive frames could be observed which decreases accuracy of estimation. Therefore, relations between following frames should be exploited to provide consistent estimates.

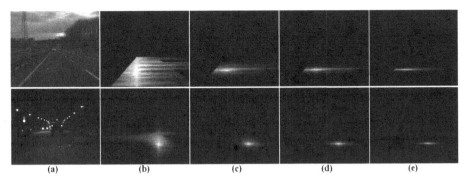

(a)	(b)	(c)	(d)	(e)

Fig. 5. (a) Intensity views; effective weight distribution for marked pixels via (b) no vertical scaling (λ=1.0) , (c) λ=0.95, (d) λ=0.9 and (e) λ=0.8

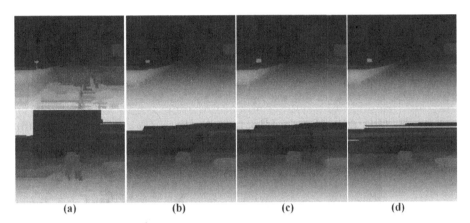

(a)	(b)	(c)	(d)

Fig. 6. Estimated disparity maps via (a) no vertical scaling, (b) λ=0.95, (c) λ=0.9 and (d) λ=0.8

Based on the analysis given in Section 3, it can be argued that instant scene changes are not expected in stereo video captured by a system installed within a car. Hence, temporal smoothness among consecutive frames is a valid assumption. On the other hand, flares or reflections, as well as windshield wiper on a vehicle, introduce observable changes in the captured video as illustrated in Figure 3. During frame-by-frame processing, these types of cases cannot be handled that degrades estimation accuracy, whereas exploiting temporal data should improve the performance.

For this purpose, two modifications are proposed in this study that aims to transfer reliable data along time axis. Stemming from the assumption of temporal smoothness, a conventional scene change analysis technique is applied by comparing histograms of two consecutive frames. Under normal conditions in which reflections, flares and other sources of disturbances do not introduce inconsistency; hence, histogram change is expected to be limited. On the other hand, there is significant difference in the histograms for unexpected scene changes. Typical frames with high histogram changes are illustrated in Figure 7 for three different stereo video.

As the first step, the percentage of histogram change is calculated between previous and current frames as follows:

$$\Delta^t = \frac{1}{N} \sum_{i=1:255} \left| Hist^t(i) - Hist^{t-1}(i) \right| \tag{6}$$

where N is the total number of pixels, $Hist^t$ is the histogram of the frame at time instant t. The rate of change (Δ) is utilized as a weighting function to model in temporal transfer of data relating permeability weights. Hence, permeability weights in the current frame are weighted by the permeability values in the previous frame as follows:

$$\overline{\mu}_t(x) = (1 - \Delta^t).\overline{\mu}_t(x) + \Delta^t.\overline{\mu}_{t-1}(x) \tag{7}$$

where $\overline{\mu}_t$ is the permeability vector involving weights in four fundamental directions for time instant t. The update formula in (7) enforces utilization of permeability weights in the current frame, as long as significant scene change is not observed. On the other hand, when there is significant scene change, which is not an expected case, permeability weights of the previous frame are utilized. Once the weights are calculated, histogram of the current frame is updated by the change factor for the analysis of the next frame as follows:

$$Hist^t(i) = (1 - \Delta^t).Hist^t(i) + \Delta^t.Hist^{t-1}(i) \tag{8}$$

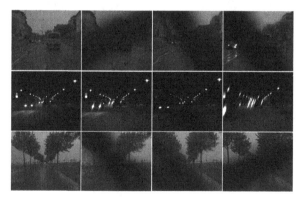

Fig. 7. Inconsistent frames yielding significant changes in histogram for three different scenes given in the first column

The histogram update in (8) provides robustness against multiple inconsistent consecutive frames. Therefore, data from the last reliable frame is transferred to the frames involving severe flares, reflections and sudden large occlusions as soon as a consistent frame is encountered with similar histogram characteristics.

The other temporal modification is provided by enforcing smoothness of disparity values along pixels with low intensity change between consecutive frames. For this purpose, temporal permeability weights are calculated for each pixel as,

$$\mu^t(x) = \exp(-|I^t(x) - I^{t-1}(x)| / \sigma), \tag{9}$$

where I^t is the intensity image for time instant t, σ is a scaling factor (set as 16). Temporal permeability relates the change of the corresponding pixel in time, which is utilized to enforce disparity values of the previous frame to the estimation of current disparity value. This is provided by including a smoothness term in the cot function as

$$C^{new}_d(x) = C_d(x) + \mu^t(x).\|d - D^{t-1}(x)\|, \tag{10}$$

where d is the candidate disparity value and $D^{t-1}(x)$ is the estimated previous disparity value of pixel x.

4   Experimental Results

The improvement of stereo matching performance is validated by utilization of a recent challenging stereo video dataset provided by [3]. Algorithm parameters are kept constant among all video sequences as well as same intermediate steps are utilized for the original and modified versions of PF based stereo matching. The evaluation of estimation performance is provided by visual comparison including spatial and temporal consistency due to lack of ground truth disparity maps. For this purpose, estimated disparity maps are illustrated in Figure 8 to Figure 11 for 4 different challenging videos. For the sake of completeness, disparity maps for five instants with 5-10 frames differences are illustrated.

In Figure 8, results of the *Crossing Cars* [3] sequence are shown, that involve consistent frames with no specific visual artifact. In the second row and third row disparity estimates with and without the proposed modifications in Sections 3.2.1. and 3.2.2 are illustrated. The effect of modifications is observable for temporal consistency of the disparity assignment of the regions below the moving car.

On the other hand, in Figure 9, for *Night and Snow* [3] sequence involving lack of texture and severe lightening changes, spatial and temporal modifications boost-up stereo matching performance. Proposed vertical damping ($\lambda=0.9$) yield spatially smooth ground plane, which is especially observable in 4th and 5th frames. Besides, estimated disparity maps are consistent among time, which is robust against changes due to headlights of cars and effects of windshield wiper.

The results of *Rain Blur* [3] sequence are illustrated in Figure 10. Lack of texture, reflections from wet road and motion of windshield wiper are the main causes of challenges in *Rain Blur* sequence. According to visual interpretation, it is obvious that modifications improve quality and consistency of disparity maps with increased disparity resolution and robustness against temporal fluctuations. However, reflections are still problematic due to insufficiency of cost function that is valid for each frame.

The effect of sun flares is observed in *Sun Flare* [3] sequence, introducing severe degradation in disparity estimation, when spatial and temporal modifications are not exploited. On the other hand, temporal modifications especially increase reliability of estimation process providing for this sequence. This improvement is clearly observable as the strength of sun flare increases.

The robustness against windshield wiper motion and rain flares is further illustrated in Figure 13 for the *Rain Flare* [3] sequence. Modifications on [10] provide obvious improvement on the estimated disparity maps.

Fig. 8. First row: 5 frames from *Crossing Cars* sequence, second row: disparity maps via [10], last row: proposed stereo matching results after spatial and temporal modifications

Fig. 9. First row: 5 frames from *Night and Snow* sequence, second row: disparity maps via [10], last row: proposed stereo matching results after spatial and temporal modifications

Fig. 10. First row: 5 frames from *Rain Blur* sequence, second row: disparity maps via [10] last row: proposed stereo matching results after spatial and temporal modifications

Fig. 11. First row: 5 frames from *Sun Flare* sequence, second row: disparity maps via [10], last row: proposed stereo matching results after spatial and temporal modifications

Apart from visual quality, the proposed approach enables prompt processing with low computational complexity and memory requirement. In this manner, temporal data is transferred by only keeping the previous disparity map rather than full cost volume that requires large memory. Besides, as shown in [10], permeability filter is one of the most efficient edge-aware filtering techniques in literature. In table 1, computation time of aggregation via permeability filter and the well known *guided filter* [7] are illustrated for a pair with resolution of (720x576) on a 3.06GHz Intel Core i7 CPU with 6 GB RAM. During experiments, the number of disparity candidates is set to 50. It is clear that, permeability filter enables almost 12 times faster operation compared to *guided filter.* This is an expected result according to the required number of additions and multiplications for aggregation, such that permeability filter exploits six additions and four multiplications, while guided filter involves 107 additions and 43 multiplications on the average.

Table 1. Computation time comparison for aggregation of 50 disparity candidates on stereo pair with size of 720x576

Computation time (msec)	Permeability Filter [10]	Guided Filter [7]
720x576x50	**1034**	**12720**

5   Conclusion

In this study, a novel approach is presented for providing spatial and temporal improvements for stereo matching algorithms that improves estimation accuracy for challenging videos. Specifically dedicated to automatic vehicle control and surveillance applications, the proposed modifications exploit general scene characteristics of stereo video captured by a camera imported in front of a car. The specifications of road plane geometry and temporal consistency between consecutive frames enable further assumptions for stereo matching to increase robustness against several imperfections, such as lack of texture, sun flare, rain flare, reflections, changing lightening and occlusions due to motion of windshield wiper. For this purpose, some modifications are provided for the stereo matching algorithm introduced in [10], that is one of the most efficient local techniques. In this manner, a vertical damping scale is included relaxing smoothness of disparity maps along vertical axis which prevents disparity resolution loss due to lack of texture. Besides, temporal consistency is enforced by scene change analysis and transfer of reliable data to consecutive frames. According to the extensive experiments on a recent challenging stereo video dataset, the proposed modifications provide reliable disparity maps under severe challenges and low texture distribution improving scene analyses for surveillance related applications.

References

[1]   Sharstein, D., Szeliski, R.: A taxonomy and evaluation of dense two-frame stereo correspondence algorithms. International Journal on Computer Vision 47, 7–42 (2002)
[2]   http://vision.middlebury.edu/stereo/
[3]   http://hci.iwr.uni-heidelberg.de//Static/challenge2012/
[4]   Yoon, K.-J., Kweon, I.S.: Adaptive support weight approach for correspondence search. IEEE Transactions on Pattern Analysis and Machine Intelligence 28(4), 650–656 (2006)
[5]   Porikli, F.: Constant time O(1) bilateral filtering. In: CVPR (2008)
[6]   Qingxiong, Y., Kar-Han, T., Ahuja, N.: Real-Time O(1) Bilateral Filtering. In: CVPR, pp. 557–564 (2009)

[7]   He, K., Sun, J., Tang, X.: Guided Image Filtering. In: Daniilidis, K., Maragos, P., Paragios, N. (eds.) ECCV 2010, Part I. LNCS, vol. 6311, pp. 1–14. Springer, Heidelberg (2010)

[8]   Rhemann, C., Hosni, A., Bleyer, M., Rother, C., Gelautz, M.: Fast cost-volume filtering for visual correspondence and beyond. In: CVPR 2011 (2011)

[9]   Zhang, K., Lu, J., Lafruit, G.: Cross based stereo matching using orthogonal integral images. IEEE Transactions on Circuits and Systems for Video Technology 19(7) (July 2009)

[10] Cigla, C., Alatan, A.A.: Efficient Edge-Preserving Stereo Matching. In: ICCV LDRMC Workshop (2011)

[11] Tombari, F., Mattoccia, S., Di Stefano, L., Addimanda, E.: Classification and Evaluation of Cost Aggregaton methods for stereo Correspondence. In: International Conference on Computer Vision and Pattern Recognition (2008)

[12] Hirschmüller, H., Scharstein, D.: Evaluation of stereo matching costs on images with radiometric differences. IEEE Transactions on Pattern Analysis and Machine Intelligence 31(9), 1582–1599 (2009)

On the Evaluation of Scene Flow Estimation

Philippos Mordohai

Stevens Institute of Technology
mordohai@cs.stevens.edu

Abstract. This paper surveys the state of the art in evaluating the performance of scene flow estimation and points out the difficulties in generating benchmarks with ground truth which have not allowed the development of general, reliable solutions. Hopefully, the renewed interest in dynamic 3D content, which has led to increased research in this area, will also lead to more rigorous evaluation and more effective algorithms. We begin by classifying methods that estimate depth, motion or both from multi-view sequences according to their parameterization of shape and motion. Then, we present several criteria for their evaluation, discuss their strengths and weaknesses and conclude with recommendations.

1 Introduction

Multiple-view reconstruction has been one of the most active areas in computer vision and, as a result, impressive 3D models can now be generated for individual objects [1–3] and large scale scenes [4–6]. Moreover, commercial entities, including Apple, Google, Nokia and Acute3D, have been able to produce accurate models from massive amounts of images and video, proving that general solutions in uncontrolled environments are possible.

This, however, is not the case for the reconstruction of dynamic scenes despite the broader spectrum of applications that would be made possible. In contrast to static 3D models used for visualization, 3D mapping, virtual tourism and measuring distances, 3D reconstructions of dynamic scenes can reach significantly more people. Applications include free-viewpoint video for 3D TV, films or video-games; markerless motion capture for entertainment, clinical medicine and biomechanical analysis; and dynamic augmented reality.

The problem of estimating 3D shape and motion from images was named *scene flow estimation* by Vedula et al. [7] who presented the first analysis of what can be estimated depending on how much about the scene is known. After a few early publications [7–9] interest in this topic waned, until recently, when it was sparked again by the growing demand for 3D content. Significant progress has been made but the problem has not been fully solved. Much better results have been obtained for humans via the use of articulated models which drastically reduces the number of parameters to be estimated [10–13]. Due to the very different nature of such strongly model-based estimation, we consider these methods out of scope here. We will, however, consider methods that do not

A. Fusiello et al. (Eds.): ECCV 2012 Ws/Demos, Part II, LNCS 7584, pp. 148–157, 2012.
© Springer-Verlag Berlin Heidelberg 2012

explicitly compute motion, such as space-time stereo [14, 15], as long as images from different time instances are used in the computation of depth for a given frame[1].

In Section 2, we present a taxonomy of the most relevant methods according to their parameterization of shape and motion. Then, in Section 3, we examine a number of criteria that have been used for evaluating these methods and discuss their strengths and weaknesses. Unlike other problems in computer vision, generating datasets with ground truth for scene flow estimation is not straightforward due to the unavailability of a suitable technology. Overcoming this challenge and generating widely used benchmarks will be instrumental for progress in this area, as it was for related problems, such as binocular [16] and multi-view [17, 18] stereo and optical flow [19].

2   A Taxonomy of the Methods

In this section, we classify dense or quasi-dense scene flow methods according to their parameterization. For example, viewpoint-based methods may parameterize each pixel using four parameters: one for depth on the ray and three for 3D motion to the next frame. On the other hand, a world-based method may endow a 3D point with six parameters: three for translational and three for rotational motion.

2.1   Temporally-Supported Depth

We begin with methods that take into account frames captured at different times to estimate depth for the pixels of the current frame. These methods do not explicitly estimate motion, because this is either not needed for the application at hand, or the computational cost of evaluating photoconsistency in 4D state spaces is too high. Space-time stereo [14, 15, 20–24] falls under this category. We note here that motion must be very small for the assumptions made by these methods to remain valid.

Methods that can handle larger motions [25–27] use optical flow to identify temporal correspondences across frames and compute the matching cost aggregating information over time. The limitations in both cases are the assumption that depth remains constant over time and that 3D motion is not estimated.

2.2   Temporally-Supported 3D Shape

Dynamic shapes can be extracted as 3D iso-surfaces in 4D spatio-temporal volumes [28, 29] or as the boundary facets of 4D Delaunay meshes [30]. A weaker form of such temporally consistent shape estimation is based on minimizing the distance between surfaces at consecutive time frames [31]. These methods are limited to sequences with very slow motion so that the bounding surfaces of the 4D volumes are smooth, while the resulting temporal correspondences are set-wise and not point-wise.

---

[1] We use the term *frames* to refer to images taken at different times.

2.3 Depth and Motion Per Pixel

This category includes viewpoint-based methods that estimate shape and 3D motion (four degrees of freedom) for each pixel of the reference view. Due to the size of the problem, early work was based on fitting parametric motion models to image segments thus drastically reducing the number of degrees of freedom to be estimated [32–34]. Isard and MacCormick [35] proposed an MRF with a 5D state space, including a flag for occlusion. Variational approaches [36–40] initialize shape by stereo matching and then estimate shape and motion jointly until convergence to the nearest local minimum of the objective function. Other methods explore the 4D search space using a winner-take-all scheme or dynamic programming [41] or by growing correspondence seeds [42].

To reduce computational complexity, several authors decouple depth and motion estimation [43–46]. Depth estimation, however, is still affected by temporal correspondences as in the methods of Section 2.1 or by predictions made using scene flow estimates of the previous frame.

2.4 3D Shape and Motion

This category includes methods that employ world-based representations and thus are not limited to $2\frac{1}{2}$-D surfaces. Initially, Vedula et al. [7] formulated and analyzed three algorithms depending on the degree to which scene geometry is known. In a separate paper, Vedula et al. [47] extended space carving to the 6D space of all shapes and flows. Other representations for joint shape and motion estimation include surface patches [8], subdivision surfaces [9], a hybrid of oriented 3D points and signed distance functions [48], probabilistic occupancy-motion grids [49] and a collection of rigid parts discovered via EM [50].

Furukawa and Ponce [51, 52] and Courchay et al. [53] estimate the scene flow of a single mesh with fixed topology. Six degrees of freedom are estimated per vertex to capture both translation and rotation.

Shape and motion estimation can be loosely coupled by reconstructing an initial 3D shape, estimating motion to the next frame and using the motion estimates to predict the shape at the next frame. Pons et al. [3] apply a variational method that minimizes the prediction error of the shape and motion estimates. Popham et al. [54] track surface patches in 3D in long sequences. Li et al. [55] extract a watertight mesh from point clouds reconstructed by variational stereo and then address scene flow as volumetric deformation.

2.5 Motion of 3D Shape

The final class of methods estimate motion between consecutive observations of shape. In other words, these algorithms consider shape estimates as input and focus on establishing temporal correspondences. More common are methods for tracking meshes with fixed topology, which are either initialized using multi-view stereo on the first frame or are externally provided. Most of these approaches use reliable, sparse features of various types [31, 56–59] to guide dense corre-spondence for all points. Cagniart et al. [60] divide the surface into elementary patches which provide integration domains for increased tolerance to noise.

These methods estimate shape independently at each time frame without the benefit of temporal correspondences, which can improve accuracy (Section 3.1). Moreover, most of them, except [60], are restricted to a single watertight mesh.

3   Evaluation Techniques

We examine several criteria that have been used to gauge the performance of scene flow estimation in the literature.

3.1   Ground Truth Depth

The easiest aspect of scene flow estimation to be evaluated is the accuracy of depth estimation. What should be measured is the improvement due to the in-clusion of temporal correspondences and not the performance of a single-frame version of the algorithm on static benchmarks. Sizintsev and Wildes [24, 46] are the only authors, to our knowledge, to perform such experiments by having cameras and scenes on motorized stages and by acquiring ground truth using structured light. These experiments show that the use of temporal information improves reconstruction accuracy. Other authors have performed similar exper-iments on synthetic data [22, 23, 26], also showing improvement.

Generating ground truth for this type of tests is feasible using LIDAR or consumer depth cameras. The latter have the advantage of capturing depth for all pixels in a single shot, while LIDAR has larger range but scans points sequentially. (Flash LIDAR does not appear to be a viable solution yet.) Despite the sparsity of LIDAR measurements, their use is fair since sampling is unbiased and no markers which would aid the algorithm under evaluation are used.

3.2   Ground Truth 2D Motion

Benchmarking motion estimation, even in 2D, is considerably harder than stereo. Baker et al. [61] had to paint hidden fluorescent texture on the scene to generate ground truth optical flow for the Middlebury Optical Flow evaluation. This tex-ture is only visible to special sensors that were used along with regular cameras. Only Li et al. [55] have measured 2D motion errors using real inputs with ground truth by clicking a small number of features in a long sequence. Quantitative optical flow results on synthetic data have been presented on a sphere [42] and a humanoid model captured by 16 virtual cameras [57].

Generating data with ground truth motion is not scalable since it requires considerable manual effort in the form of painting or clicking. The latter suffers from significant selection bias since only distinctive points can be reliably local-ized by the annotators, but these are also points on which algorithms perform well. Further, it appears that with some additional effort one could generate ground truth for 3D shape and motion by extending the annotation to more than one camera or by adding a second special sensor.

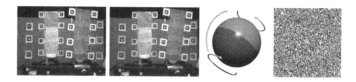

Fig. 1. Left: two frames from the left camera of the ground truth data captured by Sizintsev and Wildes [46]. The surfaces move independently, but the markers simplify matching. Right: The synthetic sphere of Huguet and Devernay [36]: a diagram showing that the two hemispheres undergo separate rotations and the texture map.

3.3   Ground Truth Scene Flow

Sizintsev and Wildes [46] present a quantitative evaluation of dense scene flow using the motorized stage described above to generate ground truth. While it is unprecedented, this experiment is not ideal since several fiducial markers had to be placed on each independently moving surface to aid motion estimation (Fig. 1). This also improves the accuracy of the algorithms being evaluated, not only on the markers themselves, but also on other pixels. Popham et al. [54] evaluated the accuracy of their algorithm over long sequences (90 frames) on a small number of points manually clicked on two images for each time frame. While the reported accuracy is high, this approach does not scale well and also suffers from selection bias as that of Li et al. [55].

The majority of scene flow estimation algorithms that include quantitative results obtain them on synthetic datasets, with the most popular being the one by Huguet and Devernay [36] (Fig. 1) which has been used by several authors [36, 38, 40, 45]. Other options include synthetic spheres, ellipses or cylinders [39, 41, 42, 45, 49, 50] or synthetic scenes [43, 45].

3.4   Image Prediction

According to Szeliski [62] and Kilner et al. [63], one can leave out one of the cameras and try to predict its images using all other available data. This test may not reveal errors in areas of low texture, but is ideal for evaluating novel view synthesis. Taking this approach a step further, Kilner et al. [63] showed that there is significant correlation between the prediction error on an existing view and the differences obtained by rendering two different real images to a virtual camera using the reconstructed surface to determine the mapping. Therefore, this test can be performed without "sacrificing" one of the input cameras, thus degrading the quality of the estimation.

To the best of our knowledge, our previous work [25] is one of the few examples in which this technique was applied. Using the calibrated and synchronized videos provided by Microsoft Research as input and the associated reconstructions [64] as the baseline, we were able to show that temporal consistency leads to lower reprojection errors. See Fig. 2(a) for some results.

Here, we propose to extend this criterion to consider not only prediction of different viewpoints, but also of images taken at the following time step using the

(a) Image prediction   (b) Background conistency

Fig. 2. Evaluation of the approach of Larsen et al. [25] on the dataset of Zitnick et al. [64]. (a) Image prediction by rendering colored depth map on a different view. Zoomed in results of [64] and [25] are shown on the left and right respectively. (b) A frame of the breakdancing sequence with row 40 highlighted and a plot of the median depth and standard deviation for all pixels under the approach of [64] in purple (top curve) and the approach of [25] in green (bottom curve). The latter has significantly smaller standard deviation for the depth of each pixel.

estimated scene flow. This type of evaluation requires minimal effort compared to the alternatives and is applicable to most methods, in particular mesh tracking methods, for which evaluation of shape is pointless. Despite not capturing errors in textureless regions well, this criterion is well-suited for applications that value novel view synthesis more than metric accuracy.

3.5   Temporal Consistency of the Background

A different criterion [25] is to evaluate the temporal consistency of at least the static parts of the scene by selecting pixels that remain static throughout the sequence and measuring the variance of the estimated depth. Small variance indicates that the algorithm maintains a consistent depth, regardless of its precision, and thus generates results with reduced jittering. We argued that for many applications, a constant, but slightly wrong, depth for the background is more visually pleasing than more accurate depth that fluctuates over time. Some results for the breakdancing sequence of [64] are shown in Fig. 2(b).

The limitation of this method is that it is inapplicable to the foreground, as well as to pixels of the background whose visibility changes during the sequence. It is also inapplicable to methods that require silhouettes as inputs.

3.6   Forward-Backward Consistency

In the absence of ground truth data, Furukawa and Ponce [51] concatenated forward and reverse videos around a common frame, creating sequences such as $f_1 f_2 f_3 f_2 f_1$, and then measured the consistency of scene flow estimates between the same pairs of frames that appear in reverse order, such as $f_1 f_2$ and $f_2 f_1$. Ideally, shape estimates should be identical and motion vectors should have the same magnitude but opposite orientation. This technique requires further analysis since certain estimators may produce consistent, but erroneous, results. On the other hand, the ease of creating the input data is a strength.

3.7   Scenes with Ground Truth Depth Undergoing Rigid Motion

The last technique of this section is to generate test sequences by acquiring videos with a moving camera rig of static scenes with ground truth depth. The ground truth depth can be acquired separately using LIDAR or consumer depth cameras and motion between frames can be estimated using the Iterative Closest Point algorithm or structure from motion. The output of this procedure is not only depth for all frames, but also ground truth dense scene flow since exact rigid transformations can be computed for all points that are visible in the range scans. As long as the algorithm under evaluation is not aware of the global rigidity of the motion and thus does not enforce the relevant constraints, the evaluation is both fair and informative. A simple form of this criterion was used by Huguet and Devernay [36] and Liu and Philomin [37] on the Middlebury data [16] using four images of each scene. Scene flow was evaluated between binocular pairs without taking into account that the true motion is pure horizontal translation. Prediction errors were also included in [37].

This technique appears to provide a good trade-off between effort required to generate the data and thoroughness of the evaluation, since, unlike image prediction, the accuracy over al pixels, textured or not, can be measured. There are at least two limitations: the technique is better suited to binocular or other narrow-baseline methods due to potential difficulties in moving a large camera rig rigidly; and the data may be unsuitable for methods that require silhouettes.

4   Conclusions

After surveying the state of the art in scene flow estimation and evaluation, the main conclusion is that the problem remains unsolved, but that it is not "unsolvable". In fact, great progress has been made in the last 3-5 years on the algorithmic front, but evaluation is still lacking.

While the generation of synthetic video sequences using proper rendering techniques seems the most practical way of producing data with ground truth, results on such sequences should be interpreted with caution. It is often very hard to capture all failure modes of stereo matching and motion estimation on synthetic data for a number of reasons including issues related to noise modeling or irregularities of camera response functions. After evaluating the criteria of Section 3, we propose the use of a combination of *image prediction* errors, which require little effort to measure and are well-suited for view synthesis tasks, and *scenes with ground truth depth undergoing rigid motions*, which require non-trivial effort to generate but capture all aspects of scene flow estimation. The *forward-backward consistency* technique is also worth further investigation.

Acknowledgement. This work was supported in part by NSF award 1217797.

References

1. Hernández Esteban, C., Schmitt, F.: Silhouette and stereo fusion for 3D object modeling. CVIU 96, 367–392 (2004)

2. Furukawa, Y., Ponce, J.: Carved Visual Hulls for Image-Based Modeling. In: Leonardis, A., Bischof, H., Pinz, A. (eds.) ECCV 2006, Part I. LNCS, vol. 3951, pp. 564–577. Springer, Heidelberg (2006)

3. Pons, J.P., Keriven, R., Faugeras, O.D.: Multi-view stereo reconstruction and scene flow estimation with a global image-based matching score. IJCV 72, 179–193 (2007)

4. Furukawa, Y., Curless, B., Seitz, S., Szeliski, R.: Towards internet-scale multi-view stereo. In: CVPR (2010)

5. Frahm, J.-M., Fite-Georgel, P., Gallup, D., Johnson, T., Raguram, R., Wu, C., Jen, Y.-H., Dunn, E., Clipp, B., Lazebnik, S., Pollefeys, M.: Building Rome on a Cloudless Day. In: Daniilidis, K., Maragos, P., Paragios, N. (eds.) ECCV 2010, Part IV. LNCS, vol. 6314, pp. 368–381. Springer, Heidelberg (2010)

6. Vu, H., Labatut, P., Pons, J.P., Keriven, R.: High accuracy and visibility-consistent dense multi-view stereo. PAMI (2011)

7. Vedula, S., Baker, S., Rander, P., Collins, R.T., Kanade, T.: Three-dimensional scene flow. In: ICCV, pp. 722–729 (1999)

8. Carceroni, R.L., Kutulakos, K.N.: Multi-view scene capture by surfel sampling: From video streams to non-rigid 3D motion, shape and reflectance. IJCV 49, 175–214 (2002)

9. Neumann, J., Aloimonos, Y.: Spatio-temporal stereo using multi-resolution subdivision surfaces. IJCV 47, 181–193 (2002)

10. Anguelov, D., Srinivasan, P., Koller, D., Thrun, S., Rodgers, J., Davis, J.: Scape: Shape completion and animation of people. ACM Trans. on Graphics 24, 408–416 (2005)

11. Cheung, K.M., Baker, S., Kanade, T.: Shape-from-silhouette across time part ii: Applications to human modeling and markerless motion tracking. IJCV 63, 225–245 (2005)

12. Starck, J., Hilton, A.: Surface capture for performance-based animation. IEEE Computer Graphics and Applications 27, 21–31 (2007)

13. Vlasic, D., Baran, I., Matusik, W., Popović, J.: Articulated mesh animation from multi-view silhouettes. ACM Trans. on Graphics 27, 1–9 (2008)

14. Zhang, L., Curless, B., Seitz, S.M.: Spacetime stereo: shape recovery for dynamic scenes. In: CVPR, pp. II:367–II:374 (2003)

15. Davis, J., Nehab, D., Ramamoorthi, R., Rusinkiewicz, S.: Spacetime stereo: A unifying framework for depth from triangulation. PAMI 27, 296–302 (2005)

16. Scharstein, D., Szeliski, R.S.: A taxonomy and evaluation of dense two-frame stereo correspondence algorithms. IJCV 47, 7–42 (2002)

17. Seitz, S.M., Curless, B., Diebel, J., Scharstein, D., Szeliski, R.: A comparison and evaluation of multi-view stereo reconstruction algorithms. In: CVPR, pp. 519–528 (2006)

18. Strecha, C., von Hansen, W., Van Gool, L.J., Fua, P., Thoennessen, U.: On benchmarking camera calibration and multi-view stereo for high resolution imagery. In: CVPR (2008)

19. Baker, S., Scharstein, D., Lewis, J., Roth, S., Black, M., Szeliski, R.: A database and evaluation methodology for optical flow. IJCV 92, 1–31 (2011)

20. Leung, C., Appleton, B., Lovell, B.C., Sun, C.: An energy minimisation approach to stereo-temporal dense reconstruction. In: ICPR, pp. IV:72–IV:75 (2004)

21. Williams, O., Isard, M., MacCormick, J.: Estimating disparity and occlusions in stereo video sequences. In: CVPR, pp. II:250–II:257 (2005)

22. Richardt, C., Orr, D., Davies, I., Criminisi, A., Dodgson, N.A.: Real-time Spatiotemporal Stereo MatchingUsing the Dual-Cross-Bilateral Grid. In: Daniilidis, K., Maragos, P., Paragios, N. (eds.) ECCV 2010, Part III. LNCS, vol. 6313, pp. 510–523. Springer, Heidelberg (2010)

23. Hosni, A., Rhemann, C., Bleyer, M., Gelautz, M.: Temporally Consistent Disparity and Optical Flow via Efficient Spatio-temporal Filtering. In: Ho, Y.-S. (ed.) PSIVT 2011, Part I. LNCS, vol. 7087, pp. 165–177. Springer, Heidelberg (2011)
24. Sizintsev, M., Wildes, R.: Spatiotemporal oriented energies for spacetime stereo. In: ICCV, pp. 1140–1147 (2011)
25. Larsen, E.S., Mordohai, P., Pollefeys, M., Fuchs, H.: Temporally consistent reconstruction from multiple video streams using enhanced belief propagation. In: ICCV (2007)
26. Bartczak, B., Jung, D., Koch, R.: Real-Time Neighborhood Based Disparity Estimation Incorporating Temporal Evidence. In: Rigoll, G. (ed.) DAGM 2008. LNCS, vol. 5096, pp. 153–162. Springer, Heidelberg (2008)
27. Yang, W., Zhang, G., Bao, H., Kim, J., Lee, H.Y.: Consistent depth maps recovery from a trinocular video sequence. In: CVPR (2012)
28. Goldluecke, B., Magnor, M.: Space-time isosurface evolution for temporally coherent 3D reconstruction. In: CVPR, pp. 350–355 (2004)
29. Sharf, A., Alcantara, D.A., Lewiner, T., Greif, C., Sheffer, A., Amenta, N., Cohen-Or, D.: Space-time surface reconstruction using incompressible flow. ACM Trans. on Graphics 27, 1–10 (2008)
30. Aganj, E., Pons, J.P., Segonne, F., Keriven, R.: Spatio-temporal shape from silhouette using four-dimensional delaunay meshing. In: ICCV (2007)
31. Starck, J., Hilton, A.: Correspondence labelling for wide-timeframe free-form surface matching. In: ICCV (2007)
32. Tao, H., Sawhney, H.S., Kumar, R.: Dynamic depth recovery from multiple synchronized video streams. In: CVPR, pp. I:118–I:124 (2001)
33. Zhang, Y., Kambhamettu, C.: On 3-D scene flow and structure recovery from multiview image sequences. PAMI 33, 592–606 (2003)
34. Li, R., Sclaroff, S.: Multi-scale 3D scene flow from binocular stereo sequences. CVIU 110, 75–90 (2008)
35. Isard, M., MacCormick, J.: Dense Motion and Disparity Estimation Via Loopy Belief Propagation. In: Narayanan, P.J., Nayar, S.K., Shum, H.-Y. (eds.) ACCV 2006, Part II. LNCS, vol. 3852, pp. 32–41. Springer, Heidelberg (2006)
36. Huguet, F., Devernay, F.: A variational method for scene flow estimation from stereo sequences. In: ICCV (2007)
37. Liu, F., Philomin, V.: Disparity estimation in stereo sequences using scene flow. In: BMVC (2009)
38. Basha, T., Moses, Y., Kiryati, N.: Multi-view scene flow estimation: A view centered variational approach. In: CVPR (2010)
39. Valgaerts, L., Bruhn, A., Zimmer, H., Weickert, J., Stoll, C., Theobalt, C.: Joint Estimation of Motion, Structure and Geometry from Stereo Sequences. In: Daniilidis, K., Maragos, P., Paragios, N. (eds.) ECCV 2010, Part IV. LNCS, vol. 6314, pp. 568–581. Springer, Heidelberg (2010)
40. Vogel, C., Schindler, K., Roth, S.: 3D scene flow estimation with a rigid motion prior. In: ICCV, pp. 1291–1298 (2011)
41. Gong, M.: Real-time joint disparity and disparity flow estimation on programmable graphics hardware. CVIU 113, 90–100 (2009)
42. Cech, J., Sanchez-Riera, J., Horaud, R.: Scene flow estimation by growing correspondence seeds. In: CVPR (2011)
43. Rabe, C., Müller, T., Wedel, A., Franke, U.: Dense, Robust, and Accurate Motion Field Estimation from Stereo Image Sequences in Real-Time. In: Daniilidis, K., Maragos, P., Paragios, N. (eds.) ECCV 2010, Part IV. LNCS, vol. 6314, pp. 582–595. Springer, Heidelberg (2010)

44. Müller, T., Rannacher, J., Rabe, C., Franke, U.: Feature- and depth-supported modified total variation optical flow for 3D motion field estimation in real scenes. In: CVPR (2011)
45. Wedel, A., Brox, T., Vaudrey, T., Rabe, C., Franke, U., Cremers, D.: Stereoscopic scene flow computation for 3D motion understanding. IJCV 95, 29–51 (2011)
46. Sizintsev, M., Wildes, R.: Spatiotemporal stereo and scene flow via stequel matching. PAMI 34, 1206–1219 (2012)
47. Vedula, S., Baker, S., Seitz, S.M., Kanade, T.: Shape and motion carving in 6D. In: CVPR, pp. 592–598 (2000)
48. Kwatra, V., Mordohai, P., Kumar Penta, S., Narain, R., Carlson, M., Pollefeys, M., Lin, M.: Fluid in video: Augmenting real video with simulated fluids. Computer Graphics Forum 27, 487–496 (2008)
49. Guan, L., Franco, J.S., Boyer, E., Pollefeys, M.: Probabilistic 3D occupancy flow with latent silhouette cues. In: CVPR (2010)
50. Franco, J.S., Boyer, E.: Learning temporally consistent rigidities. In: CVPR (2011)
51. Furukawa, Y., Ponce, J.: Dense 3D motion capture from synchronized video streams. In: CVPR (2008)
52. Furukawa, Y., Ponce, J.: Dense 3D motion capture for human faces. In: CVPR (2009)
53. Courchay, J., Pons, J.-P., Monasse, P., Keriven, R.: Dense and Accurate Spatio-temporal Multi-view Stereovision. In: Zha, H., Taniguchi, R.-I., Maybank, S. (eds.) ACCV 2009, Part II. LNCS, vol. 5995, pp. 11–22. Springer, Heidelberg (2010)
54. Popham, T., Bhalerao, A., Wilson, R.: Multi-frame scene-flow estimation using a patch model and smooth motion prior. In: BMVC Wkhp. (2010)
55. Li, K., Dai, Q., Xu, W.: Markerless shape and motion capture from multiview video sequences. IEEE Trans. on Circuits and Systems for Video Technology 21, 320–334 (2011)
56. Ahmed, N., Theobalt, C., Rossl, C., Thrun, S., Seidel, H.P.: Dense correspondence finding for parametrization-free animation reconstruction from video. In: CVPR (2008)
57. Varanasi, K., Zaharescu, A., Boyer, E., Horaud, R.: Temporal Surface Tracking Using Mesh Evolution. In: Forsyth, D., Torr, P., Zisserman, A. (eds.) ECCV 2008, Part II. LNCS, vol. 5303, pp. 30–43. Springer, Heidelberg (2008)
58. Zeng, Y., Wang, C., Wang, Y., Gu, X., Samaras, D., Paragios, N.: Dense non-rigid surface registration using high-order graph matching. In: CVPR, pp. 382–389 (2010)
59. Huang, P., Hilton, A., Budd, C.: Global temporal registration of multiple non-rigid surface sequences. In: CVPR (2011)
60. Cagniart, C., Boyer, E., Ilic, S.: Free-form mesh tracking: a patch-based approach. In: CVPR (2010)
61. Baker, S., Roth, S., Scharstein, D., Black, M.J., Lewis, J.P., Szeliski, R.: A database and evaluation methodology for optical flow. In: ICCV (2007)
62. Szeliski, R.: Prediction error as a quality metric for motion and stereo. In: ICCV, pp. 781–788 (1999)
63. Kilner, J., Starck, J., Guillemaut, J.Y., Hilton, A.: Objective quality assessment in free-viewpoint video production. Signal Processing: Image Communication 24, 3–16 (2009)
64. Zitnick, C.L., Kang, S.B., Uyttendaele, M., Winder, S., Szeliski, R.S.: High-quality video view interpolation using a layered representation. ACM Trans. on Graphics 23, 600–608 (2004)

Analysis of KITTI Data for Stereo Analysis with Stereo Confidence Measures

Ralf Haeusler and Reinhard Klette

The University of Auckland
Computer Science Department
Tamaki Campus

Abstract. The recently published KITTI stereo dataset provides a new quality of stereo imagery with partial ground truth for benchmarking stereo matchers. Our aim is to test the value of stereo confidence measures (e.g. a left-right consistency check of disparity maps, or an analysis of the slope of a local interpolation of the cost function at the taken minimum) when applied to recorded datasets, such as published with KITTI. We choose popular measures as available in the stereo-analysis literature, and discuss a naive combination of these. Evaluations are carried out using a sparsification strategy. While the best single confidence measure proved to be the right-left consistency check for high disparity map densities, the best overall performance is achieved with the proposed naive measure combination. We argue that there is still demand for more challenging datasets and more comprehensive ground truth.

1 Introduction

Computational stereo vision is in general an ill-posed problem, and solutions are approximate in some sense. Situations with no unique solutions are commonly found in recorded stereo images. Also with strong assumptions imposed to resulting disparity maps, such as piecewise smoothness, no stereo matcher can guarantee correct results.

Widely used test datasets often use input data of limited complexity [1]. On these, recently developed stereo matchers deliver dense results of satisfactory quality. However, in practice, recorded real-world data are considerably more challenging; see, e.g., [2,3]. There may be no satisfactory solution to the stereo problem in many situations displayed in these datasets. For treating unmatchable regions in disparity maps, there are some attempts to identify these using so-called confidence measures.

To evaluate quality of stereo matching results and accuracy of detected mismatches by means of confidence measures, availability of accurate ground truth is necessary. However, real-world stereo data in [2,3] are provided without ground truth. Recently published stereo-vision test data [4], in the paper briefly called *KITTI data*, show real-world scenes and come with ground truth provided by a laser range-scanner. In this paper, we try to rate the challenge given by KITTI data and quantify the value of confidence measures in dealing with such datasets.

A. Fusiello et al. (Eds.): ECCV 2012 Ws/Demos, Part II, LNCS 7584, pp. 158–167, 2012.
© Springer-Verlag Berlin Heidelberg 2012

Confidence measures can be used in stereo processing to remove spurious disparity matches and interpolate these locations with surrounding disparity values. The left-right consistency check is the most prominent example. Various confidence measures have been proposed for stereo analysis; see [5,6]. Experimental studies of quantitative evaluations of confidence measures have been conducted (on very limited datasets) in [6]. By using the KITTI data, we also discuss confidence measures on a larger set of real-world data.

Many confidence measures are derived from the graph of cost functions. For example, consider a parabola fit of the cost function at the taken minimum and its neighbourhood. The minimum of this parabola can be used to interpolate disparity with subpixel accuracy. Parameter a defines the curvature of such a parabola $ax^2 + bx + c$, and this value is often considered to be a confidence measure. In [7] it is applied with the intention to improve results for scene flow computations. An equivalent confidence measure can be defined using the slope of an Okutomi fit [8], and this may be more appropriate, depending on the stereo matching cost function used.

However, a confidence measure that only operates locally on the cost function cannot assign, for example, low confidence to ambiguous matches within repetitive textures of the source image. Improved results can be expected when the costs of all disparity values are taken into account. This was demonstrated by [9] for the 3D reconstruction of large outdoor scenes where confidence is high if the cost function has a single well-defined minimum, and low if the cost function is flat or has multiple strong local minima. It is an open question which confidence measure has the best performance in a particular matching situation.

Very little has been published on improving the accuracy of confidence measures by combining different measures. For example, see [10] for confidence measures in optical flow computations, using a supervised learning process of Gaussian mixture models with classification criteria being the magnitude of the end point error in optic flow. However, it remained open whether this confidence measure (obtained as a result of classification in feature space) could actually improve accuracy. In [11], flow data is assigned to algorithms found most suitable by classification, based on a combination of flow confidence features such as photo consistency and texture properties. [12] used similar features for detecting difficult to match flow regions in order to test whether these regions are occluded. In both, classification results are obtained using random decision forests.

In this paper we include a naive approach for confidence measure combinations for stereo, which seems to be useful in increasing accuracy, i.e. is reducing numbers of false positives. Also, we define a simple bound for limits of potential accuracy improvements by measure combinations. We apply this measure and a number of popular stereo confidence measures to the recently published KITTI dataset [4], and evaluate them using a similar sparsification strategy as used in [6].

Section 2 contains the definitions of confidence measures used in this paper, including a multiplicative combination and an upper bound for accuracy improvements. Section 3 presents the evaluation method for the performance of measures and provides details about experiments conducted. Section 4 presents results. Section 5 discusses limitations of confidence measures and of the used KITTI dataset. Section 6 concludes.

2   Confidence Measures for Stereo Analysis

For our experiments, we use *semi-global matching* (SGM) for stereo analysis [13] due to its best overall performance on synthetic and recorded outdoor data in terms of quality and computational costs. The data term in the original version of SGM stereo is derived from a mutual information measure [14]. However, [15] concludes that the census cost function leads to the best overall performance. Confidence measures used in this study are not defined on census costs directly, but on census costs aggregated using SGM with penalty parameters $p_1 = 20$ and $p_2 = 100$. In the following, we denote these aggregated cost A.

A compilation of different confidence measures can be found in [5,6]. We selected measures which appear to be pairwise "fairly different" by their definitions, with an intention to obtain the best possible performance boost by combining "orthogonal measures". This is, of course, possible only to a limited extent. All confidence measures presented here are defined pixelwise. No dependency from neighbouring pixels is introduced, except the dependency defined by cost aggregation. Contrary to the common practice, we scale values such that lower values indicate a smaller likelihood of an erroneous disparity estimate (i.e. a higher confidence).This facilitates the comparison to actual disparity errors. We define and use the following measures, with d_0 representing the estimated disparities $D(x, y)$:

- *Curvature.* Curvature derived from parabola fitting is a very popular stereo confidence measure. It is the only confidence measure in the source code of [1]. We are using the inverse of the opening parameter for scaling:

$$\Gamma_0(x, y) = \frac{1}{-2A_{(x,y)}(d_0) + A_{(x,y)}(d_0 - 1) + A_{(x,y)}(d_0 + 1)} \quad (1)$$

- *Perturbation.* The perturbation measure, introduced in [9], computes the deviation from an ideal cost function that has a single minimum at location d_0 and is very large everywhere else. Nonlinear scaling is applied:

$$\Gamma_1(x, y) = \sum_{d \neq d_0} e^{-\frac{\left(A_{(x,y)}(d_0) - A_{(x,y)}(d)\right)^2}{\varsigma^2}} \quad (2)$$

The parameter ς should be chosen such that no numerical underflows appear. A good choice depends on the range of possible valid cost values.
- *Peak ratio.* The peak ratio indicates low confidence if there are two candidates with similar matching score. It is defined as

$$\Gamma_2(x, y) = A_{(x,y)}(d_0) / A_{(x,y)}(d_1) \quad (3)$$

where d_1 is the second smallest local minimum, i.e. $A_{(x,y)}(d_1-1) > A_{(x,y)}(d_1)$ and $A_{(x,y)}(d_1+1) > A_{(x,y)}(d_1)$. Not requiring a local minimum but only the second smallest cost value yields a measure similar to parabola curvature.

- *Entropy.* Entropy defined on the disparity space was used in steering a diffusion process for cost aggregation in stereo matching [16]. It can be used as a confidence measure itself. Cost values are normalized for computing the entropy. Here, p indicates that cost values are converted into a probability distribution function:

$$\Gamma_3(x,y) = -\sum_d p(d)\log p(d) \quad \text{with} \quad p(d) = \frac{e^{-A_{(x,y)}(d)}}{\sum_{d'} e^{-A_{(x,y)}(d')}} \quad (4)$$

Similar to the perturbation measure Γ_1, cost values for all disparities influence the result. All cost values undergo nonlinear scaling, making these measures computationally rather expensive.

- *Right-left consistency check.* Right-left consistency compares the disparities of the left and right view, denoted by D and $D^{(r)}$:

$$\Gamma_4(x,y) = \left| D_{(x,y)} - D^{(r)}_{(x,y)} \right| \quad (5)$$

Large discrepancies, intuitively, should indicate a higher likelihood of an incorrect match. We are also interested in finding out whether there is confidence information extractable from disparities given with subpixel precision, i.e. for $\left| D_{(x,y)} - D^{(r)}_{(x,y)} \right| < 1$.

- *Combination of measures.* We define a measure combination Γ by multiplying all five measures defined above:

$$\Gamma(x,y) = \Gamma_0(x,y)\Gamma_1(x,y)\Gamma_2(x,y)\Gamma_3(x,y)\Gamma_4(x,y) \quad (6)$$

Note that this is not justified in the sense of joint probabilities. Measures are not pairwise independent. Correlation is quite strong as their definition is derived from same cost values A.

- *Accuracy.* Ideally confidence measures exactly predict the magnitude of the error in disparity estimation, so as to discard largest errors first. For comparison with $\Gamma_0, \ldots, \Gamma_4$ and Γ we include this ideal measure, given by the absolute difference Δ between disparity estimate D and ground truth G:

$$\Delta(x,y) = \left| D_{(x,y)} - G_{(x,y)} \right| \quad (7)$$

In practise, finding such a confidence measure was equivalent to the stereo problem being solved.

Thus, it is more realistic to compare a combination of confidence measures rather against a measure that identifies an error if at least one of the contributing confidence measures can detect it. The amount of remaining errors s is then the cardinality of the union set of all undetected erroneous pixels for a specific sparsification ϕ of the disparity map D:

$$s(\phi) = \text{card}\{D_{(x,y)} | (x,y) \in \Omega \wedge \Delta(x,y) > 3 \wedge \forall i \, (\Gamma_i(x,y) \leq \gamma_i(\phi))\} \quad (8)$$

Here, $\gamma_i(\phi)$ is the value of the confidence measure Γ_i which induces a sparsification ϕ. Note, that values from this definition cannot be derived without ground truth. It merely gives a lower limit of remaining disparity errors. The bad-pixel criterion is deviation of estimated disparities from ground truth being larger than 3. This is in accordance with the default in [4] and due to limited accuracy of laser range finder measurements.

3   Evaluation of Confidence Measures

We test SGM stereo and derived confidence measures on a small subset of the recently introduced KITTI Dataset [4]. We choose stereo frames which expose some interesting behaviour, e.g. the ones challenging for SGM stereo. Challenging are considered the frames which produce most errors in comparison to ground truth. We also include two frames where only few errors between SGM results and ground truth can be observed.

For comparisons, we use raw disparities D, i.e. do not attempt to improve results by consistency checks, interpolation, median filtering, or any other kind of postprocessing. Any such steps may introduce some bias to findings. However, we exclude such disparities from evaluation, which have been found to be occluded according to the method described in [13]. It may be beneficial, to use occlusion ground truth instead, if such was available with [4].

Furthermore, we restrict the evaluation to pixels where:

- Ground truth is available. In KITTI data there is no ground truth for upper parts of images, areas usually depicting sky in road vehicle based recordings.
- The cost function contains valid values for all possible disparities. This excludes the left image border in the left view with its width equalling the number of disparities, the reason being scaling issues in the presense of unknown cost values in the definition of confidence measures based on the entire cost function.
- Disparity estimates are supported by data term values, i.e. we do not rely on extrapolation introduced by SGM. This excludes a narrow band along the image border (e.g. 3 pixels for a 7×7 cost matching window).

A sparsification function is computed by summing the remaining errors of matching results when a certain percentile of the disparity map is filtered according to the locations having least confidence assigned. Locations with lowest confidence are removed first.

Measure comparisons often refer to the area under the sparsification curve. However, errors for very sparse maps are of little interest and should not bias a comparison of confidence measures. Thus, we do not compare the areas under the sparsification curves. We are merely interested in measure performance for disparity map densities in a range corresponding to proportions of good disparity pixels, typically between 70 % and 95 % when using the SGM stereo algorithm without postprocessing disparities on the KITTI dataset (see intersection of ground truth optimum with x-axis in Figures 2 and 3).

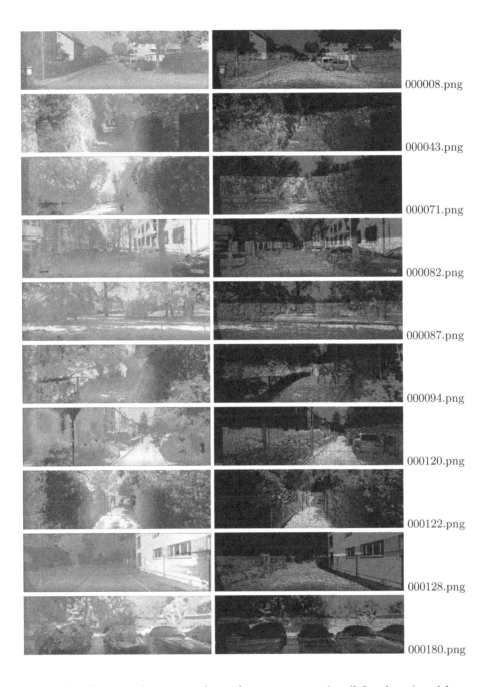

000008.png

000043.png

000071.png

000082.png

000087.png

000094.png

000120.png

000122.png

000128.png

000180.png

Fig. 1. Visualization of stereo results without postprocessing (left column) and laser range finder ground truth (right column) of frames included in this study. Close objects are red, distant objects green.

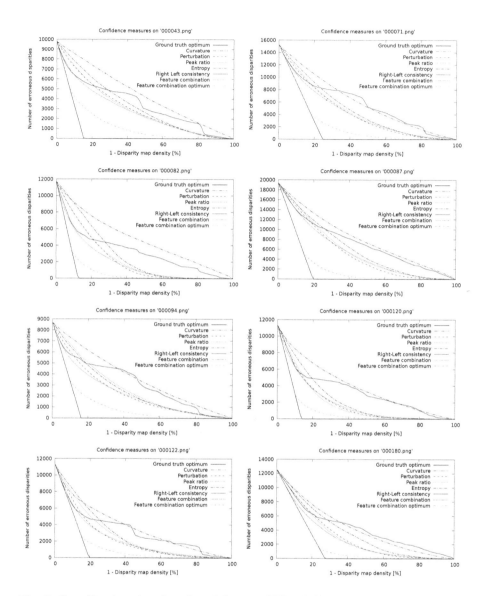

Fig. 2. Sparsification plots for selected frames of KITTI data with high amount of bad pixels in the evaluation domain excluding locations detected as being occluded by the stereo matcher. Numbers of remaining bad pixels are plotted against disparity map density.

4   Results

Recall that Frames 8 and 128 were selected due to their apparent amenability to the stereo problem. The illustration in Fig. 1, however, reveals that low error rates are only a result of missing ground truth in locations where stereo solutions

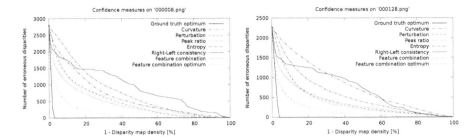

Fig. 3. Sparsification plots for selected frames of KITTI data with low amount of bad pixels in the evaluation domain excluding locations detected as being occluded by the stereo matcher. Numbers of remaining bad pixels are plotted against disparity map density.

are not accurate. Nevertheless, this may not corrupt an evaluation of confidence measures, as these areas are ignored.

Sparsification plots in Figures 2 and 3 show that the curvature confidence measure Γ_0 in general identifies disparity errors much less accurately than other confidence measures included in this study. In Frame 43 the selection of bad pixels appears to be almost random (straight line). However on Frame 43, depicting some vegetation in close proximity, other confidence measures also do not seem to work well. Useful accuracy of Γ_0, according to our experiments, can be observed in Frames 8 and 122.

The remainder of confidence measures, regarding accuracy, is almost on a par at low sparsifications. From the measures Γ_1 to Γ_4, the entropy confidence measure Γ_3 is most often the worst one. The left-right consistency check is not helpful within higher sparsifications, especially not if $\Gamma_4 < 1$.

For most frames, the naive combination Γ of confidence measures outperforms single confidence measures at a sparsification determined by numbers of bad pixels. However, the left-right consistency check Γ_4 can be on a par at this sparsification level.

Regarding the proposed bound for combined confidence measures it can be found that at the level of sparsification necessary to remove all bad pixels, there is usually a remainder of half the amount of bad pixels found by the proposed combination Γ, which cannot be identified by any confidence measure.

5   Discussion

In the following, we discuss accuracy of confidence measures on the frames included in this study and try, where possible, to link their behaviour to scene structure and quality of ground truth and stereo results.

The curvature confidence measure, although widely used, is not much better than randomly removing pixels. Reasons may include limited sharpness of recorded images. This measure only performs rather well on Frames 8 and 122. This finding may not be significant for Frame 8, due to low numbers of bad pixels involved. The reason for apparently improved accuracy of curvature on Frame 122 may be the detection of homogeneously textured areas on road surfaces, which are wrongly estimated by SGM stereo. For detection of textureless areas, however, there may exist better indicators, such as the structural tensor [17].

That, in all frames, the consistency check Γ_4 does not perform well at higher sparsifications is not surprising, as subpixel estimation only is based on interpolated cost function values and therefore compromised by so-called pixel locking. However, the consistency check is also not successful in detecting errors resulting from surface over-extension or foreground fattening [18], as these occur likewise in left-right and right-left matching.

Frame 87 visually does not seem to contain 20 percent bad pixels showing in Fig. 2. Also, confidence measures do not detect these bad pixels well. Such results pose the question whether a fixed tolerance of 3 pixel for disparity errors is appropriate. In particular, in practise, it may be advantageous to define error tolerance based on physical distance and with a lower limit in disparity space.

Another problem of the KITTI dataset is missing ground truth in large image areas. It is most often absent where image regions are challenging for stereo. This is, e.g., the case on fences (Frames 94 and 128) and car windows (Frames 82, 120 and 180). However, it should be noted that there is no agreement or even no approach regarding evaluation strategies for such image regions exposing stereo matchers to semi-transparencies.

6 Conclusion

Compared to previous benchmark data which was recorded under controlled lighting conditions, some frames of KITTI data are more challenging for computational stereo due to outdoor scenes with suboptimal lighting conditions. However, extremely difficult recordings of road scenarios are absent. To our experience, these include tunnels, back-light, night scenes with street lights and lights of other traffic participants, wet road surfaces and precipitation.

Missing ground truth at locations challenging for stereo vision reduces the significance of our findings and makes it hard to draw comprehensive conclusions.

A comprehensive analysis, however, can be conducted if sufficiently diversified datasets with ground truth are available. Apart from the low coverage with ground truth at interesting image locations, another shortcoming of the KITTI dataset is the low dynamic range and luminance resolution of the imagery. Being eight bit only, preventable stereo problems are introduced, which may disguise more interesting problems. We conclude that a sufficiently challenging and rich dataset for stereo benchmarking with ground truth is not yet available.

References

1. Scharstein, D., Szeliski, R.: A taxonomy and evaluation of dense two-frame stereo correspondence algorithms. International Journal of Computer Vision 47, 7–42 (2002)
2. The University of Auckland: .enpeda.. image sequence analysis test site (EISATS), http://www.mi.auckland.ac.nz/EISATS
3. Heidelberg Collaboratory for Image Processing: Robust Vision Challenge, http://hci.iwr.uni-heidelberg.de/Static/challenge2012/
4. Geiger, A., Lenz, P., Urtasun, R.: Are we ready for autonomous driving? The KITTI vision benchmark suite. In: Computer Vision and Pattern Recognition (CVPR), Providence, USA (2012)
5. Banks, J., Corke, P.I.: Quantitative evaluation of matching methods and validity measures for stereo vision. I. J. Robotic Res. 20, 512–532 (2001)
6. Hu, X., Mordohai, P.: Evaluation of stereo confidence indoors and outdoors. In: [19], pp. 1466–1473
7. Wedel, A., Brox, T., Vaudrey, T., Rabe, C., Franke, U., Cremers, D.: Stereoscopic scene flow computation for 3D motion understanding. International Journal of Computer Vision 95, 29–51 (2011)
8. Shimizu, M., Okutomi, M.: Precise sub-pixel estimation on area-based matching. In: ICCV, pp. 90–97 (2001)
9. Merrell, P., Akbarzadeh, A., Wang, L., Mordohai, P., Frahm, J.-M., Yang, R., Nistér, D., Pollefeys, M.: Real-time visibility-based fusion of depth maps. In: ICCV, pp. 1–8 (2007)
10. Gehrig, S.K., Scharwächter, T.: A real-time multi-cue framework for determining optical flow confidence. In: ICCV Workshops, pp. 1978–1985 (2011)
11. Aodha, O.M., Brostow, G.J., Pollefeys, M.: Segmenting video into classes of algorithm-suitability. In: [19], pp. 1054–1061
12. Humayun, A., Aodha, O.M., Brostow, G.J.: Learning to find occlusion regions. In: CVPR, pp. 2161–2168. IEEE (2011)
13. Hirschmüller, H.: Stereo processing by semiglobal matching and mutual information. IEEE Trans. Pattern Anal. Mach. Intell. 30, 328–341 (2008)
14. Egnal, G.: Mutual information as a stereo correspondence measure. Computer and Information Science, University of Pennsylvania, Philadelphia, USA, Tech. Rep. MS-CIS-00-20 (2000)
15. Hirschmüller, H., Scharstein, D.: Evaluation of cost functions for stereo matching. In: CVPR (2007)
16. Scharstein, D., Szeliski, R.: Stereo matching with nonlinear diffusion. International Journal of Computer Vision 28, 155–174 (1998)
17. Shi, J., Tomasi, C.: Good features to track. In: CVPR, pp. 593–600. IEEE (1994)
18. Okutomi, M., Katayama, Y., Oka, S.: A simple stereo algorithm to recover precise object boundaries and smooth surfaces. International Journal of Computer Vision 47, 261–273 (2002)
19. The Twenty-Third IEEE Conference on Computer Vision and Pattern Recognition, CVPR 2010, San Francisco, CA, USA, June 13-18. IEEE (2010)

Lessons and Insights from Creating a Synthetic Optical Flow Benchmark

Jonas Wulff[1], Daniel J. Butler[2], Garrett B. Stanley[3], and Michael J. Black[1]

[1] Max-Planck Institute for Intelligent Systems, Tübingen, Germany
{jonas.wulff,black}@tuebingen.mpg.de
[2] University of Washington, Seattle, WA, USA
djbutler@cs.washington.edu
[3] Georgia Institute of Technology, Atlanta, GA, USA
garrett.stanley@bme.gatech.edu

Abstract. With the MPI-Sintel Flow dataset, we introduce a naturalistic dataset for optical flow evaluation derived from the open source CGI movie Sintel. In contrast to the well-known Middlebury dataset, the MPI-Sintel Flow dataset contains longer and more varied sequences with image degradations such as motion blur, defocus blur, and atmospheric effects. Animators use a variety of techniques that produce pleasing images but make the raw animation data inappropriate for computer vision applications if used "out of the box". Several changes to the rendering software and animation files were necessary in order to produce data for flow evaluation and similar changes are likely for future efforts to construct a scientific dataset from an animated film. Here we distill our experience with Sintel into a set of best practices for using computer animation to generate scientific data for vision research.

1 Introduction

In recent years standardized datasets have been a driving force in various subfields of of computer vision such as object recognition and optical flow [1]. The benefits to the field are twofold: First, they make algorithms objectively comparable and, by creating challenges, inject a sense of competition into the community. Second, by providing a large corpus of data, ideally representative of the world, they make it possible to use learning-based techniques.

Today the Middlebury flow dataset [1] remains the most widely used optical flow benchmark. However, current top methods perform similarly on this dataset, making it hard to determine which differences in performance are significant. In this sense, the Middlebury flow dataset may no longer be challenging enough to drive continued innovation in the field.

In order to provide a more challenging optical flow benchmark, we have developed a new dataset based on the open source CGI movie Sintel[1], which we call MPI-Sintel [2]. Compared to Middlebury, it contains larger motions, non-rigidly

---

[1] http://www.sintel.org

A. Fusiello et al. (Eds.): ECCV 2012 Ws/Demos, Part II, LNCS 7584, pp. 168–177, 2012.
© Springer-Verlag Berlin Heidelberg 2012

Fig. 1. Examples. Example frames from 8 of the 35 scenes contained in our dataset. The ground truth optical flow is shown below the corresponding rendered frame. Color coding as in [1].

moving objects, and image degradations such as motion and defocus blur. Figure 1 shows 8 example scenes from our dataset and the associated ground truth optical flow. This paper serves as a companion to the primary publication introducing the dataset and benchmark [2]. Our main contributions in this paper are 1) to describe how state-of-the-art rendering software can be used to generate a high-quality synthetic optical flow dataset; 2) to point out the pitfalls that arise when using existing 3D data to generate such a dataset as well as possible solutions; and 3) to draw general conclusions relevant for users of synthetic data for computer vision applications.

1.1   The Value of Synthetic Datasets

To train and evaluate optical flow algorithms, one would ideally use a large number of natural video sequences and the corresponding ground truth optical flow. Unfortunately, no sensor currently exists that can measure optical flow directly. In some cases, one can compute the flow from auxiliary information such as special texture patterns [1] or range imagery [3,4]. Hidden texture patterns, however, can only be used in laboratory environments with controlled illumination [1]. Optical flow maps generated from depth and camera motion suffer from occlusion artifacts, noisy depth data, and interpolation error. In [4], for example, only about 50% of the pixels contain usable ground truth optical flow. Furthermore, depth-based methods only work for rigid scenes.

One of the goals of optical flow estimation is to deal with arbitrary scenes and non-rigid motions. To circumvent the problems described, we use a synthetic (computer-generated) dataset. In this case the scene geometry and its change over time are known so one can trace each pixel $\mathbf{p_t}$ from the image plane to its origin point $\mathbf{P_t}$ in the scene, track that point to its location $\mathbf{P_{t+1}}$ in the next frame, and compute the projection $\mathbf{p_{t+1}}$ in the next frame. Up to machine precision, the ground truth optical flow is then given by $\mathbf{u_t} = \mathbf{p_{t+1}} - \mathbf{p_t}$.

In addition to high accuracy, using computer-generated scenes has two further benefits. First, even realistic-looking scenes are relatively easy to create in large quantities, which is important for methods that use machine learning techniques. Second, the creator of the scene potentially has total control over all aspects of the data generation, from the raw geometry to the image rendering process. Thus, one can change aspects of the scene, such as the materials, the light, or the motion of the camera or the objects, and generate multiple renderings of the same scene using varying parameters. This allows one to evaluate the impact of individual parameters on the performance of optical flow algorithms.

The main argument against synthetic data is that the rendered images may differ from images of the real world in important ways. This critique certainly applies to previous synthetic flow benchmarks shown in Fig. 2. However, the realism and complexity of CGI that is possible today makes synthetic data worth reconsidering. Feature films, for example, often use graphics that is indistinguishable from real scenes and seamlessly combine real and CGI elements.

The dataset we propose here is derived from the CGI movie Sintel, a 14-minute short movie. It was created and rendered using the rendering software Blender[2]. Both Blender and the complete production data for Sintel are released as open source. The availability of the Blender's source code allowed us to understand and control how exactly the images were generated, something that would not have been possible using a proprietary rendering software. Furthermore, since the production data is freely available, we can modify, extend, and re-generate all parts of the movie.

2   Previous Data Sets

Datasets for optical flow evaluation can be subdivided into three categories: *natural*, containing relatively unaltered photographic images, *semi-synthetic*, containing either heavily processed or elaborately staged images, and *synthetic*, containing completely computer-generated images. Since the dataset we present here is completely synthetic, we limit this section to synthetic datasets. A review of datasets of natural and semi-synthetic datasets is given in [1].

Barron et al. [5] developed the first synthetic dataset for optical flow evaluation, which included the widely used Yosemite sequence. Yosemite is still part of the Middlebury dataset [1] but contains only grayscale images, rigid motion, no atmospheric effects such as haze, no shading, and few occlusions.

McCane et al. [6] proposed a synthetic dataset containing varying degrees of scene complexity, object motion, and camera motion, with only the highest level of scene complexity resembling a real scene (see Fig. 2). Compared to the Yosemite sequence, it contains color images and separately moving objects, but only very simple textures.

The Middlebury dataset [1], today's most widely used optical flow evaluation dataset, introduced new synthetic sequences, Urban1-3 and Grove1-3, resembling a city and natural outdoor scenes, respectively. Compared to the complex scenes

---

[2] http://www.blender.org

Fig. 2. History: Evolution of synthetic flow datasets. Example frames are shown on top, the corresponding color coded optical flow at the bottom. From left to right: Yosemite sequence from [5]; Complex sequence from [6]; Grove3 sequence from [1]; 009_Crates1 sequence from [7]; Bamboo3 sequence from MPI-Sintel [2].

from [6], these sequences contain lighting effects such as shadows, rich textures, and more complex object structure. They do not, though, contain atmospheric effects or image degradations, and display only very little independent object motion and mostly small velocities.

UCL-Flow [7] introduces 20 new image pairs with strong rigid object motion and more complex light situations with colored light sources and ambient lighting. Its intended use is to train a mechanism to locally select the best optical flow algorithm, given a set of image features.

Whether synthetic datasets are in fact realistic enough to predict performance on real images remains an open question. Vaudrey et al. [8] compare performance on synthetic and semi-synthetic sequences from Middlebury to performance on a real-world dataset, recorded from a driving car, and find that the results are worse on the natural scenes. The main differences between the synthetic Middlebury sequences and these real sequences are motion blur and violations of brightness constancy.

Meister and Kondermann [9] re-create a real scene in graphics software enabling them to compare performance on real and CGI sequences. They find that, while the locations of the errors are somewhat different, the average errors for the synthetic sequence and the real sequences are similar when using advanced rendering techniques such as global illumination and carefully selected textures.

In summary, existing synthetic datasets fall short on a number of dimensions, making them less complex than real video sequences: the rendering quality is often unconvincing, motions are limited to rigid objects and very small velocities, no degradations such as motion and focus blur are included, and the available data is often limited to image pairs.

3 Generating Synthetic Data

When generating synthetic flow data, two things are important: The *production data* that describes the 3D shape, appearance, and motion of the scenes, and the *rendering method* used to transform the production data into actual video sequences. Below we describe both components and the modifications required to make the output usable as an optical flow evaluation dataset.

3.1   Production Data

All production data (geometry, textures, compositing setups etc.) for Sintel is available as open source. We used the latest version of the data[3], which contains all the data and software used to create the original Sintel film.

Like most CGI-based films created for entertainment, Sintel contains a number of effects that help achieve a certain look, but pose problems for the scientific use of the data. In order to make the Sintel data usable for an optical flow evaluation data set, a number of changes had to be made. These changes can be subdivided into two categories: changes due to limitations of current optical flow representations, and changes due to problems with the data and/or Blender.

Changes due to Limitations of Optical Flow Representations. Optical flow is usually represented as a two-dimensional, pixel-based map, with velocities in x and y direction at each pixel. Since each pixel can only have a single motion, the complexity of the scene is limited. A transparent surface, for example, cannot be realistically captured, since a pixel cannot be assigned both the motion of the surface and the motion of the background visible through it. A similar problem arises when an object (such as a single hair) is smaller than a pixel, or when object boundaries are anti-aliased. In this case, a single pixel contains multiple, potentially different velocities. The intensity value of such a pixel might be a weighted combination of the foreground and background. In an optical flow representation, though, such a blending does not make sense, since it would assign a pixel the average velocity between the foreground and the background.

Therefore, we disable all transparencies of objects such as glass or feathering of hair, and render the optical flow without anti-aliasing. The optical flow value for a pixel is then the motion at its center. Additionally all strands of hair are set to be rendered at least 2 pixels wide. While this makes the hair appear somewhat "cartoon-y", it ensures correct optical flow at every pixel that predominantly displays hair. Fig. 3 shows an example of a scene before and after these changes.

Changes Due to Problems with the Data. Several problems were caused by bugs within Blender or by artistic "shortcuts", which go unnoticed in the movie but introduce artifacts in the still images or the optical flow fields.

Scene-wise hair problems. Rendering hair as described above effectively broke the relatively complex hair shading system[4], resulting in hair that was often lit inconsistently with respect to the rest of the scene – sometimes too bright, sometimes too dark. We solved this problem by manually adjusting the hair shading for each scene to match the ambient lighting.

---

[3] Available at `http://download.blender.org/durian/svn/`

[4] For more details on hair shading in Sintel, and the resulting difficulties, see `wiki.blender.org/index.php/Org:Institute/Openprojects/Durian/HairNotes`

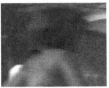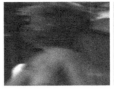

Fig. 3. Illustration of the hair transparency issue. Comparison of the rendered images and optical flow maps in the original form (left) and with our changes applied (right). Due to transparency effects, a large amount of hair is not captured in the optical flow of the original data.

Motion blur. The motion blur in Sintel is simulated using the optical flow field. The choice of the number of samples used in the blur filter represents a trade-off between accuracy and computing time. We found that in most of the scenes, it was set to a relatively low value, sometimes leading to visible artifacts. To fix this, we set the number of samples to 1024.

Texture problems. In Blender, displacement maps (i.e. textures that deform an object based on their intensity) are integrated into the scene *after* the object motion is computed. For this reason, the computed optical flow field contains the motion of the undeformed object, leading to slight inaccuracies for objects with such displacement maps. The displacement component for all textures was therefore disabled. We find that this step does not significantly impact the data, both visually and in terms of optical flow accuracy. It should be noted, though, that *bump maps* were retained, since they do not alter the rendered vertex positions, but only the normal directions. Thus, textural structure is preserved.

Animation adjustments. In Blender, it is possible to animate a change in speed of a cyclic animation (for example, to let a bird flap faster or slower). However, due to a bug in Blender, this change of motion speed is not incorporated into the optical flow field, introducing errors. We solve this by setting the speed of all cyclic animations to a constant speed.

Threading. Certain settings in the global illumination computation in Blender lead to visible tiling artifacts if different parts of the images are rendered by different threads. Since our dataset consists of a large number of scenes, we can parallelize the rendering on a (scene-)level by computing all scenes in parallel. Without a loss in performance, we can then disable multithreading for each single Blender instance, thus eliminating the tiling problem.

Halos. For dramatic effect, some scenes include relatively large, transparent halos. Besides the transparency problems described above, we found that the presence of these halos causes problems in Blender's image generation pipeline, rendering the output images unusable. Therefore, halo effects were disabled.

3.2 Generation Process

With the changes described above, the images were rendered using Blender's internal raytracing engine. It supports a number of advanced techniques, such

Fig. 4. Illustration of the optical flow interpolation problem. From left to right: The original optical flow map, containing triangulation artifacts; the same optical flow map, rendered with our modifications; a magnification of the marked region of the original rendering; the endpoint error in the marked region (difference between the correct 3D flow and the original Blender 2D flow).

as flexible material and specularity shaders, effects such as subsurface scattering, and global illumination, all of which are used heavily in Sintel. To create realistic looking images, the lighting is especially important. Blender uses ambient occlusion (causing a darkening of cavities), environment lighting (ambient light based on a sky texture), and indirect lighting. These illumination effects are computed using a Quasi-Monte-Carlo raytracing method, randomly sampling rays while trying to keep the spacing between the rays as even as possible. While this provides a good trade-off between accuracy, image quality, and computing time, it can introduce noise artifacts, as described in Sec. 4.1. Furthermore, it should be noted that, while these effects increase the perceived quality and realism of a scene, they only approximate real-world lighting.

A typical Sintel scene consists of a number of layers, defined by the artist. These layers correspond roughly to background/static and foreground/animated parts of the scene. Each layer is rendered separately and then combined with the other layers using a given compositing layout. The compositing layout defines the post-processing stages (e.g. color correction) for each layer, and how they are combined (for example based on their transparency or depth values) to form the final rendering. Since the compositing layout is mainly used for image post-processing, it cannot be used to combine the data (optical flow and depth). For example, a non-linear color correction would result in a meaningless distortion of the optical flow. When rendering the optical flow and depth, we thus collapse the whole scene onto a single layer, and render the data from that layer.

Blender computes optical flow as part of its rendering process for the purpose of simulating motion blur. Unfortunately, the computed flow is wrong, since for efficiency reasons, the computation is performed in 2D. Each vertex is projected onto the image plane in two subsequent frames, resulting in the true flow at these locations. However, the motion of pixels *inside* a triangle in between three vertices is given by linearly interpolating the *2D motions of the vertices*. The resulting inaccuracies become noticeably large in case of triangles slanted in depth. An example is shown in Fig. 4. To fix this, we modified Blender itself, and integrated a true 3D interpolation of the optical flow that is projected onto the image plane after the interpolation. Fig. 4 shows an example.

Using our modified version of Blender, the data was rendered into OpenEXR files. These files contain different layers: the data, such as the depth and flow information, as floating point values, and the images from the individual render passes as linear values. The images are then gamma-corrected using $\gamma = 0.4641$, the power Blender uses to generate standard image data (such as PNG files).

3.3 Data Selection

Without producer credits, the full movie has a length of approximately 18,000 frames, each of which has a size of about 7 MB (including depth and optical flow), amounting to a total data volume of 123 GB. We felt this was too large to be practical and use a subset of the movie containing 1628 frames from 35 scenes, chosen based on the following criteria:

Rendering consistency. Despite the efforts described above, some sequences remained problematic. In a few sequences, the depth ordering of the layers in the composite layout was inconsistent with the actual scene geometry. This leads to an object being in front of another in the images, but behind that same object in the flow and depth data, which are generated from the scene collapsed onto a single layer. Scenes where this posed a problem were excluded from the dataset.

Variability. Since the ultimate goal of this dataset is to evaluate optical flow algorithms, we wanted the contained data to be as varied and interesting as possible. We therefore exclude scenes that are mostly static, or that have similar optical flow to scenes already in the dataset.

Difficulty. One motivation for this dataset is to be more challenging than Middlebury. However, we also do not want it to be impossible to get good results. Therefore, scenes that are too easy (i.e. contain constant or very small motion) or too hard (scenes for which a human can not identify what is happening, based on an isolated, two-second snippet) are discarded.

4 Description of the Dataset

The final MPI-Sintel dataset contains 35 scenes, between 20 and 50 frames long, for a total of 1628 frames. The rendered images have a resolution of 1024 x 436 pixels at 24 frames per second. Extending previous synthetic datasets, it contains atmospheric effects, motion and defocus blur, and large velocities. The scenes span a large variety of environments, characters, and actions.

To investigate when optical flow algorithms break, we render each frame in three different passes: the *Albedo* pass contains no shading and satisfies brightness constancy everywhere except in occlusion regions, the *Clean* pass, which contains shading, but no image degradations, and the *Final* pass, which additionally includes motion blur, defocus blur, and atmospheric effects, and corresponds to the final movie. Fig. 5 shows examples of the different passes.

The dataset is split into a 1064 frame training set and a 564 frame test set[5]. The training and test sets are balanced in terms of first-order statistics of the

---

[5] All data can be obtained from `http://sintel.is.tuebingen.mpg.de`

Fig. 5. Render passes. Two examples for the different passes contained in the proposed dataset. From left to right: Albedo pass, Clean pass, Final pass

images and optical flow maps, and their respective spatial and temporal derivatives. For the training set, we provide ground truth optical flow, depth information, masks of invalid pixels, extrinsic and intrinsic camera data, maps of occluded regions, and motion boundaries. For the test set, this data is withheld for evaluation. Fig. 1 shows frames from 8 example scenes and their corresponding optical flow maps. A detailed investigation of the realism of the dataset, as well as the performance of optical flow algorithm, can be found in [2].

4.1   Remaining Problems

We took great care to eliminate problems with the data as much as possible. However, a few issues remain. The most obvious of these are occasional interpenetrations of objects, for example the main character's hair going through her collar. While comparable situations can in theory appear in the real world (for example, if a sharp object cuts through a piece of fabric), one expects these to appear far less often than in our dataset. We would advise against learning a physics-based world model from the data we present here.

In some cases, specular, highly structured textures contain too much high-frequency information for the anti-aliasing to work properly, causing a "sparkling" appearance. A similar effect with a different cause is a faint low-frequency noise in some textures. This is caused by the Global Illumination algorithm, which uses a limited, random sampling of light rays bouncing back from surfaces. Since the random sampling changes with each frame, the surfaces are effectively illuminated by a noisy light source. Both of these effects are quite subtle, and we believe that optical flow algorithms should be robust against them.

Another rendering-related issue is visible when an object of single pixel width is motion-blurred. Since foreground and background optical flow cannot be meaningfully blended, the flow is aliased. When part of an object has a width of less than a pixel, it my not be assigned a foreground flow value since the background flow is dominant. This causes the affected area to not be motion-blurred resulting in thin objects that can be partially motion blurred and partially sharp. To eliminate this effect, we rendered the affected scenes with double the resolution, and downscaled the images afterwards. This mostly eliminated the effect and, where it remains, it is confined to a very small spatial area.

5   Conclusion

We described the detailed process of generating the MPI-Sintel optical flow dataset from the open source CGI movie Sintel. This required several modifications to the data and the rendering method to to make the data suitable for use in such a benchmark. Summarizing, we find 3 key issues in using synthetic data: **1. Physical implausibilities.** Synthetic movies are made to look good, not to be physically accurate. They only roughly approximate the real world and we think it is important to compare them statistically with natural scenes to validate how realistic they are. **2. Control.** To make data usable in a scientific environment, it is important to have full control over the production data as well as the mechanisms and software used to generate or transform this data. **3. Representation.** Optical flow is usually represented as a two-dimensional motion vector field, which cannot model multiple motions at the same point. This representation limits the possible contents and complexity of the dataset. Future work should address richer representations, and evaluation measures, to allow datasets to include more complex phenomena.

With these principles, and progress in photorealistic rendering, we believe that synthetic data can play an increasing role in computer vision.

Acknowledgments. We thank T. Roosendaal for his assistance. MJB and GBS were supported in part by NSF CRCNS Grant IIS-0904630.

References

1. Baker, S., Scharstein, D., Lewis, J.P., Roth, S., Black, M.J., Szeliski, R.: A Database and Evaluation Methodology for Optical Flow. Int. J. Comput. Vision 92, 1–31 (2011)
2. Butler, D.J., Wulff, J., Stanley, G.B., Black, M.J.: A Naturalistic Open Source Movie for Optical Flow Evaluation. In: Fitzgibbon, A., Lazebnik, S., Perona, P., Sato, Y., Schmid, C. (eds.) ECCV 2012, Part VI. LNCS, vol. 7577, pp. 611–625. Springer, Heidelberg (2012)
3. Roth, S., Black, M.: On the spatial statistics of optical flow. In: ICCV 2005, vol. 1, pp. 42–49 (2005)
4. Geiger, A., Lenz, P., Urtasun, R.: Are we ready for Autonomous Driving? The KITTI Vision Benchmark Suite. In: CVPR 2012 (2012)
5. Barron, J.L., Fleet, D.J., Beauchemin, S.S.: Performance of optical flow techniques. Int. J. Comput. Vision 12, 43–77 (1994)
6. McCane, B., Novins, K., Crannitch, D., Galvin, B.: On benchmarking optical flow. Comput. Vis. Image Underst. 84, 126–143 (2001)
7. Mac Aodha, O., Humayun, A., Pollefeys, M., Brostow, G.J.: Learning a Confidence Measure for Optical Flow. IEEE Trans. Pattern Anal. Mach. Intell. 34 (to appear, 2012)
8. Vaudrey, T., Rabe, C., Klette, R., Milburn, J.: Differences between stereo and motion behavior on synthetic and real-world stereo sequences. In: 23rd International Conference of Image and Vision Computing New Zealand (IVCNZ 2008), pp. 1–6 (2008)
9. Meister, S., Kondermann, D.: Real versus realistically rendered scenes for optical flow evaluation. In: CEMT 2011, pp. 1–6. IEEE (2011)

Modeling and Detection of Wrinkles in Aging Human Faces Using Marked Point Processes

Nazre Batool* and Rama Chellappa

Department of Electrical and Computer Engineering and the Center
for Automation Research, UMIACS, University of Maryland,
College Park, MD 20742, USA

Abstract. In this paper we propose a new generative model for wrinkles on aging human faces using Marked Point Processes (MPP). Wrinkles are considered as stochastic spatial arrangements of sequences of line segments, and detected in an image by proper localization of line segments. The intensity gradients are used to detect more probable locations and a prior probability model is used to constrain properties of line segments. Wrinkles are localized by sampling MPP using the Reversible Jump Markov Chain Monte Carlo (RJMCMC) algorithm. We also present an evaluation setup to measure the performance of the proposed model. We present results on a variety of images obtained from the Internet to illustrate the performance of the proposed model.

Keywords: Modeling of wrinkles, Markov Point Process, Reversible Jump Markov Chain Monte Carlo, stochastic geometrical model.

1 Introduction

Wrinkles and fine lines are important facial features present in most aging faces. An accurate image-based analysis of these features can play an important role in relevant aging applications. Much of the work done in aging applications, e.g. age estimation and simulation, is based on the incorporation of wrinkles as texture features [1,2,3]. A few attempts have been made to evaluate wrinkles as edges [4,5]. However, image-based detection and analysis of wrinkles has mostly remained unaddressed. This can probably be attributed to the nature of the artifacts associated with wrinkles as well as the challenges posed by drastically varying skin appearance in images with variations in illumination and acquisition angles [6]. In this paper, we propose a model to detect and analyze wrinkles explicitly. The basis for our methodology is based on the following observations. First, wrinkles create the appearance of texture on skin, but at high resolution, wrinkles do not depict any repetitive/homogeneous pattern. Second, wrinkles cannot be categorized as boundaries between multiple textures. Third, a wrinkle is usually a discontinuity

---

* The first author would like to acknowledge the support of Fulbright/HEC(Pakistan)/USAID PhD Scholarship. However, the contents of this publication have not been approved by the respresenting agencies/governments of the USA/Pakistan.

A. Fusiello et al. (Eds.): ECCV 2012 Ws/Demos, Part II, LNCS 7584, pp. 178–188, 2012.
© Springer-Verlag Berlin Heidelberg 2012

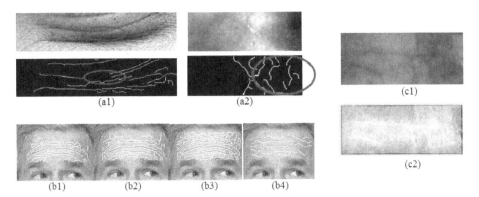

Fig. 1. (Left) Results with the Canny edge detector - (a1) Wrinkles as broken edges (a2) False edges due to illumination (b1) threshold=0.3 (b2) threshold=0.2 (b3) threshold = 0.1 (b4) wrinkles detected as line segments (Right) LoG filtering (c1) Original Image (c2) Filtered image with $\sigma = 0.5$

in background inhomogeneous skin texture. And finally, wrinkles do not always appear as continuous edges.

It can be argued that an accurate edge detector can detect wrinkles. We present some typical results using the Canny edge detector in Figure 1. In Figure 1(a1) the encircled edge is disconnected despite the original wrinkle being continuous. In Figure 1(a2) illumination discontinuities are marked as edges. Figure 1(b1-b3) show the erroneous edges if the threshold of edge detector is set too low. To explain our motivation, Figure 1(b4) shows the results of our model for comparison. A lower number of erroneous edges as well as conitnutity of edges representing detected wrinkles can be observed. In short, although intensity gradients are well picked up as edges by an edge detector, no distinction is made between intensity gradients due to wrinkles, illumination discontinuities or other factors. A method capable of filtering intensity gradients based on the probability of their being wrinkles is needed. We propose to incorporate prior semantic information available from typical appearances of wrinkles on human faces for that purpose. Wrinkles are modeled as a stochastic spatial process of 'line segments' in a Bayesian framework using Marked Point Process (MPP) [7]. In terms of methodology, our work is related to the work by Soitca et al. [8] for detection of road networks in satellite images. The main contribution of our work is the modeling of wrinkles as a spatial line process to incorporate prior information about wrinkles and detection of wrinkles explicitly as line segments. Also, as compared to the work reported in [4,5], we experiment with a larger variety of images obtained from the Internet.

2   Marked Point Process (MPP)

A spatial point process is a random process of occurrence of points in space defined with respect to a Poisson measure. Normally a set of random parameters

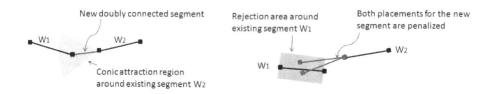

Fig. 2. (a)Attraction interaction creates doubly connected segment (b) Rejection interaction

is also associated with a point, called *mark*, describing its specific properties. In this work, the marked points represent line segments. Two segments can interact with each other due to spatial proximity in the image plane. An attraction interaction results in interconnection of line segments whereas a rejection interaction prevents overlappping or congested parallel segments. A resulting sequence of interconnected line segments represents a wrinkle. An MPP model consists of a prior probability model and a data likelihood term. The prior model imposes geometric constraints on the spatial arrangements of line segments whereas the data likelihood determines the probability of occurrence of line segments depending on the intensity gradients at image sites. A marked point is given by $w_i = (s_i, m_i)$ where $s_i = (x_i, y_i) \in S \subset \mathbb{R}^2$ is the location of center of the segment and $m_i = (l_i, \theta_i) \in M$ is the mark consisting of two parameters denoting the length and orientation of the segment, respectively. The continuous space for parameters is given by $M = [l_{min}, l_{max}] \times [\theta_{min}, \theta_{max}]$. The line segments $\{\mathbf{w} = w_i, i = 1, ..., n\}$ can be considered as a realization of the MPP on the space $S \times M$. For further details on MPP, the interested reader is referred to [7]. The probability density of MPP can be represented by the Gibbs distribution:

$$f(\mathbf{w}) = c\beta^{n(\mathbf{w})} \exp(-U(\mathbf{w})) \text{ where } U(\mathbf{w}) = U_P(\mathbf{w}) + U_D(\mathbf{w}). \qquad (1)$$

The term c is the normalizing constant, β is the intensity of the point process, $n(\mathbf{w})$ and $U(\mathbf{w})$ are the number of line segments and the total energy of the realization $\mathbf{w}$, respectively. The terms $U_P(\mathbf{w})$ and $U_D(\mathbf{w})$ correspond to the energies contributed by the prior model and the data likelihood term, respectively.

2.1   Prior Model

The prior model determines more likely geometric properties of the line segments and spatial interactions between neighboring line segments. The parameters $\{l_i, \theta_i\}$ are sampled from a uniform distribution where the parameters of the uniform distribution set limits on the geometric properties of the line segments:

$$l_i \sim \mathcal{U}([l_{min}, l_{max}]) \text{ and } \theta_i \sim \mathcal{U}([\theta_{min}, \theta_{max}]). \qquad (2)$$

Under the prior model, two segments can interact with each other in spatial domain i.e. the segments can influence each other's probability of being included in a realization of the MPP due to their spatial proximity. We propose a rejection interaction which penalizes the birth (addition) of overlapping or congested segments. Let the rejection interaction between two segments $\{w_i, w_j\}$ be denoted by $w_i \overset{r}{\sim} w_j$. A rectangular rejection region of a certain width exists around each existing segment in the configuration. Figure 9(b) shows the rectangular rejection interaction region around an existing segment $\mathbf{w}_1$. The new segment is penalized if it overlaps with the rejection region of any existing segment. The rejection interaction is modeled through the term $q(w_i, w_j)$ as follows. The parameter γ determines the penalty assigned to the interacting new segment.

$$q(w_i, w_j) = \gamma \times \mathbb{I}_{(w_i \overset{r}{\sim} w_j)} \text{ where } \mathbb{I}_{(w_i \overset{r}{\sim} w_j)} = \begin{cases} 1 \text{ if } w_i \overset{r}{\sim} w_j \\ 0 \text{ if } w_i \overset{r}{\nsim} w_j \end{cases} \tag{3}$$

The total energy for the prior model is given by:

$$U_P(\mathbf{w}) = \sum_{\substack{(w_i, w_j) \in \mathbf{w} \\ w_i \overset{r}{\sim} w_j}} q(w_i, w_j). \tag{4}$$

2.2 Data Likelihood Energy

The data likelihood determines the probability of occurrence of line segments at image sites. An image is filtered with a Laplacian of Gaussian (LoG) filter to highlight the intensity gradients caused by wrinkles. Figure 1(c1, c2) shows the LoG filter response to a low resolution forehead image. We selected the standard deviation ($\sigma = 0.5$) for LoG filters. Let D_i denote the pixels corresponding to the segment w_i and d_{min} denote the minimum filter response observed in the given image. Then the likelihood energy for the segment w_i is given by

$$U_D(w_i) = -\left[\alpha \sum_{d \in D_i} (d - d_{min})^2 \right]. \tag{5}$$

3 Simulation of the Marked Point Process

For an MPP, the number of objects is not known a priori and the Metropolis-Hastings algorithm cannot be used to sample from distributions. Green [9] presented the Reversible Jump Markov Chain Monte Carlo (RJMCMC) algorithm to allow configurations of different dimensions, i.e. different numbers of line segments. The algorithm allows jumps between states in configurations of different dimensions. Given that the state $\mathbf{w}$ is changed to $\mathbf{w}'$, the algorithm requires the matching of dimensions for two configurations. This is achieved by using an auxiliary random variable ω, sampled from an arbitrary distribution $g(\omega)$, and a bijective transformation $\mathcal{T}$ such that $\mathbf{w}' = \mathcal{T}(\mathbf{w}, \omega)$. The acceptance probability ϕ of a jump modifying configuration $\mathbf{w}$ to the configuration $\mathbf{w}'$ is then modified by the Jacobian of the transformation, $\left| \frac{\partial \mathcal{T}}{\partial (\mathbf{w}, \omega)} \right|$, as follows.

$$\phi(\mathbf{w} \to \mathbf{w}') = \min\{1, R\} \text{ where } R = \frac{f(\mathbf{w}')}{f(\mathbf{w})g(\omega)} \left| \frac{\partial \mathcal{T}}{\partial (\mathbf{w}, \omega)} \right| \times \frac{prob(\text{reverse jump})}{prob(\text{forward jump})}. \tag{6}$$

Original Image ⇨ Seed Segments ⇨ After 5000 iterations ⇨ After 15000 iterations ⇨ RJMCMC Output

Fig. 3. Step-by-step process for the detection of wrinkles in an image

The term R is called the acceptance ratio and needs to be calculated for every move under RJMCMC. Furthermore, simulated annealing is used to reach the global minimum of the Gibbs energy $U(\mathbf{w})$ in equation (1) by replacing the probability density $f(\mathbf{w})$ by $f(\mathbf{w})^{\frac{1}{T}}$ in RJMCMC algorithm. The cooling schedule for T is given by $T = \frac{T_0}{\log(1+i)}$ where i denotes the current iteration and T_0 is selected to be 10. The simulation of point processes involves birth and death moves, where points are either added to or deleted from the configuration, changing its dimension. The reverse jumps (death) ensure the reversibility of the Markov chain (See Geyer [10] for a proof and further discussion).

3.1   Birth and Death of Singly/Doubly Connected Segments

A new segment is sampled from the distribution $g(\omega)$ and connected to a randomly selected segment from the configuration with at least one free end. This move can add a singly or doubly connected segment based on spatial interactions among segments. Figure 2(a) shows an example of birth of a doubly connected segment as a result of attraction interaction. The left end of the existing segment w_2 is selected to be connected to the new segment. An attraction interaction region is defined to be a conic region connected to that end point. An existing segment in that region (w_1 in this case) results in the new segment being connected at both sides between the two existing segments. A segment is not allowed to be connected to more than one segment at either end point. Let $\{n_{c0}, n_{c1}, n_{c2}\}$ be the number of line segments with both ends free, connected at one end and connected at both ends respectively. Let (x_e, y_e) be the coordinates of a free end point selected randomly out of $2n_{c0} + n_{c1}$ available free end points in the current configuration. Let us assume that this is going to be a singly connected segment and let $\omega = (\theta_\omega, l_\omega)$ be the random vector sampled from mark space M with density function:

$$g(\omega) = \frac{1}{l_{max} - l_{min}} \times \frac{1}{\theta_{max} - \theta_{min}} \tag{7}$$

Then the new segment w is given by:

$$w(\omega) = \left[x(x_e, \theta_\omega, l_\omega) \; y(y_e, \theta_\omega, l_\omega) \; \theta_\omega \; l_\omega \right]^T \tag{8}$$

and the configuration changes to:

$$\mathbf{w}' = \mathcal{T}(\mathbf{w}, \omega) = \left[\mathbf{w} \; w(\omega) \right]^T \tag{9}$$

Let $P_{C,birth}$ and $P_{C,death}$ be the probabilities of choosing the birth and death of connected segments respectively. Then $P_{C,birth}/(2n_{c0} + n_{c1})$ is the probability

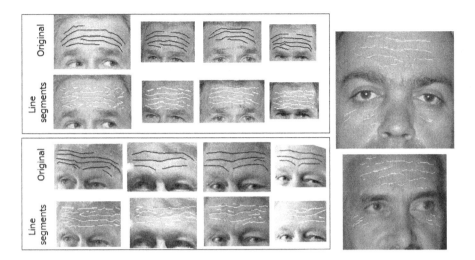

Fig. 4. Detection of wrinkles as line segments for two subjects

Fig. 5. Detection of wrinkles around eyes

of the selection of a particular free end point (x_e, y_e) for the birth of a singly connected segment, and $P_{C,death}/n_{c1}$ is the probability of the reverse jump of death (deletion) of a connected segment. The Jacobian of bijective transformation, in case of singly connected segments, is equal to one (See Appendix I for derivation). Then the acceptance ratio for this birth move is as follows:

$$R = \frac{2n_{c0} + n_{c1}}{P_{C,birth}} \times \frac{P_{C,death}}{n_{c1}} \times (l_{max} - l_{min})(\theta_{max} - \theta_{min}) \times \frac{f(\mathbf{w}')}{f(\mathbf{w})}. \qquad (10)$$

where the ratio $\frac{f(\mathbf{w}')}{f(\mathbf{w})}$ is given as:

$$\frac{f(\mathbf{w}')}{f(\mathbf{w})} = \frac{f(\mathbf{w} \cup w)}{f(\mathbf{w})} = \beta \exp\left(\alpha \sum_{d \in w} (d - d_{min})^2 - \sum_{\substack{w_i \in \mathbf{w} \\ w_i \overset{r}{\sim} w}} q(w_i, w) \right). \qquad (11)$$

In the case of the birth of a doubly connected segment, the parameter vector ω for the new line segment w is simply a function of the neighboring two segments and is not sampled randomly. In this case $g(\omega) = 1$ and $w = \omega$ which reduces the Jacobian of the bijective transformation to one. Then the acceptance ratio for the birth of a doubly connected segment is given as:

$$R = \frac{2n_{c0} + n_{c1}}{P_{C,birth}} \times \frac{P_{C,death}}{n_{c2}} \times \frac{f(\mathbf{w}')}{f(\mathbf{w})}. \qquad (12)$$

The acceptance ratios for the death of connected segments are simply the inverse of the acceptance ratios $1/R$ for the birth of these segments.

3.2   Seed Segments

The connected segments connect to pre-existing segments with free end points. This makes the placement of the first few free segments critical in the evolution of the Markov Chain in the RJMCMC algorithm. For faster convergence towards the minimum, we propose a favorable initial state by introducing 'seed' segments. The image sites with the highest filter responses are selected while keeping a minimum distance r_{seed} among them. Seed segments are then placed on these sites in the direction perpendicular to the highest intensity gradient. This results in the placement of seed segments uniformly with inter-seed distance r_{seed}. Figure 3 includes an example of seed segments. Let a seed segment be given as $w(\theta) = \begin{bmatrix} x_{seed} & y_{seed} & l_{seed} & \theta \end{bmatrix}^T$ and the corresponding set of pixels be $D(w(\theta))$. Then the optimal direction of the seed segment θ^* is found as follows.

$$\theta^* = \arg\max_{\theta \in [\theta_{min}, \theta_{max}]} \sum_{d \in D(w(\theta))} d. \tag{13}$$

4   Experiments and Discussion

For assessing the performance of the detection algorithm on uncontrolled image settings, images were selected from the Internet and the FG-NET database [11]. Aging results in wrinkles at several regions of a face i.e. forehead, eye, mouth and nose corners as well as at sagging contours of the skin. For this work, we restricted to the detection of wrinkles on forehead for two reasons (a) generating the ground truth by hand-drawing of wrinkles on the foreheads was easier and (b) wrinkles were more obvious on the forehead in most of the images. Nevertheless, with slight change of parameters in prior model, the wrinkles in other parts of the face can also be detected. For example Figure 5 shows results of detection wrinkles around eye area for two subjects. For each image, the forehead was hand cropped to a rectangle and input to the detection algorithm. It should be mentioned here that the detection of forehead area was not considered under the scope of this work and user-provided cropping was considered sufficient. In total we used 36 images with hand-drawn wrinkles as the ground truth. Where most of the wrinkles were obvious, some were less apparent and posed difficulty even for hand-drawing. The image size varied from 86 x 37 as minimum to 290 x 110 as maximum. Resizing images was not considered as we wanted to assess the performance of the detection algorithm on images of different sizes and resolutions.

Evaluation Setup. Since localization of wrinkles is a new application in image-based analysis of aging skin, we propose an evaluation setup to assess the performance of detection algorithms as well. The terms 'detected', 'original' and 'well-localized' wrinkles are used. The detected wrinkles are the output of the algorithm. The original wrinkles are those hand-drawn by a user and the well-localized wrinkles are wrinkles detected at correct locations. A margin of $m = 3$ pixels is allowed in localization i.e. a detected wrinkle is considered well-localized

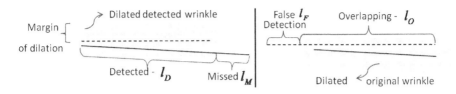

Fig. 6. Evaluation Setup, (left) Calculation for r_{detect}, (right) Calculation for r_{false}

if it is within the distance of m pixels from the hand drawn wrinkle. This way the margin accounts for small inaccuracies in the hand-drawing of wrinkles or small displacements in maximum gradient locations. Morphological dilation with the margin m is used to define the overlap area. A detected wrinkle is considered well-localized if it lies in the overlap area. Let n_W and n_D be the total number of hand drawn and detected wrinkles respectively. We propose the following ratios for evaluation. Figure 6 shows the detailed procedure for determining the ratios.

1. Detection Ratio ($\mathbf{r_{detect}}$): The ratio of the total length of original wrinkles within the overlap region of detected wrinkles to the total length of the original wrinkles.

$$r_{detect} = \frac{\sum_{n_W} l_{overlap}}{\sum_{n_W} (l_{overlap} + l_{miss})} \qquad (14)$$

2. False Alarm Ratio ($\mathbf{r_{false}}$): The ratio of the total length of falsely detected wrinkles to the background area with no wrinkles ($\nu(S)$ represents the measure on image space).

$$r_{false} = \frac{\sum_{n_D} l_{false}}{\nu(S) - \sum_{n_W} l_{original}} \qquad (15)$$

3. Miss Ratio ($\mathbf{r_{miss}}$): The ratio of the total length of missed original wrinkles to the total length of original wrinkles.

$$r_{miss} = \frac{\sum_{n_W} l_{miss}}{\sum_{n_W} (l_{overlap} + l_{miss})} \quad \text{where } r_{miss} = 1 - r_{detect} \qquad (16)$$

The cropped forehead images were input to the RJMCMC algorithm. It was observed that 2×10^4 iterations were sufficient for the Markov Chain, with the selected cooling schedule, to become stable with almost equal number of birth and death moves. The probabilities $P_{C,birth}$ and $P_{C,death}$ were set equal to 0.5 each. The seed parameters $\{r_{seed}, l_{seed}\}$ were fixed at 9 and 4 pixels respectively. However, a better approach in future work would be to select the two parameters based on image resolution. The parameters γ and α were selected heuristically. A large value of γ, 150 in this case, suffices to penalize overlapping or congested segments. The parameter α favors the birth of new segments. Figure 7(b) shows a plot of results with α varying over a scale of 10^6 for an image (Note that the x-axis has logarithmic scale). The number of segments increases with α increasing both

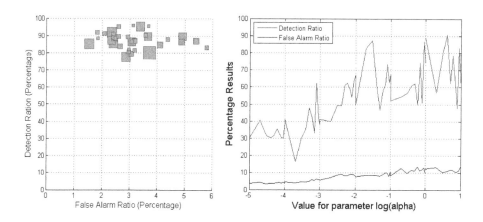

Fig. 7. (a) Detection and False alarm ratios for 36 images of different sizes (b) Effect of value α on detection and false alarm ratios

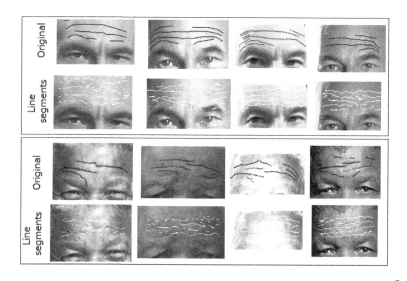

Fig. 8. Detection of wrinkles as line segments for two subjects

detection and false alarm ratios. The optimal values for α were in the range of 0.001-0.03 for smaller images and in the range of 0.00008-0.0005 for larger images. An unsupervised estimation technique for the parameters, however, is required. The dynamics of the Markov Chain were similar for every image where the total number of segments increased sharply in the beginning and then became stable with equal proportion of birth and death moves. Figure 3 shows the different steps in the algorithm. The increased number of line segments from the initial state of seed segments can be seen after 5000 iterations. Figure 7(a) shows the ROC points for the images. Each plot point is represented by a square whose

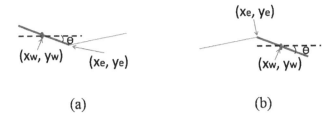

Fig. 9. Calculation for center coordinates of singly connected segment

size is proportional to the size of the image. Most of the images have detection rates greater than 80% and false alarm rates around 2.5% on average. It can be obsereved that the results are independent of the image size. The images on the right side of the plot have relatively lower detection and higher false alarm rates. These are the cases where the algorithm performed relatively poorly because of three reasons (a) some of the wrinkles were not obvious and had lower intensity gradients and, as a result, data likelihood energy values (b) wrinkles were mixed with other skin irregularities and (c) the subject had relatively discontinuous wrinkle curves. Overall, the detection rates were better in subjects with deeper and continuous wrinkles.

5 Conclusion and Future Work

In this paper we presented a novel modeling technique for wrinkles based on spatial marked point processes. The model can allow the incorporation of wrinkles, otherwise difficult features to capture, explicitly in future applications. This work will be extended to include estimation of model parameters based on image resolution and representation of wrinkles as curve patterns. The detected wrinkles as spatial curve patterns can be incorporated in biometric applications. Finally, the presented detection algorithm can enable the use of a large set of images with baseline wrinkles for that purpose.

6 Appendix I

Let the newly connected segment w be given as:

$$w = \left[x_w(x_e, \theta_w, l_w) \; y_w(y_e, \theta_w, l_w) \; \theta_w \; l_w\right]^T = \mathcal{T}(\mathbf{w}, \omega) \qquad (17)$$

where $\theta_w \in [\theta_{min}, \theta_{max}] \subseteq [-\frac{\pi}{2}, \frac{\pi}{2}]$. From Figure 9(a), when the new segment is connected to the left end point, the relationship between (x_w, y_w) and (x_e, y_e) can be written as:

$$x_w(x_e, \theta_w, l_w) = x_e - \frac{l_w}{2}cos(\theta_w). \qquad (18)$$

$$y_w(y_e, \theta_w, l_w) = y_e - \frac{l_w}{2}sin(\theta_w). \qquad (19)$$

And from Figure 9(b), when the new segment is connected to the right end point, the relationship between (x_w, y_w) and (x_e, y_e) can be written as:

$$x_w(x_e, \theta_\omega, l_\omega) = x_e + \frac{l_\omega}{2}cos(\theta_\omega). \tag{20}$$

$$y_w(y_e, \theta_\omega, l_\omega) = y_e + \frac{l_\omega}{2}sin(\theta_\omega). \tag{21}$$

Then the Jacobian factor of bijective tranformation is given as:

$$\left| \frac{\partial \mathcal{T}(\mathbf{w}, \omega)}{\partial(\mathbf{w}, \omega)} \right| = \left| \frac{\partial w}{\partial(x_e, y_e, \theta_\omega, l_\omega)} \right|$$

$$= \begin{vmatrix} \frac{\partial x_w}{\partial x_e} & \frac{\partial y_w}{\partial x_e} & \frac{\partial \theta_\omega}{\partial x_e} & \frac{\partial l_\omega}{\partial x_e} \\ \frac{\partial x_w}{\partial y_e} & \frac{\partial y_w}{\partial y_e} & \frac{\partial \theta_\omega}{\partial y_e} & \frac{\partial l_\omega}{\partial y_e} \\ \frac{\partial x_w}{\partial \theta_\omega} & \frac{\partial y_w}{\partial \theta_\omega} & \frac{\partial \theta_\omega}{\partial \theta_\omega} & \frac{\partial l_\omega}{\partial \theta_\omega} \\ \frac{\partial x_w}{\partial l_\omega} & \frac{\partial y_w}{\partial l_\omega} & \frac{\partial \theta_\omega}{\partial l_\omega} & \frac{\partial l_\omega}{\partial l_\omega} \end{vmatrix}$$

$$= \begin{vmatrix} 1 & 0 & 0 & 0 \\ 0 & 1 & 0 & 0 \\ \pm\frac{l_\omega}{2}sin(\theta_\omega) & \mp\frac{l_\omega}{2}cos(\theta_\omega) & 1 & 0 \\ \mp\frac{1}{2}cos(\theta_\omega) & \mp\frac{1}{2}sin(\theta_\omega) & 0 & 1 \end{vmatrix} \tag{22}$$

$$= 1 \tag{23}$$

References

1. Fu, Y., Guo, G., Huang, T.: Age synthesis and estimation via faces: A survey. PAMI 32, 1955–1976 (2010)
2. Luu, K., Bui, T.D., Suen, C.Y., Ricanek, K.: Combined local and holistic facial features for age-determination. In: ICCARV, pp. 900–904 (2010)
3. Suo, J., Min, F., Zhu, S., Shan, S., Chen, X.: A multi-resolution dynamic model for face aging simulation. In: CVPR, pp. 1–8 (2007)
4. Kwon, Y.H., Lobo, N.D.V.: Age classification from facial images. In: CVPR (1999)
5. Cula, G.O., Bargo, P.R., Kollias, N.: Assessing facial wrinkles: automatic detection and quantification, vol. 7161, pp. 71610J–71610J–6 (2009)
6. Cula, O.G., Dana, K.J., Murphy, F.P., Rao, B.K.: Skin texture modeling. IJCV 62, 97–119 (2005)
7. Lieshout, M.N.M.: Markov Point Processes and their Applications. Imperial College Press/World Scientific Publishing, London, Singapore (2000)
8. Stoica, R., Descombes, X., Zerubia, J.: A Gibbs point process for road extraction from remotely sensed images. IJCV 57, 121–136 (2004)
9. Green, P.: Reversible jump MCMC computation and Bayesian model determination. Biometrika 82, 711–732 (1995)
10. Geyer, C.J., Moller, J.: Simulation procedures and likelihood inference for spatial point processes. Scandinavian Journal of Statistics 21, 359–373 (1994)
11. Available: The FG-net aging database, http://www.fgnet.rsunit.com/

How Does Aging Affect Facial Components?

Charles Otto, Hu Han, and Anil Jain

Michigan State University
{ottochar,hhan,jain}@cse.msu.edu

Abstract. There is growing interest in achieving age invariant face recognition due to its wide applications in law enforcement. The challenge lies in that face aging is quite a complicated process, which involves both intrinsic and extrinsic factors. Face aging also influences individual facial components (such as the mouth, eyes, and nose) differently. We propose a component based method for age invariant face recognition. Facial components are automatically localized based on landmarks detected using an Active Shape Model. Multi-scale local binary pattern and scale-invariant feature transform features are then extracted from each component, followed by random subspace linear discriminant analysis for classification. With a component based representation, we study how aging influences individual facial components on two large aging databases (MORPH Album2 and PCSO). Per component performance analysis shows that the nose is the most stable component during face aging. Age invariant recognition exploiting demographics shows that face aging has more influence on females than males. Overall, recognition performance on the two databases shows that the proposed component based approach is more robust to large time lapses than FaceVACS, a leading commercial face matcher.

Keywords: face recognition, aging, facial components, demographics.

1 Introduction

Automatic face recognition has attracted much attention due to its widespread potential applications in homeland security and law enforcement [1]. Major challenges in designing a robust face recognition system include variations in lighting, expression, head pose, and age. A number of approaches have been proposed to achieve lighting and/or pose invariant face recognition. Among these methods, novel appearance synthesis and discriminative feature extraction are two of the popular approaches [2–5].

Unlike other sources of variation (lighting, pose, and expression) which can be controlled during face image acquisition, face aging is an unavoidable natural process during the lifespan of a person. There has been growing interest in achieving age invariant face recognition to meet the requirements of several applications in law enforcement and forensic investigation (e.g. de-duplication of driver's licenses, identifying missing children). In these applications, the age

A. Fusiello et al. (Eds.): ECCV 2012 Ws/Demos, Part II, LNCS 7584, pp. 189–198, 2012.

Fig. 1. Face aging of a subject in the FG-NET [15] database. (a) Face aging across several decades. (b) Face aging within a decade.

difference between probe and gallery face images from the same subject becomes one of the main challenges for face verification.

Age variation in face recognition can be handled in a manner similar to illumination and pose variations by using novel appearance synthesis or discriminative feature extraction [6]. For example, synthesis methods can eliminate age gaps between face images by synthesizing facial appearances via learning the face aging process [7–9]. One disadvantage of this approach is that the synthesized face image is just a pseudo-photo due to its inferred content, and the low quality of that inferred content can limit recognition performance. Discriminative feature extraction methods seek to extract facial features that are robust to age variations [10–13]. In these methods [7, 8, 10], faces are usually represented holistically. However, intrinsic and extrinsic factors have varying influence on different facial components [14]. This suggests that a component based face representation should provide better understanding of the face aging process, and facilitate an analysis of the role of individual facial components in age invariant face recognition.

While there are large variations in facial appearance across decades (see Figure 1 (a)), facial appearance within a decade may not always be clearly visible (see Figure 1 (b)). This observation suggests learning an age gap specific model for robust face recognition [10, 16]. However, other demographic factors, e.g. gender and race, which can also be inferred from faces, have not been adequately exploited in age invariant face recognition. In this paper, we present a study on the influence of aging on different facial components and demographic groups.

2   Data Sets

We use two face data sets in our study: the public domain MORPH album 2 data set [17], and a dataset comprised of mug shots collected in the state of Florida by the Pinellas County Sheriff's office (referred to here as the PCSO data set). The PCSO dataset was acquired in the public domain through Florida's "Sunshine" laws. Both data sets provide ground truth information on the race and gender

Group	PCSO			MORPH	
	0-1	1-5	5-10	0-1	1-5
White-Male	2,000	2,000	2,000	900	450
White-Female	2,000	2,000	2,000	900	450
Black-Male	2,000	2,000	2,000	900	450
Black-Female	2,000	2,000	2,000	900	450
Hispanic-Male	2,000	2,000	557	900	450
Total	10,000	10,000	8,557	4,500	2,250

(a)   (b)

Fig. 2. Numbers of subjects sampled from different demographic categories and age gaps (a), and (b) example images from MORPH (left) and PCSO (right) databases

of subjects, and contain significant age gaps between multiple face images of a given subject.

In order to study the influence of face aging on different facial components and demographic groups, we constructed subsets of the MORPH and PCSO databases containing specific age lapses between the probe and gallery sets. Subjects were further restricted by demographics to build data sets containing relatively balanced numbers of samples from several race and gender categories: white male, white female, black male, black female, and Hispanic male. The number of samples available for other demographic groups fell off sharply, leaving too few subjects to perform reasonable training and evaluation for our study.

We used data sets exhibiting 0-1, 1-5, and 5-10 year age gaps, and randomly sampled subjects from each demographic category. The numbers of subjects sampled from each demographic category are shown in Figure 2. MORPH Album2 contained no subjects exhibiting an age gap larger than 5 years, so we could only build 0-1 and 1-5 year age gap subsets for MORPH. For each subject, we sampled two images with the desired age gap. Half of the subjects in each subset are used for training and the rest are used for evaluation.

3   Face Representation

Our representation is a combination of random subspace linear discriminant analysis (RS-LDA) based classifiers [18] trained on two types of local descriptors, and is generally analogous to the multi-feature discriminative analysis (MFDA) scheme proposed in [13]. In contrast to MFDA, we apply RS-LDA to local features extracted from explicitly detected facial components (following the component localization scheme described in [19]), rather than horizontal slices of the face. Following RS-LDA for each component and feature type, we perform PCA and then train multiple LDA classifiers on subspaces sampled from the PCA dimensions. For computational efficiency we train a single LDA classifier for each sampled PCA subspace rather than using bagging to train multiple LDA classifiers per PCA subspace, as done in MFDA.

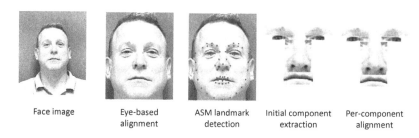

Face image | Eye-based alignment | ASM landmark detection | Initial component extraction | Per-component alignment

Fig. 3. Component extraction stages

3.1   Component Localization

Figure 3 shows the stages of our component localization process, which is essentially the same as the one described in [19]. We start by aligning all face images based on their eye locations, which we detect using the FaceVACS SDK [24]. After the initial alignment, we detect 76 facial landmarks automatically using Stasm [20], an open source Active Shape Model (ASM) [21] implementation. Stasm is designed to work on upright frontal faces, and while we are working with frontal face images, they do exhibit minor pose variations. The goal of our initial alignment step is to eliminate those pose variations, thereby improving Stasm's landmark detection accuracy.

We localize components based on subsets of landmarks corresponding to the eyes, nose, mouth, and eyebrows. Due to the initial normalization step, the eyes are typically well aligned, but the remaining three components (nose, mouth, and eyebrow) are not. We, therefore, perform a Procustes alignment for each component on the corresponding subset of landmarks across all images. This per-component normalization results in fixed-size sub-images for each component.

Figure 4 shows component sub-images averaged across all subjects in the PCSO 0-1 year age gap subset. The blue and green ellipses in Figure 4 illustrate differences between the average components across different races and genders, respectively. The sharpness of the average component images for different demographic categories demonstrates the effectiveness of per-component alignment.

3.2   Feature Extraction

For each facial component, we densely sample both MLBP [22] and SIFT [23] descriptors, using a patch size of 16x16 with 8 pixels overlap between neighboring patches. For a given feature type (MLBP or SIFT), features extracted from all patches are concatenated. Thus, a face image is represented by 8 different feature vectors (4 components × 2 feature descriptors).

3.3   Training

We use random subspace linear discriminant analysis (RS-LDA) [18] to compensate for the small number of samples per subject, similarly to MFDA [13]. We

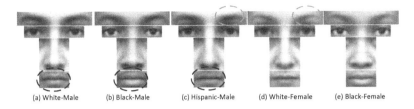

(a) White-Male   (b) Black-Male   (c) Hispanic-Male   (d) White-Female   (e) Black-Female

Fig. 4. Average component images for the subjects in the PCSO database for different demographic groups: (a) White-Male; (b) Black-Male; (c) Hispanic-Male; (d) White-Female, and (e) Black-Female. The blue and green ellipses highlight differences between the average components across different races and genders, respectively

carry out training separately for each component, and for both feature types we first apply PCA on the concatenated feature vectors in the training set for dimensionality reduction. Then we build 10 different subspaces, each with 300 dimensions by sampling from the PCA dimensions. For each subspace, the first 200 dimensions are fixed as the eigenvectors that correspond to the 200 highest eigenvalues, and the remaining 100 dimensions are randomly selected from the top 1,000 PCA eigenvectors. Finally, we perform LDA on each random subspace, leaving us with a total of 80 LDA subspaces (4 components × 2 feature descriptors × 10 random subspaces). In our experiments, training subjects are disjoint from testing subjects.

3.4   Matching

For the face images in probe and gallery sets, the extracted features are projected onto the learnt LDA subspaces. The similarity between two corresponding components is measured using the cosine similarity. To arrive at a final similarity between two faces, we first combine the scores from all LDA subspaces from a given component and descriptor type, giving us different 8 scores (one for each descriptor and component combination). We take the combined LDA subspace scores and combine both scores for each component, leaving us with 4 scores (one for each facial component). These per component scores are then combined to give a final similarity measure between two faces. We use min-max normalization followed by the sum rule for each stage of score fusion. The minimum and maximum values used in the normalization steps are the minimum and maximum scores seen when comparing all face images in the training set.

4   Results and Analysis

We evaluate our component based algorithm and FaceVACS by performing all vs. all matching, then calculating receiver operating characteristic (ROC) curves. We report either true accepts rates (TAR) attained at a fixed false accept rate (FAR), or full ROC curves. Results for specific demographic groups are based on all vs. all matching between all testing subjects within those groups.

Table 1. Per component TAR (%) at 1% FAR across time lapses on PCSO

Age gaps	Eyes	Nose	Mouth	Eyebrows
0-1 year	79.78	92.48	79.10	83.86
1-5 year	76.06	89.68	68.54	73.66
5-10 year	65.83	81.70	55.41	59.76

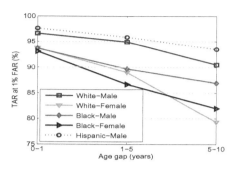

Fig. 5. Per demographic performance across three age gaps on PCSO

4.1   Per Component Performance Analysis

Table 1 shows true accept rates at 1% FAR to summarize the verification performance of individual facial components across different time lapses on the PCSO data. These results show that as the time lapse increases, the accuracy of each component decreases. The nose is the most stable component across all time lapses, which is consistent with our intuition about face aging. The influence of aging on the other components is not uniform across different time lapses. On the 0-1 year age gap set, the eyes are the second worst performing component, with a TAR less than 1% higher than the mouth's, but on the 1-5 and 5-10 year lapse data sets the eyes gain in performance relative to the other components.

4.2   Per Demographic Performance Analysis

Tables 2, 3, and 4 contain face verification results on subsets of the PCSO data sets containing only specific demographic groups. Both our method and FaceVACS generally have higher accuracy on males than females, and higher accuracy on whites and Hispanics than blacks. These results are consistent with the results reported in [24], and with most algorithms evaluated in [25]. There are a couple of exceptions to these trends, on the 0-1 year age gap FaceVACS is slightly more accurate on black females than black males, while on the 5-10 year age gap our method has higher accuracy for black females than white females. For most groups our accuracy is fairly close to FaceVACS, but the component based method performs significantly worse on white females across all time gaps. Figure 5 demonstrates the loss in verification accuracy of the component based method for each demographic group as the time lapse increases. All demographic groups lose accuracy as the age gap increases; however, males lose less accuracy than females.

Observing the performance of individual components across demographics, we see some variations along gender lines. On the 0-1 year gap set, the eyes outperform the mouth component for females, while for males the eyes are either on

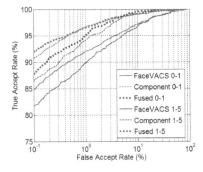

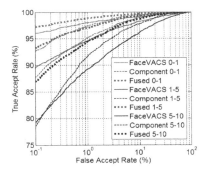

Fig. 6. MORPH results on 0-1 and 1-5 year age gap data sets

Fig. 7. PCSO results on 0-1, 1-5, and 5-10 year age gap data sets

par or better than the mouth. On the 1-5 year gap set there are again differences in the relative accuracy of components across gender lines; for females, the eyes are more accurate than the eyebrows, for males the opposite. On the 5-10 year gap set, for black and Hispanic males the eyebrows still perform better than the eyes, while for white males the eyes perform just 1% better than the eyebrows. In contrast, for females the eyes are 8-10% more accurate than the eyebrows. Across all time lapses studied, the eyes perform better for females relative to the mouth and eyebrows than they do for males.

4.3 Overall Performance

We evaluated FaceVACS and our component based system on the MORPH and PCSO data sets, and also performed a simple sum of scores fusion (with min-max normalization) on our method and FaceVACS. The ROC curves of both face recognition systems, and their fusion are shown in Figures 6 and 7.

Our component based system performs significantly better than FaceVACS on both MORPH subsets (0-1 and 1-5 year age gaps); in fact the component based system shows better performance on the 1-5 year age gap set than FaceVACS does on the 0-1 year set. On the 0-1 year age gap set the fusion of our method and FaceVACS showed minor improvement over the component based method alone on lower FAR operating points, while on the 1-5 year age gap set the fused system was consistently better than the component based method.

Table 2. Per demographic TAR (%) at 1% FAR, PCSO 0-1 year age gap set

PCSO 0-1 year	Eyes	Nose	Mouth	Eyebrows	Fused Components	FaceVACS
White-Male	74.30	89.20	74.80	82.10	96.60	98.60
White-Female	71.10	85.40	61.10	73.70	93.80	97.60
Black-Male	67.80	85.30	66.30	78.80	93.70	95.20
Black-Female	67.40	85.70	59.70	74.30	93.10	95.90
Hispanic-Male	79.60	94.80	85.90	87.30	97.60	98.70

Table 3. Per demographic TAR (%) at 1% FAR, PCSO 1-5 year age gap set

PCSO 1-5 year	Eyes	Nose	Mouth	Eyebrows	Fused Components	FaceVACS
White-Male	73.10	87.80	61.70	75.90	94.90	96.40
White-Female	64.50	79.40	53.10	57.40	89.00	93.20
Black-Male	66.00	81.20	52.90	69.50	89.70	90.30
Black-Female	62.60	80.30	55.40	56.80	86.70	87.30
Hispanic-Male	73.10	90.70	69.10	77.80	95.90	97.00

Table 4. Per demographic TAR (%) at 1% FAR, PCSO 5-10 year age gap set

PCSO 5-10 year	Eyes	Nose	Mouth	Eyebrows	Fused Components	FaceVACS
White-Male	61.20	77.20	46.80	60.00	90.50	91.90
White-Female	52.50	64.50	36.30	41.70	79.30	85.10
Black-Male	57.00	75.30	44.00	60.90	86.90	85.10
Black-Female	51.80	72.60	44.00	43.70	82.00	80.60
Hispanic-Male	62.01	86.02	56.63	63.44	93.55	92.83

Figure 8 shows some example false-reject pairs from the MORPH 0-1 year set. The left 3 pairs were falsely rejected by FaceVACS, but correctly classified by the component method. The right 2 pairs were incorrectly rejected by the component method, but accepted by FaceVACS at the 1% FAR operating point. The FaceVACS errors show its sensitivity to pose and hair variations, while the errors of component based method show its sensitivity to changes in expression (this may be the case since most facial regions we focus on are easily affected by expression changes).

The results on the PCSO subsets are mixed. FaceVACS outperforms the component based system on the 0-1 year age gap set; however, as the age gap increases the component based system performs relatively better. The component based system outperforms FaceVACS at the 1% FAR operating point on both the 1-5 and 5-10 year age gap sets, although FaceVACS has greater accuracy at lower FAR operating points. The fusion of FaceVACS and our method improved the performance on all age gap sets, with notable improvement on the larger age gaps. These results indicate that the component based method can provide complementary information to FaceVACS.

The performance of our system on complete data sets is better than its performance on most per demographic subsets because the complete data sets include cross-group matches, which are easier to reject than impostor within group matches on average. For example, on the 0-1 year age gap PCSO data set our system had 97.38% TAR at 1% FAR (better than all individual demographic groups except Hispanic males). On this data set, the mean within group impostor match score was 0.2416, while the mean cross group impostor score was 0.1273 on a score range of [0, 1].

Both our method and FaceVACS perform better on PCSO than MORPH. We attribute this to the generally lower image quality in the MORPH Album2 data set. The PCSO images have higher resolution (486×624) than MORPH (400

(a)   (b)

Fig. 8. Example false reject matches from MORPH 0-1 year age gap. (a) Pairs falsely rejected by FaceVACS but accepted by the component method at 1% FAR. (b) Pairs falsely rejected by the component method but accepted by FaceVACS at 1% FAR

$\times$ 480 or 200 $\times$ 240). Additionally, as shown in Figure 2 some MORPH images are slightly blurred, while in others the face is washed out by strong lighting. Our method's significantly better performance on MORPH than FaceVACS can be attributed to a model trained specifically on that data set compensating for the lower quality images.

5   Conclusions and Future Work

We have investigated the influence of aging on different facial components and demographic categories using a component based face representation and matching algorithm. Our experiments on the MORPH and PCSO databases show that the nose is the most stable component across face aging, and that aging has more influence on females than males. Comparisons with a leading commercial matcher (FaceVACS) show that the proposed approach is more robust to face recognition across large time lapses, while still achieving at least comparable performance to FaceVACS even across less than 1 year time lapses. Experiments also show that a score level fusion between our method and FaceVACS can improve the overall accuracy. Our future work will address how to improve face recognition accuracy by automatically estimating demographic information from face images.

References

1. Li, S.Z., Jain, A.K. (eds.): Handbook of Face Recognition, 2nd edn. Springer (2011)
2. Blanz, V., Vetter, T.: Face recognition based on fitting a 3d morphable model. IEEE Trans. PAMI 25, 1063–1074 (2003)
3. Tan, X., Triggs, B.: Enhanced local texture feature sets for face recognition under difficult lighting conditions. IEEE Trans. IP 19, 1635–1650 (2010)
4. Han, H., Shan, S., Qing, L., Chen, X., Gao, W.: Lighting Aware Preprocessing for Face Recognition across Varying Illumination. In: Daniilidis, K., Maragos, P., Paragios, N. (eds.) ECCV 2010, Part II. LNCS, vol. 6312, pp. 308–321. Springer, Heidelberg (2010)

5. Zhang, X., Gao, Y.: Face recognition across pose: A review. Pattern Recognition 42, 2876–2896 (2009)
6. Ramanathan, N., Chellappa, R., Biswas, S.: Computational methods for modeling facial aging: A survey. Journal of Visual Languages and Computing 20, 131–144 (2009)
7. Geng, X., Zhou, Z., Smith-Miles, K.: Automatic age estimation based on facial aging patterns. IEEE Trans. PAMI 29, 2234–2240 (2007)
8. Park, U., Tong, Y., Jain, A.K.: Age-invariant face recognition. IEEE Trans. PAMI 32, 947–954 (2010)
9. Suo, J., Zhu, S.C., Shan, S., Chen, X.: A compositional and dynamic model for face aging. IEEE Trans. PAMI 32, 385–401 (2010)
10. Ramanathan, N., Chellappa, R.: Face verification across age progression. IEEE Trans. IP 15, 3349–3361 (2006)
11. Mahalingam, G., Kambhamettu, C.: Age invariant face recognition using graph matching. In: Proc. BTAS, pp. 1–7 (2010)
12. Ling, H., Soatto, S., Ramanathan, N., Jacobs, D.: Face verification across age progression using discriminative methods. IEEE Trans. IFS 5, 82–91 (2010)
13. Li, Z., Park, U., Jain, A.K.: A discriminative model for age invariant face recognition. IEEE Trans. IFS 6, 1028–1037 (2011)
14. AgingSkinNet: Causes of aging skin (2010), http://www.skincarephysicians.com/agingskin-net/basicfacts.html
15. Face and Gesture Recognition Research Network: FG-NET AGING DATABASE (2010), http://www.fgnet.rsunit.com
16. Klare, B., Jain, A.K.: Face recognition across time lapse: On learning feature subspaces. In: Proc. IJCB, pp. 1–8 (2011)
17. Ricanek, K.J., Tesafaye, T.: Morph: A longitudinal image database of normal adult age-progression. In: Proc. AFGR, pp. 341–345 (2006)
18. Wang, X., Tang, X.: Random sampling lda for face recognition. In: IEEE CVPR, vol. 2, pp. 259–265 (2004)
19. Klare, B., Paulino, A.A., Jain, A.K.: Analysis of facial features in identical twins. In: Proc. IJCB, pp. 1–8 (2011)
20. Milborrow, S., Nicolls, F.: Locating Facial Features with an Extended Active Shape Model. In: Forsyth, D., Torr, P., Zisserman, A. (eds.) ECCV 2008, Part IV. LNCS, vol. 5305, pp. 504–513. Springer, Heidelberg (2008), http://www.milbo.users.sonic.net/stasm
21. Cootes, T., Taylor, C., Cooper, D., Graham, J.: Active shape models-their training and application. CVIU 61, 38–59 (1995)
22. Ojala, T., Pietikainen, M., Maenpaa, T.: Multiresolution gray-scale and rotation invariant texture classification with local binary patterns. IEEE Trans. PAMI 24, 971–987 (2002)
23. Lowe, D.G.: Object recognition from local scale-invariant features. In: Proceedings of the Seventh IEEE International Conference on Computer Vision, 1999, vol. 2, pp. 1150–1157 (1999)
24. Klare, B., Burge, M., Klontz, J., Bruegge, R.W.V., Jain, A.K.: Face recognition performance: Role of demographic information (2012), http://www.mitre.org/work/tech_papers/2012/11_4962/
25. Grother, P.J., Quinn, G.W., Phillips, P.J.: MBE 2010: Report on the evaluation of 2D still-image face recognition algorithms. NIST Report (2010)

Spatio-Temporal Multifeature for Facial Analysis

Zahid Riaz and Michael Beetz

Intelligent Autonomous Systems (IAS), Technical University of Munich,
Karlstr. 45, D-80333 Munich, Germany
{riaz,beetz}@in.tum.de

Abstract. Human faces are 3D complex objects consisting of geometrical and appearance variations. They exhibit local and global variations when observed over time. In our daily life communication, human faces are seen in actions conveying a set of information during interaction. Cognitive science explains that human brains are capable of extracting this set of information very efficiently resulting in a better interaction with others. Our goal is to extract a single feature set which represents multiple facial characteristics. This problem is addressed by the analysis of different feature components on facial classifications using a 3D surface model. We propose a unified framework which is capable to extract multiple information from the human faces and at the same time robust against rigid and non-rigid facial deformations. A single feature vector corresponding to a given image is representative of person's identity, facial expressions, gender and age estimation. This feature set is called spatio-temporal multifeature (STMF) extracted from image sequences. An STMF is configured with three different feature components which is tested thoroughly to evidence its validity. The experimental results from four different databases show that this feature set provides high accuracy and at the same time exhibits robustness. The results have been discussed comparatively with different approaches.

1 Introduction

In our daily life human faces are generally observed in action and convey a large set of information at a glance. On the other hand human brains have the ability to process this information very quickly and extract a distinct set of feature to classify various facial attributes. We build our concept on the fact from cognitive science study that facial features are processed holistically [1]. For example, instead of calculating local descriptor from facial geometry, color and corners, human brains process this information rather holistically. In general, we come across different people especially in social gatherings, meetings, markets and public places. With a first glance at their faces, we acquire a set of information about them even without interaction. This information contains gender, facial behavior, age estimation, ethnic origin and identity of the person if known before. This can be seen in Figure 1. Our goal is to find a single feature set which is representative of these facial attributes. We provide a feature set which

A. Fusiello et al. (Eds.): ECCV 2012 Ws/Demos, Part II, LNCS 7584, pp. 199–209, 2012.

generates high accuracy and at the same time is robust against currently out-
standing challenges like varying head poses and facial expressions. This feature
set is extracted using a 3D face model and mainly consists of spatio-temporal
components of the faces. A 3D model is computed from a single image of a human
face. We term the extracted feature set spatio-temporal multifeature (STMF)
because it is composed of multiple facial parameters which include geometrical, appearance and deformation components. This benefits in controlling the
spatial variation in the form of structure and texture whereas, motion pattern
in the form of temporal features which jointly provides sufficient strength over
different facial dynamics. The major contributions of this paper are; (i) to provide a unified feature set which is representative of facial expressions, gender,
facial age and identity of a person, (ii) to show that the extracted feature set
is robust against varying facial poses and expressions for face recognition applications, (iii) to comparatively study 2D and 3D face models showing that a 3D
model outperforms 2D model, (iv) and finally 3D models are capable to remove
perspective distortions in texturing a face which provide improved results. The
results have been extracted on four different benchmark datasets in comparison
to different state-of-the-art approaches.

The remaining part of this paper is divided in four sections. Section 2 discusses
some of the related work in face image analysis. Section 3 explains problem
statement in detail and configuration of our feature set. Section 4 describes
detailed feature extraction approach. Finally, section 5 evaluates the calculated
features on three different databases with various experimentations.

- Identity
- Facial Expressions
- Gender
- Age Estimation
- Ethnic Origin

Fig. 1. With a glance at a face, humans are capable to classify different facial attributes.
Our goal is to find a single feature set which is representative of these facial attributes.

2   Related Work

One of the major applications of human face image analysis is person identification. Over the efforts of a couple of decades, researchers are able to develop
commercial systems for face recognition. Many industries are providing solution
for facial biometrics [2]. Another important representation of the faces is the
behavior of the persons, which is interpreted in the form of facial expressions.
Other facial traits which do not directly represent person identity are categorized
as soft-biometrics [3]. These include facial expressions, gender, age estimation
and ethnicity. In the literature of face modeling, some useful face models are
point distribution models (PDM), 3D morphable models, photorealistic models,
deformable models and wireframe models [4]. Our proposed features consist of

model parameters which fulfill a model's key requirements of dealing with non-rigidness, deformation and capability to synthesize novel views. 3D morphable models [5], which are available with different variants [6][7] are useful in synthesizing novel views however are not efficient and require a manual intervention in preprocessing step. These models are dense and finer than 2D active appearance models (AAM) [8] and suitable for facial synthesis and animation. We use rather a coarser model called Candide-III [9] which is defined with 184 triangular surfaces. This model is supported by action units and MPEG-4 animation units [10] which makes it useful for facial expressions analysis. Candide-III is a shape model but can be rendered with texture.

We emphasize on 3D modeling for the faces because of several benefits. One of the major advantages of model parameters is the better control over facial dynamics, structure and appearance. Model parameters have been varied by Vetter et al [5] to control expressions and gender. Our system solve similar problem but using very coarser model with normal camera images and achieve high accuracy, robustness as well as fully automatic [11]. Multifeature fusion approach has also been used by Riaz et. al. [12] however robustness of the system against facial poses and expressions is not studied. In [13] authors have tested several techniques toward model fitting and their performance for facial expressions on Cohn-Kanade database. We compare our results with their [13] results but using different model fitting methodology. Hadid et al [14] discuss manifold learning for gender classification and results are obtained on different databases. However, with model based approach better accuracy is reported since model parameters contain more detail. In this paper, we extend the approach presented in [15] and apply a similar system for person identification, facial expressions, gender and estimation about aging. In addition to that we study effect of perspective distortion on human faces as compared to conventional AAM.

3   Spatio-Temporal Multifeature (STMF)

In this section, we configure a feature set which is representative of multiple facial attributes. Currently available systems for facial classification lack the property of multifeature representation of the faces. A major reason is that the most of the research work suggests to isolate the sources of variations while focusing on a particular application. For example, in face recognition application, it is a general practice to normalize the faces in order to remove facial expressions variations to stabilize face recognition results against unwanted facial expressions. Hence the extracted features do not contain facial deformation. We address an idea to develop a unified feature set which contain information regarding face recognition, facial expressions, facial aging and gender classification.

For face recognition textural information plays a key role in features extraction [16][10] whereas facial expressions are mostly person independent and require motion and structural components [17]. Similarly facial structure and texture vary significantly between gender and age classes. On the basis of this knowledge and literature survey we categorize three major feature components

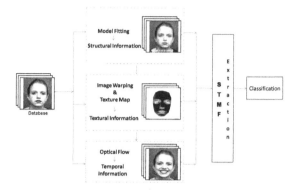

Fig. 2. Our Approach: Sequential flow toward feature extraction

Table 1. Contribution of different components to an STMF, p = primary contribution, s = secondary contribution, na = not applicable. This configuration is provided by a thorough literature survey. The experimental evidence of this configuration is provided in section 5.

	Identity	Expressions	Gender	Ethnicity	Age
Structural	p	p	p	p	p
Textural	p	s	p	p	p
Temporal	s	p	s	s	na

as primary and secondary contributor to five different facial classifications. Table 1 summarizes the significance of these constituents of the feature vector with their primary and secondary contribution toward the feature set formation. Since our feature set consists of all three kinds of information hence it can successfully represent facial identity, expressions, age, ethnicity and gender. The results are discussed in detail in section 5. Since in real world faces are seen from different views under varying poses and deformations therefore we use 3D modeling of the faces. However, any other approach can also be applied here with similar feature configuration. The approach presented in this paper is shown in Figure 2.

4   Features Extraction

In this section we explain our approach in different modules including shape model fitting, texture extraction and generating undistorted texture map and finally temporal parameters to finalize an STMF. The system initializes with a localization of a face in an image. We apply the algorithm by Viola and Jones [18] to detect and locate the face position within the image.

4.1   Structural Features

Structural features are obtained after fitting the model to the face image. For model fitting, local objective functions are calculated using haar-like features.

Face detector localizes the face region within a window. We use a state-of-the-art approach for model fitting using best objective functions. This approach is less prone to errors because of better quality of annotated images which are provided to the system for training. Further, this approach is less laborious because the objective function design is replaced with automated learning. For details we refer to [19][11]. The geometry of the model is controlled by a set of action units and animation units. Any shape s can be written as a sum of mean shape $\bar{s}$ and a set of action units and shape units.

$$s(\alpha, \sigma) = \bar{s} + \phi_a \alpha + \phi_s \sigma \tag{1}$$

Where ϕ_a is the matrix of action unit vectors and ϕ_s is the matrix of shape vectors. Whereas α denotes action units parameters and σ denotes shape parameters [10]. Model deformation governs under facial action coding systems (FACS) principles [20]. The scaling, rotation and translation of the model is described by

$$s(\alpha, \sigma, \pi) = mRs(\alpha, \sigma) + t \tag{2}$$

Where $\mathbf{R}$ and $\mathbf{t}$ are rotation and translation matrices respectively, m is the scaling factor and π contains six pose parameters plus a scaling factor. By changing the model parameters, it is possible to generate some global rotations and translations.

Fig. 3. Model fitting to two example images and texture projection on 3D surface after perspective correction. Images are taken from CMU-PIE database [21].

4.2 Textural Features

We take benefit of the 3D model to get texture projected to 3D surface and store undistorted texture in the form of texture map. The robustness of textural parameters depends upon the quality of the input texture image. Generally the effects of perspective distortions in the face images are ignored because the distance between the camera and the face is larger than the face size. We consider this effect because affine warping of the rendered triangle is not invariant to 3D rigid transformations. Since most of the triangles on the rotated faces and the face edges are tilted, therefore texture is heavily distorted in these triangles. In order to solve this problem we first apply perspective transformation followed by affine transformation to store texture in texture maps. The final transformation M is given by:

$$M = AK \left[R - Rt \right] \tag{3}$$

Where K, R and t denotes the camera matrix, rotation matrix and translation vector respectively. Whereas A is affine transformation of extracted texture to texture map. For further details, refer [22].

Figure 4 shows the texture map for a single image along with a synthesized face with smiling action using this texture. The extracted texture coefficients are parametrized using PCA with mean vector g_m and matrix of eigenvectors P_g to obtain the parameter vector b_g [15].

$$g = g_m + P_g b_g \tag{4}$$

Where g is the texture vector.

Fig. 4. Synthesized novel view from Figure 3 and its texture map

4.3   Temporal Features

Further, temporal features of the facial deformation are also calculated which consider motion over time. Local motion of feature points is observed using Lucas-Kanade pyramidal optical flow [23] on the model points. Figure 5 shows the motion patterns from image sequences in our database. We again use PCA over the velocity vectors obtained from the motion of feature points. If t is the velocity vector,

$$t = t_m + P_t b_t \tag{5}$$

Where temporal parameters b_t are computed using matrix of eigenvectors P_t and mean velocity vectors t_m.

We combine all extracted features into a single feature vector. Single image information is considered by the structural and textural features whereas image sequence information is considered by the additional temporal features. The overall feature vector becomes:

$$u = (b_{s1}, ..., b_{sm}, b_{g1}, ..., b_{gn}, b_{t1}, ..., b_{tp}) \tag{6}$$

Where b_s, b_g and b_t are shape, textural and temporal parameters respectively with m, n and p being the number of parameters retained from subspace in each

Fig. 5. Motion patterns from an image sequences. Initial image (left), landmark points using model fitting (middle), motion of the landmark points (right).

Table 2. Comparison of traditional AAM approach and rectified texture. The results are shown for textural parameters and combined structural and textural parameters. Face recognition on PIE dataset (above row), age estimation on FG-NET dataset (below row).

Database	2D Texture parameters	Rectified Textural Parameters	AAM	3D Structural + Textural Parameters
PIE	63.02%	**69.64%**	79.93%	**84.15%**
FG-NET	51.35%	**54.09%**	51.15%	**55.39%**

case. Equation 6 is called an *STMF vector*. We extract 85 structural features, approximately 200 textural features and 12 temporal features to form a combined feature vector for each image. All the subjects in the database are labeled for classification. All three individual components are normalized to one before fusion.

5   Experimentation

In order to validate the extracted features, we have used different subjects from four different databases called, CMU-PIE database [21], MMI database [24], Cohn-Kanade facial expressions database (CKFED) [25] and FG-NET database [26]. The texture extracted in each case is stored as a texture map after removing perspective distortion. During all experiments, we use two-third of the feature set for building the classifier model with 10-fold cross validation to avoid over fitting. The remaining feature set is used for testing purpose. We use all subjects from MMI, CKFED and FG-NET databases and partially use PIE database. We extract temporal features only from image sequences. For example, in case of FG-NET database no temporal information is available and hence we use only structural and textural components of the feature vector.

Since STMF set arises from different sources, so decision tree (DT) is applied for classification. However, other classifiers can also be applied here depending upon the application (Support Vector Machine (SVM) and Bayesian Networks (BN) were also used with comparable results during experimentation). We choose J48 decision tree algorithm for experimentation which uses tree pruning called subtree raising and recursively classifies until the last leave is pure. We use same

Table 3. Facial expressions recognition using different combinations of the feature sets. It can be seen that the optimal performance is obtained using all three components. These results conform to concept of feature configuration given in Table 1 (Left) Confusion matrix from our results (Right).

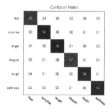

Feature type	% Recog
Shape + temporal	92.2%
Shape + Texture	83.3%
Shape + Texture + Temporal	96.4%

configuration for all classifiers trained during the experiments. The parameters used in decision tree are: confidence factor C = 0.25, with two minimum number of instances per leaf and C4.5 approach for reduced error-pruning [27].

5.1   Face Recognition

Face recognition experiments are performed on the aforementioned databases which contain images with six different facial expressions, frontal and profile faces and normal talking faces. We use all subjects from MMI and CKFED and 34 subjects with approximately 5000 images from two different sessions of the PIE database. The results of face recognition in the presence of varying poses are performed on PIE dataset and are shown in Table 2 in comparison to AAM. These results show that the removal of perspective distortions improves the classification rate. The classification rates for CKFED and MMI have been 99.59% and 99.29% respectively.

Table 4. Comparison of gender classification in comparison to different approaches [14]

Approach	Classification rate
Pixels + SVM + Fusion	88.5%
LBP + SVM + Fusion	92.1%
VLBP + SVM	84.5%
EVLBP + AdaBoost	84.6%
STMF + DT	**94.8%**

5.2   Facial Expressions Recognition

Facial expressions recognition is performed on CKFED with six universal facial expressions: anger, disgust, fear, laugh, sadness and surprise. We exclude neutral expression during the experiments, however a neutral expression can also be considered as a seventh expression during classification. An STMF feature set with three constituents (structural, textural and temporal) are used for experiments. The results are shown in Table 3 with different feature components along with the confusion matrix from our experiments. It can be seen that the results on left column of Table 3 coincide with our initial concept presented in Table 1 which shows the validity of our feature configuration.

5.3   Gender and Age Classification

We use same set of STMF for gender classification on CKFED. The results are shown in Table 4 in comparison to other approaches. (The results in Table 4 are not reproduced and use 10-fold cross validation as that of 5-fold cross validation described in [14]). The classification results may vary with choice of different classifier. For instance, we obtained 96.8% accuracy using random forests classifier instead of decision trees. This classification rate is comparable to the best reported result in [14] which is 97.2%. In order to verify our feature configuration concept, we further study age classification from all subjects of FG-NET database. This database consists of 1002 images of 62 subjects with age ranging from 0 − 69 years. We divide the database in seven groups with 10 years band. The results are shown in Table 2 in comparison to AAM and with and without structural components.

6   Conclusions and Future Work

In this paper we have experimented 3D model based STMF extraction approach. Our aim is to find the feature configuration which directly reflects human perception about the faces. Different researchers have used model based approaches and found different solutions to biometric and soft-biometric traits using various features. However, concrete research under such scenarios is still required. Moveover model fitting and efficiency of the algorithm are challenges. So far we have studied four different traits of human faces called person identity, gender, facial expressions and aging however it can further be applied to ethnicity classification. Our future goal is to consider these traits on a large variability by further enhancing our feature set for interactive systems.

Acknowledgments. This research work is funded by German Academic Exchange Service (DAAD) under the project ID-54378355 on *Context Aware Perception for Assistive Intelligent Robots*, between German and Pakistani universities (2011-2013).

References

1. Sinha, P., Balas, B., Ostrovsky, Y., Russell, R.: Face recognition by humans: Nineteen results all computer vision researchers should know about. Proceedings of IEEE 94, 1948–1962 (2006)
2. Zhao, W., Chellappa, R., Phillips, P.J., Rosenfeld, A.: Face recognition: A literature survey (December 2003)

3. Jain, A.K., Dass, S.C., Nandakumar, K.: Soft Biometric Traits for Personal Recognition Systems. In: Zhang, D., Jain, A.K. (eds.) ICBA 2004. LNCS, vol. 3072, pp. 731–738. Springer, Heidelberg (2004)

4. Abate, A., Nappi, M., Riccio, D., Sabatino, G.: 2d and 3d face recognition: A survey. Pattern Recognition Letters 28, 1885–1906 (2007)

5. Blanz, V., Vetter, T.: Face recognition based on fitting a 3D morphable model. IEEE Transactions on Pattern Analysis and Machine Intelligence 25(9), 1063–1074 (2003)

6. Huang, J., Heisele, B., Blanz, V.: Component-based Face Recognition with 3D Morphable Models. In: Kittler, J., Nixon, M.S. (eds.) AVBPA 2003. LNCS, vol. 2688, pp. 27–34. Springer, Heidelberg (2003)

7. Romdhani, S.: Face Image Analysis using a Multiple Feature Fitting Strategy. PhD thesis, Computer Science Department, University of Basel, Basel Switzerland (2005)

8. Cootes, T.F., Edwards, G.J., Taylor, C.J.: Active Appearance Models. In: Burkhardt, H., Neumann, B. (eds.) ECCV 1998. LNCS, vol. 1407, pp. 484–498. Springer, Heidelberg (1998)

9. Ahlberg, J.: An experiment on 3D face model adaptation using the active appearance algorithm. Image Coding Group, Deptt of Electric Engineering, Linköping University (2001)

10. Ahlberg, J., Dornaika, F.: Parametric Face Modeling and Tracking. In: Li, S.Z., Jain, A.K. (eds.) Handbook of Face Recognition. Springer (2005)

11. Mayer, C., Wimmer, M., Stulp, F., Riaz, Z., Roth, A., Eggers, M., Radig, B.: A real time system for model-based interpretation of the dynamics of facial expressions. In: Proc. of the International Conference on Automatic Face and Gesture Recognition (FGR 2008), Amsterdam, Netherlands (September 2008)

12. Riaz, Z., Mayer, C., Beetz, M., Radig, B.: Model Based Analysis of Face Images for Facial Feature Extraction. In: Jiang, X., Petkov, N. (eds.) CAIP 2009. LNCS, vol. 5702, pp. 99–106. Springer, Heidelberg (2009)

13. Asthana, A., Saragih, J., Wagner, M., Goecke, R.: Evaluating aam fitting methods for facial expression recognition. In: Affetive Computing and Intelligent Interaction, vol. 1, pp. 598–605 (September 2009)

14. Hadid, A., Pietikäinen, M.: Manifold Learning for Gender Classification from Face Sequences. In: Tistarelli, M., Nixon, M.S. (eds.) ICB 2009. LNCS, vol. 5558, pp. 82–91. Springer, Heidelberg (2009)

15. Riaz, Z., Gedikli, S., Beetz, M.: Spatio-temporal facial features for hri scenarios. In: CRV. IEEE (2011)

16. Zhao, W., Chellappa, R.: Face Processing: Advanced Modeling and Methods. Elsevier Inc. (2005)

17. Fasel, B., Luettin, J.: Automatic facial expression analysis: A survey. Pattern Recognition 36(1), 259–275 (2003)

18. Viola, P., Jones, M.J.: Robust real-time face detection. International Journal of Computer Vision 57, 137–154 (2004)

19. Wimmer, M., Stulp, F., Tschechne, S., Radig, B.: Learning robust objective functions for model fitting in image understanding applications. In: Proceedings of the 17th British Machine Vision Conference, pp. 1159–1168 (2006)

20. Ekman, P., Friesen, W.: The facial action coding system: A technique for the measurement of facial movement. Consulting Psychologists Press (1978)

21. Terence, S., Baker, S., Bsat, M.: The cmu pose, illumination, and expression (pie) database. In: FGR 2002: Proceedings of the Fifth IEEE International Conference on Automatic Face and Gesture Recognition, p. 53. IEEE Computer Society Press, Washington, DC (2002)
22. Riaz, Z., Beetz, M.: On the effect of perspective distortion on face recognition. In: 12th International Conference on Vision Applications (VISAPP) (February 2012)
23. Bouguet, J.-Y.: Pyramidal implementation of the lucas kanade feature tracker (2000)
24. Pantic, M., Valstar, M., Rademaker, R., Maat, L.: Web-based database for facial expression analysis (July 2005)
25. Kanade, T., Cohn, J., Tian, Y.: Comprehensive database for facial expression analysis. In: Proceedings of Fourth IEEE International Conference on Automatic Face and Gesture Recognition, pp. 46–53 (2000)
26. `http://www.fgnet.rsunit.com/`
27. Witten, I.H., Frank, E.: Data Mining: Practical machine learning tools and techniques. Morgan Kaufmann, San Francisco (2005)

The Role of Facial Regions
in Evaluating Social Dimensions

David Masip Rodo[1], Alexander Todorov[2], and Jordi Vitrià Marca[3]

[1] Universitat Oberta de Catalunya
[2] Princeton University
[3] Universitat de Barcelona
dmasipr@uoc.edu, atodorov@princeton.edu, jordi.vitria@ub.edu

Abstract. Facial trait judgments are an important information cue for people. Recent works in the Psychology field have stated the basis of face evaluation, defining a set of traits that we evaluate from faces (e.g. dominance, trustworthiness, aggressiveness, attractiveness, threatening or intelligence among others). We rapidly infer information from others faces, usually after a short period of time ($< 1000ms$) we perceive a certain degree of dominance or trustworthiness of another person from the face. Although these perceptions are not necessarily accurate, they influence many important social outcomes (such as the results of the elections or the court decisions). This topic has also attracted the attention of Computer Vision scientists, and recently a computational model to automatically predict trait evaluations from faces has been proposed. These systems try to mimic the human perception by means of applying machine learning classifiers to a set of labeled data. In this paper we perform an experimental study on the specific facial features that trigger the social inferences. Using previous results from the literature, we propose to use simple similarity maps to evaluate which regions of the face influence the most the trait inferences. The correlation analysis is performed using only appearance, and the results from the experiments suggest that each trait is correlated with specific facial characteristics.

1 Introduction

Humans continuously infer social judgments from the people surrounding us. One of the most important sources of social information is the face, specially in the first impression, and these impressions have been shown to be pervasive in many situations in our daily life [1, 2]. In spite of its questionability [3], facial trait judgments influence important social outcomes, such as the success in elections [4, 5] or court room decisions [6]. Surprisingly, this social evaluations are performed rapidly [7], and do not involve a deep thought. During the last decade, facial trait judgments have been an important research topic in Social Psychology. Currently, there exist psychological models of facial trait evaluation [8, 9] and these social evaluations have been successfully related to the amygdala, a specific brain region located deep in the medial temporal lobes [10, 11].

A. Fusiello et al. (Eds.): ECCV 2012 Ws/Demos, Part II, LNCS 7584, pp. 210–219, 2012.

This field of research has also attracted scientists from computer science, and computational models to automatically predict facial trait judgments have been developed. Facial inferences can be computationally modeled from the image stimuli, and computer vision techniques have been applied to the problem of facial trait judgments prediction. Specifically, two different descriptors have been developed: a structural modeling of the facial geometry using a set of predefined landmarks [12] and an appearance descriptor of the holistic internal region of the face [13]. The comparative studies favor the appearance over the structure, and some trait judgments can be predicted with high accuracy (80 − 90%).

In this paper we provide more insights about the specific zones of the face that influence the facial trait judgments. We present a study that aims to answer the questions: Which parts of the face play a more active role in the face evaluation? What a makes a person look more dominant, aggressive or trustworthy? Using a labeled dataset, we propose the use of simple statistical measures to build correlation maps among pixels and behavioral data. Some traits are strongly correlated with specific regions of the face, and facial trait judgments have also important dependencies on the gender.

The paper is organized as follows: section two describes the basic psychological modeling of facial evaluation, the main trait judgments are enumerated and a brief review of the main previous works is performed. Section three presents the methodology used in this study. Section four shows the experimental results, and section five discusses relevant insights from these results. Finally section six concludes this paper.

2   Basis of Face Evaluation

We constantly evaluate faces in multiple trait dimensions. In [8], Oosterhof and Todorov defined a 2D model of the facial trait judgments we perform in our daily life. The data collected in this seminal work constitutes the base corpus of our study. In this section, we will briefly review the basic notions underlying the trait judgments and the labeled facial dataset used in this paper.

In a first step (see supporting information in [8] for more details), 55 participants in the experiment were asked to write unconstrained descriptions from a set of faces. Participants were instructed to write "everything that came to their mind about the person shown in the screen". This textual information (1134 descriptions) was analyzed and classified by two researchers in fourteen trait categories (accounting for 68% of the textual statements). These 14 trait categories were: Attractive, caring, aggressive, mean, intelligent, confident, emotionally-stable, trustworthy, responsible, sociable, weird, unhappy, dominant and threatening.

In this paper, we will use the same list of trait categories. In [13], some of these traits were computationally learnt using both a structural and appearance descriptors. Besides the trait judgments learnability, authors also suggested that some regions of the face are more significant for facial trait classification. A set of predefined landmark locations were used to correlate facial geometry and facial evaluations. In this paper we propose a computational study that aims to

Fig. 1. Examples from male and female images used in the rating experiments from the Karolinska data set

analyze which regions or parts of the facial appearance are more useful for trait inferences. This study complements the initial findings in [13], given that the holistic appearance is used instead of the simple geometry of the landmarks.

2.1 Annotated Database

In the second experiment from [8], 327 undergraduate students rated a set of 66 images from the Karolinska data set [14] (half of them from males and half from females). Students were instructed to answer relying in their first impressions, and the ratings were performed in a 1 to 9 scale (where 1 meant "not at all [trait]" and 9 meant "extreme [trait]"). Each face was exposed for about 1000 ms.

Using these ratings, the researchers submitted the data to a Principal Component Analysis (PCA). The first component accounted for 63% of the data variance, and the second for 18%. Positive judgments (intelligent, attractive, responsible,...) had positive loading in the first PC and negative judgments (aggressive, mean, threatening,...) had negative loadings in the same first PC. Authors named this first axis as **valence**. The second PC was named **dominance** given the high loadings of the dominant, aggressiveness and confidence traits on this axis. In the light of these results, they suggested that the underlying dimensionality of face evaluation is 2.

In this paper we used the same 66 face images from the Karolinska data base, and we also used the normalized ratings from the previously described paper [8][1]. Figure 1 shows some samples from the database. Images have been previously converted from RGB to gray scale by averaging the 3 color planes, and each image has been centered and aligned using and Ad hoc coded GUI[2] and a manually annotated set of landmarks.

---

[1] The evaluations of the 14 traits are available for research purposes in http://webscript.princeton.edu/~tlab/databases/ from the authors of [8] upon request.

[2] A Matlab R2010b script has been used for the registration and normalization purposes.

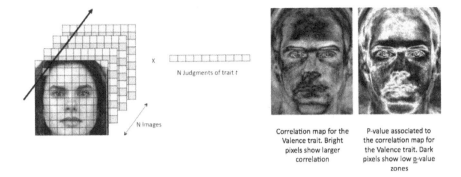

Correlation map for the Valence trait. Bright pixels show larger correlation

P-value associated to the correlation map for the Valence trait. Dark pixels show low p-value zones

Fig. 2. Scheme of the correlation computation at pixel (i,j) and the resulting maps from the valence trait. The image shows the correlation maps, where light pixels show high correlation with the trait judgment, and the p-vale map, where dark values show low p-values in the analyzed zone.

3   Facial Zones in Social Face Evaluation

The human evaluation of the facial trait judgments is not performed uniformly on the face images. Different facial zones play crucial roles in the ratings depending on the trait analyzed. In this study, we propose a methodology to evaluate the visual importance of each region of the face in the human trait judgments inferences. The problem of evaluating the saliency in images has been previously tackled in the object recognition literature [15–17]. Several approaches have been followed, usually filtering the image using: Laplacian, Gaussian, Gabor filters and steerable wavelets [18]. The appropriate scale (coarse or fine) has also been studied in object recognition and perception publications [19, 20]. Moreover, the appropriate scale has also been shown to influence face classification tasks such as face recognition [21]. In this study, a fine strategy has been followed. The trait inferences are studied in a pixel based approach correlating the image information with the behavioral data.

3.1   Similarity Maps Using Correlation

Given a data set consisting of N images represented as $\{\mathbf{X}\}_{1\ldots N}$, where the pixel (i, j) of the image a is denoted as $\{X_{ij}\}_a$; and a set of trait judgments $\mathbf{T}$, where the value T_{tk} denotes the mean value of tth trait for image k, we define the similarity operator between the image zone and the trait judgments as the correlation:

$$\rho(\mathbf{X}_{ij}, \mathbf{T}_t) = \frac{cov(\mathbf{X}_{ij}, \mathbf{T}_t)}{\sigma_{\mathbf{X}_{ij}}\sigma_{\mathbf{T}_t}} \tag{1}$$

We define the similarity map between the trait judgment t and the pixel images as a new image $\mathbf{M}$ that has at each pixel $\mathbf{M}_{ij}$ the result of $\rho(\mathbf{X}_{ij}, \mathbf{T}_t)$. i.e. the similarity in terms of correlation between the N values of the pixel at the position (i,j) and the N mean judgments of the trait analyzed. Figure 2 summarizes the algorithm.

Pseudocode of similarity maps construction

```
Given the set of face images X, and the mean trait judgments T:
begin
    for i:=1 to image height H do
        for j:=1 to image width W do
            Mij := ρ( Xij, Tt)
    endfor
endfor
end
```

Facial images usually suffer from noise artifacts related to the acquisition process or the posterior alignment step. In addition, pixel locations far from the landmarked regions are more prone to small errors. Although visually, the resulting correlation maps convey interesting information about the facial zones of interest according to the trait judgments, we used a filtered version of the face images in the experiment. Briefly, a Gaussian filter with parameter $\sigma = 5$ has been convolved with each original image, obtaining a filtered image where each pixel is the average of its environment. The resulting correlation maps are used as a similarity scores to evaluate the significance of each region of the face.

4   Experiments

The experiments use the Karolinska data set, and the ratings obtained in [8]. Figure 3 graphically shows the results for each one of the 14 facial trait judgments.

Dominance, aggressiveness, and threatening traits show positive correlation (> 0.3) specifically in the chin region (with p-vale < 0.05) and forehead (p-vale < 0.1). This result is consistent with the intuitive idea of dominance and the prototypical synthetic images of these traits developed in [8] [3].

On the other hand, attractiveness, caring, sociable and trustworthiness show positive correlation in the cheek region (> 0.3, p-vale < 0.1). These traits are correlated to the first PC (Valence axis), and the results are consistent with [13] where the upper half of the facial geometric information was found to be strongly related to these traits (specially eyes and eyebrows).

Caring, emotionally-stable, responsible and sociable show high correlations also in the eyebrow regions (with p-value < 0.1), while unhappy and weird traits do not show relevant correlations in any specific zones.

The same experiment has been repeated but using as a labels set the Valence and Dominance. To obtain these artificially generated dimensions, the same procedure as in [8] has been followed. The trait ratings have been submitted to a

---

[3] See visual animations in
http://webscript.princeton.edu/~tlab/demonstrations/ for more details.

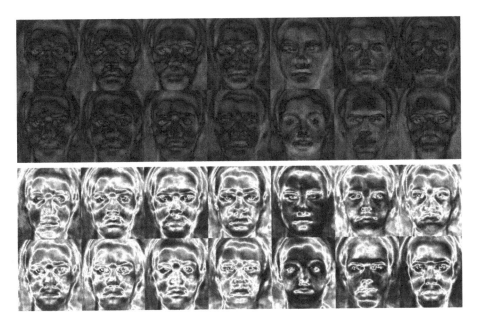

Fig. 3. Similarity maps obtained and their associated p-values. From from left to right and up to down , the traits evaluated are: attractive, trustworthy, caring, responsible, aggressive, sociable, mean, weird, intelligent, confident, unhappy, dominant, emotionally-stable, and threatening. Bright values denote high correlation (and p-value), and darker values low correlation (and p-value)

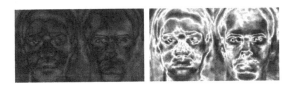

Fig. 4. Similarity maps for the dominance (2nd Principal Component) and Valence (1st Principal Component)

Principal Component Analysis, and the first two components scores (accounting for 63 and 18% of the variance respectively) have been used as ratings for the proposed 2-Dimensional model of face evaluation. Figure 4 shows the resulting similarity maps obtained from the correlation of these scores (resulting from the dimensionality reduction) and the pixel values of the images. Consistently with the previous findings, dominance shows significant correlation in the chin region (p-value < 0.1), and valence shows positive correlations in the eye-brows (p-value < 0.03) and cheek (p-value < 0.1), which is consistent with the results of the structural descriptor presented in [13].

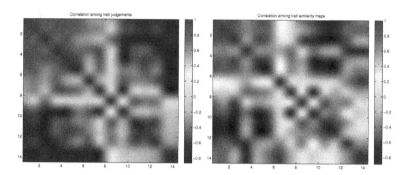

Fig. 5. Correlation among the 14 facial traits ratings representing the behavioral data and the 14 correlation maps representing the most active facial zones of each trait

4.1   Relative Correlation among Traits

In the second experiment, we explore the relationship between the different facial traits using the behavioral data and the image-based representation. It has been shown that the 14 traits selected are highly correlated, and only two orthogonal dimensions may be sufficient to model face evaluation. This redundancy in the evaluations can be analyzed by computing the correlation among the different trait judgments. We conjecture that similar correlation measures should be found using the behavioral data and the information extracted from the similarity maps.

The experimental evaluation has been performed in two phases, using different data sets at each one. The original database has been randomly split in two independent sets (D_1 and D_2), balancing the presence of male and females at each subset. In the first stage, we used the set D_1 to compute the 14×14 similarity matrix C_b, where each cell (i,j) encodes the correlation between the trait judgments i and j from the behavioral data (mean ratings).

In the second stage, we used the set D_2 to compute the 14×14 similarity matrix C_m, where each cell (i,j) encodes the correlation between the similarity maps M obtained from the traits i and j. This similarity matrix contains the relationships between the different regions of the faces that convey useful information for each trait judgment. Notice that the splitting protocol assures independence in the construction of both similarity matrices, no behavioral data from the set D_1 is used in the computation of the similarity maps (pixel space) from D_2

The figure 5 illustrates the resulting 14×14 correlation matrices from the behavioral and pixel domains at the two independent stages. For the sake of clarity, the trait judgments have been sorted in increasing weight order in the PCA decomposition of the mean ratings of the whole image set. Notice that although the similarity between judgments is not exactly the same in magnitude, they are similarly related even when the data sets have been independently extracted.

5   Discussion

The similarity maps developed show significant correlations between facial trait judgments and specific regions of facial images. Although this work is preliminary, and the availability of labeled data is scarce, some of the conclusions are consistent with previous works and also with the intuitive idea of the social appearance we infer for some of these traits.

An important remark must be performed regarding to the gender topic. Some of the correlation maps depicted in figure 3 show strong similarities with female images, and others look more similar to male images (usually related to mean, threatening and aggressive traits). Some of this relations can be found in the behavioral data collected in the facial ratings. Figure 6 shows the mean judgments of each trait using the male images (red) and the female images (blue). Notice that prior to the similarity computation there is a strong bias in the initial ground truth behavioral data. Participants in the study rated faces taking into account the gender topic.

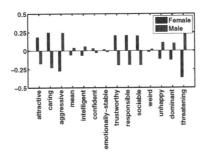

Fig. 6. Mean trait judgements (mean score of the students ratings) of each one of the 14 traits in the male (red) and female (blue) samples

6   Conclusions and Future Work

In this paper, an experimental evaluation of social values inferred from face images is performed. Taking previous works from Psychology as a starting point, and using previous published results on a specific dataset, we used simple similarity measures to evaluate which facial zones convey more information regarding to the facial traits judgments inferred. We propose the use of correlation maps to perform this experimental evaluation. The main contribution of the paper is therefore methodological. Nevertheless, the results of these trait evaluations could be used in multiple applications. The appropriate evaluation of the specific features that make look a face less trustworthy, or more aggressive, could be used in domains where static images should be corrected to improve the inferred first impression. Typical examples could be the pictures in magazines publicity, or improving candidates image in election campaigns.

The paper performs a first exploratory study on the topic. The availability of labeled data determines the statistical significance of the results. Larger image sets (> 500 images) and larger trait evaluations (using > 1000 graduate students for rating) would increase the significance. Nevertheless, we conjecture that the best improvement in the facial zones evaluation could be achieved by means of using eye tracker data [22, 23]. We plan as a future work to acquire a new data set of trait judgements. In addition to the trait ratings, information from the eye tracker should be recorded from each participant and for each trait. Previous works in visual attention and object recognition [24, 25] define specific criteria to evaluate image zones in terms of visual attention. Specifically, the notion of *fixation* is defined as specific zones where eyes are fixed between two saccades, and its position is obtained by weighted sums of pixel locations within fixations (averaged by their duration) [26].

We also plan as a future work to explore more robust hybrid approximations (using both appearance and eye tracking information). Object recognition literature shows successful attempts in relating visual attention and image saliency in the context of object detection and classification [27]. A similar Bayesian approach to take into account both sources of information could be used for the facial trait inference problem.

Acknowledgements. This research was partially supported by MEC grants TIN2009-14404-C02-01 and CONSOLIDER-INGENIO 2010 (CSD2007-00018).

References

1. Zebrowitz, L.: Reading faces: Window to the soul? Westview Press (1997)
2. Montepare, J., Zebrowitz, L.: Person perception comes of age: The salience and significance of age in social judgments. Advances in Experimental Social Psychology 30, 93–161 (1998)
3. Eagly, A., Ashmore, R., Makhijani, M., Longo, L.: What is beautiful is good, but: A meta-analytic review of research on the physical attractiveness stereotype. Psychological Bulletin; Psychological Bulletin 110(1), 109 (1991)
4. Ballew, C., Todorov, A.: Predicting political elections from rapid and unreflective face judgments. Proceedings of the National Academy of Sciences 104(46), 17948 (2007)
5. Little, A., Burriss, R., Jones, B., Roberts, S.: Facial appearance affects voting decisions. Evolution and Human Behavior 28(1), 18–27 (2007)
6. Blair, I., Judd, C., Chapleau, K.: The influence of afrocentric facial features in criminal sentencing. Psychological Science 15(10), 674 (2004)
7. Willis, J., Todorov, A.: First impressions making up your mind after a 100-ms exposure to a face. Psychological Science 17(7), 592–598 (2006)
8. Oosterhof, N., Todorov, A.: The functional basis of face evaluation. Proceedings of the National Academy of Sciences 105(32), 11087 (2008)
9. Todorov, A., Said, C., Engell, A., Oosterhof, N.: Understanding evaluation of faces on social dimensions. Trends in Cognitive Sciences 12(12), 455–460 (2008)
10. Phelps, E.A., LeDoux, J.E.: Contributions of the amygdala to emotion processing: from animal models to human behavior. Neuron 48(2), 175–187 (2005)

11. Adolphs, R., Tranel, D., Damasio, A., et al.: The human amygdala in social judgment. Nature, 470–473 (1998)
12. Rojas, Q., Masip, D., Todorov, A., Vitria, J., et al.: Automatic point-based facial trait judgments evaluation. In: 2010 IEEE Conference on Computer Vision and Pattern Recognition (CVPR), pp. 2715–2720. IEEE (2010)
13. Rojas, M., Masip, D., Todorov, A., Vitria, J.: Automatic prediction of facial trait judgments: Appearance vs. structural models. PloS one 6(8), e23323 (2011)
14. Lundqvist, D., Flykt, A., Ohman, A.: Karolinska Directed Emotional Faces: Database of standardized facial images. Psychology Section, Department of Clinical Neuroscience, Karolinska Hospital, S-171 76 Stockholm, Sweden (1998)
15. Torralba, A.: Contextual priming for object detection. International Journal of Computer Vision 53(2), 169–191 (2003)
16. Torralba, A.: Modeling global scene factors in attention. JOSA A 20(7), 1407–1418 (2003)
17. Itti, L., Koch, C., Niebur, E.: A model of saliency-based visual attention for rapid scene analysis. IEEE Transactions on Pattern Analysis and Machine Intelligence 20(11), 1254–1259 (1998)
18. Simoncelli, E., Freeman, W.: The steerable pyramid: A flexible architecture for multi-scale derivative computation. In: Proceedings of the International Conference on Image Processing, vol. 3, pp. 444–447. IEEE (1995)
19. Schyns, P., Oliva, A.: Flexible, diagnosticity-driven, rather than fixed, perceptually determined scale selection in scene and face recognition. Perception 26, 1027–1038 (1997)
20. Oliva, A., Schyns, P.: Coarse blobs or fine edges? evidence that information diagnosticity changes the perception of complex visual stimuli. Cognitive Psychology 34, 72–107 (1997)
21. Keil, M.S., Lapedriza, A., Masip, D., Vitria, J.: Preferred spatial frequencies for human face processing are associated with optimal class discrimination in the machine. PloS one 3(7), e2590 (2008)
22. Rayner, K.: Eye movements in reading and information processing: 20 years of research. Psychological Bulletin 124(3), 372 (1998)
23. Rao, R., Zelinsky, G., Hayhoe, M., Ballard, D.: Eye movements in iconic visual search. Vision Research 42(11), 1447–1463 (2002)
24. Henderson, J., Pollatsek, A., Rayner, K.: Covert visual attention and extrafoveal information use during object identification. Attention, Perception, & Psychophysics 45(3), 196–208 (1989)
25. Kowler, E., Anderson, E., Dosher, B., Blaser, E.: The role of attention in the programming of saccades. Vision Research 35(13), 1897–1916 (1995)
26. Henderson, J., McClure, K., Pierce, S., Schrock, G.: Object identification without foveal vision: Evidence from an artificial scotoma paradigm. Attention, Perception, & Psychophysics 59(3), 323–346 (1997)
27. Torralba, A., Oliva, A., Castelhano, M.S., Henderson, J.M.: Contextual guidance of eye movements and attention in real-world scenes: the role of global features in object search. Psychological Review 113(4), 766 (2006)

Illumination Normalization Using Self-lighting Ratios for 3D2D Face Recognition

Xi Zhao, Shishir K. Shah, and Ioannis A. Kakadiaris

Computational Biomedicine Laboratory, Department of Computer Science, University of Houston, 4800 Calhoun, Houston, TX 77204
zhaoxi1@gmail.com, shah@cs.uh.edu, ioannisk@uh.edu

Abstract. 3D-2D face recognition is beginning to gain attention from the research community. It takes advantage of 3D facial geometry to normalize the head pose and registers it into a canonical 2D space. In this paper, we present a novel illumination normalization approach for 3D-2D face recognition which does not require any training or prior knowledge on the type, number, and direction of the lighting sources. Estimated using an image-specific filtering technique in the frequency domain, a self-lighting ratio is employed to suppress illumination differences. Experimental results on the UHDB11 and FRGC databases indicate that the proposed approach improves the performance significantly for face images with large illumination variations.

Keywords: Lighting ratio, illumination suppression, 3D-2D face recognition.

1 Introduction

The research on 3D-2D Face Recognition has rapidly increased in recent years. Since the facial geometry is invariant to camera viewpoints, 3D facial data can be used to overcome the difficulties of head pose variations. Currently, limited by the high cost of 3D face scanners, it is impractical to deploy a large number of 3D scanners in real world face recognition applications. This emphasizes the advantage of using the alternative approach of 3D-2D face recognition setups, which use 3D + 2D facial data as the gallery and 2D facial images as the probe. An excellent survey of face recognition was presented by Bowyer *et al.* [1]. Recent reviews are included in [2][24][3][4]. Illumination variations remain a challenge for improving the overall robustness and performance of 3D-2D FR systems. In this paper, we provide an efficient solution for illumination normalization to enhance the performance of 3D-2D face recognition systems.

The basic idea of our method is to relight the input images to a preset texture with a constant value so that the relit input images are symmetric and close to each other. This is achieved by computing the point-wise division between the original texture and the *lighting ratio*, an estimate of the illumination conditions. Assuming that most of the illumination effects vary slowly on the facial textures, and that the majority of the energy of illumination is distributed among the low

A. Fusiello et al. (Eds.): ECCV 2012 Ws/Demos, Part II, LNCS 7584, pp. 220–229, 2012.

frequencies, we estimate the lighting ratios via low-pass filtering in the frequency domain. In order to choose the cut-off frequency for the filter so that it can be adaptively used for images under various lighting conditions, we propose an image-specific low-pass filtering technique. The lighting ratio is adjusted to minimize the L_2 norm between the outcome of the division and the preset texture to further reduce the contrast and exposure difference on faces due to skin type, camera parameters, and lighting conditions.

Our main contributions are: (i) developed a novel illumination normalization method based on self-lighting ratio with the aim of enhancing face recognition performance; (ii) developed an image-specific low-pass filtering method that does not require preset parameters; (iii) proposed to use a preset texture with a constant value as the reference for illumination suppression.

The rest of the paper is organized as follows: Section 2 discusses the related work in the literature. Section 3 provides an overview of a 3D-2D face recognition system. The proposed method is detailed in Section 4. Section 5 presents the experimental results. Section 6 summarizes our findings.

2 Literature Reviews

The illumination normalization methods for face recognition can be generally divided into two catogories: (i) normalizing the lighting conditions for a pair of images (relighting) [5][6][7][8][9][10], (ii) normalizing the lighting effects for a set of images (unlighting) [11][12][13][14]. To estimate the lighting effects, either subspace-based models or image processing techniques have been adopted.

Subspace-based methods model the lighting in a low-dimensional space. Shim et al. [5] built a subspace model for each pixel under various lighting conditions per subject and per pose. The lighting, pose, and reflectance were jointly inferred using an EM-like process. Zhang and Samaras [15] recovered person-specific basis images by combining spherical harmonics illumination representation with 3D morphable models. The basis images were subdivided into small regions and incorporated into an MRF framework to remove the lighting and relit faces under arbitrary unknown lighting conditions in [7]. Blanz and Vetter [16] imposed linear constraints on both the albedo and the shape of the face. They proposed a 3D morphable model to represent each face as a linear combination of 3D basis exemplars. The recovery of lighting parameters was realized as an optimization problem that aimed to minimize the difference between the input and the reconstructed image. Sungho et al. [13] minimized the L_1-norm between an image and a linear combination of principal lighting eigenvectors for unlighting. The lighting eigenvectors were obtained using PCA on eight illumination maps with eight light sources distributed evenly. Kumar et al. [6] built eight-dimensional subspace models for texture and illumination, respectively.

Image processing based methods estimate the lighting mainly via spatial smooth filtering or using Quotient image approaches. Quotient Image [17] is the ratio between an image and a linear combination of three images lit by independent light sources. Wang et al. [18] proposed the Self-Quotient image

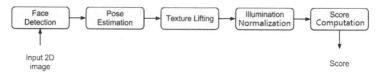

Fig. 1. Flowchart of the 3D-2D face recognition pipeline

which replaced the linear combination of three images by the smoothed input image to ease the assumptions posed in Quotient image and presented preliminary results on face recognition. Han *et al.* [8] computed illuminations using a homomorphic wavelet filtering and computed the Quotient image between two illumination images for relighting. Chen *et al.* [10] used edge-preserving filters to obtain the large-scale layers of two images and then convolved them to compute the ratio coefficients for relighting. Biswas *et al.* [11] added a signal-dependent non-stationary noise term to the Lambertian model and hence, computed albedo as the Linear Minimum Mean Square Error estimate of the true albedo. The noise incorporated the errors in surface normal and illumination estimation and thus resulted in obtaining a more realistic albedo using their methods. Vural *et al.* [14] applied the Ayofa-filters to filter out the illumination effect on faces.

3 Overview of a 3D-2D Face Recognition System

The face recognition experiments are conducted using the 3D-2D face recognition system proposed by Toderici *et al.* [3]. The facial data in the gallery include both a mesh and a texture while the facial data in the probe includes only texture. For each 3D mesh in the gallery, the Annotated Facial Model (AFM) [19] is fit to establish a person-specific point-to-point correspondence mapping of the 3D mesh to the UV space. For the 2D image in the gallery, each fitted model is transformed and projected to the pose appearing in the texture image using a set of landmarks. Then, using the previously established correspondences, the texture is lifted to a two-dimensional (UV) space with pose normalized to be frontal. The self-occluded parts of the face in the original pose are masked out. For each texture in the probe dataset, the same process is repeated using the fitted model from the gallery dataset that it is compared with. After processing textures in both gallery and probe, the illumination is normalized either by relighting [3] or unlighting (illumination normalization) as proposed in this paper, and a correlation-coefficient-based distance metric is computed for each pair of textures from the gallery and the probe. A flowchart of the system is presented in Fig. 1.

4 Minimizing Illumination Differences Using the Self-lighting Ratio

4.1 Definition of the Self-lighting Ratio

The self-quotient image Q is defined as an intrinsic property of a face image I of an individual [18], by $Q = \frac{I}{\hat{I}}$, where $\hat{I}$ is the smoothed version of I, F is the smoothing kernel, and the division is pixel-wise. Wang *et al.* [18] used a Gaussian filter F to obtain the $\hat{I}$.

The self-quotient image method has demonstrated its capability in improving face recognition performance via reducing illumination differences. However, during its computation the range of self-quotient image spans from zero to infinite, since it is computed from a pixel-wise division. A small variation on the smoothed value may lead to large variations on the self-quotient image. Therefore, while this method reduces the illumination on the facial texture, it also introduces numerical artefacts, especially in the shadowed regions. For example, obvious noise can be observed on the shadow region of the face in Fig. 2 in [18]. Meanwhile, using a spatial filter to obtain the smoothed version of I raises two different problems. First, it is hard to determine the appropriate sliding window size for filtering since the size depends on the face scale and the lighting conditions. Second, there is no consensus on the appropriate kernel in the spatial domain to obtain the lighting conditions on the face. Nevertheless, a smoothing kernel in the spacial domain has the effect of a low-pass filter in the frequency domain removing high frequencies (mostly edges) while enhancing low frequencies. This is consistent with the statement in [20], where under the Lambertian assumption, the low frequency part in the image captures mostly the lighting condition on the facial image. Thus, an alternative way to overcome the aforementioned problems is to estimate the self-lighting ratio (Eq. 1). This can be written as:

$$T = \left(\alpha \frac{1}{\hat{I}} + \beta\right)I = \left(\alpha \frac{1}{\mathcal{T}^{-1}(\mathcal{T}(\xi)\mathcal{T}(I))} + \beta\right)I = L_R I \qquad (1)$$

where L_R denotes the self-lighting ratio, ξ denotes a low-pass filter, $\mathcal{T}$ and $\mathcal{T}^{-1}$ is the Fourier transform and inverse Fourier transform, T is the relit image, $\hat{I}$ is the smoothed version of the image I, and α, β are scale and offset parameters. The adoption of these two parameters compensates the contrast and offset variations of facial textures I caused by lighting conditions, skin type, and camera parameters. The addition, the division, and the multiplication are pixel-wise.

4.2   Algorithm

The proposed algorithm changes the self-lighting ratio to minimize the difference between the relit image T and a predefined image I_p (set to a uniform value 60): $\arg\min \|I_p - L_R I\|_F$. Thus, the algorithm pursues the minimum Frobenius norm of the difference image between the input image $L_R I$ and I_p. There are three positive effects from this algorithm. First, all the relit images $T = L_R I$ are similar to each other in terms of global intensities since we adjust the lighting conditions according to one preset texture. Second, the lighting conditions on the relit images are more symmetric since I_p is symmetric and the parameters α, β adjust the contrast and offset variations on $\hat{I}$. Finally, the estimation of $\hat{I}$ is more accurate since it is performed using an image-specific low-pass filtering algorithm, which avoids the use of an arbitrary low-pass filtering parameter for all textures regardless of their lighting conditions.

Algorithm 1. Illumination normalization using lighting ratio

Input: Facial texture I and low-pass filter ξ

Output: Normalized texture T

1: Convert the texture I to the HSV color space and extract its V channel (V_g)
2: Obtain V_g's Fourier spectrum F_g via 2D Fast Fourier Transform
3: Compute the image-specific parameter P for ξ (Sec. 4.4)
4: Filter the magnitude of F_g by applying the low-pass filter ξ to obtain F_g'
5: Apply the inverse Fast Fourier transform on the filtered spectrum F_g' to obtain the lighting component $\hat{V}_g$
6: Minimize the L_2 norm between I_p and $(\alpha\frac{1}{\hat{V}_g} + \beta) * V_g$
7: Compute the normalized texture: $T = (\hat{\alpha}\frac{1}{\hat{V}_g} + \hat{\beta}) * V_g$

The detailed algorithm is depicted in Alg. 1. The symbols $\hat{\alpha}$ and $\hat{\beta}$ in Step 7 denote the optimized parameters. The Nelder-Meade simplex algorithm [21] is chosen for the minimization in Step 6. It is one of the best known algorithms for unconstrained optimization without derivatives and is quite simple in computation.

4.3   Illumination Estimation in the Frequency Domain

To filter the image in the frequency domain, we first apply the Fourier Transform to the image V: $F(k,l) = \sum_{s=0}^{N-1}\sum_{t=0}^{N-1} V(s,t)e^{-2\pi i(\frac{ks}{N}+\frac{lt}{N})}$, where V is the image, s, t are the indices on V, and N is the image size, F is the Fourier spectrum and k, l are the indices on F. The exponential term is the basis function corresponding to each point (k, l) on the Fourier spectrum. Then, the low-pass filter ξ which has the same size of F is multiplied with the magnitude of the spectrum F in a pixel-by-pixel fashion: $|F'(k,l)| = |F(k,l)|\xi(k,l)$, where $|F(k,l)|$ is the magnitude of the input spectrum F, $\xi(k,l)$ is the filter, and $|F'(k,l)|$ is the filtered spectrum. To obtain the lighting estimates in the spatial domain, the inverse Fourier transform is applied on the filtered spectrum F': $\hat{V}(s,t) = \frac{1}{N^2}\sum_{k=0}^{N-1}\sum_{l=0}^{N-1} F'(k,l)e^{2\pi i(\frac{ks}{N}+\frac{lt}{N})}$, where F' captures the low frequencies of the image V, and $\frac{1}{N^2}$ is a normalization term in the inverse transformation.

4.4   Image-Specific Low-Pass Filtering

It is hard to choose an arbitrary cut-off frequency for all facial images for low-pass filters since the lighting conditions vary in different facial images. Instead, we propose to compute an image-specific energy threshold P (in the range $[0,1]$) for each image automatically. The basic idea is that the number of lights, lighting direction, and intensity change the frequency distribution mostly in the low frequencies. While the portion of energy useful for identification is distributed mostly in middle frequencies, and the skin details which are distributed mostly in high frequencies remain relatively steady, the energy variations among fixed posed facial textures are highly related to the lighting conditions. Thus, by varying the cut-off energy instead of the cut-off frequency, we can estimate the lighting conditions in a more accurate manner for each image. Note that the energy in Fourier spectrum F_g is defined as the L_2 norm of the F_g magnitude and we iteratively increase the cut-off frequency until the energy of the passed frequency components is greater than a portion (P) of the energy of all frequencies of the image in the implementation.

We adaptively compute P for each image, which varies with the energy from lighting conditions in the image. Histogram equalization (HE) adjusts the intensity distributions on the histograms of the texture which is able to change the energy of the image to a level quite constant among different face textures across various lighting conditions. Thus, we approximate the P using the energy of the HE adjusted image as a reference:

$$P \propto E(I)/E(I_{eq}) \approx \kappa E(I)/E(I_{eq}), \tag{2}$$

where κ is a constant (set to 0.05), $E(I)$ is the energy of the input image I, and $E(I_{eq})$ is the energy of the input image processed by the histogram equalization I_{eq}. The energy is defined as the L_2 norm of their V_g images. Since the energy identification and the skin details are relatively constant as well as the energy of the HE adjusted image, P is able to reflect the energy variations caused by lighting conditions.

The choice of the low-pass filter is also important in estimating the lighting conditions. The ideal filter is a simple low-pass filter, which suppresses all frequencies higher than a threshold frequency C and keeps the lower frequencies unchanged. However, it introduces an ringing artefact that occurs along the edges of the filtered image in the spatial domain. Thus, we opt to use more sophisticated low-pass filters (e.g., a Gaussian filter or a Butterworth filter). The Gaussian filter has the same shape in the spatial and frequency domains and therefore does not incur the ringing artefact. The Butterworth filter is an approximation of Gaussian filter and outputs a similar result as the one obtained by the Gaussian filter. However, considering the computational complexity, the Butterworth filter is a better choice for wide low-pass filtering, while the Gaussian filter is more appropriate for narrow low-pass filtering, which is our case. Thus, we adopt a Gaussian filter ξ in this work.

5   Experimental Result

5.1   Datasets

To assess the robustness of our algorithm under various head poses and illumination conditions, we tested it on the publicly available UHDB11 [22] and FRGC v2.0 [23] datasets. The UHDB11 dataset contains 1,625 3D facial scans captured by a 3dMD scanner and 1,625 images captured by a Canon DSLR camera. Facial data from 23 different subjects were acquired under six indoor illumination conditions, four yaw rotations, and three roll rotations per subject. The head pose varies from ±50 degrees in the roll direction, and ±30 degrees in the pitch direction. We also evaluate our algorithm on the FRGC v2.0 dataset, which contains a large number of co-registered face images and 3D meshes with controlled and uncontrolled lighting conditions.

Fig. 2. Depiction of the unlighting results. The first and fourth rows depict the original face textures in the UV space. The second and fifth rows depict the self-ratio images. The third and sixth rows depict the unlit face textures using our method.

5.2   Illumination Normalization

Figure 2 depicts the comparison between the self-ratio and the proposed algorithm. It can be observed that the lighting effects on the unlit facial texture is reduced and distributed more evenly than those on the raw facial texture. When compared to the images form the self-ratio method, the lighting effects are more constant across our unlit images and the image energies of our relit textures are similar. This is because the lighting ratios adjust the overall intensity levels to the preset I_p. In addition, the low-pass filtering designates image-specific parameters for the low-pass filter leading to a more accurate estimate of the subject differences lighting conditions, thus the differences among unlit textures are mainly caused by identifications.

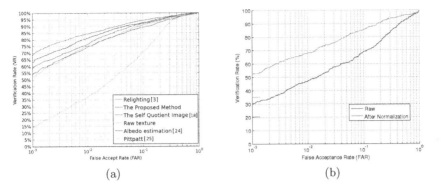

Fig. 3. Depiction of the ROC curves on the (a) UHDB11 dataset; (b) FRGC dataset

5.3   Face Recognition

Figure 3(a) depicts the ROC curves for six different methods tested on the UHDB11 dataset: (i) computing the distance metric for a relit texture using the method in [3]; (ii) computing the distance metric for the unlit texture by the proposed algorithm; (iii) computing the distance metric for the self-quotient image method proposed in [18]; (iv) computing the distance metric for the raw texture output from texture lifting; (v) computing the distance metric for the unlit texture using the albedo estimation method proposed in [25]; and (vi) using the 2D-2D PittPatt [26] face recognition system. The verification rates at 10^{-3} FAR are 64.1%, 68.9%, 61.0%, 52.3%, 54.2% and 13.8%, respectively. The gap in performance between PittPatt and other algorithms is due to pose variations in the dataset, since the other algorithms use the lifted texture in UV space with pose normalized while PittPatt recognition is performed on the face ROI detected from original images. The method proposed by Biswas *et al.* [25] results in an increased verification rate compared to the raw lifted texture. One possible reason for the relatively low performance is that their method requires a training dataset to learn the pixel intensity statistics and our training dataset is not the same as theirs. Our method has demonstrated improvement over the self-quotient method because of a better estimation of lighting conditions via the image-specific low-pass filtering and a better normalization process with the adoption of parameters α and β. Compared to the relighting method which requires the 3D face geometry, our algorithm still demonstrated its effectiveness by achieving 5% higher on verification rate.

To test the robustness of the proposed method, we also evaluated our algorithm on the FRGC v2 dataset. We used the same experimental setup as the one used in the Al-Osaimi study [4] (the same 250 facial scans from 250 subjects as the gallery and 470 facial scans as the probe). Figure 3(b) depicts the ROC curves using raw and normalized scores from our illumination normalization algorithm. Our algorithm achieves verification rates of 30.0% and 53.8% at 0.001 False Accept Rate. Compared to the verification of 20.43% and 34.89% achieved in [4], shown as the red and green dot lines in Fig.3b, the proposed approach performs better.

6   Conclusion

We proposed a novel approach to normalize illumination conditions on facial textures, without requiring 3D geometry information and prior knowledge of lighting conditions. This method has been incorporated into a 3D-2D face recognition system, thus providing the capacity to handle illumination variations on faces with different poses. We tested the algorithm on the UHDB11 and FRGC v2.0 datasets, and the results demonstrate its robustness and accuracy.

References

1. Bowyer, K., Chang, K., Flynn, P.: A survey of approaches and challenges in 3D and multi-modal 3D+2D face recognition. Computer Vision and Image Understanding 101, 1–15 (2006)
2. Zhou, Z., Ganesh, A., Wright, J., Tsai, S.F., Ma, Y.: Nearest-subspace patch matching for face recognition under varying pose and illumination. In: Proc. 8th IEEE International Conference on Automatic Face Gesture Recognition, Amsterdam, The Netherlands, pp. 1–8 (2008)
3. Toderici, G., Passalis, G., Zafeiriou, S., Tzimiropoulos, G., Petrou, M., Theoharis, T., Kakadiaris, I.: Bidirectional relighting for 3D-aided 2D face recognition. In: Proc. IEEE Computer Society Conference on Computer Vision and Pattern Recognition, San Francisco, CA, pp. 2721–2728 (2010)
4. Al-Osaimi, F.R., Bennamoun, M., Mian, A.S.: Illumination normalization of facial images by reversing the process of image formation. Machine Vision and Applications 22, 899–911 (2011)
5. Shim, H., Luo, J., Chen, T.: A subspace model-based approach to face relighting under unknown lighting and poses. IEEE Transactions on Image Processing 17, 1331–1341 (2008)
6. Kumar, R., Jones, M., Marks, T.: Morphable reflectance fields for enhancing face recognition. In: IEEE Conference on Proc. Computer Vision and Pattern Recognition (CVPR), pp. 2606–2613 (2010)
7. Wang, Y., Zhang, L., Liu, Z., Hua, G., Wen, Z., Zhang, Z., Samaras, D.: Face relighting from a single image under arbitrary unknown lighting conditions. IEEE Transactions on Pattern Analysis and Machine Intelligence 31, 1968–1984 (2009)
8. Han, H., Shan, S., Chen, X., Gao, W.: Illumination transfer using homomorphic wavelet filtering and its application to light-insensitive face recognition. In: Proc. IEEE International Conference on Automatic Face and Gesture Recognition, Amsterdam (2008)
9. Chen, J., Su, G., He, J., Ben, S.: Face Image Relighting using Locally Constrained Global Optimization. In: Daniilidis, K., Maragos, P., Paragios, N. (eds.) ECCV 2010, Part IV. LNCS, vol. 6314, pp. 44–57. Springer, Heidelberg (2010)
10. Chen, X., Chen, M., Jin, X., Zhao, Q.: Face illumination transfer through edge-preserving filters. In: Proc. IEEE Conference on Computer Vision and Pattern Recognition, Colorado Springs CA (2011)

11. Biswas, S., Aggarwal, G., Chellappa, R.: Robust estimation of albedo for illumination-invariant matching and shape recovery. IEEE Transactions on Pattern Analysis and Machine Intelligence 31, 884–899 (2009)
12. Zou, X., Kittler, J., Hamouz, M., Tena, J.: Robust albedo estimation from face image under unknown illumination. In: Proc. SPIE Biometric Technology for Human Identification, Orlando, FL, p. 69440A (2008)
13. Suh, S., Lee, M., Choi, C.H.: Robust albedo estimation from a facial image with cast shadow. In: Proc. 18th IEEE International Conference on Image Processing, Brussels, Belguim, pp. 873–876 (2011)
14. Vural, S., Mae, Y., Uvet, H., Arai, T.: Illumination normalization for outdoor face recognition by using ayofa-filters. Journal of Pattern Recognition Research 6, 1–18 (2011)
15. Zhang, L., Samaras, D.: Face recognition from a single training image under arbitrary unknown lighting using spherical harmonics. IEEE Transactions on Pattern Analysis and Machine Intelligence 28, 351–363 (2006)
16. Blanz, V., Vetter, T.: Face recognition based on fitting a 3D morphable model. IEEE Transactions on Pattern Analysis and Machine Intelligence 25, 1063–1074 (2003)
17. Shashua, A., Riklin-Raviv, T.: The quotient image: class-based re-rendering and recognition with varying illuminations. IEEE Transactions on Pattern Analysis and Machine Intelligence 23, 129–139 (2001)
18. Wang, H., Li, S., Wang, Y., Zhang, J.: Self quotient image for face recognition. In: Proc. IEEE International Conference on Image Processing, vol. 2, pp. 1397–1400 (2004)
19. Kakadiaris, I., Passalis, G., Toderici, G., Murtuza, M.N., Lu, Y., Karampatziakis, N., Theoharis, T.: Three-dimensional face recognition in the presence of facial expressions: An annotated deformable model approach. IEEE Transactions on Pattern Analysis and Machine Intelligence 29, 640–649 (2007)
20. Basri, R., Jacobs, D.: Lambertian reflectance and linear subspaces. IEEE Transactions on Pattern Analysis and Machine Intelligence 25, 218–233 (2003)
21. Nelder, J.A., Mead, R.: A simplex method for function minimization. Computer Journal 7, 308–313 (1965)
22. UH Computational Biomedicine Lab: UHDB11 face database (2009), http://cbl.uh.edu/URxD/datasets/
23. Phillips, P., Flynn, P., Scruggs, T., Bowyer, K., Chang, J., Hoffman, K., Marques, J., Min, J., Worek, W.: Overview of the face recognition grand challenge. In: Proc. IEEE Computer Society Conference on Computer Vision and Pattern Recognition, San Diego, CA, vol. 1, pp. 947–954 (2005)
24. Phillips, P.J., Scruggs, W.T., O'Toole, A.J., Flynn, P.J., Bowyer, K.W., Schott, C.L., Sharpe, M.: FRVT 2006 and ICE 2006 Large-Scale Experimental Results. IEEE Transactions on Pattern Analysis and Machine Intelligence 32, 831–846 (2010)
25. Biswas, S., Chellappa, R.: Pose-robust albedo estimation from a single image. In: Proc. IEEE Conference on Computer Vision and Pattern Recognition, San Francisco, CA, pp. 2683–2690 (2010)
26. Pittsburgh Pattern Recognition: PittPatt face tracking & recognition Software Development Kit 5.1 (2011)

Robust Learning from Normals for 3D Face Recognition

Ioannis Marras[1], Stefanos Zafeiriou[1,*], and Georgios Tzimiropoulos[1,2]

[1] Department of Computing, Imperial College London,
180 Queen's Gate. London SW7 2AZ, U.K.
[2] School of Computer Science, University of Lincoln,
Lincoln LN6 7TS, U.K.
{i.marras,s.zafeiriou,gt204}@imperial.ac.uk
http://ibug.doc.ic.ac.uk

Abstract. We introduce novel subspace-based methods for learning from the azimuth angle of surface normals for 3D face recognition. We show that the normal azimuth angles combined with Principal Component Analysis (PCA) using a cosine-based distance measure can be used for robust face recognition from facial surfaces. The proposed algorithms are well-suited for all types of 3D facial data including data produced by range cameras (depth images), photometric stereo (PS) and shade-from-X (SfX) algorithms. We demonstrate the robustness of the proposed algorithms both in 3D face reconstruction from synthetically occluded samples, as well as, in face recognition using the FRGC v2 3D face database and the recently collected Photoface database where the proposed method achieves state-of-the-art results. An important aspect of our method is that it can achieve good face recognition/verification performance by using raw 3D scans without any heavy preprocessing (i.e., model fitting, surface smoothing etc.).

1 Introduction

3D face recognition from 3D surface information has witnessed very rapid development over the past decade due to the low cost of 3D digital acquisition devices and the need of secure biometrics. Facial surface information has the obvious advantage that it is an intrinsic property of the face and hence more robust to illumination changes than appearance information. On the other hand, 3D face recognition algorithms must be able to handle many challenges such as inaccurate face alignment, pose variations, measurement noise, missing data, facial expressions and partial occlusion.

Many different approaches were proposed for dealing with the aforementioned problems [4,2,6,7,5,12]. Early approaches, such as [6], use specific face regions that are not affected by the presence of facial deformations caused by facial expressions, such as the nose and the area around it. An investigation on which face regions should be used for robust 3D face recognition was conducted in [7].

Many methods assume that facial expressions can be modeled, up to a certain extend, as isometries of the facial surfaces [2,16,5]. That is, geodesics of the facial surface are

* The work of Stefanos Zafeiriou has been partially funded by the Junior Research Fellowship of Imperial College London.

A. Fusiello et al. (Eds.): ECCV 2012 Ws/Demos, Part II, LNCS 7584, pp. 230–239, 2012.

approximately preserved in expressive faces. Following this line of research, the algorithms [2,16] compare 3D facial surfaces by computing of iso-geodesic stripes or geodesic lengths between closed curves on the facial surface. Under the same assumption, 3D face recognition methods that embed the facial surface into a Euclidean space and replace the geodesic distances by Euclidean ones were proposed in [5]. Using such an embedding, facial surfaces can be matched using conventional methods. The major drawback of these methods is the high computational complexity related to the computation of geodesics. Another solution is to an annotated morphable model [12,14,3]. One of the drawbacks of these methods is that performance depends on the success of the fitting algorithm which often fails in cases of large expressions or occlusions.

Subspace learning algorithms for normals, such as Principal Component Analysis (PCA), employ low-dimensional representation of surfaces [9,11,17,18]. In its simplest form, PCA on surface normals has been applied on the concatenation of normal coordinates [11]. One attempt to exploit the special structure of normals (i.e., that lie on a sphere) was conducted in [17]. In this paper the Azimuthal Equidistance Projection (AEP) was proposed and applied to surface normals prior to the application of PCA. Furthermore, in order to take into consideration the non-Euclidean actual manifold of objects' surfaces, Principal Geodesic Analysis (PGA) has been proposed [9] for nonlinear statistical analysis.

In this paper, motivated by the recent developments in robust 2D subspace learning from image gradient orientations [19], we propose a simple, efficient and robust subspace learning based on the azimuth angle of face surface normals. We develop a PCA in a space where the normal azimuth angles are mapped by a complex transform into a high-dimensional unit sphere and we demonstrate its robust properties.

The major advantages of the proposed methodology are:

- low-computational complexity. Our algorithms require the eigen-decomposition of Hermitian matrices for training and use simple projections for testing;
- good recognition rates without heavy preprocessing of the 3D meshes (without fitting a model). Comparable performance to state-of-the-art was also achieved when combined with this kind of preprocessing;
- state-of-the-art recognition rates in surfaces produced by Shape-from-X and Photometric Stereo algorithms;
- state-of-the-art recognition rates for cases when standard approaches, such as model fitting, may fail (i.e., presence of occlusions).

2   PCA of Needle Maps

Let us define a real surface $f(\mathbf{x})$ on a lattice or a real space $\mathbf{x} = (x, y)$. The normal field (or needle map) is defined as a set of local surface normals $\mathbf{n}(\mathbf{x}) = (n_x(\mathbf{x}), n_y(\mathbf{x}), n_z(\mathbf{x}))$ that lie on the unit sphere (i.e., $\|\mathbf{n}(\mathbf{x})\| = 1$, where $\|.\|$ is the ℓ_2 norm). Mathematically, given a continuous surface $f(\mathbf{x})$, normals $\mathbf{n}(\mathbf{x})$ can be defined as

$$\mathbf{n}(\mathbf{x}) = \frac{1}{\sqrt{1 + \frac{\partial f}{\partial x}^2 + \frac{\partial f}{\partial y}^2}} \left(-\frac{\partial f}{\partial x}, -\frac{\partial f}{\partial y}, 1 \right)^T.$$

Normals $\mathbf{n} \in \Re^3$ do not lie on a Euclidean space but on a spherical manifold $\eta \in \mathcal{S}^2$, where $\mathcal{S}^2$ is the unit 2-sphere and there is a continuous map Φ such that $\mathbf{n} = \Phi(\eta)$ where

$\Phi : \mathcal{S}^2 \mapsto \Re^3$. On the unit sphere, the surface normal $\mathbf{n}(\mathbf{x})$ at $\mathbf{x}$ has elevation angles $\theta(\mathbf{x}) = \frac{\pi}{2} - \arcsin(n_z(\mathbf{x}))$ and azimuth angle defined as $\phi(\mathbf{x}) = \arctan \frac{n_y(\mathbf{x})}{n_x(\mathbf{x})} = \arctan \frac{\frac{\partial f}{\partial y}}{\frac{\partial f}{\partial x}}$.

Methods for computing the normals of surfaces can be found in [10]. In many cases, surface reconstruction methods do not recover the actual surface but the needle map. Such methods include SfX and PS algorithms [1].

Prior to describing our algorithm, we will briefly outline two popular PCA methodologies on surface normals that take into account the special structure of surface normals (i.e., that lie in a unit sphere). The first one is based on Azimuthal Equidistant Projection (AEP) [17] and the second one on Principal Geodesic Analysis (PGA) [9,18].

For simplicity, hereinafter, we assume that we have a set $\mathcal{J} = \{\mathbf{J}_1, \ldots, \mathbf{J}_N\}$ of 3D (or 2.5D) of facial surfaces from a range camera sampled over a grid of resolution $M_1 \times M_2$. For the i-th facial surface, at each point of the grid $\mathbf{x}$, we compute the normal vector $\mathbf{G}_i = [\mathbf{n}_i(\mathbf{x})] \in \mathcal{P}^{M_1 \times M_2}$ where $\mathcal{P}$ is the pure subset of $\Re^3$ of the vector that lies on the unit sphere. In PS and SfX algorithms the set $\mathcal{G} = \{\mathbf{G}_1, \ldots, \mathbf{G}_N\}$ is computed directly.

2.1   PCA Using AEP

In order to formulate AEP we first need to define the mean elevation and azimuthal angle of $\mathcal{G}$ at each spatial location $\mathbf{x}$. In [17], the mean elevation and azimuthal angles at $\mathbf{x}$ were defined as $\tilde{\theta}(\mathbf{x}) = \frac{\pi}{2} - \arcsin(\tilde{n}_z(\mathbf{x}))$ and $\tilde{\phi}(\mathbf{x}) = \arctan \frac{\tilde{n}_y(\mathbf{x})}{\tilde{n}_x(\mathbf{x})}$, where $\tilde{\mathbf{n}}(\mathbf{x}) = (\tilde{n}_x(\mathbf{x}), \tilde{n}_y(\mathbf{x}), \tilde{n}_z(\mathbf{x}))$ is the mean representation of the normal at $\mathbf{x}$. For spherical data, such as surface normals, the intrinsic mean is in many cases represented by the spherical median [8]. For computation ease, in [17], instead of the spherical median, the average surface normal at $\mathbf{x}$ $\acute{\mathbf{n}}(\mathbf{x}) = \frac{1}{K} \sum_{i=1}^{K} \mathbf{n}_i(\mathbf{x})$, $\tilde{\mathbf{n}} = \frac{\acute{\mathbf{n}}(\mathbf{x})}{||\acute{\mathbf{n}}(\mathbf{x})||}$ was used.

In order to build the AEP, the tangent plane to the unit-sphere at the location corresponding to the mean-surface normal is computed. A local coordinate system is then established on this tangent plane. The origin is the point of contact between the tangent plane and the unit sphere. The x-axis is aligned parallel to the local circle of latitude on the unit-sphere. The AEP maps the normal $\mathbf{n}_i(\mathbf{x})$ at $\mathbf{x}$ to the new vector $\mathbf{v}_i(\mathbf{x}) = (v_x^i(\mathbf{x}), v_y^i(\mathbf{x}))$ (for more details on how to compute the AEP the interested reader may refer to [17]).

After applying the AEP transform to all the samples of $\mathcal{G}$, the matrix $\mathbf{U} = [\mathbf{u}_1 \ldots \mathbf{u}_N]$ where $\mathbf{u}_i = [v_x^i([1,1]) \ldots v_x^i([M_1, M_2]) \; v_y^i([1,1]) \ldots v_y^i([M_1, M_2])]^T \in \Re^{M_1 M_2}$ is formed. Finally, the method [17] proceeds by computing the eigenvectors of the covariance matrix $\mathbf{\Sigma}_{AEP} = \frac{1}{N} \mathbf{U}\mathbf{U}^T$. These eigenvectors $\mathbf{P}$ are used in order to represent facial shape and used as a prior for SfX algorithms. In order to project a novel sample to the subspace of $\mathbf{P}$, we first transform the test normal field $\mathcal{G}$ and $\tilde{\mathbf{n}}(\mathbf{x})$ into $\mathbf{u}$ and then project using $\mathbf{b} = \mathbf{P}^T \mathbf{u}$.

2.2   Principal Geodesic Analysis

PGA is another statistical analysis method suitable for data that do not naturally lie in a Euclidean space. In standard PCA, the lower-dimensional subspaces form a linear subspace in which the data lies. In PGA, this notion is replaced by a geodesic submanifold. In other words, while each principal axis in PCA is a straight line, in PGA each principal axis is a geodesic curve. In the spherical case this corresponds to a circle. PGA utilizes the so-called log and exponential transforms in order to map the normals, that originally lie in a unit sphere, to a space where computing linear variations from the eigenanalysis of a covariance matrix could be meaningful.

In order to formulate PGA first we need to define the exponential and log maps on the sphere and a mean representation of the normals at x. Let $\nu \in T_n\mathcal{S}^2$ be a vector on the tangent plane to $\mathcal{S}^2$ at $\eta \in \mathcal{S}^2$ and $\nu \neq 0$. The exponential map of ν, denoted by $\text{Exp}_\eta(\nu)$, is the point on $\mathcal{S}^2$ along the geodesic in the direction of ν at distance $\|\nu\|$ from η. The log map is the inverse transform of the exponential map, that is $\text{Log}_\eta(\text{Exp}_\eta(\nu)) = \nu$. The geodesic distance between two points $\eta_1 \in \mathcal{S}^2$ and $\eta_2 \in \mathcal{S}^2$ can be expressed in terms of the log map, i.e. $d(\eta_1, \eta_2) = \|\text{Log}_{\eta_1}(\eta_2)\|$.

Instead of computing the mean of spherical directional data in [9,18], PGA finds the intrinsic mean, or the so-called spherical median $\mu = [\mu(x)]$ using the Exp and Log mappings. The point μ cannot be found analytically and a gradient descent procedure was used. For details on the computation of the intrinsic mean and the spherical median, the interested reader may refer to [9].

Having computed the spherical median μ it was shown that principal geodesics can be approximated by applying linear PCA on the vectors $\mathbf{u}_\mu = [\nu_\mu(1,1)^T \ldots \nu_\mu(M_1, M_2)^T]^T \in \Re^{2M_1M_2}$ where $\nu_\mu(x) = \text{Log}_{\mu(x)}(n_i(x)) \in \Re^2$. After the transformation of the training set $\mathcal{G}$ into the matrix $\mathbf{U} = [\mathbf{u}_\mu^1 \ldots \mathbf{u}_\mu^N]$ and then we compute the principal components of $\Sigma_{PGA} = \frac{1}{N}\mathbf{U}\mathbf{U}^T$. A normal field of a novel sample $\mathbf{G}$ is transformed using Log_μ into $\mathbf{u}_\mu$ and then projected into the subspace $\mathbf{b} = \mathbf{P}^T\mathbf{u}_\mu$.

2.3   AAPCA: PCA of Azimuth Angles of Normals

The proposed PCA of azimuth angles of normals, which we call Azimuth Angle Principal Component Analysis (AAPCA) has been inspired by the use of a complex PCA of image gradient orientations for performing 2D face recognition robust to occlusions and illuminations [19]. In [19] the distribution of differences of gradient orientations between dissimilar images has been studied and it was shown, with extensive experiments, that this distribution approximately matches a uniform distribution in $[0, 2\pi)$. It was empirically shown that local orientation mismatches caused by outliers can be also well-described by a uniform distribution which, under some mild assumptions, is canceled out by applying the the cosine kernel. The use of cosine kernel then inspired a complex circular PCA. In the following, we show how this concept can be applied for the case of the azimuth angles of normals. To our knowledge, this is the first time that these concepts are introduced for 3D face recognition.

Let us first define the cosine-based dissimilarity measure between two vectors of azimuth angles $\phi_i = [\phi_i(1,1) \ldots \phi_i(M_1, M2)]^T$ and $\phi_j = [\phi_j(1,1) \ldots \phi_j(M_1, M2)]^T$ as:

$$d^2(\phi_i, \phi_j) \triangleq \sum_x \{1 - \cos[\phi_i(x) - \phi_j(x)]\} = \frac{1}{2}\left\|e^{j\phi_i} - e^{j\phi_j}\right\|^2, \qquad (1)$$

where $e^{j\phi_i} = [e^{j\phi_i(1)}, \ldots, e^{j\phi_i(p)}]^T$ where $e^{ja} = \cos a + \sqrt{-1}\sin a$. We define the mapping from $[0, 2\pi)^{M_1 M_2}$ to a subset of complex sphere with radius $\sqrt{M_1 M_2}$

$$\mathbf{z}_i(\phi_i) = e^{j\phi_i}. \tag{2}$$

After transforming the data we apply PCA on $\mathbf{z}_i$ [19], which we call it Azimuth Angle Principal Component Analysis (AAPCA).

3   Demonstrating the Robust Properties of AAPCA

In order to demonstrate the robustness of the proposed AAPCA we have conducted a series of experiments using artificially generated data. More specifically, we used 21 images of one of the subjects of the FRGC v2 database. Along with this set of images, we created a second one containing artificially occluded images. In particular, 20% of the images ware artificially occluded by a 3D cloth patch placed at random spatial locations (the cloth patch has been taken from one of the images of the FRGC v2 database).

For both the original and the corrupted set, we applied standard ℓ_2 PCA on the depth images, PGA and AEP-PCA on the normals, and the proposed AAPCA. Then, we reconstructed the depth, the normals and the azimuth angles using the first 4 principal components of the employed ℓ_2 PCA, AEP-PCA, PGE, and AAPCA, respectively. Fig. 1 illustrates the quality of reconstruction for one example. The first row of Fig. 1 shows the original images of (from left to right) depth, the first two components of the normals and the azimuth angle. The second row of Fig. 1 shows (from left to right) the corresponding occluded images (by the piece of cloth). The third row of Fig. 1 shows the reconstruction of the images in the first row using the 4 principal components of the non-corrupted subspaces. That is, the first image in the third row shows the reconstruction of the non-occluded depth image (the first image in the first row) using the 4 principal components of ℓ_2 PCA. Similarly, the second and third images of the third row show the reconstruction of the first two components of the normals (the second and third images in the first row) using PGA (we show only the PGA result due to space limitation, similar results obtained from AEP-PCA). Finally, the fourth image of the third row shows the reconstruction of azimuth angle using AAPCA. In a similar spirit, the last row of Fig. 1 shows the reconstruction of the occluded set (second row) from the subspaces learned from the corrupted set. For this case, as we may see the reconstruction results, *except for the case of the proposed AAPCA*, suffer from artifacts.

This result is well justified by looking at the first 4 principal components of each method obtained for both the original and the occluded scenarios. For the latter case, ideally, a robust method would produce eigenvectors that match as closely as possible the ones obtained from the former (original) case. As Fig. 2 shows, this is not the case however for ℓ_2 PCA using depth and PGA. More specifically, in this figure, the first and third row shows the subspace generated by the original images while the second and fourth row shows the subspace generated by the occluded data set. We may observe that in both methods, occlusions result in corrupted subspace. 2 shows also the results of the proposed AAPCA. From the sixth row, it is evident that the principal subspace appears to be artifact-free and therefore dis-occlusion is possible.

We also evaluated the robust performance of AAPCA quantitatively and compared it with that of PCA on depth values, AEP, and PGA. Because these methods operate on different domains, we used a performance measure which does not depend on the specific domain. More specifically, for each of these methods, we computed a measure of total similarity between the principal subspace for the noise-free case $\mathbf{U}_{\text{noise-free}}$ and the principal subspace for the noisy case $\mathbf{U}_{\text{noisy}}$ as follows:

$$Q = \sum_{i=1}^{k} \sum_{j=1}^{k} \cos \alpha_{ij}, \tag{3}$$

where α_{ij} is the angle between each of the k eigenvectors defining the principal components of $\mathbf{U}_{\text{noise-free}}$ and each one of $\mathbf{U}_{\text{noisy}}$ [13]. The value Q lies between k (coincident spaces) and 0 (orthogonal spaces) [13]. The mean Q values over 20 repetitions of the experiment (random placement of the occlusion) and for all tested methods are depicted in Fig. 3(a). The mean values of Q shows that the proposed AAPCA is far more robust that all the other tested methods.

Finally, we evaluated the recognition performance of our algorithm for the case of increasing synthetic occlusions. We used a set of 100 images of 50 persons from the FRGC v2 database and separated it into two sets. Each set contains one image from all 50 persons. All images of the second set (considered as the test set) were artificially occluded by a cloth patch of increasing size. Fig. 3(b) shows the best recognition rate achieved by all tested methods as a function of the percentage of occlusion. As we may observe, our method features by far the most robust performance with a recognition rate over 80% even when the percentage of occlusion is about 50%.

4   Experimental Results

4.1   FRGC V2

We used the FRGC v2 3D face database [15] for 3D face recognition experiments. The database contains 3D face scans acquired using a Minolta 910 laser scanner that produces range images with a resolution of 640×480 in pixels. Results on the database are often summarized by the verification rate (VR) at the point of receiver operating characteristic (ROC) curve where false accept rate (FAR) is equal to 0.1%. We conducted two experiments. In the first one, we fitted an annotated pre-segmented model in the data [3]. In the second one, we simply aligned the data using the eye coordinates provided by the meta-data of FRGC. The only preprocessing applied was a simple median filter on the depth data. In both types we report the VR at FAR=0.1% for the ROC III (the interested reader for more details on the ROC III may refer in [12,20]).

The best results achieved in the ROC III for all the tested methods and the state-of-the-art in 3D face recognition literature are summarized in Table 1 (the results of the other methods are directly taken from the corresponding papers). For the standard protocol test ROC III mask of FRGC v2, we obtained verification rates of around 97.4% in the first type of experiment where we fitted an annotated model. This result has been achieved by using the proposed manifold learning approach of the azimuth angles. This result is directly comparable to the best published results in ROC III.

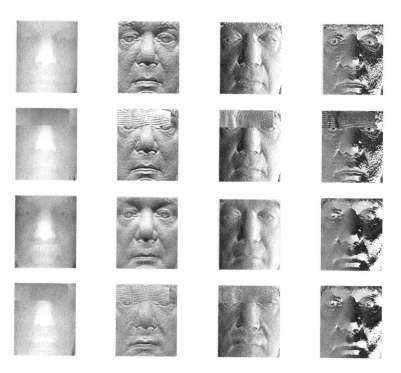

Fig. 1. Quality of reconstruction for ℓ_2 PCA, PGA, and AAPCA. **First row:** the original images of (from left to right) depth, the first two components of the normals and the azimuth angle. **Second row:** (from left to right) the corresponding occluded images (by the piece of cloth). **Third row:** the reconstruction of the images in the first row using the 4 principal components of the non-corrupted subspaces. The first image in the third row shows the reconstruction of the non-occluded depth image (the first image in the first row) using the 4 principal components of ℓ_2 PCA. Similarly, the second and third images of the third row show the reconstruction of the first two components of the normals (the second and third images in the first row) using PGA . Finally, the fourth image of the third row shows the reconstruction of azimuth angle using AAPCA. **Fourth row:** the reconstruction of the occluded set (second row) from the subspaces learned from the corrupted set. For this case, as we may see the reconstruction results, *except for the case of the proposed AAPCA*, suffer from artifacts.

In the second experiment, where little preprocessing was applied, the proposed method achieved about 85% VR at 0.1% FAR. This VR is quite good if consider that this result can be achieved in less than 0.1 msec per match, while the computational time of fitting a model is on the order of minutes [12,3] in a powerful desktop.

4.2   Photoface Database

The Photoface database consists of a total of 1.839 sessions of 261 subjects and a total of 7.356 images. In the verification protocol we applied the probe (or client set) defined by 126 persons. One image is used for training while the second is used for testing

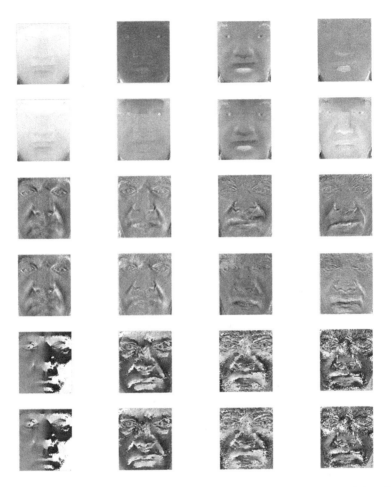

Fig. 2. The 4 principal components of ℓ_2 norm PCA on depth, **First row:** Original data, **Second row:** Corrupted data. The 4 principal components of PGA, **Third row:** Original data, **Fourth row:** Corrupted data. The 4 principal components of the proposed AAPCA, **Fifth row:** Original data, **Sixth row:** Corrupted data.

Table 1. Verification Rate for FAR=0.1% in ROC III

	Without Data Pre-processing	With Data Pre-processing
Kakadiaris et al. [12]	-	97.0%
Wang et al. [20]	-	98.04%
AAPCA	85.0%	97.4%
ℓ_2 PCA	54.2%	91.4%
PGE	68.3%	93.4%
AEP-PCA	68.3%	93.4%

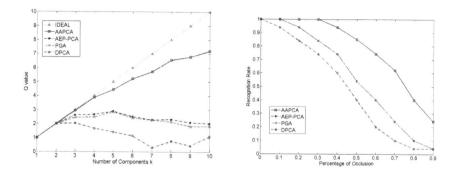

Fig. 3. (a) The Q values obtained for all methods as a function of the number of principal components, (b) Recognition rates for all methods as a function of the percentage of occlusion

client claims. The remaining 135 people in the database, with one image per person, are considered to be impostors. In order to produce the normal field, standard four lights PS was applied with no-preprocessing.

Since, the verification protocol offers only one image for training we applied only PCA-based algorithms. The best Equal Error Rate (EER) for all tested methods are summarized in Table 2. The proposed AAPCA achieved verification performance improvement of more than 40%.

Table 2. EER for the Photoface database

Methods	AEP-PCA	PGA	AAPCA
EER	8.3%	8.1%	4.9%

5   Conclusions

We introduced a new concept: PCA of 3D mesh normal orientations. Our framework is as simple as standard ℓ_2 PCA, yet much more powerful for efficient subspace-based data representation. Central to our analysis is the distribution of mesh normal orientation differences and the cosine kernel which provide us a consistent way to measure mesh dissimilarity. We showed how this dissimilarity measure can be naturally used to formulate a robust version of PCA. We demonstrated some of the favorable properties of our framework for the application of 3D face recognition. Extensions of our scheme span a wide range of theoretical topics and applications; from statistical machine learning and clustering to 3D object recognition.

References

1. Barsky, S., Petrou, M.: The 4-source photometric stereo technique for three-dimensional surfaces in the presence of highlights and shadows. IEEE T-PAMI 25(10), 1239–1252 (2003)
2. Berretti, S., Del Bimbo, A., Pala, P.: 3D face recognition using isogeodesic stripes. IEEE T-PAMI 32(12), 2162–2177 (2010)

3. Blanz, V., Scherbaum, K., Seidel, H.: Fitting a morphable model to 3D scans of faces. In: ICCV, pp. 1–8 (2007)
4. Bowyer, K., Chang, K., Flynn, P.: A survey of approaches and challenges in 3D and multi-modal 3d+ 2D face recognition. CVIU 101(1), 1–15 (2006)
5. Bronstein, A., Bronstein, M., Kimmel, R.: Expression-invariant representations of faces. IEEE T-IP 16(1), 188–197 (2007)
6. Chang, K., Bowyer, K., Flynn, P.: Multiple nose region matching for 3D face recognition under varying facial expression. IEEE T-PAMI, 1695–1700 (2006)
7. Faltemier, T., Bowyer, K., Flynn, P.: A region ensemble for 3-D face recognition. IEEE T-IFS 3(1), 62–73 (2008)
8. Fisher, R.: Dispersion on a sphere. Proceedings of the Royal Society of London. Series A. Mathematical and Physical Sciences 217(1130), 295–305 (1953)
9. Fletcher, P., Lu, C., Pizer, S., Joshi, S.: Principal geodesic analysis for the study of nonlinear statistics of shape. IEEE T-MI 23(8), 995–1005 (2004)
10. Foley, J.: Computer graphics: principles and practice. Addison-Wesley Professional (1996)
11. Gokberk, B., Dutagaci, H., Ulas, A., Akarun, L., Sankur, B.: Representation plurality and fusion for 3-D face recognition. IEEE T-SMCS, Part B 38(1), 155–173 (2008)
12. Kakadiaris, I.A., Passalis, G., Toderici, G., Murtuza, N., Lu, Y., Karampatziakis, N., Theoharis, T.: Recognition in the presence of facial expressions: An annotated deformable model approach. IEEE T-PAMI 29(4), 640–649 (2007)
13. Krzanowski, W.: Between-groups comparison of principal components. Journal of the American Statistical Association, 703–707 (1979)
14. Passalis, G., Perakis, P., Theoharis, T., Kakadiaris, I.: Using facial symmetry to handle pose variations in real-world 3D face recognition. IEEE T-PAMI 33(10), 1938–1951 (2011)
15. Phillips, P.J., Flynn, P., Scruggs, T., Bowyer, K.W., Chang, J., Hoffman, K., Marques, J., Min, J., Worek, W.: Overview of the face recognition grand challenge. In: CVPR, pp. 947–954 (2005)
16. Samir, C., Srivastava, A., Daoudi, M.: Three-dimensional face recognition using shapes of facial curves. IEEE T-PAMI 28(11), 1858–1863 (2006)
17. Smith, W., Hancock, E.: Recovering facial shape using a statistical model of surface normal direction. IEEE T-PAMI 28(12), 1914–1930 (2006)
18. Smith, W., Hancock, E.: Facial shape-from-shading and recognition using principal geodesic analysis and robust statistics. IJCV 76(1), 71–91 (2008)
19. Tzimiropoulos, G., Zafeiriou, S., Pantic, M.: Subspace learning from image gradient orientations. IEEE T-PAMI (accepted for publication, 2012)
20. Wang, Y., Liu, J., Tang, X.: Robust 3d face recognition by local shape difference boosting. IEEE T-PAMI 32(10), 1858–1870 (2010)

Coupled Marginal Fisher Analysis
for Low-Resolution Face Recognition

Stephen Siena, Vishnu Naresh Boddeti, and B.V.K. Vijaya Kumar

Carnegie Mellon University, Electrical and Computer Engineering,
5000 Forbes Avenue, Pittsburgh, Pennsylvania, USA 15213
ssiena@andrew.cmu.edu, naresh@cmu.edu, kumar@ece.cmu.edu

Abstract. Many scenarios require that face recognition be performed at conditions that are not optimal. Traditional face recognition algorithms are not best suited for matching images captured at a low-resolution to a set of high-resolution gallery images. To perform matching between images of different resolutions, this work proposes a method of learning two sets of projections, one for high-resolution images and one for low-resolution images, based on local relationships in the data. Subsequent matching is done in a common subspace. Experiments show that our algorithm yields higher recognition rates than other similar methods.

1 Introduction

Face recognition is a prevalent technology, with a wide range of applications in the public and private sectors. This is facilitated by the dramatic improvements to recognition systems in the past twenty years. Face recognition can be reliable when images are captured under controlled conditions.

Difficulties may arise in unconstrained environments where quality images are not easily collected. Oftentimes, these environments involve subjects that are uncooperative or unaware that an image is being captured. In some scenarios, it can be desirable to photograph subjects without their active participation or knowledge, such as in surveillance videos or when the subject is at a longer distance from the camera.

In these cases where the image acquisition environment is not ideal, captured faces can have a much lower resolution than faces captured in a controlled setting. Faces captured at a low resolution provide a challenge for recognition algorithms that rely on traditional feature extraction; such features can be impossible to compute on small images where facial features are represented by only a few pixels. The previously mentioned problems make it challenging to compare low-resolution (LR) images captured at testing to high-resolution (HR) images, as the LR and HR images do not share a common feature representation.

This problem has recently received increasing attention in the biometrics community. While naïve methods for matching LR images to HR images have been available for some time, algorithms tailored to LR face recognition have begun to emerge. This work introduces Coupled Marginal Fisher Analysis (CMFA), a

A. Fusiello et al. (Eds.): ECCV 2012 Ws/Demos, Part II, LNCS 7584, pp. 240–249, 2012.

new algorithm that learns projections that map HR images and LR images to a common subspace. We find projections by extending the principles of Marginal Fisher Analysis (MFA) [1], an effective linear projection method for images of the same resolution. The formulation is closest to Simultaneous Discriminant Analysis (SDA) [2], but does not make the same assumptions about how the data is distributed in the subspace. While SDA is optimal for Gaussian distributions, CMFA learns projections based on the local neighborhoods of data samples, and makes no assumptions about the global data distribution in the subspace.

Most existing methods for LR face recognition operate in the scenario where the training and testing classes are distinct. SDA and other techniques have been demonstrated to operate well in such scenarios [3], [4]. These techniques are good at modeling the relation between HR and LR images that can be extended to unseen subjects. In this process, these methods try to model the blur function between HR and LR images, but do not account for class specific details. However, in certain supervised settings, such as identifying people on a watch list, we can afford to train on the class of images used in testing. Tuning the learned projections to model class specific features along with the image formation operation is expected to result in better classification performance. Further, in this scenario, learning these projections taking advantage of the local neighborhoods of the data samples is beneficial. This is the motivation for CMFA.

2   Related Work

This work addresses the matter of matching face images of different resolutions. When pixels are used as the feature representation of the face, images of different resolutions have feature vectors of different lengths. In this section, we discuss different approaches to transforming images so that all data samples have a feature vector of the same size.

A simple approach to matching LR probe images is to reduce the size of the gallery images. Once gallery images are downsampled, traditional linear projection methods for face recognition, including Principal Component Analysis (PCA) [5], [6], Linear Discriminant Analysis (LDA) [7], and MFA [1], can be used. While these approaches can be effective for comparing images of the same resolution, downsampling the gallery images needlessly discards information in the data.

The opposite approach is to increase the resolution of the probe images. Performing some form of super-resolution makes the probe images the same dimensionality as the gallery images, and standard single resolution methods can once again be used. Simple methods such as bilinear or bicubic interpolation do not require any training. Other super-resolution methods can be trained to learn face priors [8] or the relationship between high and low-resolution images [9]. These approaches can be effective for reconstructing HR images, and while they can produce visually appealing results, they often lack the high frequency components of true HR images to be very effective for recognition tasks.

Finally, methods that truly attempt to match images of different resolutions have emerged. Hennings-Yeoman et al. present a method of super-resolution that simultaneously includes feature extraction to guide the process towards recognition instead of only reconstruction [10]. The methods closest to our proposed algorithm map images from both the high and low-resolutions to a common subspace. Li et al. learn a set of projections for each resolution using Coupled Mapping, and also use a penalty matrix to preserve local relationships [3]. Zhou et al. proposed Simultaneous Discriminant Analysis (SDA) to learn two sets of projections in a similar way while adding within-class scatter and between-class scatter to the objective function, much like LDA in the single resolution case [2]. Biswas et al. map images to a common subspace such that the distances between HR and LR images approximate the distances between two HR images [4].

3   Coupled Marginal Fisher Analysis

3.1   Problem Statement

Assume we have a gallery of HR images $\mathbf{H} = [h_1, h_2, \ldots, h_N]$, $h_i \in \Re^M$, where N is the number of gallery images and M is the feature dimension. Provided with each gallery image h_i is a class label π_i. Given a m-dimensional LR probe image x, where $m << M$, we want to assign it to class

$$\pi_i \text{ where } i = \arg\min_i d(f_h(h_i), f_l(x)), \tag{1}$$

where $d(\cdot, \cdot)$ is a distance metric and $f_h(\cdot)$ and $f_l(\cdot)$ are functions that map HR and LR images to a common subspace. If $f_h(\cdot)$ and $f_l(\cdot)$ are sets of linear projections, then Eq. 1 can be rewritten as

$$\pi_i \text{ where } i = \arg\min_i d(\mathbf{P}_H h_i, \mathbf{P}_L x), \tag{2}$$

where $\mathbf{P}_H$ and $\mathbf{P}_L$ are $\hat{m} \times M$ and $\hat{m} \times m$ matrices, respectively. The distance function $d(\cdot, \cdot)$ is therefore computed on $\hat{m}$-dimensional data, where $\hat{m} \leq m$. Euclidean distance is chosen for this work.

When learning $\mathbf{P}_H$ and $\mathbf{P}_L$, we recognize that we want $d(\mathbf{P}_H h_i, \mathbf{P}_L x)$ to be small when x belongs to the same class as h_i, and large otherwise. Therefore, our objective function is

$$J(\mathbf{P}_H, \mathbf{P}_L) = \min \frac{\sum_{\pi_i = \pi_j} \|\mathbf{P}_H h_i - \mathbf{P}_L l_j\|_2^2 w_{ij}}{\sum_{\pi_i \neq \pi_j} \|\mathbf{P}_H h_i - \mathbf{P}_L l_j\|_2^2 w_{ij}^P}, \tag{3}$$

where $\mathbf{L} = [l_1, l_2, \ldots, l_N]$ is the set of LR training images. In the absence of LR training images, HR training images can be downsampled and blurred instead. $\mathbf{W}$ and $\mathbf{W}^P$ represent intrinsic and penalty adjacency matrices, respectively, that weight image pairs to be emphasized when learning $\mathbf{P}_H$ and $\mathbf{P}_L$. For more discussion about these matrices, refer to [1]. The definitions for these matrices used in this work are provided in the next section.

If we assume that $w_{ij} = 0$ if $\pi_i \neq \pi_j$ and $w_{ij}^P = 0$ if $\pi_i = \pi_j$, then Eq. 3 can be rewritten as

$$J(\mathbf{P}_H, \mathbf{P}_L) = \\ \min \frac{Tr(\mathbf{P}_H^T \mathbf{HD}^H \mathbf{H}^T \mathbf{P}_H + \mathbf{P}_L^T \mathbf{LD}^L \mathbf{L}^T \mathbf{P}_L - \mathbf{P}_H^T \mathbf{HW}^T \mathbf{L}^T \mathbf{P}_L - \mathbf{P}_L^T \mathbf{LWH}^T \mathbf{P}_H)}{Tr(\mathbf{P}_H^T \mathbf{HD}^{\mathbf{P}H} \mathbf{H}^T \mathbf{P}_H + \mathbf{P}_L^T \mathbf{LD}^{\mathbf{P}L} \mathbf{L}^T \mathbf{P}_L - \mathbf{P}_H^T \mathbf{HW}^{\mathbf{P}T} \mathbf{L}^T \mathbf{P}_L - \mathbf{P}_L^T \mathbf{LW}^{\mathbf{P}} \mathbf{H}^T \mathbf{P}_H)} \tag{4}$$

where $\mathbf{D}^L$, $\mathbf{D}^H$, $\mathbf{D}^{\mathbf{P}L}$, and $\mathbf{D}^{\mathbf{P}H}$ are diagonal matrices defined as $d_{ii}^L = \sum_j w_{ij}$, $d_{jj}^H = \sum_i w_{ij}$, $d^{\mathbf{P}L}_{ii} = \sum_j w_{ij}^P$, and $d^{\mathbf{P}H}_{jj} = \sum_i w_{ij}^P$. $Tr(\cdot)$ represents the trace operator. Eq. 4 can be rewritten as

$$J(\mathbf{P}_H, \mathbf{P}_L) = \min \frac{Tr(\mathbf{P}^T \mathbf{XAX}^T \mathbf{P})}{Tr(\mathbf{P}^T \mathbf{XBX}^T \mathbf{P})}, \tag{5}$$

where

$$\mathbf{P} = \begin{bmatrix} \mathbf{P}_L \\ \mathbf{P}_H \end{bmatrix}, \mathbf{X} = \begin{bmatrix} \mathbf{L} & \mathbf{0} \\ \mathbf{0} & \mathbf{H} \end{bmatrix}, \mathbf{A} = \begin{bmatrix} \mathbf{D}^L & -\mathbf{W} \\ -\mathbf{W}^T & \mathbf{D}^H \end{bmatrix}, \text{and } \mathbf{B} = \begin{bmatrix} \mathbf{D}^{\mathbf{P}L} & -\mathbf{W}^P \\ -\mathbf{W}^{\mathbf{P}T} & \mathbf{D}^{\mathbf{P}H} \end{bmatrix}. \tag{6}$$

We can compute $\tilde{\mathbf{A}} = \mathbf{XAX}^T$ and $\tilde{\mathbf{B}} = \mathbf{XBX}^T$, and substituting these into Eq. 5 yields

$$J(\mathbf{P}_H, \mathbf{P}_L) = \min \frac{Tr(\mathbf{P}^T \tilde{\mathbf{A}} \mathbf{P})}{Tr(\mathbf{P}^T \tilde{\mathbf{B}} \mathbf{P})}, \tag{7}$$

which can be turned into the generalized eigenvalue problem,

$$\tilde{\mathbf{A}} \mathbf{P} = \lambda \tilde{\mathbf{B}} \mathbf{P} \tag{8}$$

3.2 Computing W and $\mathbf{W}^{\mathbf{P}}$

MFA. MFA is a discriminative projection learning algorithm designed to be effective on data irrespective of the distribution of each class [1]. On the other hand, LDA is designed to be optimal when each individual class follows a Gaussian distribution, but will not be as effective on non-Gaussian data classes. As discussed in [1], MFA does not encode global relationships between classes into the intrinsic and penalty adjacency matrices. Instead, MFA encodes the intraclass compactness and interclass separability with local relationships. The adjacency matrices are encoded using nearest neighbors as follows:

$$w_{ij} = \begin{cases} 1, \text{if } i \in N_{k_1}^+(j) \text{ or } j \in N_{k_1}^+(i) \\ 0, else. \end{cases} \tag{9}$$

$$w_{ij}^P = \begin{cases} 1, \text{if } (i, j) \in P_{k_2}^+(\pi_i) \text{ or } (i, j) \in P_{k_2}^+(\pi_j) \\ 0, else. \end{cases} \tag{10}$$

$N_{k_1}^+(i)$ represents the set of the k_1 nearest neighbors of x_i from the same class. c_i represents the class label of x_i, and $P_{k_2}^+(\pi_i)$ represents the set of the k_2 nearest pairs among the set $\{(i,j), i \in \pi_i, j \notin \pi_i\}$. In essence, MFA seeks to project data into a subspace so that a particular data sample is projected close to its local neighborhood from the same class. At the same time, it attempts to maximize the distance between the pairs of data from different classes that were originally the closest together. Note that with this formulation, MFA has two parameters which must be learned, k_1 and k_2.

CMFA. CMFA uses similar rules for defining $\mathbf{W}$ and $\mathbf{W^P}$. Initially, the same rules were used, and nearest neighbors were computed using the Euclidean distance of HR images. Tests showed that a linear combination of the Euclidean distance of HR images and LR images had a negligible effect on the nearest neighbors when the LR images were generated from corresponding HR images.

One change that was tested and retained after stronger performance was the rule for defining $\mathbf{W^P}$. We tried forming $\mathbf{W^P}$ by finding the nearest neighbors between classes of each data sample instead of the closest pairs between classes, so the penalty adjacency graph is computed as follows,

$$w_{ij}^P = \begin{cases} 1, \text{ if } i \in N_{k_2}^-(j) \text{ or } j \in N_{k_2}^-(i) \\ 0, \, else. \end{cases} \quad (11)$$

where $N_{k_2}^-(i)$ represent the of the k_2 nearest neighbors of x_i from a different class.

3.3   Regularization

Often is it desirable to add in a regularization factor when learning projections. If we consider Eq. 5, we consider that regularization can be added as follows,

$$J(\mathbf{P}_H, \mathbf{P}_L) = \min \frac{Tr(\mathbf{P}^T \mathbf{X A X}^T \mathbf{P})}{Tr(\mathbf{P}^T \mathbf{X(B + \alpha I) X}^T \mathbf{P})}, \quad (12)$$

where $\mathbf{I}$ is the identity matrix, and α is the regularization constant. If regularization is included, the derivation of the eigenvalue problem is no different, since the sum of $\mathbf{B} + \alpha\mathbf{I}$ is known.

4   Experiments

4.1   General Testing Protocols

We compare CMFA to SDA and MFA. SDA is a coupled mapping and learns projections for HR and LR probe images at the same time. On the other hand, MFA must be learned at a single dimension. Results labeled 'MFA' is a baseline using HR gallery and probe images. 'MFA-LR' uses LR gallery and probe images. Results for 'MFA-BL' use HR gallery images and learns HR projections, and

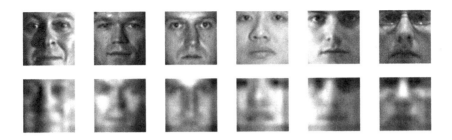

Fig. 1. HR and corresponding LR images from PIE (left 3 columns) and Multi-PIE (right 3 columns)

then uses LR probe images that are upsampled to the HR dimensionality using bi-linear interpolation.

Both MFA and CMFA require two parameters, k_1 and k_2. There is no clear method for setting these values, so a grid search is performed to find which values of k_1 and k_2 to use for each test. Similarly, different values for the regularization constant α are tested for all tested algorithms. We tested the algorithms with values of $\alpha = [10^{-6}, 10^{-5}, 10^{-4}]$, and found that in nearly all cases, $\alpha = 10^{-5}$ was optimal for the algorithms used.

In many cases, using as many projections as is possible to learn does not provide the best results. Because the 12×12 LR images used have 144 feature dimensions, we report the single best result from using $[10, 20, 30, ..., 140]$ projections.

Following projection learning, matching of probe images is done by finding the Euclidean distance nearest neighbor. Performance is measured by rank-1 identification rate, which equals the percentage of probe images that find a true match using the nearest neighbor classification.

All reported results are the average of 20 trials.

4.2   PIE / Multi-PIE

For testing we use the CMU Pose, Illumination, and Expression (PIE) database [11], and the CMU Multi-PIE database [12]. We take a part of the PIE dataset containing frontal images of 66 subjects with varying illumination, such that each subject has 21 images taken in one session. Multi-PIE addresses some concerns of the PIE dataset, and includes 337 subjects, with multiple sessions (up to 5) for most subjects. Again, frontal images with a neutral expression are used. Each of the 337 subjects has between 20 and 100 images (20 per session). Images in both datasets are registered based on eye locations. For all tests, HR images are 48×48, and in lieu of genuine LR images, they are generated by downsampling and blurring the HR images to 12×12 (see Fig. 1).

The data is split such that each subject has an equal number of images in the gallery, and the remaining images become the probe set. The gallery images are then used for training. For tests on PIE, the best parameters for CMFA

Table 1. Rank 1 identification rates when training on a set of gallery images, and testing on LR and HR probe images. The number in parentheses for Data is the number of gallery images per subject. The number in parentheses for each reported performance level is the standard deviation over 20 runs.

Data	LR Probe				HR Probe		
	SDA	CMFA	MFA-LR	MFA-BL	SDA	CMFA	MFA
PIE	75.07	78.34	**78.58**	45.13	78.68	**84.33**	83.82
(2)	(2.26)	(2.56)	(2.85)	(6.11)	(2.28)	(2.39)	(2.42)
PIE	89.87	92.66	**93.61**	38.50	92.26	**94.44**	93.30
(4)	(2.14)	(1.48)	(1.41)	(4.93)	(2.03)	(1.28)	(1.53)
PIE	95.30	97.83	**98.17**	35.10	97.45	**98.47**	98.07
(6)	(1.29)	(0.77)	(0.69)	(5.37)	(0.87)	(0.65)	(0.72)
Multi-PIE	69.71	**71.61**	65.29	9.53	74.18	**75.48**	72.08
(2)	(0.93)	(0.81)	(1.10)	(1.45)	(1.00)	(0.99)	(1.25)
Multi-PIE	94.00	**94.46**	91.80	3.58	**96.32**	96.03	87.54
(6)	(0.44)	(0.46)	(0.45)	(1.03)	(0.31)	(0.46)	(0.61)
Multi-PIE	96.46	**96.80**	95.16	2.90	**98.19**	98.13	93.85
(10)	(1.32)	(1.16)	(1.32)	(0.66)	(0.77)	(0.77)	(1.18)

was $k_1 = 2$ and k_2 set to a value between 5 and 25. For Multi-PIE, $k_1 = C$ where C equals to the number of training images per class, and k_2 was equal to roughly C^3. Small changes in the value of k_2 do not have a significant impact on performance.

Table 1 shows that CMFA and MFA both outperform SDA on the PIE dataset, and CMFA is the best performing algorithm on the Multi-PIE dataset. The table shows similar trends when testing HR probe images, but it is interesting to note that CMFA and MFA-LR both outperform the baseline MFA in some cases. Fig. 2 shows that on the Multi-PIE dataset it is not necessary to learn many projections to achieve the highest possible performance on LR probe images.

CMFA's better performance compared to SDA indicates that CMFA does a better job discriminating between classes it trains on. This is consistent with the relative performance between MFA and LDA [1].

While the difference between CMFA and SDA is approximately one to two standard deviations, given a particular amount of training, Fig. 3 shows that while the performance does vary between the 20 trials, the relative performance is much more consistent. This indicates that while the selected gallery has an impact on the performance of each algorithm, the advantage of CMFA is not tied to the particular images in the gallery. A paired t-test comparing CMFA and SDA showed that $p < .0001$ for each experiment setting reported in Table 1, indicating a significant difference in their respective performances.

4.3   LR Feature Representation

One of the benefits of coupled mapping is that it can be used for effective LR face matching when images are too small for most feature extraction techniques

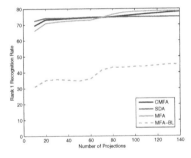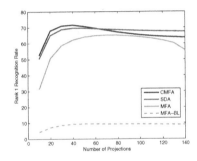

Fig. 2. Performance on LR probe images, with 2 gallery/training images per subject on the PIE dataset (left) and Multi-PIE dataset (right)

used in face recognition. Still, it is possible that some feature representations can be effective for lower resolution images.

While the previous results are based on using the pixels in the original images, we also consider two feature extraction techniques which are designed with the goal of illumination invariance. Simplified Local Binary Pattern (SLBP) considers the number of pixels in the 8-connected neighborhood that have a higher intensity than the pixel being considered [13]. The result for each pixel is an integer value between 0 and 8. We exclude pixels that on the edge of images that do not have an 8-connected neighborhood.

We also consider color ratio (CR) as a means of illumination invariance [14]. CR is defined as

$$I(x,y) = \frac{I(x,y)}{\mu(h(x,y))} \tag{13}$$

where $I(x,y)$ is the pixel in an image, and $h(x,y)$ is a window around $I(x,y)$. We only tested a window size of 3×3. As with SLBP, we do not compute the CR for the pixels on the edge of the image. Thus, for an $K \times K$ image, the corresponding SLBP and CR images used are $K - 2 \times K - 2$. An example of SLBP and CR can be seen in Fig. 5.

We tested these methods on the PIE dataset, using 2 training/gallery images per subject as in Section 4.2. We tested CMFA and SDA over a range of resolutions for the LR probe images, applying SLBP and CR to both the HR and LR images when using them. When testing with CMFA, we used the best parameters learned in earlier test, and did not relearn the values for the new feature representations. Results can be seen in Fig. 5. It is observed that at lower resolutions, just using the pixels is the most effective. However, as the resolution of the probe images become larger, the recognition rate when using pixels does not increase much at all, whereas both CR and SLBP features improve dramatically. Fig. 5 also shows that the as the resolution changes, the performance difference between CMFA and SDA stays nearly constant when using pixels. When using SLBP and CR, the difference between the two algorithms is much smaller.

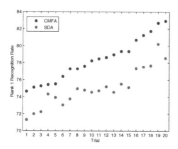
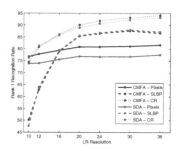

Fig. 3. Performance for each of 20 trials on PIE, using 2 training images per subject. Trials are sorted by CMFA performance.

Fig. 4. Performance of different feature representations for coupled mapping. Results are using the PIE dataset, with 2 gallery/training images per subject.

Fig. 5. Sample from PIE dataset showing the original image (left), image using Simplified LBP (center), and image using color ratio (right)

Overall, it seems that using pixels is the best of the three options at very low resolution, while color ratio helps improve performance as the probe image is a higher resolution. Finding the best feature representation for different resolutions can help systems that capture images over a range of different resolutions.

5 Conclusions

The work presents CMFA, an algorithm for performing coupled mapping to match images of different resolutions. CMFA appears to work well when it can learn from the local relationships that will be encountered in testing. CMFA thus provides an alternative solution to LR face matching that can be more desirable depending on the application. In addition, we show that some basic image processing can improve LR face recognition results. In future work we would like to more thoroughly explore different LR feature representations, as well as consider other options for learning projections with coupled mapping.

References

1. Yan, S., Xu, D., Zhang, B., Zhang, H.J., Yang, Q., Lin, S.: Graph embedding and extensions: A general framework for dimensionality reduction. IEEE Transactions on Pattern Analysis and Machine Intelligence 29, 40–51 (2007)

2. Zhou, C., Zhang, Z., Yi, D., Lei, Z., Li, S.Z.: Low-resolution face recognition via Simultaneous Discriminant Analysis. In: International Joint Conference on Biometrics (2011)

3. Li, B., Shan, S., Chen, X.: Low-resolution face recognition via coupled locality preserving mappings. IEEE Signal Processing Letters 17, 20–23 (2010)

4. Biswas, S., Bowyer, K.W., Flynn, P.J.: Multidimensional scaling for matching low-resolution face images. IEEE Transactions on Pattern Analysis and Machine Intelligence (forthcoming)

5. Sirovich, L., Kirby, M.: Low-dimensional procedure for the characterization of human faces. Journal of the Optical Society of America A 4, 519–524 (1987)

6. Turk, M., Pentland, A.: Eigenfaces for recognition. Journal of Cognitive Neuroscience 3, 71–86 (1991)

7. Belhumeur, P.N., Hespanha, J.: Eigenfaces vs. fisherfaces: Recognition using specific linear projection. IEEE Transactions on Pattern Analysis and Machine Intelligence 19, 711–720 (1997)

8. Baker, S., Kanade, T.: Hallucinating faces. In: IEEE International Conference on Automatic Face and Gesture Recognition (2000)

9. Zou, W.W.W., Yuen, P.C.: Very low resolution face recognition problem. In: IEEE International Conference on Biometrics: Theory Applications and Systems (2010)

10. Hennings-Yeoman, P.H., Baker, S., Kumar, B.V.: Simultaneous super-resolution and feature extraction for recognition of low-resolution faces. In: IEEE Conference on Computer Vision and Pattern Recognition (2008)

11. Sim, T., Baker, S., Bsat, M.: The CMU pose, illumination, and expression (PIE) database. In: IEEE International Conference on Automatic Face and Gesture Recognition (2002)

12. Gross, R., Matthews, I., Cohn, J., Kanade, T., Baker, S.: Multi-PIE. In: IEEE International Conference on Automatic Face and Gesture Recognition (2008)

13. Tao, Q., Veldhuis, R.: Illumination normalization based on simplified local binary patterns for a face verification system. In: Biometrics Symposium at The Biometrics Consortium Conference (2007)

14. Adjeroh, D.A.: On ratio-based color indexing. IEEE Transactions on Image Processing 10, 36–48 (2001)

Exploring Bag of Words Architectures in the Facial Expression Domain

Karan Sikka, Tingfan Wu, Josh Susskind, and Marian Bartlett

Machine Perception Laboratory, University of California San Diego
{ksikka,ting,josh,marni}@mplab.ucsd.edu

Abstract. Automatic facial expression recognition (AFER) has undergone substantial advancement over the past two decades. This work explores the application of bag of words (BoW), a highly matured approach for object and scene recognition to AFER. We proceed by first highlighting the reasons that makes the task for BoW differ for AFER compared to object and scene recognition. We propose suitable extensions to BoW architecture for the AFER's task. These extensions are able to address some of the limitations of current state of the art appearance-based approaches to AFER. Our BoW architecture is based on the spatial pyramid framework, augmented by multiscale dense SIFT features, and a recently proposed approach for object classification: locality-constrained linear coding and max-pooling. Combining these, we are able to achieve a powerful facial representation that works well even with linear classifiers. We show that a well designed BoW architecture can provide a performance benefit for AFER, and elements of the proposed BoW architecture are empirically evaluated. The proposed BoW approach supersedes previous state of the art results by achieving an average recognition rate of 96% on AFER for two public datasets.

1 Introduction

Automatic Facial Expression Recognition (AFER)[1,13,22,16] has been gaining momentum over the years due to its application in multiple domains such as human computer interaction, and analyzing human behavior, among others. This progress has been possible due to advancement in computer vision and machine learning, along with higher computing power.

Bag of words (BoW) models represent images as orderless collection of local features. These models have recently shown remarkable performance in multiple domains including scene recognition [11,23], object and texture categorization [5,17,27], and human activity recognition [10]. Applicability to multiple domains can be attributed to the simplicity of the BoW model along with significant research in feature extraction [18,27], codebook construction [23,9], application of fast but efficient kernels for discriminative classification [27,23], and encoding schemes [4,26]. Efficient methods for pooling and matching over spatial and temporal grids at multiple scales [10,11] has helped extend BoW to domains where spatial or temporal information is important.

A. Fusiello et al. (Eds.): ECCV 2012 Ws/Demos, Part II, LNCS 7584, pp. 250–259, 2012.

A strength that BoW brings to the table is invariance. Feature values are pooled within a specific region of space (or time) without reference to exactly where in the window the feature occurred. This gives BoW models tolerance to small perturbations in the positions of image features, making them robust to variations in the shape of a cup, for example. In contrast, facial expression is a subordinate level classification problem defined by nonrigid deformations of a basic object shape. Fundamental differences have been described between face and object recognition, in which objects can be defined by the presence of component parts with substantial tolerance to metric differences in their positions, whereas faces consist of the same parts in approximately the same relations, and detection of metric variations in a holistic representation takes on much more importance [2]. Hence the invariance structure of the facial expression task differs from those of object recognition, potentially requiring for example, information on multiple spatial scales. It therefore stands to reason that an optimal BoW architecture suited for object recognition may also differ for the AFER task.

Recently BoW has been applied to problems involving discrimination of subordinate-level categories such as flowers [17] and breeds of cats and dogs [20]. These findings further motivated us to look into BoW for the problem of facial expression recognition.

Our contribution lies in a principled exploration of BoW architectures for the AFER domain, and investigating whether the resulting BoW architecture is competitive with state-of-the-art performance for current approaches for AFER. While a small number of previous papers employed BoW for an AFER task (e.g. [14]) this is the first to present a principled exploration of BoW design in this domain. Thus a clear picture has not yet emerged of a BoW architecture best suited for the AFER domain, and how it compares to current approaches to AFER. Specifically, this paper explores BoW for an appearance-based discriminative approach to AFER. Appearance based discriminative approaches have been highly successful for face detection [25] face identification [7] and expression recognition [1] [22], and can provide person-independent recognition performance in real-time [15]. State of the art AFER performance has been shown for Gabor energy filters [1] [15], and local binary patterns (LBP) [22]. Here we compare the performance of BoW framework to state-of-the-art AFER approaches based on Gabor and LBP features.

Our **contributions** are as follows:

1. We identify inherent challenges in appearance based approaches to AFER and argue that most of these can be addressed through a suitable BoW pipeline. We highlight reasons why AFER differs from domains where BoW has been applied successfully in the past, and which would influence the architecture of our BoW model.

2. In order to address the demands of AFER task, we propose a BoW approach that combines highly discriminative Multi-Scale Dense SIFT (MSDF) features with spatial pyramid matching (SPM). To the best of our knowledge, this is the first work employing MSDF features for AFER. The spatial pyramid representation provides spatial information to BoW to maintain both

holistic and local characteristics. This is augmented with the recently proposed locality-constrained linear coding (LLC) [26] along with max-pooling, leading to a representation that is powerful even with a linear classifier.

3. We compare the BoW performance to two of the most successful algorithms for AFER: Gabor wavelets and LBP, as input to Support Vector Machines (SVM). Experiments on two public datasets demonstrate that the proposed BoW pipeline is highly effective for AFER, giving significantly better performance than approaches relying on Gabors or LBP features.

4. Experiments further demonstrate the contributions of specific components of the proposed BoW pipeline. We show that MSDF features compare favorably with Gabor and LBP features when input directly to a SVM, however a significant hike in performance is obtained by integrating them with proposed BoW architecture. We further demonstrate the advantages of employing multi-scale features, compared to single scale features, and LLC coding, compared to traditional hard coding, in our BoW pipeline.

2   Related Work

Appearance based approaches can extract features densely at every face pixel, as in gabor wavelets [1], or can pool features in certain regions of support. For instance in the case of LBP, the face is divided into regular overlapping grids [22], while for the approach in [14] features are pooled over 4 segmented facial regions around eyes, nose etc. It is possible to represent many AFER approaches through a general block-diagram as shown in Fig. 1. Strategies for each block for different methods used in this paper are given in Table. 1.

Although the Gabor energy representation possesses some shift invariance, their spatial invariance is low relative to other image features explored here. This could make them less robust to alignment errors that can result from variations such as head pose, ethnicity etc. LBP based methods achieve some invariance by employing a rectangular grid as a region of support. Selecting an apt grid pattern is a non-trivial problem for LBP based methods.

A previous paper [14] constructed a BoW representation by pooling features over 4 facial regions, which are obtained through a segmentation step. This intermediate segmentation step poses the problem of using a non-standard support region for feature pooling, and the final representation may critically depend on a good segmentation. Since the algorithm is evaluated only on a single dataset, it is unclear if the proposed segmentation works well across multiple datasets. Next, separate dictionaries were learned for each of these sub-regions, which may lack sufficient features for robust codebook construction. Moreover, the BoW representation in [14] did not achieve strong performance alone, and required the addition of pyramid histogram of gradients (PHOG) features to obtain appreciable results. This left the question open as to whether BoW itself provides coding advantages in the AFER domain. This work attempts to address this question.

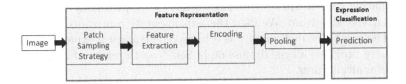

Fig. 1. General Block diagram for AFER

3   Proposed Bag of Words Approach

The AFER community follows a common practice of separating the face detection and alignment task from the task of expression recognition, factoring out rigid deformations in order to make the problem more tractable. Hence the AFER task does not typically entail invariance to transformations such as scale, translation, or in-plane rotations. The goal is to detect the appearance or texture variations in face images that result from facial expression, while allowing invariance to factors such as differences in the positions of the lip corners for a low versus high intensity smile, or differences in facial wrinkling patterns due to age or facial physiognomy, or variations due to small residual rotation and alignment errors. The invariance task therefore may be on a different scale or along different feature dimensions than for many object recognition tasks. We address these goals by exploring a BoW architecture with suitable extensions, which are mentioned in a sequential order below. The ordering adheres to the general block diagram in Fig. 1.

1. **Sampling strategy and features:** BoW represents images as collection of independent local patches. These patches can either be sampled as sparse informative points, i.e. ones extracted using various interest point detectors [5,27], or as dense patches at different locations and scales. Work in [18] pointed out that, (1) interest points based methods often saturate in performance since they can only provide limited patches, and (2) the minimum-scale of patches has a considerable influence on results because the vast majority of patches or interest points typically occur at the finest few scales. Thus, based on these findings we compute SIFT descriptors (constant orientation) densely on the image by extracting them with a stride of 2 pixels. In this paper we explore a multi-scale dense SIFT representation (MSDF) [24], which pools over multiple region sizes, retaining more spatial information at the smaller scales. Here we employed 5 different scales, defined by setting the width of the SIFT spatial bins to 4, 8, 12, 16, and 24 pixels. Empirical comparisons demonstrated that multi-scale SIFT features indeed lead to better performance than their single-scale counterpart. SIFT features have been extracted using code from author's website in [11].

2. **Codebook Construction (for encoding):** The vocabulary is constructed by quantizing SIFT descriptors randomly selected from the training images using approximate K-means clustering. This clustering approach is based on

calculating data-to-cluster distances using the Approximate Nearest Neighbor (ANN) algorithm. We used the implementation provided by authors in [4]. The size of the dictionary was set based on empirical experiments to 800. We have provided a brief discussion in Sec. 5 on the effect of vocabulary size on recognition rates.

3. **Encoding and Pooling:** The original BoW model ignores the spatial order of local descriptors. However spatial information is necessary for AFER. To address this particular limitation, we have incorporated a particular extension of BoW [11] called *spatial pyramid matching* (SPM), that has shown significant success on a number of tasks [27,20]. For our spatial pyramid representation, we partition an image into $2^l \times 2^l$ segments in different scales $l = 0, 1, 2, 3, 4$, compute the BoW histograms within these 341 segments and finally concatenate the histograms into a single feature vectors. This strategy of pooling over spatial pyramids is more structured and eliminates the need to select the right grid pattern, as was the case for LBP and the approach in [14]. Experimental results demonstrate that spatial pyramid matching contributes substantially to performance for AFER.

Recent research shows that the choice of encoding and pooling has a significant effect on the classification accuracy [4]. Hence this work employs the recently proposed LLC encoding along with max spatial pooling [26] to construct the final multi-scale representation. LLC encoding projects each descriptor to a local linear subspace spanned by some codewords by solving an optimization problem [26]. This approach is known to be more robust to local spatial translations and captures more salient properties of visual patterns as compared to the original simple histogram spatial encoding [26]. Most importantly a linear kernel is sufficient to achieve good performance with LLC encoding, thus avoiding the computational expense of applying non-linear kernels [4], as is the case with spatial histogram based encoding [11,27]. The two parameters for LLC encoding were (1) M, the number of nearest visual words to be considered, was set to 5, and (2) parameter β used in the computation of the projections was set to 10^{-4}, as done in [4].

4   Experiments

4.1   Datasets

These algorithms were evaluated on two public datasets, the Cohn-Kanade+ (CK+) [16] and Amsterdam Dynamic Facial Expression Set (ADFES) [21]. Of these, CK+ is the most widely used dataset for AFER, while ADFES as an evaluation dataset for AFER task has been introduced in this paper. The rationale behind using these two datasets is that they both consist of directed facial expressions, validated by the Facial Action Coding System (FACS).

CK+: The CK+ dataset consists of 123 subjects between the age of 18 to 50 years, of which 69% female, 81% Euro-American, 13% Afro-American, and 6% other groups. Subjects were instructed to perform a series of 23 facial displays, six of which were based on description of prototypic emotions. For our experiments, we used the 327 peak frames which had emotion labels validated by trained professionals as provided by the authors. The faces were cropped and resized as mentioned in Section 4.2. A salient feature of this dataset is that the authors have provided a standard evaluation procedure [16] so that it is possible to compare results from different works directly. The algorithms are tested on a leave-one-subject-out cross-validation experiment where an expression is classified into one of the 7 classes, namely- angry, contempt, disgust, fear, happy, sadness and surprise.

ADFES: The ADFES dataset consists of 22 subjects aged from 18 to 25 years old, of which 10 are Mediterranean and 12 are North-European, and 10 are females and 12 are males. The subjects were instructed to perform nine emotional states of which six popular *basic emotions* [8] are being used for our experiments. Again the faces were registered into 96 × 96 patches as mentioned in Section 4.2. The algorithms are evaluated on 5 fold cross-validation experiment where an expression is classified into one of the six classes

4.2 Methods

Pre-processing: Faces were detected automatically by a variant of the Viola and Jones detector [6] and normalized to 96 × 96 patches based on the location of the eyes.

The first baseline method was based on Gabor wavelets. Features were extracted using 72 Gabor filters spanning 8 orientations and 9 scales, whose parameters were selected as in [15]. The images were first convolved with each filter in the filter bank and the output magnitudes were concatenated into a feature vector. The second baseline method was LBP. Implementation of LBP features was obtained from the authors' [19] website. Normalized uniform LBP histograms were extracted with an exhaustive combination of parameters (namely neighborhood parameters (P, R), number of horizontal and vertical grids and overlap ratio between blocks) and the best results were reported. The rationale behind running the experiment with an exhaustive combination of parameters was to realize the degree to which the performance of the algorithm depends on the chosen parameters. Our experiments revealed that the best parameters for LBP were different for both datasets indicating that this method might be parameter dependent.

Classifier: As mentioned earlier a linear support vector machine (SVM) [3] was used as the classifier for the proposed BoW method as well as for the Gabor baseline. For LBP and simple BoW, SVM with a polynomial kernel of degree 2 and a histogram intersection kernel was used for consistency with previous papers employing these methods [28] [27]. To avoid over-fitting we applied a double cross-validation method. Double cross-validation is a method to estimate separate training, test, and validation set performance in small datasets. Here, the hyper-parameters for the SVM (or kernel) were obtained by selecting the parameters with best performance on a 25% subset of the training samples. For each experiment we have reported the average percentage accuracy and standard error measure.

Most of the details of the proposed BoW algorithm are described in Sec 3. Since experiments for CK+ are run in a leave-one-subject-out fashion, we chose to prevent re-clustering of data for each fold by constructing a dictionary once from samples in the ADFES dataset and using the same for each fold. This strategy also tests the generalization capability of the BoW approach, where a different dataset is used for codebook construction.

Table 1. Methods compared in this paper for AFER. All methods below the double line are based on BoW. Those above the double line are passed directly to an SVM.

Method	Pixel Sampling	Features	Encoding	Pooling Strategy
Gabor	1 Pixel	Gabor filter outputs (9 scales & 8 orient.)	No	Concatenation
LBP	1 Pixel	LBP	No	Sum-pooling over regular grids
MSDF	2 Pixel	SIFT (5 scales)	No	Concatenation
Simple BoW	2 Pixel	SIFT (5 scales)	Hard encoding	Sum-pooling over Spatial Pyramids
SS-SIFT+BoW	2 Pixel	SIFT (1 scale)	LLC	Max-pooling over Spatial Pyramids
Proposed Method (MSDF+BoW)	2 Pixels	SIFT (5 scales)	LLC	Max-pooling over Spatial Pyramids

5   Results

The performance statistics for prescribed experiments on CK+ and ADFES are shown in Table. 2. It is evident that the proposed BoW approach outperforms previous state of the art AFER approaches, Gabors and LBP, on the two recognition tasks. Moreover to the best of our knowledge these are the best publishable results for AFER on both CK+ and ADFES. This observation supports our contention that a suitable BoW architecture can indeed provide a performance benefit for AFER.

Regarding dictionary size, we found that increasing the dictionary size improved performance for small dictionary sizes, saturated at 800, and began to decrease for larger dictionary sizes. Performance started decreasing significantly at dictionary size beyond 2000.

Regarding image features, we note that raw MSDF features performed better than both Gabor and LBP on CK+, although not on ADFES. In order to support the argument that the proposed BoW architecture is responsible for boost in performance and not MSDF features alone, we extracted MSDF features as described in Section 3, concatenated all the features in an image into a single vector and passed it straight to an SVM, which is similar to that used in Gabor based methods [15]. This was compared to the same MSDF features in the proposed BoW architecture. Table. 2 shows that the proposed method contributes performance benefit beyond MSDF features alone.

Table 2. Comparison of the proposed BoW pipeline with other approaches- Gabor wavelets [15], LBP [22], MSDF consisting of vectorized MSDF features passed to a linear SVM, Simple BoW, and Single-Scale SIFT+BoW as described in Section 4.2.

DATASET	ADFES	CK+
Gabor	94.59 ± 2.61	91.81 ± 1.94
LBP	94.96 ± 1.96	82.38 ± 2.34
MSDF	92.59 ± 3.41	94.34 ± 1.62
Simple BoW	94.09 ± 2.32	92.67 ± 1.93
SS-SIFT+BoW	93.3 ± 1.13	93.28 ± 1.76
Proposed Method	**96.30 ± 1.08**	**95.85 ± 1.40**

Next, to highlight the advantage of employing multi-scale features compared to single scale features, we also ran our proposed pipeline, except with Single Scale SIFT (SS-SIFT) features instead of MSDF features. For SS-SIFT we used a spatial bin size of 4 pixels and a stride of 2 pixels. Table. 2 shows that the multiscale features in the **Proposed Method** give about a 3 percentage point advantage over the same model implemented with single scale features.

We also evaluated coding strategies. We compared the LLC encoding with max-pooling to the simple histogramming strategy [4], comprised of traditional hard quantization and sum-pooling. We refer to this as "simple BoW". By comparing the **Proposed Method** to simple BoW, we observe that selecting LLC encoding along with max pooling in our proposed method leads to consistent improvement in performance for both datasets.

The most substantial performance benefit was provided by the spatial pyramid matching. Removal of the SPM from the BoW model, eliminating all spatial information, reduced classification performance on CK+ from 95.9% to 83.1%(±2.5).

6   Conclusion

This paper explores the applications of Bags of Words, a technique highly successful in object and scene recognition community, to AFER. We first highlighted reasons that had hindered the success of BoW for AFER, and then proposed ways to tackle these issues based on recent advances in computer vision. Elements of the proposed BoW architecture were empirically evaluated.

Spatial information at multiple scales is crucial for AFER as compared to object and scene classification tasks. Hence spatial pyramid matching is recommended for the BoW architecture to preserve spatial information during matching, and we showed that performance drops substantially without it. We also discovered that multi-scale features are necessary for AFER as is the case for most object and scene categorization tasks. In particular BoW allowed us to effectively employ highly discriminative multi-scale SIFT features. We also showed that the performance benefit was not from the MSDF features alone. The BoW architecture itself contributed further to performance. Advantages of employing novel encoding and pooling strategies as compared to standard histogram of quantized descriptors was also shown for the task of AFER. The final model is a multilayered architecture with successive nonlinearities in the MSDF features, codebook, and pooling. As such, this sequence of nonlinearities bears a relationship to deep learning [12].

State of the art results on two public datasets highlight the effectiveness of this approach on AFER. In conclusion our findings support the claim that a principled BoW architecture can provide a performance benefit for the AFER task.

Acknowledgment. Support for this work was provided by NSF grant IIS-0905622. Any opinions, findings, conclusions or recommendations expressed in this material are those of the author(s) and do not necessarily reflect the views of the National Science Foundation.

References

1. Bartlett, M., Littlewort, G., Frank, M., Lainscsek, C., Fasel, I., Movellan, J.: Automatic recognition of facial actions in spontaneous expressions. Journal of Multimedia 1(6), 22–35 (2006)
2. Biederman, I., Kalocsais, P.: Neurocomputational bases of object and face recognition. Philosophical Transactions of the Royal Society of London. Series B: Biological Sciences 352(1358), 1203–1219 (1997)
3. Chang, C., Lin, C.: Libsvm: a library for support vector machines, software (2001)
4. Chatfield, K., Lempitsky, V., Vedaldi, A., Zisserman, A.: The devil is in the details: an evaluation of recent feature encoding methods. In: British Machine Vision Conference (2011)
5. Csurka, G., Dance, C., Fan, L., Willamowski, J., Bray, C.: Visual categorization with bags of keypoints. In: Workshop on Statistical Learning in Computer Vision, ECCV, vol. 1, p. 22 (2004)
6. Eckhardt, M., Fasel, I., Movellan, J.: Towards practical facial feature detection. International Journal of Pattern Recognitionand Artificial Intelligence 23(3), 379 (2009)
7. Guo, G., Li, S., Chan, K.: Support vector machines for face recognition. Image and Vision computing 19(9-10), 631–638 (2001)
8. Izard, C.: The face of emotion (1971)
9. Jurie, F., Triggs, B.: Creating efficient codebooks for visual recognition. In: Tenth IEEE International Conference on Computer Vision, ICCV 2005, vol. 1, pp. 604–610. IEEE (2005)
10. Laptev, I., Marszalek, M., Schmid, C., Rozenfeld, B.: Learning realistic human actions from movies. In: IEEE Conference on Computer Vision and Pattern Recognition, CVPR 2008, pp. 1–8. IEEE (2008)
11. Lazebnik, S., Schmid, C., Ponce, J.: Beyond bags of features: Spatial pyramid matching for recognizing natural scene categories. In: 2006 IEEE Computer Society Conference on Computer Vision and Pattern Recognition, vol. 2, pp. 2169–2178. IEEE (2006)
12. Lee, H., Grosse, R., Ranganath, R., Ng, A.: Convolutional deep belief networks for scalable unsupervised learning of hierarchical representations. In: Proceedings of the 26th Annual International Conference on Machine Learning, pp. 609–616. ACM (2009)

13. Li, S.Z., Jain, A.K., Tian, Y.-L., Kanade, T., Cohn, J.F.: Facial expression analysis. In: Handbook of Face Recognition, pp. 247–275. Springer, New York (2005)
14. Li, Z., Imai, J., Kaneko, M.: Facial-component-based bag of words and phog descriptor for facial expression recognition. In: IEEE International Conference on Systems, Man and Cybernetics, SMC 2009, pp. 1353–1358. IEEE (2009)
15. Littlewort, G., Whitehill, J., Wu, T., Fasel, I., Frank, M., Movellan, J., Bartlett, M.: The computer expression recognition toolbox (cert). In: 2011 IEEE International Conference on Automatic Face & Gesture Recognition and Workshops (FG 2011), pp. 298–305. IEEE (2011)
16. Lucey, P., Cohn, J., Kanade, T., Saragih, J., Ambadar, Z., Matthews, I.: The extended cohn-kanade dataset (ck+): A complete dataset for action unit and emotion-specified expression. In: 2010 IEEE Computer Society Conference on Computer Vision and Pattern Recognition Workshops (CVPRW), pp. 94–101. IEEE (2010)
17. Nilsback, M., Zisserman, A.: A visual vocabulary for flower classification. In: 2006 IEEE Computer Society Conference on Computer Vision and Pattern Recognition, vol. 2, pp. 1447–1454. IEEE (2006)
18. Nowak, E., Jurie, F., Triggs, B.: Sampling Strategies for Bag-of-Features Image Classification. In: Leonardis, A., Bischof, H., Pinz, A. (eds.) ECCV 2006. LNCS, vol. 3954, pp. 490–503. Springer, Heidelberg (2006)
19. Ojala, T., Pietikainen, M., Maenpaa, T.: Multiresolution gray-scale and rotation invariant texture classification with local binary patterns. IEEE Transactions on Pattern Analysis and Machine Intelligence 24(7), 971–987 (2002)
20. Parkhi, O.M., Vedaldi, A., Zisserman, A., Jawahar, C.V.: Cats and dogs. In: IEEE Conference on Computer Vision and Pattern Recognition (2012)
21. Van der Schalk, J., Hawk, S., Fischer, A., Doosje, B.: Moving faces, looking places: Validation of the amsterdam dynamic facial expression set (adfes). Emotion 11(4), 907 (2011)
22. Shan, C., Gong, S., McOwan, P.: Facial expression recognition based on local binary patterns: A comprehensive study. Image and Vision Computing 27(6), 803–816 (2009)
23. van Gemert, J.C., Geusebroek, J.-M., Veenman, C.J., Smeulders, A.W.M.: Kernel Codebooks for Scene Categorization. In: Forsyth, D., Torr, P., Zisserman, A. (eds.) ECCV 2008, Part III. LNCS, vol. 5304, pp. 696–709. Springer, Heidelberg (2008)
24. Vedaldi, A., Fulkerson, B.: Vlfeat: An open and portable library of computer vision algorithms. In: Proceedings of the International Conference on Multimedia, pp. 1469–1472. ACM (2010)
25. Viola, P., Jones, M.: Robust real-time face detection. International Journal of Computer Vision 57(2), 137–154 (2004)
26. Wang, J., Yang, J., Yu, K., Lv, F., Huang, T., Gong, Y.: Locality-constrained linear coding for image classification. In: 2010 IEEE Conference on Computer Vision and Pattern Recognition (CVPR), pp. 3360–3367. IEEE (2010)
27. Zhang, J., Marszalek, M., Lazebnik, S., Schmid, C.: Local features and kernels for classification of texture and object categories: A comprehensive study. In: Conference on Computer Vision and Pattern Recognition Workshop, CVPRW 2006, p. 13. IEEE (2006)
28. Zhao, G., Pietikainen, M.: Dynamic texture recognition using local binary patterns with an application to facial expressions. IEEE Transactions on Pattern Analysis and Machine Intelligence 29(6), 915–928 (2007)

Kernel Conditional Ordinal Random Fields for Temporal Segmentation of Facial Action Units

Ognjen Rudovic[1], Vladimir Pavlovic[2], and Maja Pantic[1,3]

[1] Computing Dept., Imperial College London, UK
[2] Dept. of Computer Science, Rutgers University, USA
[3] EEMCS, University of Twente, The Netherlands
{o.rudovic,m.pantic}@imperial.ac.uk, vladimir@cs.rutgers.edu

Abstract. We consider the problem of automated recognition of temporal segments (neutral, onset, apex and offset) of Facial Action Units. To this end, we propose the Laplacian-regularized Kernel Conditional Ordinal Random Field model. In contrast to standard modeling approaches to recognition of AUs' temporal segments, which treat each segment as an independent class, the proposed model takes into account *ordinal* relations between the segments. The experimental results evidence the effectiveness of such an approach.

Keywords: Action units, histogram intersection kernel, ordinal regression, conditional random field, kernel locality preserving projections.

1 Introduction

The dynamics of facial expressions are crucial for interpretation of observed facial behavior. For example, involuntary initiated (spontaneous) facial expressions are characterized by synchronized, smooth, symmetrical, consistent and reflex-like facial muscle movements whereas voluntary initiated (acted) facial expressions are subject to volitional real-time control and tend to be less smooth, with more variable facial dynamics [1].Facial expression dynamics can be explicitly analyzed by detecting the temporal segments (neutral, onset, apex, offset) of facial muscle actions, i.e., Action Units (AUs), and, in turn, their duration, speed and co-occurrences. Although FACS [2] teaches human coders how to identify temporal segments of specific AUs, the manual coding of these segments is labor intensive. Automating this process would make it easier and widely accessible as a research tool [3].

To date, only few works addressed the problem of automatic recognition of temporal segments of AUs in face videos - [4],[5],[6] (frontal view) and [7] (profile view). [6],[7] used rule-based reasoning and geometric based features to encode temporal segments of AUs. [5] used facial-motion-based features and a combination of gentleboost and HMM, while [4] combined SVM and HMM with geometric-based features, for the target task. Note that all these works

A. Fusiello et al. (Eds.): ECCV 2012 Ws/Demos, Part II, LNCS 7584, pp. 260–269, 2012.

approach the recognition of AUs' temporal segments as a four-class classification problem. On the other hand, by noting that the AUs' temporal segments are directly related to the intensity of AUs[1], their representation can be enriched with ordinal labels: neutral = 1 ≺ onset, offset = 2 ≺ apex = 3. These *ordinal* relations – which are ignored by the afore-mentioned works – can then be used to augment the classification of the temporal segments. To this end, we propose the Laplacian-regularized Kernel Conditional Ordinal Random Field (Lap-KCORF) model for temporal segmentation of AUs. This model is a nonlinear generalization of Conditional Ordinal Random Field (CORF) [8] and its Laplacian-regularized version (Lap-CORF) [9], recently proposed for facial expression intensity estimation. We also propose Composite Histogram Intersection kernel that automatically discovers the facial regions relevant for the classification of the AUs' temporal segmenats.

The remainder of the paper is organized as follows. We give an overview of Conditional Ordinal Random Field (CORF) in Sec. 2. We then describe the proposed Laplacian Kernel CORF model in Sec. 3, and its adaptation for recognition of AU temporal segments in Sec. 4. Sec. 5 shows the experimental results, and Sec. 6 concludes the paper.

2   Conditional Ordinal Random Field (CORF)

The goal of ordinal regression is to predict the output h that indicates the ordinal score of an item represented by a feature vector $\mathbf{x} \in \mathbb{R}^p$. Formally, we let $h = 1 \prec h = 2 \prec \ldots \prec h = R$, where R is the number of ordinal scores. Recently, a CRF-like model named CORF [8] has been proposed for dynamic ordinal regression. Similar to CRF, CORF models the distribution of a set (sequence) of random variables $\mathbf{h}$, conditioned on inputs $\mathbf{x}$. This distribution, denoted by $P(\mathbf{h}|\mathbf{x})$, has a Gibbs form clamped on the observation $\mathbf{x}$ and is defined as:

$$P(\mathbf{h}|\mathbf{x}, \boldsymbol{\theta}) = \frac{1}{Z(\mathbf{x}; \boldsymbol{\theta})} e^{s(\mathbf{x}, \mathbf{h}; \boldsymbol{\theta})}, \tag{1}$$

where $Z(\mathbf{x}; \boldsymbol{\theta}) = \sum_{\mathbf{h} \in \mathcal{H}} e^{s(\mathbf{x}, \mathbf{h}; \boldsymbol{\theta})}$ is the normalizing partition function ($\mathcal{H}$ is a set of all possible output configurations), and $\boldsymbol{\theta} = \{\mathbf{a}, \mathbf{b}, \sigma, \mathbf{u}\}$ are the parameters of the score function $s(\cdot)$, defined as

$$s(\mathbf{x}, \mathbf{h}; \boldsymbol{\theta}) = \sum_{r \in V} \boldsymbol{\Psi}_r^{(V)}(\mathbf{x}, h_r) + \sum_{e=(r,s) \in E} \mathbf{u}\, \boldsymbol{\Psi}_e^{(E)}(\mathbf{x}, h_r, h_s), \tag{2}$$

where the contribution of static $\boldsymbol{\Psi}_r^{(V)}(\mathbf{x}, h_r)$ and dynamic $\boldsymbol{\Psi}_e^{(E)}(\mathbf{x}, h_r, h_s)$ features is summed over all *node* ($r \in V$) and *edge* ($e = (r, s) \in E$) cliques in the output graph $G = (V, E)$.

---

[1] The temporal development of an AU starts with its intensity being zero (neutral), followed by the increase in its intensity (onset) until it reaches a peak (apex), from where it decreases (offset) towards zero intensity (neutral).

In contrast to standard CRF, CORF enforces ordering of $\mathbf{h}$ by using the modeling strategy of static ordinal regression methods [9]. Specifically, the probabilistic ranking likelihood, $P(h = c|f_s(x)) = P(f_s(x) \in [b_{c-1}, b_c))$, defined as

$$P(h = c|f(\mathbf{x})) = \Phi\left(\frac{b_c - f_s(\mathbf{x})}{\sigma}\right) - \Phi\left(\frac{b_{c-1} - f_s(\mathbf{x})}{\sigma}\right), \tag{3}$$

is used to set the node features as $\boldsymbol{\Psi}_r^{(V)}(\mathbf{x}, h_r) = \sum_{c=1}^{R} I(h_r = c) \cdot log(P(h_r = c|f_s(\mathbf{x})))$. Here, $\Phi(\cdot)$ is the standard normal cdf, and σ is the parameter that controls the steepness of the likelihood function. The function $f_s(\mathbf{x}) = a^T x$ projects the inputs $\mathbf{x}$ onto a line divided into R bins, where the binning parameters $\mathbf{b} = [-\infty = b_0, \dots, b_R = +\infty]^\top$ are defined so that they satisfy the ordering constraints $(b_i < b_{i+1}, \forall i)$; thus, enforcing the projected features to be sorted according to their ordinal scores h. The edge features, $\boldsymbol{\Psi}_e^{(E)}(\mathbf{x}, h_r, h_s)$, are set as

$$\left[I(h_r = k \; \wedge \; h_s = l)\right]_{R \times R} \otimes f_d(\mathbf{x}_r, \mathbf{x}_s). \tag{4}$$

$I(\cdot)$ is the indicator function that returns 1 (0) if the argument is true (false), $\otimes$ is the Kronecker delta, and $f_d(\mathbf{x}_r, \mathbf{x}_s) = |x_r - x_s|$ is the absolute difference between measurement features at adjoining nodes.

Learning of CORF parameters is typically accomplished by maximizing the conditional data likelihood objective (1). In standard log-linear CRF this results in convex optimization [10], while in CORF the objective is nonlinear and non-convex [9]. Nevertheless, in both cases it is critical to regularize the conditional data likelihood to improve the model performance and generalization. Like CRF, standard CORF [8] uses linear feature function $f_s(x)$ and L_2 regularizer for a. Lap-CORF [9] extends this model using the graph Laplacian regularization. The graph encodes long-term dependencies between the inputs x and imposes general geometric smoothness on CORF predictions. As a consequence, $f_s(x)$ becomes a linear approximation of the general (graph Laplacian) functional leading to better generalization and less sensitivity to inter-subject variations. Although the Lap-CORF representation is effective in some tasks (e.g., [9]), f_s is still constrained to the linear form. This can limit the model's performance if the mappings from the feature space to the ordinal space are highly complex. To address this, in what follows, we generalize Lap-CORF to the non-linear case that permits the use of implicit feature spaces through Mercer kernels.

3   Laplacian Kernel CORF

In this section, we first describe the Kernel CORF (KCORF) model based on the general theory of functional optimization in RKHS. We then use Kernel Locality Preserving Projections [11] to provide specific kernel regularizer for the KCORF model, which gives rise to the Laplacian-regularized KCORF (Lap-KCORF) model. Finally, we explain the learning and inference in the proposed model.

3.1 Kernel CORF

Consider a regularized loss function of the form

$$\arg\min_{\theta,\alpha,\tau} \sum_{i=1}^{N} -\ln P(h_i|f(x_i), \theta, \alpha, \tau) + \Omega_K(\theta, \alpha, \tau), \qquad (5)$$

where $\Omega_K(\theta, \alpha, \tau)$ is the (kernel-inducing) regularizer. To find an optimal functional form of $f^*(\cdot)$, Lafferty et al. [12] proposed the following Representer Theorem for conditional graphical models.

Theorem 1. *Let K be a Mercer kernel on x h_C with associated RKHS norm $\|\cdot\|_K$, and let $\Omega_K : R_+ \to R_+$ be strictly increasing. Then the minimizer f^* of optimization problem (5), if it exists, has the form*

$$f^*(\cdot) = \sum_{i=1}^{N} \sum_{c \in C^{(i)}} \sum_{h_c \in h^{|c|}} \alpha_c^{(i)}(h_c) K_c(\mathbf{x}^{(i)}, h_c^{(i)}; \cdot). \qquad (6)$$

Here, c are the vertices of cliques $C^{(i)}$ in graph G, and $h_c \in h^{|c|}$ are all possible labellings of that clique. From (6), we see that the structure in the model output is captured by the 'dual parameters' $\alpha_c^{(i)}$, which depend on all assignments of labels over the training examples. Note, however, that such a model may have an extremely large number of parameters [12]. On the other hand, CORF already models the structure in the output by means of the parametric ordinal model. It also models temporal dynamics of $\mathbf{h}$ by means of the transition matrix $\mathbf{u}$. Therefore, the functional form in (6) can be simplified by dropping dependences on labels $\mathbf{h}$, and by defining kernel K_c only on the node cliques ($r \in V$). In this way, we recover the Kernel CORF model that is the semi-parametric CORF model with static (f_s) and dynamic (f_d) feature functions defined as

$$f_s(x) = \sum_{i=1}^{N} \alpha_i K(x, x_i | \tau) \ \wedge \ f_d(x_t, x_{t-1}) = f_s(x_t) - f_s(x_{t-1}), \qquad (7)$$

where τ are the kernel parameters. Note that the above-defined dynamic feature function is defined in the ordinal space, while in the case of CORF and Lap-CORF, it is defined in the ambient space. Thus, the former uses only the relevant features, i.e., projections on the ordinal line that correlate with the segments' intensity, to quantify the temporal changes. By contrast, CORF and Lap-CORF use all (relevant and irrelevant) features to determine this change.

3.2 Regularization Using Kernel Locality Preserving Projection

KLPP is the kernel extension of Linear Locality Preserving Projection (LLPP), an optimal linear approximation to the eigenfunctions of the Laplace Beltrami operator on the manifold, that is frequently used for nonlinear dimensionality reduction [11]. KLPP uses the notion of Laplacian of the graph to learn non-linear mappings that project inputs onto a low-dimensional manifold. Formally, it first constructs an undirected graph $G = (V, E)$ [2], where each edge is associated with a weight W_{ij} that quantifies the similarity of data points (i, j). Given W, KLPP seeks to find the nonlinear function $f(\cdot)$ that is smooth on G, i.e., which minimizes

$$\Omega(\|f\|_K) = \sum_{i=1}^{N} \sum_{j=1}^{N} (f(x_i) - f(x_j))^2 W_{ij} = 2\alpha^T K L K \alpha, \qquad (8)$$

where L is graph Laplacian defined as $L = D - W$, and D is a diagonal degree matrix with $D_{ii} = \sum_j W_{ij}$. We derive the similarity measure based on the ordinal labels h as

$$W_{ij} = 1 - \frac{|h_i - h_j|}{R - 1}, \quad h_i, h_j = 1, ..., R. \qquad (9)$$

Note that when the ordinal difference between two data points increases, the extent of distance enlargement (the second term in W_{ij}) increases accordingly.

By using Laplace regulizer, $\Omega(\|f\|_K)$, in concert with other regularizers, we obtain the Laplacian-regularized KCORF model, which loss function is given by (5) but where

$$\Omega_K(\theta, \alpha, \tau) = \lambda_1 \Omega(\|f\|_K) + \lambda_2 \|\alpha\|^2 + \lambda_3 \|\theta\|^2. \qquad (10)$$

The additional regularization based on graph Laplacian incorporates geometric structure in the kernel-based regularization of the KCORF model. In other words, it constrains the conditional probability distribution $P(h|f(x), \theta, \alpha, \tau)$ to vary smoothly along the geodesics in the intrinsic geometry of $P(x, h)$, which is ignored in the CORF and standard CRF models.

3.3   Lap-KCORF: Learning and Inference

The final objective function of Lap-KCORF is obtained by plugging the kernel feature functions defined in (7), and the regularization term in (10), into (5). Note that, in addition to Laplacian regularization, we also use the L_2 regularizer for the kernel weights α, in order to avoid diverging solutions. The parameters b and σ are re-parametrized, as explained in [8], in order to arrive at the unconstrained minimization problem. The minimization of such objective is achieved using the quasi-Newton limited-BFGS method (see [8] for gradient derivations). We now describe briefly the learning strategy. Initially, we use KLPP to set the kernel weights α. Then, we set the edge parameters $u = 0$ to form a static ranking model that treats each node independently. After learning the node and kernel parameters $\{b, \sigma, \alpha, \tau\}$, we optimize the model w.r.t. u while holding the other parameters fixed. In the final step, we optimize all model parameters together. Once the parameters of the Lap-KCORF model are found, the inference of test sequences is carried out using Viterbi decoding.

---

[2] Note that this graph is different from the one defined in CORF in Sec. 2.

4   Recognition of AU Temporal Segments

In this section, we first adapt the proposed Lap-KCORF model to the target task. We then introduce Composite Histogram Intersection (CHI) kernel that we employ in the Lap-KCORF model.

4.1   Lap-KCORF for Recognition of AU Temporal Segments

Recognition of AU temporal segments (neutral, onset, apex and offset) is usually cast as a four-class classification problem. In addition to categorical labels (neutral $= 1$, onset $= 2$, apex $= 3$, offset $= 4$), we also assign ordinal labels to the temporal segments (neutral $= 1 \prec$ onset, offset $= 2 \prec$ apex $= 3$). To incorporate this into the Lap-KCORF model, we need to lower its assumption that all classes have different and monotonically increasing ranking scores. This is attained by re-defining its node features as

$$P(h = \text{onset}|f_s(x)) = P(h = \text{offset}|f_s(x)) = P(f_s(x) \in [b_0, b_1)). \quad (11)$$

Note that with such-defined node features, the Lap-KCORF model can perform classification of neutral and apex solely based on their ordinal scores. However, to differentiate between onset and offset, Lap-KCORF has to rely completely on its dynamic features, where the transition matrix u and the intensity of the appearance change, measured in the ordinal space by $f_d(x_t, x_{t-1})$, play key role in discriminating between onset and offset. Fig.1 illustrates the importance of modeling the sign in dynamic features for discerning the two phases of equal ordinal score.

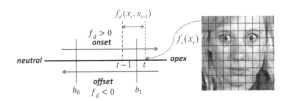

Fig. 1. Modeling of AUs' temporal segments in the ordinal space of Lap-KCORF

4.2   Composite Histogram Intersection (CHI) Kernel

For classification of the temporal segments using the Lap-KCORF, we propose the CHI kernel derived from the widely used Histogram Intersection (HI) kernel [13]. The HI kernel is specifically designed for measuring similarity between two histograms. Formally, we are given two image histograms x_i and x_j, both containing M bins, where the b-th bin has the value x_i^b and x_j^b, respectively. If we assume that x_i and x_j have the same size, i.e., $\sum_{b=1}^{M} x_i^b = \sum_{b=1}^{M} x_j^b$, then the HI kernel is given by: $k(x_i, x_j) = \sum_{b=1}^{M} \min\{x_i^b, x_j^b\}$. To compute the histograms, we employ Local Binary Patterns (LBPs) since they have been shown to be effective in the task of AU detection [14]. Specifically, we first align facial images, and then divide each image into 10x10 equally sized non-overlapping regions. LBP histograms are then extracted from each region, resulting in a 59-D feature vector per each region.

To combine information from multiple local regions, we propose the Composite Histogram Intersection (CHI) kernel:

$$k_{chi}(\mathrm{x}_i, \mathrm{x}_j) = \sum_{r=1}^{R} \beta_r \mathrm{k_r}(\mathrm{x}_i, \mathrm{x}_j), \quad \beta_r \geq 0, \quad \sum_{r=1}^{R} \beta_r = 1, \tag{12}$$

where β_r is learned from training data to reflect the relevance of region r, to which we apply the HI kernel $k_r(\cdot, \cdot)$. The positiveness constraint ensures that $k_{chi}(\cdot, \cdot)$ is positive definite, and the unitary constraint is necessary to avoid diverging solutions. To avoid constrained optimization of the kernel parameters β, we introduce re-parameterization: $\beta_r = Z_\tau^{-1} e^{\tau_r}$, where Z_τ is the normalization const. The CHI kernel automatically finds facial regions important for the classification of the AUs' temporal segments, and discards the irrelevant ones. This may help to reduce overfitting, and, thus, improve predictive accuracy of the classifier.

5   Experiments

We evaluated the proposed approach using the MMI facial expression database (MMI-db)[15], parts I and II. Specifically, we used videos depicting facial expressions of single AU activation, performed by different subjects. Furthermore, in this paper we report results only for AUs from the upper face (i.e., AU1, AU2, AU3, AU4, AU5, AU6, AU7, AU43, AU45 and AU46). The activation of each AU is manually coded per frame into one of four temporal segments (neutral, onset, apex or offset), and it is provided by the db creators. We refer our reader to [4] for more details about the db, and the AUs that we address in this paper.

We trained the proposed Lap-KCORF model for each AU separately using the corresponding image sequences. The parameter learning was done as explained in Sec.3.3. As input features, we used 5x10 LBP histograms computed from the upper face of the aligned training images (see Sec.4.2). Furthermore, we initialized the weights β_r of the CHI kernel by assuming uniform prior. To reduce the computational cost of the Lap-KCORF model, without significantly reducing the model's performance, we set the maximum number of the kernel bases to #300. The bases were sampled uniformly at random from training examples of each temporal segment.

We compared the performance of Lap-KCORF to that achieved by Lap-CORF[9] in the target task. Since Lap-CORF[9] is a regularized version of the base CORF model proposed in [8], we do not include the results for CORF in this paper. For Lap-CORF, the values of the 50 histograms of each image were concatenated to form a vector. The training set of such vectors was pre-processed

Table 1. F1-score for each AU

Method	AU1	AU2	AU4	AU5	AU6	AU7	AU43	AU45	AU46	Av.
SVM-HMM[4]	0.65	**0.69**	0.54	0.45	0.58	0.34	**0.72**	**0.78**	0.29	0.56
Lap-CORF[9]	0.67	0.64	0.52	0.55	0.59	0.54	0.57	0.65	0.48	0.58
Lap-KCORF	**0.70**	0.68	**0.58**	**0.60**	**0.63**	**0.59**	0.69	0.71	**0.62**	**0.65**

by applying PCA to reduce its dimensionality ($\sim$25) by preserving 98% of energy. Lap-KCORF used full histogram features. We also show the performance of the Hybrid SVM-HMM [4] model, the state-of-the-art approach to automatic recognition of AUs' temporal segments, which is based on geometric features. Finally, in all our experiments we applied 5-fold cross validation procedure[3], where each fold contained image sequences of different subjects. We report the accuracy using the F-1 measure, defined as $2pr/(p+r)$, where p and r represent obtained precision and recall, respectively.

Table 2. F1-score for each temporal segment

Method	neutral	onset	apex	offset
SVM-HMM[4]	**0.78**	0.45	0.57	0.44
Lap-CORF[9]	0.65	0.48	0.68	0.50
Lap-KCORF	0.72	**0.53**	**0.79**	**0.54**

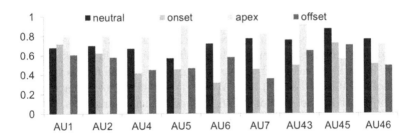

Fig. 2. Lap-KCORF: F1 score for temporal segments of different AUs

Table 1 shows the average performance of recognition of temporal segments of different AUs. SVM-HMM and Lap-CORF perform similarly on average. It is interesting to note that parametric Lap-CORF performs this well having that it uses linear feature functions, in contrast to its kernel counterparts, i.e., SVM-HMM and Lap-KCORF. Although SVM-HMM performs better than the proposed Lap-KCORF on certain AUs, the latter model exhibits better performance

---

[3] We used three folds for training, one for validation - to find the regularization parameters, and one for testing.

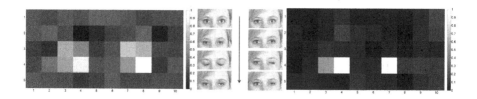

Fig. 3. The weights of the CHI kernel learned for AU45 (*left*) and AU46 (*right*)

on average. This is attributed in part to its superior recognition of AU7 and AU46. The same can be observed from the results per segment shown in Table 2. Note that both Lap-CORF and Lap-KCORF outperform SVM-HMM on all temporal segments except neutral, which signals that these models are better suited for modeling the *dynamics* of an AU activation. Since all these models model the dynamics by means of the parametric transition matrix, we attribute the better performance achieved by Lap-K/CORF to their modeling of the static ordinal constraints (important for the apex-segment recognition). Furthermore, the better performance of Lap-KCORF compared to that of Lap-CORF is in part due to Lap-KCORF's modeling of the temporal dynamics in the ordinal space as explained in Sec. 4.1 (crucial for differentiation between the onset and the offset phases), and in part due to the proposed CHI kernel, which selects 'good' features for the target task. Finally, it is interesting to note from Fig.5 that Lap-KCORF recognizes well the apex of AUs' activation in all cases except for AU45. We inspected the data of this AU, and found that there were only few examples of the apex present. Hence, Lap-KCORF did not have sufficient support of the kernel bases of the apex, which affected its performance in this particular task.

Fig.3 depicts the relevance (measured by the values β_r of the CHI kernel) of facial regions for the recognition of AU45 (blink) and AU46 (wink).The reason why in AU46 we have 'relevant' regions on both sides of the face is that we used examples of AU46L (left wink) and AU46R (right blink) together to train the model. Note that in the case of AU46 we have much sparser β's. This is due to the fact that in AU46 the closure of the eye, which is annotated as apex, lasts much longer than in AU45, and, thus, the model assigns more weight to the region where the eye stayed closed. In conclusion, these maps can be used to further analyze the dynamics of AU activations.

6   Conclusion

We proposed the Lap-KCORF model for the recognition of AUs' temporal segments. We also proposed the Composite Histogram Intersection kernel for automatic learning of relevance of the facial regions for the target task. Our experimental results suggest that ordinal relations between AUs' temporal segments play an important role in the recognition task, in addition to their temporal relations. The proposed Lap-KCORF model can also be applied to AU intensity estimation, the problem addressed in [3]. This is part of our ongoing research.

Acknowledgments. This material is based upon work supported by the European Research Council under the ERC Starting Grant agreement no. ERC-2007-StG-203143 (MAHNOB), and by the National Science Foundation under Grant No. IIS 0916812.

References

1. Pantic, M.: Machine analysis of facial behaviour: Naturalistic and dynamic behaviour. Philosophical Transactions of Royal Society B 364, 3505–3513 (2009)
2. Ekman, P., Friesen, W., Hager, J.: Facial Action Coding System (FACS): Manual. A Human Face (2002)
3. Mahoor, M., Cadavid, S., Messinger, D., Cohn, J.: A framework for automated measurement of the intensity of non-posed facial action units. In: CVPRW, pp. 74–80 (2009)
4. Valstar, M.F., Pantic, M.: Fully automatic recognition of the temporal phases of facial actions. IEEE Transactions on Systems, Man and Cybernetics 42, 28–43 (2012)
5. Koelstra, S., Pantic, M., Patras, I.: A dynamic texture based approach to recognition of facial actions and their temporal models. IEEE PAMI 32, 1940–1954 (2010)
6. Pantic, M., Patras, I.: Detecting facial actions and their temporal segments in nearly frontal-view face image sequences. In: Proc. of IEEE Int'l Conf. Systems, Man and Cybernetics, pp. 3358–3363 (2005)
7. Pantic, M., Patras, I.: Dynamics of facial expression: Recognition of facial actions and their temporal segments from face profile image sequences. IEEE Transactions on Systems, Man and Cybernetics - Part B 36(2), 433–449 (2006)
8. Kim, M., Pavlovic, V.: Structured Output Ordinal Regression for Dynamic Facial Emotion Intensity Prediction. In: Daniilidis, K. (ed.) ECCV 2010, Part III. LNCS, vol. 6313, pp. 649–662. Springer, Heidelberg (2010)
9. Rudovic, O., Pavlovic, V., Pantic, M.: Multi-output laplacian dynamic ordinal regression for facial expression recognition and intensity estimation. In: CVPR (in press, 2012)
10. Lafferty, J., McCallum, A., Pereira, F.: Conditional Random Fields: Probabilistic models for segmenting and labeling sequence data. In: ICML, pp. 282–289 (2001)
11. He, X., Niyogi, P.: Locality Preserving Projections. In: NIPS (2004)
12. Lafferty, J., Zhu, X., Liu, Y.: Kernel conditional random fields: representation and clique selection. In: ICML 2004, p. 64 (2004)
13. Barla, A., Odone, F.,, V.: Histogram intersection kernel for image classification. In: ICIP 2003, vol. 2, pp. III-513–III-516 (2003)
14. Jiang, B., Valstar, M.F., Pantic, M.: Action unit detection using sparse appearance descriptors in space-time video volumes. In: FG 2011, pp. 314–321 (2011)
15. Pantic, M., Valstar, M.F., Rademaker, R., Maat, L.: Web-based database for facial expression analysis. In: ICME 2005, pp. 317–321 (July 2005)

Exploring the Facial Expression Perception-Production Link Using Real-Time Automated Facial Expression Recognition

David M. Deriso[1], Josh Susskind[1], Jim Tanaka[2], Piotr Winkielman[3],
John Herrington[4], Robert Schultz[4], and Marian Bartlett[1]

[1] Machine Perception Laboratory, University of California, San Diego
dderiso@ucsd.edu, {josh,marni}@mplab.ucsd.edu
[2] Department of Psychology, University of Victoria
[3] Department of Psychology, University of California, San Diego
[4] Center for Autism Research, Children's Hospital of Philadelphia

Abstract. Motor production may play an important role in learning to recognize facial expressions. The present study explores the influence of facial production training on the perception of facial expressions by employing a novel production training intervention built on feedback from automated facial expression recognition. We hypothesized that production training using the automated feedback system would improve an individual's ability to identify dynamic emotional faces. Thirty-four participants were administered a dynamic expression recognition task before and after either interacting with a production training video game called the Emotion Mirror or playing a control video game. Consistent with the prediction that perceptual benefits are tied to expression production, individuals with high engagement in production training improved more than individuals with low engagement or individuals who did not receive production training. These results suggest that the visual-motor associations involved in expression production training are related to perceptual abilities. Additionally, this study demonstrates a novel application of computer vision for real-time facial expression intervention training.

1 Introduction

Facial expression production and perception are crucial components of social functioning. Disruptions in these processes limit an individual's ability to interact with others, which has negative consequences on health and quality of life [1,2]. Neurophysiological disorders such as autism spectrum disorders (ASD) are associated with reduced ability to produce [3] and perceive [4] facial expressions [5]. Recent advances in automated facial expression recognition technology open new possibilities for clinical interventions that target these deficits. The broader goal of this project is to develop an intervention based on facial expression production by leveraging automatic facial expression recognition technology to provide real-time feedback on the participants own expressions.

A. Fusiello et al. (Eds.): ECCV 2012 Ws/Demos, Part II, LNCS 7584, pp. 270–279, 2012.

The present study employs the automated expression recognition intervention to explore the link between facial expression perception and production. We examine the effect of emotional facial expression production training on the perception of dynamic facial expressions. To the best of our knowledge, this is the first paper to address the question of whether training facial expression production influences perception. Previous computer-based interventions focused on expression recognition [6,7], but not production, and the link between facial production and perception remains unclear. Practice with expression production may not only influence production itself, but may also influence perception due to possible associations between recognition and motor production.

1.1   Exploring the Expression Perception and Production Link

The recruitment of the motor system for perceptual learning is a theme that has become widespread in cognitive science, dating back to the motor theory of speech perception [8]. The theory posits that motor production plays an important role in the development of perceptual recognition capabilities. More recent evidence suggests that perceptual recognition itself involves dynamic interaction through a network of brain areas including the motor system. Neurons in a visual-motor system, called "mirror neurons," have been reported to activate during the production of specific muscle movement and also to visual display (perception) of the same muscle movement performed by another [9]. There is evidence from cognitive neuroscience and psychology that perceptual systems for facial expression recognition may be linked with motor as well as somatosensory feedback systems [10,11]. For example, facial motor interference produced by biting a pen has been shown to impair recognition of certain emotional expressions [12]. Moreover, disrupting sensory feedback from the facial region of somatosensory cortex via TMS impairs discrimination of facial expressions, but not recognition of facial identity [13].

Together, these studies suggest that perception and production may be linked through a common use of the motor system. The present study explores this link by measuring the impact of facial expression production training on the ability to recognize dynamic facial expressions. We hypothesized that training with facial expression production will improve perceptual ability to recognize dynamic facial expressions.

To study the effects of facial expression production, we employed real-time facial expression recognition within a novel intervention game called the emotion mirror. In this paradigm, subjects receive closed-loop sensorimotor feedback, where they produce facial expressions and simultaneously view their expressions mirrored by interactive animations.

2   Methods

To measure the effect of production training on perceptual ability, a pre-test post-test design was employed where perceptual ability was measured using the

Dynamic Expression Recognition Task (DERT) before and after the intervention task (Emotion Mirror) or control task (Sushi Cat).

2.1 Dynamic Expression Recognition Task ("DERT")

Social interactions demand efficient and accurate interpretations of dynamic facial expressions. However, previous studies of face perception have predominantly used static, high intensity facial stimuli, with which participants are often at ceiling recognition performance. To measure the perceptual ability for dynamic facial expressions, DERT was adapted from [14,5].

Participants were shown a human face that gradually morphed over the course of 500 ms from a neutral expression to one of four basic emotions: sad, angry, fearful, and surprised. In order to assess the perceptual limitations for identifying an emotion, the amount of information given for each decision was varied by allowing the morph to reach one of five percentages of completion (intensity): 15 (difficult), 30, 45, 60, and 75 (easy). The lowest intensity is presented first, in a block design. Participants were instructed to identify each expression as quickly and accurately as possible, while response reaction time and accuracy were recorded.

Dynamic stimuli were created by generating morphs of six actors selected from the Radboud database [15] of basic emotional expressions. Each actor's face was morphed from neutral to a high intensity expression using facial action constellations defined in the Facial Action Coding System (FACS) manual [16] as markers. Morphs were rapidly displayed as sequences that lasted a total of one second, beginning with a neutral expression that lasted for 500 msec, followed by a dynamic expression (See Figure 1).

DERT differs from [14,5] in that the dynamics are consistent across expression intensities; it does not slow down the frame rate or rate of expression production for the low intensity expressions, nor does it hold a static facial expression at the end of the dynamic display. Because the low intensity expressions had fewer frames, a one second total display time was achieved by increasing the duration of the static neutral expression before the onset of the low intensity morph (See Figure 1).

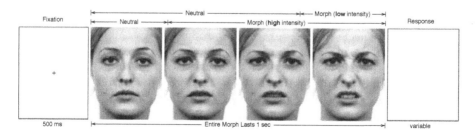

Fig. 1. Dynamic Expression Recognition Task

2.2   The Emotion Mirror

The emotion mirror is an intervention game in which an illustrated character responds to the facial expression of the subject in real-time. There are two conditions that govern the direction of the interaction: "it mimics you" and "you mimic it." In the first condition, the participant is audibly prompted to make one of six expressions. If the correct expression is produced, the character mirrors the participant's expression (ie. "it mimics you"), which is rewarding to the participant. In the second condition, the character displays and holds an expression, and participant is instructed to copy the character (ie. "you mimic it"). As the participant approximates the expression of the character, an ice-cream cone grows by increasing in units of scoops and toppings. This playful interaction is designed to appeal to children and adults.

The game includes a selection of engaging animated characters that range in visual complexity. It is well known that children with ASD tend to be more comfortable with visually simple displays, and are more comfortable with robots and animals than with human faces. Accordingly, the avatars in the intervention game range from animals, to outer-space creatures, to a more realistic human avatar for which children can choose gender, skin color, and hair color to match their own (See Figure 2). Each condition cycled through three characters (dog, girl, boy) for six emotions each (two conditions with three repetitions of six emotions). The task knits expressive production and perception as it is the participant's own face that drives the expressions shown on the avatar, and provides feedback and practice in facial expression mirroring behaviors.

The facial expression recognition engine behind the Emotion Mirror is the Computer Expression Recognition Toolbox (CERT).

(a) It Mimics You   (b) You Mimic It

Fig. 2. The Emotion Mirror

2.3   The Computer Expression Recognition Toolbox ("CERT")

CERT is a computer vision system for measuring facial expressions in real time [17,18] (See Figure 3). CERT automatically codes the intensity of six expressions of basic emotion, three dimensions of head pose (yaw, pitch, and roll, as well as the 20 facial actions from the FACS [8] most related to emotion. FACS is a system for objectively scoring facial expressions in terms of elemental movements, called action units (AUs), which roughly correspond with individual facial muscle movements. FACS provides a comprehensive description of facial expressions, providing greater specificity and diversity than emotion categories.

The technical approach to CERT is an appearance-based discriminative approach. Such approaches have proven highly robust and fast for face detection and tracking (e.g. [19], and take advantage of the rich texture information in facial expression images. This class of approaches achieves a high level of robustness through the use of large data sets for machine learning. This speed and robustness has enabled real-time analysis of spontaneous expressions. Evaluation of CERT on benchmark datasets shows state-of-the-art performance for both recognition of basic emotions and recognition of facial actions. CERT also provides information about expression intensity. See [17] for more information on system design and benchmark performance measures. CERT operates in near real-time at approximately 12-15 frames per second, and is available for academic use.

A softmax competition between CERT's six expressions of basic emotion and neutral mediates the matching signal between the prompted emotion and that of the participant. This matching signal drives the character's expression intensity or the height of the ice cream in proportion to the participant's expression intensity.

2.4 Participants

Participants were thirty-four healthy college students (M = 14, F= 19, M(age) = 20.5) who volunteered for course credit. All volunteers were instructed to bring corrective eyewear if needed. No subjects were excluded, although data from four intervention subjects sets were unusable due to recording errors. The study was approved by the Human Research Protections Program at the University of California, San Diego.

Fig. 3. The Computer Expression Recognition Toolbox ("CERT")

2.5   Experimental Design

Each participant was randomly assigned into one of two groups: intervention (N=17) and control (N=17). The intervention group received facial expression production practice, and the control group played a spatial game that does not involve expression perception or production. All participants were assessed for recognition of dynamic facial expressions before and after intervention using the Dynamic Expression Recognition (DERT) task. The intervention group performed facial expression production exercises for 20 minutes, starting first with the Emotion Mirror "it mimics you," followed by "you mimic it," and finally Face-Face-Revolution [7]. The control group played a spatial computer game that does not involve expression perception or production called "Sushi Cat" [908] for 20 minutes. The object of the game is to drop a cat from an optimal position such that as the cat falls and bounces off obstacles, it can eat the maximum amount of sushi before landing. The control task does not prompt the user to produce facial expressions.

2.6   Measures

The primary dependent measures for DERT were accuracy, and reaction time. Pre-test scores were used as a covariate to compare post-test scores across intervention and control groups. Confusion matrices were also analyzed by comparing their similarity to the identity matrix using the Backus-Gilbert spread (BGS) (Equation. (1)) [20]. The BGS measures the Euclidean distance between two vectorized matrices, normalized by the number of off-diagonal elements.

$$1 - \left[\sum_{ij} (X_{ij} - I_{ij})^2 \Big/ \sum_{mn} (1 - I_{mn})^2 \right] \qquad (1)$$

In order to determine the extent to which participants made an effort to undergo production training with the emotion mirror, a measure of engagement, or compliance, was assessed using the mean accuracy of expression production. To calculate this, a true positive was awarded for a given trial when the peak emotion measured by CERT (integrated across the duration of the trial) matched the target emotion prompted by the Emotion Mirror.

Speed of facial expression production during the emotion mirror exercise was also assessed as the time from the stimulus onset to the peak CERT value for the target emotion (time-to-peak).

3   Results

We tested the hypothesis that engagement with the emotion mirror intervention (EM) would lead to improvements in expression recognition as measured by the DERT. As predicted, there was a trend for a positive correlation between engagement with the Emotion Mirror and gain scores on the dynamic expression recognition task ($r = .517, n = 13, t(1, 11) = 2.01, p < 0.07$) as measured by a Pearson product moment correlation. The correlation was stronger for the Emotion Mirror's "you mimic it" condition ($r = .612, n = 13, t(1, 11) = 2.57, p < 0.026$). Preliminary analyses were performed to ensure no violation of the assumptions of normality, linearity, and homoscedasticity.

To investigate whether the perceptual improvement was related to intervention engagement or chance, the intervention group was split by the median level of engagement into two groups: high engagement and low engagement (abbreviated as "T_high" and "T_low"). The pre and post-test performance of these new groups were then compared against a control group, who were given the same tests.

Since our main dependent measure of accuracy has a fixed ceiling at 1.00, we employed the ANCOVA method to improve the sensitivity of our between-group comparisons [21]. A two-way mixed analysis of covariance was conducted to assess the effectiveness of the emotion mirror intervention in improving accuracy on the dynamic expression recognition task. The within-subject independent variable was the amount of facial morph (15, 30, 45, 60, 75) and the between-subject independent variable was group assignment (control, intervention with high EM accuracy, intervention with low EM accuracy). The dependent variable was pos-test DERT accuracy scores, while DERT pre-test scores were used as a covariate to control for individual differences. Checks were conducted to ensure that there were no violations of the assumptions of normality, linearity, homogeneity of variance, homogeneity of regression slopes, and reliable measurement of the covariate. After adjusting for pre-test DERT accuracy scores, there was a significant main effect of treatment group ($F(1, 2) = 3.361, p < 0.006$). There was also a significant main effect of morph level ($F(1, 4) = 13.812, p < .00001$), and an interaction of treatment group by morph level ($F(1, 8) = 3.357, p < 0.002$) (See Figure 4).

To assess whether the intervention group improved more than the control group, we compared the accuracy improvement (gain score) for each group collapsed across levels of morph. Post-hoc Welch independent two sample t-tests were performed on the adjusted post-test score. These tests revealed that the intervention group with high EM accuracy had significantly greater improvements than did the control group ($t(55.8) = -3.03, p < 0.00373$, two-sided, mean difference $= 0.02$, 95% CI: -0.0312 to -0.00635). These tests also revealed that the intervention group with high EM accuracy had significantly greater improvements than did the intervention group with low EM accuracy ($t(62.6) = 4.89, p < .00001$, two-sided, mean difference $= -0.038$, 95% CI: 0.02 to 0.05), and the control group had significantly greater improvements than did the intervention group with low EM accuracy ($t(48) = 3.02, p < 0.004$, two-sided, mean difference $= -0.019$, 95% CI: 0.006 to 0.031). These results suggest that changes in perceptual accuracy from pre-test to post-test is strongly influenced by the accuracy during the emotion mirror task. These findings support the influence of expression practice and visual-motor associations, in expression recognition.

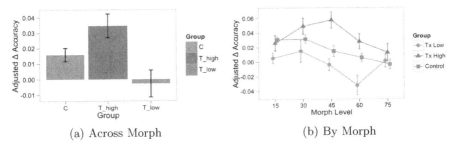

(a) Across Morph   (b) By Morph

Fig. 4. Perceptual Improvement (Post - Pre)

The relationship between the latency of production (time-to-peak) and improvement in DERT reaction time was assessed with a Pearson product moment correlation. The quicker an individual was to maximally produce the correct expression was significantly related to quicker reaction times ($r = -0.558, n = 13, t(1, 11) = -2.23, p < 0.048$). In addition, confusion matrices were quantified by measuring the similarity to the identity matrix using the Baccus-Gilbert Spread (BGS). Improvement in the BGS during the emotion mirror was significantly correlated in improvement in the BGS for recognition as measured by DERT ($r = .558, n = 13, t(1, 11) = 2.23, p < 0.048$).

4   Discussion

Consistent with the hypothesis that practice with production leads to improvements in perception, we found that greater engagement with the emotion mirror intervention improves perceptual accuracy for dynamic faces across emotions and varying levels of difficulty. The perceptual benefit was tied to expression production performance during motor training. These findings are consistent with our initial theory that the visual-motor associations gained in production training influence perceptual abilities.

In further support of the role of facial motor practice in perception, we found that the increase in speed of expression production during the Emotion Mirror was correlated with recognition performance improvement in DERT. This result demonstrates a relationship between learning in facial motor production and learning in facial expression perception that cannot be accounted for by practice recognizing facial expressions alone, and supports the hypothesis that the motor production itself contributed to perceptual improvement.

Furthermore, improvements in the confusion matrix (measured by the BGS) for facial expression production during the Emotion mirror were significantly correlated in improvement in the BGS for recognition as measured by DERT, providing further evidence that improvements in production are related to improvements in perception.

Though no significant differences were observed between engagement with the two production conditions, the "it mimics you" condition showed a stronger correlation with perceptual improvement in DERT than did "you mimic it." Though the differences between these two tasks were not explicitly studied, this correlation suggests that there may be a difference in the efficacy between the two methods of training. Further studies are needed to tease apart whether this correlational discrepancy was due to differences in the way each condition trained the participant, or if one condition had a stronger coupling between the subject and the emotion mirror

This study is not without limitations. Facial expression production training can be a tiring process, and the current methods were unable to adjust for how tired the participants were when they underwent the second, also tiring, perceptual assessment. Not all participants may have felt comfortable producing facial expressions, and some may have felt embarrassed more so than would children who may be more engaged with the illustrated characters and ice cream. CERT does not necessary work equally well for all participants, and some may have had a harder time engaging that others.

The present study is a product of a multi-disciplinary research effort to develop and evaluate a computer-aided intervention system to enhance the facial expression skills of children with ASD that merges the expertise of researchers in computer vision, face perception, autism, and social neuroscience. Recent advances in computer vision open new avenues for computer assisted intervention programs that target critical skills for social interaction, including the timing, morphology and dynamics of facial expressions. Such systems enable investigations into the learning of facial expression production that were previously not possible. The Emotion Mirror presents pioneering work to develop an engaging intervention system for facial expression processing based on automatic facial expression recognition technology. Such technology contributes not only to potential treatments, but also to the study of learning and plasticity in perception and production systems, and to understanding the cognitive neuroscience of emotion.

Acknowledgment. Support for this work was provided by NIH grant NIMH-RC1 MH088633 and NSF grant SBE-0542013. Any opinions, findings, conclusions or recommendations expressed in this material do not necessarily reflect the views of the National Science Foundation.

References

1. Eisenberger, N., Cole, S.: Social neuroscience and health: neurophysiological mechanisms linking social ties with physical health. Nature Neuroscience (2012)
2. House, J., Landis, K., Umberson, D.: Social relationships and health. Science 241, 540–545 (1988)
3. McIntosh, D., Reichmann-Decker, A., Winkielman, P., Wilbarger, J.: When the social mirror breaks: deficits in automatic, but not voluntary, mimicry of emotional facial expressions in autism. Developmental Science 9, 295–302 (2006)

4. Adolphs, R., Sears, L., Piven, J.: Abnormal processing of social information from faces in autism. Journal of Cognitive Neuroscience 13, 232–240 (2001)
5. Rump, K., Giovannelli, J., Minshew, N., Strauss, M.: The development of emotion recognition in individuals with autism. Child Development 80, 1434–1447 (2009)
6. Madsen, M., El Kaliouby, R., Goodwin, M., Picard, R.: Technology for just-in-time in-situ learning of facial affect for persons diagnosed with an autism spectrum disorder. In: Proceedings of the 10th International ACM SIGACCESS Conference on Computers and Accessibility, pp. 19–26. ACM (2008)
7. Tanaka, J., Wolf, J., Klaiman, C., Koenig, K., Cockburn, J., Herlihy, L., Brown, C., Stahl, S., Kaiser, M., Schultz, R.: Using computerized games to teach face recognition skills to children with autism spectrum disorder: the lets face it! program. Journal of Child Psychology and Psychiatry 51, 944–952 (2010)
8. Liberman, A., Mattingly, I.: The motor theory of speech perception revised. Cognition 21, 1–36 (1985)
9. Rizzolatti, G., Craighero, L.: The mirror-neuron system. Annu. Rev. Neurosci. 27, 169–192 (2004)
10. Heberlein, A., Adolphs, R.: Neurobiology of emotion recognition. Social Neuroscience: Integrating Biological and Psychological Explanations of Social Behavior 31 (2007)
11. Niedenthal, P., Mermillod, M., Maringer, M., Hess, U.: The simulation of smiles (sims) model: Embodied simulation and the meaning of facial expression. Behavioral and Brain Sciences 33, 417–433 (2010)
12. Oberman, L., Winkielman, P., Ramachandran, V.: Face to face: Blocking facial mimicry can selectively impair recognition of emotional expressions. Social Neuroscience 2, 167–178 (2007)
13. Pitcher, D., Garrido, L., Walsh, V., Duchaine, B.: Transcranial magnetic stimulation disrupts the perception and embodiment of facial expressions. The Journal of Neuroscience 28, 8929–8933 (2008)
14. Montagne, B., Kessels, R., De Haan, E., Perrett, D.: The emotion recognition task: A paradigm to measure the perception of facial emotional expressions at different intensities. Perceptual and Motor Skills 104, 589–598 (2007)
15. Langner, O., Dotsch, R., Bijlstra, G., Wigboldus, D., Hawk, S., Van Knippenberg, A.: Presentation and validation of the radboud faces database. Cognition and Emotion 24, 1377–1388 (2010)
16. Ekman, P., Friesen, W.: Facial action coding system: A technique for the measurement of facial movement (1978)
17. Galantucci, B., Fowler, C., Turvey, M.: The motor theory of speech perception reviewed. Psychonomic Bulletin & Review 13, 361–377 (2006)
18. Littlewort, G., Whitehill, J., Wu, T., Fasel, I., Frank, M., Movellan, J., Bartlett, M.: The computer expression recognition toolbox (cert). In: 2011 IEEE International Conference on Automatic Face & Gesture Recognition and Workshops (FG 2011), pp. 298–305. IEEE (2011)
19. Pelc, K., Kornreich, C., Foisy, M., Dan, B.: Recognition of emotional facial expressions in attention-deficit hyperactivity disorder. Pediatric Neurology 35, 93–97 (2006)
20. Schyns, P., Petro, L., Smith, M.: Transmission of facial expressions of emotion co-evolved with their efficient decoding in the brain: behavioral and brain evidence. PLoS One 4, e5625 (2009)
21. Cribbie, R., Jamieson, J.: Decreases in posttest variance and the measurement of change. Methods of Psychological Research Online 9, 37–55 (2004)

Understanding Critical Factors
in Appearance-Based Gender Categorization

Enrico Grosso, Andrea Lagorio, Luca Pulina, and Massimo Tistarelli

POLCOMING – University of Sassari
Viale Mancini, 5 – 07100 Sassari, Italy
{grosso,lagorio,lpulina,tista}@uniss.it

Abstract. Gender categorization, based on the analysis of facial appearance, can be useful in a large set of applications. In this paper we investigate the gender classification problem from a non-conventional perspective. In particular, the analysis will aim to determine the factors critically affecting the accuracy of available technologies, better explaining differences between face-based identification and gender categorization.

A novel challenging protocol is proposed, exploiting the dimensions of the Face Recognition Grand Challenge version 2.0 database (FRGC2.0). This protocol is evaluated against several classification algorithms and different kind of features, such as Gabor and LBP. The results obtained show that gender classification can be made independent from other appearance-based factors such as the skin color, facial expression, and illumination condition.

1 Introduction

It can be rather difficult to reliably categorize the gender of an unknown individual from its exterior appearance. Humans can perform this task pretty well on the basis of a number of independent features, not limited to the facial appearance. The tone of the voice, the gait, the hair style and dressing are all factors which strongly affect our judgement of gender. Yet, in some cases, gender categorization can be difficult for humans as well. For these reasons, gender categorization, posed as a binary classification problem from a number of face samples, is a very challenging task, but with a strong application potential [1,2]. A successful gender classification system can boost a large number of applications, such as search engines, surveillance systems, and interfaces, and it may help to better tailor public services to the user's needs. In the last two decades, the computer vision community has proposed several approaches to face-based gender classification. Starting from the seminal work of Golomb, Lawrence, and Sejnowski [3], key contributions are due to Cottrell and Metcalfe [4] – who proposed a multi-layer neural network approach – and Brunelli and Poggio [5], who detailed in the early 90s a system based on HyperBF networks. More recently, Moghaddam et al. [6] proposed a methodology based on Support Vector Machines (SVM). Mäkinen and Raisamo [7] surveyed several methodologies based on Multilayer Neural Network, SVM and Discrete AdaBoost. Lapedriza and

A. Fusiello et al. (Eds.): ECCV 2012 Ws/Demos, Part II, LNCS 7584, pp. 280–289, 2012.

colleagues [8] investigated the usage of boosting classifiers, like AdaBoost and JointBoosting. Shobeirinejad and Gao [9] presented a technique in which a histogram intersection is used as a measure of similarity for classification.

Most of the contributions listed above agree on a generic processing scheme composed of a preliminary feature extraction step, followed by a classification algorithm. This scheme proved to be effective in face recognition and the extension to gender classification has been quite straightforward and equally effective. In fact, these two steps are semantically very different: feature extraction has to do with image signals which are considered relevant for the problem (for instance the skin color could be extremely relevant for race detection) whilst classification has to do with the optimal partition of the feature space, possibly taking into account existing constraints.

In this paper we investigate gender categorization by means of an extended empirical analysis on the Face Recognition Grand Challenge version 2.0 (FRGC2.0) dataset [10]. To this extent, a **first contribution** concerns the proposal of a challenging experimental protocol for gender categorization. Inspired by the above feature extraction-classification dichotomy and from the experiments detailed in [10], a procedure is described based on exploiting the dimensions embedded in the data collected in FRGC2.0 – i.e. identity, facial expression, skin color, and environmental conditions. The proposed protocol is for general purpose, and it can be easily extended to other datasets and to different features and classifiers.

A second, and more relevant contribution, concerns the application of the proposed protocol to a significant set of features and classifiers, proving that gender classification should be treated as a very different problem from face classification. In our experiments 1-Nearest-Neighbour [11], Aggregation Pheromone density based pattern Classification (APC) [12], and Support Vector Machines [13] are used as classifiers. Feature extraction is based on Gabor features – see, e.g., [14] –, Local Binary Patterns (LBP) [15] and raw pixel values with histogram equalization.

Notably external factors critically affecting the accuracy of face recognition like race, expressions and environmental conditions, are almost irrelevant for gender categorization. This fact is in agreement with the human ability to judge a person's gender from the facial appearance only. We also report interesting insights related to the feature extraction step. Particularly, Gabor features turn to be an effective choice in uncontrolled environment, while, in the case of controlled environment raw pixel values perform equally well.

The paper is structured as follows. In Section 2 we introduce the notation used and we give a brief description of the FRGC2.0 dataset. We also briefly introduce both the classification algorithms and the feature extraction methods herewith employed. In Section 3 we describe our experimental setup, detailing the experimental protocol. Section 4 shows the results of the experimental protocol applied to a selected set of features and classifiers. Finally, in Section 5 conclusions are drawn.

Fig. 1. Images samples from the FRGC2.0 database. Neutral, smiling and different light conditions images from the same person are depicted in the first row. In the second row, they are depicted images related to the different races, namely Asian, Asian Middle Eastern, Asian Southern, Black or African American, Hispanic, and White.

2   Data, Algorithms, and Features

2.1   The FRGC2.0 Dataset

The proposed computational analysis of gender categorization is based on processing 2D face images comprised in the Face Recognition Grand Challenge dataset, version 2.0. The dataset is composed of more than 50,000 images (see Figure 1), divided into a training and a validation set [10], denoted as Γ and Σ, respectively.

As both Γ and Σ include all subjects (males and females) involved in the images collections, the FRGC2.0 training set can be regarded as a set $\Gamma = \{\underline{\gamma}_1, \ldots, \underline{\gamma}_n\}$, with $n = 291$ (the total amount of involved subjects), in which each $\underline{\gamma}_j$ denotes the pool of images related to the subject j. Each image $\gamma_{jk} \subset \underline{\gamma}_j$ is characterized by a tuple of three elements $< C, E, R >$, where:

- $C = \{c2l, c3l, u\}$ denotes the types of control, i.e., controlled images with two or three studio lights ($c2l$ and $c3l$, respectively), and uncontrolled images (denoted as u).
- $E = \{BlankStare, Happiness\}$ denotes the facial expressions in the dataset images, i.e., neutral and smiling, respectively.
- $R = \{A, AME, AS, BAA, H, U, W\}$ denotes the race of the subject, where, following the categorization of FRGC2.0, A stands for "Asian", AME for "Asian Middle Eastern", AS for "Asian-Southern", BAA for "Black or African American", H for "Hispanic", while U stands for "Unknown", and, finally, W denotes "White" race.

The same categorization can be applied to the test set $\Sigma = \{\underline{\sigma}_1, \ldots, \underline{\sigma}_n\}$, with $n = 466$.

2.2   Algorithms

In this paper, gender categorization is modeled as a binary pattern classification problem. In binary classification, a set of patterns is given, i.e., input vectors

$X = \{\underline{x}_1, \ldots \underline{x}_k\}$ with $\underline{x}_i \in \mathbb{R}^n$, and a corresponding set of labels, i.e., output values $Y \in \{0, 1\}$ – in this case, male and female. The labels as generated by some unknown function $f : \mathbb{R}^n \rightarrow \{0, 1\}$ applied to the patterns, i.e., $f(\underline{x}_i) = y_i$ for $i \in \{1, \ldots, k\}$ and $y_i \in \{0, 1\}$. The task of a binary classifier c is to extrapolate f given X and Y, i.e., to construct c from X and Y so that when given some $\underline{x}^\star \in X$, $c(\underline{x}^\star)$ will equal $f(\underline{x}^\star)$; such task can be achieved *training an inductive model* of c.

In the following, the classifiers applied for gender categorization analysis are briefly reviewed.

- **1-nearest-neighbor** (1-NN): this classifier yields the label of the training instance which is closer to the given test instance, whereby closeness is evaluated using some proximity measure, e.g. Euclidean distance; we use the method described in [11] to store the training instances for fast look-up.
- **Aggregation Pheromone density based pattern Classification** (APC): this is a pattern classification algorithm modeled on the ants colony behavior and distributed adaptive organization in nature. Each data pattern is considered as an ant, and the training patterns (ants) form several groups or colonies depending on the number of classes present in the data set. Each colony releases a quantity of pheromones proportional to the population of ants. A new test pattern (ant) will move along the direction where the average aggregation pheromone density (at the location of the new ant) is higher and eventually it will join that colony [12].
- **Support Vector Machines** (SVM): this is a supervised learning algorithm used for both classification and regression tasks. Roughly speaking, the basic training principle of SVMs is finding an optimal linear hyperplane such that the expected classification error for (unseen) test patterns is minimized [13].

2.3 Features

Different input vectors X are extracted from Γ and Σ either as raw pixel values, Gabor or LBP features. In order to avoid registration errors, all images are first aligned according to the positions of the eyes.

The most elementary features used are the raw pixel values (denoted as PV), extracted from the image matrix (re-scaled to 64x64 pixels) and aligned in a mono-dimensional vector. To compensate for illumination changes, histogram equalization is first applied.

Gabor features are extracted by applying a standard bank of Gabor kernels with 5 scales and 8 orientation. For each image, a feature vector of 2560 elements is extracted by sampling the filters outputs on the 64 nodes of a uniform 8×8 grid. All processing is based on the Feature Extraction Library (FELib) [16].

A modified version of the original Local Binary Pattern operator (LBP) has been also applied. The LBP operator is denoted as $LBP_{P,R}$, where P is the number of sampling points on a circle of radius R. An interesting extension of LBP takes into account the bitwise transitions of the obtained binary pattern [15]. In order to obtain a good trade-off between description performance and feature

Table 1. Synopsis of training, validation and test sets. The table is structured as follows. The first column shows the name of set (in the case of test sets, we report groups only), and it is followed by three columns. The first column ("#") reports the total amount of images in the set, while the remaining two ("F" and "M") report the percentage of the images in the set, labeled as female and male, respectively.

	#	F	M
Γ_t	1027	42.65%	57.35%
Σ_v	1292	43.19%	56.61%
Σ_a	1262	45.01%	54.99%
Σ_b	1958	50.56%	49.45%
Σ_c	1958	50.56%	49.45%

vector length, the $LBP_{8,2}^{u2}$ operator has been used [17]. Each image is divided into a a uniform 7×7 grid and the $LBP_{8,2}^{u2}$ is applied to each resulting subwindow. The histograms are computed within each window independently and concatenated. The resulting histogram has size $m \times n$ where m is the number of windows (49 in this case) and n is the length of a single $LBP_{8,2}^{u2}$ histogram (10 in this case). Therefore, the total histogram is composed of 490 buckets.

3   Experimental Setup

In order to evaluate the gender categorization capability of the chosen classifiers on the given feature sets, an experimental protocol has been devised, based on the FRGC2.0 dataset. The dataset is composed of about 40,000 images from 466 subjects of different races, 43.93% are female and 56.07% are male. Images were taken at different illumination conditions, and with different facial expressions.

The aim of the experimental trial is to compute the classification models trained on data having specific values of C, E, and R. Towards this end, the algorithms described in Section 2.2 are trained selecting controlled images – two studio lights – related to "Caucasian" subjects (the most recurrent in the FRGC2.0) showing a neutral expression. In other words, the classifiers are trained on a set Γ_t in which, for each subject j, $|\gamma_j|$ is equal to the total amount of images $\gamma_{jk} \subset \gamma_j$ such that $(C = c2l) \wedge (E = BlankStare) \wedge (R = W)$.

It is well-known, from machine learning literature, that classifiers performance may vary with different parametrization tunings. In order to provide a fair comparison among classifiers, the FRGC2.0 validation set Σ is divided into two parts. The first part is composed of the images related to the 291 subjects also occurring in Γ. This partition – denoted as Σ_v – is used just for parameter tuning. Σ_v is established with the same criteria applied for Γ:

$$\Sigma_v : \text{for each subject } j, \sigma_{jk} \subset \sigma_j \text{ such that } (C = c2l) \wedge (E = BlankStare) \wedge (R = W)$$

Concerning the test set, we consider the partition of Σ composed of the images from the 175 subjects *not occurring* in Γ. Nine different test sets are extracted and organized in three groups:

- Σ_a: for each subject j, $\forall \sigma_{jk} \subset \sigma_j \in \Sigma$ such that $\gamma_j \notin \Gamma$ and $(E = BlankStare) \wedge (R = W)$. The rationale is to have the same facial expression and race of the training set, in order to have a baseline for the comparisons. This group is composed of three test sets, i.e., $\Sigma_{a,c2l}$, $\Sigma_{a,c3l}$, $\Sigma_{a,u}$, representing test sets in which σ_{jk} has a value of C equal to $c2l$, $c3l$, and u, respectively.
- Σ_b: for each subject j, $\forall \sigma_{jk} \subset \sigma_j \in \Sigma$ such that $\gamma_j \notin \Gamma$ and $(E = BlankStare)$. In this group are involved images that are not constrained to a particular value of R. The rationale is to compare the accuracy of the classifiers with respect to the race. Also this group if composed of three test sets, i.e., $\Sigma_{b,c2l}$, $\Sigma_{b,c3l}$, $\Sigma_{b,u}$.
- Σ_c: for each subject j, $\forall \sigma_{jk} \subset \sigma_j \in \Sigma$ such that $\gamma_j \notin \Gamma$ and $(E = Happiness)$. The rationale is to compare the accuracy of the classifiers with respect to different facial expressions. Also this group is not constrained by a particular value of R. It is composed of three test sets: $\Sigma_{c,c2l}$, $\Sigma_{c,c3l}$, $\Sigma_{c,u}$.

Cardinalities and label distributions of the sets are reported in Table 1.

4   Experimental Results

The first experimental trial is aimed to train a gender categorization model based on 1-NN, APC, and SVM. A parameter grid search involving both APC and SVM is performed, as follows:

- Concerning APC, we explore the parameter δ related to the pheromone intensity as described in [12].
- Concerning SVM, we consider a C-SVC with a Radial Basis Function (RBF) kernel. In particular, we explore the parameter space related to both cost c and the parameter g of the kernel RBF.

We test the obtained models on Σ_v, and the results of these experiments with the best parameter configuration – in terms of accuracy – are shown in Table 2. For all experiments described, when referring to APC and SVM, the parametrization in Table 2 was applied.

In the next experiment, the performance of 1-NN, APC, and SVM, trained on Γ_t using PV features, and tested on the test sets described in Section 3 are evaluated. The obtained results are summarized in Table 3.

From table 3, SVM outperforms all classifiers, reporting an accuracy greater than 90% on all test sets with $C = c2l$ and $C = c3l$ in both groups Σ_a and Σ_b. SVM is also the best performing classifier for $C = u$. Concerning $\Sigma_{a,c2l}$, the SVM accuracy is more than 10% higher than both 1-NN and APC. The classification results related to $\Sigma_{a,c2l}$ can be regarded as a reference, because it is composed of images having the same value of C, E, and R used to compute Γ_t.

Considering the results related to $\Sigma_{a,c3l}$, the accuracy of all classifiers is very close to the one reported for $\Sigma_{a,c2l}$. As a consequence, we can conjecture that

Table 2. Parameter optimization for the considered algorithms. The table is organized as follows: The first column shows the name of the algorithms, and it is followed by three groups of columns, reporting the results of the optimization considering PV, Gabor and LBP features. Each group of columns is composed of two subcolumns, reporting the accuracy (column "Acc.") of the computed model, and the related parameters (column "Par.").

Classifier	PV		Gabor		LBP	
	Acc.	Par.	Acc.	Par.	Acc.	Par.
1-NN	97.54%	–	98.99%	–	96.59%	–
APC	95.90%	$\delta = 2$	99.07%	$\delta = 0.1$	94.27%	$\delta = 50$
SVM	98.80%	$c = 2, g = 0$	99.46%	$c = 2, g = 2$	97.29%	$c = 16, g = 2\text{e-}06$

Table 3. Evaluation results using PV features. The table is composed of four columns. The first one ("Test set") denotes the test set on which classifiers has been evaluated. The three following columns report the accuracy performance (in percentage) related to 1-NN, APC, and SVM (columns "1-NN", "APC", and "SVM", respectively).

Test set	1-NN	APC	SVM
$\Sigma_{a,c2l}$	83.60%	84.86%	95.80%
$\Sigma_{a,c3l}$	81.70%	84.15%	95.01%
$\Sigma_{a,u}$	64.10%	67.99%	76.39%
$\Sigma_{b,c2l}$	81.31%	82.38%	91.37%
$\Sigma_{b,c3l}$	81.10%	82.69%	91.78%
$\Sigma_{b,u}$	63.89%	66.70%	75.49%
$\Sigma_{c,c2l}$	80.03%	80.54%	88.07%
$\Sigma_{c,c3l}$	81.00%	81.15%	89.07%
$\Sigma_{c,u}$	65.83%	68.08%	78.19%

all considered classifiers are robust with respect to controlled illumination variations. From the results obtained from images captured in an uncontrolled environment – $\Sigma_{a,u}$ –, the performances of the classifiers decrease. SVM still provides the best classification performance, but its accuracy is about 20% lower than the one reported for both $\Sigma_{a,c2l}$ and $\Sigma_{a,c3l}$.

Considering the results related to Σ_b, the same results described for Σ_a hold: SVM outperforms the other classifiers, and there is a lack of performance for $C = u$. The resulting accuracy of all classifiers is very close to that reported for Σ_a. However, as discussed in Section 3, the images comprised in such test sets are not constrained from a particular value of R. As a consequence, we can conjecture that classifiers performance are not affected by race variations. The same conclusions can be drawn from the results related to the group Σ_c, in which also E (facial expression) is not constrained.

As for Gabor features, the results of the performed experiments are summarized in Table 4. Also in this case SVM outperforms the other classifiers, reaching an accuracy greater than 90% on all test sets having $C = c2l$ and $C = c3l$. SVM is also the best performing classifier for $C = u$. Concerning $\Sigma_{a,c2l}$, SVM accuracy is more than 5% greater than APC accuracy, and about 9% greater than 1-NN

Table 4. Evaluation results using Gabor features. The table is organized as Table 4.

Test set	1-NN	APC	SVM
$\Sigma_{a,c2l}$	82.88%	86.53%	91.92%
$\Sigma_{a,c3l}$	83.44%	87.48%	92.95%
$\Sigma_{a,u}$	64.66%	68.70%	78.68%
$\Sigma_{b,c2l}$	83.20%	86.57%	90.60%
$\Sigma_{b,c3l}$	83.71%	87.13%	91.62%
$\Sigma_{b,u}$	65.37%	68.18%	77.99%
$\Sigma_{c,c2l}$	74.44%	80.75%	90.14%
$\Sigma_{c,c3l}$	74.11%	81.61%	90.81%
$\Sigma_{c,u}$	63.48%	64.86%	71.12%

Table 5. Evaluation results using LBP features. The table is organized as Table 3.

Test set	1-NN	APC	SVM
$\Sigma_{a,c2l}$	79.63%	81.93%	90.89%
$\Sigma_{a,c3l}$	81.30%	81.06%	91.36%
$\Sigma_{a,u}$	53.80%	51.34%	51.98%
$\Sigma_{b,c2l}$	82.79%	85.03%	91.73%
$\Sigma_{b,c3l}$	82.53%	83.76%	92.13%
$\Sigma_{b,u}$	49.08%	52.35%	54.44%
$\Sigma_{c,c2l}$	80.08%	81.97%	90.40%
$\Sigma_{c,c3l}$	77.43%	78.65%	89.32%
$\Sigma_{c,u}$	56.84%	54.70%	55.41%

accuracy. Considering the results related to $\Sigma_{a,c3l}$, the accuracy of all classifiers is very close to the one reported for $\Sigma_{a,c2l}$. Also for $\Sigma_{a,u}$, a lack of classifiers performance is reported. SVM still produces the best classification results, but its accuracy is about 14% smaller than the one reported for both $\Sigma_{a,c2l}$ and $\Sigma_{a,c2l}$. The performance of both 1-NN and APC also decrease of about 20%. Considering the results related to Σ_b, the same results described for Σ_a hold: SVM outperforms the other classifiers, and there is a lack of performance for $C = u$. The accuracy reported for all classifiers is very close to that reported for Σ_a.

The last experiment performed is similar to the previous one, but LBP features were used instead of Gabor features. The obtained results are reported in Table 5.

Also in this case, SVM is the best performing classifier – in terms of accuracy. From the results related to Σ_a, Σ_b, and Σ_c, the same conclusions made for both PV and Gabor features can be drawn. This fact confirm our conjecture that gender classification is independent from the values of E (facial expression) and R (race), and also from controlled illumination variations. However, differently from the previous experiments, LBP features are almost useless in the uncontrolled cases $\Sigma_{a,u}$, $\Sigma_{b,u}$, and $\Sigma_{c,u}$.

5   Conclusions

The gender categorization problem has been analyzed trying to understand which factors critically affect the accuracy of available technologies. The proposed protocol exploited the dimensions of the FRGC2.0 database, analyzing the sensitivity of a two-steps feature extraction-classification approach with respect to three different classifiers and three orthogonal types of features.

The results of our empirical analysis can be summarized as follows:

- Gender categorization is independent from the race of the subjects. Our results show that training an inductive model on a set of images composed of subject of only one race, the accuracy of the classifiers is about the same if in the test set we involve subjects of different races.
- The accuracy in gender categorization does not change in a noticeable way for controlled changes of illumination. We showed that, training classifiers on FRGC2.0 controlled images with two studio lights, and testing them on controlled images with three studio lights, the accuracy result is almost the same of the test performed on controlled images with two studio lights.
- Different facial expressions do not influence in a noticeable way the gender categorization accuracy applying SVM to Gabor and LBP features. A marginal degradation is reported for PV features, starting from a 96% accuracy obtained for $\Sigma_{a,2cl}$. This fact is probably related to the iconic information content of PV features, while both Gabor and LBP features are mainly related to the frequency image content.

As a final comment, our analysis confirms that race, facial expression, and illumination condition are almost irrelevant for gender categorization from human faces. Obviously, relaxing the constraints for race and expression, the identification performance decreases. But this finding is independent from both classifiers and features.

Concerning the adopted classifiers, SVMs always outperform the other classifiers. The analysis performed in this paper confirms that Gabor features are an effective choice in the case of uncontrolled environments. Moreover, elementary features such as raw pixel values can be usefully applied for gender categorization.

As future work, we are planning to investigate additional dimensions of FRGC2.0, e.g. age, and to extend our analysis to other datasets, including masking and face occlusions. In addition, we plan to extend our analysis to additional feature representation and state-of-the-art gender classification methods, and carefully consider the statistical significance of the classifier results.

Acknowledgments. This research has received funding from Autonomous Region of Sardinia (Italy), L.R. 07/08/2007, n. 7, under grant agreement CP 2_442, "Adaptive Biometric Systems: Methodologies, Models, and Algorithms".

References

1. Shan, C.: Learning local binary patterns for gender classification on real-world face images. Pattern Recognition Letters 33, 431–437 (2012)
2. Lian, H.-C., Lu, B.-L.: Multi-view Gender Classification Using Local Binary Patterns and Support Vector Machines. In: Wang, J., Yi, Z., Żurada, J.M., Lu, B.-L., Yin, H. (eds.) ISNN 2006. LNCS, vol. 3972, pp. 202–209. Springer, Heidelberg (2006)
3. Golomb, B., Lawrence, D., Sejnowski, T.: Sexnet: A neural network identifies sex from human faces. In: Advances in Neural Information Processing Systems, vol. 3, pp. 572–577 (1991)
4. Cottrell, G., Metcalfe, J.: Empath: Face, emotion, and gender recognition using holons. In: Proceedings of the 1990 Conference on Advances in Neural Information Processing Systems, vol. 3, pp. 564–571. Morgan Kaufmann Publishers Inc. (1990)
5. Brunelli, R., Poggio, T.: Hyperbf networks for gender classification. In: Proceedings of the DARPA Image Understanding Workshop, San Diego, CA, vol. 314 (1992)
6. Moghaddam, B., Yang, M.: Learning gender with support faces. IEEE Transactions on Pattern Analysis and Machine Intelligence 24, 707–711 (2002)
7. Makinen, E., Raisamo, R.: Evaluation of gender classification methods with automatically detected and aligned faces. IEEE Transactions on Pattern Analysis and Machine Intelligence 30, 541–547 (2008)
8. Lapedriza, A., Marin-Jimenez, M., Vitria, J.: Gender recognition in non controlled environments. In: 18th International Conference on Pattern Recognition, ICPR 2006, vol. 3, pp. 834–837. IEEE (2006)
9. Shobeirinejad, A., Gao, Y.: Gender classification using interlaced derivative patterns. In: 2010 20th International Conference on Pattern Recognition (ICPR), pp. 1509–1512. IEEE (2010)
10. Phillips, P., Flynn, P., Scruggs, T., Bowyer, K., Chang, J., Hoffman, K., Marques, J., Min, J., Worek, W.: Overview of the face recognition grand challenge. In: IEEE Computer Society Conference on Computer Vision and Pattern Recognition, CVPR 2005, vol. 1, pp. 947–954. IEEE (2005)
11. Aha, D., Kibler, D., Albert, M.: Instance-based learning algorithms. Machine Learning 6, 37–66 (1991)
12. Halder, A., Ghosh, A., Ghosh, S.: Aggregation pheromone density based pattern classification. Fundamenta Informaticae 92, 345–362 (2009)
13. Cortes, C., Vapnik, V.: Support-vector networks. Machine Learning 20, 273–297 (1995)
14. Shen, L., Bai, L.: A review on gabor wavelets for face recognition. Pattern Analysis & Applications 9, 273–292 (2006)
15. Ojala, T., Pietikainen, M., Maenpaa, T.: Multiresolution gray-scale and rotation invariant texture classification with local binary patterns. IEEE Transactions on Pattern Analysis and Machine Intelligence 24, 971–987 (2002)
16. Zhu, J., Hoi, S., Lyu, M., Yan, S.: Near-duplicate keyframe retrieval by nonrigid image matching. In: Proceeding of the 16th ACM International Conference on Multimedia, pp. 41–50. ACM (2008), http://www.vision.ee.ethz.ch/~zhuji
17. Ahonen, T., Hadid, A., Pietikainen, M.: Face description with local binary patterns: Application to face recognition. IEEE Transactions on Pattern Analysis and Machine Intelligence 28, 2037–2041 (2006)

Facial Landmarking: Comparing Automatic Landmarking Methods with Applications in Soft Biometrics

Amrutha Sethuram, Karl Ricanek, Jason Saragih, and Chris Boehnen

Face Aging Group, UNCW, U.S.A.
{sethurama,ricanekk}@uncw.edu, jason.saragih@csiro.au, boehnencb@ornl.gov
http://www.faceaginggroup.com

Abstract. Registration is a critical step in computer-based image analysis. In this work we examine the effects of registration in face-based soft-biometrics. This form of soft-biometrics, better termed as facial analytics, takes an image containing a face and returns attributes of that face. In this work, the attributes of focus are gender and race. Automatic generation of facial analytics relies on accurate registration. Hence, this work evaluates three techniques for dense registration, namely AAM, Stacked ASM and CLM. Further, we evaluate the influence of facial landmark mis-localization, resulting from these techniques, on gender classification and race determination. To the best of our knowledge, such an evaluation of landmark mis-localization on soft biometrics, has not been conducted. We further demonstrate an effective system for gender and race classification based on dense landmarking and multi-factored principle components analysis. The system performs well against a multi-age face dataset for both gender and race classification.

Keywords: facial landmarking, auto-landmarking methods, gender classification, race determination.

1 Introduction

Automatic facial landmarking is a very important step that precedes any task involving face recognition or analysis. These landmarks, also referred to as fiducial points or anchor points, are used for accurate registration of faces and have a significant effect on the impending analysis. While some applications, such as, face recognition and tracking use a few landmarks like the eye and eyebrow corners, centers of the iris, corners of the mouth, tip of the nose and chin for registration, other applications like age estimation, expression analysis, detection of intent or facial aging require a greater number of landmarks for analysis. Further, it is important that the detection of these points be accurate and robust to environmental variables e.g. illumination, occlusion, expression, pose, etc. It has been shown that precise landmarks are essential for face-recognition performance and that more landmarks results in higher recognition performance. However, under various conditions of image acquisition, automatic facial landmarking becomes

A. Fusiello et al. (Eds.): ECCV 2012 Ws/Demos, Part II, LNCS 7584, pp. 290–299, 2012.
© Springer-Verlag Berlin Heidelberg 2012

a challenging task. There exist many automatic registration algorithms which perform well in detecting the internal landmarks e.g., the eye corners, centers of the iris and the corners of the mouth. More often, performance of these algorithms are reported solely on a few such, well-defined points, which artificially inflate the performance of algorithms in a real-world application. However, in this paper, we consider an extremely dense scheme consisting of 252-points on the face that includes internal and boundary points. Such a dense scheme is helpful in applications in soft biometrics such as expression recognition, detection of micro gestures, age estimation, gender and race classification, facial aging etc. While one can argue that accurate detection of a few internal points is sufficient for many tasks, it is often necessary that features such as the boundary of the face must be accurately detected for applications that involve facial synthesis or off-pose face recognition. The main contributions of this paper are: (1) Provide a set of baseline algorithms and performance metrics for extremely dense registration. (2) Evaluate the influence of automatic detection of landmarks on gender classification and race determination. The remainder of this paper is organized as follows: A background on existing automatic landmarking methods and those considered for this work is discussed in section 2. Experiments and Results are presented in section 3. Conclusion and future work is discussed in section 4.

2   Background

Algorithms proposed for automatic facial landmarking can be broadly classified into two categories: image-based methods and structure-based methods. In image-based methods, faces are treated as vectors in high dimensional space, which are then modeled as a manifold. The variability in facial features is captured through popular transformations like the Principal Components Analysis, Independent Components Analysis, Gabor Wavelets, Discrete Cosine Transforms and Gaussian derivative filters. The appearance of each landmark is then learned through the use of machine learning approaches like support vector machines, boosted cascade detectors and multi-layer perceptrons [1] [2][3].

Structure-based methods use prior knowledge about facial landmark positions, and constrain the landmark search using heuristic rules that involve angles, distances and areas. Very popular methods in this category are Active Shape Models (ASM) [4], Active Appearance Models (AAM) [5] and Elastic Bunch Graphing Methods. ASMs model textures of small neighborhoods around landmarks and iteratively minimizes the differences between landmark points and their corresponding models. The AAM typically looks at the convex hull of landmarks, synthesizes a facial image from a joint appearance and shape model, and seeks to minimize similarity to the target face iteratively. Cristinacce et al. [6] proposed the Constrained Local Model (CLM) approach that uses a set of local feature templates for detection of landmarks. There have been many variants and improvements on these classic ASM, AAM and CLM approaches. By fitting more landmarks and stacking two ASMs in series, Milborrow and Nicolls [7] locate features in frontal views of faces. In [8], Saragih *et al.* propose a regularized mean-shift algorithm to the CLM approach. Due to their widespread use in various automatic landmarking applications, the availability of their actual implementations and also flexibility to train the algorithms using our dense scheme, the following three automatic landmarking methods are considered for this work.

Active Appearance Models: Active appearance models (AAM), a group of flexible deformable models, have been widely used for automatic landmarking. First proposed by Cootes et. al [5], AAM decouples and models shape and pixel intensities of an object. As described in [5], the AAM model can be generated in three main steps: (1) A statistical shape model is constructed to model the shape variations of an object using a set of annotated training images. (2) A texture model is then built to model the texture variations, which is represented by intensities of the pixels. (3) A final appearance model is then built by combining the shape and the texture models. The AAM software used for this work was obtained from [9].

Constrained Local Models: Constrained Local Models are a derivative of Active Shape Models (ASM). These are methods that make independent predictions regarding locations of the model's landmarks, which are combined by enforcing a prior over their joint motion. Most CLM variants implement a two step fitting strategy, where an exhaustive local search is first performed to obtain a response map for each landmark. Optimization is then performed using strategies to maximize the responses of the landmarks. In this paper, one such strategy that uses a gaussian prior over the model's PCA parameters is implemented as an automatic method to be compared against. The algorithm is itself presented by Saragih et al. in [8]

STASM: STASM or Stacked Active Shape Model [7] is an extension of active shape model proposed by Cootes [4]. As described in [7], STASM extends the active shape model by fitting more landmarks than actually needed, by selectively using two-instead of one-dimensional landmark templates and stacking two active shape models in series. The C++ software library to train and test the models for this work was obtained from [10]

3   Experiments and Results

3.1   Design of Experiments

Databases Used The automatic landmarking algorithms were trained using images obtained from MORPH [11] (a publicly available mugshot database), the PAL database [12] and the Pinellas County database (mugshot database with limited distribution). In addition, the data was formulated with distribution of images over four ethno-gender groups: African American Male (AAM), African American Female (AAF), Caucasian American Male (CAM) and Caucasian American Females (CAF), and age ranges as shown in Table 1 and Table 2 for training the general model. A total of 1155 images were used for training.

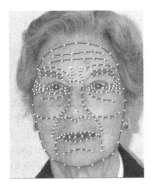

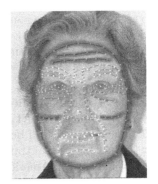

Fig. 1. Example of dense annotation map

Fig. 2. Component scheme adopted for landmarking. Each expert was trained on annotating a color coded feature

Table 1. Training Data: Distribution based on ethno-gender groups and age ranges

Age Range	AAM	AAF	CAM	CAF
18-30	50	50	50	50
31-40	50	50	50	50
41-50	50	50	50	50
51-60	50	50	49	50
61-70	50	50	48	50
71+	38	21	49	50

Table 2. Training Data: Distribution based on databases

Database	AAM	AAF	CAM	CAF
Pinellas	88	62	104	180
MORPH	200	199	149	67
PAL	0	10	43	53

Obtaining Ground-Truth Data Obtaining ground truth coordinates for points on an image is not only tedious but also a time-consuming task. Great effort must be taken to get the annotators to consistently locate and label the right features on the image. In addition, to account for inter-observer variability in obtaining gold standard points requires that the images be annotated by at least 3 or more trained annotators for each image [13]. Thus it has become customary for researchers to report the performance of their algorithms on datasets that have ground truth as part of their distribution. However, since this work is based on a dense 252 landmark scheme for the face, which is not available in any face datasets, it was necessary that we generated the ground truth in-house. Given the large number of training and testing data and the density of the annotation scheme itself, it was not practical, both in terms of time and resources, to obtain repeat measurements for the ground truth data by 4 or 5 well-trained annotators. Instead, a component scheme was developed, in which, experts were trained to annotate a specific region or component of the face. Each expert annotated a specific feature/component of the face as color coded in Figure 2 across all the images in the training and testing data. This ensured that variations in annotating features of the face were kept at a minimum.

Training and Testing Methodology. For purposes of evaluation and comparison, each of the automatic landmarking methods were trained on the entire set of 1155 images, which will be henceforth termed as *general* model.

Similar to the collection of training data, testing data from the various ethno-gender groups i.e. African American Females (AAF), Caucasian American Males (CAM), African American Males (AAM) and Caucasian American Females (CAF) were formulated to evaluate the performance of the algorithms. In addition to the 1155 images that were manually annotated to train the models, ground truth for test images for the AAF, CAM, AAM and CAF ethno-gender groups were obtained using the same component scheme. The distribution of test images used in this work is as shown in Table 3 and Table 4.

For testing the performance of the landmarking algorithms, each of the algorithms were trained on the general model and automatic landmarks were obtained for the general test set. These detected landmarks were then compared to the ground truth that was generated for the testing data.

Table 3. Testing Data: Distribution based on ethno-gender groups and age ranges

Age Range	AAF	CAM	AAM	CAF
18-30	50	50	50	50
31-40	44	49	50	50
41-50	41	50	50	50
51-60	49	50	50	50
61-70	11	50	43	50
71+	0	50	2	26

Table 4. Testing Data: Distribution based on databases

Database	AAF	CAM	AAM	CAF
Pinellas County	103	240	140	244
MORPH	80	44	101	6
PAL	12	15	4	26

3.2   Performance Measures

In our experiments, we evaluate the efficiency of the AAM, CLM and STASM landmarking algorithms in a two step process. First, the actual error in point detection is evaluated on all of the 252 points,by comparing the points detected by the algorithms with the ground-truth available on the testing data. Next, the influence of these detected landmark points is quantified when applied to gender classification and race determination as shown in Figure 3

Error Analysis of Automatic Point Detection. The efficiency of the algorithms are evaluated by analyzing the errors associated with the detected points

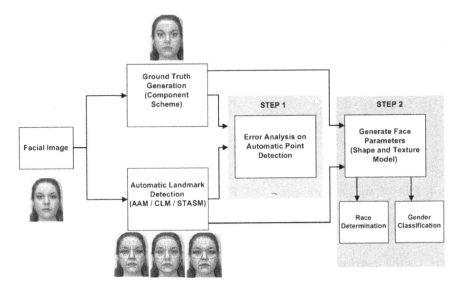

Fig. 3. Evaluation of automatic landmarking methods

when compared to the ground-truth. The interocular distance d_{io} is used as a normalization factor for computing error measures. Interocular distance is the distance between the centers of left and right eye and is often used in state-of-the art studies in 2-D facial landmarking. Since the distance error measure is scaled by the interocular distance, it is invariant to the variation in size of each individual face, which allows scaled comparison of point to point errors between images. The interocular distance varied between 48.8 and 130.11 pixels for the test data.

The detection error of a point i is defined as the Euclidean point to point distance between the ground-truth point T_i and detected point $\hat{T}_i$:

$$e_i = \frac{||T_i - \hat{T}_i||}{d_{io}} \qquad (1)$$

An *average error per annotation point p*, across all the images in the test set was computed using the formula

$$m_p = \frac{1}{md_{io}} \sum_{i=1}^{m} d_i \qquad (2)$$

where d_i are the Euclidean point to point errors for each individual annotation point and m is the number of images in the test data set. The average error for each of these individual points is as shown in Figure 4 for the test data.

The classification rate C_i can be defined as:

$$C_i = \frac{\sum_{j=1}^{m} e_i^j < 0.1}{m} \qquad (3)$$

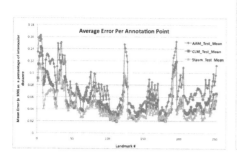

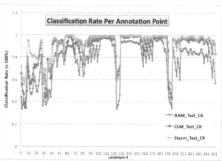

Fig. 4. Plot of average error per annotation point as a percentage of interocular distance vs. landmark

Fig. 5. Plot of average error per annotation point as a percentage of interocular distance vs. landmark

where j is the image number and m is the total number of images in the dataset. The classification rate for the test data is as shown in Figure 5.

The average image error on an image I can be defined as

$$m_I = \frac{1}{nd_{io}} \sum_{i=1}^{n} d_i \qquad (4)$$

where n denotes the number of landmarks (252) and d_i values are the Euclidean point-to-point distances for each individual landmark location. The average image error for the different algorithms for the general model is as shown in Figure 6.

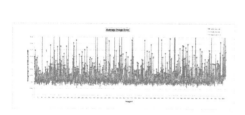

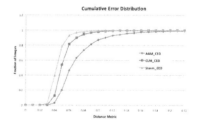

Fig. 6. General Test Data: Average Image Error

Fig. 7. Comparison of cumulative error distribution of point to point error

The cumulative error distribution of point to point error measured on the test set is as shown in Figure 7.

Also, to compare the errors associated with the individual physical features of the face, average errors were computed on the set of landmarks that make up the physical feature. Results are as shown in Table 5 for the general model.

Table 5. General Model: Average Error Associated With Physical Features (as a percentage of interocular distance)

Algorithm	Face Outline	Eyebrow (L)	Eyebrow (R)	Eye (L)	Eye (R)	Nose	Mouth	Soft Tissue
AAM	12.1	7.9	7.0	3.6	3.3	4.4	6.3	8.2
CLM	9.2	5.5	**5.0**	**2.5**	**2.4**	3.2	3.9	5.7
STASM	**7.2**	**5.2**	5.3	2.6	2.6	**2.7**	**2.9**	**4.7**

In the analysis of the average image error on our data, a Kruskal-Wallis H test was performed. It was found that there was a statistically significant difference between the different algorithms (H(2) = 980.88, P < 0.01) with a mean rank of 2151.69 for AAM, 1480.72 for CLM and 932.09 for STASM. Since STASM and CLM have relatively lower mean errors, their performance is better than AAM. From Figure 4, it can be seen that STASM has the lowest average error per annotation point. From Figure 5, it is seen that the average error per annotation point is comparable in both CLM and STASM on all points other than the boundary points on the face. In addition, the average image error on each of the training images were lower for STASM and CLM as shown in Figure 6. Also, Figure 7 shows that STASM has a higher fraction of images on which the error was below 10% of the interocular distance. At 10% of the inter ocular distance, STASM and CLM perform better than the AAM. It is evident from Table 5 that, STASM and CLM have lower errors on individual facial features when compared to the AAM. It can be seen from Figure 4 and Table 5, that errors associated with points on the soft tissue are larger than the errors associated with points on an actual facial feature e.g. left eye, right eye, nose and the mouth. This may be also due to the fact that it is a challenging task for the algorithms to detect the points when the actual trait of the soft tissue e.g. creases on the forehead, nasiolabial lines or the crows feet, is not very well defined across all faces, i.e. these creases and lines are not apparent on young faces. Future experiments will delve into quantifying the errors on older faces. The primary errors are found on the face boundary. Further, the left face boundary–chin to the ear–generates the most errors. This is helpful for applications where automatic detection of the outline of the face is also important, in addition to the internal features. Finally, although the time taken to train the models and time to automatically detect these landmarks were not quantified directly from the experiments performed, it was observed that STASM and CLM have much lower training and detection times when compared to the AAM. This suggests that STASM and CLM are better methods for automatic landmarking on realtime application, e.g. face tracking on video or large-scale batch analysis of faces, which may be executed in cloud based systems.

Application to Soft Biometrics. In practice, automatic landmark detection leads to mis-localization of a few annotation points. An evaluation of the influence of this mis-localization was performed on gender classification and race determination. For each of these classifiers, an active appearance model (AAM) was trained on the set of training images and the corresponding combined appearance parameters were used to train a Support Vector Machine (SVM). All face parameters, except the four, which explains rotation, translation, and scale, were used to train each (gender and race) classifier. The trained SVM classifiers were then used to determine the gender and race of the images in the hold out testing data. The results are as shown in Table 6 and Table 7 below. It can be seen that, performance of CLM and STASM on gender and race classification are comparable and better than AAM. Also, comparing the difference between the efficiencies of classifiers on ground truth and auto-detected points, gender classification is more sensitive to automatic landmarking errors than race determination. An example of an image in which race was falsely misclassified to be caucasian by all the three algorithms is as shown in Figure 8. Similarly, an example in which the gender was misclassified to be a female by all the three algorithms is as shown in Figure 9. In both the examples the classification was correct, when the face parameters were generated from the groundtruth points.

Table 6. Gender Determination Classification Accuracy (%)

Ground Truth	AAM	CLM	STASM
96.8	83.3	85.9	85.8

Table 7. Race Classification Accuracy (%)

Ground Truth	AAM	CLM	STASM
99.2	96.5	97.9	98

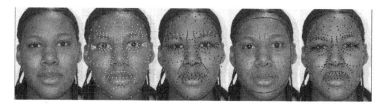

Fig. 8. Race Classification: Source Image, Ground-truth Annotations (✓), AAM detected(X), CLM detected(X), STASM detected points(X)

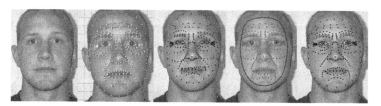

Fig. 9. Gender Determination: Source Image, Ground-Truth Annotations (✓), AAM detected(X), CLM detected(X), STASM detected points(X)

3.3   Conclusion and Future Work

In this paper, three state-of-the art algorithms - AAM, CLM and STASM, are compared for automatic landmark detection on a set of dense landmarks on the face. The performance of each of the algorithms are evaluated both in terms of actual errors in landmark detection and consequently by their ability in gender classification and race determination. A particular strength of the CLM algorithm is its performance in the presence of occlusions. Future evaluations will include performance of these registration techniques in the presence of noise and occlusions. From the experiments that were conducted, it can be concluded from this paper that: (1) CLM and STASM are better algorithms to be used for automatic landmarking on a dense landmarking scheme in terms of accuracy, time taken to train the model and detection of landmarks. (2) The influence of mis-localization of annotation points, resulting from automatic landmarking algorithms, is pronounced on race determination and gender classification. The efficiency of the classifiers decreases with the degree of inaccuracy in the landmarks detected. However, while manual landmarks are still the best for gender and race classification, automatic detection algorithms such as STASM and CLM are viable surrogates.

Acknowledgments. This work was partially funded by ongoing efforts with National Institute of Justice, Oakridge National Labs, and Federal Bureau of Investigations Biometric Center of Excellence.

References

1. Viola, P., Jones, M.: Robust real-time object detection. International Journal of Computer Vision (2001)
2. Vukadinovic, D., Pantic, M.: Fully automatic facial feature point detection using gabor feature based boosted classifiers. In: IEEE International Conference on Systems, Man and Cybernetics, vol. 2, pp. 1692–1698 (2005)
3. Dibeklioglu, H., Salah, A., Gevers, T.: A statistical method for 2-d facial landmarking. IEEE Transactions on Image Processing 21, 844–858 (2012)
4. Cootes, T.F., Taylor, C.J., Cooper, D.H., Graham, J.: Active shape models-their training and application. Computer Vis. and Image Under. 61, 38–59 (1995)
5. Cootes, T.F., Edwards, G.J., Taylor, C.J.: Active appearance models. In: Proc. Eur. Conf. Comput. Vis., vol. 2, pp. 484–498 (1998)
6. Cristinacce, D., Cootes, T.: Feature detection and tracking with constrained local models. In: BMVC, pp. 929–938 (2006)
7. Milborrow, S., Nicolls, F.: Locating Facial Features with an Extended Active Shape Model. In: Forsyth, D., Torr, P., Zisserman, A. (eds.) ECCV 2008, Part IV. LNCS, vol. 5305, pp. 504–513. Springer, Heidelberg (2008)
8. Saragih, J., Lucey, S., Cohn, J.: Deformable model fitting by regularized landmark mean-shift. International Journal of Computer Vision 91, 200–215 (2011)
9. AAM, http://sourceforge.net/projects/asmlibrary/files/
10. Stasm, http://www.milbo.users.sonic.net/stasm/download.html
11. Ricanek, K., Tesafaye, T.: Morph: A longitudinal image database of normal adult age-progression. In: 7th Int. Conf. on Auto. Face and Gesture Recog., pp. 341–345 (2006)
12. Minear, M., Park, D.: A lifespan database of adult facial stimuli. Behavior Research Methods, Instruments and Computers: A Journal of the Psychonomic Society, Inc. 36, 630–633 (2004)
13. Vučinić, P., Trpovski, Ž., Šćepan, I.: Automatic landmarking of cephalograms using active appearance models. European Journal of Orthodontics 32, 233–241 (2010)

Gender Recognition Using Cognitive Modeling

Jens Fagertun, Tobias Andersen, and Rasmus Reinhold Paulsen

Technical University of Denmark
Department of Informatics and Mathematical Modelling
Lyngby, Denmark

Abstract. In this work, we use cognitive modeling to estimate the *"gender strength"* of frontal faces, a continuous class variable, superseding the traditional binary class labeling. To incorporate this continuous variable we suggest a novel linear gender classification algorithm, the Gender Strength Regression. In addition, we use the gender strength to construct a smaller but refined training set, by identifying and removing ill-defined training examples. We use this refined training set to improve the performance of known classification algorithms. Also the human performance of known data sets is reported, and surprisingly it seems to be quite a hard task for humans. Finally our results are reproduced on a data set of above 40,000 public Danish LinkedIN profile pictures.

Keywords: Gender recognition, Linear Discriminant Analysis, Support Vector Machines, Cognitive Modeling, Linear Regression.

1 Introduction

Determining gender is a natural, subconscious task performed everyday in human interaction. By continuously training of this task on a daily basis, the human mind is shaped to become a gender recognition expert. Despite the strong belief that this is the case, there are very few scientific studies to support this. The studies that make a comparison between human vs. machine gender recognition performance are nearly two decades old, such as [1]. However, it is probably safe to assume that we humans do perform well as gender recognition experts, even with limited scientific documentation of the subject. This gives rise to some interesting questions: "Can we understand how humans perform the task of gender recognition?" and "Can we use this information to enhance machine learning models?".

It should be noted, that when confined only to non-intrusive data (such as visual or audio data) the two populations (male and female) cannot be perfectly separated. There are border-line cases where determining gender is also extremely hard for humans; cases where sports athletes need to undergo a DNA test to exactly determine the gender, come to mind.

The problem of automatic gender classification has been studied for years. Many algorithms have been proposed that employ different methods, including Linear Discriminant Analysis (LDA) [2], Haar-like wavelets [3], Locally Binary

A. Fusiello et al. (Eds.): ECCV 2012 Ws/Demos, Part II, LNCS 7584, pp. 300–308, 2012.

Patterns (LBP) [3] and Support Vector Machines (SVM) [4]. All these methods work on a binary understanding of class association, which does not necessarily enable the method to exclude ill-defined samples that could lead to a performance decrease. This work tries to address this shortcoming by analyzing how humans perform gender classification and incorporating this information into both a novel and well-known pattern recognition algorithms.

Obviously, humans perform gender recognition based on a variety of data, such as face, hair style, clothes, height, voice and movement patterns. In this article we look exclusively at faces. To address the previously posed questions, this work will look into the human performance. We estimate a continuous *"gender strength variable"* and use it to construct a novel linear gender classification algorithm, the Gender Strength Regression (GSR). In addition, we look into using this gender strength variable to construct a smaller but refined training set, by identifying and removing ill-defined training examples. We then assess if this refined training set improves performance of known classification algorithms.

The structure of the paper is as follows. Section 2 introduces the data sets used in this work. Section 3 describes the cognitive test that estimates the gender strength variable. Section 4 presents the Gender Strength Regression method. Section 5 presents the experiments and the obtained results. Finally, Section 6 presents a discussion and conclusion on this work.

2   Data Sets

In this work we use four data sets in order to ensure that our results are not biased towards a single protocol of acquiring facial images. The data sets are subsets of publicly available data, filtered so that they only contain frontal images with no extreme lighting or extreme facial expressions. The images have been cropped and rotated to only show the central face, excluding outer cheeks, lower chin and hair. Every image has been converted to gray scale and standardized by a histogram equalization. Furthermore, the data sets include the same number of males and females. This should motivate the observer to employ a response criterion that is not biased towards one of the two response categories. The data sets used are described in Table 1 with random samples shown in Figure 1.

3   Cognitive Test

The object of the cognitive test is to estimate the gender strength of each sample. The gender strength variable is defined as a variable in the interval [0 1] where close to zero signifies belonging poorly to the sample's group, whereas one signifies belonging strongly to the sample's group. To encode the gender in the variable, females will be denoted in the negative interval [-1 0] and males in the positive interval [0 1].

In order to estimate the gender strength variable, two cognitive user tests were devised and conducted on four and six test participants, respectively. The gender strength variable is estimated as a latent variable encoded by the time it takes participants to perform the gender classification task.

Table 1. Data sets used in this work

Data set	Total number of images used
AR [6]	298
XM2VTS [7]	552
FERET [8]	836
Public Danish LinkedIN profile pictures	200

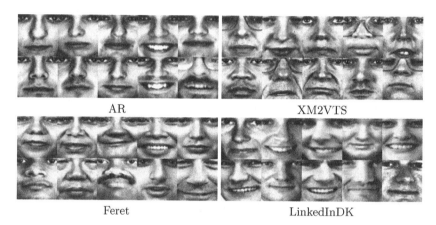

AR   XM2VTS

Feret   LinkedInDK

Fig. 1. Random sample images from the four data sets, with females and males in the first and second row, respectively

The cognitive test is conducted with the psychtoolbox for matlab [9], to ensure precise exposure/answer times. In the first test (time limited) every facial image is shown for precisely 200 ms, followed by a scrambled image of the original image (also shown for 200 ms) to disrupt the after image, which is sustained neural activity in the visual system following a visual stimulus. In the second test (not time limited) every facial image is shown until the user makes the classification. A graphical illustration of the tests is shown in Figure 2.

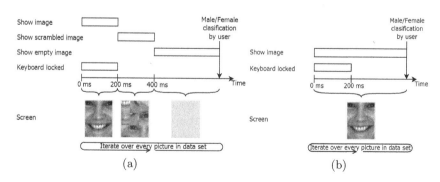

(a)   (b)

Fig. 2. Timeline for the cognitive tests, (a) time limit and (b) no time limit. There is a 550 ms delay from a user classification to the next picture is shown.

The gender strength variable is estimated by standardizing the test persons answer times, so that all answer times from one test person (per data set) has mean zero and unit variance. Then, a pooling of the standardized answer times from all test persons is performed. Finally, the pooled answer times below the mean are encoded to one, the outliers (above three standard deviations) are encoded to zero and the remaining are linearly encoded between the values zero and one.

4 Gender Strength Regression

In classification problems, training data is usually only labeled with which class it belongs to. As a result, classifiers, such as LDA and SVM, have only a binary understanding of class membership, which they use in the objective function to construct the classification method. LDA seeks to minimize the within class variance while maximizing the between class variance, whereas SVM tries to maximize the margin (distance) between classes. Due to this binary understanding of class, these methods work on the complete data set. The performance of methods such as LDA and SVM depends solely on the given training data, where more training data does not necessarily yield a better performance.

In this paper we suggest enhancing the performance of classifiers such as LDA and SVM by removing ill-defined training samples. In this work, ill-defined samples are defined as cases where more than 50% of the test participants in the the human cognitive tests fail to perform a correct classification.

Furthermore, we suggest a new classifier that seeks to estimate the gender strength variable by regression. A linear least squares regression has the objective function

$$\min_{\beta} \| \beta \mathbf{X} - \mathbf{y} \|^2, \tag{1}$$

with the closed form solution

$$\beta = (\mathbf{X}^T \mathbf{X})^{-1} \mathbf{X}^T \mathbf{y}, \tag{2}$$

where $\mathbf{X}$ is a matrix with samples and variables in the rows and columns, respectively. $\mathbf{y}$ is a vector with the gender strength scores, also called the response variable. β is the coefficient for the regression line. In an optimal system ((1) is small) the decision threshold would be zero in accordance with how we encoded the response variable in the regression, see Section 3. However, this will not always be the case. A more accurate decision threshold can be calculated by

$$\frac{\sum_{i=1}^{k} \beta \mathbf{x}_i}{2k} + \frac{\sum_{j=1}^{l} \beta \mathbf{x}_j}{2l}, \tag{3}$$

where i and j belong to samples of class male and female, respectively. k and l are the sizes of the two classes. This assumes that the two classes have the same distributions.

5 Experiments

5.1 Cognitive Test

In the cognitive test, the False Classification Rate (FCR) is reported in Table 2. It can be seen that in the first test where participants only saw the central face for a fraction of a second the performance was not bad, in the sense that it is clearly better than guessing (test participants reported that they felt like they were guessing most of the time). When the time constraint was removed, the performance increased. Also it seems that the individuals in the AR and Feret data sets had a bias toward masculinity, resulting in more females that were wrongly classified as a male than compared to the two other data sets.

Table 2. False classification rates for the cognitive test with standard deviations

Data set		Test with time constraint	Test without time constraint	Combined
AR	Male*	0.068 ± 0.047	0.006 ± 0.008	0.031 ± 0.042
	Female**	0.107 ± 0.062	0.164 ± 0.070	0.141 ± 0.070
	Total	**0.174 ± 0.096**	**0.169 ± 0.066**	**0.171 ± 0.074**
XM2VTS	Male*	0.084 ± 0.054	0.035 ± 0.015	0.055 ± 0.042
	Female**	0.097 ± 0.045	0.053 ± 0.030	0.071 ± 0.041
	Total	**0.181 ± 0.050**	**0.088 ± 0.025**	**0.126 ± 0.059**
Feret	Male*	0.048 ± 0.052	0.027 ± 0.009	0.035 ± 0.033
	Female**	0.163 ± 0.131	0.079 ± 0.039	0.112 ± 0.092
	Total	**0.211 ± 0.121**	**0.106 ± 0.043**	**0.148 ± 0.094**
LinkedInDK	Male*	0.059 ± 0.038	0.038 ± 0.020	0.046 ± 0.029
	Female**	0.104 ± 0.048	0.028 ± 0.019	0.058 ± 0.050
	Total	**0.163 ± 0.053**	**0.065 ± 0.028**	**0.104 ± 0.063**

* Male wrongly classified as a female.
** Female wrongly classified as a male.

5.2 Projection Lines

To obtain an understanding of how GSR classifies gender, all samples in the data sets are projected onto the respective GSR line. Only the time limited test is used as we want to see the first features we as humans use to perform gender classification. The estimated Gaussian distribution of these projections is shown in Figure 3, together with synthesized faces corresponding to points on the regression line.

5.3 Recognition Results

Cross-Validation Evaluation Gender classification was performed for all data sets using GSR and compared to LDA and SVM[3] with a linear kernel in a leave-one-out cross-validation scheme (Train on all data, except one sample. Then

---

[3] Matlab implementation of LDA and SVM is used.

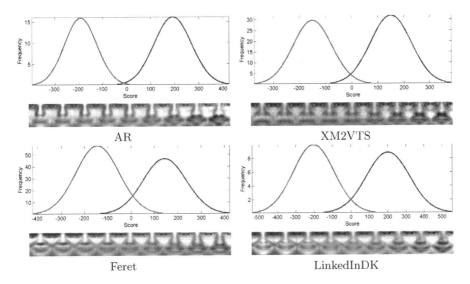

Fig. 3. The estimated gaussian distribution of the data sets projected to the GSR projection line, with synthesized faces corresponding to points on the regression line

test on this "unseen" sample and iterate this process over all samples in the given data set). Three experiments were conducted where the gender strength variable and the ill-defined samples were estimated by (case 1) only the time-limited test, (case 2) only the non-time-limited test and (case 3) by both the time-limited and non-time-limited test combined. The results are presented in Table 3. As the dimension of the variables is much higher than the samples for all data sets, a dimensionality reduction by Principal Component Analysis (PCA) [5] was preformed prior to building the models. The PCA was set to retain 95% of the data set variance.

Generalization Evaluation. To see how the algorithms perform on images not included in four data sets, an experiment was conducted, where all four data sets were collapsed into one training set of 1886 images and these were tested on a data set consisting of 40,692 images from public Danish LinkedIN profiles (LinkedInDKFULL). In this experiment we used a radial basis function kernel for SVM. Finding the optimal parameters for a non-linear SVM is still an open problem, therefore we employ a gridsearch strategy to determine the C and γ, in the grid $[10^{-2}10^5]$ and $[10^{-5}10^1]$, respectively. It was found that $C = 10^4$ and $\gamma = 10$ was the optimal setup. The results are presented in Table 4, where it can be seen that removing ill-defined training samples had a huge impact.

6   Discussion and Conclusion

In this work we have presented the gender strength variable, a new way of determining class membership that supersedes the conventional binary classes

Table 3. FCR obtained by a leave-one-out cross-validation scheme for case 1 to 3, including (full training set) or excluding (refined training set) ill-defined training examples. Bold signifies lowest FCR for a data set in the corresponding test and green signifies lowest FCR for a data set between tests in (full training set) and (refined training set).

Full training set | | | | **Refined training set** | | |

Case 1

Data set	LDA	SVM	GSR	Data set	LDA	SVM	GSR
AR	0.0604	0.0604	**0.0570**	AR	0.0537	0.0537	0.0671
XM2VTS	0.1304	0.1304	0.1250	XM2VTS	0.1286	0.1286	0.1250
Feret	**0.1364**	**0.1364**	0.1495	Feret	0.1280	0.1292	0.1388
LinkedInDK	**0.1950**	0.2000	0.2000	LinkedInDK	0.1800	0.1800	0.2000

Case 2

Data set	LDA	SVM	GSR	Data set	LDA	SVM	GSR
AR	0.0604	0.0604	0.0638	AR	0.0604	0.0604	0.0839
XM2VTS	0.1304	0.1304	**0.1232**	XM2VTS	0.1196	0.1196	0.1304
Feret	0.1364	0.1364	**0.1304**	Feret	0.1244	0.1256	0.1292
LinkedInDK	**0.1950**	0.2000	0.2050	LinkedInDK	0.1900	0.1900	0.1950

Case 3

Data set	LDA	SVM	GSR	Data set	LDA	SVM	GSR
AR	0.0604	0.0604	0.0570	AR	0.0570	0.0570	0.0638
XM2VTS	0.1304	0.1304	**0.1268**	XM2VTS	0.1159	0.1159	0.1232
Feret	**0.1364**	**0.1364**	0.1376	Feret	0.1232	0.1184	0.1352
LinkedInDK	**0.1950**	0.2000	0.2100	LinkedInDK	0.1700	0.1700	0.2100

Table 4. FCR obtained by training on all four data sets and testing on 40,692 public Danish LinkedIN profile pictures, including (a) or excluding (b) ill-defined training examples. Bold signifies lowest FCR for a data set in the corresponding test and green signifies lowest FCR for a data set between tests in (a) and (b).

Data set	LDA	SVM	GSR	Data set	LDA	SVM	GSR
LinkedInDKFULL	0.3762	**0.3227**	0.3521	LinkedInDKFULL	0.2520	0.2172	0.2373
(a)				(b)			

normally used in gender recognition. We have assessed the benefit of the gender strength variable by identifying and removing ill-defined training samples to improve existing methods such as LDA and SVM. Employing the refined training set on LDA and SVM (both in a linear and non-linear version) gave a significant improvement. We could see a performance increase when pooling answers from both cognitive tests (with and without time constraints) probably due to the fact that we obtained a more robust estimation of ill-defined training samples. This indicates that not only the volume of the training data is important but also the quality of the training data. However, how to optimally determine ill-defined training samples is still an open question.

Interestingly we also observed an improvement with SVM. As SVM manly focuses on samples close to the decision boundary one could expect that removing ill-defined samples would lead to a decrease in performance. However, here we should remember that the two populations (male and female) cannot be perfectly separated, and ill-defined samples my not lie adjacent to the decision boundary, which results in the observed performance increase.

A new method was also devised - the Gender Strength Regression. Results indicate that without removing ill-defined training samples GSR performs similarly to or better than the LDA and SVM (in a linear version). However, when using the refined training set, LDA and SVM outperforms GSR. Also the complexity of the data seems to be best modeled by non-linear methods, however these methods need more tuning of parameters.

Human performance was reported, to the authors' knowledge for the first time, on the four data sets. When comparing the performance of human vs. automatic machine learning algorithms, it can be seen that the machine learning algorithms outperform humans on the AR data set. Machine learning algorithms perform only 1-3% worse than humans on the Feret and XM2VTS data sets. But when going from the relatively constrained data sets (similar frontal poses) to the more unconstrained data set of Danish LinkedIN profile pictures, humans outperform the machine learning algorithms. It should be kept in mind that all tests were performed on the central face in gray scale images.

Finally, the results obtained for the four data sets were validated by reproducing the trend that a performance boost was achieved when removing ill-defined training samples, by collapsing the four training sets and testing them on a data set of 40,692 public Danish LinkedIN profile pictures.

It should be noted that the gender strength variable seems to be well estimated by a linear encoding of the gender classification response times, however it is not known if this is the optimal encoding.

References

1. Bruce, V., Burton, A., Hanna, E., Healey, P., Mason, O., Coombes, A., Fright, R., Linney, A.: Sex discrimination: how do we tell the difference between male and female faces? Perception 22(2), 131–152 (1993)
2. Bekios-Calfa, J., Buenaposada, J.M., Baumela, L.: Revisiting Linear Discriminant Techniques in Gender Recognition. IEEE Transactions on Pattern Analysis and Machine Intelligence 33(4), 858–864 (2011)
3. Mäkinen, E., Raisamo, R.: Evaluation of Gender Classiffcation Methods with Automatically Detected and Aligned Faces. IEEE Transactions on Pattern Analysis and Machine Intelligence 30(3), 541–547 (2008)
4. Moghaddam, B., Yang, M.-H.: Learning Gender with Support Faces. IEEE Transactions on Pattern Analysis and Machine Intelligence 24(5), 707–711 (2002)
5. Kirby, M., Sirovich, L.: Application of the Karhunen-Loeve procedure for the characterization of human faces. IEEE Transactions on Pattern Analysis and Machine Intelligence 12, 103–108 (1990)
6. Martinez, A.M., Benavente, R.: The AR Face Database. Technical Report, Computer Vision Center Purdue University (1998)

7. Messer, K., Matas, J., Kittler, J., Luettin, J., Maitre, G.: XM2VTSDB: The Extended M2VTS Database. In: Second International Conference on Audio and Videobased Biometric Person Authentication (1999)
8. Phillips, H., Moon, P., Rizvi, S.: The FERET evaluation methodology for face recognition algorithms. IEEE Transactions on Pattern Analysis and Machine Intelligence 22(10) (2000)
9. Brainard, D.H.: The Psychophysics Toolbox. Spatial Vision 10(4), 433–436 (1997)

Periocular Recognition Using Retinotopic Sampling and Gabor Decomposition

Fernando Alonso-Fernandez and Josef Bigun

Halmstad University. Box 823. SE 301-18 Halmstad, Sweden
{feralo,josef.bigun}@hh.se
http://islab.hh.se

Abstract. We present a new system for biometric recognition using periocular images based on retinotopic sampling grids and Gabor analysis of the local power spectrum. A number of aspects are studied, including: 1) grid adaptation to dimensions of the target eye vs. grids of constant size, 2) comparison between circular- and rectangular-shaped grids, 3) use of Gabor magnitude vs. phase vectors for recognition, 4) rotation compensation between query and test images, and 5) comparison with an iris machine expert. Results show that our system achieves competitive verification rates compared with other periocular recognition approaches. We also show that top verification rates can be obtained without rotation compensation, thus allowing to remove this step for computational efficiency. Also, the performance is not affected substantially if we use a grid of fixed dimensions, or it is even better in certain situations, avoiding the need of accurate detection of the iris region.

Keywords: Biometrics, periocular, eye, iris, Log-Polar mapping, Gabor decomposition.

1 Introduction and Related Work

Periocular recognition has gained attention recently in the biometrics field [1–9] due to demands for increased robustness of face or iris systems. Periocular refers to the face region in the immediate vicinity of the eye, including the eye, eyelids, lashes and eyebrows. Faces and irises have been extensively studied [10, 11], but periocular recognition has received revived attention recently, with suggestions that it may be as discriminative by itself as the face as a whole [5, 8]. Periocular region can be easily obtained with existing setups for face and iris, and the requirement of high user cooperation can be relaxed. An evident advantage is its availability over a wide range of acquisition distances even when the iris texture cannot be reliably obtained (low resolution, off-angle, etc.) [12] or under partial face occlusion (close distances). Most face systems use a holistic approach, requiring a full face image, so the performance is negatively affected in case of occlusion [10]. Also, the periocular region appears in iris images, so fusion with the iris texture has a potential to improve the overall recognition [9].

Most of the studies for periocular recognition have used Local Binary Patterns (LBP) [13] and, to a lesser extent, gradient orientation (GO) histograms [14] and

A. Fusiello et al. (Eds.): ECCV 2012 Ws/Demos, Part II, LNCS 7584, pp. 309–318, 2012.

Scale-Invariant Feature Transform (SIFT) keypoints [15]. The best performance is consistently obtained with SIFT features (rank-one recognition accuracy: 81-94%, EER: 7%), followed by LBPs (rank-one: 74-87%, EER: 19%) and GO (rank-one: 67-90%, EER: 22%) [3, 7]. Comparison with face or iris is also done in some cases. For example, Park et al. [3] reported a rank-one accuracy of 99.77% using the whole face, but when the full face is not available (simulated by synthetically masking the face below the nose region), accuracy fell to 39.55%. This points out the strength of periocular recognition when only partial face images are available, for example in criminal scenarios with surveillance cameras, where it is likely that the perpetrator masks parts of his face. In the same direction, Miller et al. [5] found that, at extreme values of blur or down-sampling, periocular recognition performed significantly better than face. On the other hand, both face and periocular matching using LBPs under uncontrolled lighting were very poor, indicating that LBPs are not well suited for this scenario. Finally, Woodard et al. [9] fused periocular and iris information from near-infrared (NIR) portal data finding that periocular identification performed better than iris, and the fusion of the two modalities performed best. In most of these studies, periocular images were acquired in the visible range. Periocular on visible light works better than on NIR, because it shows melanin-related differences [7]. On the other hand, many iris systems work with NIR illumination due to higher reflectivity of the iris tissue in this range [16]. Unfortunately, the use of more relaxed scenarios will make NIR light unfeasible (e.g. distant acquisition, mobile devices, etc.) so there is a high pressure to the development of algorithms capable of working with visible light [17].

Here, we come up with a periocular recognition system based on retinotopic sampling grids positioned in the pupil center, followed by Gabor decomposition at different frequencies and orientations. This setup have been used in texture analysis [20], facial landmark detection and face recognition [2], and real-time face tracking and liveness assessment [1, 21], with high discriminative capabilities. We use the CASIA-IrisV3-Interval database [18] (2,655 eye images, 249 contributors), and the BioSec database [19] (3,200 images, 200 contributors). Although not directly comparable, our system achieves competitive verification rates in comparison with existing periocular recognition approaches [3, 7].

2   Recognition System

In our recognition system, input images are analyzed with a retinotopic sampling sensor, whose receptive fields consist in a set of modified Gabor filters designed in the log-polar frequency plane [1, 2]. The system is described next.

2.1   Sampling Grid

Our recognition strategy is based on a sparse retinotopic sampling grid obtained by log-polar mapping [1, 2], which is positioned in the pupil center (Figure 1, left). The grid has log-polar geometry, meaning that the density of sampling

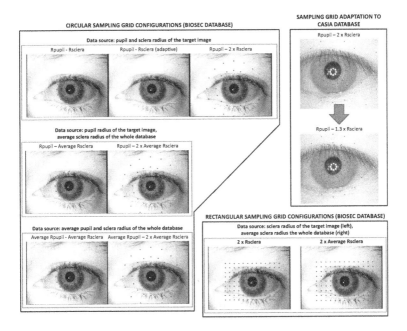

Fig. 1. Left: Circular sampling grid with different configuration of radius of the innermost and outermost circles. **Bottom right:** Uniform rectangular grids. Image is from the BioSec database. **Top right:** Sampling grid adaptation to the smaller images of CASIA database.

points decreases exponentially with the distance from the center. Such non-uniform sampling, with frequency decreasing from the center to the periphery, imitates the arrangement of photoreceptors in the human retina [22]. Each point of the grid is associated with a receptive field of the human eye. At each point, a Gabor decomposition of the image is performed to the effect that they mimic the simple cells of the primary visual cortex having the same receptive field but different spatial directions and frequencies [23]. The sparseness of the sampling grid allows direct filtering in the image domain without needing the Fourier transform, with significant computational savings [2] and even feasibility in real time [21]. In our experiments, we use a grid of 81 points arranged in 5 concentric circles, with 16 points per circle plus the point at the grid center. We also consider one case of non-concentricity between pupil and sclera circles (see the "adaptive" configuration in Figure 1, left, 1st row). For similitude with other previous works [3, 7], we also use a rectangular grid of 117 points, distributed uniformly in 9 rows and 13 columns (Figure 1, bottom right).

The circular grid is configured in several ways, employing different values of radius of the innermost and outermost circles: i) using pupil and sclera radius of the target image (Figure 1, left, 1st row), ii) using pupil radius of the target image only (2nd row), or iii) no usage of the pupil or sclera radius (3rd row). In cases ii) and iii), the average pupil and/or sclera radius of the whole database is used. This way, we evaluate the potential benefit of adapting the grid to the

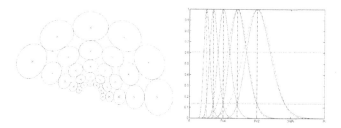

Fig. 2. Left: Iso-curves of the modified Gabor filters. Right: radial cross-sectional plot. Two standard Gabor filters are superimposed with dashed lines. Modified filters have a steeper cut-off on the low-frequency side, reducing overlap towards low frequencies. Image from [2].

dimensions of the target eye, compared with placing a grid of constant size. Similarly, width of the rectangular grid is built with two different configurations (Figure 1, bottom right), one using the sclera radius of the target image and the second using the average sclera radius. Height of the rectangular grid is 4/6 of its width [3]. Figure 1, left and bottom right, shows grid configurations with the BioSec database. Due to smaller image size, there is less periocular region available in CASIA database, thus some configurations of the sampling grid has to be reduced accordingly to ensure that it is mostly contained in the image (Figure 1, top right).

2.2   Log-Polar Sampling in the Fourier Domain

The local power spectrum of the image is sampled at each point of the grid by a set of Gabor filters that constitute the associated receptive field. The simple cells are modeled with 30 Gabor filters, organized in 5 frequency channels and 6 equally spaced orientation channels (Figure 2, left). When only a small number of frequency channels is used, the (standard) Gaussian spectrum of Gabor filters produces a non-uniform frequency coverage. Given that the central frequency of the filters increases exponentially, a symmetric Gaussian shape results in excessive overlap towards the low (densely sampled) frequencies and poor coverage of high frequencies. To solve that, a set of modified Gabor filters is used [1] defined as Gaussians in the log-polar frequency plane. For a filter tuned to orientation φ_0 and angular frequency $\omega_0 = \exp(\xi_0)$:

$$G(\xi, \varphi) = A \exp\left(-\frac{(\xi - \xi_0)^2}{2\sigma_\xi^2}\right) \exp\left(-\frac{(\varphi - \varphi_0)^2}{2\sigma_\varphi^2}\right) \qquad (1)$$

where A is a normalization constant and (ξ, φ) are the log-polar frequency coordinates $left((\xi, \varphi) = (\log|\vec{\omega}|, \tan^{-1}(\omega_x, \omega_y))$. This way, filters are designed by arranging a set of identical Gaussians in a rectangular lattice in the log-polar frequency plane. When seen in the standard Fourier plane, the overlap in low frequencies is significantly reduced (Figure 2, right). Filter wavelengths span the range from 4 to 16 pixels in half-octave intervals.

The Gabor responses are grouped into a single complex vector, which is used as identity model. Matching between two images is using either the magnitude of complex values or a binary vector obtained by phase binary quantization to 4 levels. Prior to matching with magnitude vectors, they are normalized to a probability distribution (PDF), and matching is done using the χ^2 distance [24]. Matching between binary vectors is done using the Hamming distance [16]. Rotation is accounted for by shifting the grid of the query image in counter- and clock-wise directions, and selecting the lowest distance, which corresponds to the best match between two templates.

Table 1. Verification results in terms of EER (CASIA database). The best case of each column is marked in bold. Results with rotation compensation: the relative EER variation with respect to no rotation compensation is given in brackets. R_p=pupil radius. R_s=sclera radius.

			Circular geometry - EER (%)			
			No rotation compensation		Rotation compensation	
	innermost circle	outermost circle	Gabor magnitude	Gabor phase	Gabor magnitude	Gabor phase
1	R_p	R_s	6.13	19.75	**5.85** (-4.59%)	6.88 (-65.17%)
2	R_p	R_s (adaptive)	**5.96**	**18.91**	5.68 (-4.66%)	**5.66** (-70.04%)
3	R_p	$1.3 \times R_s$	6.95	21.55	6.73 (-3.05%)	10.45 (-51.48%)
4	R_p	avg(R_s)	6.33	20.25	6.18 (-2.38%)	7.52 (-62.85%)
5	R_p	$1.3 \times$avg(R_s)	7.22	22.13	6.97 (-3.48%)	10.90 (-50.75%)
6	avg(R_p)	avg(R_s)	7.53	25.40	7.32 (-2.79%)	19.57 (-22.95%)
7	avg(R_p)	$1.3 \times$avg(R_s)	7.99	26.28	7.68 (-3.96%)	22.18 (-15.60%)

			Rectangular geometry - EER (%)			
			No rotation compensation		Rotation compensation	
	height	width	Gabor magnitude	Gabor phase	Gabor magnitude	Gabor phase
1	$1.3 \times (4/6) \times R_s$	$1.3 \times R_s$	**7.89**	23.40	**7.81** (-1.11%)	15.83 (-32.37%)
2	$1.3 \times (4/6) \times$avg(R_s)	$1.3 \times$avg(R_s)	8.37	**23.23**	8.20 (-2.05%)	**15.64** (-32.66%)

3   Experiments

3.1   Databases and Protocol

We use the CASIA-IrisV3-Interval [18] and the BioSec baseline [19] databases. CASIA has 2,655 NIR images of 280×320 pixels (height×width) from 249 contributors in 2 sessions, with 396 different eyes (the number of images per contributor and per session is not constant, and not all the individuals have images of the two eyes). The BioSec database has 3,200 NIR images of 480×640 pixels from 200 individuals in 2 sessions. Each person contributes with 4 images of the two eyes per session (thus, 400 different eyes). We have manually annotated all images of the database, computing the radius and the center of the iris and sclera circles, which are used as input for the experiments.

Table 2. Verification results in terms of EER (BioSec database). The best case of each column is marked in bold. Results with rotation compensation: the relative EER variation with respect to no rotation compensation is given in brackets. R_p=pupil radius. R_s=sclera radius.

	innermost circle	outermost circle	Circular geometry - EER (%)			
			No rotation compensation		Rotation compensation	
			Gabor magnitude	Gabor phase	Gabor magnitude	Gabor phase
1	R_p	R_s	18.71	28.38	18.47 (-1.30%)	15.78 (-44.39%)
2	R_p	R_s (adaptive)	18.69	**27.52**	18.52 (-0.91%)	**13.88** (-49.56%)
3	R_p	$2 \times R_s$	16.67	32.76	16.86 (+1.11%)	25.36 (-22.58%)
4	R_p	avg(R_s)	19.09	29.39	18.66 (-2.23%)	16.34 (-44.37%)
5	R_p	$2 \times$avg(R_s)	16.84	32.94	16.59 (-1.49%)	25.46 (-22.73%)
6	avg(R_p)	avg(R_s)	17.46	38.93	17.49 (+0.20%)	31.10 (-20.12%)
7	avg(R_p)	$2 \times$avg(R_s)	**15.25**	37.88	**15.08** (-1.14%)	33.66 (-11.16%)

	height	width	Rectangular geometry - EER (%)			
			No rotation compensation		Rotation compensation	
			Gabor magnitude	Gabor phase	Gabor magnitude	Gabor phase
1	$2 \times (4/6) \times R_s$	$2 \times R_s$	**15.25**	**35.76**	**15.18** (-0.46%)	**29.97** (-16.19%)
2	$2 \times (4/6) \times$avg(R_s)	$2 \times$avg(R_s)	15.56	38.34	15.41 (-0.94%)	32.95 (-14.06%)

We consider each eye as a different user. Verification performance experiments with the CASIA database are as follows. Genuine matches are obtained by comparing each image of a user to the remaining images of the same user, avoiding symmetric matches. Impostor matches are obtained by comparing the 1st image of a user to the 1st image of the next 100 users. With this procedure, we obtain 9,018 genuine and 31,477 impostor scores. With the BioSec database, genuine matches for a given user are obtained by comparing the 4 images of the 1st session to the 4 images of the 2nd session. Impostor matches are obtained by comparing the 2nd image of the 1st session of a user to the 2nd image of the 2nd session of all the remaining users. With this, we obtain $400 \times 4 \times 4 = 6,400$ genuine and $400 \times 399 = 159,600$ impostor scores. Note that experiments with the BioSec database are made by matching images of different sessions, but these inter-session experiments are not possible with CASIA-IrisV3-Interval, since it does not contain session information.

We conduct matching experiments of iris texture using 1D log-Gabor filters [25]. The iris region is unwrapped to a normalized rectangle using the Daugman's rubber sheet model [16] and next, a 1D Log-Gabor wavelet is applied plus phase binary quantization to 4 levels. Matching is done using the Hamming distance. Rotation is accounted for with the same procedure of Section 2.2.

Some fusion experiments are also done. Prior to fusion, scores of the individual systems are normalized to log-likelihood ratios. Given a score s_i, normalization is achieved as $f_i = a_0 + a_1 \cdot s_i$. Weights a_0, a_1 are trained via logistic regression as in [26]. This is done separately for each system. Normalized scores from each system are then summed for the fusion. This trained fusion approach it has shown superior performance than other fusion rules [26, 28].

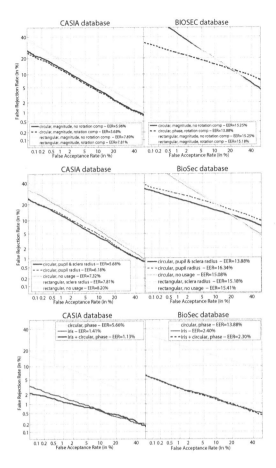

Fig. 3. First row: Circular vs. rectangular grid (best cases of Tables 1 and 2, with and w/o rotation compensation). **Second row**: Grid adaptation to the target image (best cases of Tables 1 and 2 depending whether the sampling grid makes use of the pupil and/or sclera radius values of the target image, with rotation compensation). **Third row**: Comparison of iris and periocular recognition (best cases of Tables 1 and 2, with rotation compensation). The best fusion combination found between our periocular system and the iris matcher is also shown.

3.2   Results

EER results with the different sampling grid configurations are given in Tables 1 and 2. It is observed that rotation compensation does not have appreciable effects in the Gabor magnitude (EER is reduced up to 4.7% in the best case), but there is a substantial improvement with phase vectors (up to 50% with BioSec, 70% with CASIA). The positive result, however, is that Gabor magnitude without rotation compensation performs similar to phase vectors after rotation compensation with circular grids, and even much better if we use square grids (EER is about 50% less). This would allow to save computational time by suppressing rotation compensation.

Comparing circular and rectangular grids (Figure 3, 1st row), there is no clear winner. With CASIA, circular grids perform slightly better, but with BioSec, the best geometry depends on the DET region. Also remarkably, BioSec database has higher error rates than CASIA. Apart from differences given by the sensor (which cannot be assessed with the information available), one reason could be that experiments with BioSec are inter-session. On the contrary, one can think that BioSec images are bigger (480×640 vs. 280×320 pixels) with more periocular region available, so error rates should be lower. One way to assess the latter would be to increase the density and number of grid points with Biosec, a direction that we are currently exploring.

We now evaluate the effect of adapting the grid to the dimensions of the target eye (Figure 3, 2nd row). With CASIA and circular grids, adaptation both to the pupil and sclera radius is always best. However, if the outer dimension of the grid is fixed, performance is not too much affected (EER from 5.68% to 6.18%). With rectangular grids on CASIA, using a grid of constant dimensions does not have a dramatic impact neither (EER from 7.81% to 8.20%). Concerning BioSec database, the best case depends on the region of the DET. For low FAR, adaptation both to the pupil and sclera radius is always best. For low FRR however, both circular and rectangular grids with fixed dimensions are able to give the best performance.

Finally, we compare the performance of our periocular system with the iris expert (Figure 3, 3rd row). We also assess its fusion. We have tested all the fusion possibilities between the iris expert and the cases (rows) of Tables 1 and 2 (with rotation compensation only), reporting in Figure 3, 3rd row, the combination with the lowest EER. The best fusion on CASIA is with case 4 (phase) of Table 1. With BioSec, the best fusion is with case 6 (phase). As it can be observed, the dedicated iris machine expert works much better than our periocular approach. In addition, the fusion results in a relatively appreciable improvement on CASIA at low FAR, but no improvement is observed on BioSec.

4   Conclusion

We propose the use of retinotopic sampling grids positioned in the pupil center for recognition using periocular images. The local power spectrum is sampled at each grid point by a set of Gabor filters tuned to different frequencies and orientations [1, 2]. The system is evaluated with two databases acquired using iris sensors. One advantage of periocular systems is that existing setups for face and iris can be used for recognition purposes.

We compare the use of Gabor magnitude and phase vectors. We also carry out rotation compensation experiments by shifting the grid of the query image to find the best match with the test image. Results show that rotation compensation does not have appreciable effects in the Gabor magnitude, but produces a significative performance improvement with phase vectors. In any case, Gabor magnitude without rotation compensation already performs at similar or better levels than phase vectors after rotation compensation.

Depending on the database, it is better to use circular or rectangular grids. We also evaluate the effect of adapting the grid to the dimensions of the target eye. Although adaptation is the optimal solution in most cases, the performance is not too much affected if we use a grid of fixed dimensions, or it is even better in certain situations. The only requirement of our system is the availability of the center of the eye and, in some cases, of the pupil radius. These are available even when the iris texture is difficult to extract [12]. Finally, we compare our system with a dedicated iris expert using 1D Log-Gabor wavelets [25]. We observe that the iris expert works much better than our periocular approach, and the fusion of the two results in a slight improvement with one of the databases.

Future work includes comparison and fusion of our approach with other existing periocular recognition algorithms [7] and evaluation on images in the visual spectrum [3]. Also, existing works do not focus on detection of the periocular region (it is manually extracted), but on texture analysis only. Only Park et al. [3] used a Viola-Jones face detector plus heuristics measurements to extract the periocular region, so successful extraction relies on an accurate detection of the (whole) face. We will explore the use of eye detectors that does not need the whole face. In this sense, the sampling grid and Gabor decomposition used in this work has been already used for the task of facial landmark detection [1, 2, 21], and it will be the source of future work.

Acknowledgments. Author F. A.-F. thanks the Swedish Research Council and the EU for for funding his postdoctoral research. Authors also acknowledge the CAISR research program of the Swedish Knowledge Foundation, the EU BBfor2 project (FP7-ITN-238803) and the EU COST Action IC1106 for its support. Authors also would like to thank L.M. Tato-Pazo for her valuable work in annotating the iris database, and to the Biometric Recognition Group (ATVS-UAM) for making the iris part of the BioSec database available for our experiments.

References

1. Smeraldi, F., Carmona, O., Bigün, J.: Saccadic search with gabor features applied to eye detection and real-time head tracking. IVC 18 (2000)
2. Smeraldi, F., Bigün, J.: Retinal vision applied to facial features detection and face authentication. Pattern Recognition Letters 23 (2002)
3. Park, U., Jillela, R.R., Ross, A., Jain, A.K.: Periocular biometrics in the visible spectrum. IEEE TIFS 6 (2011)
4. Miller, P.E., Rawls, A.W., Pundlik, S.J., Woodard, D.L.: Personal identification using periocular skin texture. In: Proc. ACM SAC (2010)
5. Miller, P.E., Lyle, J.R., Pundlik, S.J., Woodard, D.L.: Performance evaluation of local appearance based periocular recognition. In: Proc. IEEE BTAS (2010)
6. Bharadwaj, S., Bhatt, H.S., Vatsa, M., Singh, R.: Periocular biometrics: When iris recognition fails. In: Proc. IEEE BTAS (2010)

7. Hollingsworth, K., Darnell, S.S., Miller, P.E., Woodard, D.L., Bowyer, K.W., Flynn, P.J.: Human and machine performance on periocular biometrics under near-infrared light and visible light. IEEE TPAMI 7 (2012)
8. Woodard, D.L., Pundlik, S.J., Lyle, J.R., Miller, P.E.: Periocular region appearance cues for biometric identification. In: Proc. IEEE CVPR Biometrics Workshop (2010)
9. Woodard, D.L., Pundlik, S.J., Miller, P., Jillela, R., Ross, A.: On the fusion of periocular and iris biometrics in non-ideal imagery. In: Proc. ICPR (2010)
10. Li, S., Jain, A. (eds.): Handbook of Face Recognition. Springer (2004)
11. Bowyer, K., Hollingsworth, K., Flynn, P.: Image understanding for iris biometrics: a survey. Computer Vision and Image Understanding 110 (2007)
12. Matey, J., Ackerman, D., Bergen, J., Tinker, M.: Iris recognition in less constrained environments. In: Advances in Biometrics: Sensors, Algorithms and Systems (2008)
13. Ojala, T., Pietikainen, M., Maenpaa, T.: Multiresolution gray-scale and rotation invariant texture classification with local binary patterns. IEEE TPAMI 24 (2002)
14. Dalal, N., Triggs, B.: Histograms of oriented gradients for human detection. In: Proc. IEEE CVPR (2005)
15. Lowe, D.: Distinctive image features from scale-invariant key points. International Journal of Computer Vision 60 (2004)
16. Daugman, J.: How iris recognition works. IEEE TCSVT 14 (2004)
17. NICE II. Noisy Iris Challenge Evaluation, Part II (2010), http://nice2.di.ubi.pt/
18. CASIA Iris Image Database, http://biometrics.idealtest.org
19. Fierrez, J., Ortega-Garcia, J., Torre-Toledano, D., Gonzalez-Rodriguez, J.: BioSec baseline corpus: A multimodal biometric database. Patt. Recogn. 40 (2007)
20. Bigün, J., du Buf, J.M.H.: N-folded symmetries by complex moments in gabor space and their application to unsupervised texture segmentation. IEEE TPAMI 16 (1994)
21. Bigun, J., Fronthaler, H., Kollreider, K.: Assuring liveness in biometric identity authentication by real-time face tracking. In: Proc. CIHSPS (2004)
22. Bigun, J.: Vision with Direction. Springer (2006)
23. Hubel, D.H.: Eye, brain, and vision. Scientific American Library. Distributed by W.H. Freeman, New York (1988)
24. Gilperez, A., Alonso-Fernandez, F., Pecharroman, S., Fierrez, J., Ortega-Garcia, J.: Off-line signature verification using contour features. In: Proc. ICFHR (2008)
25. Masek, L.: Recognition of human iris patterns for biometric identification. Master's thesis, School of Computer Science and Software Engineering, Univ. Western Australia (2003)
26. Alonso-Fernandez, F., Fierrez, J., Ramos, D., Gonzalez-Rodriguez, J.: Quality-based conditional processing in multi-biometrics: Application to sensor interoperability. IEEE TSMC-A 40(6) (2010)
27. Duda, R., Hart, P., Stork, D.: Pattern Classification, 2nd edn. (2004)
28. Poh, N., Bourlai, T., Kittler, J., Allano, L., Alonso-Fernandez, F., Ambekar, O., Baker, J., Dorizzi, B., Fatukasi, O., Fierrez, J., Ganster, H., Ortega-Garcia, J., Maurer, D., Salah, A., Scheidat, T., Vielhauer, C.: Benchmarking Quality-dependent and Cost-sensitive Score-level Multimodal Biometric Fusion Algorithms. IEEE TIFS 4(4) (2009)

Exploiting Perception for Face Analysis: Image Abstraction for Head Pose Estimation

Anant Vidur Puri and Brejesh Lall

Indian Institute of Technology, New Delhi, India
http://www.ee.iitd.ac.in

Abstract. We present an algorithm to estimate the pose of a human head from a single, low resolution image in real time. It builds on the fundamentals of human perception i.e. abstracting the relevant details from visual cues. Most images contain far too many cues than what are required for estimating human head pose. Thus, we use non-photorealistic rendering to eliminate irrelevant details like expressions from the picture and accentuate facial features critical to estimating head pose. The maximum likelihood pose range is then estimated by training a classifier on scaled down abstracted images. The results are extremely encouraging especially when compared with other recent methods.Moreover the algorithm is robust to illumination, expression, identity and resolution.

Keywords: Face, Head Pose, Non Photorealistic Rendering, Abstraction.

1 Introduction

Head pose estimation is an intriguing and actively addressed problem in computer vision[1]. The reason for this is the application potential of an accurate pose estimation system in Human Computer Interaction, which is one of the most upcoming research areas in recent times. Some of the applications in this field are emotion recognition, unobtrusive customer feedback, biological pose correction, and interactive gaze interfaces. Knowledge of head pose is also extremely useful in a host of other head and face related computer vision applications including surveillance and avatar animation. More recently, a lot of research has been done on facial expression recognition which is highly simplified if head pose is known apriori. Recognition is also benefitted by prior knowledge of head pose.

In view of all this, highly accurate systems have been proposed, including 3D models[2], fiducial point fitting[3], and machine learning (ML)[4] [5] techniques. But, the major challenge that thee methods face is pose estimation in the presence of extreme facial expressions. This is a pertinent problem as in any real-life setting, the human-face is seldom without any facial expressions. Also, a critical use of pose is in facial expression recognition. So any solution which is not reasonably robust to expression is futile. Most of these methods also suffer from one or more drawbacks such as high computational complexity[3], requirements for huge training sets[5], tedious alignment issues[4] [5], sensitivity to illumination[5] [2], personalized initialization, and non-scalability to estimate

A. Fusiello et al. (Eds.): ECCV 2012 Ws/Demos, Part II, LNCS 7584, pp. 319–329, 2012.

pose for multiple subjects[3] [2]. It is thus with an aim to simplify the problem and to seek an easy, fast, and accurate solution that we propose our algorithm.

Our approach is essentially to seek appropriate features that can be leveraged by statistical learning techniques. The unique part is that it takes advantage of the fact that most images have a level of detail that is much more than what is required to estimate pose. So, we abstract the image using non-photorealistic rendering (NPR)[5]. NPR reduces the complexity of analysis while sending the information across in a better and easier form. This approach leads to a computationally light system suitable for real time use and scalable to multiple subjects. Abstraction affords robustness to identity and facial expressions. Also, our approach is relatively insensitive to skin and lighting variations. The obtained features lead to considerably fewer alignment issues than other ML techniques for head pose estimation. The method's accuracy and computational lightness make it ideal as a first step to estimate finer head pose. Fig. 1 illustrates the excellent performance of our algorithm showing the results on certain random images from the Internet.

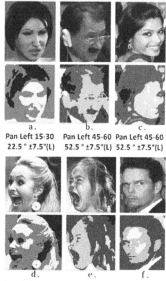

Fig. 1. Successful examples

The rest of the paper is organized as follows. Section 2 describes image abstraction while section 3 describes the NPR algorithms used in our system. Sections 4 and 5 focus on the training and testing pipelines, respectively. We present our results in section 6, where we also describe a heuristic to estimate a usable output range of pose. The final section is the conclusion describing future scope and possible modifications to the algorithm.

2   Image Abstraction

The reason behind abstraction can be best understood through a series of examples shown in Fig.2. It shows the actual image of a person followed by the same image after it has undergone different forms of abstraction. These include segmentation of the color regions, identification of prominent contours, isolation of the skin region or viewing only very few features of the face like hairline and eyes.

Fig. 2. Various forms of image abstraction (left to right): original image, color segmentation image, contours image, skin detector output, cropped upper face

The thing common to all these images is that they contain far less detail (information) than the original image. While one has lesser colors, another has no colors but only strokes and one even has parts of the face missing. Yet they can all be used to infer pose. The crucial fact here is that our brain seldom needs so much detail to estimate pose. Similar claims of the brain using limited information from an image have been verified in works on perception and imaging. [6] shows how people can interpret shapes from line drawings just as well as they can from shaded images. Experiments have been conducted which show that humans take lesser response time to analyze a scene when shown cartoon drawings rather than real pictures [7]. Cavanagh [8] proposes that though we think we are seeing a complete person, we actually just see a line diagram of the person i.e. Fig.3.

This brings us to the next important fact that even though our eyes see the complete image our brain uses only what is bare minimum required to perform the given task (in this case - estimate pose). A machine lacks this ability to filter out unnecessary details. However, if we can do the abstraction prior to analysis by a learning algorithm, it is possible to increase the efficiency and overall performance of many such algorithms. The lesser a machine has to learn the less confused it will get and the easier it will be to obtain results.

Fig. 3. What we see(left) and what we think we see

Abstraction, however, is a subjective term and can be taken to have many meanings. In our system, we achieve abstraction using non-photorealistic rendering techniques. In the next section, we describe NPR and how it leads to image abstraction.

3 Non-photorealistic Rendering

As the name suggests, non-photorealistic rendering of images seeks to give an artistic impression to images. This may be by simulating paintbrush strokes, creating segments of uniform colour, introducing a pen and ink illustration effect etc. Stylizing the image to make it look like a painting has an effect akin to that of abstraction i.e. to preserve necessary information while doing away with unnecessary details. The earliest well-documented experiments in this area were conducted as long as half a century ago [14]. These showed the clear advantage of non-photo realistically rendered images over real life pictures as far as speed of perception is concerned. [9] also presents a perceptual experiment that illustrates the mutual beneficence of NPR and perception. It also states, 'Artists have long realized that complex scenes, and even abstract ideas or concepts can often be visualized more effectively with simple images that hide much of the complexities of the physical interaction between light and matter[10]. Indeed, much of the work in non-photorealistic rendering is motivated by exactly this potential for effective visual communication [11].' This same fact can also be inferred from a simple observation: *most real life paintings lack extensive detail yet manage to draw attention to key features.* Paintings like the Mona Lisa (Da Vinci) or

The Potato Eaters (van Gogh) have not been painted with intricate detail yet they draw attention to salient features better than even high resolution images. The style and organization is such that they are rendered with meaningful abstraction to achieve more effective visual communication. Another notable example is the poster of Moulin Rouge by Toulouse-Lautrec (Fig. 4), which draws the viewer's attention to meaningful parts through abstraction (Refer [12] for a discussion on this work).

NPR can thus reduce complexity of a computer vision algorithm by accentuating salient information. To investigate this prospect, we use two simple forms of NPR to simplify and abstract features of the head so as to make pose estimation easier. These are:

Fig. 4.   Henri   de   Toulouse-Lautrec's 'Moulin Rouge'

1) Regional Segmentation
2) Stroke Rendering

Both methods are explained in the following subsections.

3.1   Regional Segmentation

The method is essentially color based segmentation: seed growing followed by refinement steps. First, a seed is planted, and a region is grown by adding all neighborhood pixels with RGB values within a certain threshold. The algorithm then recursively calls itself on the neighbors of the last added pixel(s). Whenever the threshold is violated, a new seed is planted, and a new region is grown. This continues until every pixel is a part of some segment. This process is illustrated through Fig. 5.

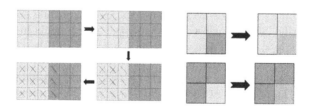

Fig. 5. (Left: Region growing using initial seed. The single line denotes pixels being processed in current step. Crossed pixels have been analyzed and are part of current segment. Right:Refining segments by smoothing out edges.

Refinement of segments happens in two steps. The first step involves smoothing the segment boundaries. This is done by considering four pixels of the initially segmented image at a time. If three out of four pixels belong to one segment then all four are merged into the same segment by filling the fourth pixel with an intensity value that is intermediate between that pixel and the others, as shown in Fig. 5.

The second refinement step is repeated segmentation, i.e., segmentation and refinement are done repeatedly until the number of segments becomes constant. This ensures that the image cannot now be divided into more segments with that threshold value.

Fig. 7 shows similar results for images from the Pointing Database [13] (which is used for training and testing our pose estimation system). As can be seen, unnecessary irregularities in the image are smoothed out and important patches emerge.

We undertake two steps to make the system robust to illumination and skin color. First, we have used histogram equalization on the original images. Further, we normalize the pixel values of the NPR image i.e. $p_i = (p_i - \mu)/\sigma$, where μ and σ are the mean and standard deviation of that NPR image.

It is noticed in the results, that, any facial contortions or extreme expressions are smoothed out and only blobs remain. Hairlines show up in all cases; eyes also result in distinct blobs. Often these two alone are sufficient to determine pose. The algorithm also detects mouth and nose as distinct blobs. Moreover, hair and skin can show up as different segments. Thus, the approach is adaptable to a wide range of people, environmental conditions, and facial expressions.

These observations are strengthened by the mean and variance images, shown in Fig. 8 (derived during training).The NPR images are converted to gray scale and used by the system during training and testing. The locally uniform regions in the mean images show that the images are smoothened to uniform color segments. We also get some regions of very low variance, which implies that critical features of the face are strongly captured. Often, shadows are visible on the face, and this may initially seem like a deterrent. On observing the learned model, however, we realize that the shadows and where they lie (which side below the chin, etc) are themselves cues for pose and are learned by the system. *Since only the basic features of the face, which remain more or less same throughout the dataset, are retained, the algorithm learns lesser but more relevant information and is thus able to respond better.*

3.2 Stroke Rendering

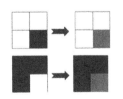

Fig. 6. Edge Refinement

The second method involves rendering the image using strokes like in line drawings. First, edges are detected using simple Sobel masks of size 3X3. These edges are then thresholded to retain only those edges which define major segments in the image. These edges are then refined by considering four pixels at a time; if three of them are black (i.e., they form an edge), the fourth one is given half the maximum grayscale value. Similarly if only one is black, it is reassigned half the maximum grayscale value. This is illustrated in Fig. 6.

The edges detected by using this method are, however, very thin. It could be difficult to train a system on such thin edges as the amount of data would be too little. So we do a thickening operation on the edges, similar to dilation. The mean and variance images for stroke rendering are shown in Fig. 8.

While the mean images do show some clarity in terms of making out the face and pose, there are very few smooth, low variance regions. This could challenge a system to learn a suitable pattern. However, the images become better as the pan angle becomes more acute. As far as computational performance is concerned, a Python implementation is cur-

Fig. 7. NPR results for Pointing Database (top to bottom): original image, region segmented image, stroke rendered image

rently able to non-photorealistically render at 3 fps (for both region segmentation and strokes) with image size 96X96 pixels while running on a 2.4 GHz Intel 3 Processor.

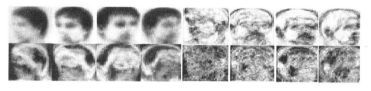

Fig. 8. Mean (top) and variance (bottom) images for different poses for regional segmentation(left) and stroke rendering(right)

4 Training

A learning-based system is expected to perform well if trained on abstracted images of human heads. We have explored this idea using a naive Bayes classifier. As mentioned before, we have used images from the Pointing Database (30 different images are available for each pose) for training our system. The training procedure is explained below:

(i) Images are cropped according to the boundary of the head and the cropped images are histogram equalized to be robust to illumination effects.

(ii) A non-photorealistic rendering algorithm is applied to generate abstracted images. The same parameters are maintained during training and testing.

(iii) The result is then converted to a gray scale, 32X32 frame. This step helps in normalizing the locations of the abstract regions across various head shapes. It also saves computations during both training and testing.

(iv) A statistical model is learned (Section 5) at each pixel i for a given pose textitj(p_{ij}), by computing the mean μ_{ij} and standard deviation σ_{ij} of pixel values x_{ij} , as shown in equations (1) and (2). Here, each pixel is assumed to be statistically independent, which makes the computation easy because the probabilities across all pixels can be just multiplied to obtain the total probability; at the same time, the learned model is accurate enough for pose estimation. Separate models are trained for both NPR techniques. Currently, the system learns models from frontal, $0°$, to $90°$ in steps of $15°$ for pan right and left. Also, for certain pan angle ranges($< 60°$), models for tilt up $30°$ and tilt down $30°$ are learned.

$$\mu_{ij} = \Sigma x_{ij}/N \tag{1}$$

$$\sigma_{ij}^2 = \Sigma(x_{ij} - \mu_{ij})^2/N \tag{2}$$

5 Estimating Pose

In a test image, the head region is first cropped. To the best of our knowledge several machine learning techniques impose a strict requirement on the cropped face. For example, in Huang et al. (2011), the crop is according to the positions of fiducial points. Finding these facial features itself is difficult, leading to a chicken-or-egg problem. Our method is suited for images cropped along the head boundary, which is a much easier requirement on any system. Obtaining this cropped image requires a foreground/background separation technique. We have used GrabCut[14], available as an OpenCV function, on the output of a head tracker. For tracking, we have implemented a variation of the elliptical head tracker [15], which uses image gradient and color histogram for tracking a head through different poses in a video. A typical result from our tracker is shown in Fig. 9. Definite foreground and background regions are automatically marked for GrabCut, and we get cropped images as shown. Once the image is cropped along the head boundary, the same NPR technique used during training is applied, with the same threshold setting. The probability $P(ij)$ that any pixel i of value x_i belongs to a specific pose j can be found using equation (3).

$$P_{ij} = \frac{1}{\sigma_{ij}\sqrt{\pi}}e^{-\frac{(x_{ij} - \mu_{ij})^2}{2\sigma_{ij}^2}} \tag{3}$$

$$P_{j*} = max_j \prod_i P_{ij} \tag{4}$$

The estimated pose $j*$ maximizes the product of probabilities across all pixels according to equation (4). The same result can be achieved by finding the minimum log likelihood sum and thus saving on computation, as shown in equation (5).

$$L_{j*} = min_j \Sigma_i \frac{(x_{ij} - \mu_{ij})^2}{2\sigma_{ij}^2} \tag{5}$$

6   Results and Discussions

We feel that coarse pose is best expressed as lying in a window, rather than one angle with an unknown associated uncertainty. Thus, the results of the maximum likelihood estimation can be further interpreted as follows:

(i) First, the log likelihood sums for frontal, pan 30°, 60°, and 90° are considered, and the least among these fixes one end of the output pose range.
(ii) Next, the log likelihood sums for pan 15°, 45°, and 75° are considered, and the least among these fixes the other end.

For instance, if pan right 30° had the least log likelihood sum in step (i), and pan right 15° had the least log likelihood sum in step (ii), the pose is classified as between 15° to 30° turned right, i.e., 22.5° ± 7.5° pan right. Given the pan window, we compare the tilt-up and tilt-down log likelihood sums at that pan window to estimate tilt angle. For the window of 0° to 30°, tilt models are built at pan 15°; for the window of 30° to 60°, at pan 45°; and for the window of 60° to 90 at pan 75°.

Fig. 9. Using the tracker (left); real life results after using the tracker(right)

6.1   Performance Evaluation

The results we obtain for five-fold cross validation on the Pointing Database are encouraging, as shown in Tables 1 and 2. We show results for both methods i.e. regional segmentation and stroke rendering. The results show that regional segmentation works much better at pan angles less than 60°, implying that rough regional information corresponding to hair and facial features (e.g., eyes, and mouth) are the more appropriate features for head pose estimation in this range.However, at extreme pan angles, stroke rendering seems to perform better. This seems strange but actually at extreme side poses, there are not many regions which can be segmented out. The edges(eg jaw line) however become more prominent in the profile. So, stroke rendering performs better. [15] suggests that colour and gradient data are complimentary to one another. So we tried a third method wherein we multiplied the probabilities obtained using Regional Segmentation and Stroke Rendering and then rank ordered the now obtained probabilities in the same way as described above. As expected, these results are consistently accurate throughout the span of angles.

6.2   Comparisons with Other Approaches

To prove that an appropriate form of image abstraction is essential for a problem, we present cross-validation results without any form of abstraction i.e. direct down sampling of the image to size 32X32. Comparing with these results, the better performance of the abstraction methods is evident. Wu and Toyama (2000)[12] have also used Naive Bayes for estimating coarse head pose. Their method uses features extracted by three Gabor filters and a Gaussian filter, which is computationally much more expensive than our regional segmentation method, whose complexity is only of the order of the number of image pixels. We present cross validation results for our implementation of their system in Table 1. As we can see out system outperforms them in almost all cases. We also obtained Mean Average Errors and compared them with those of 3 other approaches. Since other approaches express it as the error w.r.t ($\pm$ 0°), and ours is w.r.t ($\pm$ 7.5°), we added half of 7.5 i.e. 3.75 to our errors(assuming a mean average error of 3.5 each time). This is shown in Table 3. Note that our approach performs consistently across all pan angles upto 90° and all tilt angles upto 60°

Table 1. Results for Pan(0°-90°) with tilt between 0°-30°

	0°-15°	15°-30°	30°-45°	45°-60°	60°-75°	75°-90°	Avg
Colour Segmentation	92	92	96	88	82	80	92
Stroke Rendering	76	72	84	60	92	88	79
Toyama et al[16]	90	85	71	52	51	45	70
Hybrid	87	85	88	80	86	84	87
Unabstracted Images	85	80	80	71	70	65	77

Table 2. Results for Tilt(0°-60°)given pan angle range

Pan Angle Range	0°-15°	15°-30°	30°-45°	45°-60°	60°-75°	75°-90°	Avg
Colour Segmentation	80	84	87	84	82	80	84
Stroke Rendering	72	70	74	76	78	82	75
Hybrid	78	80	82	82	80	80	82

Table 3. Mean Average Error°

Method	Pan	Tilt
Colour Segmentation	4.95	6.15
Stroke Rendering	6.85	7.5
Hybrid	5.65	6.55
Tu et al[17]	14.1	14.9
Gourier et al [18]	10.1	15.9
Dahmane et al[19]	5.7	5.3

7   Conclusion and Future Work

We have discussed how the human brain uses much less information than what is actually available to it for processing images. We have tried to replicate the same and, in specific, demonstrated how NPR based image abstraction can be very useful for rough head pose estimation. Our algorithm is robust to illumination, expressions and identity and works successfully even at low resolutions, making it suitable for surveillance based applications. Moreover, it has little training effort or constraints and works in real time, enabling use on mobile platforms. This can also benefit fine pose estimation algorithms by providing them with an initial rough pose window. For instance, certain ML-based fine pose methods cannot be used practically because they need good initialization eg.bunch graphs [5].We believe that a technique with better color segmentation or other suitable forms of stylization and more sophisticated classifiers will further enhance these results and applications.

References

1. Murphy-Chutorian, E., Trivedi, M.: Head pose estimation in computer vision: A survey. IEEE Transactions on Pattern Analysis and Machine Intelligence 31, 607–626 (2009)
2. Cai, Q., Sankaranarayanan, A., Zhang, Q., Zhang, Z., Liu, Z.: Real time head pose tracking from multiple cameras with a generic model. In: 2010 IEEE Computer Society Conference on Computer Vision and Pattern Recognition Workshops (CVPRW), pp. 25–32 (2010)
3. Saragih, J., Lucey, S., Cohn, J.: Face alignment through subspace constrained mean-shifts. In: 2009 IEEE 12th International Conference on Computer Vision, pp. 1034–1041 (2009)
4. Huang, D., Storer, M., De la Torre, F., Bischof, H.: Supervised local subspace learning for continuous head pose estimation. In: 2011 IEEE Conference on Computer Vision and Pattern Recognition (CVPR), pp. 2921–2928 (2011)
5. Fu, Y., Huang, T.: Graph embedded analysis for head pose estimation. In: 7th International Conference on Automatic Face and Gesture Recognition, FGR 2006, pp. 3–8 (2006)
6. Cole, F., Sanik, K., DeCarlo, D., Finkelstein, A., Funkhouser, T., Rusinkiewicz, S., Singh, M.: How well do line drawings depict shape? In: ACM SIGGRAPH 2009 papers, SIGGRAPH 2009, pp. 28:1–28:9. ACM, New York (2009)
7. Ryan, T.A., Schwartz, C.B.: Speed of perception as a function of mode of representation. American Journal of Psychology 69, 60–69 (1956)
8. Cavanagh, P.: Vision is getting easier everyday. Perception 24, 1227–1232 (1995)
9. Winnemöller, H., Feng, D., Gooch, B., Suzuki, S.: Using npr to evaluate perceptual shape cues in dynamic environments. In: Proceedings of the 5th International Symposium on Non-photorealistic Animation and Rendering, NPAR 2007, pp. 85–92. ACM, New York (2007)
10. Zeki, S.: A vision of the brain. Blackwell Scientific Publications, Oxford (1993)
11. Strothotte, T., Schlechtweg, S.: Non-photorealistic computer graphics: Modeling, rendering, and animation. Morgan Kaufmann (2002)

12. DeCarlo, D., Santella, A.: Stylization and abstraction of photographs. In: Proceedings of the 29th Annual Conference on Computer Graphics and Interactive Techniques, SIGGRAPH 2002, pp. 769–776. ACM, New York (2002)

13. Gourier, N., Hall, D., Crowley, J.L.: Estimating face orientation from robust detection of salient facial features. In: Proceedings of Pointing, ICPR, International Workshop on Visual Observation of Deictic Gestures, vol. 1, pp. 617–622 (2004)

14. Rother, C., Kolmogorov, V., Blake, A.: "grabcut": interactive foreground extraction using iterated graph cuts. ACM Trans. Graph. 23, 309–314 (2004)

15. Birchfield, S.: Elliptical head tracking using intensity gradients and color histograms. In: Proceedings of the 1998 IEEE Computer Society Conference on Computer Vision and Pattern Recognition, pp. 232–237 (1998)

16. Wu, Y., Toyama, K.: Wide-range, person- and illumination-insensitive head orientation estimation. In: Proceedings of the Fourth IEEE International Conference on Automatic Face and Gesture Recognition, pp. 183–188 (2000)

17. Tu, J., Fu, Y., Hu, Y., Huang, T.: Evaluation of Head Pose Estimation for Studio Data. In: Stiefelhagen, R., Garofolo, J.S. (eds.) CLEAR 2006. LNCS, vol. 4122, pp. 281–290. Springer, Heidelberg (2007)

18. Gourier, N., Maisonnasse, J., Hall, D., Crowley, J.L.: Head Pose Estimation on Low Resolution Images. In: Stiefelhagen, R., Garofolo, J.S. (eds.) CLEAR 2006. LNCS, vol. 4122, pp. 270–280. Springer, Heidelberg (2007)

19. Dahmane, M., Meunier, J.: Object representation based on gabor wave vector binning: An application to human head pose detection. In: 2011 IEEE International Conference on Computer Vision Workshops (ICCV Workshops), pp. 2198–2204 (2011)

Complex Bingham Distribution for Facial Feature Detection

Eslam Mostafa[1,2] and Aly Farag[1]

[1] CVIP Lab, University of Louisville, Louisville, KY, USA
[2] Alexandria University, Alexandria, Egypt
{eslam.mostafa,aly.farag}@louisville.edu

Abstract. We present a novel method for facial feature point detection
on images captured from severe uncontrolled environments based on a
combination of regularized boosted classifiers and mixture of complex
Bingham distributions. The complex Bingham distribution is a rotation-
invariant shape representation that can handle pose, in-plane rotation
and occlusion better than existing models. Additionally, we regularized a
boosted classifier with a variance normalization factor to reduce false positives. Using the proposed two models, we formulate our facial features
detection approach in a Bayesian framework of a maximum a-posteriori
estimation. This approach allows for the inclusion of the uncertainty
of the regularized boosted classifier and complex Bingham distribution.
The proposed detector is tested on different datasets and results show
comparable performance to the state-of-the-art with the BioID database
and outperform them in uncontrolled datasets.

1 Introduction

The face analysis pipeline usually consists of four modules: face detection, face
alignment, feature extraction and face matching. Face detection is the first step
in this process since it segments the facial region from the background before
further processing is performed. The next stage is face alignment, where facial
components, such as the eyes, nose, and mouth and facial outline, are located.
Accurate detection of these facial components is crucial to the success of the
later stages of the pipeline.

Valstar et al. [1] describe the difference between facial component detection,
where entire facial features (e.g., mouth region) are detected, and feature point
detection, where more detailed points inside the facial features (e.g., mouth corners) are located. Tasks such as face recognition, gaze estimation, facial expression analysis, gender and ethnicity classification often rely on these finer points.
In this work, we propose a novel facial feature point detector that will locate 15
feature points, as illustrated in Fig. 1.

There have been a number of recent methods that have shown great accuracy
in locating feature points in mostly frontal images and controlled environments.
Our immediate goal is facial feature point detection in challenging real-life situations such as face recognition at-a-distance, where there are different illumination

A. Fusiello et al. (Eds.): ECCV 2012 Ws/Demos, Part II, LNCS 7584, pp. 330–339, 2012.

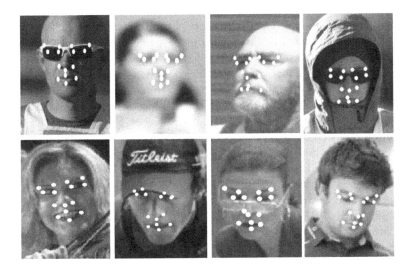

Fig. 1. Sample of results of the proposed facial feature detector on our collected outdoor at-a-distance images (**Top row**) and Labeled Faces in the Wild (LFW) dataset (**Bottom row**)

conditions, variability in pose and expression, existence of occlusion and image acquisition of faces is performed outdoor and at-a-distance (50m to 150m) from the camera. Moreover, we have taken into consideration the speed of this facial feature point detection approach to approach real-time.

Since no public dataset is available with these requirements, we have acquired a database for testing our detector besides the existing databases in the literature. Our collected images, as shown in Fig. 1(**Top row**), are taken in uncontrolled environments at far distances, where instances such as heavy shadowing across the feature points may occur and parts of the face can be occluded (e.g., by sunglasses, hair, or scarf). Pose is also varied from near frontal to severe pose (±45%), where some feature points are occluded.

Previous work on facial features detectors can be classified into two main groups : (a) view-based and (b) 3D-based detectors. View-based approaches train on a set of 2D models; each model can cope with shape or texture variation within a small range of pose. 3D-based approaches [2] can handle multiple views using only a single 3D model but can be sensitive to initialization and computationally expensive. View-based approaches are widely used compared to its 3D counterpart.

The texture and shape prior models are the main components for building a view-based detector. For the texture model, the local texture around given facial feature is modeled,(i.e., the pixels intensity in a small region around the feature point), while for the shape model, the relationship among facial features are modeled. Both models are learned from labeled exemplar images.

Texture-based detectors aim to find the best suitable point in the face that matches the texture model. The texture model can be constructed using different descriptors such as Haar-like [3], local binary pattern (LBP) [4] , Gabor [5], scale-invariant feature transform (SIFT) [6] features. The search problem can be formulated either as a regression or classification. For the classification problem, a sliding window runs through the image to determine if each pixel is a feature or non-feature. For the regression problem, the displacement vector from an initial point to the actual feature point is estimated.

Texture-based detectors are imperfect for many reasons; visual obstructions such as hair, glasses,and hands can greatly affect the results. The detection of each facial feature is also independent from others and it ignores the relation among these facial feature points. To overcome the disadvantages of texture-based detectors, constraints related to the relative location of facial features from each other can be established from the shape model. The relationship among facial feature positions is commonly modeled as a single Gaussian distribution function [7,8], which is the model used by the Active Appearance Model (AAM) and Active Shape Model (ASM) algorithms.

Cristinacce et al. [9] modeled the relative positions of facial features by a pairwise reinforcement of feature responses, instead of a Gaussian distribution while Valstar et.al [1] modeled shape using the Markov Random Field (MRF). These two approaches use a single distribution, which is not suitable for modeling a wide range of poses. Everingham et.al [10] extended the model of a single Gaussian distribution into a mixture of Gaussian trees. Belhumeur et.al [6] used a non-parametric approach, using information from their large collection of diverse, labeled exemplars.

In this work, we propose a novel view-based detector based on a regularized boosted classifier coupled with a mixture of complex Bingham distributions. The following are the contributions of this paper: (a) use of a mixture of complex Bingham distributions to model various viewpoints, (b) regularizing a boosted classifier with a variance normalization factor to reduce false positives, and (c) a new energy function for facial features detection combining two uncertainty terms related to (a) and (b).

The complex Bingham distribution is more robust in modeling the joint probability of the location of facial features than existing models; existing models need a preprocessing step before using the shape prior to filter out scale, translation, and rotation using least-square approaches (e.g., Procrustes analysis), which can introduce errors to the system due to noise and outliers. Since the probability distribution function (PDF) of a complex Bingham has a symmetric property, there is no need to filter out rotation. Scale and translation can be easily removed by a simple mean and normalization step [11].

We propose to regularize the output of the boosted classifier to handle false positives in the classification step of each pixel in a certain neighborhood as feature or non-feature. The output of the classifier should give a high response in the actual facial feature position and decrease smoothly going away from the actual position. If the neighborhood variance is low, it is certain that one pixel position is the actual feature point; otherwise, if the neighborhood variance is high, i.e., all classifier outputs in the neighborhood have combined high or low scores, the classifier is uncertain if a feature point exists in the area. Regularization is performed by dividing a normalization term to the classifier output related to the standard deviation of the output probability scores in the search neighborhood.

Finally, we formulate the facial feature point detection problem as an energy minimization function that incorporate information from both texture and shape models simultaneously, while most of the state-of-the-art approaches use the shape model to improve the results of texture-based methods. The proposed method is compared with existing algorithms on different datasets. Figure 1 shows a sample results of our facial features detector method on a sample of tested images.

2   Facial Feature Extraction

In this section, we describe our texture and shape prior models and how the problem of facial feature point detection is formulated as an energy minimization function that incorporates the uncertainty of the texture model response and the shape prior model.

2.1   Texture Model

In this work, Haar-like features are chosen as the descriptor of local appearance. The first real-time face detector used these features for detection in [12]. The main advantage of Haar-like features over most other features is in the calculation speed. Using integral images, a Haar-like feature of any size can be computed in constant time.

For all training samples, we rescale the images such that the face bounding box is 80×80. The optimal patch size around a given facial feature position has been empirically determined to be 16×16. Positive samples are taken at manually annotated locations. Negative samples are taken at least 20 pixels away from the annotated locations. For each facial feature, a feature/non-feature classifier was trained using the AdaBoost learning algorithm on the positive and negative samples.

Given the face detection bounding box of an input image, we extract sub-images for each facial feature point; each sub-image is the search space of a given facial feature point. The center of this sub-image is the mean position of the feature point in all training images after filtering translation, scale and rotation. The width and height of the sub-image is based on the variance of the feature position. A sliding window is run over the sub-image and the AdaBoost classifier assigns a score for each pixel to be the correct position of the facial feature. The score at position Z is given by $S(D_{Z_i}) = \sum_{t=1}^{r} \alpha_{t_i} F_{t_i}(Z_i)$ where α_{t_i} is the weight of weak classifier t for the feature i and F_{t_i} is the binary response of weak classifier.

In the case of a perfect texture-based detector, the classifier response is homogenous as the probability of the pixel being a feature is high at the true position and decreases smoothly going away from this position. Therefore, we regularize the output of the classifier with a variance normalization factor by dividing the output probability of classifier with $\sigma_{\aleph(Z)}$. $\sigma_{\aleph(Z)}$ is the standard deviation of the output probability among the neighborhood $\aleph(Z)$. Thus, the probability of position Z is the position of the feature i based on the texture detector can be written as

$$P(D_{Z_i}) = \frac{K}{\sigma_{\aleph(Z_i)}} \sum_{t=1}^{r} \alpha_{t_i} F_{t_i}(Z_i)$$

where K is the normalization constant.

Since each feature has a corresponding sub-image that has a sliding window classifier running over it, the output of each texture detector can be considered independent from others. Therefore, the overall probability of $\mathbf{Z} = [Z_1, Z_2...Z_N]$ is the positions vector of N facial features based on the texture-based detector is given by $P(D_{\mathbf{Z}}) = \prod_{i=1}^{N} P(D_{Z_i})$

2.2   Shape Prior Model

Faces come in various shapes due to differences among people, pose, or facial expression of the subject. However, there are strong anatomical and geometric constraints that govern the layout of facial features. The representation of shape, i.e., joint distribution between facial feature points, is described by various models in the literature. The active shape model (ASM) is one example, which is based on a single Gaussian distribution.

Typically, one would like to have a shape representation that is invariant to translation, scale and rotation. A common way to address this problem is to use least-squares (LS) fitting methods, .e.g., Procrustes analysis [11], where misalignments due to noise and outliers may happen [13]. Moreover, an iterative procedure is needed to align multiple shapes.

We propose to use the complex Bingham distribution [14] for our facial feature detection approach. The advantage of using this distribution is that shapes do not need to be aligned with respect to rotation parameters. The probability distribution function of the complex Bingham is

$$P(Y) = c(A)^{-1} exp(Y^* A Y) \tag{1}$$

where $c(A)$ is a normalizing constant.

Since the complex Bingham distribution is invariant to rotation, it is suitable to represent shape in the pre-shape domain, the domain where shapes are zero-offset and unit-scale. In our work, we use the classical way of transforming from the original shape vector to the pre-shape domain by simply multiplying with Helmert sub-matrix(H) to the original shape vector the (matrix) and then performing[11].

Multiplying the original shape vector with the Helmert sub-matrix (H) will project the original facial features position vector $Z \in C^n$ to C^{n-1}. Then, the shape representation using complex Binghanm is

$$P(\mathbf{Z}) = c(A)^{-1} exp(\frac{H\mathbf{Z}}{\| H\mathbf{Z} \|}^* A \frac{H\mathbf{Z}}{\| H\mathbf{Z} \|}) \tag{2}$$

where A is a $(N-1) * (N-1)$ Hermitian parameter matrix, N is number of landmarks or facial feature points. The spectral decomposition can be written as $A = \mathbf{U}\Lambda\mathbf{U}^*$, where $\mathbf{U} = [U_1 U_2 \cdots U_{N-1}]$ is a matrix whose columns U_i correspond to the eigenvectors of A and $\Lambda = diag(\lambda_1, \cdots, \lambda_{N-1})$ is the diagonal matrix of corresponding eigenvalues.

The normalization constant $c(A)$ is given by $c(A) = 2\pi^{N-1} \sum_{i=1}^{N-1} a_i \exp(\lambda_i)$ where $a_i^{-1} = \prod_{m \neq i}(\lambda_i - \lambda_m)$ The log likelihood of parameters is

$$L(\Lambda, \mathbf{U}) = \sum_{i=1}^{N-1} \lambda_i U_i^* S U_i - N \log c(A) \tag{3}$$

where the matrix S is a $N-1 \times N-1$ matrix denoting the auto correlation matrix for manually annotated shapes that have zero mean and unit scale. The maximum likelihood estimators are given by [11]

$$U_i = G_i \quad i = 1, 2, \cdots, N-1 \tag{4}$$

and the solution to

$$\frac{d \log c(\Lambda)}{d\lambda_i} = \frac{l_i}{N} \tag{5}$$

where $\mathbf{G} = [G_1 G_2 \cdots G_{N-1}]$ denotes the corresponding eigenvector of S and $L = diag(l_1, l_2 \cdots l_{N-1})$ is the diagonal matrix of corresponding eigenvalues.

Since no exact solution exists, we estimate λ by minimization of function F

$$F_i = \frac{d \log c(\Lambda)}{d\lambda_i} - \frac{N}{l_i} \tag{6}$$

This function is linearly approximated and solved iteratively using gradient descent. The update equation of parameter λ is given by

$$\lambda_i^{t+1} = \lambda_i^t - \kappa \frac{a_i + \lambda_i^t \sum_{m=1}^{N-2} \prod_{i \neq m \neq k}(\lambda_i - \lambda_k)}{\sum_{i=1}^{N-1} a_i \lambda_i^t} \tag{7}$$

Using the above equation, the parameters of complex Bingham distribution A and $c(A)$ can be estimated off-line from the training shapes examples which are manually annotated from the MUCT dataset. Since the deformation of shape due to different poses is large and cannot be handled by a single distribution [10], [15], we divide the training annotated shapes into M classes. Each class carries a small range of poses and has its own parameters A_m and $c(A_m)$ and a

Bayes classifier rule is used to determine which class the test image belongs to. In this work , we use $M = 5$ which correspondence to poses $-45°, -25°$, frontal, $25°$,and $45°$ The index of class is given by

2.3   Combining Texture and Shape Model

In facial feature detection problems, we try to recover numerous of hidden variables (position of facial features) based on observable variables (image gray level). This problem can be formulated as a Bayesian framework of maximum a-posteriori (MAP) estimation. We want to find the vector Z, which maximizes the response probability for the texture model and shape model.

$$\hat{Z} = \arg \max P(I|Z)P(Z). \tag{8}$$

$P(I|Z)$ represents the probability of similarity between the texture of the face to off-line model given the facial feature vector. Since the similarity of the face can be expressed in the similarity of the windows around each facial feature, it can be written as $P(W(Z_i), W(Z_2) \cdots W(Z_N)|Z)$. Where $W(Z_i)$ is the image window around the facial point Z_i. The windows around each facial point can be considered independent from each others. Therefore

$$P(I|Z) = \prod_{i=1}^{N} P(W(Z_i)|Z_i), \tag{9}$$

where $P(W(Z_i)|Z_i)$ can be interpreted as the probability of a pixel being feature based on the texture model. Based on boosted classifier and Haar-like feature vector the probability can be written as

$$P(W(Z_i)|Z_i) = P(D_{Z_i}) = \frac{K}{\sigma_{\aleph(Z_i)}} \sum_{t=1}^{r} \alpha_{t_i} F_{t_i}(Z_i) \tag{10}$$

Therefore, the maximum-a-posteriori estimate of facial features can be formulated as an energy minimization of function $E(Z)$

$$E(\mathbf{Z}) = -\frac{H\mathbf{Z}^* AH\mathbf{Z}}{\| H\mathbf{Z} \|^2} - \sum_{i=1}^{N} \log P(D_{Z_i}) \tag{11}$$

This energy function is non-linear and not amenable to gradient descent-type algorithms. It is solved by a classical energy minimization technique, which is simulated annealing where maximum number of iterations is empirically set to 100 iterations.

$$m^* = \arg_m \min \frac{H\mathbf{Z}}{\| H\mathbf{Z} \|}^* A_m \frac{H\mathbf{Z}}{\| H\mathbf{Z} \|} + \log(c_m(A)) \tag{12}$$

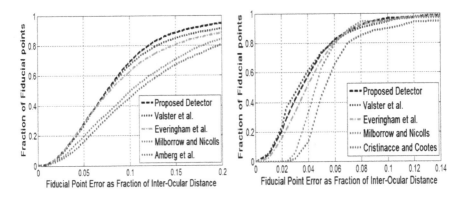

Fig. 2. A comparison of the cumulative error distribution measured on our collected images dataset(Left) and BIO-ID(Right)

3   Experiments

Our work focuses on facial feature extraction in severe uncontrolled environments, pose, existence of shadow, presence of occlusion objects as sunglasses or subject's hand, existence of in-plane rotation, and blurred images at range distances in real time. Existing available public databases for evaluation facial feature extraction do not consider long distance, above 50 meters, and blurred images. So we collected 1541 faces for 55 subjects. These images are taken at distances of 30, 50, 80, 100, 150 meters with a Canon 7D camera attached to a 800mm telephoto lens. Furthermore, most of the researchers about facial features detection in the literature reported results on the BiOID database,therefore we also included it to test the proposed detector. The BiOID dataset [16] contains 1521 images, each showing a near frontal view of a face in controlled indoor environments with no illumination and occlusion problems for 23 distinct subjects.

In our experiment, we compare proposed detector with existing algorithms which are the extended Active shape Model (STASM) [17], compositional image alignment (AAM) [18], the detector proposed by Everingham et al. [10], and the detector proposed by Valster et al.[1]. STASM shows good performance in locating facial features on various datasets and most researchers use this detector for comparison, e.g., [18], [1]. The compositional image alignment approach is a modification of the original AAM and has better results than its predecessor. The detector proposed by Everingham et al. [10] shows competitive results for the commercial product COTS on a LFPW dataset [6]. The detector proposed by Valster et al shows the best results on BioID dataset. We excluded from our comparison the detector which is proposed in [6]; however, they reported excellent results on LFPW dataset. Since this task need to be as fast as possible due to being part of real time system, our detector takes on average 0.47 seconds on an Intel Core $i7$ 2.93 GHz machine for locating all facial feature points. Figure 2 shows the cumulative error distribution of me_{17} defined by [19] for our detector compared to those reported by [19],[1], [5],[17] on collected image at distance and BIO-ID.

For investigation, the effect of the regualized boosted classifier as texture model and the complex bingham as shape model, we conduct an experiment from four tests on our collected images in an uncontrolled environment. First, The boosted classifier without the regulairzed term is used as texture model along with the gaussian distribution as a shape model. Second, the regularized term is added to the boosted classifier while keeping the shape model as gaussian. Third,the regularized term is kept while changing the shape model to complex bingham distribution. Last, the regularized term is discarded while keeping the shape model as complex bingham distribution, as shown in figure 3 (b). It shows that each of regularized term and the complex bingham improves the result especially when the detected facial features are far from the correct one. However,the effect of complex bingham distribution is more significant than the regularized term.

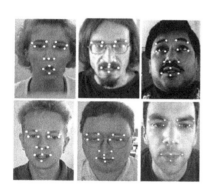 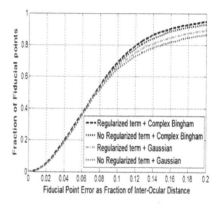

Fig. 3. (a) Some results of our proposed detector on the BioID dataset. (b) The Evaluation of the effect of regularized term in the texture model and complex bingham as shape model on our collected images dataset.

4   Conclusion

We have described a new approach for facial features detection based on complex Bingham distribution and regularized boosted classifier. We combine the uncertainty of the response of complex Bingham and boosted classifier is an energy minimization function. Our detector is robust under a variation of pose, in-plane rotation, expression, occlusion, and illumination. It shows that we outperform existing facial detector in uncontrolled environment images and achieve a comparable results in the less challenging dataset BIO-ID.

References

1. Valstar, M., Martinez, B., Binefa, X., Pantic, M.: Facial point detection using boosted regression and graph models. In: Proceedings of IEEE Int'l Conf. Computer Vision and Pattern Recognition (CVPR 2010), San Francisco, USA, pp. 2729–2736 (2010)
2. Zhang, Z., Liu, Z., Adler, D., Cohen, M.F., Hanson, E., Shan, Y.: Robust and rapid generation of animated faces from video images: A model-based modeling approach. Int. J. Comput. Vision (2004)
3. Eckhardt, M., Fasel, I.R., Movellan, J.R.: Towards practical facial feature detection. IJPRAI
4. Shan, C., Gong, S., Mcowan, P.: Facial expression recognition based on local binary patterns: A comprehensive study. Image and Vision Computing, 803–816 (2009)
5. Vukadinovic, D., Pantic, M.: Fully automatic facial feature point detection using Gabor feature based boosted classifiers. In: IEEE Int'l Conf. on Systems, Man and Cybernetics 2005, pp. 1692–1698 (2005)
6. Belhumeur, P.N., Jacobs, D.W., Kriegman, D.J., Kumar, N.: Localizing parts of faces using a consensus of exemplars. In: The 24th IEEE Conference on Computer Vision and Pattern Recognition, CVPR (2011)
7. Cristinacce, D., Cootes, T.: Facial feature detection using adaboost with shape constraints. In: 14th British Machine Vision Conference, Norwich, England, pp. 231–240 (2003)
8. Cristinacce, D., Cootes, T.: Boosted regression active shape models. In: 18th British Machine Vision Conference, Warwick, UK, pp. 880–889 (2007)
9. Cristinacce, D., Cootes, T., Scott, I.: A multi-stage approach to facial feature detection. In: 15th British Machine Vision Conference, London, England, pp. 277–286 (2004)
10. Everingham, M., Sivic, J., Zisserman, A.: "Hello! My name is... Buffy" – automatic naming of characters in TV video. In: Proceedings of the British Machine Vision Conference (2006)
11. Dryden, I., Mardia, K.V.: The statistical analysis of shape. Wiley, London (1998)
12. Viola, P., Jones, M.J.: Robust real-time face detection. Int. J. Comput. Vision, 137–154 (2004)
13. Hamsici, O., Martinez, A.: Rotation invariant kernels and their application to shape analysis. IEEE Transactions on Pattern Analysis and Machine Intelligence, 1985–1999 (2009)
14. Bingham, C.: An antipodally symmetric distribution on the sphere. The Annals of Statistics, 1201–1225 (1974)
15. Saragih, J.M., Lucey, S., Cohn, J.: Face alignment through subspace constrained mean-shifts. In: International Conference of Computer Vision, ICCV (2009)
16. Frischholz, R.W., Dieckmann, U.: Bioid: A multimodal biometric identification system. Computer, 64–68 (2000)
17. Milborrow, S., Nicolls, F.: Locating Facial Features with an Extended Active Shape Model. In: Forsyth, D., Torr, P., Zisserman, A. (eds.) ECCV 2008, Part IV. LNCS, vol. 5305, pp. 504–513. Springer, Heidelberg (2008)
18. Brian Amberg, A.B., Vetter, T.: On compositional image alignment with an application to active appearance models. In: Proceedings of IEEE Int'l Conf. Computer Vision and Pattern Recognition (CVPR 2009) (2009)
19. Cristinacce, D., Cootes, T.: Feature detection and tracking with constrained local models. In: 17th British Machine Vision Conference, Edinburgh, UK, pp. 929–938 (2006)

Estimating Surface Normals from Spherical Stokes Reflectance Fields

Giuseppe Claudio Guarnera[1,*], Pieter Peers[2],
Paul Debevec[1], and Abhijeet Ghosh[1]

[1] USC Institute for Creative Technologies, Playa Vista, CA, USA
[2] The College of William & Mary, Williamsburg, VA, USA

Abstract. In this paper we introduce a novel technique for estimating surface normals from the four Stokes polarization parameters of specularly reflected light under a single spherical incident lighting condition that is either unpolarized or circularly polarized. We illustrate the practicality of our technique by estimating surface normals under uncontrolled outdoor illumination from just four observations from a fixed viewpoint.

1   Introduction

Accurate shape and appearance estimation is a crucial component in many computer vision applications. Despite being at the focal point of intense research, shape and appearance estimation remains a challenging problem, especially under uncontrolled real-world conditions. Estimation of both small-scale surface shape as well as surface reflectance greatly benefits from accurate knowledge of surface orientation. In this work, we propose a novel method for estimating surface orientation from the Stokes polarization vector under a *single* spherical incident illumination condition that is either circularly polarized (Fig. 1,c-d) or unpolarized (Fig. 1, e-f).

Polarization cues have previously been employed to separate diffuse and specular reflectance components (e.g., [1–4]), to classify materials (e.g., [1, 5]), to estimate reflectance properties (e.g., [6, 7]), and to estimate surface normals (e.g., [8–12]). Motivated by the polarization characteristics of natural lighting, which is either unpolarized (overcast sky) or linearly polarized (sunlight), most of these methods, with exception of [2, 4, 10] focus solely on linear polarization cues. In contrast, in this work we leverage observations of the view-independent symmetric Stokes reflectance field – which encodes the impact of unpolarized, linearly polarized, as well as circularly polarized reflected light – for estimating surface normals under *constant* incident spherical illumination. We show that for many dielectric materials, a non-negligible circularly polarized reflectance is observed, not only under circularly polarized incident lighting, but also for unpolarized lighting. Leveraging these circular polarization cues greatly improves normal estimation for front facing surfaces. We demonstrate that both types of incident lighting can be used to reliably estimate surface normals from observations of the Stokes reflectance field, and show how this theory can be applied to normal estimation under uncontrolled outdoor illumination.

---

* Currently at the Department of Mathematics and Computer Science, University of Catania, Italy.

A. Fusiello et al. (Eds.): ECCV 2012 Ws/Demos, Part II, LNCS 7584, pp. 340–349, 2012.
© Springer-Verlag Berlin Heidelberg 2012

(a) Subject   (b) Photometric Normals (c) Circular Stokes Param.   (d) Circ. Pol. Normals   (e) Unpol. Stokes Param.   (f) Unpol. Normals

Fig. 1. Estimating surface normals (encoded as $\frac{1}{2}(\mathbf{x}+1) \rightarrow R$, $\frac{1}{2}(\mathbf{y}+1) \rightarrow G$, and $\frac{1}{2}(\mathbf{z}+1) \rightarrow B$) from Stokes parameters (encoded as $|s_3| \rightarrow R$, $|s_1| \rightarrow G$, and $|s_2| \rightarrow B$) of specularly reflected incident spherical illumination. Surface normals inferred from circularly polarized illumination (c-d), and unpolarized illumination (e-f), compared to surface normals obtained from a photometric stereo variant [2](b). Top-row: Plastic orange - ϕ-ambiguity resolved by growing normals inward. Bottom-row: Marble statue - ϕ-ambiguity resolved using an additional measurement.

2   Related Work

The seminal work by Woodham [13] on photometric stereo, which proposes to estimate surface normals from single viewpoint images of diffuse surfaces lit from different lighting directions, has inspired much research since its introduction in 1978. While recent advances do not require the incident lighting to be known beforehand [14], these methods still require multiple lighting conditions to accurately estimate surface orientation. In contrast the proposed method requires just a *single* lighting condition, making it better suited for normal estimation in uncontrolled outdoor environments.

Shape estimation under fixed lighting can be obtained from specular cues. Roth and Black [15] introduce the concept of specular flow and illustrate how such specular flow relates to shape under general environmental illumination for surfaces that exhibit (binary) mixtures of diffuse and specular materials. Vasilyev et al. [16] extend specular flow to general unconstrained surface shapes. However, estimating specular flow from multiple viewpoints is a difficult and complex problem. While the proposed method also relies on specular reflections, it only needs four observations from a *single* viewpoint under constant illumination, avoiding complex specular flow and/or correspondence computations. Furthermore the proposed method naturally handles per-pixel mixtures of diffuse and specular.

Polarization cues have also been used extensively for estimating surface normals. Most methods exploit the property that the *angle of polarization* relates to the surface normal direction perpendicular to the plane of incidence. The direction within the plane of incidence is found by either observing the surface from multiple viewpoints [17–20], or from the *degree of polarization* [11, 12, 21–23]. The majority of the above methods infer surface information from a series of photographs of the surface while rotating a linear polarizer in front of the camera. The proposed method does not only rely on linear polarization cues, but instead infers surface information from the full characterization of the reflectance (i.e., the Stokes reflectance field), that can be captured in just four photographs with different polarizers in front of the camera (i.e., three linear polarizers rotated 0, 45, and 90 degrees, and a (left) circular polarizer). Furthermore, we show that even under unpolarized incident lighting, some non-negligible circularly polarized reflectance is present, which impacts the accuracy of the estimated normals if ignored.

Ma et al. [2] propose a photometric stereo variant that employs either linear or circular polarization for separating diffuse and specular reflections, and compute accurate surface normals from the specular component. However, unlike the proposed method, they rely on photometric cues for estimating the surface normal.

Koshikawa [10] estimate the surface normal of a *single* surface point from the Stokes vector, measured using a ellipsometer, under a single directional circularly polarized light source. They assume known index of refraction, and estimate the normal from the Fresnel equations. However, they ignore the ambiguity in the azimuthal angle of the surface normal. In contrast, the proposed method employs a standard DSLR camera instead of an ellipsometer and considers both circularly polarized *and* unpolarized incident lighting, and explicitly handles the azimuthal ambiguity.

3   Surface Normal Estimation from Stokes Vectors

Background: Mueller Calculus.   Before detailing how surface normals can be estimated from measurements of the Stokes reflectance field under a single spherical illumination condition, we first give a brief overview of the related theory on Stokes parameters and Mueller calculus. A more detailed description can be found in [24]. In what follows we assume that the surface consists of a homogeneous dielectric material, and the coordinate frame is that of the camera, i.e., the camera looks down the -Z axis, the X axis points right, and the Y axis points up.

The polarization state of light can be described by the 4-element Stokes vector $\mathbf{s} = (s_0, s_1, s_2, s_3)$, where: s_0 represents the total power, s_1 is the power of the $0°$ linear polarization, s_2 is the power the $+45°$ linear polarization, and s_3 is the power of right circular polarization. The degree of polarization, or ratio of the power of polarized light versus the total power equals: $DOP = \sqrt{s_1^2 + s_2^2 + s_3^2}/s_0$. When a polarized ray hits a reflective surface (i.e., specular), the resulting change to Stokes vector is predicted by Mueller calculus: $\mathbf{s}' = \mathbf{C}(\phi)\mathbf{D}(\delta;\mathbf{n})\mathbf{R}(\theta;\mathbf{n})\mathbf{C}(-\phi)\mathbf{s}$. Each of the linear operators $\mathbf{C}$, $\mathbf{D}$ and $\mathbf{R}$ can be compactly represented by a matrix. $\mathbf{C}$ is the Mueller rotation that brings the linear polarization parameters into a canonical frame:

$$\mathbf{C} = \begin{pmatrix} 1 & 0 & 0 & 0 \\ 0 & \cos 2\phi & -\sin 2\phi & 0 \\ 0 & \sin 2\phi & \cos 2\phi & 0 \\ 0 & 0 & 0 & 1 \end{pmatrix}, \tag{1}$$

where ϕ is the angle between the camera's $\mathbf{x}$ axis and the incident plane determined by the surface normal $\mathbf{n}$ and incident direction (i.e., $\arccos(\mathbf{n} \cdot \mathbf{x})$). $\mathbf{R}$ is the Mueller reflection matrix:

$$\mathbf{R} = \begin{pmatrix} \frac{\mathbf{R}_\| + \mathbf{R}_\perp}{2} & \frac{\mathbf{R}_\| - \mathbf{R}_\perp}{2} & 0 & 0 \\ \frac{\mathbf{R}_\| - \mathbf{R}_\perp}{2} & \frac{\mathbf{R}_\| + \mathbf{R}_\perp}{2} & 0 & 0 \\ 0 & 0 & \sqrt{\mathbf{R}_\| \mathbf{R}_\perp} & 0 \\ 0 & 0 & 0 & \sqrt{\mathbf{R}_\| \mathbf{R}_\perp} \end{pmatrix}, \qquad (2)$$

where $\mathbf{R}_\|$ and $\mathbf{R}_\perp$ are the Fresnel equations for the parallel and perpendicular components, respectively, as functions of the incident angle θ (i.e., $\arccos(\mathbf{n} \cdot \mathbf{z})$). Finally, $\mathbf{D}$ is the Mueller retardation matrix. For dielectric materials, this essentially flips the signs of s_2 and s_3 over the Brewster angle.

Finally, the Stokes reflectance field [6] is defined as the description of the Stokes vectors resulting from a single surface interaction, under a user-defined incident light field, computed for every surface normal direction.

Uniform Circularly Polarized Incident Lighting. We will develop our theory first on the case where the incident illumination has power Φ over the sphere of incident directions and is circularly polarized. In other words $\mathbf{s}(\omega) = \mathbf{s} \sim (\Phi, 0, 0, \Phi)$. Applying Mueller calculus for diffuse and specular surface interactions yields the Stokes reflectance vector $\mathbf{s}'$:

$$\begin{aligned} \mathbf{s}' &= (s_0', s_1', s_2', s_3') \\ &= \left(\rho_s \Phi \frac{\mathbf{R}_\perp + \mathbf{R}_\|}{2} + \rho_d \Phi, \rho_s \Phi \frac{\mathbf{R}_\perp - \mathbf{R}_\|}{2} \cos 2\phi, \rho_s \Phi \frac{\mathbf{R}_\perp - \mathbf{R}_\|}{2} \sin 2\phi, \mp \rho_s \Phi \sqrt{\mathbf{R}_\| \mathbf{R}_\perp} \right), \end{aligned} \qquad (3)$$

where ρ_d and ρ_s are the diffuse and specular albedo of the dielectric material. Note that s_0' is the result of both specular as well as diffuse reflectance. While the impact of diffuse reflectance can be easily removed from s_0' using the degree of polarization [6], we avoid using this component in our computations to minimize the impact of potential diffuse pollution (e.g., due to suboptimal polarizers). Note that s_1', s_2' and s_3' are the result of specular reflections only, and hence unaffected by any diffuse pollution.

To compute θ, we establish a relation χ between the Stokes components s_1', s_2' and s_3' that is independent of specular albedo ρ_s and the power of the incident light source Φ:

$$\chi = \arctan \left(\frac{s_3'}{\sqrt{s_1'^2 + s_2'^2}} \right) = \arctan \left(\mp 2 \frac{\sqrt{\mathbf{R}_\| \mathbf{R}_\perp}}{\mathbf{R}_\perp - \mathbf{R}_\|} \right). \qquad (4)$$

Note that χ is implicitly related by a non-linear one-to-one mapping to θ via the Fresnel equations $\mathbf{R}_\perp$ and $\mathbf{R}_\|$. We invert this non-linear mapping by precomputing a lookup table that maps χ to θ, obtained by evaluating Eq. (4) for a dense sample of θ, and assuming a fixed index of refraction of 1.4. Fig. 2 illustrates the impact of on the accuracy of the recovered θ when the true index of refraction differs from the fixed index. As can be seen, the error remains below $5°$ for moderate indexes of refraction and for $\theta < 60$. Alternatively, the index of refraction can also be computed using the method described in [6].

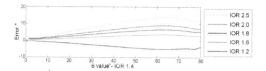

Fig. 2. Error plots for θ estimated with a fixed index of refraction of 1.4 for materials with increasing index of refraction

The remaining azimuthal angle ϕ can be directly computed from the linear components s_1' and s_2':

$$\arctan\left(\frac{s_2'}{s_1'}\right) = \arctan\left(\frac{\sin 2\phi}{\cos 2\phi}\right) = 2\phi. \qquad (5)$$

Note that this is exactly the same as the *angle of polarization* used in prior work. Similarly as in prior work, this relation is ambiguous: ϕ and $\phi + \pi$ both satisfy the above equation. Resolving this ambiguity as been the focus of many prior work. In this work, we employ two alternative strategies:

1. For convex objects, we can grow the normals in from the silhouette, assuming that the normals at the silhouette are orthogonal to silhouette edge and the view direction. This strategy was also employed in prior work such as [21].
2. Alternatively, we can capture an additional photograph of the surface while lit by another known spherical illumination condition $I(\cdot,\cdot)$ such that $I(\phi,\theta) \neq I(\phi + \pi,\theta)$. This strategy is useful when incident lighting can be precisely controlled (e.g., laboratory setting). We will also employ a variant of this for normal estimation in uncontrolled outdoor lighting.

Uniform Unpolarized Incident Lighting. In the case that the incident lighting is unpolarized (i.e., the Stokes vector is $(\Phi,0,0,0)$), Mueller calculus for diffuse and specular surface interactions predicts the following resulting reflected Stokes vector:

$$\mathbf{s}' = \left(\rho_s \Phi \frac{\mathbf{R}_\perp + \mathbf{R}_\parallel}{2} + \rho_d \Phi, \rho_s \Phi \frac{\mathbf{R}_\perp - \mathbf{R}_\parallel}{2} \cos 2\phi, \rho_s \Phi \frac{\mathbf{R}_\perp - \mathbf{R}_\parallel}{2} \sin 2\phi, 0\right). \qquad (6)$$

Observe that s_1' and s_2' are solely due to specular reflections. ϕ can be computed similarly as before using Eq. (5). However, Eq. (4) cannot be employed for estimating θ, because the circular Stokes component s_3' differs. While a relation can be expressed in terms of s_1' and s_2' (e.g., $\sim s_1'^2 + s_2'^2$), such a relation will suffer from a low SNR when $\mathbf{R}_\perp \approx \mathbf{R}_\parallel$. While no circular polarization is predicted by Eq. (6), we experimentally detected a small quantity of left circularly polarized reflectance under unpolarized incident illumination. We observe that, while fairly constant for different angles of θ, it is stronger than the observed amount of linearly polarized reflectance near normal incidence (Fig. 3, (a)) . This provides a means to improve the accuracy of surface normals for front facing surfaces. We believe that this observed circularly polarized reflectance is due to polarization preserving (subsurface) scattering, which was not taken into account when computing Eq. (6). Fig. 3, (b-e) shows an experimental validation that indicates that the observed circularly polarized reflectance is not due to specular reflections (i.e., non-zero s_3' is observed between the sharp highlights). Furthermore, it

(a) Circular vs Linear mag.   (b) Black ball   (c) Black ball Unpol. Stokes   (d) Blue ball   (e) Blue ball Unpol. Stokes

Fig. 3. (a) Plot of reflected circular vs linear polarization under uniform spherical illumination as function of θ. (b - e) Stokes parameters of two sharp specular balls under uniform spherical illumination (emitted from a LED sphere with 346 lights) showing circular polarization (red) between the observed specular highlights which are linearly polarized.

has been shown that scattering from randomly oriented particles can give rise to circular polarization (see [25], p.451), and that polarization is preserved for an average of 2.5 scattering events [26]. Exact modeling of the corresponding Mueller matrix, and thus the resulting s_3', for polarization preserving scattering is difficult due to the many unknown factors. Instead of relying on an exact formulation of s_3' for computing θ, an example-based strategy is employed. The Stokes reflectance field of a dielectric object with known shape (e.g., a sphere) is recorded under unpolarized incident lighting. To account for differences in specular albedo and scattering properties, a first-order correction is performed by scaling the maximum of $\sqrt{s_1'^2 + s_2'^2}$ and of s_3' in the target dataset to match those of the exemplar dataset. This first-order correction works well for objects that exhibit a rich variation in surface normals. Finally, the normal of a surface point is computed by finding the best matching $\sqrt{s_1'^2 + s_2'^2}$ and s_3' pair on the exemplar.

Uncontrolled Outdoor Illumination. The extension of the proposed method to uncontrolled outdoor environments builds on two observations:

– We observe that overcast sky is unpolarized, and the content varies approximately as: $I(\phi, \theta) \sim sin(\phi)$. Such an illumination condition is slowly varying, and fulfills the condition that $I(\phi, \theta) \neq I(\phi + \pi, \theta)$, and thus it is suitable for resolving the ϕ-ambiguity.

– Furthermore, if the content of the environment lighting varies slowly in comparison to the sharpness of the specular reflection (which is the case for overcast sky), then we can approximate the intensity of incident lighting over the solid angle of significant specular response as a constant scale factor s_ω. Hence, for every surface point, the specular response is similar (up to a scale factor s_ω) as if it was captured under a constant lighting condition. However, care has to be taken when performing the first-order correction of $\sqrt{s_1'^2 + s_2'^2}$ and s_3' since different surface points' specular reflections are possibly scaled by a different scale factor s_ω. We propose to either capture the exemplar in the same environment (and hence it includes s_ω), or alternatively perform a first-order correction on the ratio $s_3'/\sqrt{s_1'^2 + s_2'^2}$ instead of the individual components (effectively dividing out s_ω). The latter is similar to the ratio used in Eq. (4).

Again, we can readily apply the theory outlined for the uniform unpolarized incident lighting case to compute surface normals under uncontrolled overcast illumination.

The inclusion of circular polarization yields a more robust estimation of surface normals compared to prior work such as [11, 12, 21–23] which rely solely on linear polarization cues to estimate the in-plane incident angle from the *reduced* degree of polarization: $DOP' = \sqrt{s_1^2 + s_2^2}/s_0$ (i.e., s_3 is implicitly assumed to be zero). We found the estimation error to reduce by $5°$ close to normal incidence with the inclusion of circular polarization.

4 Results

We validate our theory in both controlled and uncontrolled lighting conditions. We follow the acquisition scheme of [6] to capture the Stokes reflectance field. Specifically, four photographs of a surface are recorded with four different polarizers in front of the camera: a linear polarizer rotated $0°$ (P_H), $45°$ (P_{45}), $90°$ (P_V), and a (left) circular polarizer ($P_\circ$). We can then robustly compute the Stokes vector components as: $s_0 = P_H + P_V$, $s_1 = P_H - P_V$, $s_2 = 2P_{45} - s_0$, and $s_3 = s_0 - 2P_\circ$. This scheme has the advantage that any unpolarized light that passes through the polarizers will be canceled out in the computation of s_1, s_2, and s_3. While s_0 may overestimate the unpolarized power, it is not used in any of our computations.

Fig. 1 shows surface normal estimation results for a convex plastic orange (top row) under controlled incident lighting generated by an LED sphere with 346 lights. We compare the estimated surface normals under circularly polarized and unpolarized spherically uniform incident lighting to surface normals obtained by the photometric method of Ma et al. [2]. The ϕ ambiguity is handled by growing the normals in from the silhouette. Fig. 1 (bottom row) presents the results under similar conditions of a more complex marble statue with concavities. The ϕ-ambiguity is solved by capturing an additional lighting conditions: $I(\phi, \theta) = (\sin(\phi) + 1)/2$.

Fig. 4 gives a quantitative error analysis of the surface normal estimation for an object with known shape (i.e., sphere). As can be seen the quality of the estimated normals is good, except close towards extreme angles due to reflection occlusion. Furthermore, the surface normals estimated under circular incident lighting exhibit a better SNR for front facing surfaces compared to those acquired under unpolarized incident lighting. The mean angular error is around $7°$ for incident angles less than $75°$. Note that normals towards the bottom of the sphere exhibit a larger error due to reflection occlusion from the stand supporting the ball.

Fig. 5 shows normal estimation results under a spherical linear intensity gradient in the top-down direction: $I(\phi, \theta) = (\sin(\phi) + 1)/2$, which simulates an idealized outdoor overcast condition. Fig. 5 (top row) show the estimated normals of a plastic maquette under this simulated lighting condition. The ϕ-ambiguity was handled by growing in the normals from the silhouette. Fig. 5 center and bottom row, show a marble statue and a plaster bas relief respectively captured under the same single simulated lighting condition. For these two cases, the ϕ-ambiguity was solved using the intensity information of the incident lighting condition.

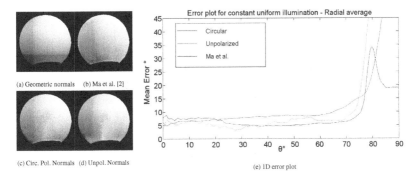

(a) Geometric normals   (b) Ma et al. [2]

(c) Circ. Pol. Normals   (d) Unpol. Normals

(e) 1D error plot

Fig. 4. Surface normals of a spherical ball estimated from Stokes parameters of incident spherical illumination. Surface normals inferred from circularly polarized illumination (c), and unpolarized illumination (d), compared to known ground truth geometric normals (a), and compared to normals obtained from linearly polarized incident lighting using the method of [2] (b).

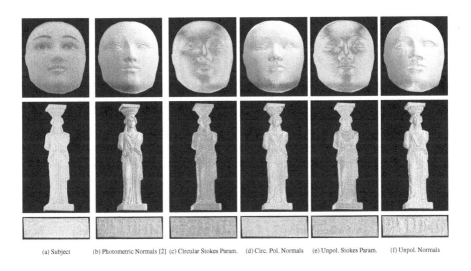

(a) Subject   (b) Photometric Normals [2]   (c) Circular Stokes Param.   (d) Circ. Pol. Normals   (e) Unpol. Stokes Param.   (f) Unpol. Normals

Fig. 5. Estimated surface normals from Stokes parameters under idealized simulated outdoor lighting conditions. Surface normals inferred from circularly polarized illumination (c-d), and unpolarized illumination (e-f), compared to photometric normals [2] (b). Top-row: Plastic maquette - surface normal map of face grown inward from the silhouette. Center-row: Marble statue - ϕ ambiguity resolved using directional cues from the incident illumination. Bottow-row: Plaster bas relief.

Fig. 6 shows results of surface normal estimation from outdoor illumination on a cloudy day for the convex plastic orange as well as a jade Confucius statue with several concavities. The exemplar sphere was captured under the same lighting condition.

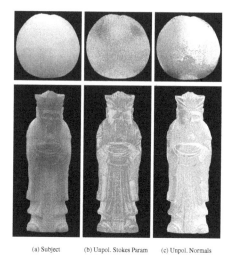

(a) Subject   (b) Unpol. Stokes Param   (c) Unpol. Normals

Fig. 6. Estimated surface normals from Stokes parameters of diffuse outdoor illumination. Top-row: Plastic orange. Bottom-row: Confucius statue.

5   Conclusion

We presented a novel technique for estimating surface normals from polarization cues obtained from the Stokes reflectance field captured in just four photographs from a single viewpoint and under a single (unpolarized or cicularly polarized) constant spherical incident lighting. While the theory is based on Meuller calculus and is strictly for homogeneous dielectric materials with a constant specular roughness, we found it to work well in practice for both dielectrics as well as dielectric-metal composites. We validated the proposed technique in both controlled as well as uncontrolled outdoor lighting conditions.

Acknowledgments. We would like to thank Jay Busch, Santa Datta, Saskia Mordijck, Kathleen Haase, Bill Swartout, Randy Hill, and Randolph Hall for their support and assistance with this work. This work was sponsored in part by NSF grants IIS-1016703 and ISS-1217765, the University of Southern California Office of the Provost and the U.S. Army Research, Development, and Engineering Command (RDECOM). The content of the information does not necessarily reflect the position or the policy of the US Government, and no official endorsement should be inferred.

References

1. Wolff, L.B., Boult, T.E.: Constraining object features using a polarization reflectance model. PAMI 13, 635–657 (1991)
2. Ma, W.C., Hawkins, T., Peers, P., Chabert, C.F., Weiss, M., Debevec, P.: Rapid acquisition of specular and diffuse normal maps from polarized spherical gradient illumination. In: Rendering Techniques, pp. 183–194 (2007)

3. Nayar, S., Fang, X., Boult, T.: Removal of Specularities using Color and Polarization. In: CVPR (1993)
4. Ghosh, A., Fyffe, G., Tunwattanapong, B., Busch, J., Yu, X., Debevec, P.: Multiview face capture using polarized spherical gradient illumination. In: Proceedings of the 2011 SIGGRAPH Asia Conference, SA 2011, pp. 129:1–129:10. ACM, New York (2011)
5. Tominaga, S., Yamamoto, T.: Metal-dielectric object classification by polarization degree map. In: CVPR, pp. 1–4 (2008)
6. Ghosh, A., Chen, T., Peers, P., Wilson, C.A., Debevec, P.: Circularly polarized spherical illumination reflectometry. ACM Trans. Graph. 29, 162:1–162:12 (2010)
7. Cula, O.G., Dana, K.J., Pai, D.K., Wang, D.: Polarization multiplexing and demultiplexing for appearance-based modeling. PAMI 29, 362–367 (2007)
8. Wolff, L.B., Lundberg, A., Tang, R.: Image understanding from thermal emission polarization. In: CVPR, p. 625. IEEE Computer Society, Washington, DC (1998)
9. Miyazaki, D., Ikeuchi, K.: Inverse polarization raytracing: Estimating surface shapes of transparent objects. In: CVPR, pp. 910–917 (2005)
10. Koshikawa, K.: A polarimetric approach to shape understanding of glossy objects, 190–192 (1992)
11. Atkinson, G.A., Hancock, E.R.: Shape estimation using polarization and shading from two views. PAMI 29, 2001–2017 (2007)
12. Saito, M., Sato, Y., Ikeuchi, K., Kashiwagi, H.: Measurement of surface orientations of transparent objects by use of polarization in highlight. J. Opt. Soc. Am. A 16, 2286–2293 (1999)
13. Woodham, R.J.: Photometric stereo: A reflectance map technique for determining surface orientation from image intensity. In: Proc. SPIE's 22nd Annual Technical Symposium, vol. 155 (1978)
14. Basri, R., Jacobs, D.W.: Photometric stereo with general, unknown lighting. In: CVPR, pp. 374–381 (2001)
15. Roth, S., Black, M.J.: Specular flow and the recovery of surface structure. In: Proceedings of the 2006 IEEE Computer Society Conference on Computer Vision and Pattern Recognition, CVPR 2006, vol. 2, pp. 1869–1876 (2006)
16. Vasilyev, Y., Zickler, T., Gortler, S., Ben-Shahar, O.: Shape from specular flow: Is one flow enough?, pp. 2561–2568 (2011)
17. Rahmann, S., Canterakis, N.: Reconstruction of specular surfaces using polarization imaging. In: CVRP, vol. 1, p. 149 (2001)
18. Atkinson, G.A., Hancock, E.R.: Multi-view surface reconstruction using polarization. In: ICCV, pp. 309–316 (2005)
19. Miyazaki, D., Kagesawa, M., Ikeuchi, K.: Transparent surface modeling from a pair of polarization images. PAMI 26, 73–82 (2004)
20. Wolff, L.B.: Surface orientation from two camera stereo with polarizers. In: Proc. SPIE Conf. Optics, Illumination and Image Sensing for Machine Vision IV, vol. 1194, pp. 287–297 (1989)
21. Miyazaki, D., Kagesawa, M., Ikeuchi, K.: Polarization-based transparent surface modeling from two views. In: ICCV, p. 1381 (2003)
22. Atkinson, G.A., Hancock, E.R.: Two-dimensional brdf estimation from polarisation. Comput. Vis. Image Underst. 111, 126–141 (2008)
23. Miyazaki, D., Ikeuchi, K.: Shape estimation of transparent objects by using inverse polarization ray tracing. PAMI 29, 2018–2030 (2007)
24. Collett, E.: Field Guide to Polarization, SPIE Field Guides, vol. FG05. SPIE (2005)
25. Bohren, C., Huffman, D.R.: Absorption and Scattering of Light by Small Particles. Wiley Science Paperback Series (1998)
26. Tuchin, V.V.: Light scattering study of tissues. Physics-Uspekhi 40, 495 (1997)

Base Materials for Photometric Stereo

David Tingdahl[1], Christoph Godau[2], and Luc Van Gool[1]

[1] Katholieke Universiteit Leuven, ESAT/IBBT/VISICS, Belgium
[2] Technische Universität Darmstadt, IDD, Germany

Abstract. Image-based capture of material appearance has been extensively studied, but the quality of the results and generality of the applied methods leave a lot of room for improvement. Most existing methods rely on parametric models of reflectance and require complex hardware systems or accurate geometric models that are not always available or practical. Rather than independently estimating reflectance properties for each surface point, it is common to express the reflectance as a combination of base materials inherent to each particular object or scene.

We propose a method for efficient and automatic extraction of base materials in a photometric stereo system. After jointly estimating per-pixel reflectances and refined surface normals using these materials, we can render photo-realistic images of complex objects under novel lighting conditions in real time.

1 Introduction

After decades of development, the acquisition of object geometry using specialized scanners and image-based methods is now a relatively mature technology. The accurate capture of surface appearance and reflectance on the other hand, remains a major challenge for all but the simplest materials. Image-based capture of material appearance has been extensively studied [1], but the quality of the results and generality of the applied methods leave a lot of room for improvement. In particular, most existing methods rely on parametric models of reflectance and require complex hardware systems or accurate geometric models that are not always available.

Leaving aside the complex effects of subsurface scattering, transparency and inter-reflections, the appearance of a homogeneous material can be accurately described by its bidirectional reflectance distribution function (BRDF). This four-dimensional function defines the percentage of light reflected for every possible combination of incoming and outgoing light directions.

The acquisition of an independent BRDF for each surface location is not practical. A high enough sample density would require thousands of images for a single object. Rather than estimating a full BRDF for each surface point, we can express the reflectance as a combination of BRDFs from base materials inherent to each particular object. The variation of materials and surface geometry across the object allows for a reasonably dense sampling of these base materials from a relatively small number of images. This concept is illustrated in Fig. 1, where a strawberry is reconstructed using the method presented in this paper.

A. Fusiello et al. (Eds.): ECCV 2012 Ws/Demos, Part II, LNCS 7584, pp. 350–359, 2012.

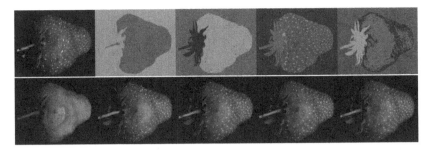

Fig. 1. Material clusters and reconstructed images with the number of base materials varying from 1 (left) to 5 (right). The ground truth image is in the top-left.

After reviewing related works in Section 2, we propose a method for efficient and automatic extraction of base materials from images in Section 3, which are then used to enhance results obtained from a traditional photometric stereo system in Section 4. We show that our conceptually simple, data-driven reflectance descriptor outperforms model-based approaches for material segmentation in terms of robustness to errors in the estimated geometry (Section 5.2). Using the captured reflectance and geometry information, we can produce photo-realistic renderings under arbitrary lighting conditions in real time (Section 5.3).

2   Background and Related Works

Photometric stereo infers information about a surface from images taken under varying light directions. The traditional approach [2] assumes Lambertian reflectance because of its simplicity and linearity. Surfaces violating this assumption can still be reconstructed by employing robustification to detect and discard outliers such as shadows and specular highlights [3,4]. More recent photometric stereo algorithms attempt to go beyond the Lambertian model by estimating a full bidirectional reflectance distribution function (BRDF) [5,6].

A BRDF describes the reflectance characteristics of a surface for varying directions of incoming (v_{in}) and outgoing (v_{out}) light and can capture complex phenomena including off-specular highlights and iridescence (goniochromatism).

BRDFs are commonly parametrized in spherical coordinates over the four-dimensional domain ($\theta_{in}, \phi_{in}, \theta_{out}, \phi_{out}$), where the surface normal is at the north pole ($\theta_{normal} = 0$) and the surface tangent (at $\phi = 0$) defines the orientation of an anisotropic surface.

We use the reparameterization proposed by Rusinkiewicz [7] based on half and difference angles: ($\theta_h, \phi_h, \theta_d, \phi_d$). The halfway vector ($\theta_h, \phi_h$) is the vector bisecting v_{in} and v_{out}. The difference angles (θ_d, ϕ_d) are the spherical coordinates of v_{in} after rotating the halfway vector to the north pole.

Exploiting the symmetries and isotropy in commonly encountered materials Romeiro et al. [8,9] propose discarding the azimuthal components. This results in a bivariate BRDF representation using only (θ_h, θ_d), as illustrated in Fig. 2.

Fig. 2. Left: The bivariate BRDF model is parameterized by θ_h and θ_d with the normal pointing towards the north pole. Right: Base materials extracted from a strawberry, represented with the bivariate model.

They show that this simplification only results in a small decrease in rendered image quality for a wide range of materials.

Sophisticated hardware systems like the multi-camera, multi-projector system constructed by Weinmann et al. [10] achieve impressive results, but they are expensive, and their size makes them unusable for on-site acquisition. Fortunately, most real-world objects are composed of a limited number of base materials. The variation of normals and materials across the surface makes it possible to obtain a large number of samples for each base material from a relatively small number of images. As shown by Lensch et al. [11], combinations of these materials can describe the reflectance at each surface point. Additional constraints can impose spatial smoothness or limit the number of base materials for each combination [5,12,6,13].

In order to obtain reflectance data for these base materials, some methods make use of reference objects [5] or custom-made material charts [14] that have to be included in the scene, but this is not always possible or practical. Goldman et al. [6] cluster the albedos obtained from photometric stereo to obtain an initial set of base materials, but this is not directly applicable for specular surfaces [15], as their albedo is poorly defined. Other approaches [6,11,15] try to fit analytic reflectance models such as Ward's and Lafortune or hemispherical harmonics basis functions to each surface element and apply a clustering algorithm to their parameters. These models can be highly non-linear, and the resulting complexity and sensitivity to noise can be problematic, especially when geometry and lighting are not precisely known. Alldrin et al. [13] make use of the bivariate BRDF representation by globally optimizing for base materials, weights and normals. By employing a non-parametric reflectance descriptor for robust material clustering, we extend on their work by separating the tasks of material classification and optimization into two. This allows us to reconstruct high-resolution images of complex samples within an hour on a desktop PC.

3   Extracting Base Materials

The input to our algorithm is a set of M photometrically calibrated images $\mathcal{I}_1, ...\mathcal{I}_M$ acquired with a static camera and varying but known lighting directions. We assume an orthographic projection model and point-like light sources at infinity. These assumptions hold for objects which are small in comparison to the distance to both the light source and the camera. We also assume that the target surface can be described with the bivariate BRDF model described in Section 2.

We find initial surface normals $\mathcal{N} = \{n_1, n_2, ..., n_N\}$ using Lambertian photometric stereo. Our implementation is robust to non-Lambertian characteristics and produces a usable, albeit noisy normal map even for specular and other intricate surface effects. In theory, the method can recover the normal if a surface point exhibits Lambertian characteristics for at least three of the images, which is the case for most materials [5].

Before we can extract full BRDFs for the base materials, we need to cluster the surface points into groups of similar reflectance. This requires a compact and robust representation of the local reflectance characteristics at each point, as well as a suitable distance measure.

3.1 Describing Local Reflectance

For every pixel, we have a series of RGB measurements $\mathcal{P} = \{p_1, ..., p_M\}$, one for each of the M light directions. The incoming light intensity varies with geometry and is compensated for by dividing each measurement with $\cos(\alpha)$, where α is the angle between incoming light and surface normal.

We now sample individual bivariate BRDF descriptors for each surface element (pixel) from the set of RGB values in $\mathcal{P}$. First, the M light directions and the camera direction (v_{in} resp. v_{out} in Fig. 2) are rotated such that the normal is pointing towards the north pole. This gives us a pair of angular coordinates (θ_h, θ_d) for each measurement in $\mathcal{P}$. We sample $\mathcal{P}$ on a grid of $u \times v$ bins over the angular space by computing the average measurement for each bin. This is done separately for each color channel. Finally, we transform each sampled bin into the $L^*a^*b^*$ color space to render distance measurements more perceptually meaningful. One material descriptor d thus consists of a vector of $3 \times u \times v$ elements. The whole BRDF domain is rarely sampled at any one pixel and d is thus usually a sparse vector.

3.2 Clustering into Base Materials

We use k-means to cluster the descriptors into k clusters $\{c_1, c_2, ..., c_k\}$ of similar reflectance. For the moment, assume that k is known. Starting from a random labeling, we compute each cluster center as the mean of all its descriptors, discarding any missing values. For element j in cluster c, we have:

$$c_j = \frac{1}{\sum_{d \in c} g(d_j)} \sum_{d \in c} g(d_j) d_j, \quad j = [1, ..., 3uv]. \tag{1}$$

where $g(d_j)$ is an indicator function, returning 1 if element j exists in descriptor d and 0 otherwise. The dissimilarity between descriptor d and cluster c is computed as the mean squared euclidean distance between their overlapping elements:

$$dist(d, c) = \frac{1}{\sum_j [g(d_j)g(c_j)]} \sum_{j=1}^{3uv} g(d_j)g(c_j)(d_j - c_j)^2. \tag{2}$$

As d is sparse, Equation 2 is not suitable for directly computing the dissimilarity between two descriptors. However, since k-means only requires the distance between d and the denser c, this measure is applicable as long as the angular span of c is large enough to include d. To reduce the sparseness of d, we use a relatively small dimensionality of the sample grid ($u = v = 3$ in all our experiments). As our results show, this low angular resolution still allows for an efficient clustering of the reflectance space.

Since the output of k-means depends on the initial labeling, we run the clustering 25 times and select the labeling with the lowest error, measured as the accumulated distance between the descriptors and their corresponding cluster centers:

$$E = \sum_d dist(d, c_d). \tag{3}$$

Note that the clusters themselves are not used as base material BRDFs due to their low angular resolution. Instead, we use the resulting labeling to sample high-resolution BRDFs, as explained in Section 4.1.

3.3   How Many Base Materials?

The number of base materials obviously varies depending on the object. Fig. 1 shows the reconstruction of a strawberry for various number of base materials, rendered using the output from our photometric stereo pipeline (as described in Section 4). Intuitively, this scene seems to consist of four materials: background cloth, red body, green leaf and yellow seed capsules. However, the visual quality for three and even two base materials is surprisingly realistic, while adding a fifth material does not appear to significantly improve the result. To determine the number of base materials, we use down-sampled (300×300 pixels) versions of the original images. Starting with a single material ($k = 1$), we increase k until convergence, i.e. until $E_{k+1}/E_k > 0.9$ using the error measure from Equation 3. This algorithm detects five base materials for the strawberry.

4   Photometric Stereo

4.1   BRDF Sampling

The low resolution BRDF descriptors are efficient for classification, but do not provide enough angular resolution for realistic rendering. To this end, we sample a high resolution BRDF from each detected cluster. Again, we use the bivariate representation over (θ_h, θ_d), but this time with a larger grid size (50×50 in our experiments). This results in a set of base material BRDFs: $\mathbf{B} = \{B_1, B_2, ..., B_k\}$. We interpolate empty bins and smooth the BRDF with a Gaussian kernel. Examples of extracted base materials can be seen in Fig. 2.

4.2 Computing Weight Map and Normals

We express each surface point as a linear combination of the base materials by computing a weight vector $w = [w_1, w_2, ..., w_k]^T$ for each pixel. The RGB values for base material j are given as a function $\mathbf{b}_j(n, l)$ of surface normal n (depending on the pixel) and light direction l (depending on the image). We can then render a pixel as a function of surface normal, light direction and material weights:

$$\hat{p}(n, l, w) = \sum_{j=1}^{k} \mathbf{b}_j(n, l) w_j \cos(\alpha). \qquad (4)$$

For each pixel, we then define a cost function C based on the ΔE_{ab}^* color difference between predicted ($\hat{p}$) and measured (p) values in each of the M images:

$$C(n, w) = \sum_{m=1}^{M} \Delta E_{ab}^*(\hat{p}(n, w, l_m), p) \qquad (5)$$

where l_m is the (known) light direction in image m.

For each pixel, Equation 5 is minimized with respect to n and w using Levenberg-Marquard. The normals are initialized from the Lambertian reconstruction and the weights are initialized according to the k-means labeling: unity for the labeled material and zero for all others. We obtain the surface normals and material weight vectors that result in the lowest color difference across all images. Since the calculations are independent for each pixel, the computations are simple to parallelize.

5 Results

5.1 Acquisition System

We captured all images using a custom-built dome-shaped acquisition device. The device consists of 260 LEDs placed on a hemisphere, and a downward-looking camera at the top. Note that our method is not tied specifically to this device, for example reflective spheres could be used to obtain the light directions. For each sequence, we recorded 260 images. All images were used for the Lambertian initialization, while it proved sufficient to only use every third image for the remainder of the algorithm (87 images), significantly reducing computation time.

5.2 Robustness to Noise

In order to test the robustness of our algorithm, we use a simple object with only two materials: a matte piece of paper with a grid-like pattern of transparent glue shown in Fig. 3. The perceived color of the painted grid is very close to the original paper surface, but with severe specular highlights. Material clustering that takes into account the full BRDF should be able to separate these materials.

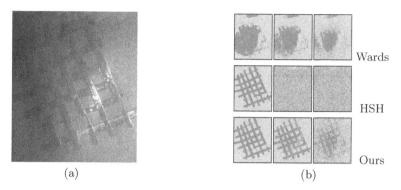

(a)   (b)

Fig. 3. Noise robustness of material clustering with three different reflectance models. (a) One of the input images, shown with increased contrast. (b) Clustering results with increasing normal noise, from left to right: no added noise, $\sigma = 0.05$ and $\sigma = 0.1$. Ward's model (top) does not result in a usable clustering, while HSH (middle) fails for even small amounts of noise. Our parameter-free description (bottom) exhibits graceful degradation for increasing levels of noise.

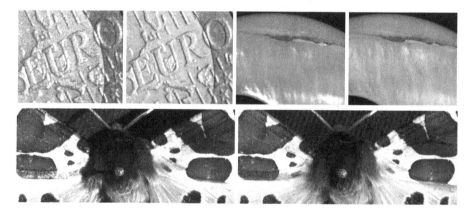

Fig. 4. Views of reconstruction results. The original image (left) was removed from the input set, its light direction was then used in the reconstructions (right).

We compare our non-parametric model to two others that have previously been used for material classification: Ward's anisotropic model [16], and hemispherical harmonics (HSH) [17,15]. For both of these models, we independently fit a BRDF to each color channel. We use the three-parameter version of Ward's model as in [16], computed using Levenberg-Marquard with analytic Jacobian. The HSH model is of second degree, resulting in 9 coefficients per color channel, computed using linear least squares.

Fig. 3 shows the resulting labeling from k-means with the number of materials fixed to $k = 2$. HSH and our model perform similarly without added noise, while Ward's model apparently not well suited for this clustering approach. When adding Gaussian noise to the normals, our method shows a graceful degradation

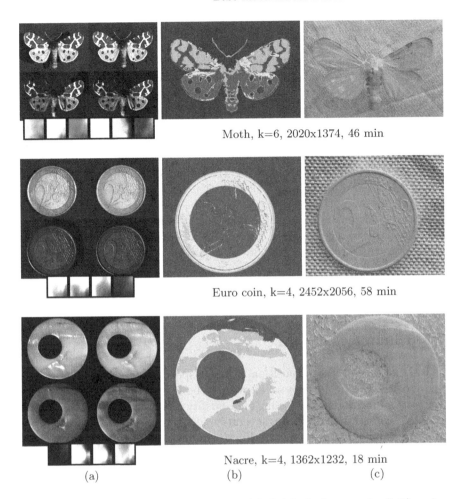

Moth, k=6, 2020x1374, 46 min

Euro coin, k=4, 2452x2056, 58 min

Nacre, k=4, 1362x1232, 18 min

(a)   (b)   (c)

Fig. 5. Photometric stereo results showing: (a) Original photographs (left) and rendered results (right) for two novel light directions, along with the set of extracted base materials. (b) Final material labels. (c) Surface normals. The rendered results are all visually convincing. The piece of nacre is translucent and highly specular, showing the robustness of the proposed method to violations of the underlying reflectance model.

with increasing levels of noise, while HSH performance decreases dramatically even for low levels of noise. This illustrates the difficulty of fitting non-linear, analytic BRDF models to noisy measurements.

5.3   Material Clustering and Reconstruction Results

Using our enhanced photometric stereo system, we acquire and reconstruct three objects: A Euro coin, a Garden Tiger moth, and a small ornamental piece of nacre (mother of pearl). All experiments were executed and timed on a desktop PC with a Quad Core Intel i7 CPU. Fig. 5 shows the rendered output, material segmentation, surface normals and computation time for each object. The simplicity of the bivariate BRDF model allows for fast rendering: our single-core CPU based renderer easily achieves real-time performance for all our examples. The rendered images are obtained for a novel light direction that was removed from the input set of images. Our model convincingly reproduces the iridescence of the moth wings (Fig. 5a, top row) where the hue changes from yellow to red when the incoming light angle increases. This behavior can also be seen in the captured base materials. In the images of the Euro coin, mutual interference of reflected wavefronts create a noisy speckle pattern in the image, visible in in the close-up of Fig. 4, while the rendered image is virtually noise-free. The correct locations of shadows show that the estimated geometry is true to the original, even for small details such as the individual countries. Nacre is a particularly challenging material due to its combination of translucency and strong specularities. Nevertheless, the rendered output is visually acceptable, which demonstrates the robustness of our algorithm to violations of the bivariate BRDF model. Overall, the reconstructions are of high quality, except for highly specular details which are difficult to capture with low dynamic range input images.

6   Concluding Remarks

We have shown that the acquisition of scene-specific base materials using a non-parametric BRDF descriptor can reliably be used to enhance a traditional photometric stereo system, providing high-quality rendered results, material segmentations and normal maps for several challenging objects. The results are surprisingly robust to noise and violations of the underlying assumptions about reflectance that cause difficulties for approaches based on non-linear analytic reflectance models.

A dedicated acquisition device such as our dome allows for rapid capture of 260 images. However, such a large number is likely to be redundant; it is well worth investigating how to adaptively reduce the number while maintaining high photometric and geometric fidelity. Note also that our fixed-camera setup limits the domain of the sampled BRDFs which may prohibit novel-viewpoint rendering.

Going forward, there are numerous possible generalizations: multi-view environments, unknown lighting, multi-spectral and HDR imaging, uncalibrated cameras, and even more general reflectance models including anisotropic materials. New developments in BRDF acquisition and representation may provide possibilities beyond those of existing approaches.

Acknowledgments. We gratefully acknowledge support from the EC 7th Framework Program under grant agreement n. 231809 (IP project 3D-COFORM) and the KULeuven Research Council grant Center for Archaeological Studies.

References

1. Weyrich, T., Lawrence, J., Lensch, H., Rusinkiewicz, S., Zickler, T.: Principles of Appearance Acquisition and Representation. Foundations and Trends in Computer Graphics and Vision 4(2), 75–191 (2007)
2. Woodham, R.J.: A Photometric Method for Determining Surface Orientation from Multiple Images. Optical Engineering 19(1), 139–144 (1980)
3. Chandraker, M., Agarwal, S., Kriegman, D.: ShadowCuts: Photometric Stereo with Shadows. In: CVPR, pp. 1–8 (2007)
4. Verbiest, F., Van Gool, L.: Photometric stereo with coherent outlier handling and confidence estimation. In: CVPR, pp. 1–8 (2008)
5. Hertzmann, A., Seitz, S.M.: Example-based photometric stereo: shape reconstruction with general, varying BRDFs. PAMI 27(8), 1254–1264 (2005)
6. Goldman, D.B., Curless, B., Hertzmann, A., Seitz, S.M.: Shape and Spatially-Varying BRDFs from Photometric Stereo. PAMI 32(6), 1060–1071 (2010)
7. Rusinkiewicz, S.: A new change of variables for efficient BRDF representation. In: Rendering Techniques, pp. 11–22 (1998)
8. Romeiro, F., Vasilyev, Y., Zickler, T.: Passive Reflectometry. In: Forsyth, D., Torr, P., Zisserman, A. (eds.) ECCV 2008, Part IV. LNCS, vol. 5305, pp. 859–872. Springer, Heidelberg (2008)
9. Romeiro, F., Zickler, T.: Blind Reflectometry. In: Daniilidis, K., Maragos, P., Paragios, N. (eds.) ECCV 2010, Part I. LNCS, vol. 6311, pp. 45–58. Springer, Heidelberg (2010)
10. Weinmann, M., Schwartz, C.: A multi-camera, multi-projector super-resolution framework for structured light. In: 3DIMPVT, pp. 397–404 (2011)
11. Lensch, H.P.A., Goesele, M., Kautz, J., Heidrich, W., Seidel, H.-P.: Image-based reconstruction of spatially varying materials. In: Eurographics Workshop on Rendering Techniques, pp. 103–114 (2001)
12. Haber, T., Fuchs, C., Bekaer, P., Seidel, H., Goesele, M., Lensch, H.: Relighting objects from image collections. In: CVPR, pp. 627–634 (2009)
13. Alldrin, N., Zickler, T.: Photometric stereo with non-parametric and spatially-varying reflectance. In: CVPR (2008)
14. Ren, P., Wang, J., Snyder, J., Tong, X., Guo, B.: Pocket reflectometry. ACM Transactions on Graphics 30(4), 45:1–45:10 (2011)
15. Wang, O., Gunawardane, P., Scher, S., Davis, J.: Material classification using BRDF slices. In: CVPR, pp. 2805–2811 (2009)
16. Chung, H.: Efficient photometric stereo on glossy surfaces with wide specular lobes. In: CVPR (2008)
17. Gautron, P., Krivanek, J., Pattanaik, S.: A novel hemispherical basis for accurate and efficient rendering. In: Eurographics Symposium on Rendering (2004)

Robust Luminance and Chromaticity for Matte Regression in Polynomial Texture Mapping

Mingjing Zhang and Mark S. Drew

School of Computing Science,
Simon Fraser University
{mza44,mark}@cs.sfu.ca

Abstract. Polynomial Texture Mapping (PTM) is a technique employed in a variety of settings, from museums to in-the-field image capture to multi-illuminant microscopy. It consists of illuminating the surface in question with lights from a collection of light directions, each light in turn. To date, the most accurate interpolation employed in PTM consists of two stages: a matte regression stage followed by a further specularity/shadow interpolation. For the first stage, recovering an underlying matte model so as to acquire surface albedo, normals and chromaticity, PTM employs polynomial regression at each pixel, mapping light-direction to luminance. A more accurate model excludes outlier values deriving from specularities and shadows by employing a robust regression from 6-D polynomials to 1-D luminance. Robust methods are guaranteed to automatically find the best representation of the underlying matte content. Here, we retain the idea of using robust methods but instead investigate using a much simpler robust 1-D mode-finder, acting on luminance and on chromaticity components. We then go on to increase accuracy by carrying out 3-D to 1-D regression: this strikes a balance between the best method and the fastest method, with greatly diminished complexity and another large speedup. We show that little accuracy is lost using this much simpler method, and demonstrate the effectiveness of the new method on several image datasets.

1 Introduction

Polynomial Texture Maps (PTM) [1] use a single fixed digital camera at constant exposure, with a set of n images captured using lighting from different directions. A typical rig would consist of a hemisphere of xenon flash lamps imaging an object, where directions to each light is known. The basic idea in PTM is to improve on a simple Lambertian model for matte content, whereby the three components of the light direction are mapped to luminance, by extending the model to include a low-order polynomial of lighting-direction components. The strength of PTM, in comparison to a simple Lambertian Photometric Stereo (PST) [2] is that, in its original Least Squares (LS) formulation at least, PTM can better model real radiance and to some extent grasp intricate dependencies due to self-shadowing and interreflections. Usually, some 40 to 80 images are

A. Fusiello et al. (Eds.): ECCV 2012 Ws/Demos, Part II, LNCS 7584, pp. 360–369, 2012.

captured. The better capture of details is the driving force behind the interest in this technique evinced by many museum professionals, with the original LS-based PTM method already in use at major museums in the U.S. including the Smithsonian, the Museum of Modern Art, and the Fine Arts Museums of San Francisco, and is planned for the Metropolitan and the Louvre [3].

PTM generates a matte model for the surface, where luminance (or RGB) is modelled at each pixel via a polynomial regression from light-direction components to luminance. Say, e.g., there are $n = 50$ images, with n known normalized light-direction 3-vectors a . Then in the original embodiment, a 6-term polynomial model is fitted at each pixel separately, regressing onto that pixel's n luminance values using LS regression. The main objectives of PTM are recovery of surface properties – surface normal, colour, and albedo – plus the ability to *re-light* pixels using the regression parameters obtained. For re-lighting, the idea is simply that if the regression from in-sample light-directions a to luminance values L is known then substituting a new a will generate a new L, thus yielding a simple interpolation scheme for new out-of-sample directions.

In [4], we extend PTM in two ways: (1) First, the LS regression for the underlying matte model is replaced by a robust regression, the Least Median of Squares (LMS) method [5]. This means that only a majority of the n pixel values obtained at each pixel need be actually matte, with specularities and shadows automatically identified as outliers. With knowledge of correctly matte pixels in hand, surface normals, albedos, and pixel chromaticity are more accurately recovered; (2) Secondly, [4] furthers adds an additional interpolation level by modelling the part of in-sample pixel values that is not completely explained by the matte PTM model via a Radial Basis Function (RBF) interpolation. The RBF model takes care of features such as specularities and shadows that change abruptly with lighting direction. The interpolation is still local to each pixel, and thus does not attempt to bridge non-specular locales as in Reflectance Sharing, for example [6,7]. In Reflectance Sharing a *known* surface geometry is assumed, as opposed to the present paper. Here, we rely on the idea that there is at least a small contribution to specularity at any pixel, e.g. the sheen on skin or paint-work, so that we need not share across neighbouring pixels and can employ the RBF approach from [4].

The main contribution of this paper is to investigate replacing the robust regression from polynomials in a onto L by two far simpler but still robust methods: first we apply a robust mode-finder to either the components of chromaticity – the pixel colour independent of brightness – or the luminance. The result is a fast identification of outliers, as opposed to a very slow such identification in 6-D to 1-D robust regression. If we are willing to tolerate more time complexity, but with more accuracy, then we can use a 3-D to 1-D robust regression. This reduces PTM to PST but with an essential difference: we use a fully robust method. We found that this simplification introduced little reduction in accuracy compared to a full-polynomial robust version but with a large speedup. Exact solutions for LMS estimation require $O(n^d \log n)$ time. Here we have $n \approx 50$ and either $d = 6$ or $d = 3$ or, in the case of mode-finding, $d = 1$;

the lower bound on algorithmic implementations of LMS have complexity $O(n^d)$ (cf. [5], p. 206), meaning a reduction of 5 (for $d = 3$) and then a further 3 (for $d = 1$) orders of magnitude.

With robust outlier identification in hand, we can then go on to apply a full 6-D to 1-D regression as usual in PTM, but using only (all) the light direction information for inlier directions, resulting in a much simpler technique overall.

For the fastest, robust-mode based method the insight here is that, inside specular or shadow areas, the pixel colour or brightness changes abruptly from some approximate form of a matte colour to instead a chromaticity/luminance associated with shadows or specularities, which will be near the unsaturated region of colour space.

By examining pixel reconstruction error compared to the best, robust 6-D method, we found in fact that for a mode-based method, purely using luminance without chrominance was best. Using mode-finding for 1-D data, in essence we are inverting the process of the robust version of PTM: in the method [4], the robust regression randomly suggests sets of 6 lighting directions and solves for regression coefficients. The optimum set is that regression delivering the minimum robust error, with residuals identified as too large (according to another robust measure) flagged as outliers. Here, in contrast, we do not first seek potential regression parameters but, instead, simply flag outliers as light-directions giving chromaticities/luminances not near the mode value for that pixel. Then we go on to find a 6-D to 1-D regression as usual, but using a simple trimmed LS method and all the inlier directions at once. The 3-D to 1-D linear robust regression stands between the two extremes of best- and simplest-regression.

2   Matte Modelling Using PTM

2.1   Luminance

PTM models smooth dependence of images on lighting direction via polynomial regression. Here we briefly recapitulate PTM as amended by [4]. Suppose n images of a scene are taken with a fixed-position camera and lighting from $i = 1..n$ different lighting directions $a^i = (u^i, v^i, w^i)^T$. Let each RGB image acquired be denoted ρ^i, and we also make use of luminance images, $L^i = \sum_{k=1}^{3} \rho_k^i$. Colour is re-inserted later, below.

Robust 6-D Regression. With [4] we use a 6-D vector p for each light direction 3-vector a as follows:

$$p(a) = (u, v, w, u^2, uv, 1), \quad \text{where } w = \sqrt{1 - u^2 - v^2} \tag{1}$$

Then at each pixel (x, y) separately, we can seek a polynomial regression 6-vector of coefficients $c(x, y)$ in a simple model

$$\begin{bmatrix} p(a^1) \\ p(a^2) \\ ... \\ p(a^n) \end{bmatrix} c(x, y) = \begin{bmatrix} L^1(x, y) \\ L^2(x, y) \\ ... \\ L^n(x, y) \end{bmatrix} \tag{2}$$

E.g., if $n = 50$ then we could write this as

$$\underset{50 \times 6}{\boldsymbol{P}} \quad \underset{6 \times 1}{\boldsymbol{c}} (x, y) = \underset{50 \times 1}{\boldsymbol{L}} (x, y) \tag{3}$$

The original PTM [1] solves a similar equation, using LS; the recent version [4] solves eq. (3) using a robust LMS regression [5] from matrix $\boldsymbol{P}$ to vector $\boldsymbol{L}$.

Robust Modes. In a mode-finder based approach, we adopt (3), but solve for $\boldsymbol{c}$ using only inlier directions $\boldsymbol{a}$, with the decision of whether a direction is an inlier based not on the relation of luminance to light direction as in PTM but instead on whether chrominance or luminance is in the cluster around the mode colour over n lights, for this pixel, or is instead excluded from that cluster. This is a far simpler problem. For reference, we call this method Method:MODE.

The simple method outlined in [8] is similar in a sense. That method simply drops the top 10-percentile of luminance values associated with lights (at the current pixel) and also drops the bottom 50% of luminances. Then, coefficient values sought are found using a triangular function to weight lighting directions in the resulting range. Along with [4] we refer to this simple method as Method:QUANTILE, and denote the original PTM method as Method:LS. The robust method [4] based on 6-D LMS is denoted Method:LMS. The difference from [8] in this paper is that, in keeping with the most accurate method, Method:LMS, here we seek a *robust* way to identify outliers, rather than simply using a heuristic. That is, we let the data itself dictate what are in- and outliers.

Robust Linear-PTM. Instead of eq. (3) we could use only the *linear* part of $\boldsymbol{p}$, i.e., the lighting directions $\boldsymbol{a}$ themselves; however here we apply a *robust* regression, and solve for new, 3-D coefficients $\boldsymbol{c}$ in

$$\boldsymbol{A} \; \boldsymbol{c} (x, y) \; = \; \boldsymbol{L} (x, y) \tag{4}$$

where the entire collection of light directions $\boldsymbol{a}$ is given by the $n \times 3$ matrix $\boldsymbol{A}$. This 3-D approach turns out to be remarkably successful and accurate, notwithstanding a large reduction in complexity compared to 6-D. Let us call this Method:LINEAR.

Re-lighting. For the above methods, we obtain regression coefficients $\boldsymbol{c}$ directly from robust LMS, from Method:LMS or Method:LINEAR. For Method:MODE, we use a trimmed version of (3), wherein we drop outliers identified by the mode-finder, to obtain 6-D $\boldsymbol{c}$. For all methods, matte interpolation proceeds by generating a new luminance value L for new light direction $\boldsymbol{a}'$ via interpolation $L(x, y) = \max[\boldsymbol{p}(\boldsymbol{a}') \boldsymbol{c}(x, y), 0]$ or the dimension-3 version for Method:LINEAR, with negative values set to zero. Colour is re-introduced by multiplying by the chromaticity times the albedo as follows.

2.2   Colour, Normals, Albedo

The luminance L consists of the sum of colour components: $L = R + G + B$. Luminance is given by the shading s (e.g., this could be Lambertian shading, meaning surface normal dotted into light direction), times albedo α: i.e., $L = s\alpha$. The chromaticity χ is *defined* as RGB colour ρ independent of intensity:

$$\rho = L\chi, \quad L = s\alpha, \quad \chi \equiv \{R, G, B\}/(R + G + B) \tag{5}$$

Suppose our robust regression below delivers binary weights ω, with $\omega = 0$ for outliers. With [4], we recover a robust estimate of chromaticity χ as the median of inlier values, for $k = 1..3$:

$$\chi_k = \underset{i \in (\omega \equiv 1)}{\mathrm{median}} \left(\rho_k^i / L^i \right) \tag{6}$$

And an estimate of surface normal n is given by a trimmed PST: with the collection of directions a stored in the $n \times 3$ matrix A, suppose ω^0 is an index variable giving the inlier subset of light directions: $\omega^0 - (\omega \equiv 1)$. Using just the inlier subset, a trimmed version of PST gives an estimate of normalized surface normal $\widehat{n}$ and albedo α via

$$\tilde{n} = \left(A \left(\omega^0 \right) \right)^+ L \left(\omega^0 \right); \quad \alpha = \|\tilde{n}\|, \quad \widehat{n} = \tilde{n}/\alpha \tag{7}$$

where A^+ is the Moore-Penrose pseudoinverse. Method:QUANTILE instead uses matrices weighted by the triangular functions.

With chromaticity χ in hand, eq. (5) gives RGB pixel values ρ for the interpolated luminance L. And (7) above also gives us the properties albedo α and surface normal $\widehat{n}$ intrinsic to the surface.

3   Robust Chromaticity/Luminance Modes

Firstly, let us start by using Method:LMS, regressing from 6-D $p(a)$ to luminance L [4]. That is, we are solving eq. (3) for c, by robustly finding the best slope. Fig. 1(a) displays one image from a dataset of images taken from $n = 50$ angles.[1] Here, a yellow x shows a single pixel, one that takes on matte, shadowed, and specular values depending on the lighting direction. Fig. 1(b) shows luminance values L at this pixel, in sorted-L order, for $n = 50$. LMS regression automatically identifies outliers, here shadows and specularities, that do not adhere closely enough to a matte model (3). However the objective of LMS is mainly to trim outlier values so as to obtain the best possible values of slopes $c(x, y)$. LMS is guaranteed to perform optimally provided at least $\lfloor n/2 \rfloor + 1$ values are indeed inliers. Here we also flag as outliers any unphysical negative values $\hat{L}$.

Thus in our situation we are using LMS to perform a regression from 6-D values P onto 1-D luminance values L. The band shown in Fig. 1(a) is automatically chosen by LMS such that within the band, residuals $\hat{L} - L$ that are too large in absolute value are flagged as outliers. The figure shows measured luminance values as black dots, regression estimates $\hat{L}$ as blue circles, and outliers with a red box.

---

[1] Data courteously supplied by Tom Malzbender, HP.

The complexity of LMS is high, but has strong mathematical guarantees. The advantage of using a robust mechanism for finding slopes is that we will then also find demonstrably best estimates of surface normals and albedo [4]. How LMS proceeds is repeatedly sub-sampling to get best slope parameters c, establishing an initial set of inliers, and then re-calculating the inlier band using only the previous set of survivors.

Alternatives could be: ignoring the problem of outliers (e.g., [1]); or perhaps applying a heuristic, as in [8], and making a simple guess for potential outliers.

3.1   Luminance Modes

In this paper we wish to strike a balance between a simple but fast method, on the one hand, and a best-accuracy but high-complexity regression on the other. Since regression (3) is aimed at luminance, let us consider what we can learn from luminance alone, without regard for an underlying matte model. Since luminance is scalar, what we require in this simpler approach is a *robust* method of flagging luminance values that are potential shadows or specular highlights. Therefore we make use of the much simpler robust LMS regression denoted "location finding" [5], meaning determining the location of the *mode* of scalar values. Fig. 1(c) again shows sorted-luminance values, but now the inlier band and outlier determination is determined simply using the luminance values themselves, without regard to the 6-D to 1-D matte model. Outliers are initially determined simply by whether L values are sufficiently close to the mode value, shown as a horizontal line. The inlier band is indicated by another two horizontal lines bracketing this mode value.

Again, negative approximations $\hat{L}$ are deemed outliers. In order to obtain luminance approximations we go back to the full regression model (3) but restrict the calculation of slopes c to a trimmed LS calculation as follows:

$$c = (P(\omega))^+ L(\omega), \qquad \hat{L} = P c \qquad (8)$$

where now ω are binary weights from the much simpler, 1-D LMS location finder.

3.2   Chromaticity Modes

Another approach might be to use the observation that in fact in a shadow or specularity, the colour of the pixel changes substantially. Consider again the chromaticity χ in eq. (5). Suppose we carry out our 1-D LMS mode-finder idea simply on the scalar green-chromaticity value χ_2. Plotting red-green 2-D chromaticity values in Fig. 1(d), we show outlier values circled in red. Indeed, this idea does determine outlier chromaticities.

So in this case we would carry out the indicated 1-D regression, followed by generation of inlier slopes and approximations of matte luminance $\hat{L}$ just as in (8) above, but now for inliers determined by chromaticity, not luminance. And, of course, we can also combine Luminance and Chromaticity to use both kinds of mode-finder to help identify outliers.

We found that in order of accuracy for such 1-D estimation approaches, for generating $\hat{L}$ compared to the best method, Method:LMS, we have an order Lum > (Green & Red & Lum) > Green > (Green & Red) > Method:QUANTILE where ">" means better accuracy. I.e., using Luminance alone is always best, (R & G) seems to be slightly worse than Green, and (G & R & Lum) is between Green and Lum; Method:QUANTILE is worst.

Therefore, Method:MODE comes down to using the considerably faster 1-D robust mode-finder as a new mechanism for determining matte image output as per eq. (8). To encompass both matte plus specular/shadow information, we then go on to include RBF networks for modelling this non-smooth information, as in [4].

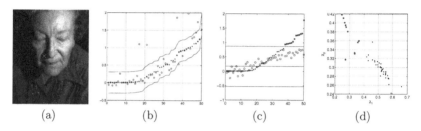

(a)   (b)   (c)   (d)

Fig. 1. (a): One original image, with light with spherical angles $\{\theta, \phi\}= \{39.8°, -0.4°\}$. (b): 6-D to 1-D LMS regression: black dots are measured data, blue circles are regression estimates $\hat{L}$, and outliers are indicated with a red box. (c): Using mode of Luminance: mode value is center horizontal line, bracketed by horizontal inlier band; inliers include negative-$\hat{L}$ lights. (d): Red vs. Green chromaticity, with outliers for Green mode in red.

4   Specularities and Shadows

Following [4] we adopt an RBF network approach for the remaining luminance not explained by the matte model (3). The "excursion" η is defined as the set of $(N \times 3 \times n)$ non-matte colour values not explained by the $\boldsymbol{R}_{matte}$ given by the basic PTM matte equation (3), now extended to functions of the colour channel as well: the approximated colour matte image is given by

$$\boldsymbol{R}_{matte} = \boldsymbol{P} \, \boldsymbol{C} \, \chi \, , \quad \text{or} \quad \boldsymbol{R}_{matte} = \boldsymbol{A} \, \boldsymbol{C} \, \chi \text{ in Method:LINEAR} \qquad (9)$$

where $\boldsymbol{C}$ is the collection of all luminance-regression slopes. Including colour, all RBF quantities become functions of the colour channel as well.

Then an $(N \times 3 \times n)$ set of non-matte excursion colour values η is defined for our input set of colour images, via $\eta = \boldsymbol{R} - \boldsymbol{R}_{matte}$ where $\boldsymbol{R}$ is the $(N \times 3 \times n)$ set of input images. We follow [4] in carrying out RBF interpolation for interpolant light directions. But here we use the much faster luminance-mode approach Method:MODE or Method:LINEAR for generating matte images and also for recovering the surface chromaticity, surface normal, and albedo.

For a particular input dataset, the RBF network models the interpolated excursion solely based on the direction to a new light a': an estimate is given by $\hat{\eta} = RBF(a')$. Thus one arrives at an overall interpolant

$$\hat{R} = \hat{R}_{matte}(a') + \hat{\eta}(a') \tag{10}$$

5   Accuracy

We can determine the best balance to strike between simplicity and accuracy by challenging each method using Gaussian noise added to synthetic data, thus with ground truth known. Let us use the synthetic-Mozart image dataset ($n = 50$ images), comprised of (inherently noisy) range-finder data with Lambertian shading plus specularity.

Fig. 2 shows results for four methods comparing both accuracy of recovery of surface normals as well as albedo, for this dataset. We see that the fastest method, Method:MODE, does not compare well, whereas the more costly but still relatively   fast Method:LINEAR compares well with ostensibly the most accurate Method:LMS and a good deal better than the simple Method:QUANTILE. What we learn here is that a robust approach does pay, but we can use a simpler (albeit still robust) method, at least for such basically Lambertian plus shadows plus specularity data.

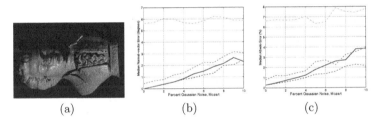

| (a) | (b) | (c) |

Fig. 2. Gaussian-noise sensitivity for synthetic Mozart image set: (b): One example out of 50 input images. (b): Median angular error for recovered surface normal – blue is Method:LMS, green is Method:MODE, magenta is Method:QUANTILE, and red is Method:Linear. (c): Median percent albedo error.

6   Results and Conclusions

Interpolation results, along with matte image and normal vectors recovered, are shown in Fig. 3. [2] Given the success and speed of Method:Linear in Fig. 2, in this paper we adopt that method for generating the matte part of interpolants.

[2] Row 2: Data courteously supplied by Roberto Scopigno, Visual Computing Laboratory, ISTI-CNR, Pisa, Italy; Rows 3-7: Data courteously supplied by Mark Mudge of Cultural Heritage Imaging.

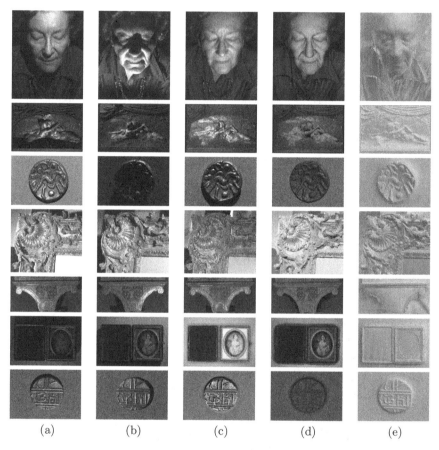

(a)   (b)   (c)   (d)   (e)

Fig. 3. (a,b): Input images with lighting directions to be interpolated; (c): interpolants for direction given by the mean of directions for (a,b); (d): robust matte image for interpolated angle; (e): normals. Directions for (a,b,c) are row 1: $\{\theta, \phi\} = \{24.5°, 58.7°\}, \{90.0°, -90.0°\} \rightarrow \{36.8°, -71.6°\}$; row 2: $\{52.2°, -63.4°\}$, $\{83.0°, 134.5°\} \rightarrow \{25.0°, 179.9°\}$; row 3: $\{23.3°, 85.1°\}, \{75.3°, 80.8°\} \rightarrow \{49.3°, 82.1°\}$; row 4: $\{39.2°, -177.1°\}, \{23.5°, 32.4°\} \rightarrow \{11.6°, 148.3°\}$; row 5: $\{34.7°, -142.9°\}, \{42.4°, -31.4°\} \rightarrow \{24.3°, -80.1°\}$; row 6: $\{75.3°, -99.2°\}$, $\{62.2°, 100.1°\} \rightarrow \{24.0°, -164.8°\}$; row 7: $\{36.6°, -30.5°\}, \{36.7°, -120.5°\} \rightarrow \{27.7°, -75.48°\}$;

The importance of achieving a good model for the matte surface cannot be overstressed, in that the underlying matte foundation gives us the surface properties desired – surface normals, albedo, chromaticity. On top of that fundamental structure, we also wish to derive convincing, accurate, and informative interpolants. To date, the RBF approach is the most straightforward, in that it involves no (spatial) Reflectance Sharing [6], which needs geometric knowledge.

From the results, one can see that a combination of using a fast matte model, as proposed here for the first part of the interpolation process, along with accurate RBF modelling, does generate interpolants with useful specular and shadow information. Further work will entail approaches to speed up the second part of the interpolation as well.

References

1. Malzbender, T., Gelb, D., Wolters, H.: Polynomial texture maps. In: Computer Graphics, SIGGRAPH 2001 Proceedings, pp. 519–528 (2001)
2. Woodham, R.J.: Photometric method for determining surface orientation from multiple images. Optical Engineering 19, 139–144 (1980)
3. Mudge, M.: Cultural Heritage Imaging.: Personal Communication (2010)
4. Drew, M., Hel-Or, Y., Malzbender, T., Hajari, N.: Robust estimation of surface properties and interpolation of shadow/specularity components. Image and Vision Computing 30, 317–331 (2012)
5. Rousseeuw, P.J., Leroy, A.M.: Robust Regression and Outlier Detection. Wiley (1987)
6. Zickler, T., Enrique, S., Ramamoorthi, R., Belhumeur, P.: Reflectance sharing: image-based rendering from a sparse set of images. In: Eurographics Symposium on Rendering, pp. 253–265 (2005)
7. Zickler, T., Ramamoorthi, R., Enrique, S., Belhumeur, P.: Reflectance sharing: Predicting appearance from a sparse set of images of a known shape. IEEE Trans. on Patt. Anal. and Mach. Intell. 28, 1287–1302 (2006)
8. Wenger, A., Gardner, A., Tchou, C., Unger, J., Hawkins, T., Debevec, P.: Performance relighting and reflectance transformation with time-multiplexed illumination. ACM Trans. Graph. 24, 756–764 (2005)

Illuminant Estimation from Projections on the Planckian Locus

Baptiste Mazin, Julie Delon, and Yann Gousseau

LTCI, Télécom-ParisTech, CNRS,
46 rue Barault, Paris 75013, France
{baptiste.mazin,julie.delon,yann.gousseau}@telecom-paristech.fr

Abstract. This paper deals with the automatic evaluation of the illuminant from a color photography. While many methods have been developed over the last years, this problem is still open since no method builds on hypotheses that are universal enough to deal with all possible situations. The proposed approach relies on a physical assumption about the possible set of illuminants and on the selection of grey pixels. Namely, a subset of pixels is automatically selected, which is then projected on the Planckian locus. Then, a simple voting procedure yields a robust estimation of the illuminant. As shown by experiments on two classical databases, the method offers state of the art performances among learning-free methods, at a reasonable computational cost.

1 Introduction

Human vision has the ability to perceive colors in a stable way under light sources having very different spectral contents. In contrast, cameras capture colors differently depending on the illuminant. Automatically canceling out this dependence is a difficult problem that is not yet fully solved. Specifically, the problem of estimating the illuminant of a scene has been the subject of a large body of works, as detailed for instance in the recent paper [1]. A classical application of such an estimation is the automatic correction of scenes acquired under non-standard illuminants. In a different context, color is an important feature for many computer vision tasks such as image comparison, object detection or motion estimation, tasks for which robustness to a change in illuminant may be achieved by a preliminary estimation.

The illumination estimation problem, where one tries to separate the intrinsic color of objects and the content of the illuminant, is basically an underconstrained problem. Indeed, a change in measured colors can be caused by a change in object colors or by a change of illuminant. As a consequence, automatically achieving color constancy necessitates some supplementary assumptions.

The first type of assumptions is based on scene composition. The most obvious one is to assume the presence of a white object in the scene [2], the so-called White-Patch assumption. This assumption is generally weakened to the presence of a perfectly reflective surface, yielding the Max-RGB algorithm. Another well known hypothesis is that the average world is grey, resulting in the Grey-World algorithm [3].

A. Fusiello et al. (Eds.): ECCV 2012 Ws/Demos, Part II, LNCS 7584, pp. 370–379, 2012.

An alternative approach is to use physical models to constrain the problem. Forsyth [4] first proposed to use the fact that under a given illuminant, the range of observable colors is limited. This approach was followed by many improvements over the last years [5,6].

While most algorithms described above rely on a Lambertian assumption, other algorithms involve a dichromatic model assuming that measured light is composed of both a Lambertian and a specular components [7,8]. These methods are often complemented by the assumption that feasible illuminant colors are limited [5,7].

Despite offering correct estimations in a large number of situations, none of the previously mentioned hypotheses is universal and satisfied for all scene-illuminant combinations. Moreover, failure situations vary from one hypothesis to the other. For this reason, interesting results have been obtained by combining the joint use of several basic methods and of learning procedures [9].

In this paper, we present a new learning-free method for the automatic estimation of the illuminant. The method relies on a physical *a priori*, building on the Planckian locus, on the possible set of illuminants. It also involves a simple voting procedure from a selected subset of pixels. Experiments on two widely used databases and comparisons with results provided by Gijsenij and al. [1] show that this approach outperforms standards methods without requiring any learning step.

2   Background

In this section, we give some background on the formation of color images, on the distribution of illuminants under a black body assumption and on the use of chromaticity diagrams. We also summarize previous works on the problem of illuminant estimation.

Illuminant estimation is the first and the toughest nut to crack for color constancy. The second aspect of color constancy is image correction, for which various methods can be used [1]. This paper only deals with the first step of the process.

2.1   Color Image Acquisition

Most approaches used to solve the illuminant estimation problem rely on a dichromatic model [10] for image formation, simplified with a Lambertian assumption. In these conditions, for a pixel $\mathbf{x}$, values $\mathbf{p}(\mathbf{x}) = (p_R(\mathbf{x}), p_G(\mathbf{x}), p_B(\mathbf{x}))$ depend on the spectral distribution of the light source $L(\lambda)$, the spectral distribution of surface reflectance $S(\lambda, \mathbf{x})$, and the camera sensitivities functions $\rho(\lambda) = (\rho_R(\lambda), \rho_G(\lambda), \rho_B(\lambda))$:

$$p_c(\mathbf{x}) = \int_\omega L(\lambda)S(\lambda, \mathbf{x})\rho_c(\lambda)d\lambda, \tag{1}$$

where $c = \{R, G, B\}$, and ω is the visible spectrum.

Assuming that camera sensitivity functions are Dirac delta functions associated to the wavelengths λ_R, λ_G and λ_B, Equation (1) can be rewritten as follows,

$$p_c(\mathbf{x}) = L(\lambda_c)S(\lambda_c, \mathbf{x}).$$ (2)

The illuminant estimation problem amounts to retrieve $L = (L_R, L_G, L_B) := (L(\lambda_R), L(\lambda_G), L(\lambda_B))$. This would for instance allows to render the scene under a given canonical illuminant L^u. Once the illuminant has been computed, the correction can be made using Von Kries model or more complex models. The main difficulty arises from the fact that measured pixel values $L(\lambda)$ depend on both the surface reflectance function and the spectrum of the light source.

2.2   Distribution of Feasible Illuminants

Grey-World and White-Patch hypotheses [2] (that will be recalled in the next paragraph) are certainly the most used assumptions to achieve illuminant estimation. There are, however, many situations in which these hypotheses are false and yield incorrect estimation. One of their limitation is that no *a priori* information on the chromaticity of the feasible illuminants is used. For instance, an image filled with a saturated green will lead to estimate a saturated green illuminant even though this is very unlikely.

Therefore, additional constraints are often added to limit the set of feasible illuminants. The blackbody radiator hypothesis is one of the most commonly used assumption. This hypothesis is based on the Planck model, which states that the spectrum of light emitted by an idealized physical body heated at a given temperature is given by

$$L(T, \lambda) = c_1 \lambda^{-5} \left[\exp\left(\frac{c_2}{\lambda T} \right) - 1 \right]^{-1},$$ (3)

where T is the temperature in kelvins, λ is the wavelength and $c_1 = 3.74183 \times 10^{16}$ Wm^2 and $c_2 = 1.4388 \times 10^{-2}$ mK are two constants.

Planck's formula is an accurate estimation of the spectrum of most illuminants including daylight [11]. It results that under the blackbody hypothesis, the possible colors of a grey pixel are limited. This can be conveniently visualized in a chromaticity diagram, the definition of which we now recall. A chromaticity diagram is a 2D projection of 3D color information discarding the intensity component. The CIE 1931 xy chromaticity diagram is the best known of such diagrams. It is derived from an RGB colorspace through an XYZ colorspace. This first step can be done by applying a device dependent matrix to RGB triplets. The xy chromaticities are then obtained by normalizing the vector XYZ such that $x + y + z = 1$. The relation between the Planckian locus and common illuminants (obtained from the database described in [12]) is illustrated on Figure 1.

2.3   Previous Work

In the context of illuminant estimation and color constancy, the most simple and widely used approaches are based on the White-Patch and on the Grey-World assumptions. The White-Patch assumption assumes that a surface with a perfect reflectance is present in the scene. This hypothesis yields the well known Max-RGB algorithm which presumes that the brighter point corresponds to a perfect reflective surface. The Grey-World hypothesis is that the average reflectance of the scene is achromatic. Both assumptions have been combined by Finlayson [13], proposing the framework described by the following equation:

$$L_c = \left(\frac{\int p_c(\mathbf{x})^n d\mathbf{x}}{\int d\mathbf{x}} \right)^{1/n} . \tag{4}$$

When $n = \infty$, this equation yields the Max-RGB algorithm and when $n = 1$, it yields the Grey-World algorithm. A classical variant of this method, called general Grey World [14], consists in performing a preliminary convolution of the image with a Gaussian kernel.

This framework was extended by van de Weijer [15]. This extension includes the Grey-Edge hypothesis that the average of reflectance differences is achromatic, leading to the equation:

$$L_c = \left(\int \left| \frac{\partial^k p_c(\mathbf{x})^n}{\partial \mathbf{x}^k} \right| d\mathbf{x} \right)^{1/n} . \tag{5}$$

All algorithms given by Equation (5) use all pixels to identify the white point. As noticed in [16], a more intuitive approach is to first detect potentially grey surfaces and then to estimate the illuminant from the corresponding pixels. Several algorithms using this procedure have recently been proposed.

Li and al. [16] propose an algorithm which iteratively estimates a white point maximizing the number of grey pixels. This algorithm takes as a starting point the estimation given by Equation 5 and therefore aims at refining this estimation. However, this estimation can be inaccurate and as noticed by the authors this step is especially touchy.

Another way to detect potentially grey pixels is to select points that are close to the Planckian locus in a chromaticity space and then to average them [17]. While inconsistent estimations (such as a purple illuminant) can be avoided this way, the approach may fail in the case where there is two potentially grey surfaces in the scene. Indeed, in this case, the resulting estimation will be made of the midway point between these surfaces. In the spirit of this approach, we define a simple pixel based voting procedure to estimate the illuminant chromaticity.

Many voting procedures permitting to choose between concurrent solutions to the color constancy problem were proposed in the literature. Since the same pixels values can be obtained by different combinations of illuminant and reflectance, Sapiro proposes a voting procedure [18] where each pixel votes for a set of parameters defining the reflectance of the illuminant functions. A Hough transform is then used to select the best parameters set. Riess et al. [19] propose another voting procedure. Roughly, many patches are selected and for each of them an illuminant is estimated by using an inverse chromaticity space. All patches for which the estimation succeeds vote and the illuminant is selected from these votes.

Very recently Vasquez-Corral *et al.* [20] propose to refine such voting approaches by incorporating perceptual constraints. In their approach, illuminants are weighted by "their ability to map the corrected image onto specific colors". These colors being chosen as universal color categories, this technique does not require any learning step.

3   Illuminant Selection via Grey Pixel Identification

Our illuminant selection algorithm draws on the assumption that most light sources are close to the Planckian locus. This hypothesis is well founded, as shown for instance by the experiment illustrated on Figure 1. Relying on this observation, our algorithm starts by finding pixels close to the Planckian locus in a well chosen color space. These pixels can be considered as the "most probably grey" in **p**. We then find the color temperature of all these pixels by projecting them on the Planckian locus. We build the histogram of this set of temperatures and apply a voting procedure in order to determine the most probable temperature T^0 for our illuminant. Finally, the complete illuminant is estimated by computing the barycenter of all pixels p that voted for the temperature T^0 in the histogram (see Algorithm 1 for a complete description of the procedure).

The color space used in the whole algorithm is the CIE 1960 uv diagram, as recommended by the CIE. Indeed, in this space, isotherms are defined as the lines perpendicular to the Planckian locus [21]: the correlated color temperature (CCT) of a pixel is thus the one of its closest black body radiator. Also, the temperature scale used in the voting procedure must be chosen carefully. Indeed, the Kelvin temperature scale does not yield a regular sampling of the Planckian locus [22]. The correlated color temperature $T(p)$ of a each pixel p is thus converted into the MIRED (Micro Reciprocal Degree) scale $T_{Mired}(p) = 10^6/T(p)$ before computing the histogram. This conversion was found by Priest [22] as a better way to sample color temperature according to human perception. This MIRED scale is illustrated by Figure 1, right. Finally, in order to give a greater importance to brighter pixels in the voting procedure, the contribution of each pixel in the histogram is weighted by a power of its luminance in **p**. This weighting limits the influence of dark pixels and can be seen as a trade off between the Grey-World and the White-Patch hypotheses [13]. An example of application of the method may be seen on Figure 1.

4   Algorithm Evaluation

In this section, we compare our algorithm to classical and recent state of the art approaches on two different databases, drawing from the results and codes from the recent evaluation paper [1]. These databases contain both indoor and outdoor scenes, taken under a large variety of illuminants.

The first database is the SFU grey-ball database [23], composed of 11,346 images and reprocessed in order to work on linear images, as explained in [1].

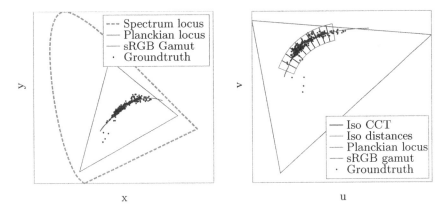

Fig. 1. Left: CIE 1931 chromaticity diagram. Right: CIE 1960 uv chromaticity diagram. On both diagrams, the green line represents the Planckian locus, and blue points correspond to the groundtruth illuminants of the Gehler database [12]. On the right, some isotemperatures curves are plotted in the CIE 1960 uv chromaticity diagram, with a maximum distance to the Planckian locus equal to 0.02.

input : Image **p** in the space sRGB, threshold δ, bin number N, standard deviation σ, power n, canonical illuminant $(u^{\mathrm{ref}}, v^{\mathrm{ref}})$.
output: Illuminant (u^0, v^0) in the CIE uv diagram.
Initialize histogram $H = 0$ on N bins;
for *each pixel p* **do**
    $p_{uv} = Convert_{sRGB \to uv}(p)$;
    $[p_{Planck}, T(p)] = Proj_{Planck}(p_{uv})$;
    `// ` p_{Planck} ` is the projection of ` p_{uv} ` on the Planckian locus in the`
        `CIE 1960 uv diagram and ` $T(p)$ ` is the temperature (in Kelvins)`
        `of the projection;`
    $d = \mathrm{distance}(p_{uv}, p_{Planck})$;
    if $d < \delta$ **and** $2000K \le T(p) \le 20000K$ **then**
        $T_{MIRED}(p) = 10^6/T(p)$;
        $weight(p) = luminance(p)^n$;
        Add $weight(p)$ to bin $T_{MIRED}(p)$ in H;
    end
end
if $H == \emptyset$ **then**
    return $(u^0, v^0) = (u^{\mathrm{ref}}, v^{\mathrm{ref}})$;
end
Filter histogram H with a normalized Gaussian of standard deviation σ;
Find $T^0 = \arg\max(H)$;
Find the barycenter of $H[T^0 - \sigma, T^0 + \sigma]$;
$\mathcal{L}$ = list of pixels p such that $T_{MIRED}(p)$ is in $[T^0 - \sigma, T^0 + \sigma]$;
return $(u^0, v^0) = Barycenter(\mathcal{L}, weight(\mathcal{L}))$;

Algorithm 1. Illuminant selection algorithm. In practice, the parameters used in the experimental section are $\delta = 0.01$, $N = 1000$, $\sigma = 2$ and $n = 3$.

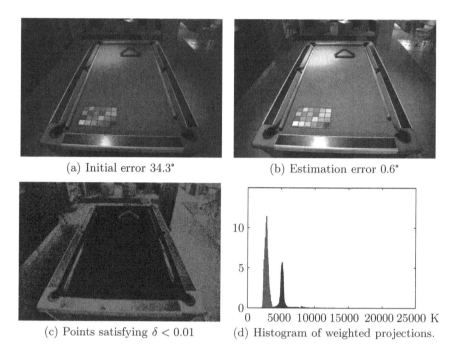

(a) Initial error 34.3°   (b) Estimation error 0.6°

(c) Points satisfying $\delta < 0.01$ (d) Histogram of weighted projections.

Fig. 2. Illustration of method results (for (a) and (b) errors are computed in the sRGB colorspace). (c) shows points close to the Planckian locus and (d) shows the histogram built from their projection on the Planckian locus, weighted by the luminance. On (c) and (d), red points correspond to a CCT < 4000 and blue points to a CCT $\in [4000, 6000]$.

The second is the Gehler database, composed of 568 images. Gehler *et al.* [24] provide both RAW and TIFF versions of each image. TIFF images are generated automatically by the camera and hence contain many non-linear corrections (demosaicing, clipping, gamma correction). In order to avoid the influence of these corrections, we choose, as in [24] to rely only on RAW versions. In our experiments, we provide two different evaluations, each one relying on a different reprocessing of RAW images. In the first one, images are reprocessed in the color space of the camera, as in [1]. In the second one, images are reprocessed in the sRGB colorspace, which is a less arbitrary choice, as explained below. This linear transformation is enabled by the fact that we know the cameras used to create the database [1].

For each database, the experimental protocol is then exactly as described in [1] and consists in computing for each image of the database some similarity measure between the estimated illuminant $\mathbf{I}^e$ and the groundtruth illuminant $\mathbf{I}^g$. Both illuminants define a "grey" axis in the color space of the image. The quality of the estimation is then measured by using the angle between these axes, *i.e.*

---

[1] The conversion from the camera colorspace to sRGB is specific to the camera and involves the use of the intermediary space XYZ.

$$E_a(\mathbf{I}^e, \mathbf{I}^g) = \cos^{-1}\left(\frac{\mathbf{I}^e \cdot \mathbf{I}^g}{||\mathbf{I}^e|| \cdot ||\mathbf{I}^g||}\right). \tag{6}$$

For the images of the SFU grey-ball database, this error is computed directly in the sRGB colorspace. For the Gehler database, this error can also be computed in the camera RGB colorspace, as chosen in [1]. This choice presents two problems. First, the three color components of a camera have very different dynamic ranges, which makes the error computation somehow biased. Most importantly, two different cameras are used to create the database, and averaging errors obtained in two different colorspaces seems inconsistent. This further motivates the use of the sRGB space, both for the developing and for the error computation.

Table 1. Performances on the colorchecker dataset in sRGB space. Results against learning-free methods ([2,3,14,15]) and methods involving a training phase ([4,6,8]).

Method	Mean	Median	Trimean	Best-25%(μ)	Worst-25%(μ)
White-Patch [2]	9.6°	7.7°	8.6°	2.2°	20.3°
Grey-World [3]	9.1°	8.6°	8.8°	2.9°	16.2°
general Grey-World [14]	6.7°	4.9°	5.4°	1.4°	14.9°
1st − order Grey-Edge [15]	7.0°	6.3°	6.4°	2.8°	12.5°
Pixel-based Gamut Mapping [4]	5.8°	3.4°	4.1°	0.7°	14.4°
Edge-based Gamut Mapping [6]	10.1°	7.4°	8.2°	2.8°	21.7°
ML (category-wise prior) [8]	4.3°	3.6°	3.7°	1.4°	8.4°
Our method	4.1°	2.9°	3.4°	0.7°	12.8°

Table 2. Performances on the colorchecker dataset in camera RGB space

Method	Mean	Median	Trimean	Best-25%(μ)	Worst-25%(μ)
White-Patch [2]	7.5°	5.7°	6.4°	1.5°	16.2°
Grey-World [3]	6.4°	6.3°	6.3°	2.3°	10.6°
general Grey-World [14]	4.7°	3.5°	3.8°	1.0°	10.2°
1st − order Grey-Edge [15]	5.4°	4.5°	4.8°	1.9°	10.0°
Pixel-based Gamut Mapping [4]	4.2°	2.3°	2.9°	0.5°	10.8°
Edge-based Gamut Mapping [6]	6.7°	5.0°	5.5°	2.0°	14.0°
ML (category-wise prior) [8]	3.1°	2.3°	2.5°	0.9°	6.5°
Our method	4.1°	3.1°	3.3°	0.9°	9.0°

We compare our algorithm against standards learning-free illuminant estimation schemes and against some of the best methods requiring a training phase. Results are summarized in Table 1,2 and 3 . The first Table shows the results obtained in the sRGB colorspace [2] for the Gehler database. The same comparisons performed in the camera RGB space are given in Table 2, enabling a direct comparison with the results from [1]. Table 3 provides the results on the SFU

---

[2] In order to compute errors in sRGB for other approaches, we project the illuminant estimations provided by [1] in sRGB. This may differ from a direct estimation of the illuminant in sRGB.

Table 3. Performances on the linear SFU grey-ball database in sRGB space

Method	Mean	Median	Trimean	Best-25%(μ)	Worst-25%(μ)
White-Patch [2]	12.7°	10.5°	11.3°	2.5°	26.2°
Grey-World [3]	13.0°	11.0°	11.5°	3.1°	26.0°
general Grey-World [14]	12.6°	11.1°	11.6°	3.8°	23.9°
1st – order Grey-Edge [15]	11.1°	9.5°	9.8°	3.2°	21.7°
Pixel-based Gamut Mapping [4]	11.8°	8.9°	10.0°	2.8°	24.9°
Edge-based Gamut Mapping [6]	13.7°	11.9°	12.3°	3.7°	26.9°
ML [8]	10.3°	8.9°	9.2°	2.8°	20.3°
Our method	10.9°	8.5°	9.1°	2.2°	23.5°

grey-ball database. Our approach shows better results than standard, learning-free methods, both in sRGB and in the camera colorspace, and both in term of mean and median of errors. The method is quite stable, providing good results on two databases with the same set of parameters. Our results are also not far from those obtained with more complex learning-based methods, at a very reasonable computational cost. Observe that errors in the sRGB colorspace are higher than those obtained in the camera colorspace. This can be explained by the reduced dynamic range of the camera color component.

5   Conclusion

In this paper, we have presented an automatic method for the estimation of the illuminant from a digital image. The method relies on projections on the Planck locus and on a voting scheme. Its efficiency has been demonstrated through various comparisons on two classical databases. One of the main interests of the method is a detailed analysis of the informative points in the image, obtained through a histogram of weighted projections on the Planckian locus. An interesting perspective of the work is a finer analysis of this histogram, an application of which could be the estimation of multiple illuminants of a scene.

Aknowledgement. This work is partially founded by the ANR projects Callisto and FUI project CEDCA.

References

1. Gijsenij, A., Gevers, T., van de Weijer, J.: Computational color constancy: Survey and experiments. IEEE Trans. Image Process. 20, 2475–2489 (2011)
2. Land, E., McCann, J.J.: Lightness and retinex theory. J. Opt. Soc. Am. 61, 1–11 (1971)
3. Buchsbaum, G.: A spatial processor model for object colour perception. J. Franklin Inst. 310, 1–26 (1980)
4. Forsyth, D.A.: A novel algorithm for color constancy. Int. J. Comput. Vision 5, 5–36 (1990)

5. Finlayson, G.D., Hordley, S.D.: Gamut constrained illuminant estimation. Int. J. Comput. Vision 67 (2006)
6. Gijsenij, A., Gevers, T., van de Weijer, J.: Generalized gamut mapping using image derivative structures for color constancy. Int. J. Comput. Vision 86, 127–139 (2010)
7. Finlayson, G.D., Schaefer, G.: Solving for colour constancy using a constrained dichromatic reflection model. Int. J. Comput. Vision 42, 127–144 (2001)
8. Chakrabarti, A., Hirakawa, K., Zickler, T.: Color constancy with spatio-spectral statistics. IEEE Trans. Pattern Anal. Mach. Intell. (2012)
9. Gijsenij, A., Gevers, T.: Color constancy using natural image statistics and scene semantics. IEEE Trans. Pattern Anal. Mach. Intell. 33, 687–698 (2011)
10. Shafer, S.A.: Using color to separate reflection components, pp. 43–51 (1992)
11. Judd, D.B., Macadam, D.L., Wyszecki, G., Budde, H.W., Condit, H.R., Henderson, S.T., Simonds, J.L.: Spectral distribution of typical daylight as a function of correlated color temperature. J. Opt. Soc. Am. 54, 1031–1036 (1964)
12. Gehler, P.V., Rother, C., Blake, A., Minka, T., Sharp, T.: Bayesian color constancy revisited. In: Conference on Computer Vision and Pattern Recognition, pp. 1–8 (2008)
13. Finlayson, G.D., Trezzi, E.: Shades of gray and colour constancy. In: Color Imaging Conference, pp. 37–41 (2004)
14. Barnard, K., Martin, L., Coath, A., Funt, B.: A comparison of computational color constancy algorithms. IEEE Trans. Image Process. 11, 2002 (2002)
15. Van De Weijer, J., Gevers, T., Gijsenij, A.: Edge-based color constancy. IEEE Trans. Image Process. 16, 2207–2214 (2007)
16. Li, B., Xu, D., Xiong, W., Feng, S.: Color constancy using achromatic surface. Color Res. Appl. 35, 304–312 (2010)
17. Kwon, H.J., Lee, S.H., Bae, T.W., Sohng, K.I.: Compensation of de-saturation effect in hdr imaging using a real scene adaptation model. J. Visual Commun. Image Represent. (2012)
18. Sapiro, G.: Color and illuminant voting. IEEE Trans. Pattern Anal. Mach. Intell. 21, 1210–1215 (1999)
19. Riess, C., Eibenberger, E., Angelopoulou, E.: Illuminant estimation by voting (2009)
20. Vazquez-Corral, J., Vanrell, M., Baldrich, R., Tous, F.: Color constancy by category correlation. IEEE Transactions on Image Processing 21, 1997–2007 (2012)
21. Wyszecki, G., Stiles, W.S.: Color Science: Concepts and Methods, Quantitative Data and Formulae, 2nd edn. Wiley-Interscience (2000)
22. Priest, I.G.: A proposed scale for use in specifying the chromaticity of incandescent illuminants and various phases of daylight. J. Opt. Soc. Am. 23, 41–45 (1933)
23. Ciurea, F., Funt, B.: A large image database for color constancy research (2003)
24. Shi, L., Brian: Re-processed version of the gehler color constancy dataset of 568 images (2010)

Lighting Estimation in Indoor Environments from Low-Quality Images

Natalia Neverova, Damien Muselet, and Alain Trémeau

Laboratoire Hubert Curien – UMR CNRS 5516, University Jean Monnet,
Rue du Professeur Benoît Lauras 18, 42000 Saint-Étienne, France
natalia.neverova@etu.univ-st-etienne.fr,
{damien.muselet,alain.tremeau}@univ-st-etienne.fr
http://laboratoirehubertcurien.fr

Abstract. Lighting conditions estimation is a crucial point in many applications. In this paper, we show that combining color images with corresponding depth maps (provided by modern depth sensors) allows to improve estimation of positions and colors of multiple lights in a scene. Since usually such devices provide low-quality images, for many steps of our framework we propose alternatives to classical algorithms that fail when the image quality is low. Our approach consists in decomposing an original image into specular shading, diffuse shading and albedo. The two shading images are used to render different versions of the original image by changing the light configuration. Then, using an optimization process, we find the lighting conditions allowing to minimize the difference between the original image and the rendered one.

Keywords: light estimation, depth sensor, color constancy.

1   Introduction

Nowadays, there are growing demands in the context of augmented reality applications, which is a subject of enormous attention of researchers and engineers. The ability to augment real scenes with arbitrary objects and animations opens up broad prospects in the areas of design, entertainment and human-computer interaction. In this context, correct estimation of lighting conditions (3D positions and colors) inside the scene appears to be a crucial step in making the rendering realistic and convincing.

Today, there exist solutions that require complex hardware setup with high dynamic / high resolution cameras and light probes [1]. Instead, our goal is to design a system that can be used at home by any user owning a simple and cheap RGB-D sensor. In this context, a nice solution has been proposed in [2] but that solution requires the user to specify the geometry of the scene, the object interactions and the rough positions and colors of the light sources. Furthermore, that approach is adapted to simple scene geometries since the environment is represented as a cube.

A. Fusiello et al. (Eds.): ECCV 2012 Ws/Demos, Part II, LNCS 7584, pp. 380–389, 2012.

In this paper, we show that using cheap depth sensors (such as Microsoft Kinect) allows to avoid these requirements of light probes, multiple user interactions and simple geometries. Indeed, from the rough geometric information provided by such a sensor, we can simulate different versions of an observed scene under different lighting conditions. Then, we can estimate the light conditions that minimize the difference between the rendered image (with estimated light) and the target image (i.e. the original one).

The contributions of our approach are threefold. First, we propose a new iterative algorithm allowing to estimate light colors in low-quality images. Second, unlike the classical approaches, we account the specular information in the rendering process and show in the experiments that this information improves the light estimation. Finally, we propose a rough light position estimation that is used for the initialization of the optimization process.

The rest of the paper is organized as follows: first we will provide a brief overview of state-of-the-art methods of light estimation and image decomposition. Then in Section 3 we will describe the main ideas of the proposed method and justify it from the physical point of view. In Section 4 we propose a way to initialize the optimization problem introduced in Section 3. Section 5 contains some experimental results and Section 6 concludes the paper and provides some details on future works.

2   Related Work

Light Estimation. Light estimation is one of the most challenging problems in computer vision, especially when it comes to indoor scenes. Presence of multiple light sources of different sizes and shapes, intensities and spectral characteristics is a typical situation for this kind of environments. The image based lighting approach described in [1] is one of the most advanced techniques of light modeling that allows to obtain high quality results but at cost of processing time. The main limitations of this approach are that it requires a complex hardware setup with additional cameras and/or light probes and is based on high dynamic and high resolution imaging. A modified approach proposed in [3] allows to directly estimate positions of light sources but is also based on using cumbersome hardware. One of the most popular alternatives to image-based lighting approaches aims on detection and direct analysis of shadings. These techniques are generally more suitable for outdoor environments with strong casts, directed light sources and simple geometry. An exhaustive survey of cast detection methods in different contexts is provided in [4], while [5] explores the possibility of their integration in real-time augmented reality systems. Finally, we must mention a recent work [2] exploiting an idea of light estimation and correction through rendering-based optimization procedure. This approach is the closest to the one proposed in this paper, therefore we will address to some parts of their work in the following sections.

Intrinsic Images. In order to render the image with estimated lighting, it is recommended to decompose the color of each pixel into albedo and shading [6,7].

Land and McCann proposed in 1975 the Retinex theory assuming that albedo is characterized by sharp edges while shading varies slowly [8]. Inspired by this work, some papers have tried to improve the decomposition results [9]. Most of the intrinsic image decompositions assume diffuse reflection and neglect the specular reflection. Using jointly segmentation and intrinsic image decomposition, Maxwell et al. [10] account the specularities in the decomposition but this kind of approach is not adapted to low-quality images acquired under uncontrolled conditions [7]. Thus, to overcome the presence of highlights, a preliminary step consists in separating specular and diffuse reflection [11] and then applying the intrinsic decomposition on the diffuse image. In order to decompose an image into diffuse and specular components we take advantage of the simplicity of the method proposed by Shen et al. [12]. However, since they assumed known illuminant, we propose to modify their approaches in order to estimate the light color during the process.

3   Light Estimation through Optimization

3.1   Assumptions and Workflow

In the first step, in order to simplify the estimation lighting process, we have considered the following assumptions. First, we assume that all light sources illuminating a scene have the same chromaticity. Second, we assume that the specular reflectance distribution (ρ_s in eq. 1) is the same over all the surfaces in a scene. This assumption which is not true from a theoretical point of view does not disturb the light estimation in practice. However, for the rendering of synthetic object, we can account different specular reflectance distributions. Moreover, we assume that the lights are planar and of negligible sizes. And last, we assume dichromatic reflection model as presented in Fig. 1.

As can be seen on Fig. 1, our approach consists in decomposing a color image into three images. First, we use a similar approach as [12] in order to separate diffuse and specular reflections. However, we modify the original process in order to evaluate the overall light color that we assume constant over the whole image. Then, from the diffuse reflection image, we apply a Retinex based decomposition [13] since Retinex has been shown to provide nice results in [6]. This intrinsic decomposition provides the shading and albedo images. The obtained specular A^0 and diffuse B^0 shading images are the inputs of the optimization process. They are independently compared with the rendered specular A and diffuse B shading images, which are obtained from geometric information provided by the Kinect and from the initial light condition estimation L^0. Then the light conditions L are iteratively updated until the difference between real and rendered images is minimum.

3.2   Reflection Model

Thanks to the depth information provided by the Kinect, we are able to account both diffuse and specular reflection in the rendering images used during the optimization. Consequently, we can consider the dichromatic reflection model [14]

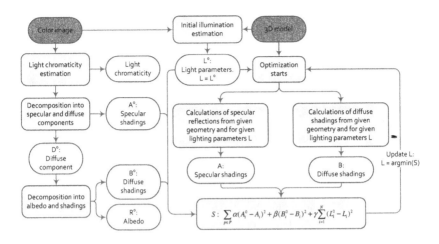

Fig. 1. Workflow of the proposed method

and more specifically, the Phong model [15] that estimates the spectral power distribution of the light reflected by a given surface point illuminated by N light sources $I_{0,i}(\lambda)$ as:

$$I(\lambda, p)_N = -\rho_d(\lambda, p) \sum_{i=1}^{N} I_{0,i}(\lambda) \frac{(\mathbf{n_{s,i}}, \mathbf{d_i})(\mathbf{n}, \mathbf{d_i})}{||\mathbf{d_i}||^4} + \tag{1}$$

$$\rho_s \sum_{i=1}^{N} I_{0,i}(\lambda) \frac{(\mathbf{n_{s,i}}, \mathbf{d_i})}{||\mathbf{d_i}||^{k+1}} (\mathbf{v}, (\mathbf{d_i} - 2(\mathbf{n}, \mathbf{d_i})\mathbf{n}))^k,$$

where $\rho_d(\lambda, p)$ is the diffuse reflectance of the considered surface point, the brackets model the dot product, k is a coefficient that can be defined and set experimentally (in our implementation we set $k = 55$), $\rho_s(\lambda, p)$ is the specular reflectance and all the other parameters ($\mathbf{n_s}$, $\mathbf{n}$, $\mathbf{d}$, $\mathbf{v}$) are introduced in Fig. 2. Assuming neutral specular reflection, as it is usually done, and constant maximum specular reflectance over the scene, $\rho_s(\lambda, p) = \rho_s$ is a constant in a given scene.

From this equation, we propose to extract two terms that only depend on the geometry of the scene (viewing direction, surface orientation and light position) and not on the reflection properties of the surfaces:

$$B(p) = \left[\frac{(\mathbf{n_{s,i}}, \mathbf{d_i})(\mathbf{n}, \mathbf{d_i})}{||\mathbf{d_i}||^4} \right] \text{ called diffuse shading;} \tag{2}$$

$$A(p) = \left[\frac{(\mathbf{n_{s,i}}, \mathbf{d_i})}{||\mathbf{d_i}||^{k+1}} (\mathbf{v}, (\mathbf{d_i} - 2(\mathbf{n}, \mathbf{d_i})\mathbf{n}))^k \right] \text{ called specular shading.} \tag{3}$$

Starting from depth images, the only unknowns in these equations are the light positions and orientations. So, given an image provided by the Kinect, we can

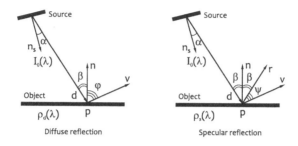

Fig. 2. Diffuse and specular reflections. $\mathbf{n_s}$ – normal vector to the surface of the planar light source ($|\mathbf{n_s}| = 1$), $\mathbf{d}$ – vector connecting the light source with the given object point ($|\mathbf{d}| = d$); α – angle between vectors $\mathbf{n_s}$ and $\mathbf{d}$, $\mathbf{n}$ – normal vector to the surface of the object ($|\mathbf{n}| = 1$), β – angle of incident light (between vectors $\mathbf{n_s}$ and $\mathbf{n}$), $\mathbf{v}$ – viewing direction ($|\mathbf{v}| = 1$), φ – angle between the surface normal and the viewing direction, $I_0(\lambda)$ – intensity of the light source in the direction perpendicular to its surface, $\rho_d(\lambda)$ – diffuse reflectance, $\rho_s(\lambda)$ – specular reflectance.

render these two shading images (A and B) for all light geometries we want. The idea of the next step is to be able to extract these shading images (A^0 and B^0) from the original color image in order to find the best light geometries that minimize the differences between the rendered images A and B and their corresponding original images A^0 and B^0 (see Fig. 1).

3.3   Color Image Decomposition

To decompose an image into diffuse and specular components we consider and improve the method proposed in [12]. In this paper, the authors generated a specular-free image from a color image by subtracting from each pixel the minimum of its RGB values and adding a pixel-dependent offset. This simple approach provides good results when the light color is known and the image is normalized with respect to this color and rescaled to the range $[0, 255]$. In our case, the light color is unknown and we propose to estimate it during the process. Thus, in the first step, we assume white light and we run the algorithm on the original image. Then, once the specular component is separated from the diffuse one, the chromaticity of the illuminants is estimated as the mean chromaticity of the detected specular pixels. After that the original image can be normalized with respect to the "new" light color and specular component can be recalculated using the same formula. Consequently, we propose an iterative process that successively applies specular detection and light chromaticity estimation until convergence. Today we have no proof about the convergence properties but in practice, a maximum of 3 iterations are required to obtain stable specular image and light chromaticity on the tested images.

After running this algorithm, we obtain the light chromaticity, the specular shading image called A^0 and the diffuse image called D^0. The diffuse image can be further decomposed into diffuse shading and albedo terms. It can be done in different ways, but in this work we use the Retinex theory [8] that proved to

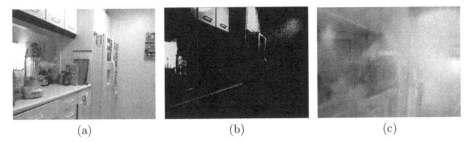

(a)   (b)   (c)

Fig. 3. Decomposition of a color image (a) into specular (b) and diffuse (c) components

be a state-of-the-art method of intrinsic image decomposition [6]. Here we use a fast implementation of Retinex proposed in [13]. The diffuse shading image is called B^0. The decomposition is illustrated in Fig. 3.

3.4 Optimization

In the previous sections, we have explained how to render diffuse (B) and specular (A) shadings using the equations (2) and (3) respectively and how to obtain the corresponding original images B^0 and A^0 from the considered color image. The idea of the optimization step is to evaluate the light conditions that minimize the differences between these images:

$$L = \arg\min \left\{ \sum_{p \in P} \alpha [A^0(p) - A(p)]^2 + \beta [B^0(p) - B(p)]^2 + \gamma \sum_{i=1}^{N} [L_i^0 - L_i]^2 \right\},$$

$$(4)$$

where α, β and γ are coefficients set experimentally (in our implementation we set $\alpha = 1$, $\beta = 0.75$, $\gamma = 30 M_x M_y$, where $M_x \times M_y$ is the size of the image).

The last term $(L_i^0 - L_i)$ of the equation (4) constraints the process not to move far away from the initial light position estimation L_i^0. Indeed, in a preprocessing step (detailed in the next section), we can roughly estimate the potential 3D position L_i^0 of all the lights i in the scene and the value of the coefficient γ depends on how confident we are in this first estimation. The next section explains different ideas on how to perform this estimation.

It is important to note here that the previous equation is used to optimize the light positions, but it could be easily extended to optimize both the positions and the colors of the lights. In this case, we would have to render the color image with equation (1) and compare it with the original color image.

4 Discussion about Initialization

For initialization, we need to specify the number of light sources and their approximate positions. By detecting the areas of maximum intensities in specular

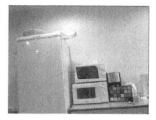

Fig. 4. Some images used for light color estimation

Table 1. Mean angular error obtained on the images of Fig. 4

Grey-world	MaxRGB	Shades of grey	Grey edge	our proposition
1.10	0.96	2.84	1.03	0.43

spots and knowing the surface orientation of these areas and the position of the camera, we can estimate the direction of reflected light. That gives an approximate direction of light sources locations. By specifying several points of specular reflections on different surfaces and finding the intersection points of corresponding lines, we can also find the distances to the sources. If there are several light sources illuminating the scene, different specular reflections will correspond to different positions. In this case all rays can be combined in several groups and number of sources and their directions can be roughly defined. We propose to do it with a greedy algorithm based on a voting scheme consisting of accumulation and search steps.

5   Experiments

5.1   Light Color

In order to check the results of our iterative process that allows to estimate the light color, we have acquired a set of images, containing color target as ground truth (see Fig. 4). We have mentioned that the color images provided by the Kinect device are noisy and of low resolution. Therefore we wanted to assess the quality of the results provided by the classical color constancy algorithms in this context. We have tested the following algorithms [16]: Grey-world, MaxRGB, Shades of grey, Grey edge and our proposition. For each algorithm, we have evaluated the mean angular error as recommended in [16].

The results are displayed in table 1. We can see that algorithms based on the analysis of the edges do not perform well on this low-quality images. MaxRGB that is the nearest approach to our proposition provides good results but our approach outperforms all the tested methods. The advantage of our method compared to MaxRGB is that it is based on the detection of specular areas by using a pixel-dependent offset and this can help in the case of low-quality images [16]. The use of our iterative process also helps in this detection step.

5.2   Light Positions

We tested our method on some color images from NYU Depth V1 dataset [17]. This dataset contains 2284 VGA-resolution images of various indoor environments together with corresponding depth maps taken with the Kinect sensors. Since there are no other works trying to estimate light conditions from depth sensors, we can not show comparison results. Instead, we propose to show one convincing example illustrating how our approach is improving the state-of-the-art method [2], while not requiring any user interaction. Let us consider the top color image from Fig. 5. We have run different optimization procedures on this image, starting from the same initial 3D light positions:

- Method 1: we first apply our decomposition (specular vs. diffuse and then albedo vs. shading on the diffuse) and consider only the diffuse shading image B^0 for optimization, i.e. we optimize only $[B^0(p) - B(p)]^2$,
- Method 2: same as method 1 but considering only the specular shading image A^0 for optimization, i.e. we optimize only $[A^0(p) - A(p)]^2$,
- Method 3: same as method 1 but considering both the specular shading image A^0 and the diffuse shading image B^0 for optimization, i.e. we optimize equation (4),
- Method 4: we neglect the specular reflection and just decompose the original color image into albedo and shading and we optimize the shading part (similar to [2]).

On Fig. 5, for each method (from 1 to 4), we have plotted a cross corresponding to the center of the highlight that would be obtained if the light position was returned by this method. This is a good way to compare the returned position estimations from the different methods. On the image, we can see that crosses corresponding to methods 2 and 3 are the nearest to the real highlight. Since the cross 4 is very far from the real highlight, we can conclude that the specular reflection should not be neglected during the optimization process. Indeed, in this case, the highlight is considered as a diffuse spot and the algorithm try to optimize the light position so that we obtain this diffuse spot, leading to a high position error. This illustration validates the importance to apply first the multiple decompositions and to optimize both specular and diffuse shadings. Then, we show on the second and third rows of this figure the diffuse and specular rendering of each method (column j corresponds to method j). We can see that by only considering the specular component (column 2), the diffuse rendering is not correct because the distance between the light and the wall is hard to estimate from specularities only. Fortunately, the third column (proposed method) displays the best results, showing that both specular and diffuse components have to be used for the estimation.

Thus, this illustration shows that our approach is able to better estimate positions of light source present in the scene using color and depth data provided by a depth sensor.

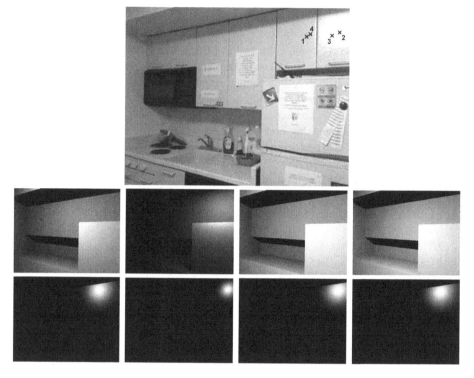

Fig. 5. First row: light position results in case of specular reflection. See text for details. Second row: diffuse rendering. Third row: specular rendering. Each column corresponds to one method from method 1 (left) to method 4 (right).

6   Conclusion

In this paper, we have proposed an approach to cope with the problem of lighting estimation from low-quality color images. First, we have used an iterative process that allows to well estimate the light color of the scene. Second, thanks to a multiple decompositions of the image, we have run an optimization framework that leads to fine estimation of light positions. In our experiments we used a depth sensor providing information exploited for the rendering of the different decompositions. We have shown that our light color estimation outperforms state-of-the-art methods and that accounting specular reflection during the optimization process improves the results over methods that just assume lambertian reflection. As future works, we propose to extend the approach to lights with different colors. In real indoor environments, the colors of the lights do not vary significantly within a scene, but it would help to detect even slight spatial variation and by this way refine the color of each individual light. Indeed, the correct estimation of the light color can also help in the specularity detection. Second, we could add one term in the final objective function that represents the final color rendering of the image. Thus, we could minimize the difference between this image and the original color one and by this way also optimize the color of the light (instead of only the position). Finally, there is still a large possibility of improvement of the specularity detection if we consider the geometry information during this step. Until now, just pixel chromaticities were considered.

References

1. Debevec, P.: Image-based lighting. IEEE Computer Graphics and Applications 22, 26–34 (2002)
2. Karsch, K., Hedau, V., Forsyth, D., Hoiem, D.: Rendering synthetic objects into legacy photographs. In: SIGGRAPH Asia Conference, pp. 157:1–157:12. ACM Press, New York (2011)
3. Frahm, J.-M., Koeser, K., Grest, D., Koch, R.: Markerless augmented reality with light source estimation for direct illumination. In: 2nd IEEE European Conference on Visual Media Production (CVMP), pp. 211–220. IEEE Press, New York (2005)
4. Al-Najdawi, N., Bez, H.E., Singhai, J., Edirisinghe, E.A.: A survey of cast shadow detection algorithms. Pattern Recognition Letters 33, 752–764 (2012)
5. Jacobs, K., Loscos, C.: Classification of illumination methods for mixed reality. Computer Graphics Forum 25, 29–51 (2006)
6. Grosse, R., Johnson, M.K., Adelson, E.H., Freeman, W.T.: Ground truth dataset and baseline evaluations for intrinsic image algorithms. In: 12th IEEE International Conference on Computer Vision (ICCV), pp. 2335–2342. IEEE Press, New York (2009)
7. Shida, B., van de Weijer, J.: Object Recoloring based on Intrinsic Image Estimation. In: 13th IEEE International Conference on Computer Vision (ICCV), pp. 327–334. IEEE Press, New York (2011)
8. Land, E.H., McCann, J.J.: Lightness and retinex theory. Journal of the Optical Society of America 61, 1–11 (1971)
9. Horn, B.K.P.: Determining lightness from an image. Computer Graphics and Image Processing 3, 277–299 (1974)
10. Maxwell, B.A., Shafer, S.A.: Segmentation and Interpretation of Multicolored Objects with Highlights. Computer Vision and Image Understanding 77, 1–24 (2000)
11. Artusi, A., Banterle, F., Chetverikov, D.: A Survey of Specularity Removal Methods. Computer Graphics Forum 30, 2208–2230 (2011)
12. Shen, H.-L., Cai, Q.-Y.: Simple and efficient method for specularity removal in an image. Applied Optics 48, 2711–2719 (2009)
13. Limare, N., Petro, A.B., Sbert, C., Morel, J.-M.: Retinex Poisson Equation: a Model for Color Perception. Image Processing On Line (2011), http://www.ipol.im/pub/algo/lmps_retinex_poisson_equation/
14. Shafer, S.A.: Using color to separate reflection components. Color Research and Application 10, 210–218 (1984)
15. Phong, B.T.: Illumination for computer generated pictures. Communications of the ACM 18, 311–317 (1975)
16. Gijsenij, A., Gevers, T., van de Weijer, J.: Computational Color Constancy: Survey and Experiments. IEEE Transactions on Image Processing: A Publication of the IEEE Signal Processing Society 20, 2475–2489 (2011)
17. Silberman, N., Fergus, R.: Indoor scene segmentation using a structured light sensor. In: 13th IEEE International Conference on Computer Vision Workshops (ICCV Workshops), pp. 601–608. IEEE Press, New York (2011)

Color Constancy Using Single Colors

Simone Bianco

University of Milano-Bicocca, Italy

Abstract. This work investigates if the von Kries adaptation can be generalized to deal with single colored patches. We investigate which colored patches can give statistically equivalent performance to a white patch for von Kries adaptation. The investigation is then extended to couples of colors, and the analysis of the characteristics of the colors forming the couples is carried out. We focus here on single and couples of colors since common objects and logos are usually composed by a small number of colors.

1   Introduction

Computational color constancy aims to estimate the actual color in an acquired scene disregarding its illuminant. Many illuminant estimation solutions have been proposed in the last few years [1,2], although it is known that the problem addressed is actually ill-posed as its solution lacks uniqueness and stability [3]. A recent research area which has shown promising results aims to improve illuminant estimation by using visual information automatically extracted from the images. The existing algorithms exploit both low-level [4,5], intermediate-level [6] and high-level [7] visual information.

In [7] several illuminant estimation approaches are applied to compute a set of possible illuminants. For each of them an illuminant color corrected image is evaluated on the likelihood of its semantic content: is the grass green, the road grey, and the sky blue, in correspondence with our prior knowledge of the world. The illuminant resulting in the most likely semantic composition of the image is selected as the illuminant color. In [8] an object-based approach is used for illuminant classification: only the pixel associated to an object are considered in the illuminant classification process using the object's spectral characteristics.

It has been shown that memory colors could be used as hints to give a more accurate estimate of the illuminant color in the scene. For example, Moreno et al. [9] obtained memory colors for three different objects (grass, snow and sky) using psychophysical experiments. A different approach has been used in [10] where a face detector was used to find faces in the scene, and the corresponding skin colors were used to estimate the chromaticity of the illuminant.

In this work we investigate if single colors can be used to estimate the illuminant color in the scene. We focus here on single colors since common objects (see Fig. 1.a which contains some examples extracted from the ALOI dataset [11]) and logos (see Fig. 1.b) are usually composed by a small number of colors. The idea is that if we are able to automatically recognize objects and logos that have

A. Fusiello et al. (Eds.): ECCV 2012 Ws/Demos, Part II, LNCS 7584, pp. 390–400, 2012.
© Springer-Verlag Berlin Heidelberg 2012

Fig. 1. a) Examples of common objects extracted from the ALOI dataset [11]; b) examples of common logos (http://www.flickr.com/photos/27845211@N02/2662264721/sizes/l/in/pool-75819424@N00/)

intrinsic colors, we could use them for color constancy. If the reflectance of the color and the sensor transmittance curves are known, it is possible to recover the illuminant power spectrum distribution in the set of a finite-dimensional linear model [12]. If the same color has been acquired under different illuminants, it is possible to classify the scene illuminant in one of the known illuminant classes [13]. We want here to relax these requirements: we assume to only know the sensor response of a reference colored patch under a canonical illuminant and under the scene illuminant. We investigate here for which colors the illuminant can be estimated as the ratio of the sensor response of the reference patch under the canonical illuminant and the sensor response of the same patch under the scene illuminant, giving statistically equivalent color constancy performance to those that would be obtained in the case of the classical von Kries white-patch normalization [14,15] (i.e. the reference patch is white). This investigation is then extended to couples of colors, analyzing the characteristics of the forming colors.

The procedure proposed can be applied to any colors, and is here illustrated for both the Gretag Macbeth ColorChecker DC chart and the Munsell atlas.

2   Problem Formulation and Proposed Solution

The image values for a Lambertian surface located at the pixel with coordinates (x, y) can be seen as a function $\rho(x, y)$, mainly dependent on three physical factors: the illuminant spectral power distribution $I(\lambda)$, the surface spectral reflectance $S(\lambda)$ and the sensor spectral sensitivities $\mathbf{C}(\lambda)$. Using this notation $\rho(x, y)$ can be expressed as

$$\rho(x, y) = \int_{\omega} I(\lambda) S(x, y, \lambda) \mathbf{C}(\lambda) \mathrm{d}\lambda, \qquad (1)$$

where ω is the wavelength range of the visible light spectrum, ρ and $\mathbf{C}(\lambda)$ are three-component vectors.

The aim of any color constancy algorithm [16] is to transform the color observation vector ρ to its corresponding illuminant-independent descriptor $\mathbf{d}$:

$$\mathbf{d} = \mathcal{Q}\rho, \qquad (2)$$

where $\mathcal{Q}$ is a linear transform. Following [16], we constrain $\mathcal{Q}$ to be diagonal. In this work the Forsyth's definition of descriptor is used [17], which is defined as the observation of a surface seen under a canonical illuminant.

$$\mathbf{d}_i^c \equiv \boldsymbol{\rho}_i^c = \int_\omega I_c(\lambda)S_i(\lambda)\mathbf{C}(\lambda)d\lambda, \tag{3}$$

In the von Kries adaptation [14], or white-patch normalization, the descriptor for a surface i acquired under an unknown illuminant e is obtained as follows:

$$\mathbf{d}_i^e = \mathcal{D}^{e,c}\boldsymbol{\rho}_i^e \tag{4}$$

with

$$\mathcal{D}^{e,c} = [\mathrm{diag}\,(\boldsymbol{\rho}_w^e)]^{-1} \tag{5}$$

where $\boldsymbol{\rho}_w^e$ corresponds to the image values of a white surface acquired under the unknown illuminant.

Since a white surface is not always available in the acquired scene, in this work we want to see if other colors can be used to obtain the illuminant compensation matrix $\mathcal{D}^{e,c}$. This would enable to use colored objects (eventually automatically detected in the scene), to be used to derive the diagonal mapping $\mathcal{D}^{e,c}$ given only their representation under a canonical illuminant c, without further knowledge of both the object spectral reflectance and the camera sensor transmittances.

Given only $\boldsymbol{\rho}_i^e$ and its acquired values under a canonical illuminant $\boldsymbol{\rho}_i^c$, $\mathcal{D}^{e,c}$ can be obtained as

$$\mathcal{D}^{e,c} = \frac{\mathrm{diag}\,(\boldsymbol{\rho}_i^c/\boldsymbol{\rho}_i^e)}{||\,(\boldsymbol{\rho}_i^c/\boldsymbol{\rho}_i^e)\,||_\infty} \tag{6}$$

which for the case of a white surface corresponds to the white-patch normalization [14,15].

The estimation described in Eq. 6 can be extended to two or more colors in different ways [13,17]. In this work we consider the easiest extension: given n corresponding colors seen under the canonical and the scene illuminant, the diagonal mapping is estimated as the average of the single estimations given by each color taken individually, i.e.

$$\mathcal{D}^{e,c} = \frac{1}{n}\sum_{i=1}^n \frac{\mathrm{diag}\,(\boldsymbol{\rho}_i^c/\boldsymbol{\rho}_i^e)}{||\,(\boldsymbol{\rho}_i^c/\boldsymbol{\rho}_i^e)\,||_\infty} \tag{7}$$

Furthermore, the estimation described in Eq. 5 can be extended to the case of generalized diagonal transforms which are able convey higher color constancy performance [16]. Let $\mathcal{T}$ be the sensor sharpening transformation, than Eq. 5 becomes

$$\mathcal{D}^{e,c} = \mathcal{T}^{-1}[\mathrm{diag}\,(\mathcal{T}\boldsymbol{\rho}_w^e)]^{-1}\mathcal{T} \tag{8}$$

The extensions of Eq.6 and 7 for the case of generalized diagonal transforms are straightforward.

Given a set of colors $i = 1, \ldots, m$, we want to find those which can be used to estimate a diagonal mapping $\mathcal{D}^{e,c}$ with statistically equivalent color constancy performance to those that would be obtained using a white surface. The color constancy performance are measured for each color of the set using the normalized distance (ND) metric [16], which is defined as

$$\text{ND} = 100 * \frac{||\mathbf{d}_i^e - \mathbf{d}_i^c||}{||\mathbf{d}_i^c||} \qquad (9)$$

where $\mathbf{d}_i^c$ denotes the canonical descriptor and $\mathbf{d}_i^e$ denotes the descriptor for the scene illuminant e. The cumulative ND histograms are calculated on all the color set, using each of the colors at turn to estimate the diagonal mapping $\mathcal{D}^{e,c}$, resulting in a total of m cumulative histograms. In order to determine if there are colors that can be used to obtain color constancy performance statistically equivalent to what can be obtained using a perfect white patch (i.e. perfectly spectrally flat reflectance spectrum), the Wilcoxon Signed-Rank Test [18] is used: a color is considered equivalent to an ideally white surface for von Kries adaptation, if the respective ND cumulative histograms are considered statistically equivalent by the Wilcoxon test.

3   Experimental Results

The experimental results are obtained with simulated data using the theoretical model of image formation reported in Eq. 1. For the sensor spectral sensitivities $\mathbf{C}(\lambda)$, 7 different filter sets are used: 6 correspond to measured sensor sensitivities of digital cameras (i.e. Nikon D1, Nikon D70, Nikon D100, Nikon D5000, Canon 500D, and Sony DXC930); the remaining one are the XYZ color matching functions. The illuminant spectral power distributions are the same 14 used in [19], i.e.: six CIE daylight illuminants (D48, D55, D65, D75, D100, D200), three CIE standard illuminants (A, B, C), a 2000 K Planckian blackbody radiator, a uniform white (UW), and three fluorescent illuminants (F2, F7, F11). The surface spectral reflectances are those of the Gretag Macbeth ColorChecker DC chart (MDC), which is composed of 180 different colored patches.

The color constancy performance are measured using the normalized distance (ND) metric (see Eq.9), choosing the white-patch descriptor vectors calculated for D65 as the canonical descriptor vectors. We consider a color equivalent to an ideally white surface for von Kries adaptation, if the respective ND cumulative histograms are considered statistically equivalent by the Wilcoxon test under all the 14 illuminants considered. As an example, the ND cumulative histrograms under all the 14 illuminants using the XYZ color matching functions are reported in Fig. 2. Each line corresponds to a different color of the MDC. The red lines correspond to the colored patches considered statistically equivalent to an ideally white surface for von Kries adaptation.

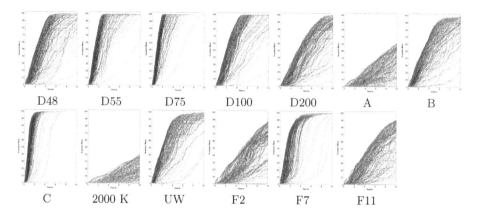

Fig. 2. ND cumulative histrograms under all the 14 illuminants using the XYZ color matching functions. The red lines correspond to the colored patches considered statistically equivalent to an ideally white surface for von Kries adaptation.

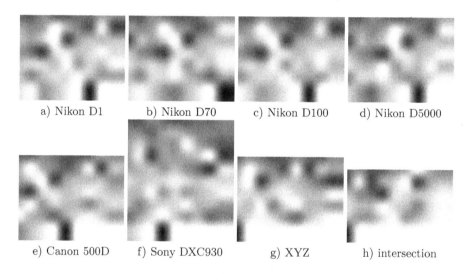

Fig. 3. Patches of the MDC chart considered statistically equivalent to an ideally white surface for von Kries adaptation under all the 14 illuminants for each of the sensor filter sets considered (a-g); intersection of all the patches extracted (h)

In Fig. 3 the patches of the MDC chart considered statistically equivalent to an ideally white surface for von Kries adaptation under all the 14 illuminants are reported for each of the sensor filter sets considered. The intersection of all the patches extracted are also reported.

In Fig. 4 the patches of the MDC chart are plotted in the CIEL*a*b* color space. They are plotted distinguishing the patches considered statistically equivalent to an ideally white surface (black crosses) from those which are not (red dots).

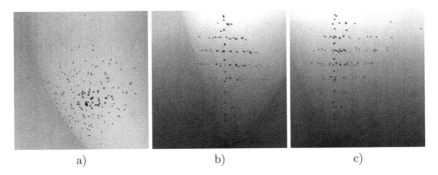

a)   b)   c)

Fig. 4. Patches of the MDC chart reported in the CIEL*a*b* color space: a*b* plane (a), a*L* plane (b), b*L* plane (c). Black crosses: patches considered statistically equivalent to an ideally white surface; red dots: the remaining patches.

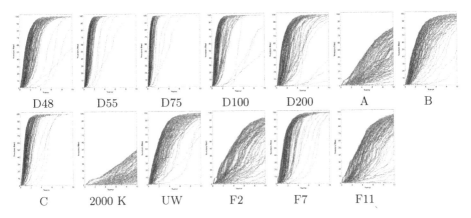

Fig. 5. ND cumulative histrograms under all the 14 illuminants using the XYZ color matching functions with the CAT02 chromatic adaptation transform. The red lines correspond to the colored patches considered statistically equivalent to an ideally white surface for von Kries adaptation.

Since it is known that generalized diagonal transforms are able to convey higher color constancy performance [16], we investigate how the use of the CAT02 chromatic adaptation transform [20] modifies the ND cumulative histograms (Fig. 5) and the extracted patches (Fig.6.a) when the XYZ color matching functions are used. In order to have a more compact representation of which hues are most present among the extracted patches, we also plot their color names histogram [21] where to each patch the name with the highest probability is assigned (Fig.6.b); the 11 color names considered are the same used in [21], i.e.: black, blue, brown, gray, green, orange, pink, purple, red, white, and yellow. In the case of sensor transmittances different from the XYZ, it is still possible to compute a sharpening transform using for example the method described in [22].

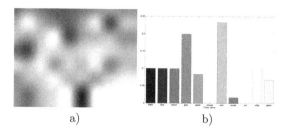

a)   b)

Fig. 6. Patches of the MDC chart considered statistically equivalent to an ideally white surface for von Kries adaptation under all the 14 illuminants using the XYZ color matching functions with the CAT02 chromatic adaptation transform (a). Their color names histogram (b).

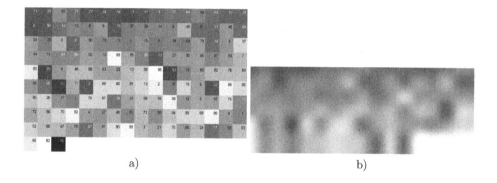

a)   b)

Fig. 7. Patches composing the couples that considered statistically equivalent to a white patch (a). Remaining patches after removing all the couples containing one of the patches reported in Fig. 3.h.

From the comparison of Fig. 5 and Fig. 2 it is possible to notice how all the ND cumulative histograms have been moved towards the upper left corner of the plot, indicating higher color constancy performance under all the illuminants considered. Together with the increase in color constancy performance, the use of the chromatic adaptation transform is also able to increase the number of colored patches considered statistically equivalent to an ideally white surface for von Kries adaptation: using the CAT02 the number of extracted patches is 60, while using only the XYZ CMF it was 55, which is almost a 9.1% increase.

The analysis on single colors is now extended to couples of colors using Eq. 7 for the computation of the diagonal mapping. In Fig. 7 the patches that compose the couples considered statistically equivalent to an ideally white surface for von Kries adaptation under all the 14 illuminants with all the filter sets considered are reported. In the upper right corner of each colored patch is reported the number of extracted couples in which it appeared.

In Fig. 8 the patches of the MDC chart are plotted in the CIEL*a*b* color space. They are plotted distinguishing the patches which formed couples

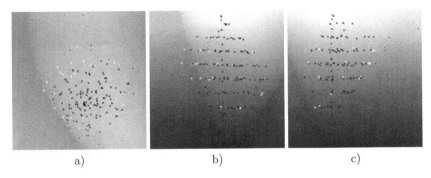

Fig. 8. Patches of the MDC chart reported in the CIEL*a*b* color space: a*b* plane (a), a*L* plane (b), b*L* plane (c). Black crosses: patches in couples considered statistically equivalent to an ideally white surface and appeared in more than 10 couples; yellow stars: patches appeared in less than 10 couples; red dots: the remaining patches.

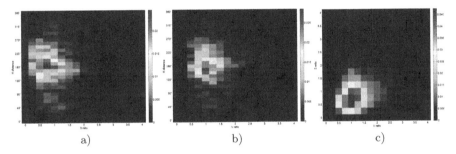

Fig. 9. 2D histograms of the angular distance between the hues, the ratio of the saturations, and the ratio of the values for the colors forming the couples.

considered statistically equivalent to an ideally white surface and appeared in more than 10 couples (black crosses), from those in couples statistically equivalent but appeared in less than 10 couples (yellow stars), from those in couples not statistically equivalent (red dots).

In order to investigate how the couples are composed, we first eliminate all the couples in which at least one of the colors is one of those reported in Fig. 3.h. The remaining colors are reported in Fig. 7.b. The couples formed by the colors in Fig. 7.b are then analyzed as follows: the two colors are converted into the HSV color space and then the angular distance between the hues, the ratio of the saturations, and the ratio of the values are computed. The 2D histograms of these 3 quantities are reported in Fig. 9.

From the histograms reported in Fig. 9 it is possible to see that the couples are mostly composed of opponent colors (the H distance is mainly included in the $[135°, 270°]$ interval); it is also possible to note that there is a number of couples that satisfy the gray world assumption [23] (i.e. their average color is gray): they correspond to the bin in the histogram with H distance equal to $180°$ and S ratio equal to 1.

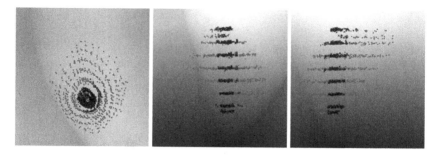

Fig. 10. Patches of the Munsell atlas reported in the CIEL*a*b* color space: a*b* plane (a), a*L* plane (b), b*L* plane (c). Black crosses: patches considered statistically equivalent to an ideally white surface; red dots: the remaining patches.

a)   b)

Fig. 11. Patches of the Munsell atlas considered statistically equivalent to an ideally white surface for von Kries adaptation under all the illuminants and sensor filter sets considered (a). Their color names histogram (b).

In order to have a more populated plots than those reported in Fig. 4, the same analysis carried out for the MDC chart, is now applied to the Munsell atlas. The single colors considered statistically equivalent to an ideally white surface for von Kries adaptation are reported in Fig. 10 and 11.a. In Fig.11.b their color names [21] histogram are also reported, where to each patch the name with the highest probability is assigned.

4   Conclusions

In this work it has been investigated if the von Kries adaptation can be generalized to colored patches. In fact von Kries adaptation is a channel-independent scaling where each component is the reciprocal of the sensor response induced from a reference patch, which is usually white. This paper gives a procedure to determine which colored patches can give statistically equivalent performance to a white patch for von Kries adaptation. The simulations have been carried out 14 different illuminants and 7 different sensor sets. The investigation is then extended to couples of colors, and the analysis of the characteristics of the colors forming the extracted couples is carried out. The procedure can be applied to color sets of any cardinality; the results can not be given here due to the lack of space.

References

1. Hordley, S.D.: Scene illuminant estimation: past, present, and future. Color Research & Application 31(4), 303–314 (2006)
2. Gijsenij, A., Gevers, T., van de Weijer, J.: Computational color constancy: survey and experiments. IEEE TIP 20(9), 2475–2489 (2011)
3. Funt, B., Barnard, K., Martin, L.: Is Machine Colour Constancy Good Enough? In: Burkhardt, H.-J., Neumann, B. (eds.) ECCV 1998. LNCS, vol. 1406, pp. 445–459. Springer, Heidelberg (1998)
4. Bianco, S., Ciocca, G., Cusano, C., Schettini, R.: Automatic Color Constancy Algorithm Selection and Combination. Pattern Recognition 43(3), 695–705 (2010)
5. Gijsenij, A., Gevers, T.: Color Constancy using Natural Image Statistics and Scene Semantics. IEEE TPAMI 33(4), 687–698 (2011)
6. Bianco, S., Ciocca, G., Cusano, C., Schettini, R.: Improving Color Constancy Using Indoor-Outdoor Image Classification. IEEE TIP 17(12), 2381–2392 (2008)
7. van de Weijer, J., Schmid, C., Verbeek, J.: Using High-Level Visual Information for Color Constancy. In: IEEE ICCV, pp. 1–8 (2007)
8. Hel-Or, H.Z., Wandell, B.A.: Object-based illuminant classification. Pattern Recognition 35(8), 1723–1732 (2002)
9. Moreno, A., Fernando, B., Kani, B., Saha, S., Karaoglu, S.: Color Correction: A Novel Weighted Von Kries Model Based on Memory Colors. In: Schettini, R., Tominaga, S., Trémeau, A. (eds.) CCIW 2011. LNCS, vol. 6626, pp. 165–175. Springer, Heidelberg (2011)
10. Bianco, S., Schettini, R.: Color constancy using faces. In: IEEE CVPR, pp. 65–72 (2012)
11. Geusebroek, J.M., Burghouts, G.J., Smeulders, A.W.M.: The Amsterdam library of object images. IJCV 61(1), 103–112 (2005)
12. Wandell, B.A.: The synthesis and analysis of color images. IEEE TPAMI 9(1), 2–13 (1987)
13. Finlayson, G.D., Hordley, S.D., Hubel, P.M.: Color by correlation: a simple, unifying framework for color constancy. IEEE TPAMI 23(11), 1209–1221 (2001)
14. West, G., Brill, M.H.: Necessary and sufficient conditions for von Kries chromatic adaptation to give colour constancy. J. of Math. Biol. 15, 249–258 (1982)
15. Land, E.H.: The retinex theory of color vision. Scientific American 237(6), 108–128 (1977)
16. Finlayson, G.D., Drew, M.S., Funt, B.V.: Color constancy: generalized diagonal transforms suffice. JOSA A 11(11), 3011–3019 (1994)
17. Forsyth, D.: A novel algorithm for color constancy. IJCV 5, 5–36 (1990)
18. Wilcoxon, F.: Individual comparisons by ranking methods. Biometrics 1, 80–83 (1945)
19. Bianco, S., Bruna, A., Naccari, F., Schettini, R.: Color space transformations for digital photography exploiting information about the illuminant estimation process. JOSA A 29(3), 374–384 (2012)

20. Moroney, N., Fairchild, M.D., Hunt, R.W.G., Li, C., Luo, M.R., Newman, T.: The CIECAM02 Color Appearance Model. In: Proc. of the 10th CIC, pp. 23–27 (2002)
21. van de Weijer, J., Schmid, C., Verbeek, J., Larlus, D.: Learning Color Names for Real-World Applications. IEEE TIP 18(7), 1512–1524 (2009)
22. Chong, H.Y., Gortler, S.J., Zickler, T.: The von Kries hypothesis and a basis for color constancy. In: IEEE ICCV, pp. 1–8 (2007)
23. Buchsbaum, G.: A spatial processor model for object color perception. Journal of Franklin Institute 310, 1–26 (1980)

An Effective Method for Illumination-Invariant Representation of Color Images

Takahiko Horiuchi[1], Abdelhameed Ibrahim[1,2],
Hideki Kadoi[1], and Shoji Tominaga[1]

[1] Graduate School of Advanced Integration Science, Chiba University,
Yayoi-cho 1-33, Inage-ku, Chiba 263-8522, Japan
[2] Faculty of Engineering, Mansoura University, Mansoura, Egypt
{horiuchi,shoji}@faculty.chiba-u.jp

Abstract. This paper proposes a method for illumination-invariant representation of natural color images. The invariant representation is derived, not using spectral reflectance, but using only RGB camera outputs. We suppose that the materials of target objects are composed of dielectric or metal, and the surfaces include illumination effects such as highlight, gloss, or specularity. We preset the procedure for realizing the invariant representation in three steps: (1) detection of specular highlight, (2) illumination color estimation, and (3) invariant representation for reflectance color. The performance of the proposed method is examined in experiments using real-world objects including metals and dielectrics in detail. The limitation of the method is also discussed. Finally, the proposed representation is applied to the edge detection problem of natural color images.

Keywords: Illumination-invariant, color image, highlight detection, spectral reflectance estimation.

1 Introduction

Color information observed from object surfaces provides crucial information in computer vision and image analysis which include the essential problems of feature detection, image segmentation, object recognition, and image retrieval. However, in real-world applications there are various illumination factors that can affect the appearance of color images captured from object surfaces. The captured images do not only depend on surface-spectral reflectances and illuminant spectrum, but also include reflection effects such as shading, gloss, and highlight, which mainly depend on illumination geometries and surface materials. Therefore, image representations invariant to shading, shadow, lighting, and specularity have been proposed for color images [1-4] and for spectral images [5, 6] so far in several ways. However, most of the illumination-invariant methods used the standard dichromatic reflection model by Shafer [7]. This model is valid for such limited materials of inhomegeneous dielectrics as plastics and paints. It should be noted that there are metallic objects in real-world scenes, which cannot be described by the standard dichromatic reflection model.

A. Fusiello et al. (Eds.): ECCV 2012 Ws/Demos, Part II, LNCS 7584, pp. 401–410, 2012.

In our previous studies, we proposed an invariant representation for a variety of real-world objects including metals and dielectrics [8]. We showed that the normalized surface spectral reflectance by the minimum reflectance was invariant to illumination effects and the representation was effective to spectral imaging applications [9]. However, the method requires an expensive and special measurement device such as a spectral imaging system and a standard white reference. Furthermore, long measurement time is necessary due to acquisition of the high-dimensional spectral data.

The present paper proposes a method for illumination-invariant representation of natural color images captured by an off-the-shelf RGB camera, and its application to image processing. The illumination-invariant representation of spectral reflectance is not available directly for this problem because the illuminant spectrum is unknown. We derive the invariant representation by not using spectral reflectance, but using only three sensor outputs. Estimation of illumination (light source) color is required separately. We suppose that the materials of target objects are composed of dielectric or metal, and the surfaces include illumination effects such as highlight, gloss, or specularity. We propose an algorithm for realizing the invariant representation for color images in three steps: (1) detection of specular highlight, (2) illumination color estimation, and (3) invariant representation for object color.

2   Invariant Representation for Spectral Reflectances

The illuminant-invariant representation for surface-spectral reflectances can be derived from the standard dichromatic reflection model for dielectric and the extended reflection model for metal [8]. The spectral reflectances of object surfaces in a scene are observed by specific devices such as a spectral imaging system, a standard white reference, and a spectroradio/photometer. The typical imaging system consists of a liquid crystal tunable (LCT) filter and a monochrome camera. Then it is found that the normalized surface-spectral reflectances by the minimum reflectance among the observed spectral reflectances are invariant to highlight, shading, surface geometry, and illumination intensity. The invariant representation for spectral reflectance is described as

$$S'(\theta, \lambda) = \frac{S(\theta, \lambda) - \min\{S(\theta, \lambda)\}}{\sqrt{\int_{400}^{700} (S(\theta, \lambda) - \min\{S(\theta, \lambda)\})^2 d\lambda}}, \tag{1}$$

where $S(\theta, \lambda)$ is the spectral reflectance function of the wavelength λ, observed in the range of a visible wavelength [400, 700 nm], and the geometric parameters θ, including the direction angles of the viewing angle and the phase angle. For precise spectral representation, spectral images are usually captured at equal interval of 5nm or 10 nm in the visible range. The imaging system using a LCT filter takes more than 150 second to capture 31-band images at 10 nm interval. Therefore, use of expensive devices and long measurement time are bottleneck towards practical use.

3   Principle of Invariant Representation for Color Images

3.1   Dichromatic Reflection Models

The standard dichromatic reflection model suggests that light reflected from the surface of an inhomogeneous dielectric object is composed of interface reflection and body reflection.

Let $\mathbf{C}_S = \left[C_S^{(R)}, C_S^{(G)}, C_S^{(B)} \right]^T$ be a 3-D column vector representing the red, green, and blue sensor responses of a color imaging system. The sensor outputs can be expressed as

$$\mathbf{C}_S = m_I \mathbf{C}_I + m_B \mathbf{C}_B, \tag{2}$$

where the vectors $\mathbf{C}_I$ and $\mathbf{C}_B$ are the color vectors representing, respectively, the interface and body reflection components of the color signal reflected from the object. The weights m_I and m_B are the geometric scale factors.

The standard model incorporates the neutral interface reflection (NIR) assumption which states that the interface reflection component is coincident with the color of light source. This allows Eq.(2) to be written as

$$\mathbf{C}_S = m_I \mathbf{C}_L + m_B \mathbf{C}_B, \tag{3}$$

where $\mathbf{C}_L$ is a constant color vector of light source. It is shown that this ref lection model is valid for a variety of natural and artificial dielectric objects includi ng plastic and paint.

Metal is a homogeneous material that indicates essentially different reflection properties from the dielectric materials. It consists of only interface reflection with the Fresnel reflectance. So, if the surface is shiny and stainless, the body reflection component is negligibly small. A sharp specular highlight is observed only at the viewing angle of the mirrored direction. Thus the surface reflection depends on the incident angle of illumination.

Tominaga [10] shows that the spectral reflection of metal surface can be approximated by a linear combination of only two interface reflection components. This type of surface reflection is called the extended dichromatic reflection model. The color model can be expressed as

$$\mathbf{C}_S = m_{I1} \mathbf{C}_{I1} + m_{I2} \mathbf{C}_{I2}, \tag{4}$$

where the first term in the right hand side corresponds to the specular color component at the normal incident and the second corresponds to the grazing color component at the horizontal incident. It is noted that surface-spectral reflectance is whitened at the grazing angle. Therefore, the observed color vector can be expressed in a linear combination of the metal color at the normal incident and the light source color $\mathbf{C}_L$ as follows

$$\mathbf{C}_S = m_{I1} \mathbf{C}_{I1} + m_{I2} \mathbf{C}_L. \tag{5}$$

3.2   Illuminant-Invariant Representation

We briefly explain an illumination-invariant representation, which is limited to the standard dichromatic reflection model for inhomogeneous dielectric objects, and then extend the invariant representation for all materials including dielectric and metal. We focus on the 3-D RGB-space. Let us consider that illumination is not white but colored without $C_L^{(R)} = C_L^{(G)} = C_L^{(B)}$. Let $\hat{\mathbf{C}}_L$ be an estimate of the illumination color vector obtained in a separate way. Then the influence of illumination color is reduced from the sensor outputs as

$$\hat{\mathbf{C}}_S = \mathbf{C}_S / \hat{\mathbf{C}}_L, \tag{6}$$

where the division "/" is done in element-wise operation. The above equation means the sensor output for the same object surface under a standard white illumination and the transformed color $\hat{\mathbf{C}}_S$ is named "reflectance color" in this paper. With a reliable estimate $\hat{\mathbf{C}}_L$, the standard reflection model in Eq.(3) allows Eq.(6) to be written in the following form

$$\hat{\mathbf{C}}_S = m_I \mathbf{I} + m_B (\mathbf{C}_B / \hat{\mathbf{C}}_L), \tag{7}$$

where $\mathbf{I}$ is a unit vector with $[1/3, 1/3, 1/3]^T$. Thus the sensor vector $\hat{\mathbf{C}}_S$ has a constant specular reflection component. Let $\hat{\mathbf{C}}_B = \mathbf{C}_B / \hat{\mathbf{C}}_L$ be the body color normalized by the light source color, which means the object color observed under white illumination (canonical color). Then, subtraction of one color component from another component provides a representation independent of the specular reflection component as follows

$$\hat{C}_S^{(R)} - \hat{C}_S^{(G)} = (m_I + m_B \hat{C}_B^{(R)}) - (m_I + m_B \hat{C}_B^{(G)}) = m_B (\hat{C}_B^{(R)} - \hat{C}_B^{(G)}), \tag{8}$$

where the geometric weighting coefficient m_I is eliminated. In this case, the ratio of two subtractions between color components can be illumination-invariant, that is, invariant to highlight, shading, and surface geometry by eliminating the remaining weighting coefficient m_B.

$$\frac{\hat{C}_S^{(R)} - \hat{C}_S^{(G)}}{\hat{C}_S^{(G)} - \hat{C}_S^{(B)}} = \frac{m_B (\hat{C}_B^{(R)} - \hat{C}_B^{(G)})}{m_B (\hat{C}_B^{(G)} - \hat{C}_B^{(B)})} = \frac{\hat{C}_B^{(R)} - \hat{C}_B^{(G)}}{\hat{C}_B^{(G)} - \hat{C}_B^{(B)}}. \tag{9}$$

Next, we consider the image sensor outputs for a metal object. In a similar way, the normalization of Eq.(6) is applied to the extended reflection model Eq.(5). We obtain

$$\hat{\mathbf{C}}_S = m_{I1} (\mathbf{C}_{I1} / \hat{\mathbf{C}}_L) + m_{I2} \mathbf{I}. \tag{10}$$

Note that, Eq.(10) for the extended reflection model is the mathematically same fashion as Eq.(7) for the standard model, although the two equations have different physical meaning. Therefore, we derive a unified invariant representation for all materials including dielectric and metal. In fact, an invariant equation for metal is derived from Eq.(10) with $\hat{\mathbf{C}}_{I1} = \mathbf{C}_{I1} / \hat{\mathbf{C}}_L$ as

$$\frac{\hat{C}_S^{(R)} - \hat{C}_S^{(G)}}{\hat{C}_S^{(G)} - \hat{C}_S^{(B)}} = \frac{m_{I1}(\hat{C}_{I1}^{(R)} + m_{I2}) - (m_{I1}\hat{C}_{I1}^{(G)} + m_{I2})}{m_{I1}(\hat{C}_{I1}^{(G)} + m_{I2}) - (m_{I1}\hat{C}_{I1}^{(B)} + m_{I2})} = \frac{\hat{C}_{I1}^{(R)} - \hat{C}_{I1}^{(G)}}{\hat{C}_{I1}^{(G)} - \hat{C}_{I1}^{(B)}}. \tag{11}$$

where the geometric weighting coefficients m_{I1} and m_{I2} are eliminated. We note that the operation of Eq.(11) results in an equivalent operation to Eq.(9), that is invariant to highlights, shading, and geometries.

4   Procedure for Invariant Representation

4.1   Detection of Specular Highlight

It is well-known that specular highlight is useful for illuminant estimation because the spectral reflectance of the interface reflection component is constant over the visible range and the color vector is coincident with illumination color as in Eq.(3). So far, several methods were presented for detecting bright specular highlights on the observed object surfaces (e.g., see [11]). However, note that this illuminant estimation method is available for dielectrics at any incidence angle of illumination, but available for metals at a limited angle with incidence near the grazing angle.

In this paper, we use a highlight detection method based on variable luminance thresholding. First, we calculate the luminance value from the captured RGB image at every pixel and make a luminance histogram for the entire image. Second, highlight candidates are extracted using a single threshold value, which corresponds to the luminance at a clear valley in the distribution curve of the luminance histogram. Third, the extracted candidate areas are labeled based on connectivity of pixels. If the connected pixel count is small, the area is eliminated. Then the connected areas with enough pixel counts are reserved as the highlight areas. Fourth, each highlight area is narrowed by increasing the threshold value, in order to determine precisely the highlight area. The above process is repeated for the respective target regions.

It should be noted that the detection algorithm is very simple, although the detection accuracy is not so high. However, the detection of a few high lights is enough for estimating the illumination color. Therefore, an accurate detection algorithm is not necessary for this purpose. We verified that this detection algorithm was effective empirically.

4.2   Illumination Color Estimation

Considering the dichromatic reflection property, the image data in each detected highlight area of object surfaces are projected onto a 2-D space using two principal components by

$$\begin{bmatrix} \xi_1 \\ \xi_2 \end{bmatrix} = \begin{bmatrix} \mathbf{V}_1^T \\ \mathbf{V}_2^T \end{bmatrix} \mathbf{C}_S \tag{12}$$

where $\mathbf{V}_1$ and $\mathbf{V}_2$ denote the first and second principal component vectors, which are computed from the image data set $\{\mathbf{C}_S\}$ belonging to the highlight area. A histogram of the projected 2-D image data (ξ_1, ξ_2) consists of two clusters for the specular reflection component and the diffuse reflection component according to the dichromatic reflection model. Then, the cluster of specular reflection component indicating the light-source color is extracted to estimate illuminant. Note that the histogram is divided into two linear clusters. Then, the specular cluster corresponds to highlight pixels by the specular reflection.

If the specular highlight area is much brighter than the matte area, the linear highlight cluster is much longer than the linear cluster of the diffuse component, so that the highlight cluster is regarded as a single linear cluster. In this case, the first principal component vector of the highlight cluster corresponds to the directional vector representing the illumination. The illumination color vector can be recovered by extracting the first principal component vector of the highlight cluster and transforming it inversely into the original 3-D color space.

Let $(\hat{\xi}_1, \hat{\xi}_2)$ be the directional vector extracted from the specular highlight cluster. Then the illumination color vector $\hat{\mathbf{C}}_L$ is estimated as follows:

$$\hat{\mathbf{C}}_L = \hat{\xi}_1 \mathbf{V}_1 + \hat{\xi}_2 \mathbf{V}_2. \tag{13}$$

If the object color is similar to the illumination color, the estimation accuracy may decrease.

4.3   Invariant Representation for Reflectance Color

We can generalize the invariant expressions in Eq.(11) to a stable expression based on the subtraction between any color component and the minimal component. The generalized representation for the reflectance color $\hat{\mathbf{C}}_S$ is given as

$$\hat{C'}_S^{(i)} = \frac{\hat{C}_S^{(i)} - \min\{\hat{C}_S^{(R)}, \hat{C}_S^{(G)}, \hat{C}_S^{(B)}\}}{\sqrt{\sum_{j \in \{R,G,B\}} \left(\hat{C}_S^{(j)} - \min\left\{\hat{C}_S^{(R)}, \hat{C}_S^{(G)}, \hat{C}_S^{(B)}\right\}\right)^2}}. \tag{14}$$

This representation is effective in the sense of measurement and computation time.

5   Experiments

Figure 1(a) shows an experimental scene, including a metal object of copper and two dielectric objects of ceramic (cup) and plastic (frog), which are illuminated with the light source of an incandescent lamp. The color images were captured using a Canon 5D Mark II digital camera. We assume that the specular highlight pixels are not clipped. The image with 445×273 pixels in Fig.1 (a) was analyzed.

First, four areas surrounded by yellow rectangles in Fig.1 (a) are the detection results of specular highlight areas. Second, the illumination color vector $\hat{\mathbf{C}}_L$ was estimated at each decected highlight region by the principal component analysis of highlight clusters in 2D histogram of these areas, as shown in Sec.4.2. Then the estimated color vectors were averaged. The estimated illumination color vector was then compared with a direct measurement using a standard white reference. A fairly good coincidence between the estimate and the measurement was obtained with the RMSE of 0.044. Figs. 1(b) and 1(c) show the surface

color image corrected from the observed image using the white reference and
the surface color image corrected using the estimated illumination color vector,
respectively. These corrections were done by element-wise division as indicated
in Eq.(6). These results suggest that the influences of illumination color are
reduced in the surface color images corrected using the estimated illumination
color vector $\hat{\mathbf{C}}_L$.

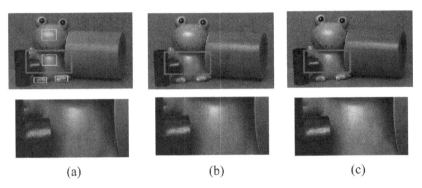

(a)   (b)   (c)

Fig. 1. Color image correction: (a) observed color image and detected highlight regions;
(b) corrected image using the white reference; (c) corrected image using the estimated
illumination color vector

Figure 2(a) depicts a 3-D view of a single channel image (R channel) for
the small rectangular area including metal and dielectrics. That is, the figure
represents the R component of reflectance. Note that the reflectance color image
has the influences of shading and specularity. In contrast, 2(b) shows the 3-D
view of the illumination-invariant representation for the same part at the R-
channel. Note that all shadows and highlights disappear from the original color
image, so that the invariant image is composed of only the reflection component
inherent to each object surface.

It is obvious that the proposed invariant method for color images is simpler
and faster than the invariant method for spectral images in Ref. [8]. However,
the proposed method based on color images has a limitation. It is the problem
of metamer. For instance, our invariant representation may become the same
between two object surfaces, even if those are different spectrally. Figure 3(a)
shows a test scene, which has two plastic objects with similar object colors but
slightly different surface spectral reflectances as shown in Fig. 3(b). Figures 4(a)
and 4(b) show the invariant representations using the spectral image and the
color image, respectively. Figures 4(c) and 4(d) shows their region classification
results using the normalized cut approximated by the Nyström method. Two
objects are segregated in Fig. 4(c) and not segregated in Fig. 4(d), although
illumination effects disappear from both objects. An additional processing may
be required for such an object classification.

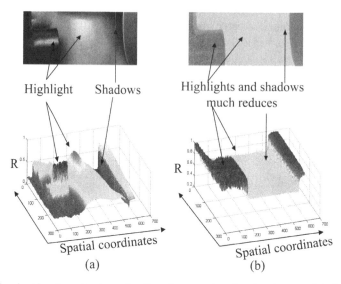

Fig. 2. Illumination-invariant evaluation for a natural color image. (a) 3-D view of the component image at the R-channel; (b) 3-D view of the illumiantion-invariant representation for the same part at the R-channel.

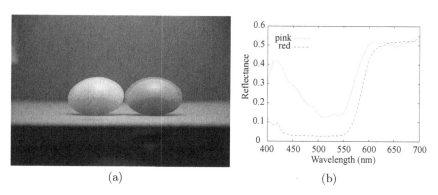

Fig. 3. A test scene. (a) original color image. (b) Surface-spectral reflectances for two plastic objects in (a).

Fig. 4. Experimental results for Fig. 3(a). (a) Invariant representation from the spectral image. (b) Invariant representation from the color image. (c) Object classification result from the spectral image. (d) Object classification result from the color image.

6   Applications to Edge Detection

Let us consider the edge detection problem of natural color images based on the proposed illumination-invariant representation. We calculate the gray-scale edge strength using the Gaussian color model [2] from the normalized color values and the illumination-invariant representation to show the effectiveness of the reflectance color images in reducing the illumination conditions. A white light source is assumed in the present experiment. Figure 5(a) shows a color test scene used in Ref. [3]. Figure 5(b) depicts the gray-scale edge strength of the original tested part. The binary edges are automatically calculated by Otsu's method from the gray-scale image. The upper images and lower images indicate gray-scale images and binary images, respectively. The result contains many shadows and highlights effects. Figure 5(c) shows the gray-scale edges of the proposed representation. The edges clearly separate different materials of metal and dielectric. Thus the proposed representation is independent of the illumination effects of highlight and shadow, and the geometry of object shape. To confirm the usefulness of the proposed method, the first results using the photometric quasi-invariant method [3] are shown in Fig. 5(d) with binary edges. The second result using the color invariance method [2] are shown in Fig. 5(e).

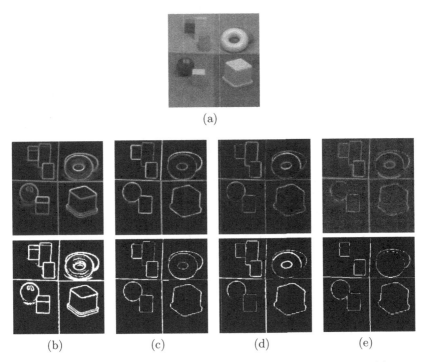

(a)

(b)   (c)   (d)   (e)

Fig. 5. Edge detection evaluation; (a) a color test scene [3], (b) all edges, (c) proposed invariant method (d) quasi-invariant method [3], (e) color invariant method [2]

7 Conclusion

This paper has proposed a method for illumination-invariant representation of natural color images. The target objects were supposed to be dielectric and metal, and the surfaces included illumination effects such as highlight, gloss, or specularity. The procedure for realizing the invariant representation consisted of three steps: (1) detection of specular highlight, (2) illumination color estimation, and (3) invariant representation for reflectance color. The performance of the proposed method was examined in experiments using real-world objects including metals and dielectrics in detail. The results showed that the proposed representation was invariant to highlight, shadow, object surface geometry, and illumination intensity. Moreover, we applied the invariant representation to the edge detection problem successfully.

We also explore as a future work an objective evaluation of the proposed invariant representation for complex scenes including noise.

References

1. Burghouts, G.J., Geusebroek, J.-M.: Performance Evaluation of Local Colour Invariants. Computer Vision and Image Understanding 113, 48–62 (2009)
2. Geusebroek, J.M., Boomgard, R.V., Smeulders, A.W.M., Geerts, H.: Color Invariance. IEEE Trans. Pattern Analysis and Machine Intelligence 23, 1338–1350 (2001)
3. van de Weijer, J., Gevers, T., Geusebroek, J.M.: Edge and Corner Detection by Photometric Quasi-Invariants. IEEE Trans. Pattern Analysis and Machine Intelligence 27, 625–630 (2005)
4. van de Weijer, J., Gevers, T., Smeulders, A.W.M.: Robust Photometric Invariant Features from the Color Tensor. IEEE Trans. Image Processing 15, 118–127 (2006)
5. Stokman, H.M.G., Gevers, T.: Detection and Classification of Hyper-spectral Edge. In: Proc. 10th British Machine Vision Conference, pp. 643–651 (1999)
6. Montoliu, R., Pla, F., Klaren, A.K.: Multispectral invariants. Technical Report, DLSI, Universitat Jaume I (2004)
7. Shafer, S.A.: Using Color to Separate Reflection Components. Color Research and Applications 10, 210–218 (1985)
8. Ibrahim, A., Tominaga, S., Horiuchi, T.: A spectral Invariant Representation of Spectral Reflectance. Optical Review 18, 231–236 (2011)
9. Ibrahim, A., Tominaga, S., Horiuchi, T.: Invariant Representation for Spectral Reflectance Images and Its Application. EURASIP Journal on Image and Video Processing 2011 (2011)
10. Tominaga, S.: Dichromatic Reflection Models for a Variety of Materials. Color Research and Applications 19, 277–285 (1994)
11. Imai, Y., Kato, Y., Kadoi, H., Horiuchi, T., Tominaga, S.: Estimation of Multiple Illuminants Based on Specular Highlight Detection. In: Schettini, R., Tominaga, S., Trémeau, A. (eds.) CCIW 2011. LNCS, vol. 6626, pp. 85–98. Springer, Heidelberg (2011)

Specularity, the Zeta-image, and Information-Theoretic Illuminant Estimation

Mark S. Drew[1], Hamid Reza Vaezi Joze[1], and Graham D. Finlayson[2]

[1] School of Computing Science,
Simon Fraser University
{mark,hrv1}@cs.sfu.ca
[2] School of Computing Sciences,
University of East Anglia
graham@cmp.uea.ac.uk

Abstract. Identification of illumination is an important problem in imaging. In this paper we present a new and effective physics-based colour constancy algorithm which makes use of a novel log-relative-chromaticity planar constraint. We call the new feature the Zeta-image. We show that this new feature is tied to a novel application of the Kullback-Leibler Divergence, here applied to chromaticity values instead of probabilities. The new method requires no training data or tunable parameters. Moreover it is simple to implement and very fast. Our experimental results across datasets of real images show the proposed method significantly outperforms other unsupervised methods while its estimation accuracy is comparable with more complex, supervised, methods. As well, the new planar constraint can be used as a post-processing stage for any candidate colour constancy method in order to improve its accuracy.

1 Introduction

Identification of illumination is an important problem in image processing for digital cameras, for both still images and video. In a scene consisting of dielectric materials (e.g., plastics, and indeed most non-metals) there is typically substantive specular content. This does not necessarily mean extremely bright mirror-like reflection, but can consist for example of the glint of light reflected from blades of grass, or the sheen of light reflected from a desk surface. For non-metals, this very common specular content is an important indicator of the colour of the lighting in a scene.

Many colour constancy algorithms have been proposed (see [1, 2] for an overview). The foundational colour constancy method, the so-called White-Patch or Max-RGB method, estimates the light source colour from the maximum response of the different colour channels. Another well-known colour constancy method is based on the Grey-World hypothesis, which assumes that the average reflectance in the scene is achromatic. Grey-Edge is a recent version of the Grey-World hypothesis that says: the average of the reflectance differences in a

A. Fusiello et al. (Eds.): ECCV 2012 Ws/Demos, Part II, LNCS 7584, pp. 411–420, 2012.

scene is achromatic [3]. The Gamut Mapping algorithm, a more complex and more accurate algorithm, was introduced by Forsyth [4]. It is based on the assumption that in real-world images, for a given illuminant one observes only a limited number of colours. Several extensions have been proposed.

Lee [5] proposed a method which uses specularity to compute illumination by using the fact that in the CIE chromaticity diagram the coordinates of the colours from different points from the same surface will fall on a straight line connected to the specular point. This is the case when the light reflected from a uniform surface is an additive mixture of the specular component and the diffuse component. This seminal work initiated a substantial body of work on identifying specular pixels and using these to attempt to discover the illuminant (e.g. [6, 7]). Although these works are theoretically strong, none of them reports performance over real world datasets of images with and without specularities.

In this paper, we set out a new discovery, consisting of a planar constraint that must be obeyed, in a certain standard model of reflectance, by specular or near-specular pixels in an image. The new feature involved we call the Zeta-image,[1] and below we show that this feature is tied to the information-theoretic concept of applying one distribution to generate bitstring codes for another; here we view chromaticity components, which add to 1, in the role of probabilities. We present a novel physics-based colour constancy algorithm based on a log-relative-chromaticity planar constraint, which requires no training data or tunable parameters. It is easy to implement and very fast compared to more complex colour constancy methods such as gamut mapping. Our experimental results over three large datasets of both laboratory and real world images show that the proposed method significantly outperforms other unsupervised methods while its accuracy of estimation is comparable with more complex methods that need training data and tunable parameters.

2   Relative Chromaticity Near Specular Point

2.1   Image Formation Model and Relative Chromaticity

Let the RGB 3-vector at each pixel be denoted $\boldsymbol{R}$, with components $R_k, k = 1..3$. Let the RGB 3-vector for the light itself as seen by the camera be e_k, and let the 3-vector for the reflectance at a pixel as seen by the camera, under equi-energy white light, be s_k. Now in a product-of-vectors simple model [8] we approximately have the matte ("body", i.e., non-specular) RGB value at that pixel equal to

$$R_k \simeq \sigma s_k e_k / q_k \tag{1}$$

where σ is shading. In the standard Lambertian model for matte shading, σ equals lighting-direction dotted into surface normal. Here, q_k is a triple giving the overall (integrated) camera sensor strength [9].

If we also consider an additional specular component, this equation becomes

$$R_k \simeq \sigma s_k e_k / q_k + \beta e_k \tag{2}$$

---

[1] Patent applied for.

where β represents the amount of specular component at that pixel. The value of β for a pixel will depend upon the lighting direction, the surface normal, and the viewing geometry. Here, the specular component βe_k is simply assumed to be the same colour as the light itself, in a Neutral Interface Model [5] for dielectrics. For purposes of discovering properties of this equation, let us assume for the time being that β is simply a constant — in actuality it will be a scalar property of each pixel and this issue is further discussed below in §2.3. Let us lump values $\sigma s_k/q_k$ into a single quantity and for convenience call this simply s_k. Now we have

$$R_k = s_k e_k + \beta e_k \qquad (3)$$

The chromaticity ρ_k is colour without magnitude, in an L_1 norm: $\rho = \{R, G, B\}/(R + G + B)$, so here we have

$$\rho_k = \frac{s_k e_k + \beta e_k}{\sum_{j=1}^{3}(s_j e_j + \beta e_j)} \qquad (4)$$

Let the chromaticity of the light itself be denoted $\rho_k^e = e_k/\sum_j e_j$. Now here we wish to examine the properties of the Relative Chromaticity, which we define to be the chromaticity divided by the chromaticity of the light, ρ_k^e. Let us call this quotient chromaticity χ_k, so that

$$\chi_k = \frac{\rho_k}{\rho_k^e} = \frac{s_k e_k + \beta e_k}{\sum_{j=1}^{3}(s_j e_j) + \beta \sum_{j=1}^{3} e_j} \cdot \frac{\sum_{j=1}^{3} e_j}{e_k} \qquad (5)$$

where all divisions are taken to be component-wise. Dividing by the light chromaticity is the main innovative step in this paper: it is an *ansatz* that we claim will bear fruit by generating a constraint on the illuminant colour.

For convenience, let $E \equiv \sum_{j=1}^{3} e_j = |e|$ where $|\cdot|$ is the L_1 norm. Then we arrive at

$$\chi_k = \frac{s_k + \beta}{\frac{(\sum_j s_j e_j)}{E} + \beta} \qquad (6)$$

So, for a pixel with no matte component s_k but only a purely specular component, we would have $\chi_k \equiv 1$ for all 3-vector elements $k = 1..3$.

2.2   Log-Relative-Chromaticity and Planar Constraint

Next we show that in fact log values are preferable, in that a simple planarity constraint falls out of the formulation once we move to the log domain.

Let us define a new quantity, ψ, which is the logarithm of the ratio χ defined above: we call this the Log-Relative-Chromaticity:

$$\psi_k = \log(\chi_k) = \log(\rho_k/\rho_k^e) \qquad (7)$$

Now *near* a specular point, we can take the limit as $(1/\beta) \to 0$. Let $\alpha = 1/\beta$. Then in the limit as specularity increases, ψ goes to

$$\psi_k = \lim_{\alpha \to 0} \log\left\{(\alpha s_k + 1)/\left(\alpha \sum_j(s_j e_j)/E + 1\right)\right\}$$

Using a Maclaurin series,

$$\psi_k = \alpha \left(s_k - \frac{\sum_j s_j e_j}{E} \right) + O\left(\alpha^2\right) \tag{8}$$

Omitting $O\left(\alpha^2\right)$, we note by inspection that the quantity ψ_k is *orthogonal to the illuminant vector*:

$$\sum_k \psi_k e_k \equiv 0 \text{ , so also } \sum_k \psi_k \rho_k^e = 0 \tag{9}$$

Therefore we have a planar constraint on image pixels that are near-specular:

Planar Constraint: *For near-specular pixels, Log-Relative-Chromaticity values are orthogonal to the light chromaticity.*

Note that in eq. (8) above we have expressed this orthogonality in a different way than the usual, Euclidean-norm based calculation of the part of the vector *s* that is orthogonal to vector *e* , *viz.* $(s_k - \boldsymbol{s} \cdot \hat{\boldsymbol{e}} \, \hat{e}_k)$ for normalized light vector $\hat{\boldsymbol{e}}$. Nevertheless, it is easy to verify that eq. (9) does indeed hold. Eq. (8) means an L_1-based projection onto the plane orthogonal to the light.

2.3   Varying Specular Factor β

The fact that specular scalar factor β is not a constant makes no difference to the argument: for near-specular pixels any value of β still leads to quantity ψ_k lying in the plane orthogonal to the illuminant.

3   Planar Constraint Method

Here we begin construction of an algorithm by considering first a simple search method as motivation, and then stating an analytic solution.

3.1   Global Search

The planar constraint suggests that the dot product for near-light-colour (e.g., specular) pixels is minimized for the correct illuminant. This points to a useful descriptor for finding the specular point.

Suppose we were to assume that for any candidate illuminant the lowest 10-percentile, say, of dot-product values (9) could be near-specular pixels. Now, to find the correct illuminant, we need to minimize dot-product values (9) over candidate illuminants for those lowest 10-percentile pixels. Thus an optimization can be stated as follows:

Define the **Zeta-image** ζ as the dot-product of the log-relative-chromaticity ψ , eq. (7), with a putative light direction:

$$\zeta = -\psi \cdot \boldsymbol{\rho}^e = -\log(\boldsymbol{\rho}/\boldsymbol{\rho}^e) \cdot \boldsymbol{\rho}^e \tag{10}$$

$$Minimize: \qquad \min_{\rho^e} \; \mathcal{I} = \sum_{\psi \in \Psi_0} |\zeta|$$

$$\text{subject to } \sum_{k=1}^{3} \rho_k^e = 1, \; 0 < \rho_k^e < 1, \; k = 1..3 \tag{11}$$

where Ψ_0 is the set of pixel dot-product values (9) with the candidate illuminant chromaticity ρ^e that are in the lowest 10-percentile.

The meaning of eq. (11) is that we first carry out a search, over possible illuminant chromaticities ρ^e. This can be phrased as either an optimization-based approach or, as here, a simple hierarchical grid search. Then we adopt a heuristic that says that the lowest 10-percentile of values of dot-products with the candidate illuminant could be specular or in general illuminant-coloured. For these pixels we calculate the sum of absolute values of dot-products and take as the best candidate light that which delivers the minimum sum.

Fig. 1(a) shows an input image, and Fig. 1(b) shows a boolean map of the lowest 10-percentile of dot-product values (9) with the correct illuminant chromaticity of that image. In contrast, if we show the lowest 10-percentile of dot products with the chromaticity of an incorrect light, where ψ values are constructed using that incorrect light, the boolean map identifying putative specular/light-coloured pixels is as displayed in Fig. 1(c). We see that using the correct light produces a much more plausible map of possible pixels that will help identify the light.

The float-valued Zeta-image is displayed in Fig. 1(d). We show next that we can directly use the Zeta-image to analytically find the correct illuminant.

3.2 Analytic Solution

Having motivated the method, we now state an analytic solution that in fact produces excellent results and is very simple and fast. Suppose we identify a possible set Ψ_0 of specular pixels by any convenient method — e.g., we could simply take the top 5% of brightness.

Let the number of bright pixels be N. Then our analytic solution is as follows: **Theorem:** Up to an L_1 normalization, **the light colour is given by the geometric mean**

$$\rho_k^e = g(\rho_k) \equiv \left(\prod_{i=1}^{N} \rho_k^i \right)^{1/N}, \; k = 1..3 \tag{12}$$

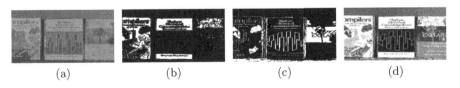

(a)	(b)	(c)	(d)

Fig. 1. (a): Image taken under measured illuminant. (b): Light-coloured pixels identified using planar constraint, when correct illuminant is chosen. (c): Putative light-coloured pixels for incorrect illuminant. (d): Analytic Zeta-image (float, 1-intensity).

To prove this, let us first solve an auxiliary optimization replacing (11). For physical lights, we expect ζ from eq. (10) to be non-negative, so [with no absolute-value bars as in $\mathcal{I}$ in eq. (11)] we first solve

$$\min_{\boldsymbol{\rho}^e} \sum_i \zeta_i + \lambda \left(\sum_{k=1}^3 \rho_k^e - 1\right) \tag{13}$$

where $i = 1..N$ ranges over the N pixels in $\boldsymbol{\psi} \in \Psi_0$, and λ is a Lagrange multiplier enforcing that $\boldsymbol{\rho}^e$ is a chromaticity. Taking partial derivatives with respect to ρ_k^e we have the normal equations

$$-\sum_i \left[\log\left(\rho_k^i\right) - \log\left(\rho_k^e\right) - 1\right] + \lambda = 0, \text{ with solution } \rho_k^e = g(\boldsymbol{\rho}_k) \cdot \exp(-(N+\lambda)/N).$$

The meaning of (13) then is: **The planarity constraint yields the geometric mean of the chromaticities as the solution for the light,** up to trivial scaling of the L_1-norm.

However so far we have omitted absolute value bars, with a full optimization minimizing $\mathcal{I} = \sum_i |\zeta_i|$. We now observe that the form (10) formally has the structure of the Kullback-Leibler Divergence from information theory, in that chromaticities for image, ρ_k^i, and light, ρ_k^e all add to unity: $\sum_{k=1}^3 \rho_k = 1$. We are minimizing $\sum_{i=1}^N [\sum_{k=1}^3 -\rho_k^e \log(\rho_k^i/\rho_k^e)]$, which has the K-L structure except that instead of summing over probabilities for symbols we are here summing over colour-channels. Thus each dot product (the sum over k at each pixel) is necessarily nonnegative since it represents the extra bits required to code samples from ρ_k^e when using a code based on ρ_k^i. Hence we can simply consider the minimization (13), with solution (12) up to scaling. □

As a final step, we calculate a final value for ρ_k^e by trimming pixels to the least-10% values of the Zeta-image ζ and recalculating the geometric mean (12).

Areas of images that are specular tend to be bright. According to our theory the geometric mean of pixels in these bright (generally, specular) regions is the optimal estimate for the illuminant. Our insight is in contradistinction to the work of Choudhury and Medioni [10] and Funt and Shi [11] which proposed finding the max after a local mean calculation (e.g. after local blurring). In the presence of specular highlights we instead claim that illuminant estimation is the mean of the max, not the converse. Indeed, using the correct ordering is crucial (a fact borne out by our experiments reported below).

3.3   2nd Algorithm: Planar Constraint Applied as Post-processing

Suppose we have an estimate $\boldsymbol{\rho}^{e\star}$ of the correct illuminant, from any colour constancy algorithm. If our estimate is indeed near the correct illuminant we can then identify as near-specular pixels those whose absolute value of dot-product eq. (9) with the candidate light chromaticity falls in the lowest 10-percentile, say (i.e., nearest to zero). Forming a Singular Value Decomposition of $\boldsymbol{\psi}$ values for those pixels determines the best-fit plane. Within the model presented here that normal should be close to the illuminant chromaticity in direction. Because of the additional evidence brought to bear by eq. (9) we expect the estimate to improve. If instead the illuminant estimate is wrong, then we have found that the above SVD step will almost always not change it much and no harm is done by carrying out this post-processing step. We carry out

$$
\begin{aligned}
\psi_k &= \log\left(\frac{\rho_k}{\rho_k^{e\star}}\right), \ k = 1..3; \quad \Psi = \psi^T \rho^{e\star} ; \\
\psi(\Psi_0) &= SVD(\psi(\Psi_0)) = U\, diag(d)\, V^T ; \\
\rho^e &= V_3/|V_3| ; \quad \text{success} = (d_3 \text{ small}) \& (\rho^e \simeq \rho^{e\star})
\end{aligned}
\tag{14}
$$

where $\rho^{e\star}$ is the estimate of the illumination provided by a colour constancy method, Ψ_0 is the lowest 10-percentile of Ψ, and ρ^e is the estimate of the illumination based on the planar constraint.

The meaning of eq. (14) is that, for any estimate $\rho^{e\star}$ of the light chromaticity ρ^e, if the model (9) is obeyed around the light point then SVD should produce an estimate of the light that agrees with $\rho^{e\star}$.

We demonstrate below that this planar constraint does indeed improve the estimate of ρ^e, verifying the suitability of the plane constraint applied as a post-processing step, for any candidate colour constancy algorithm. In the next section we will demonstrate the substantial improvement delivered by this simple planar constraint when added to each of several well-known colour constancy algorithms as a post-processing step.

4   Experiment Results

4.1   Datasets

We apply our proposed method to three different real-image datasets [12–14] and compare our results to other colour constancy algorithms.

Our first experiment uses the Barnard dataset [12], denoted the SFU Laboratory dataset, which contains 321 measured images under 11 different measured illuminants. The scenes are divided into two sets as follows: minimal specularities (22 scenes, 223 images – i.e., 19 missing images); and non-negligible dielectric specularities (9 scenes, 98 images – 1 illuminant is missing for 1 scene).

For a more real-world (out of the laboratory) image experiment we used the re-processed version of the Gehler colour constancy dataset [15], denoted the ColorChecker dataset [13]. This dataset consists of 568 images, both indoor and outdoor. The illuminant ground truth for these images is known because each image has a Macbeth ColorChecker placed in the scene. The ColorChecker is masked off in tests.

Ciurea and Funt [14] introduced the GreyBall dataset, which contains 11346 images extracted from video recorded under a wide variety of imaging conditions. The images are divided into 15 different clips taken at different locations. The ground truth was acquired by attaching a grey sphere to the camera, displayed in the corner of the image. This grey sphere must be masked during experiments.

4.2   Previous Methods

To compare, we use the standard well-known colour constancy methods: White-Patch, Grey-World, and Grey-Edge implemented by [3]. For Grey-Edge we use optimal settings, which differ per dataset [16] ($p = 7$, $\sigma = 4$ for the SFU Laboratory dataset and $p = 1$, $\sigma = 6$ for the ColorChecker dataset). We also use the result provided by Gijsenij and et al. [17] for pixel-based gamut mapping, using the best general gamut mapping setting, which is for *1st-jet* as reported in [17] (although we could not precisely match their exact results using the code they released). For other methods we use results as provided by Gijsenij [2, 16].

For methods which need training data, such as the gamut mapping methods, in the SFU Laboratory dataset 31 images (all images recorded under the *syl-50MR16Q*-illuminant) were used for computation of the canonical gamut, and subsequently these were omitted from the test set. For the ColorChecker dataset, three-fold cross-validation was used to learn the canonical gamut (with the folds as well as the ground truth supplied with the original dataset). Testing for supervised methods is as described in [2], §VII-A.

4.3   Post-processing

Table 1 shows the accuracy of the plane constraint eq. (14) in §3.3 as a post-processing step applied to the results of each of well-known colour constancy algorithms, in order to improve the estimate.

Table 1. Median of angular errors for well-known colour constancy algorithms for the SFU Laboratory [12] dataset and ColorChecker dataset [13], plus result after post-processing with planar constraint eq. (14) for each colour constancy algorithm

Method	SFU Lab.	ColorChecker
White-Patch	6.5°	5.7°
White-Patch + Planar Con.	5.1°	4.4°
Grey-World	7.0°	6.3°
Grey-World + Planar Con.	5.0°	4.3°
Grey-Edge	3.2°	4.3°
Grey-Edge + Planar Con.	2.7°	3.8°

4.4   Global Search and Analytic Solution Experiment

Table 2 indicates the accuracy of the proposed methods for the SFU Laboratory dataset [12], the ColorChecker dataset [13] and the GreyBall dataset [14], in terms of the mean and median of angular errors, for several colour constancy algorithms applied to these datasets. For those methods which need data-dependent tunable parameters, we utilize optimal parameters for their dataset. For an overview of results of different algorithms on these datasets refer to [2, 16].

To our knowledge, for the SFU Laboratory dataset the Planar Constraint Search eq. (11) does best in terms of median angular error compared to any reported colour constancy method, even those needing training data. We do note that for this dataset the Planar Constraint Search eq. (11) is not the best for the ColorChecker dataset, with Gamut Mapping methods performing better. However, both Planar Search and the Analytic method of §3.2 (Geomean) do as well or better than the other relatively fast methods for the GreyBall dataset, and are only bested by the much more complex method [18].

Run-times average 5.2s for Planar-Constraint Search and 415ms for the Analytic method, compared to 617ms for the GreyEdge algorithm and 63.2s for 1st-Jet Gamut Mapping, operating on the SFU Laboratory dataset using (unoptimized) Matlab.

Table 2. Angular errors for several colour constancy algorithms for SFU Laboratory dataset [12], ColorChecker dataset [13] and GreyBall dataset [14]

Dataset Methods	SFU Labratory		Color Checker		Gray Ball	
	Median	Mean	Median	Mean	Median	Mean
White Patch	6.5°	9.1°	5.7°	7.4°	5.3°	6.8°
Gray World	7.0°	9.8°	6.3°	6.4°	7.0°	7.9°
Gray Edge	3.2°	5.6°	4.5°	5.3°	4.7°	5.9°
Bayesian [15]	-	-	3.5°	4.8°	-	-
Gamut Mapping	2.3°	3.7°	2.5°	4.1°	5.8°	7.1°
Gamut Mapping 1jet [17]	2.1°	3.6°	2.5°	4.1°	5.8°	6.9°
Natural Image Statistics	-	-	3.1°	4.2°	3.9°	5.2°
Planar Constraint Search	1.9°	4.3°	2.8°	4.1°	4.6°	5.9°
Geomean	2.1°	6.2°	2.7°	4.2°	4.7°	5.8°

5   Conclusions

In this paper we present a novel physics-based insight regarding a plane constraint that obtains for log-relative-chromaticity values near the illuminant point (for white surfaces, or specularities in the neutral-interface model). This insight provides a useful and very simple method for identifying the illuminant chromaticity. Experiment results over datasets consisting of laboratory images and of real-world images demonstrate that the proposed method significantly outperforms other unsupervised methods while its accuracy of illuminant estimation is comparable with the best (supervised) methods but much faster. As well, the plane constraint can also be brought to bear to improve estimates provided by other illuminant estimation algorithms, in a post-processing step; experimental results indicate that estimate errors can be reduced by some 15 percent by this simple and very fast mechanism.

References

1. Hordley, S.D.: Scene illuminant estimation: past, present, and future. Color Research and Application 31, 303–314 (2006)
2. Gijsenij, A., Gevers, T., van de Weijer, J.: Computational color constancy: Survey and experiments. IEEE Trans. on Image Proc. 20 (2011)
3. van de Weijer, J., Gevers, T.: Color constancy based on the grey-edge hypothesis. In: Int. Conf. on Image Proc., pp. II:722–II:725 (2005)
4. Forsyth, D.: A novel approach to color constancy. In: Int. Conf. on Computer Vision, pp. 9–18 (1988)
5. Lee, H.: Method for computing the scene-illuminant chromaticity from specular highlights. J. Opt. Soc. Am. A 3, 1694–1699 (1986)
6. Lehmann, T.M., Palm, C.: Color line search for illuminant estimation in real-world scenes. J. Opt. Soc. Amer. A 18, 2679–2691 (2001)
7. Tan, R., Nishino, K., Ikeuchi, K.: Color constancy through inverse-intensity chromaticity space. J. Opt. Soc. Am. A 21, 321–334 (2004)
8. Borges, C.: Trichromatic approximation method for surface illumination. J. Opt. Soc. Am. A 8, 1319–1323 (1991)
9. Drew, M., Finlayson, G.: Multispectral processing without spectra. J. Opt. Soc. Am. A 20, 1181–1193 (2003)
10. Choudhury, A., Medioni, G.: Perceptually motivated automatic color contrast enhancement. In: Color and Reflec. in Imaging and Comp. Vis. Workshop, pp. 1893–1900 (2009)
11. Funt, B.V., Shi, L.: The rehabilitation of MaxRGB. In: 18th Color Imaging Conf., pp. 256–259 (2010)
12. Barnard, K., Martin, L., Funt, B.V., Coath, A.: A data set for colour research. Color Res. and Applic. 27, 147–151 (2002)
13. Shi, L., Funt, B.V.: Re-processed version of the Gehler color constancy dataset of 568 images (2010), http://www.cs.sfu.ca/~colour/data/
14. Ciurea, F., Funt, B.V.: A large image database for color constancy research. In: Color Imag. Conf., pp. 160–164 (2003)
15. Gehler, P., Rother, C., Blake, A., Minka, T., Sharp, T.: Bayesian color constancy revisited. In: Comp. Vis. and Patt. Rec. (2008)
16. Gijsenij, A.: Color constancy: Research website on illuminant estimation (2012), http://staff.science.uva.nl/~gijsenij/colorconstancy/
17. Gijsenij, A., Gevers, T., Weijer, J.: Generalized gamut mapping using image derivative structures for color constancy. Int. J. of Comp. Vis. 86, 127–139 (2008)
18. Gijsenij, A., Gevers, T.: Color constancy using natural image statistics and scene semantics. Trans. on Patt. Anal. and Mach. Intell. 33, 687–698 (2011)

Robust Estimation of Pigment Distributions from Multiband Skin Images and Its Application to Realistic Skin Image Synthesis

Motonori Doi[1], Masahiro Konishi[1], Akira Kimachi[1],
Shogo Nishi[1], and Shoji Tominaga[2]

[1] Osaka Electro-Communication University, Osaka, Japan
[2] Chiba University, Chiba, Japan

Abstract. This paper describes a robust method for estimating pigment distributions on a skin surface from multiband images. The spatial distributions of the pigments such as melanin, oxy-hemoglobin and deoxy-hemoglobin give rise to a color texture. The distributions are estimated by using the Kubelka-Munk theory. The accuracy of estimating the pigment distributions is affected by a fine texture of sulcus cutis and a broad texture of shade caused by three-dimensional body shape. In order to separate these textures from the color texture, wavelet-based multi-resolution analysis (MRA) is applied to the multiband images before the pigment estimation, because the textures of sulcus cutis and shade predominantly have low and high spatial frequency components in the multiband skin images, respectively. Realistic skin image is synthesized from modified pigment distributions with additional features such as stain, inflammation and bruise by changing the concentrations of melanin, oxy-hemoglobin and deoxy-hemoglobin, respectively. The experimental results of skin image synthesis show good feasibility of the proposed method.

Keywords: Skin, Pigment distribution estimation, Multiband image, The Kubelka-Munk theory, Multi-resolution analysis, Skin image synthesis.

1 Introduction

Various texture patterns appear on the surface of human skin. For example, we perceive moles, veins, inflammation and bruise as skin surface textures of dark brown spots, bluish streaks, and red and purple marks, respectively. These color features are caused by high concentration of pigments in the skin. Specifically, melanin, oxy-hemoglobin, and deoxy-hemoglobin make the skin look brownish, reddish, and purplish, respectively. The skin surface also has a fine texture caused by minute grooves called sulcus cutis, and a broad texture of shade caused by three-dimensional body shape. These textures are superimposed on the pigment derived texture.

A. Fusiello et al. (Eds.): ECCV 2012 Ws/Demos, Part II, LNCS 7584, pp. 421–430, 2012.

The analysis and synthesis of these texture features on human skin are important in several research areas, such as computer graphics, medical imaging and cosmetics development. Especially, in computer graphics, the detailed description of human skin is essential for realistic image rendering. It is difficult to generate photorealistic skin image, because the skin surface includes various textures. When we put a conspicuous pattern on a skin image, it is difficult to match its skin color and texture to the color and texture of the surrounding area. Therefore the skin image rendering includes precise color reproduction and synthesis of the complicated tissue patterns. For the realistic skin image rendering, the decomposition of real skin image into texture components and the reconstruction of modified texture components into skin image are required. Our previous work[1] decomposed RGB color image of skin into texture components. Then, images with enhanced texture components were synthesized. However, the method cannot control each texture with different pigment distribution. Tsumura et al. proposed a method for skin texture analysis and synthesis of facial images based on independent component analysis[2]. Their work considered neither the deoxy-hemoglobin absorption nor the texture of sulcus cutis on the skin surface. The skin color image analysis requires accurate estimation of the pigment distributions from real images. It is difficult, however, to distinguish the concentration of oxy-hemoglobin and deoxy-hemoglobin in the RGB color space. Moreover, the superimposed textures of sulcus cutis and shade introduce additional spatial variation in a skin image, hindering accurate estimation of the pigment distributions.

To solve these problems, the present paper proposes a method for robustly estimating the pigment distributions on a human skin surface from multiband images, and synthesizing realistic skin color images using the estimation results. We apply the estimation method of spectral reflectance of skin surface based on the Kubelka-Munk theory[3] to estimate the pigment distributions from multiband images. This method can estimate the concentrations of oxy-hemoglobin and deoxy-hemoglobin, as well as melanin, separately by taking account of the spectral absorption of these pigments. To improve the estimation accuracy, multiresolution analysis (MRA) is adopted to the multiband images as a pre-image processing. The MRA effectively separates the textures of sulcus cutis and shade from the color texture associated with the pigment distributions. At the image synthesis stage, artificial images of human skin with additional features such as stain, inflammation and bruise are realistically produced in combination with the separated textures of sulcus cutis and shade, by changing the estimated distributions of melanin, oxy-hemoglobin and deoxy-hemoglobin.

2   Features of Skin Surface

Skin surface consists of layers of turbid medium. Fig.1(a) shows the rough sketch of skin surface. Top layer of horny substance is almost transparent and has fine grooves of skin surface. Fig.1(b) shows the texture of fine grooves by sulcus cutis. Skin surface roughness by sulcus cutis gives fine texture to skin. Epidermis

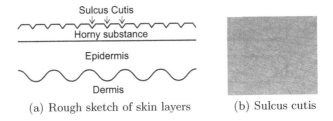

Sulcus Cutis

Horny substance

Epidermis

Dermis

(a) Rough sketch of skin layers   (b) Sulcus cutis

Fig. 1. Skin layers and sulcus cutis

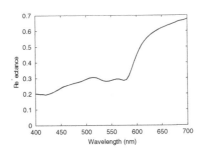

Fig. 2. Spectral reflectance of skin

includes pigments of melanin, and dermis includes oxy-hemoglobin and deoxy-hemoglobin. The spatial color distribution on skin surface is determined by these pigment concentrations. Shade appears on the skin surface of curved body shape.

Surface reflectances of natural objects including human skin are spectrally high-dimensional[4]. However, the conventional three-channel color cameras often cannot capture small color differences on object surfaces. The analysis of concentration of each pigment requires precise color information. In such a case, a multiband imaging system with more than three different spectral bands is useful to detect the difference in pigmentation.

The spectral reflectance of skin is influenced by the interaction of pigments inside the skin tissue. Fig.2 shows spectral reflectance curves of skin. A basic feature of the reflectance curves is that the reflectance increases almost monotonically as the wavelength increases. A special feature is the "W" shaped or "U" shaped hollow in the range from 500nm to 600nm. This change in reflectance is caused by the absorption of oxy-hemoglobin. Thus, the narrow band imaging is required to capture the hollow of skin reflectance curve.

3   Estimation of Pigment Distributions from Multiband Skin Images

We propose a multispectral analysis method of pigment distributions on skin surface. Fig.3 shows the scheme of pigment distribution estimation. First of all,

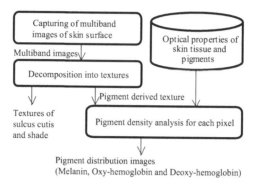

Fig. 3. Scheme of pigment distribution estimation

the multiband images of skin are captured. The captured images are decomposed into texture components by the MRA. The shade texture and sulcus cutis texture are separated from multiband images for accurate pigment density estimation. Then, pigment density for each pixel is estimated. As the result of the estimation, pigment distribution images are obtained.

3.1   Capturing Multiband Images

In the multiband imaging of skin, we select suitable spectral bands to capture the absorbance of pigments. The present multiband imaging system is composed of a monochrome camera and a programmable light source (Gooch&Housego, OL490), which can emit light with arbitrary spectral-power distribution. The programmable light source is useful for the band selection. The spectral reflectance of skin shows the W shaped or U shaped hollow by the absorption of hemoglobin in the range from 500nm to 600nm. Therefore, the spectral image in this range is captured with narrow band width of 10nm. In the other range, the band width is set to 30nm. In all, 17 band images are captured. The exposure time for each band is controlled for sufficient contrast. The output of the camera is normalized by a standard white.

3.2   Decomposing Images into Textures

The MRA with wavelet functions[5] is applied for the decomposition of images. The MRA is done as follows. First, an image is decomposed into four components as shown in Fig.4(a). These are components of low frequency for column and row (LL), low frequency for column and high frequency for row (LH), high frequency for column and low frequency for row (HL), and high frequency for column and row (HH). This is the decomposition at level depth -1. Then, the LL component for column and row is decomposed into four components again as shown in Fig.4(b). This is the decomposition at level depth -2. By repetition of the decomposition, the levels are from 0 for the original image to -m for the

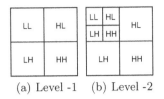

(a) Level -1   (b) Level -2

Fig. 4. Multi-resolution analysis

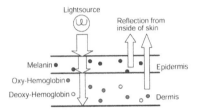

Fig. 5. Skin optics model

DC component in the case of a square image with 2m-by-2m pixels. This image analysis is useful for the separation of some texture patterns.

Sulcus cutis texture is included in high frequency levels. The shade caused by body shape appears in low frequency levels. We detect the shade from low frequency levels of the image taken under long wavelength illumination. The skin image doesn't contain clear pigment absorbance and fine grooves under long wavelength illumination. Then, the shade and sulcus cutis pattern are separated from multiband images.

3.3 Skin Reflectance Analysis Based on the Kubelka-Munk Theory

The relationship between spectral reflectance of skin and pigment concentrations is studied using the Kubelka-Munk theory[6,7]. It is known that the Kubelka-Munk theory is available for calculating the optical values of reflectance and transmittance within a layer consisting of turbid materials. A method based on the Kubelka-Munk theory was presented to estimate the density parameters of pigments and the skin surface reflectance[3].

The skin optics model for the skin spectral reflectance is assumed. The skin model is the two turbid layers of the epidermis including melanin and dermis including hemoglobin as shown in Fig.5. Horny substance that doesn't contain pigments is not considered in this model. The incident light penetrating the skin surface is absorbed and scattered in these two layers. The body reflectance function of the skin surface $R_b(\lambda)$ is described as a function of wavelength as

$$R_b(\lambda) = R_e(\lambda) + \frac{T_e^2(\lambda)R_{dt}(\lambda)}{1-R_e(\lambda)R_{dt}(\lambda)}$$
$$R_{dt}(\lambda) = R_d(\lambda) + \frac{T_d^2(\lambda)}{1-R_d(\lambda)}$$

$$(1)$$

where $R_e(\lambda)$ and $T_e(\lambda)$ are, respectively, the spectral reflectance and transmittance of the epidermis, $R_d(\lambda)$ and $T_d(\lambda)$ are the spectral reflectance and transmittance of the dermis, respectively. The reflectance of tissues under dermis is regarded as 1.

The spectral reflectances and transmittances of the respective layers are given as follows:

Epidermis:

$$R_e(\lambda) = \frac{1}{a_e(\lambda)+b_e(\lambda)\coth b_e(\lambda)S_e(\lambda)D_e}$$

$$T_e(\lambda) = \frac{b_e(\lambda)}{a_e(\lambda)\sinh b_e(\lambda)S_e(\lambda)D_e+b_e(\lambda)\cosh b_e(\lambda)S_e(\lambda)D_e} \tag{2}$$

$$u_e(\lambda) = \frac{S_r(\lambda)+K_r(\lambda)}{S_e(\lambda)}, b_e(\lambda) = \sqrt{a_e^2(\lambda)-1}$$

Dermis:

$$R_d(\lambda) = \frac{1}{a_d(\lambda)+b_d(\lambda)\coth b_d(\lambda)S_d(\lambda)D_d}$$

$$T_d(\lambda) = \frac{b_d(\lambda)}{a_d(\lambda)\sinh b_d(\lambda)S_d(\lambda)D_d+b_d(\lambda)\cosh b_d(\lambda)S_d(\lambda)D_d} \tag{3}$$

$$a_d(\lambda) = \frac{S_d(\lambda)+K_d(\lambda)}{S_d(\lambda)}, b_d(\lambda) = \sqrt{a_d^2(\lambda)-1}$$

where $S_e(\lambda)$ and $S_d(\lambda)$ are spectral scattering coefficients in epidermis and dermis, respectively. The spectral absorption coefficients $K_e(\lambda)$ and $K_d(\lambda)$ in the two layers are determined by the pigments in the following forms:

$$K_e(\lambda) = w_m K_m(\lambda)$$
$$K_d(\lambda) = w_h K_h(\lambda) + w_{dh} K_{dh}(\lambda) \tag{4}$$

where $K_m(\lambda)$, $K_h(\lambda)$, and $K_{dh}(\lambda)$ represent the spectral-absorption coefficients of melanin, oxy-hemoglobin, and deoxy-hemoglobin, respectively. The constant coefficients w_m, w_h, and w_{dh} represent the weights of the pigment absorption coefficients.

For applying the estimation algorithm to real measurements, we need the optical and histological data of skin tissue. The spectral absorption data, the spectral scattering data, and the layer thickness values published in Refs[8,9] are used in this paper.

4   Skin Image Synthesis

Realistic skin image is synthesized from modified pigment distributions. Fig.6 shows the scheme of skin image synthesis.

First, the pigment density at a certain area in the pigment distribution image is modified by image editing software. Then, the multispectral pigment derived texture is generated from the modified pigment distribution image by the method based on the Kubelka-Munk theory. Next, the multispectral pigment derived texture, the sulcus cutis texture and shade texture are composed into multiband

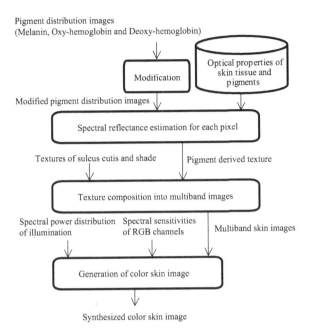

Pigment distribution images
(Melanin, Oxy-hemoglobin and Deoxy-hemoglobin)

Modification

Optical properties of
skin tissue and
pigments

Modified pigment distribution images

Spectral reflectance estimation for each pixel

Textures of sulcus cutis and shade   Pigment derived texture

Texture composition into multiband images

Spectral power distribution   Spectral sensitivities
of illumination   of RGB channels   Multiband skin images

Generation of color skin image

Synthesized color skin image

Fig. 6. Scheme of skin image synthesis

skin images by the MRA. Finally, an RGB color image of skin is produced from a set of multiband skin images. We should note that color appearance of the skin image depends on the RGB spectral-sensitivity functions of the camera used.

5   Experiments

5.1   Spectral Image of Skin

We captured multiband images of skin surface on inner forearm (Male, 41 years old). A square area of 2cm × 2cm was extracted from the multiband image as an image of 256 × 256 pixels. Fig.7 shows an image sequence of 17 bands and the RGB image. The extracted area included mole and vein.

5.2   Analysis Results of Skin Image

The MRA was applied to all band images. We used the Daubechies wavelet with wavelet order equal to 10 for the MRA. The wavelet order was determined empirically. Images were decomposed into 8-level texture component. We determined three high frequency levels (Level 1, 2, 3) as sulcus cutis texture. The shade caused by body shape was extracted from Level 7 and 8 of the image taken under long wavelength illumination. Then, the shade and sulcus cutis patterns

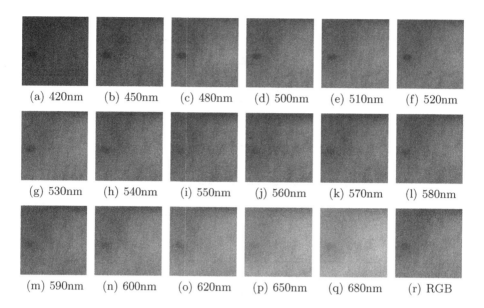

(a) 420nm   (b) 450nm   (c) 480nm   (d) 500nm   (e) 510nm   (f) 520nm

(g) 530nm   (h) 540nm   (i) 550nm   (j) 560nm   (k) 570nm   (l) 580nm

(m) 590nm   (n) 600nm   (o) 620nm   (p) 650nm   (q) 680nm   (r) RGB

Fig. 7. Image sequence of 17 bands and the RGB image including mole and vein

Fig. 8. Band image without shade and sulcus cutis texture patterns(550nm)

were separated from multiband image. Fig.8 shows an example of spectral image without shade and sulcus cutis patterns. Then, the pigment density analysis based on the Kubelka-Munk theory was done for multiband images.

The pigment distribution images are shown in Fig. 9. In these images, bright pixels shows high pigment density and dark pixels shows low pigment density. Mole showed the high concentration of melanin. Vein appeared in deoxy-hemoglobin distribution image. The distributions of oxy-hemoglobin and deoxy-hemoglobin are detected independently.

5.3   Synthesis Results of Skin Image

In the synthesis, we generated three types of images; 1) addition of melanin spot (stain), 2) addition of oxy-hemoglobin spot (inflammation), 3) addition of deoxy-hemoglobin spot (bruise). Fig.10 shows the modified pigment distribution image with the high concentration spot of each pigment. Fig.11 shows the synthesized skin color images. The CIE D65 was supposed as the illumination in

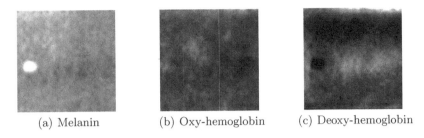

(a) Melanin   (b) Oxy-hemoglobin   (c) Deoxy-hemoglobin

Fig. 9. Pigment distribution images. (Bright pixels show high pigment density.)

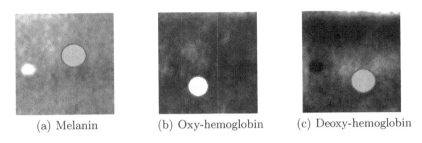

(a) Melanin   (b) Oxy-hemoglobin   (c) Deoxy-hemoglobin

Fig. 10. Modified pigment distribution images with pigment concentration area

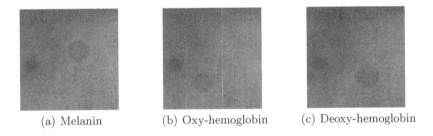

(a) Melanin   (b) Oxy-hemoglobin   (c) Deoxy-hemoglobin

Fig. 11. Results of texture synthesis for the addition of pigment concentration area

the synthesis. The colors of added spots are realistic, and the textures of the spots are matched to the textures of the surrounding area. These images show the feasibility of the proposed method.

6   Conclusions

This paper proposed a method for the estimation of pigment distributions from multiband skin images, and synthesizing realistic skin images including high concentrations of pigments. By using multiband images, pigment distribution of melanin, oxy-hemoglobin and deoxy-hemoglobin are estimated by the method based on the Kubelka-Munk theory. For accurate estimation, textures of shade and sulcus cutis are separated from multiband images by the MRA in advance of the estimation. Realistic skin image is synthesized from modified pigment distributions by changing the estimated distributions of melanin, oxy-hemoglobin and deoxy-hemoglobin. Experimental results showed that synthesized skin images for the addition of pigment concentrations of stain, inflammation and bruise were realistic. The results showed good feasibility of the proposed method.

Acknowledgments. This work was supported by Grants-in-Aid for Scientific Research (KAKENHI) (No. 23135529).

References

1. Doi, M., et al.: Image Analysis and Synthesis of Skin Color Textures by Wavelet Transform. In: Proceedings of IEEE Southwest Symposium on Image Analysis and Interpretation 2006, pp. 193–197 (2006)
2. Tsumura, N., et al.: Image-based skin color and texture analysis/synthesis by extracting hemoglobin and melanin information in the skin. In: Proceedings of SIGGRAPH 2003, pp. 770–779 (2003)
3. Doi, M., et al.: Spectral Reflectance Estimation of Human Skin and Its Application to Image Rendering. Journal of Image Science and Technology 49, 574–582 (2005)
4. Tominaga, S.: Spectral imaging by a multi-channel camera. Journal of Electronic Imaging 8, 332–341 (1999)
5. Mallat, S.G.: A theory for multiresolution signal decomposition: the wavelet representation. IEEE Transactions on Pattern Analysis and Machine Intelligence 11, 674–693 (1989)
6. Kubelka, P.: New Contributions to the Optics of Intensely Light-Scattering Materials. Part I. Journal of the Optical Society of America 38, 448–457 (1948)
7. Kubelka, P.: New Contributions to the Optics of Intensely Light-Scattering Materials. Part II. Journal of the Optical Society of America 44, 330–335 (1954)
8. Anderson, R.R., Parrish, J.A.: The Optics of Human Skin. Journal of Investigative Dermatology 77, 13–19 (1981)
9. Van Gemert, M.J.C., et al.: Skin Optics. IEEE Transactions on Biomedical Engineering 36, 1146–1154 (1989)

A Fisheye Camera System for Polarisation Detection on UAVs

Wolfgang Stürzl[1,2] and Nicole Carey[2]

[1] Institute of Robotics and Mechatronics, German Aerospace Center (DLR)
[2] Center of Excellence Cognitive Interaction Technology
and Department of Neurobiology, Bielefeld University, Germany
wolfgang.stuerzl@dlr.de, nicole.carey@uni-bielefeld.de

Abstract. We present a light-weight polarisation sensor that consists of four synchronised cameras equipped with differently oriented polarisers and fisheye lenses allowing us to image the whole sky hemisphere. Due to its low weight and compact size it is well-suited as a biomimetic sensor on-board a UAV. We describe efficient methods for reconstruction of the full-sky polarisation pattern and estimation of sun position. In contrast to state-of-the art polarisation systems for UAVs that estimate sun azimuth only, our approach can determine sun elevation as well, even in the presence of clouds and for significant pitch and roll angles of the UAV. The calibration and registration of the four fisheye cameras is achieved by extending an existing omni-directional calibration toolbox to multi-camera calibration. We present examples of full-sky reconstruction of the polarisation pattern as well as an analysis of the error in the sun position estimate. In addition, we performed a preliminary test on-board a quadcopter.

1 Introduction

The polarisation pattern in the sky is caused by scattering of sunlight in the atmosphere of the earth. Since it is symmetrical with respect to the observer-sun axis it can be used as a compass cue and it has long been known that skylight polarisation is used by insects for navigation [1–3]. In this paper we present a compact sensor that is well-suited to enable polarisation-based navigation of small UAVs or mobile robots. Due to its large field of view it also allows detailed full-sky reconstruction of the polarisation pattern.

Previous implementations of detailed full-sky polarimetry, notably Gal et al. [4], North and Duggin [5], Voss and Liu [6], and Miyazaki et al [7] have been large and require rotation of the polariser, making them not suited to implementation on small autonomous vehicles, much less flying ones. Conversely, mobile platforms employing polarisation detection such as that described by Lambrinos et al [8], Pandian [9] and Chahl and Mizutani [10] tend to have narrower viewing fields, and are more interested in gross attitude estimation than reconstructing the finer structure of the polarisation properties of the sky hemisphere and landscape.

A. Fusiello et al. (Eds.): ECCV 2012 Ws/Demos, Part II, LNCS 7584, pp. 431–440, 2012.

Fig. 1. The four-camera polarisation sensor mounted on a quadrotor (AscTec Pelican)

2   Polarisation Sensor and Calibration

Fig. 1 shows our wide-angle polarisation sensor consisting of four small camera units with fisheye lenses. Each is equipped with a differently oriented polariser placed between lens and CMOS sensor. Images are captured synchronously and transmitted serially via USB 2.0 by means of a multi-sensor board (VRmMFC, VRmagic).

2.1   Intensity and Polariser Orientation Calibration

If placed behind a linear polariser oriented at angle ϕ_k, the response of the camera sensor to partially linearly polarised light is given by [11]

$$I = f[Q_0(1 + \delta \cos(2\phi - 2\phi_k))] \; , \tag{1}$$

where Q_0 is the energy of the unpolarised light absorbed by a sensor pixel during camera exposure, δ its degree of polarisation and ϕ its polarisation angle. In the simplest case, the function $f[]$ consists of a linear gain followed by analog-to-digital conversion, which we disregard in the following,

$$I = g \, Q_0 \left(1 + \delta \cos(2\phi - w\phi_k)\right) \; . \tag{2}$$

To estimate the polariser orientation, we used a known polarised light source – an LCD computer monitor set to display a simple white background – and using a relatively long exposure (to maximise the sensitivity to minor intensity changes) we rotated the camera system around its central axis in increments of one degree. We then calculated the mean intensity of a central group of pixels for each camera at each rotational position. The angle corresponding to the lowest mean intensity was assumed to be the long anti-preferred axis of the polariser.

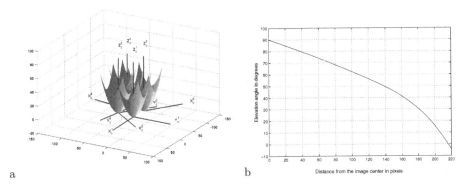

a   b

Fig. 2. a) Illustration of the estimated poses of the four fisheye cameras. b) Radial mapping function of camera 1.

To calibrate the intensity gain function for the cameras, we used the same light source and conducted four independent calibrations with the screen aligned with the centre of the viewing angle of the camera being calibrated. We also ensured that each camera had the same polariser orientation relative to the screen, and increased the exposure time gradually. In this way, we could verify that the gain function of each camera was linear across the image, and adjust for any discrepancies in the slopes of the different cameras.

Remark: We did not compensate for "radial intensity fall-off" induced by the fisheye lenses, since we were mainly interested in polarisation angle and degree of polarisation and not intensity.[1] All four lenses were assumed to have very similar fall-off functions and for estimating polarisation, similar positions in the four cameras are used.

2.2 Geometrical Calibration: Intrinsic Camera Parameters and Registration of Reference Frames

In order to obtain a full calibration of the four fisheye cameras, i.e. estimation of four sets of intrinsic camera parameters and rigid-body transformations between the camera reference frames, we extended the "Omnidirectional Camera Calibration Toolbox (OCamCalib)" [12] to multi-camera calibration. In addition to providing transformation parameters, our approach improves the estimation of intrinsic camera parameters since the number of necessary pose estimations of the calibration board per camera is reduced.[2]

---

[1] Radial intensity fall-off can be modelled by a multiplicative function.

[2] If N_I is the number of images per camera used for calibration and N_{ip} the number of internal parameters per camera, then we have to estimate just $4 \times N_{ip} + (N_I + 3) \times 6$ parameters compared with $4 \times N_{ip} + N_I \times 4 \times 6$ parameters when using the single-camera calibration framework for each of the four cameras.

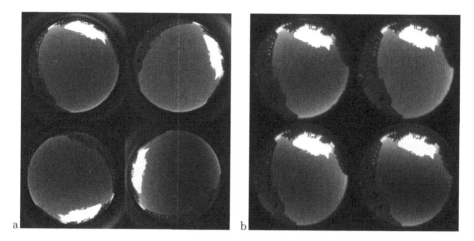

Fig. 3. Using the calibration results, the four cameras images shown in (a) are remapped to the same orientation and with corresponding pixels having identical viewing directions (b). An equidistant angular mapping is employed radially, i.e. the elevation angle depends linearly on the distance from the image center, el $= 90° - k\sqrt{(u - u_c)^2 + (v - v_c)^2}$.

The estimated relative poses of the four camera reference frames and a typical radial mapping function (elevation angle in dependence on the distance from the estimated image center in pixels) are shown in Fig. 2. For the calibration, we used 10 sets of four synchronously captured images and a 4th order polynomial for the radial projection function.

As shown in Fig. 3, after geometrical calibration, the four simultaneously captured camera images can be remapped in such a way that each viewing direction corresponds to the same pixel coordinates in each of the four remapped images.

3   Estimating Local Polarisation

After calibration of the four camera system, the polarisation angle ϕ and the degree of polarisation δ for each viewing direction can be estimated from the pixel values I_k of the $K = 4$ sensors by minimising the following error function, deduced from Eq. (2):

$$
\begin{aligned}
E(A, B, Q_0) &= \sum_{k=1}^{K} \left(Q_0(1 + \delta\cos(2\phi - 2\phi_k)) - g_k^{-1}I_k\right)^2 \\
&= \sum_k \left(Q_0 + Q_0\delta\left(\cos(2\phi)\cos(2\phi_k) + \sin(2\phi)\sin(2\phi_k)\right) - g_k^{-1}I_k\right)^2 \\
&= \sum_k \left(Q_0 + Ac_k + Bs_k - J_k\right)^2 \ ,
\end{aligned}
\tag{3}
$$

where we have substituted $A = Q_0\delta\cos(2\phi)$, $B = Q_0\delta\sin(2\phi)$, $c_k = \cos(2\phi_k)$, $s_k = \sin(2\phi_k)$, and $J_k = g_k^{-1}I_k$.

$$0 = \frac{\partial}{\partial Q_0}E(\phi,\delta,Q_0) \quad\Longrightarrow\quad Q_0^* = \bar{J} - A\bar{c} - B\bar{s} \ , \tag{4}$$

where $\bar{c} = \frac{1}{K}\sum c_k$, $\bar{s} = \frac{1}{K}\sum s_k$ and $\bar{J} = \frac{1}{K}\sum J_k$. Substituting this into (3),

$$\tilde{E}(A,B) = E(A,B,Q_0^*) = \sum_k \left(A\tilde{c}_k + B\tilde{s}_k - \tilde{J}_k\right)^2 \ , \tag{5}$$

where $\tilde{c}_k = c_k - \bar{c}$, $\tilde{s}_k = s_k - \bar{s}$, $\tilde{J}_k = J_k - \bar{J}$.

The solution of $0 = \frac{\partial}{\partial A}\tilde{E}(A,B)$ and $0 = \frac{\partial}{\partial B}\tilde{E}(A,B)$ is

$$A = \frac{N_A}{D_{AB}} \ , \quad B = \frac{N_B}{D_{AB}} \ , \tag{6}$$

$$N_A = \overline{\tilde{s}^2}\,\overline{\tilde{c}\tilde{J}} - \overline{\tilde{c}\tilde{s}}\,\overline{\tilde{s}\tilde{J}} \ , \quad N_B = \overline{\tilde{c}^2}\,\overline{\tilde{s}\tilde{J}} - \overline{\tilde{c}\tilde{s}}\,\overline{\tilde{c}\tilde{J}} \ , \quad D_{AB} = \overline{\tilde{c}^2}\,\overline{\tilde{s}^2} - \overline{\tilde{c}\tilde{s}}^2 \ , \tag{7}$$

where $\overline{\tilde{s}^2} = \frac{1}{K}\sum(s_k - \bar{s})^2$, $\overline{\tilde{c}^2} = \frac{1}{K}\sum(c_k - \bar{c})^2$, $\overline{\tilde{c}\tilde{s}} = \frac{1}{K}\sum(c_k - \bar{c})(s_k - \bar{s})$, $\overline{\tilde{c}\tilde{J}} = \frac{1}{K}\sum(c_k - \bar{c})(J_k - \bar{J})$, $\overline{\tilde{s}\tilde{J}} = \frac{1}{K}\sum(s_k - \bar{c})(J_k - \bar{J})$.

From A and B we can estimate the polarisation angle,

$$\tan(2\phi) = \frac{B}{A} = \frac{N_B}{N_A} \quad\Longrightarrow\quad \phi = \tfrac{1}{2}\mathrm{atan2}(N_B, N_A) \tag{8}$$

and the degree of polarisation

$$\delta = \frac{\sqrt{A^2 + B^2}}{Q_0} = \frac{\sqrt{A^2 + B^2}}{\bar{J} - A\bar{c} - B\bar{s}} = \frac{\sqrt{N_A^2 + N_B^2}}{D_{AB}\bar{J} - N_A\bar{c} - N_B\bar{s}} \ . \tag{9}$$

Note that if the angles of the K polarisers are equally distributed, i.e. $\phi_k = \frac{k-1}{K}180° + \phi_1$, $k = 1, 2, \dots, K$, then the equations above are simplified to be[3]

$$A = \frac{2}{K}\sum_k \cos(2\phi_k)J_k \ , \quad B = \frac{2}{K}\sum_k \sin(2\phi_k)J_k \ , \tag{10}$$

$$\phi = \tfrac{1}{2}\mathrm{atan2}\left(\sum_k \sin(2\phi_k)J_k, \sum_k \cos(2\phi_k)J_k\right) \ , \tag{11}$$

$$\delta = \frac{2\sqrt{(\sum_k \cos(2\phi_k)J_k)^2 + (\sum_k \sin(2\phi_k)J_k)^2}}{\sum_k J_k} \ . \tag{12}$$

Finally, the polarisation angle with respect to the local meridian in the camera centered reference frame is computed,

$$\alpha[u,v] = \phi[u,v] - \mathrm{az}[u,v] \ . \tag{13}$$

---

[3] ϕ_1 is the orientation angle of the polariser in the first camera with respect to the camera reference frame.

The polarisation vector in 3D for a viewing direction given by azimuth angle 'az' and elevation angle 'el' is then

$$\boldsymbol{p}[u,v] = \cos(\alpha[u,v])\boldsymbol{e}_{el}[u,v] + \sin(\alpha[u,v])\boldsymbol{e}_{az}[u,v] \ , \qquad (14)$$

where $\boldsymbol{e}_{el} = \frac{\partial \boldsymbol{e}}{\partial el} = (-\sin(el)\cos(az), -\sin(el)\sin(az), \cos(el))^\top$, $\boldsymbol{e}_{az} = \frac{1}{\cos(el)}\frac{\partial \boldsymbol{e}}{\partial az}$
$= (-\sin(az), \cos(az), 0)^\top$, and $\boldsymbol{e} = (\cos(el)\cos(az), \cos(el)\sin(az), \sin(el))^\top$ is the unit vector pointing into the direction given by (az, el).

4   Estimation of Sun Position from Polarisation

According to the single-scattering Rayleigh model, all polarisation vectors are orthogonal to the sun direction vector $\boldsymbol{e}_S$, i.e. $\boldsymbol{p}[u,v]^\top \boldsymbol{e}_S = 0$ for all u, v. We thus estimate the sun direction by minimising the deviation from orthogonality, i.e.

$$E(\boldsymbol{e}_S, \lambda) = \sum_{uv} w[u,v](\boldsymbol{p}[u,v]^\top \boldsymbol{e}_S)^2 - \lambda(\|\boldsymbol{e}_S\|^2 - 1) \ . \qquad (15)$$

$w[u,v]$ is an optional weighting factor that can be set, for instance, proportional to the degree of polarisation $\delta[u,v]$, and the term $-\lambda(\|\boldsymbol{e}_S\|^2 - 1)$ ensures that $\boldsymbol{e}_s$ is a unit vector. Minimising (15) leads to

$$\lambda \boldsymbol{e}_S = \sum_{uv} w[u,v]\boldsymbol{p}[u,v]\boldsymbol{p}[u,v]^\top \boldsymbol{e}_S \ . \qquad (16)$$

Thus, $\boldsymbol{e}_S$ is eigenvector of matrix $P = \sum_{uv} w[u,v]\boldsymbol{p}[u,v]\boldsymbol{p}[u,v]^\top$ corresponding to the smallest eigenvalue $\lambda_{\min}$.

4.1   Direct Estimation of Sun Azimuth

In case only the azimuthal angle of the sun is of interest, we can simplify our approach by projection onto the x-y plane, i.e. $\boldsymbol{p}[u,v]) = (p_x[u,v]), p_y[u,v]))^\top$, $\boldsymbol{e}[u,v]) = (e_x[u,v]), e_y[u,v]))^\top = (\cos(el[u,v])\cos(az[u,v]), \cos(el[u,v])\sin(az[u,v]))^\top$, $\boldsymbol{e}_S = (e_{xS}, e_{yS})^\top$, and minimise

$$E(\boldsymbol{e}_S) = \sum_{uv} w[u,v]\Big(\boldsymbol{p}[u,v]^\top (\boldsymbol{e}[u,v] - \boldsymbol{e}_S)\Big)^2 \ . \qquad (17)$$

Note that in the 3-dimensional case, (17) is equivalent to (15) since $\boldsymbol{p}[u,v]^\top \boldsymbol{e}[u,v] = 0$. The explicit solution of (17) is given by

$$\boldsymbol{e}_S = D^{-1}(N_x, N_y)^\top \ , \qquad (18)$$

$$N_x = (\sum w[u,v]p_y^2[u,v])P_x - (\sum w[u,v]p_x[u,v]p_y[u,v])P_y \ ,$$

$$N_y = (\sum w[u,v]p_x^2[u,v])P_y - (\sum w[u,v]p_x[u,v]p_y[u,v])P_x \ ,$$

$$P_x = \sum w[u,v](\boldsymbol{p}[u,v]^\top \boldsymbol{e}[u,v])p_x[u,v] \ , \quad P_y = \sum w[u,v](\boldsymbol{p}[u,v]^\top \boldsymbol{e}[u,v])p_y[u,v] \ ,$$

$$D = (\sum w[u,v]p_{xi}^2)(\sum w[u,v]p_{yi}^2) - (\sum w[u,v]p_{xi}p_{yi})^2 \ .$$

and thus $azi_S = \text{atan2}(N_y, N_x)$.

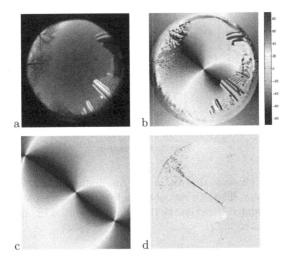

Fig. 4. Comparison of sky polarisation reconstructed using our four-lens system and the theoretical pattern predicted by the single-scatter model for the same sun placement. a) Remapped image of camera 1. b) Corresponding sky reconstruction with polarisation direction mapped to colour. c) Single-scatter polarisation model for the same sun position. d) Error between theoretical and estimated polarisation map.

4.2   Sky Reconstruction and Sun-Finding

Strictly speaking, the above method has two possible solutions under the single-scattering model: one at the sun position, and one diametrically opposite at the anti-solar position. However it is relatively trivial to distinguish between these possibilities; one may use the gravity vector to determine the most likely sun candidate, the chromatic gradient of the relative blue intensity of the sky [13], or even a simple intensity calculation.

In figure 4 we compare the sky pattern resolved by our sensor system with that predicted by the single scatter polarization model. The two are closely aligned (Fig. 4d) apart from some minor discrepancies. Using sky maps of this form, we tested our sun finding algorithm at various times of day. The results can be seen in figure 5. The azimuthal angle is resolved very precisely; the elevation estimation has a wider variance, possibly due to a higher sensitivity to atmospheric distortion [14].

Note that a more accurate sky model can be obtained via a double scattering formula [14], however our investigations showed the error between model and sky was not significantly reduced by incorporating these additional neutral points; moreover the inversion required to find the sun position becomes significantly more laborious.

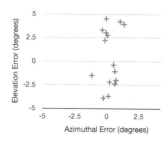

Fig. 5. Azimuth and elevational error in the sun-finding algorithm when tested on 15 images on a clear day. The sun was not visible due to horizon obstruction, but its position could be calculated based on the time, date, and lat./long. of the experimental location (Bielefeld, March 2012)

5   Discussion

The lightweight and speedy nature of this imaging system makes it well-suited to implementation on UAVs or small ground-based robots. Moreover, the wide-field visual sensors mean we can obtain a very accurate impression of the polarisation properties of natural scenes. This makes the system ideal for biomimetic investigations, such as tracing insect paths through canopied areas or cluttered environments, and reconstructing their visual input. Figure 6 demonstrates a sequence of images reconstructed from the system moving along a simulated 'bee-path' under a tree canopy. The sun is not visible and is difficult to pinpoint based on pure intensity information, however the sky pattern is clear even under hazy, nonoptimal conditions.

We also tested our polarisation sensor mounted on a quadcopter and compared the estimations from the sun finding algorithms described in section 4

Fig. 6. Extracts from video footage taken on a hazy evening under heavy canopy. The poor atmospheric conditions attenuate the polarisation pattern around the horizon, however through gaps in the foliage around the zenith point, the solar meridian is clear and distinct.

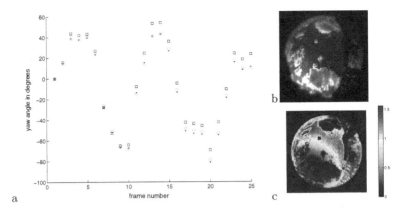

a   c

Fig. 7. a) Comparison of estimated yaw angles. Shown are values from the on-board
IMU (squares), azimuth values of the sun vector calculated using either the eigenvector
method described in section 4 (circles) or the direct approach, section 4.1 (dots). b) The
first image of the sequence (remapped image of camera 1). c) The corresponding weight
map $w[u, v]$. The weighting function was chosen to be $w[u, v] = B[u, v]/(R[u, v] + 1) \times \delta[u, v] \times \theta(\text{ele}[u, v] > 10°)$, where $B[u, v]$ and $R[uv]$ are the blue and red pixel values at
position $[u, v]$, $\delta[u, v]$ the degree of polarisation and $\theta(\text{ele}[u, v] > 10°)$ is a step function
that is $= 1$ for elevation angle larger than $10°$ and $= 0$ otherwise.

with yaw angle estimations of the on-board IMU. The results of 25 yaw-angle
estimates during a 35 s segment of a flight with significant yaw-turns are shown
in figure 7a. The flight was performed on a sunny day with clouds (see Fig. 7b).
To reduce the effect of clouds, which can disrupt the polarisation pattern of the
sky, we applied a weighting function that emphasises bluish parts with strong
polarisation (Fig. 7c). The IMU data was obtained by interpolating the estimations from the quadcopter's autopilot that were recorded with 10 Hz. While the
overall course matches, there a noticeable differences in the yaw value estimates
between the IMU and the polarisation sensor. As the autopilot had no magnetic
compass, slight drift in the yaw angle estimate might have occurred.

An integration of our polarisation system with other sensors on the quadcopter, in particular the IMU, is planned for future work.

Acknowledgements. We thank Michal Smíšek and Klaus Strobl for help with
the extension of the calibration toolbox.

References

1. von Frisch, K.: The Dance Language and Orientation of Bees. Harvard University
   Press (1967)
2. Wehner, R.: Polarized-light navigation by insects. Scientific American 235, 106–115
   (1976)

3. Srinivasan, M.V.: Honeybees as a model for the study of visually guided flight, navigation, and biologically inspired robotics. Physiological Reviews 91, 413–460 (2011)
4. Gal, J., Horvath, G., Meyer-Rochow, V.B., Wehner, R.: Polarization patterns of the summer sky and its neutral points measured by full-sky imaging polarimetry in finnish lapland north of the arctic circle. Proceedings of the Royal Society of London A 457, 1385–1399 (2001)
5. North, J.A., Duggin, M.J.: Stokes vector imaging of the polarized sky-dome. Applied Optics 36, 723–730 (1997)
6. Voss, K.J., Liu, Y.: Polarized radiance distribution measurements of skylight i. System description and characterisation. Applied Optics 36, 6083–6094 (1997)
7. Miyazaki, D., Ammar, M., Kawakami, R., Ikeuchi, K.: Estimating sunlight polarization using a fish-eye lens. IPSJ Transactions on Computer Vision and Applications 1, 288–300 (2009)
8. Lambrinos, D., Kobayash, H., Pfeifer, R., Maris, M., Labhart, T., Wehner, R.: An autonomous agent navigating with a polarized light compass. Adaptive Behavior 6, 131–161 (1997)
9. Pandian, A.: Robot navigation using stereo vision and polarization imaging, Masters Thesis, Institut Universitaire de Technologie IUT Le Creusot, Universite de Bourgogne (2008)
10. Chahl, J., Mizutani, A.: Biomimetic attitude and orientation sensors. IEEE Sensors Journal 12, 289–297 (2012)
11. Berry, H.G., Gabrielse, G., Livingston, A.E.: Measurement of the stokes parameters of light. Applied Optics 16, 3200–3205 (1977)
12. Scaramuzza, D., Siegwart, R.: A practical toolbox for calibrating omnidirectional cameras. In: Vision Systems Applications (2007)
13. Coemans, M., vos Hzn, J., Nuboer, J.: The relation between celestial colour gradients and the position of the sun, with regard to the sun compass. Vision Research 34, 1461–1470 (1994)
14. Berry, M.V., Dennis, M.R., Lee Jr., R.L.: Polarization singularities in the clear sky. New Journal of Physics 6, 162 (2004)

Time-Lapse Image Fusion

Francisco J. Estrada

University of Toronto at Scarborough,
1265 Military Trail,
M1C 1A4, Toronto, On., Canada
http://www.cs.utoronto.ca/~strider

Abstract. Exposure fusion is a well known technique for blending multiple, differently-exposed images to create a single frame with wider dynamic range. In this paper, we propose a method that applies and extends exposure fusion to blend visual elements from time sequences while preserving interesting structure. We introduce a time-dependent decay into the image blending process that determines the contribution of individual frames based on their relative position in the sequence, and show how this temporal component can be made dependent on visual appearance. Our time-lapse fusion method can simulate on video the kind visual effects that arise in long-exposure photography. It can also create very-long-exposure photographs impossible to capture with current digital sensor technologies.

1 Introduction

The problem of blending visual information from multiple source frames for the purpose of creating high dynamic range (HDR) images has been studied at great depth over the past two decades. The seminal work by Debevec and Malik [1] first proposed a sound framework for recovering a camera's response curve, for using this curve to generate a high-dynamic range radiance map from a set of differently exposed shots of a scene, and for rendering a single image from the radiance map that more faithfully approximates the perceived visual qualities of scenes with extreme illumination variations. Since then, a large volume of research on algorithms and techniques for HDR has been published. Thorough studies of existing techniques can be found in [2], [3], while [4] provides a sample of current research.

HDR techniques are typically complex as they are concerned with photometric accuracy and, in order to produce an image that can be displayed on a typical computer screen, require an additional and often computationally expensive step of tone mapping ([5], [6], [7], [8], [9]) during which the HDR information is appropriately compressed into the available dynamic range (typically that of an 8-bit RGB image).

Recently, exposure fusion ([10] and [11]) has been proposed as a faster, simpler alternative to HDR based on the argument that as long as we are interested only in the final blended image, neither radiance map estimation nor tone mapping

A. Fusiello et al. (Eds.): ECCV 2012 Ws/Demos, Part II, LNCS 7584, pp. 441–450, 2012.

Fig. 1. Time-lapse fusion result on a sequence of 219 photographs taken over a period of 2 hours around sunset. Four of the source frames are also shown. The blended image contains visual elements and detail from all source frames, while softening the appearance of moving scene structure.

are required. Instead, exposure fusion produces an image by blending pixels from all source frames with suitable weighting for each pixel. The weight of each pixel depends on how valuable its visual information is for the final blend. Exposure fusion results in [11] show that it can yield images of comparable visual quality to those created from HDR techniques while greatly simplifying the image processing pipeline.

Until now, HDR and image fusion have been concerned with the blending of multiply-exposed shots to increase the dynamic range of the scene. Here we propose that image fusion can also be used to blend images taken over a (possibly very long) interval of time, blending visual information from a dynamically changing scene while preserving detail and interesting structure. We focus on two problems: Simulating long-exposure effects on motion video, which constrains the exposure time to be no longer than that allowed by the framerate; and the creation of very-long-exposure photographs such as that shown in Fig. 1 which are beyond what is possible to capture in practice with a camera. In what follows, we describe first the original exposure fusion formulation, then we introduce the temporal component that is the basis for time-lapse fusion, and finally show results of the algorithm on video and time-lapse photographic sequences.

2   Exposure Fusion

There is a wide array of existing algorithms that blend multiple images to enhance particular aspects of visual structure. Laplacian pyramid blending [12], for example, demonstrated early on that by properly mixing the coefficients of the Laplacian pyramids of two images, a single, blended frame could be created that preserved sharp detail from both source images. In the interval since the pyramid blending method was introduced, algorithms have been proposed to blend information from images taken at different apertures [13], for fusing multi-spectral data for image enhancement [14], [15], for seamlessly inserting components of one image into another [16], [17], and for removing undesired image content by replacing it with suitable regions taken from images in a large database [18]. These are just a handful of representative examples. In this paper we explore a specific problem in image blending, namely, that of combining images taken at different points in time for photographic and video applications.

Our method is based on the exposure fusion algorithm of Mertens et al. [11]. The original exposure fusion method provides an alternative to complicated and computationally expensive HDR processing. The exposure fusion method takes as input a set of images $\{I_1, I_2, \ldots, I_K\}$, and generates a single output image by computing a weighted sum of corresponding pixel values over the input image set. The weight of each pixel is based on three properties: Contrast, saturation, and well-exposedness, and it is assumed that the images are aligned.

Contrast computation is based on local edge energy provided by a Laplacian pyramid decomposition of the source images. Saturation is defined as the standard deviation of the RGB colour components of each pixel, and well-exposedness gives higher weights to pixels away from brightness extremes. Given these components, pixel weights are computed as:

$$W_{i,j,k} = C_{i,j,k}^{\alpha_c} + S_{i,j,k}^{\alpha_s} + E_{i,j,k}^{\alpha_e}, \tag{1}$$

where the indices i, j, k refer to pixel (i, j) in image k, $C_{i,j,k}$, $S_{i,j,k}$, and $E_{i,j,k}$ are the pixel's contrast, saturation, and well-exposedness values respectively, and the α exponents control the influence of each of these terms. Pixel weights are normalized to that the weight of pixels at (i, j) across all frames sums to 1: $\hat{W}_{i,j,k} = \frac{W_{i,j,k}}{\sum_{k'=1}^{K} W_{i,j,k'}}$. Given the pixel weights for all pixels in all source frames, the simplest exposure fusion algorithm would compute the colour of the final blended pixel $R(i, j)$ as:

$$\hat{R}_{i,j} = \sum_{k=1}^{K} \hat{W}_{i,j,k} I_{i,j,k}. \tag{2}$$

However, this can lead to artifacts around image edges and other fine structures due to high frequency variations in the weight maps themselves. To avoid this problem, Eq. 2 is actually implemented using pyramid blending similar to that described in [12]. Each input image is processed to obtain a Laplacian $L\{I_k\}$ pyramid with d levels. The corresponding weight map is processed to obtain a Gaussian pyramid $G\{\hat{W}_k\}$ with the same number of levels d. From these Laplacian and Gaussian pyramids, each level $l = \{d, d-1, \ldots, 1\}$ of the blended Laplacian pyramid for the result frame is computed as

$$L_l\{R_{i,j}\} = \sum_{k=1}^{K} G_l\{\hat{W}_{i,j,k}\} L_l\{I_{i,j,k}\}. \tag{3}$$

The result frame R is finally obtained by pyramid reconstruction from $L\{R\}$.

Exposure fusion was shown to produce blended images of a visual quality similar to those produced by more complicated HDR/tone-mapping algorithms. Given its relative simplicity, it has been adopted in applications such as panoramic imaging, through an open source project called *enfuse*. It should be noted that the exposure fusion algorithm in no way constrains the source images to be taken under different exposure settings. In fact, if the parameters of the method are set to ignore the well-exposedness term, standard exposure fusion can be used to blend any set of aligned photographs of the same scene.

However, for video applications such as video processing we would like to be able to control the contribution of each pixel not only through its photometric properties, but also through its relative position within the sequence of frames. To this end, we expand the original formulation of exposure fusion to include a temporal decay term. This time decay can be applied in a per-frame manner to achieve visual effects similar to those in long-exposure photography, or it can be made structure dependent so that the specific image structure is highlighted in the blended frames.

3   Time-Lapse Fusion

Exposure fusion provides a way to extend the dynamic range of still photographs. We are interested in extending the temporal range of the events that can be recorded in photographs and video. There are two factors that limit exposure length: First, the need for short exposure times under bright illumination conditions. This applies to both still photography and video, and though it can be controlled to a certain degree through the use of appropriate filters and small apertures, it is still technically not feasible to obtain exposure times in the order of tens of minutes or even hours under daylight. Secondly, for motion video, the longest exposure achievable using a video camera is limited by the frame rate. This is an unavoidable limitation of video processing and places a hard upper-bound on the maximum exposure time for each frame.

Here we introduce time-lapse fusion as a means for artificially extending the exposure time of both still photography and motion video. The process takes as input a sequence of frames $I_1, \ldots, L_K$ either from a video, or from a time-lapse photographic sequence in which photographs are taken at regular intervals over an arbitrarily long period. We assume the sequence is taken with the camera mounted on a sturdy tripod so that static structure in the scene remains aligned.

Time-lapse fusion produces an output sequence $R_1 \ldots R_K$ in which image R_t is produced by blending source frames $I_t, I_{t-1}, \ldots, I_{t-\tau}$ effectively incorporating visual components from τ previous frames as well as the current one. The value of τ is set by the user, and controls the length of the virtual exposure time for each result frame. For motion video the virtual exposure time (VET) of each frame is given by $VET = \tau/\text{framerate}$. For time-lapse sequences, the virtual exposure time is dependent on the interval between shots. At first sight, it may seem reasonable to simply average frames $I_t, I_{t-1}, \ldots, I_{t-\tau}$ into the result frame; however, averaging over time tends to weaken and blur fast-moving structure, losing detail and giving a large weight to uniform backgrounds as seen in Fig. 2. Careful blending is required to preserve detail and produce the desired long-exposure effects.

We modify the pixel weight equation 1 to include a time-decay factor that modulates the overall contribution of pixels to the final blended image R_t:

$$W_{i,j,k} = (C_{i,j,k}^{\alpha_c} + S_{i,j,k}^{\alpha_s} + E_{i,j,k}^{\alpha_e})T(k,t). \quad (4)$$

Here, $T(k,t)$ is a Gaussian-shaped envelope with $\sigma = \tau/3$

$$T(k,t) = e^{-\frac{(t-k)^2}{2*\sigma^2}}, \quad (5)$$

with t the index of the current frame. The motivation for a Gaussian envelope is that it provides smooth transitions between consecutive output frames. A box window would be simpler, but would result in visible changes between frames especially for time-lapse sequences with large intervals between shots.

Figure 2 shows the output of time-lapse fusion for two frames from a fireworks sequence. The output frames clearly show the effects of having a long virtual exposure. Structure and fine detail are well preserved, and unlike frame averaging, time-lapse fusion does not create a blurry output that blends heavily with the black background. Figure 3 shows another example of time-lapse fusion with different virtual exposure times.

Fig. 2. Left: Original input frames from a movie sequence of fireworks. Middle: Results of averaging each frame with the previous 25 in the sequence. Right: Time-lapse fusion results with $\tau = 25$ for a virtual exposure time of .83 seconds. Averaging generates blur and blends structure with the background. Time-lapse fusion produces a pleasing long-exposure effect and preserves sharp detail.

For very-long-exposure photography, we follow the same process with the exception that only the last output frame R_K is computed, and we set τ to be very large so that effectively the entire sequence contributes to the final frame. The blended image in Figure 1 was produced in this way for a virtual exposure time of about 2 hours. Very long exposures are thus possible even under bright daylight conditions. During the process, the photographer retains full control over focus, aperture, and hence depth of field. With careful implementation, it is possible to process pixel weights frame-by-frame, making arbitrarily long exposures possible. Figure 4, for example, shows long exposure results from long time-lapse sequences, including a portrait produced by blending photos of the same person taken over a period of 1 year.

Fig. 3. Left: Original input frame from a movie sequence of waves. Middle: Time-lapse fusion results for $\tau = 7$ (virtual exposure time .23 seconds). Left: Time-lapse fusion with $\tau = 25$ (virtual exposure time .83 seconds).

While the use of Gaussian envelope is appropriate for simulating long exposure effects, the time decay factor can be an arbitrary function of relative frame position. In particular, structure-dependent envelopes that highlight specific image content are possible. In the following section we show how to make time-lapse fusion structure dependent, so that the decay time varies spatially over individual frames.

4   Stretch the Sunset

In the previous section we explored the use of a time decay factor that applies to entire frames in a sequence. However, the time decay factor can vary spatially over an image providing control at the pixel level of how long individual pixels will contribute toward the resulting blend. In this section we show that through the use of a structure-dependent time decay, computed independently for each pixel in each frame of the sequence, we can produce images that highlight specific image structure. The example we use is that of extending the duration of sunset colours over a time-lapse sequence taken at dusk.

Under this scheme, a time-decay map $D_{i,j,k}$ is computed for each frame k in the sequence. This map contains at each pixel location (i, j) a constant that controls how quickly the influence of the pixel will decay over time. To maintain consistency with the frame-wise time decay discussed in the previous section, we also model each pixel's temporal weight as a Gaussian envelope:

$$T(i, j, k, t) = e^{-\frac{(t-k)^2}{2 * D_{i,j,k}^2}}, \qquad (6)$$

Fig. 4. Very-long exposure photography. The portrait on the left is the result of blending images of the same person taken over a period of 1 year. The subject's face is carefully aligned in each source frame but the clothing, hair style, and background are otherwise unconstrained (source images from **clickflashwhirr.me**). Right side: Additional examples of very-long exposures from time-lapse sequences. Virtual exposure times range in the tens to hundreds of minutes.

where t is the current time index, k is the frame's time index, $D_{i,j,k} \in [\sigma_{min}, \sigma_{max}]$ is the decay constant for the pixel, and the parameters σ_{min} and σ_{max} determine the minimum and maximum intervals, respectively, over which pixels will contribute to the blended result.

In order to understand what Eq. 6 is doing, we need to specify how the time decay map $D_{i,j,k}$ is computed in the first place. This will depend on the input sequence and what the user wishes to accomplish through the blending. As a concrete example, here we use the same sequence of 219 images from which Figure 1 was generated. The sequence includes an interval covering about 2 hours around sunset.

We will generate an output sequence through time-lapse fusion so that the duration of the sunset colours is stretched. We also want some temporal smoothing over all other elements of the scene so that the different frames, which were taken about 30 seconds apart from each other, blend seamlessly. To detect sunset colours we rely on a simple measure of saturation. The time decay value for each pixel is given by: $D_{i,j,k} = \sigma_{min} + (S_{i,j,k} * (\sigma_{max} - \sigma_{min}))$, where $S_{i,j,k}$ is the saturation for the pixel in $[0, 1]$, and we set $\sigma_{min} = 7$ and $\sigma_{max} = 500$ which in effect means high-saturation pixels contribute all the way through the end of the sequence.

Figure 5 shows four frames from the sequence as well as their contribution over time as given by Eq. 6. Here t stands for the age of the frame, so the

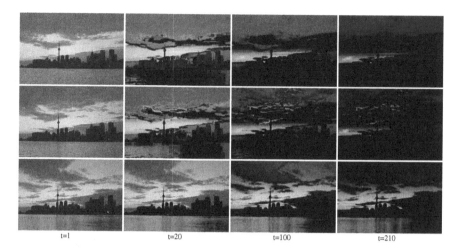

t=1   t=20   t=100   t=210

Fig. 5. The leftmost column shows four frames of the input sequence. Each successive column then shows the temporal blending weights for pixels in the corresponding image depending on the age of the frame. For example, the third column shows the blending weights for pixels once the image is 100 frames old.

images show how strongly different pixels contribute to a blended image as the frame ages. By the time a frame is $3 * \sigma_{min}$ frames old, the contribution of non-saturated pixels has faded to almost zero. Saturated pixels have large temporal blending weights all through the sequence. Note that for each frame the regions that persist change in shape, and that indeed the regions that contain sunset-like colours fade the slowest.

Figure 6 shows the results of structure-dependent time-lapse fusion compared against the standard time-lapse fusion described in the previous section (i.e. using a single time decay value per frame, with a fixed $\tau = 25$). Results are similar for the earlier parts of the sequence; however, as the sequence moves along the standard time-lapse fusion method loses the sunset colours in the clouds. The structure-dependent version, on the other hand, preserves the red glow in the clouds and the colours reflected in the water for much longer. The resulting sequence does indeed produce the illusion of a longer sunset full of reds and oranges.

A final example is shown in Fig. 7 which shows selective smoothing of water-fall structure. In this case standard time-lapse fusion causes blurring of people walking through the sequence which is not desirable. A simple threshold on distance from pure white was used to automatically obtain a coarse segmentation of the waterfall structure in each frame. Waterfall regions are given $\sigma_{max} = 11$ for a virtual exposure time of 1.16 seconds. The rest of the scene is assigned $\sigma_{min} = .33$ so that non-waterfall pixels contribute only while the frame is the current frame. This effectively renders the moving water smooth while leaving the rest of the scene untouched. In the above examples no user interaction was required.

Fig. 6. Stretched sunset sequence. The top row shows four of the original sequence frames. The middle row shows the result of applying standard time-lapse fusion (as in Section 3). The bottom row shows blended results using the structure dependent decay map described in this Section.

Fig. 7. Selective smoothing of water. The left column shows two frames from motion video containing waterfalls. The middle column shows standard time-lapse fusion results which blur everything in the scene. The right column shows structure-dependent fusion which selectively smooths over the waterfall regions leaving the rest of the scene unchanged.

5   Conclusion

In this paper we proposed a time-lapse fusion algorithm that extends the exposure fusion framework to blend images taken at different points in time. We showed that a simple temporal decay factor with a Gaussian profile can be used to simulate long exposure effects on video, and that arbitrarily long exposures not physically realizable with a real camera are possible while allowing the photographer to maintain control of focus, aperture, and depth of field. We then extended the method to allow for pixel-level control of time-decay so that specific image content can be highlighted in the final blend. At the pixel level, time-lapse fusion allows for the creation of video sequences that change the temporal profile of events in the scene to produce visually striking results. Time-lapse fusion can, in this way, provide photographers with a tool to expand their ability to create depictions of the world that are beyond physical or practical limitations.

References

1. Debevec, P., Malik, J.: Recovering high dynamic range radiance maps from photographs. In: SIGGRAPH, pp. 369–378 (1997)
2. Bloch, C.: The HDRI Handbook: High Dynamic Range Imaging for Photographers and CG Artists. Rocky Nook (2007)
3. Hoefflinger, B. (ed.): High-Dynamic-Range (HDR) Vision. Springer (2005)
4. Hasinoff, S., Durand, F., Freeman, W.: Noise-optimal capture for high dynamic range photography. In: CVPR, pp. 553–560 (2010)
5. Reinhard, E., Devlin, K.: Dynamic range reduction inspired by photoreceptors. IEEE Transactions on Visualization and Computer Graphics 11, 13–24 (2005)
6. Durand, F., Dorsey, J.: Fast bilateral filtering for the display of high-dynamic-range images. ACM Transactions on Graphics 21, 257–266 (2002)
7. Fattal, R., Lischinski, D., Werman, M.: Gradient domain high dynamic range compression. ACM Transactions on Graphics 21, 249–256 (2002)
8. Mantiuk, R., Myszkowski, K., Seidel, H.: A perceptual framework for contrast processing of high dynamic range images. ACM Transactions on Applied Perception 3, 286–308 (2006)
9. Kim, M., Kautz, J.: Characterization for high dynamic range imaging. Eurographics 27, 691–697 (2008)
10. Goshtasby, A.: Fusion of multi-exposure images. Image and Vision Computing 23, 611–618 (2005)
11. Mertens, T., Kautz, J., Van Reeth, F.: Exposure fusion. In: Pacific Conference on Computer Graphics and Applications, pp. 382–390 (2007)
12. Burt, P., Adelson, E.: A multi-resolution spline with application to image mosaics. ACM Transactions on Graphics 2, 217–236 (1983)
13. Hassinof, S., Kutulakos, K.: A layer-based restoration framework for variable apperture photography. In: ICCV, pp. 1–8 (2007)
14. Schaul, L., Fredembach, C., Süsstrunk, S.: Color image dehazing using the near-infrared. In: ICIP, pp. 1629–1632 (2009)
15. Bennet, E., Mason, J., McMillan, L.: Multispectral bilateral video fusion. IEEE Transactions on Image Processing 16, 1185–1194 (2007)
16. Kwatra, V., Schödl, A., Essa, I., Turk, G., Bobick, A.: Graphcut textures: Image and video synthesis using graph cuts. In: SIGGRAPH, pp. 277–286 (2003)
17. Pérez, P., Gangnet, M., Blake, A.: Poisson image editing. In: SIGGRAPH, pp. 313–318 (2003)
18. Hays, J., Efros, A.: Scene completion using millions of photographs. In: SIGGRAPH (2007)

HDR Imaging under Non-uniform Blurring

C.S. Vijay, Paramanand Chandramouli, and Rajagopalan Ambasamudram

Department of Electrical Engineering,
Indian Institute of Technology Madras, Chennai 600 036, India
{csv2000,paramanand}@gmail.com, raju@ee.iitm.ac.in

Abstract. Knowledge of scene irradiance is necessary in many computer vision algorithms. In this paper, we develop a technique to obtain the high dynamic range (HDR) irradiance of a scene from a set of differently exposed images captured using a hand-held camera. Any incidental motion induced by camera-shake can result in non-uniform motion blur. This is particularly true for frames captured with high exposure durations. We model the motion blur using a transformation spread function (TSF) that represents space-variant blurring as a weighted average of differently transformed versions of the latent image. We initially estimate the TSF of the blurred frames and then estimate the latent irradiance of the scene.

1 Background

The irradiance from a real world scene incident on a camera could range from very small to very large values. This variation is termed as the dynamic range. However, the CCD/CMOS sensors used in today's cameras are unable to accommodate the entire range. Over the past decade, this limitation has increasingly drawn the attention of vision researchers for applications in computer graphics, visual effect production etc. [1]. A widely followed approach for inferring scene irradiance is to optimally combine information from multiple images captured with different exposure times [2–6]. The focus in these methods is on modeling the camera pipeline and estimating the camera response function (CRF) to find the high dynamic irradiance of the scene. Another approach for HDR imaging is based on image fusion [7–9]. Here the focus is on obtaining a well-composed low dynamic range (LDR) image by finding a weighted average of the differently exposed intensity images.

For a real world scene, the exposure times can vary from values as small as $1/500s$ to as high as $5s$. Although the camera can be held still for the lower exposures, it would be an incredible feat for any photographer to hold the camera steady for long exposure times while taking multiple shots of a static scene. One could resort to tripods but they are bulky and difficult to carry around and setup. The issue of motion blurring has recently attracted a lot of attention. The restoration of uniformly blurred images was considered in [10, 11]. Fergus et al. [12] consider single image blind-deblurring for uniformly blurred images using natural image priors. However, as shown in [13, 14], camera rotation which induces space-variant blurring cannot be ignored in camera-shake.

A. Fusiello et al. (Eds.): ECCV 2012 Ws/Demos, Part II, LNCS 7584, pp. 451–460, 2012.

Fig. 1. Multiple exposed images where higher exposures are motion-blurred

The works in [14–16] consider single image deblurring of space-variantly motion-blurred images. Interestingly, none of the above works address the high dynamic (HD) nature of scenes. One of the effects of HD scenes is pixel saturation which causes ringing effects while deblurring. This problem was addressed in [17, 18] by masking outliers. Lu et al. [19] discuss the problem of obtaining HDR images from motion blurred observations and jointly estimate the CRF, blur kernels and the latent scene irradiance. However, they consider a space-invariant blur model which restricts the camera motion to in-plane translations. Though, this is a good step forward, it is limited in scope as the effect of rotation on blur is greater than that of translation [14] and hence cannot be ignored.

In this paper, we discuss a method to obtain the HDR image from a set of differently exposed images that are likely to be non-uniformly blurred. While capturing images with hand-held cameras, one can safely assume that no blurring will occur for low exposure times since the displacement of the camera in this short duration will be negligible. Hence, we consider a scenario with access to both blurred higher exposures and non-blurred lower exposures. The scene is assumed to be distant enough to preclude any parallax effects. The higher exposures (though blurred) contain information not present in the less-exposed images. Fig. 1 shows one such image set. One simplistic solution is to deblur the images and then reconstruct the HDR using existing methods. This is, of course, subject to the effectiveness of deblurring of these over-exposed images which i) may not be very accurate, and ii) may also contain artifacts. Here, we adopt the transformation spread function (TSF) [20] aka motion density function [15] to model space-variant blur. The TSF describes the blurring process as a weighted average of differently transformed versions of the latent scene irradiance. Studies have revealed that a general camera motion can be well-approximated by a 3D TSF (in-plane translation and rotation) when the depth variations are not significant [14, 15]. For the estimation of these TSFs, we assume that the blur is uniform locally, and use the local point spread functions (PSFs) of the blurred (high exposure) images, which are derived using patches of blurred and non-blurred (lower exposure) image pairs centered at the same location. The scene irradiance is then estimated using least square minimization along with total variation regularization. Thus, we simultaneously achieve the twin objectives of deblurring and HDR imaging.

We list below the main contributions of this work:

1. This is the first attempt of its kind for recovering HDR from *non-uniformly* blurred images.
2. We propose TSF estimation in the irradiance domain in order to handle

in-plane translation as well as rotation. This is a generalization of Lu et al.'s work [19] which allows for only simple translations since it uses uniform PSF.
3. We use locally estimated PSFs to arrive at the TSF which has not been attempted before.

2   Blur Model and TSF

During the image formation process, the scene radiance passes through a camera pipeline [2], before getting converted into intensity values. The pixel intensity value in an image is a monotonic but nonlinear function of the irradiance and the exposure period. The light energy accumulated can be described as

$$X = \int_{t=0}^{\Delta t} E \ dt + n \tag{1}$$

where E is the latent irradiance, Δt is the exposure time and n is additive noise. This accumulated energy undergoes several nonlinear conversions before being represented as pixel intensity value. These nonlinearities collectively are termed as the CRF, resulting in the intensity $Z = f(X)$. Given the exposure time and the CRF, the irradiance can be obtained as $B = f^{-1}(Z)/\Delta t$ where f^{-1} is the inverse CRF. It is important to note that this inverse mapping is not linear. Since the CRF maps the response of a particular camera setting, it is independent of the scene and can be calculated off-line.

When there is camera motion, the latent irradiance image (considering a static scene) can be viewed as undergoing a series of transformations. The final observation is an accumulation of the result of all these transformations. i.e.,

$$Z = f\left(\int_{t=0}^{\Delta t} \mathbf{\Gamma}_t(E) \ dt\right) + n \tag{2}$$

where $\mathbf{\Gamma}_t$ refers to the homography transformation operation at instant t, and $\mathbf{\Gamma}_t(E)$ denotes the outcome of applying $\mathbf{\Gamma}_t$ on E. Each of these transformations contributes according to the time spent in that state (exposure time), and is represented by suitably derived weights. While averaging over time, the temporal information is lost. In the TSF model, the result (blurred image) is the average over all possible transformations.

The general camera motion can be well approximated by 3 degrees of motion (in-plane translation and rotation) [15] when depth variations in the scene are minimal. The transformation space can be sampled to obtain a finite set $\mathbf{H}$ of $N_{\mathbf{H}}$ different transformations, which contains the transformations to approximately form the blurred image. The TSF h_T is a function that maps the finite set of transformations $\mathbf{H}$ to a non-negative real number i.e., $h_T : \mathbf{H} \to \mathbf{R}$. For each transformation $\mathbf{\Gamma} \in \mathbf{H}$, the value of the TSF $h_T(\mathbf{\Gamma})$ denotes the fraction of the total exposure duration for which the camera stayed in the position that caused the transformation $\mathbf{\Gamma}$. The final blurred intensity image in terms of the TSF is

$$Z = f\left(\sum_{k=1}^{N_{\mathbf{H}}} h_T(\mathbf{\Gamma}_k) \mathbf{\Gamma}_k(E)\right) \tag{3}$$

2.1   TSF Estimation

In this work, the input consists of a set of differently exposed images with non-uniformly blurred higher exposures. The differently exposed images are obtained from the same scene irradiance. Hence, the inverse map of each intensity image to the irradiance domain will be comparable. The image intensity and irradiance are related by $B^i = f^{-1}(Z^i)/\Delta t^i$, where i takes values $1 \dots N_E$ for N_E differently exposed images, Z^i is the ith observation, and B^i is the corresponding irradiance map. Because of the non-linearity of the CRF, irradiance values obtained from pixels with very high or very low intensities may not be comparable. The influence of such pixels is restricted using a mask whose weights are obtained from a 256-point Tukey window.

While estimating the TSF, we first estimate the PSF at local patches where the blur may be assumed to be locally uniform. The estimation is carried out with respect to a non-blurred lower exposure by minimizing

$$\underset{h}{\operatorname{argmin}} \left\| \left(m_p \cdot B_{\mathbf{p}}^s - m_p \cdot \left(h * E_{\mathbf{p}}^r \right) \right) \right\|_2 \tag{4}$$

where h is a local PSF to be estimated, s is the observation index corresponding to one of the blurred higher exposures, r is the index of highest exposed non-blurred observation, $B_{\mathbf{p}}^s$ is the blurred irradiance patch of an exposure corresponding to s, $E_{\mathbf{p}}^r$ is the the non-blurred irradiance patch of an exposure corresponding to r, and m_p is the mask applied at location $\mathbf{p}$. We estimate $N_{\mathbf{p}}$ such PSFs $h_{\mathbf{p}_1} h_{\mathbf{p}_2} \dots h_{\mathbf{p}_{N_{\mathbf{p}}}}$ at image locations $\mathbf{p}_1 \mathbf{p}_2 \dots \mathbf{p}_{N_{\mathbf{p}}}$. If any misalignment is present among the observations, it is implicitly accounted for in the estimated TSF (globally) and PSF (locally).

Fig. 2 demonstrates PSF estimation for a non-uniformly blurred image captured with a hand-held camera. The space-variant nature of the blur is evident from the estimated PSFs. A PSF at a pixel (i, j) is related to TSF as

$$h(i, j; m, n) = \sum_{k=1}^{N_{\mathbf{H}}} h_T(\mathbf{\Gamma}) \, \delta_d \left(m - (i_{\mathbf{\Gamma}} - i), n - (j_{\mathbf{\Gamma}} - j) \right) \tag{5}$$

where $(i_{\mathbf{\Gamma}}, j_{\mathbf{\Gamma}})$ denotes the co-ordinates of the point when a transformation $\mathbf{\Gamma}^{-1}$ is applied on (i, j), and δ_d denotes the 2D Kronecker delta function. Each local PSF $\mathbf{p}_l$ can be considered as a weighted sum of the components of the TSF of the image. Such a linear relation can be expressed as $h_{\mathbf{p}_l} = M_l h_T$ for $l = 1 \dots N_p$, where M_l is a matrix whose entries are determined by the location $\mathbf{p}_l$ of the blur kernel and the interpolation coefficients. All the M_ls and $\mathbf{p}_l$s for $l = 1 \dots N_p$ can be stacked and related to the TSF as

$$\overline{h} = \mathbf{M} h_T \tag{6}$$

where $\overline{h}$ is a stack of the estimated blur kernels. A typical value for N_p is 5. To get an estimate of the sparse TSF that is consistent with the observed blur kernel, we minimize the following cost function

$$\underset{h_T}{\operatorname{argmin}} \left\| \overline{h} - \mathbf{M} h_T \right\|_2 + \lambda_s \left\| h_T \right\|_1 \tag{7}$$

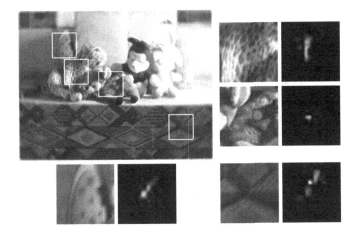

Fig. 2. The blurred image and some select patches are shown. The estimated PSFs are shown along-side each patch.

where a sparsity constraint is enforced by the l_1-norm term. To minimize the cost function, we use the toolbox available at [21]. The TSFs of all the blurred higher exposures are obtained using this method. For a detailed explanation of TSF estimation, we refer the reader to our supplementary material [22].

3   Scene Irradiance Estimation

Having obtained the TSFs of the blurred images, we proceed to invert the blurring process to obtain the actual scene irradiance which is present in the different exposures. We pose this as an optimization problem, where the solution can be obtained by minimizing the cost function

$$\sum_{i=1}^{N_E} \|K^i E - B^i\|^2 \tag{8}$$

Here E and B^i are the latent irradiance and the given i^{th} image irradiance of the scene, expressed in vector form and the sum is over all the observations. K^i is a large but sparse matrix, which represents the space-variant blurring operation and whose rows are a local blur filter acting on E.

The CRF of cameras is highly nonlinear at very high and very low pixel intensities. In order to restrict the influence of these nonlinearities, we mask these pixels from contributing to the estimation process. This is done to emphasize the usage of the linear part of the CRF. The mask is derived from a Tukey window, which has a smooth transition from 0 to 1. The mask applied is common to all 3 channels. This is done so as to maintain color balance. The parameter of the window used to obtain the mask depends on the CRF and image histogram (intensity distribution). This mask also acts as a pixel weighting function for different exposures. The summation can be removed from equation (8) by stacking all the irradiance images (B^is) into a single matrix $\widetilde{B}$ and the K^i matrices into a single matrix $\widetilde{K}$ and can be expressed in a single matrix equation

$$\|\overline{m}\widetilde{K}E - \overline{m}\widetilde{B}\|^2 \tag{9}$$

where E is the latent irradiance to be estimated and $\overline{m}$ is a large diagonal matrix which is a collection of all the masks applied to different exposures. The mask values are arranged along the diagonal. While optimizing the above cost, total variation regularization is used to stabilize the solution, thus giving the energy

$$O = \underset{E}{\text{argmin}} \ \|\overline{m}.\widetilde{K}E - \overline{m}.\widetilde{B}\|^2 + \lambda_{TV} \int |\nabla E| \tag{10}$$

We solve the above equation iteratively using conjugate gradient method. The derivative of the cost function is

$$\frac{\partial O}{\partial E} = \overline{m}.\widetilde{K}^T \left(\overline{m}. \left(\widetilde{K}E - \widetilde{B} \right) \right) + \lambda_{TV} \left(\nabla \frac{\nabla E}{|\nabla E|} \right) \tag{11}$$

where E is the irradiance image in t^{th} iteration, λ_{TV} is the total variation regularization parameter, and K^T represents the adjoint of the blurring operation and corresponds to inverse warping [16]. The term $\widetilde{K}E$ is obtained by blurring E using TSFs that are present in $\widetilde{K}$.

4   Experimental Results

For the synthetic case, we captured a set of observations at different exposures from a still camera. The higher exposures from this non-blurred dataset were subject to non-uniform motion blurring. The real data was captured with a hand-held DSLR Sony α and a compact Fujifilm HS10. While the blurring was found to be negligible for lower exposures, it was significant at higher exposures. All the datasets were captured from a sufficiently long distance. The CRF of these cameras were derived off-line using the code of [2] from images captured using a tripod (for stability) and for identical camera settings as used in the experiments. To recover the HDR image from the given set (which includes blurred observations), we first convert the intensities to irradiances. Next, we select patches in a blurred image and corresponding patches in a non-blurred frame (with maximum exposure) to evaluate the local PSFs. Using these estimated PSFs, the TSF corresponding to each of the blurred images is determined by solving Eqn.(7). The scene irradiance is finally estimated by minimizing Eqn.(10). For viewing purpose, the estimated irradiance image was tone-mapped using the technique of [23]. The quality of the final LDR image is subject to tone-mapping.

We initially applied our scheme on the synthetic image set shown in Fig. 3. The higher exposures (Fig. 4(a) and (b)) of $\frac{1}{2}s$ and $2s$ are blurred using known TSFs. These TSFs were chosen along the lines of blurs caused by real camera-shake in hand-held cameras so as to simulate a real-world scenario. The TSF dimensions t_x and t_y took integer values $\in$ [-12,12], and θ_z ranged $\in$ [-1.5,1.5]

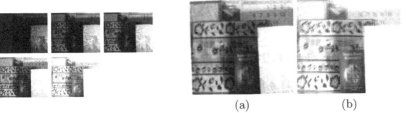

	(a) (b)
Fig. 3. Synthetic image set	**Fig. 4.** Synthetically blurred higher exposures

(a)   (b)   (c)   (d)

Fig. 5. (a) Original tone-mapped HDR image derived from non-blurred images. (b) HDR obtained from individually deblurred images. (c) Result obtained using [19]. (d) Estimated HDR tone-mapped image using our method.

degrees in steps of 0.25 degrees. The blurred images have visible regions that are not apparent in lower exposures. We hope to recover these while estimating the HDR irradiance but without blur.

Fig. 5(a) shows the tone-mapped HDR image obtained from the original set of non-blurred images using [2]. This result is used for comparison and to evaluate the performance of our method. Fig. 5(b) shows the HDR image obtained from a set of deblurred images. The deblurring was performed using the code provided by Whyte et al. [14]. It is quite apparent that the image is still blurred to some extent (as can be seen around the numbers) and it contains artifacts along the edges. This is understandable as [14] is not designed for the HDR problem. Hence a naive and computationally intensive solution of deblurring images and finding the HDR is not very effective. Fig. 5(c) shows the result obtained using [19] for our non-uniformly blurred data. Although the image has been deblurred in certain regions such as the illuminated parts and the book title, residual blur can be seen in the outer region where the effect of rotation is more. For instance, the digits in the calender and the flower pattern near the left-hand-side boundary of the image appear blurred. This is not surprising since [19] is not equipped to handle non-uniform blur. Fig. 5(d) shows the recovered HDR image using our method. The details in the scene become more apparent in our output. The front-illuminated part is visible and so are the darker regions in the scene such as the book title and the top image on the booklet. The numbers which become better visible with increased exposure have been uniformly lit. The result is in-fact comparable to Fig. 5(a) which was obtained without any blur.

(a)   (b)

Fig. 6. Two different real data sets

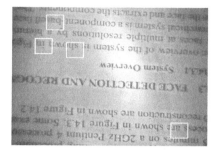

Fig. 7. Recovered HDR images for the datasets in Fig. 6. using our method

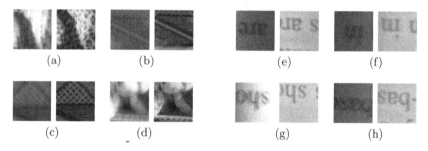

(a)   (b)   (e)   (f)

(c)   (d)   (g)   (h)

Fig. 8. Close-up of blurred data (available only in the higher exposures) and the corresponding patch in the output image

Fig. 6 shows two real image sets with the highest exposure being $2s$. The first set shown in Fig. 6(a) has images of size 640×480 captured at exposure times $\frac{1}{15}, \frac{1}{8}, \frac{1}{2}$ and 2s. The two highest exposures are motion-blurred. These frames contain information about the lower portion of the scene that is not visible in the less-exposed frames. The second set in Fig. 6(b) shows images captured with exposure durations $\frac{1}{8}, \frac{1}{3}$ and 1s. The observations corresponding to $\frac{1}{3}$ and 1s are blurred. The difference in the information available among these observations is clearly evident.

In Fig. 7, the HDR outputs of both the sets are shown for our model. The results have been rid of saturation effects and the darker regions are well-lit. The blurred information in the higher exposures has been restored while retaining the information from lower exposure, such as the illuminated regions in the scene. In Fig. 8, we show close-up patches from the most exposed images and the estimated result (side-by-side). Figs. 8(a-d) correspond to the first set while Figs. 8(e-h) correspond to the second. Fig. 8(a) reveals reduced smudging in the image. Also, the texture on the toy has been recovered. Patch sets 8(b) and (c) bring out the pattern present in the lower part of the scene clearly. These

(a)   (b)   (c)   (d)

Fig. 9. (a) Our Result. (b) Result of [19]. (c) Close-ups of (a). (d) Close-ups of (b).

patterns are not quite visible in the lower exposures. From Fig. 8(d), we can also observe that the result is shifted with respect to the input blur patches. This shift is due to the compensation for the misalignment between input patches. Fig. 8(e-h) further reinforce the fact that our method satisfactorily achieves the twin objectives of HDR imaging and deblurring.

In Fig. 9, we give a comparison of the results obtained by our method (Fig. 9(a)) with that of [19] (Fig. 9(b)) on the dataset of Fig. 6(a). Both the results are well lit but Fig. 9(b) has significant residual blur. While Fig. 9(c) shows the close-up patches from our result, those obtained using [19] are shown in Fig. 9(d). Since the upper portion of the scene is well illuminated, the non-blurred lower exposures contribute to the final result. Hence, in the first patch, we see that the outputs from both the algorithms are focused. However, since [19] uses a convolution model, blur persists in their result as highlighted in second and third patches of Fig. 9(d). In contrast, the corresponding patches from our output in Fig. 9(c), show that the latent irradiance image has been completely recovered. This example serves to clearly bring out the advantages of our approach over the state-of-the-art [19] in HDR imaging with blur.

5   Conclusions

In this paper, we proposed an approach to obtain high dynamic scene irradiance from a set of frames captured with a hand-held camera, where the higher exposures are non-uniformly blurred due to camera-shake. A two-step procedure was proposed in which we first obtain the TSF of each blurred image followed by regularization to solve for scene irradiance. The method was validated on both synthetic and real datasets. It will be interesting to extend our framework to include the possibility of all the frames being blurred (as in the case of night scenes) and for dynamic scenarios.

References

1. Reinhard, E., Heidrich, W., Pattanaik, S., Debevec, P., Ward, G., Myszkowski, K.: High dynamic range imaging: acquisition, display, and image-based lighting. Morgan Kaufmann (2010)

2. Debevec, P.E., Malik, J.: Recovering high dynamic range radiance maps from photographs. In: ACM SIGGRAPH (1997)
3. Mann, S., Picard, R.W.: On being 'undigital' with digital cameras: Extending dynamic range by combining differently exposed pictures. Citeseer (1995)
4. Mitsunaga, T., Nayar, S.K.: Radiometric self calibration. In: Proc. CVPR (1999)
5. Fattal, R., Lischinski, D., Werman, M.: Gradient domain high dynamic range compression. ACM Trans. on Graph. 21 (2002)
6. Reinhard, E., Ward, G., Pattanaik, S., Debevec, P.: High dynamic range imaging. Elsevier (2006)
7. Mertens, T., Kautz, J., Van Reeth, F.: Exposure fusion. In: Pacific Conf. on Computer Graph. and App. (2007)
8. Raskar, R., Ilie, A., Yu, J.: Image fusion for context enhancement and video surrealism. In: ACM SIGGRAPH 2005 Courses (2005)
9. Ward, G.: Fast, robust image registration for compositing high dynamic range photographs from hand-held exposures. Journal of Graphics Tools 8, 17–30 (2003)
10. Rav-Acha, A., Peleg, S.: Two motion-blurred images are better than one. Pattern Recognition Letters 26 (2005)
11. Yuan, L., Sun, J., Quan, L., Shum, H.: Image deblurring with blurry/noisy image pairs. ACM Trans. Graph. (26)
12. Fergus, R., Singh, B., Hertzmann, A., Roweis, S.T., Freeman, W.T.: Removing camera shake from a single photograph. ACM Trans. on Graphics 25 (2006)
13. Levin, A., Weiss, Y., Durand, F., Freeman, W.T.: Understanding and evaluating blind deconvolution algorithms. In: Proc. CVPR (2009)
14. Whyte, O., Sivic, J., Zisserman, A., Ponce, J.: Non-uniform deblurring for shaken images. In: Proc. CVPR (2010)
15. Gupta, A., Joshi, N., Lawrence Zitnick, C., Cohen, M., Curless, B.: Single Image Deblurring Using Motion Density Functions. In: Daniilidis, K., Maragos, P., Paragios, N. (eds.) ECCV 2010, Part I. LNCS, vol. 6311, pp. 171–184. Springer, Heidelberg (2010)
16. Tai, Y., Tan, P., Brown, M.S.: Richardson-lucy deblurring for scenes under projective motion path. IEEE Trans. PAMI 33 (2011)
17. Whyte, O., Sivic, J., Zisserman, A.: Deblurring shaken and partially saturated images. In: IEEE Workshop CPCV, with ICCV (2011)
18. Cho, S., Wang, J., Lee, S.: Handling outliers in non-blind image deconvolution. In: Proc. ICCV (2011)
19. Lu, P.Y., Huang, T.H., Wu, M.S., Cheng, Y.T., Chuang, Y.Y.: High dynamic range image reconstruction from hand-held cameras. In: Proc. CVPR (2009)
20. Chandramouli, P., Rajagopalan, A.N.: Inferring image transformation and structure from motion-blurred images. In: Proc. of the BMVC (2010)
21. Liu, J., Ji, S., Ye, J.: Slep: sparse learning with efficient projections (2009), http://www.public.asu.edu/~jye02/Software/SLEP
22. Supplementary material: Transformation spread function estimation (2012) Supplied as additional material SupMaterial.pdf
23. Reinhard, E., Stark, M., Shirley, P., Ferwerda, J.: Photographic tone reproduction for digital images. ACM Transactions on Graphics 21 (2002)

Semantic Image Segmentation
Using Visible and Near-Infrared Channels*

Neda Salamati[1,2], Diane Larlus[2], Gabriela Csurka[2], and Sabine Süsstrunk[1]

[1] IVRG, IC, École Polytechnique Fédérale de Lausanne, Switzerland
[2] Xerox Research Centre Europe, 6, Chemin de Maupertuis, Meylan, France

Abstract. Recent progress in computational photography has shown that we can acquire physical information beyond visible (RGB) image representations. In particular, we can acquire near-infrared (NIR) cues with only slight modification to any standard digital camera. In this paper, we study whether this extra channel can improve semantic image segmentation. Based on a state-of-the-art segmentation framework and a novel manually segmented image database that contains 4-channel images (RGB+NIR), we study how to best incorporate the specific characteristics of the NIR response. We show that it leads to improved performances for 7 classes out of 10 in the proposed dataset and discuss the results with respect to the physical properties of the NIR response.

1 Introduction

Semantically segmenting a scene given an image is one of the eminent goals in computer vision. While we have seen a lot of progress in recent years using sophisticated image descriptors [1,2] and better machine learning techniques [3,4], segmentation still remains challenging. Whereas humans have no difficulties performing semantic image interpretation, machine vision systems still struggle mainly because of the ambiguity of the influence of light and surface reflectance on a given pixel value. For example, a dark pixel can either result from a dark surface reflectance under normal lighting conditions or a light surface reflectance under shadow. Decoding the contributions of light and reflectance from an image is an ill-posed problem [5]. To solve it, we either need to make assumptions about the world, or to capture more information.

In this paper, we study semantic segmentation using the latter approach. Specifically, we propose to use near-infrared (NIR) images in addition to visible (RGB) images as input. Silicon sensors of digital cameras are naturally sensitive in the NIR wavelengths range (750-1100nm). By removing the NIR blocking filter affixed to the sensor, digital cameras can capture both RGB and NIR images [6]. RGB and NIR cues have been successfully combined in many applications like dehazing [7], dark flash photography [8], and scene categorization [9,10].

We believe that the intrinsic properties of NIR images make them relevant for semantic segmentation. First, due to the NIR radiation being adjacent to the visible spectrum, NIR images share many characteristics with visible images. In

* This work was supported by the Swiss National Science Foundation under grant number 200021-124796/1 and Xerox foundation.

A. Fusiello et al. (Eds.): ECCV 2012 Ws/Demos, Part II, LNCS 7584, pp. 461–471, 2012.

particular, the shapes of objects in the scene are preserved, *i.e.*, borders of physical objects in the visible images match the borders in the NIR image, which is necessary for segmentation. Second, the intensity values in the NIR images are more consistent across a single material, and consequently across a given class region, due to the unique reflectances of certain natural and man-made composites to NIR radiation [11]. For instance, vegetation is consistently "bright", and sky and water are "dark". Third, texture in NIR images is more intrinsic to the material. This is partly due to the transparency of most colorants and dyes in NIR; texture introduced by (color) patterns on a surface is less dominant in NIR. Additionally, there is generally less haze present in NIR images [7]. Consequently in landscape scene images, distant regions appear sharper (see Figure 1).

These properties of NIR images have been used by the remote sensing and military communities for years to detect and classify natural and/or man-made objects [12]. However, in this paper we approach semantic image segmentation from a different point of view. First, as opposed to the aerial photography, we address images in typical street and landscape photography. Second, most remote sensing applications use true hyper-spectral capture, with several bands in the NIR and even the IR. Our framework only uses a single channel that integrates all NIR radiation, and that can be captured by a standard sensor of any digital camera. This is in-line with the recent developments in computational photography, where different camera set-ups are proposed to concurrently capture three visible (RGB) and one NIR channel, either on two sensors with a beam splitter [13] or on a single sensor [14]. To this end, we apply a state-of-the-art segmentation framework to the task. Our proposed system is based on a Conditional Random Field (CRF) model [15], where we exploit different possibilities of combining the visible and NIR information in the recognition part and in the regularization part of the model.

The contributions of this paper are three-fold. First, we study how to best use NIR in a CRF based segmentation framework, exploring different options for both recognition and regularization parts of the model. Second, we provide a new semantic segmentation dataset that contains images having both visible and NIR channels (RGB+NIR) and pixel-level annotations. Finally, we discuss the results obtained with both cues for different classes and connect our observations with material characteristics and other properties of NIR radiation.

1.1 Previous Work

Semantic Image Segmentation is the process of partitioning an image into regions, where each region corresponds to a semantic class within a predefined list. The appearance of these classes are learned using labeled images. Methods usually fuse two sub-tasks: a recognition part, responsible for the labeling, and a regularization part that enforces neighboring pixels to belong to the same class. The recognition part is based on the local appearance that is considered at the pixel [1], or at the patch level [3]. Different features are used to describe the local appearance, among them texture (filter banks), color statistics, and SIFT [16]. The low-level features are often transformed into higher-level features, such as the Bag-of-Visual-Words [17] or the Fisher Vector (FV) representations [18], before feeding them into a classifier. In our work, we follow [2] for local representation and use FVs for recognition. The local consistency is usually enforced by pairwise constraints between neighboring pixels. The local appearance and the local consistency are often combined using Markov random fields (MRF) [3] or conditional random fields (CRF) [1]. In this paper, we use a CRF model.

NIR. The spectral signature of different materials in the NIR part of the spectrum is the foundation for most of remote sensing applications. In such tasks, to achieve a successful classification, data with high spectral resolution is required [12]. On the contrary, [19] exploits the material-based low-level segmentation task using the 4-channel images that can be potentially captured by any digital camera. Incorporating this freely available data, we are going one step further and not only segment the scene but also semantically label every region of the image. For that purpose, we explore a framework using supervised classifiers that learn the relation between visible and NIR information given a class.

The rest of this article is organized as follows. The CRF model we used is described in Section 2. The various experiments are described in Section 3. Finally, a discussion is proposed in Section 4.

2   Model

Semantic segmentation is formulated as a discrete labeling problem that assigns each pixel $i \in \{1, ..., N\}$ to a label from a fixed set Ψ. Given the observations $\mathbf{x} = \{x_1, ..., x_N\}$, the task is to estimate a set of random variables $\mathbf{Y} = \{Y_1, ..., Y_N\}$, taking values in Ψ^N. We employ a CRF that considers the posterior distribution to define the Gibbs energy: $E(y) = -\log P(Y = y \mid X = x) - \log Z$, where Z is a normalization constant. The maximum a posteriori (MAP) labeling y^* of the random field is defined as:

$$y^* = \mathrm{argmax}_{y \in \Psi^N} P(Y = y \mid x) = \mathrm{argmin}_{y \in \Psi^N} E(y) \tag{1}$$

The labeling is formulated as a pairwise CRF, whose energy can be written as:

$$E(y) = E_{unary}(y) + \lambda E_{pair}(y), \tag{2}$$

and is composed of a unary and a pairwise term. As in [20], we assign a weight λ to E_{pair} that models the trade-off between recognition and regularization.

The Unary Term is responsible for the recognition part of the model and uses the probability for each pixel to belong to a class. E_{unary} is considered as the cost of assigning labels y to observations x, and is defined as: $E_{unary} = \sum_i -\log(p(Y_i = y_i | \mathbf{x}))$. We used a patch based representation, since patches contain more information than pixels. Low-level descriptors are computed for each patch, and transformed into Fisher Vectors (FV) [18]. FVs computed on the patches of the training images and their labels are used to train linear SVM classifiers. For a test image, FV representations of patches are given to the

Fig. 1. Examples of 4 channel images (visible = RGB, left and NIR, middle) and their ground truth (right) from our dataset

classifiers, a score is inferred for each patch, and for each class. The scores can be transformed into probabilities at the pixel level [2], yielding probability maps.

The Pairwise Term regularizes the pixel labeling, neighboring pixels are encouraged to share labels. We used a 4-neighbor system ν (each pixel is connected to its 4 direct neighbors). We relax the regularization constraints along the edges, using a contrast sensitive Potts model: $E_{pair} = \sum_{(i,j)\in\nu} \delta_{y_i,y_j} \exp(-\beta||p_i - p_j||^2)$ where δ_{y_i,y_j} is the Kronecker delta and $\beta = \frac{1}{2<||p_i-p_j||^2>}$ as in [20]. This potential penalizes disagreeing neighboring pixel labels, and the penalty is lower were pixel values change. That way, borders between regions are encouraged to follow edges. The pixel value p_i can be considered in the visible domain $(p_i = \{r_i, g_i, b_i\})$, in the NIR domain $(p_i = n_i)$ or in both (4 dimensions).

Model Inference is carried out by the multi-label graph optimization library of [21,22] using α-expansion.

3   Experiments

First we present our dataset and the implementation details (Sec. 3.1). We then compare different descriptors for the model recognition part (Sec. 3.2), and the regularization part (Sec. 3.3) is then studied for the most promising ones.

3.1   Proposed Dataset and Technical Details

Our dataset is based on a previously released scene dataset [9], where images are composed of 3 visible (RGB) channels and a NIR channel. To the best of our knowledge, that is the only set of diverse natural images for which both visible and NIR channels have been recorded. The original dataset consists of 477 images, divided into 8 outdoor and 1 indoor scenes. We discarded the indoor and old building classes, whose appearance is too different from the other classes[1].

The remaining 370 images were manually segmented and annotated at the pixel level with the following classes: *Building, Cloud, Grass, Road, Rock, Sky, Snow, Soil, Tree, Water*. We followed the MSRC annotation style [1], pixels are labeled as one of these classes or as *void* class. *Void* corresponds to pixels whose class is not defined as part of our classes of interest, or are too ambiguous to be labeled (see Figure 1).

We extract patches of size 32×32 on a regular grid (every 10 pixels) at 5 different scales. To extract different scales the images are resized by factors of

---

[1] Keeping these scene classes would have resulted in images with only (or mostly) void regions, according to our 10 pre-selected semantic classes.

Table 1. Left: evaluation (average of per-class and overall accuracies) of the segmentation for different local descriptors and their combinations. Right: p-value for the paired t-test, for the overall accuracy per image of different strategy pairs.

Descriptor	Per-class	Overall
COL_{rgb}	71.78	77.05
COL_{rgbn}	74.00	79.47
COL_{p1234}	72.50	77.09
$SIFT_l$	65.62	72.89
$SIFT_n$	66.18	73.82
$SIFT_{p1}$	65.80	73.07
$SIFT_{rgb}$	72.94	78.68
$SIFT_{rgbn}$	74.77	81.70
$SIFT_{p1234}$	75.09	81.77
$COL_{rgb} + SIFT_l$	77.36	82.55
$COL_{rgbn} + SIFT_n$	**78.88**	**84.26**
$COL_{p1234} + SIFT_n$	77.57	82.85

Strategy A	Strategy B	p-value
COL_{rgb}	COL_{rgbn}	3.10^{-4}
$COL_{rgb} + SIFT_l$	$COL_{rgbn} + SIFT_n$	1.10^{-4}
$SIFT_{p1234}$	$COL_{rgbn} + SIFT_n$	3.10^{-6}
$SIFT_{rgbn}$	$COL_{rgbn} + SIFT_n$	5.10^{-7}
$SIFT_{rgbn}$	$SIFT_{p1234}$	7.10^{-7}
$SIFT_n$	$SIFT_l$	9.10^{-2}

1, 0.7, 0.5, 0.35, and 0.25. We consider two different features. The SIFT feature ($SIFT$) [16] encodes texture using histograms of oriented gradients for each bin of a 4×4 grid covering the patch. The color feature (COL) encodes the intensity values in each image channel using mean and standard deviation in each bin of the same grid covering the patch. Low-level descriptors are computed for each patch and their dimensionality is reduced by PCA to 96. A visual codebook with 128 Gaussians is built in the projected space, and each patch is transformed into a FV. By using the same PCA dimension and the same codebook size, the FV representation of all descriptors has the same dimensionality.

We randomly split our dataset into 5 sets of images (5 folds) and define 5 sets of experiments. For each experiment, one fold is used for validation, one is used for testing, and the remaining images are used for training the model. Results for the 5 test-folds are grouped and evaluated at once, producing a single score for the dataset for each evaluation measure.

We consider two measures that evaluate the segmentation as a pixel level categorization problem. The first one (**overall**) is the overall accuracy (*i.e.*, the number of correctly classified pixels divided by the total number of pixels), the second one (**per-class**) is the average of the per-class accuracy (*i.e.*, average over the classes of the ratio between true positives and positives). The pixels labeled as *void* in the ground truth are not considered for evaluation.

3.2   Descriptor Comparison

This set of experiments evaluates the recognition part of our model. As described in Section 2, each pixel is associated with a probability of belonging to each of the classes. We produce a semantic segmentation by assigning pixels to their most likely label, $y^* = \text{argmax}_{y \in L} P(Y = y|\mathbf{x})$. This is equivalent to our full model, using $\lambda = 0$. In other words, only the unary term is considered here.

First, we compare different COL and $SIFT$ features. COL extracts statistics over RGB channels, consequently we call it COL_{rgb}. The standard SIFT, computed on the luminance channel (visible image) is called $SIFT_l$. The color descriptor can be extended to 4-channel images (RGB+NIR), defining COL_{rgbn}.

We also consider the alternative 4-D color space proposed by [9], and introduce COL_{p1234}, that concatenates COL features computed on each of the 4 alternative channels $p1$, $p2$, $p3$, and $p4$, that are obtained from PCA applied to RGBN. We propose to examine $SIFT_n$, a SIFT descriptor computed on the NIR image. The $SIFT_{p1}$ descriptor, computed only on the first channel ($p1$) of the alternative color space, is also considered.

As color and texture are complementary, we look at different ways to combine them. The first one, proposed initially for visible images by [23], is a multispectral SIFT, $SIFT_{rgb}$, that concatenates $SIFT$ descriptors computed on the R, G, and B channels. This can be extended in a straightforward manner to 4-dimensional images, defining $SIFT_{rgbn}$, and $SIFT_{p1234}$ respectively. To combine color and texture, we also consider combinations of $SIFT$ and COL descriptors, by averaging the relevant probability maps. Results are reported for $COL_{rgb} + SIFT_l$ that contains only visible information, and for $COL_{rgbn} + SIFT_n$ and $COL_{p1234} + SIFT_n$ that also include NIR.

Table 1 (left) compares the segmentation accuracy obtained by these descriptors and their combination. In order to get an intuition whether results are significantly different, we computed statistical significance using the paired t-test on overall results per image for the most interesting pairs of descriptors. Results are reported in Table 1 (right). A p-value smaller than 0.05 means the descriptors are statistically different from each other, with a 5% confidence level.

From Table 1, we can make the following observations. First, COL descriptors using NIR information outperform the visible only COL_{rgb}. The original 4-D color space (COL_{rgbn}) performs better than the de-correlated space (COL_{p1234}). For the SIFT descriptor, $SIFT_n$ does slightly better than $SIFT_l$, as we expected due to the material dependency of the NIR response, but the difference is not significantly different on this dataset, at the 5% confidence level. The same applies when comparing $SIFT_n$ and $SIFT_{p1}$.

The best single descriptor is $SIFT_{p1234}$, as already shown for image classification in [9]. This descriptor encodes texture for the different color channels, visible and NIR. Still, this best descriptor is outperformed by the late fusion of COL and single-channel $SIFT$ descriptors.

As main conclusions, the best visible only approach for recognition is $COL_{rgb} + SIFT_l$. We will use this descriptor as our visible-only baseline for the rest of the paper. According to our study, the best way to include the NIR information for local recognition is through $COL_{rgbn} + SIFT_n$. It outperforms the best visible method ($COL_{rgb} + SIFT_l$) by almost 2% (+1.71 overall accuracy).

3.3 Graph Model

In the previous section, we studied the recognition part of our model, and acknowledged the gain obtained using NIR together with the 3 visible channels to build local descriptors. For the regularization part, we use the previously obtained probability maps per class, and apply them in the full model described in Section 2. The resulting energy function is optimized using the library of [21,22]. λ is fixed to 5 for all the experiments.

Table 2. Results for the full CRF model

Descriptor	Pairwise	Per-class	Overall
	VIS	78.45	83.82
$COL_{rgb} + SIFT_l$	NIR	78.48	83.71
	$VIS + NIR$	78.58	83.94
	VIS	80.10	85.50
$COL_{rgbn} + SIFT_n$	NIR	80.01	85.38
	$VIS + NIR$	**80.30**	**85.72**
	VIS	78.68	84.21
$COL_{p1234} + SIFT_n$	NIR	78.76	84.20
	$VIS + NIR$	78.87	84.34
	VIS	76.68	83.41
$SIFT_{p1234}$	NIR	76.76	83.37
	$VIS + NIR$	76.81	83.50

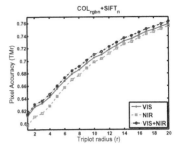

Fig. 2. Trimap accuracy, for varying radius (size of the band around the border considered for evaluation)

We focus on the most promising combinations of descriptors from the recognition part: $COL_{rgbn} + SIFT_n$, $COL_{p1234} + SIFT_n$, and $SIFT_{p1234}$. We compare them to our visible only baseline $COL_{rgb} + SIFT_l$. For the pairwise potential, the Potts model is extracted on the visible image (VIS), the NIR one (NIR) and the full 4-channel image ($VIS + NIR$). This means that the pixel intensity difference is computed for pixel values p_i being of dimension 3, 1 and 4 respectively. Results are presented in Table 2.

First, we note that regularization always improves segmentation accuracy (comparing Table 1 and 2), this improvement is modest (between 1% and 1.7%).

Second, we observe that visible only pixel information (VIS) for the pairwise potential is comparable to the NIR Potts model (none of the difference is statistically significant). Nevertheless, combination of both ($VIS + NIR$) is always slightly better than any of the individual pairwise models, and this is statistically different at the 5% confidence level.

To better understand the role of the regularization, we also consider a third evaluation measure, *trimap accuracy* [24] that considers the overall classification accuracy for pixels in a narrow band around borders between two regions in the ground truth. Results for the $COL_{rgbn} + SIFT_n$ descriptors, and the different pairwise potentials are shown in Figure 2[2]. These results support our previous claim that the 4D pixel representation leads to better results[3].

The best results using visible only information were obtained by the full model, with $COL_{rgb} + SIFT_l$ as descriptors for recognition and a regularization using the RGB image. This is our visible baseline, referred to as VB. The best results for RGB+NIR images were obtained by $COL_{rgbn} + SIFT_n$ and $VIS + NIR$ for regularization. Our best strategy is referred as BS in the following discussion.

4   Result Analysis and Discussion

In this section, we analyze and compare the segmentation results obtained with the two strategies VB and BS based on the confusion matrices reported in Table 3 and sample images in Figure 3.

---

[2] Curves for the other descriptors look similar, and have been omitted.

[3] Statistical significance is obtained for this measure as well.

Table 3. Confusion matrices for i) descriptor $COL_{rgbn} + SIFT_n$ and 4-dimentional pairwise (BS) on top and ii) $COL_{rgb} + SIFT_l$ with visible-only pairwise (VB) below

		Tree	Grass	Soil	Build.	Road	Rock	Snow	Water	Sky	Cloud
VISIBLE + NIR	Tree	**94.3**	2.4	0.3	1.1	0.1	1.1	0.1	0.1	0.2	0.3
	Grass	13.4	**81.0**	1.0	0.4	0.7	2.4	0.0	1.0	0.0	0.1
	Soil	10.5	9.3	**64.6**	1.0	6.3	5.6	1.1	1.3	0.1	0.0
	Build.	4.7	0.4	0.4	**89.6**	2.9	0.6	0.0	0.2	0.2	1.1
	Road	1.1	1.4	1.5	8.7	**84.2**	0.5	1.7	0.8	0.0	0.0
	Rock	23.4	1.9	2.2	1.4	0.3	**64.3**	4.5	1.0	0.4	0.6
	Snow	0.8	0.0	1.6	1.4	4.2	20.0	**69.6**	0.6	0.0	1.8
	Water	4.4	0.5	1.5	4.9	0.2	1.6	0.5	**83.2**	0.9	2.4
	Sky	1.5	0.0	0.0	2.0	0.2	0.1	0.0	0.1	**78.6**	17.5
	Cloud	0.9	0.0	0.0	0.4	0.0	0.6	0.2	0.1	4.3	**93.5**
VISIBLE ONLY BASELINE	Tree	**91.8**	3.7	0.5	2.0	0.2	0.9	0.1	0.1	0.2	0.4
	Grass	12.6	**80.6**	0.9	0.7	0.7	3.2	0.0	1.2	0.0	0.0
	Soil	11.9	10.7	**60.5**	0.3	6.9	5.5	1.8	2.2	0.1	0.0
	Build.	3.6	0.4	0.7	**89.8**	2.9	0.3	0.5	0.4	0.3	1.1
	Road	1.4	1.5	1.6	8.0	**83.0**	1.0	2.3	1.1	0.0	0.0
	Rock	21.2	1.3	1.7	2.1	0.1	**66.3**	5.2	1.4	0.4	0.3
	Snow	0.2	0.0	0.1	1.3	2.1	20.0	**72.7**	0.0	0.0	3.7
	Water	5.8	2.0	1.2	6.6	1.8	2.9	0.5	**73.4**	0.5	5.3
	Sky	1.6	0.0	0.0	1.8	0.2	0.1	0.1	0.5	**73.5**	22.3
	Cloud	0.6	0.0	0.0	0.7	0.0	0.3	0.8	0.1	4.5	**92.9**

From Table 3, we note that the almost 2% overall difference between BS and VB relates to an improvement for 7 classes out of 10. The largest improvement is observed for classes *water* (+9.8%), *sky* (+5.1%), *soil* (+4.1%). *Trees, clouds,* and *grass* are improved by 2.5%, 0.6%, and 0.4%, respectively. On the other hand, the performance on classes *building, rock* and *snow* were slightly lower (less than 2% except for the class *snow*).

Haze Effect. First, we observe the benefit of NIR in the presence of haze. As stated by Rayleigh's law, the light scattered from small particles ($< \lambda/10$) is inversely proportional to the wavelength λ ($1/\lambda^4$) [6]. Particles in the air (haze) satisfy this condition and are scattered more in the short-wavelength range of the spectrum. Thus, when images are captured in the NIR, atmospheric haze is less visible and the sky becomes darker (see image 5 in Figure 3). The "haze transparency" characteristic of NIR results in sharper images for distant objects (see images 3 or 5). In particular, vegetation and mountains at a distance in the visible image is smoothed and bluish, which may affect classification results. The sharper and haze-free appearance in NIR helps classification and leads to better segmentation, such as for the class *rock* in image 2.

Border Accuracy. For some images, we observed that borders are more precisely detected while incorporating NIR in the pairwise potential. This can be explained by the material dependency of NIR responses that may reduce wrong edges due to clutter, or may result in more contrasted edges between classes. This information, used in the regularization part of our model, helps to align borders between regions with a change of material (see images 3, 4, 5, and 6).

Water. The class *water* exhibits the largest improvement. Since water absorbs radiation in the NIR, this class appears very dark and becomes very distinctive.

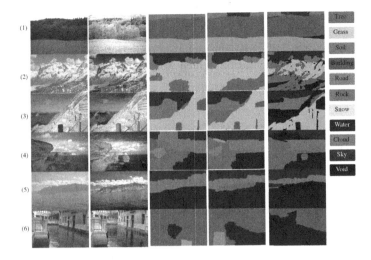

Fig. 3. Visible and NIR images (1st and 2nd column), segmentation results for visible only ($COL_{rgb}+SIFT_l$ and pairwise on VIS, 3rd column) and NIR+visible ($COL_{rgbn}+SIFTn$ and pairwise on $VIS+NIR$ 4th column) methods. Ground truth (5th column)

Even if in visible images, the blue color can be confused with other classes (sky, far away mountains), it has a unique 4-D appearance that lead to 10% improvement compared to the visible baseline. Errors due to reflection are also reduced, for instance in the image 6 in Figure 3.

Clouds and Sky. The classes *cloud* and *sky* are better segmented in the BS scenario, and, more importantly, are less confused. Sky is dark in NIR, due to Rayleigh's scattering mentioned above, while clouds remain white. As clouds are formed from particles larger than $\lambda/10$, Mie scattering [6] that is independent of wavelength applies. Thus, the contrast between these two classes are higher in NIR images, allowing more accurate segmentation (see images 2, 5 of Figure 3).

Tree and Grass. Vegetation is better predicted when NIR information is present due to the unique value of chlorophyll in NIR. Both *tree* and *grass* accuracies are improved. However, as both contain chlorophyll, classes *tree* and *grass* have similar responses in NIR and becomes more confused when NIR is present.

Building. The accuracy of the class *building* stays approximately the same for VB and BS. This class is not made of a homogeneous material, hence, material based information does not bring any advantage.

Conclusions. In this paper, we presented a framework for semantic image segmentation using the RGB and NIR information captured by any ordinary digital camera. Segmentation was formulated using a CRF model, and we studied how to incorporate the NIR cue, either in the recognition or in the regularization parts of our model, and showed that integrating NIR along with conventional RGB images improves the segmentation results. In particular, we observed that the overall improvement is due to a large improvement for some classes whose response in the NIR domain is particularly discriminant, as water, sky or cloud. The use of this potentially free additional information is a promising direction to improve semantic segmentation, which we plan to test on a broader range of classes.

References

1. Shotton, J., Winn, J.M., Rother, C., Criminisi, A.: *TextonBoost*: Joint Appearance, Shape and Context Modeling for Multi-class Object Recognition and Segmentation. In: Leonardis, A., Bischof, H., Pinz, A. (eds.) ECCV 2006, Part I. LNCS, vol. 3951, pp. 1–15. Springer, Heidelberg (2006)
2. Csurka, G., Perronnin, F.: An efficient approach to semantic segmentation. IJCV 95 (2011)
3. Verbeek, J., Triggs, B.: Region classification with markov field aspects models. In: CVPR (2007)
4. Ladicky, L., Russell, C., Kohli, P., Torr, P.H.S.: Graph Cut Based Inference with Co-occurrence Statistics. In: Daniilidis, K., Maragos, P., Paragios, N. (eds.) ECCV 2010, Part V. LNCS, vol. 6315, pp. 239–253. Springer, Heidelberg (2010)
5. Finlayson, G.D., Drew, M.S., Funt, B.V.: Color constancy: generalized diagonal transforms suffice. Journal of the Optical Society of America 11, 3011–3019 (1994)
6. Fredembach, C., Süsstrunk, S.: Colouring the Near-infrared. In: CIC (2008)
7. Schaul, L., Fredembach, C., Süsstrunk, S.: Color image dehazing using the Near-infrared. In: ICIP (2009)
8. Krishnan, D., Fergus, F.: Dark flash photography. In: SIGGRAPH (2009)
9. Brown, M., Süsstrunk, S.: Multispectral SIFT for scene category recognition. In: CVPR (2011)
10. Salamati, N., Larlus, D., Csurka, G.: Combining visible and Near-infrared cues for image categorisation. In: BMVC (2011)
11. Salamati, N., Fredembach, C., Süsstrunk, S.: Material classification using color and NIR images. In: CIC (2009)
12. Zhou, W., Huang, G., Troy, A., Cadenasso, M.L.: Object-based land cover classification of shaded areas in high spatial resolution imagery of urban areas: A comparison study. Remote Sensing of Environment 113, 1769–1777 (2009)
13. Zhang, X., Sim, T., Miao, X.: Enhancing photographs with NIR images. In: CVPR (2008)
14. Kermani, Z., Lu, Y., Süsstrunk, S.: Correlation-based joint acquisition and demosaicing of visible and Near-infrared images. In: ICIP (2011)
15. Lafferty, J., McCallum, A., Pereira, F.: Conditional random fields: probabilistic models for segmenting and labeling sequence data. In: ICML (2001)
16. Lowe, D.: Distinctive image features from scale-invariant keypoints. IJCV (2004)
17. Csurka, G., Dance, C., Fan, L., Willamowski, J., Bray, C.: Visual categorization with bags of keypoints. In: ECCV SLCV Workshop (2004)
18. Perronnin, F., Dance, C.: Fisher kernels on visual vocabularies for image categorization. In: CVPR (2007)
19. Salamati, N., Süsstrunk, S.: Material-based object segmentation using Near-infrared Information. In: CIC (2010)
20. Rother, C., Kolmogorov, V., Blake, A.: "GrabCut": interactive foreground extraction using iterated graph cuts. In: SIGGRAPH (2004)

21. Boykov, Y., Kolmogorov, V.: An experimental comparison of min-cut/max-flow algorithms for energy minimization in vision. IEEE TPAMI 26, 1124–1137 (2004)
22. Kolmogorov, V., Zabih, R.: What energy functions can be minimized via Graph Cuts? IEEE TPAMI 26, 147–159 (2004)
23. van de Sande, K.E.A., Gevers, T., Snoek, C.G.M.: Evaluating color descriptors for object and scene recognition. IEEE TPAMI 32, 1582–1596 (2010)
24. Kohli, P., Ladický, L., Torr, P.H.S.: Robust higher order potentials for enforcing label consistency. IJCV 82, 302–324 (2009)

Utilization of False Color Images in Shadow Detection

Yagiz Aksoy and A. Aydin Alatan

Electrical and Electronics Engineering Department
Middle East Technical University
06800, Ankara, Turkey
{yaksoy,alatan}@eee.metu.edu.tr

Abstract. Shadows are illuminated as a result of Rayleigh scattering phenomenon, which happens to be more effective for small wavelengths of light. We propose utilization of false color images for shadow detection, since the transformation eliminates high frequency blue component and introduces low frequency near-infrared channel. Effectiveness of the approach is tested by using several shadow-variant texture and color-related cues proposed in the literature. Performances of these cues in regular and false color images are compared and analyzed within a supervised system by using a support vector machine classifier.

1 Introduction

In natural outdoor and satellite images, shadows are illuminated as a result of atmospheric scattering of sunlight. There are several scattering phenomenons modeled in the literature [1] and in this work, Rayleigh scattering is assumed to be the most dominant one.

In the atmosphere, the amount a light beam is scattered depend on the fourth negative power of the wavelength(λ^{-4})[2]. Consecutively, light with shorter wavelengths, such as blue and violet colors, are the most scattered and light with longer wavelengths, such as red color and near-infrared (NIR) illumination, are the least scattered components of the sunlight. Actually, NIR, with a wavelength of around 1000 nm, is scattered 40 times less than blue, with a wavelength of around 400 nm [2]. The main conclusion about shadows one can make from this phenomenon is the saturation of shadows with blue channel.

This phenomenon forms the basic assumption of color-related cues for shadow detection proposed in the literature. HSV color space gives important information on shadows. Since blue is the dominant channel in shadow regions, hue channel appears with higher values; whereas saturation channel yields larger intensities due to the saturation of shadows with blue; and value channel results with smaller terms as shadows appear darker. Several shadow maps have been proposed on these assumptions [1,3,4]. As NIR light is scattered the least, color-to-NIR ratios also give important cues on shadows [5].

False color transformation is defined as the use of near-infrared, red and green channels to form a 3-channel image instead of red, green and blue channels.

A. Fusiello et al. (Eds.): ECCV 2012 Ws/Demos, Part II, LNCS 7584, pp. 472–481, 2012.

Hence, frequency spectrum of each channel of a 3-channel color image is shifted towards lower frequencies. An image with its false color version can be examined in Figure 1. Since Rayleigh scattering is more effective for high frequencies of light, illumination on shadows is smaller in false color images and shadows are expected to appear more characteristic. As the main contribution of this paper, we propose the use of false color images, instead of regular red - green - blue images, to improve the shadow segmentation performance.

(a) Original Image   (b) False Color Image

Fig. 1. A satellite image and corresponding false color image

Apart from selection of an appropriate color space, another issue is to determine correct features for shadow detection. The main cue for shadows is that shadows appear darker. When illumination is computed as the mean value of three channels for each pixel in a color image, one should expect to have "more darker" shadows in false color images compared to regular images. As another important property, shadows also have important textural characteristics [6]. Since illumination is suppressed in shadows, they are expected to appear smoother than their surroundings. Moreover, they differ from dark-colored objects, as dark objects appear textureless. We also expect to have more characteristic textural properties for shadows, when false color images are utilized.

In this effort, we test the effectiveness of proposed approach by utilizing several features proposed in the literature for false color images. A system is constructed to achieve the segmentation in a supervised manner by using a conventional support vector machine classifier.

The document is organized as follows. A literature survey is presented in Section 2. Utilized shadow-related cues are detailed in Section 3. Results are shared and discussed in Section 4 and the work is concluded in Section 5.

2   Related Work

Polidorio et al. [1] create the shadow map by using the difference between saturation and value channels of HSV color-space image by exploiting the fact that shadows have higher saturation with blue and violet wavelength due to atmospheric scattering. When image channels are in the range [0-1], they threshold the difference between saturation and value channels at zero for airborne sensors and at 0.2 for orbital sensors to get the final shadow map. The values of these thresholds are set globally, and unfortunately, performance of their algorithm highly depends on these values. Vegetation and dark objects are often falsely segmented as shadows in this approach.

Tsai [3] uses a hue based approach to identify shadows. By using the same fact about high saturation of shadows with blue and violet colors, Tsai uses HSV color space and assumes hue of shadow pixels will appear high to propose the ratio map (R) seen in (1).

$$R = \frac{Hue + 1}{Value + 1} \ where \ Hue, Value \in [0 - 1] \tag{1}$$

This map is thresholded by Otsu's method to compute the final shadow map. However, Tsai's method suffers from being unable to differentiate dark objects, such as roads, from shadows, since hue is not very sensitive in darker areas.

Chung, Lin and Huang [4] modifies Tsai's shadow map by using hue and value components scaled to be in the range [0-255] and applying an exponential function shown in (2) to the resultant ratio map to get the modified ratio map R':

$$R'(x, y) = \begin{cases} exp\left(-\left(\frac{Hue(x,y)}{Value(x,y)+1} - T_S\right)^2 / 4\sigma_2\right) * 255 & if \ \frac{Hue}{Value+1} < T_S \\ 255 & otherwise \end{cases} \tag{2}$$

where, T_S is determined by checking at which value of T_S the condition $\sum_{i=0}^{T_S} P(i) = P_S$ holds, in which $P(i)$ represents the probability of the value i in the ratio image histogram. P_S is set to 0.95 empirically and σ is calculated as $\sqrt{\sum_{i=0}^{T_S-1} P(i)i - T_S^2}$. They also apply Otsu thresholding to the image and continue with a successive thresholding scheme. They dilate the resultant candidate shadow results by a 3x3 square structuring element and analyze each candidate region iteratively by using a separability factor SB, and if SB is greater than a threshold, which is again set empirically, the resultant region is marked as shadow.

Fredembach and Süsstrunk [5] propose the use of color-to-NIR ratios together with a darkness map to identify shadows automatically. They define their temporary darkness maps as in (3) and (4) by red, green, blue and NIR channels that are scaled to be in the interval [0-1]. Then, relation in (5) is applied to the temporary maps and final darkness map (D) is computed as in Equation 6.

$$D_{VIS} = 1 - \sqrt{R^2 + G^2 + B^2} \tag{3}$$

$$D_{NIR} = 1 - NIR \tag{4}$$

$$f(x) = \frac{1}{1 + e^{-0.5(x-0.25)}} \tag{5}$$

$$D = f(D_{VIS})f(D_{NIR}) \tag{6}$$

The authors [5] integrate color information to the system by defining a Color-to-NIR ratio image (F), shown in (7), and multiplying darkness and ratio maps to get the final shadow metric (M, seen in (8)). This metric map is then binarized by setting the threshold to the first valley in the histogram of the final shadow map.

$$F = min\left(max\left(\frac{Red}{NIR}, \frac{Green}{NIR}, \frac{Blue}{NIR} \right), 1 \right) \tag{7}$$

$$M = DF \tag{8}$$

Although Color-to-NIR ratios give important information on shadows, the method [5] might typically result in many falsely labeled shadow pixels, especially in aerial and satellite images.

Finlayson, Hordley and Drew [7] remove shadows by a scalar function of a three-channel image, which depends only on the reflectance of a surface. By exploiting the fact that the shadow edges will appear on the regular image, but not in the reflectance-only image, they use the edge map differences of two images to locate shadows. One shortcoming of their approach is the necessity for calibration of cameras. In order to derive the reflectance-only map, their method needs camera calibration and this process needs multiple shots of the static scene in different daylight conditions.

In a different approach, Zhu et al. [6] takes the challenge of segmenting shadows from monochromatic images. They propose several textural features, some of which are detailed here, to differentiate shadows from darker objects. The authors [6] claim that smoothness is a shadow-variant feature, since shadows tend to suppress local illumination changes due to low illumination, and hence, appear as smoothed versions of their neighbors. Moreover, local maximum, computed in 3x3 neighborhood, is also an indicator of shadow regions. To differentiate dark objects from shadows, they realize that most of the darker objects appear textureless and propose discrete entropy (E) as a near-black feature, computed by the formula:

$$E_i = \sum_{i \in w} -p_i log_2(p_i) \tag{9}$$

where w is 3x3 neighborhood of pixel i and p_i is the probability of the histogram counts at pixel i. They train their system using binary conditional random fields and boosted decision trees and reach up to a high recognition rate. However, since their approach does not utilize color information, the performance is limited.

3   Shadow Cues

As the main shadow cue, one might use illumination that is computed as the mean value of the three channels that form the image. Illumination of a regular and a false color image can be seen in Figure 2. It can be easily observed that shadows appear darker in the false color image.

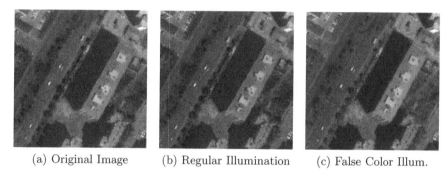

(a) Original Image   (b) Regular Illumination   (c) False Color Illum.

Fig. 2. Illumination component in regular and false color images

As texture-based cues, entropy, smoothness and local maximum are utilized as proposed in [6]. Entropy is calculated by (9). Smoothness is calculated by taking the absolute difference between the original illumination scaled to be in the range [0-1] and a Gaussian-smoothed version and subtracting the result from 1. Finally, local maximum is computed as the maximum illumination in a 3x3 neighborhood of each pixel. The resultant maps can be examined in Figure 3.

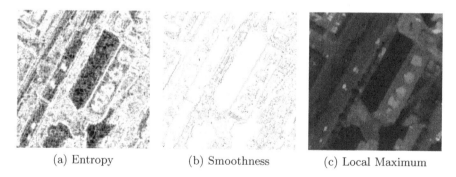

(a) Entropy   (b) Smoothness   (c) Local Maximum

Fig. 3. Texture-based shadow cue maps of the image in Figure 2a

As color-based cues, difference between saturation and value [1], as well as the ratio between hue and value ratio are utilized. As a final, the relation in (1) is also exploited [3]. The resultant maps are presented in Figure 4.

We also use the cue extracted from color-to-NIR ratios that are proposed in [5]. F metric, containing information about only color-to-NIR ratios (see (7)),

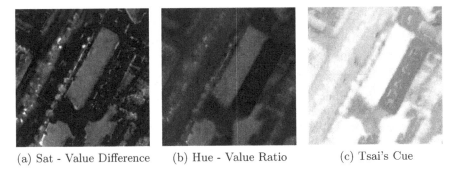

(a) Sat - Value Difference   (b) Hue - Value Ratio   (c) Tsai's Cue

Fig. 4. Color-based shadow cue maps of the image in Figure 2a

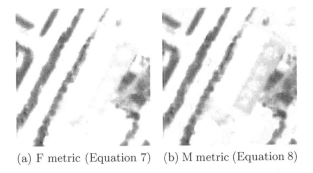

(a) F metric (Equation 7)   (b) M metric (Equation 8)

Fig. 5. Color-to-NIR ratio-based cue maps of the image seen in Figure 2a (The results are stretched to [0-255] scale for visualization)

and M metric, the main shadow map proposed (see (8)), were used in the tests. Corresponding maps can be seen in Figure 5.

4   Results

The tests are conducted by training the support vector machine classifier using a total of 400 marked shadow and non-shadow samples and quantitative results are result of a 500x500 test image. These images are obtained from the satellite IKONOS at 1-meter resolution.

In order to measure performance, we use precision and recall metrics. Precision, defined in (10), measures the percentage of the successfully classified shadows in the true shadow pixels, where recall, defined in (11), yields the percentage of the successfully classified shadow pixels among all that are classified as shadow. The performance is high when both metrics are as close to one hundred as possible.

Table 1. Feature Performances

Features	RGB		False-Color	
(w/ Illumination)	Precision	Recall	Precision	Recall
Entropy	97.3	93.9	98.8	96.1
Smoothness	89.4	96.9	97.0	97.9
Local Max	92.2	97.0	97.8	97.8
Sat - Val Difference	88.8	95.9	93.6	98.6
Hue - Val Ratio	81.0	94.6	95.7	97.7
Tsai's Ratio	94.9	96.3	95.7	97.1
F	96.5	98.4	97.3	98.3
M	96.7	98.4	97.3	98.3
Entropy and M	98.4	97.5	98.7	97.2

$$Precision \ (\%) = \frac{True \ Positive}{True \ Positive + False \ Negative} * 100 \qquad (10)$$

$$Recall \ (\%) = \frac{True \ Positive}{True \ Positive + False \ Positive} * 100 \qquad (11)$$

In these relations, *True Positive* denotes the true shadows that are classified successfully, *False Negative* denotes the true shadows that were erroneously classified as non-shadow and *False Positive* denotes the true non-shadow pixels that are erroneously classified as shadows.

We trained and tested our system by using illumination together with each one of the selected features for both RGB and false color images. Performance of each feature can be seen in Table 1.

Notice that for each metric, performance increases with the use of false color image. Textural features and use of color-to-NIR ratios appear to be superior to HSV color space based features.

Next, we combine the most successful texture-based feature, entropy, and the most successful color-based feature, M, to achieve a better performance. The maximum performance we could obtain is 98.7 precision and 97.2 recall by the use of illumination, entropy and M in false color.

Our test system can easily be utilized as a shadow recognition system initialized with minimal user interaction. Especially in false color, as shadows and non-shadows are easily and linearly separable in the constructed system, with minimal user interaction in one of the images in a database, an effective classifier can be constructed. Figure 7 shows shadow segmentation results in several other images in the same database as the image where the classifier was trained.

The results of the algorithms by Polidorio et al. [1], Tsai [3], Chung et al. [4] and Fredembach and Süsstrunk [5] together with the results of the proposed algorithm can be observed in Figure 6. The performance of the cited algorithms are presented in Table 2. As large regions, such as roads, are segmented falsely as shadows in Tsai's and Fredembach's algorithms, they come up with lower

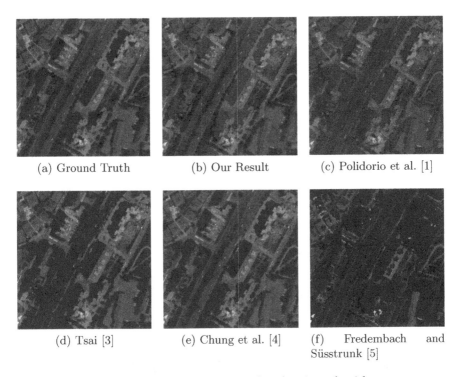

(a) Ground Truth   (b) Our Result   (c) Polidorio et al. [1]

(d) Tsai [3]   (e) Chung et al. [4]   (f)   Fredembach   and Süsstrunk [5]

Fig. 6. Shadow segmentation results of various algorithms

Table 2. Performances of various algorithms

Algorithm	Precision	Recall
Polidorio et al. [1]	82.4	97.8
Tsai [3]	53.7	99.5
Chung et al. [4]	78.4	99.1
Fredembach and Süsstrunk [5]	53.3	97.9
Proposed	98.7	97.2

precision values. Polidorio's and Chung's algorithms perform better; however, as some regions, such as vegetation, are falsely segmented as shadows in these approaches, the precision values are not high. The proposed approach results in quite high precision compared to aforementioned approaches, since challenging regions, such as roads and vegetation, could be eliminated in three dimensional space by a linear classifier. Achieving such a high precision might result in slight decrease in recall.

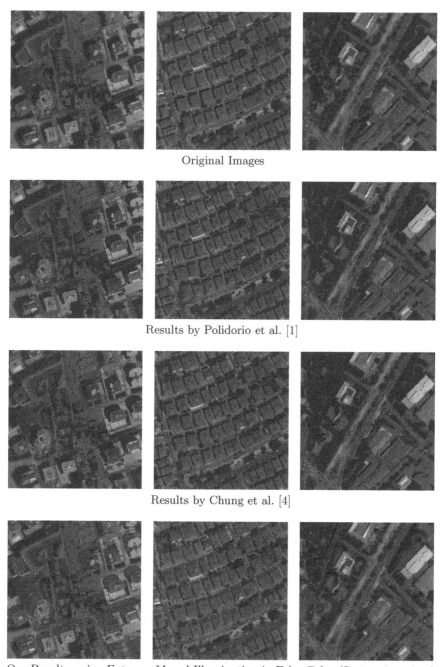

Original Images

Results by Polidorio et al. [1]

Results by Chung et al. [4]

Our Results, using Entropy, M and Illumination in False Color (System is trained
from the same 400 samples taken from the image in Figure 2a)

Fig. 7. Shadow segmentation results of various algorithms in several images

5 Conclusion

This paper proposes the use of false color images for efficient segmentation of shadows. This claim is tested by using a supervised approach with several shadow-related features and it is shown that for any of the utilized features, use of false color images increases performance remarkably. Moreover, a supervised approach to segment shadows is also proposed and shown to be effective and superior to other state-of-the-art approaches.

Acknowledgments. This work is partially supported by HAVELSAN Inc.

References

1. Polidorio, A., Flores, F., Imai, N., Tommaselli, A., Franco, C.: Automatic shadow segmentation in aerial color images. In: XVI Brazilian Symposium on Computer Graphics and Image Processing (SIBGRAPI), pp. 270–277 (2003)
2. Fredembach, C., Süsstrunk, S.: Colouring the near infrared. In: Proceedings of the IS&T/SID 16th Color Imaging Conference, pp. 176–182 (2008)
3. Tsai, V.: A comparative study on shadow compensation of color aerial images in invariant color models. IEEE Transactions on Geoscience and Remote Sensing 44, 1661–1671 (2006)
4. Chung, K.L., Lin, Y.R., Huang, Y.H.: Efficient shadow detection of color aerial images based on successive thresholding scheme. IEEE Transactions on Geoscience and Remote Sensing 47, 671–682 (2009)
5. Fredembach, C., Süsstrunk, S.: Automatic and accurate shadow detection from (potentially) a single image using near-infrared information. Technical report, EPFL (2010)
6. Zhu, J., Samuel, K., Masood, S., Tappen, M.: Learning to recognize shadows in monochromatic natural images. In: IEEE Conference on Computer Vision and Pattern Recognition (CVPR), pp. 223–230 (2010)
7. Finlayson, G.D., Hordley, S.D., Drew, M.S.: Removing Shadows from Images. In: Heyden, A., Sparr, G., Nielsen, M., Johansen, P. (eds.) ECCV 2002, Part IV. LNCS, vol. 2353, pp. 823–836. Springer, Heidelberg (2002)

High Information Rate and Efficient Color Barcode Decoding

Homayoun Bagherinia and Roberto Manduchi

University of California, Santa Cruz, Santa Cruz, CA 95064, USA
{hbagheri,manduchi}@soe.ucsc.edu
http://www.ucsc.edu

Abstract. The necessity of increasing information density in a given space motivates the use of more colors in color barcodes. A popular system, Microsofts HCCB technology, uses four or eight colors per patch. This system displays a color palette of four or eight colors in the color barcode to solve the problem with the dependency of the surface color on the illuminant spectrum, viewing parameters, and other sources. Since the displayed colors cannot be used to encode information, this solution comes at the cost of reduced information rate. In this contribution, we introduce a new approach to color barcode decoding that uses 24 colors per patch and requires a small number of reference colors to display in a barcode. Our algorithm builds groups of colors from each color patch and a small number of reference color patches, and models their evolution due to changing illuminant using a linear subspace. Therefore, each group of colors is represented by one such subspace. Our experimental results show that our barcode decoding algorithm achieves higher information rate with a very low probability of decoding error compared to systems that do display a color palette. The computational complexity of our algorithm is relatively low due to searching for the nearest subspace among 24 subspaces only.

1   Introduction

Color barcodes are becoming one of the technologies to embed information in recent years. The information density of conventional 1-D and 2-D barcodes is much lower than color barcodes in a limited area. The use of colors creates more symbols that lead to larger data capacity within the same symbol size.

One of the popular color barcodes in the market is HCCB (Microsoft's High Capacity Color Barcode) [8]. HCCB uses a grid of colored triangles with four or eight colors to encode data. The necessity of increasing information density in a given space encourages the idea of using more colors in color barcodes. For instance, using 24 colors instead of 8 would increase the information rate by 1.5 times in the same barcode area.

Decoding large number of colors is a challenging task. One of the main problems is that an observed color patch depends on the surface reflectance and unknown illuminant spectrums. One way to overcome this problem is to apply a

A. Fusiello et al. (Eds.): ECCV 2012 Ws/Demos, Part II, LNCS 7584, pp. 482–491, 2012.

pre-processing step such as color constancy operation to compensate with varying and unknown illuminants ([3], [5], [6], [7]). Another strategy is the clustering of a number of colors in color space [10]. Modeling the changes of the observed color due to changing illuminant could also solve this problem [1].

In this contribution, our focus is a solution for decoding the color information in a barcode. We consider color barcodes that can be decoded under multiple illuminants with small number of reference patches of known colors, seen under the same illuminant as the color to be decoded. The use of reference color patches enables robust decoding with relatively low computational complexity which is suitable for implementation on a low powered mobile device. Our algorithm considers each color patch and a set of reference color patches as a group of color patches, and models their evolution due to changing illuminant using a linear subspace. Therefore, each group of colors (one color and one or more reference patches) is represented by one such subspace. When a color barcode is observed, our algorithm decodes each color independently by building a group from the color and a set of reference color patches. Then, each group is decoded by finding the nearest subspace among all subspaces. Our experiments show that our approach produces higher information rate than existing technology such as HCCB and the works described in [1] and [8] with a very low probability of incorrect decoding using small number of reference color patches.

2   Related Work

There are limited numbers of research work in the literature on the topic of color barcode decoding. The common approach to color barcode decoding (e.g. [8], [10]) assumes that all N colors that are used to generate a color barcode are available in the barcode itself. HCCB technology also assumes that all colors in the palette are available. This makes the decoding task simpler by comparing the color of the patches in the barcode against the colors of N patches. However, since the N color patches are not information-carrying patches, the information rate will be reduced.

The method of Sali and Lax [10] uses a k-means classifier to assign the (R,G,B) value of a color patch to one reference color. Similarly, the HCCB detection algorithm [8] identifies a set of clusters in color space using mean shift clustering, and assigns each cluster center to one of the reference colors in a palette, contained in the barcode itself. These strategies usually work well for the limited number of colors in a barcode. Color clustering is not guaranteed to work well when many more colors are used. Moreover, these strategies only work for dense barcodes, with the number of patches considerably larger than the number of colors N, so that the attachment of the color palette to the barcode has insignificant impact on the spatial density of information.

Wang and Manduchi [12] studied the problem of information embedding via printed color. Their algorithms used one or more reference color patches of known colors, observed under the same unknown illuminant as the colors to be decoded. Known reference color patches enable an estimate of illuminant as a parametric color transformation between a canonical illuminant and the unknown illuminant. This transformation is used to render the unknown color patch under the canonical illuminant, which can be decoded using the training data.

Recent work by Bagherinia and Manduchi [1] showed a study of the variation of small groups of printed colors and modeled their evolution due to changing illuminant using a low-dimensional linear subspace. Their approach decodes length k barcode elements of a color barcode, and does not use reference colors. They showed that by carefully selecting a subset of barcode elements, it is possible to achieve good information rate at low decoding error probability. Since their system uses a subset of barcode elements and does not allow the repeat of colors within a barcode element, maximum information rate for N colors cannot be achieved. The number of subspaces also increases with the length k of barcode elements which leads to high computational complexity for large barcodes. Thus, this approach is not suitable for low powered mobile device implementation.

This contribution builds on the work by Bagherinia and Manduchi [1]. However, rather than considering groups of k color patches, we concentrate on the variation of one color patch and r reference patches as a group of color patches to model their evolution due to changing illuminant.

3   Information Rate and Probability of Decoding Error

The patches in a color barcode are created from a set $\mathcal{C}_N \subset \mathcal{C}$ of N color patches and $\mathcal{C}_M \subset \mathcal{C}$ of M reference color patches. A color barcode can be defined as the juxtaposition of n color bars for information encoding and r reference colors in any spatial pattern, resulting in a $K = n + r$ length barcode.

As defined in [1], the information rate R of a barcode (reference colors are not used) is defined by the logarithm base 2 of the number of different symbol that can be represented by the barcode and measured in bits per bar. The information rate for a barcode of K bars and r reference patches is defined as:

$$R(K, r) = \left(1 - \frac{r}{K}\right) \log_2 N \tag{1}$$

An approach to color barcode decoding assumes that r reference patches in the barcode are attached to the barcode. This may allow for more robust decoding. However, this solution comes at the cost of reduced information rate, since r reference patches cannot be used to encode information.

Fig. 1 illustrates the information rate for $N = 24$, $K = 120$ bars and varying r from 0 to 24. For example, the information rate of a length 120 barcode that displays all $r = 24$ reference colors is 3.67 bits/bar. The information rate using $r = 2$ reference colors is 4.51 bits/bar. A color barcode system that uses two reference colors can pack about 0.84 additional bits per bar (or 100 bits overall) than systems that use 24 reference colors ($r = N$). Thus, it is highly beneficial to use small number of reference colors.

The probability of decoding error $P(r)$ is important to consider for a generic barcode with N colors and r reference colors. This is defined as the average probability of decoding error of a color patch over all colors. As described in [1], the

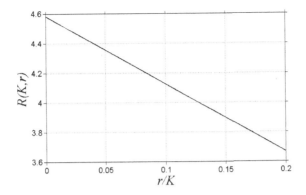

Fig. 1. The information rate for $N = 24$, a length $K = 120$ barcode, and varying r from 0 to 24 reference colors

probability of decoding error for a barcode of length K, assuming that decoding errors for the individual colors in the barcode are statistically independent events, is:

$$P_E(K, r) = 1 - (1 - P_E(r))^K \qquad (2)$$

The probability of incorrect decoding grows with the number of bars K in the barcode. The dependence $P_E(K, r)$ on r can be determined experimentally as described in Sec. 5.

4   Color Barcode Decoding

4.1   Decoding Approach

Let the $3(1 + r)$-dimensional vector $\mathbf{e} = [c, d_1, \ldots, d_r]^T$ be the measured color of a surface for information decoding and r reference surfaces (a reference color group of r colors), where $c = [c^R, c^G, c^B]^T$ and $d_j = [d_j^R, d_j^G, d_j^B]^T$ $(j = 1 \ldots r)$ are (R, G, B) color vectors. A model to describe the observed color of Lambertian surfaces assumes that the spectra of the surface reflectances and of the illuminants live in finite-dimensional spaces of dimension N_{ref} and N_{ill} respectively [7]. Hence, the observed group of colors under a given illuminant is equal to

$$\mathbf{e} = \mathbf{\Phi} v \qquad (3)$$

$\mathbf{\Phi}$ is a $3(1 + r) \times N_{\text{ill}}$ full-rank matrix whose entries are a function of the illumination and reflectance basis vectors as well as of the spectral sensitivities of the camera assuming Lambertian characteristics of surfaces. $v = [v_1, v_2, \ldots, v_{N_{\text{ill}}}]^T$ is a vector of length N_{ill} containing the coefficients of the illuminant with respect to the chosen basis.

The observed color c of a single surface under a given illuminant is equal to $c = \mathbf{\Phi}_c v$. The decoding of c would be very difficult if no reference color is used. This is due to the fact that $N_{\text{ill}} \geq 3$ in general ([4], [9]), and the rank of $\mathbf{\Phi_c}$ would be 3 which makes $rank(\mathbf{\Phi_c})$ smaller than N_{ill}. If, however, a color along with multiple reference colors seen under the same illuminant is decoded at once, the probability of correct decoding will be higher due to $\mathbf{e} \in \mathbb{R}^{3(1+r)}$ and $rank(\mathbf{\Phi}) = min(3(1+r), N_{\text{ill}})$. The vector $\mathbf{e}$ is constrained to live in a subspace S of dimension of at most N_{ill}.

Let S be the linear subspaces in $\mathbb{R}^D$ spanned by $\mathbf{e}^i$ over varying illuminant i. The decoding algorithm for an individual color represented by $\mathbf{e}$ begins by modeling the subspaces S_k of N colors ($k = 1 \ldots N$). Similar to the work described in [1], we have considered two approaches to build these subspaces. In the first case, the subspaces of suitable dimension D are built from observations under verity of illuminants via Principal Component Analysis (PCA). The second approach is based on the diagonal model of color changes, which assumes that each color channel changes as a result of an illuminant change by a multiplicative factor. The matrix $\mathbf{\Phi}$ is formed based on a single color and r reference color patches under a single illuminant as follows

$$\mathbf{\Phi}^T = \begin{bmatrix} c^R & 0 & 0 & d_1^R & 0 & 0 & d_2^R \ldots \\ 0 & c^G & 0 & 0 & d_1^G & 0 & 0 \ldots \\ 0 & 0 & c^B & 0 & 0 & d_1^B & 0 \ldots \end{bmatrix} \tag{4}$$

The subspace modeling based on diagonal model is less accurate. However, it allows a fast calibration procedure (since it requires a single image of N colors and r reference colors under a single illuminant) and is suitable for the situation when a different camera is used or the colors are printed with a different printer.

Once N subspaces are built, we decode an observed color vector $\mathbf{e}$ by assigning it to the subspace that minimizes the distance to $\mathbf{e}$. The distance is defined as the distance between $\mathbf{e}$ and its projection onto S_k.

4.2   Reference Color and Subspace Selection

To produce a certain $P_E(r)$ smaller than desired, one needs to define reference colors within a set of colors. Selection of r number of reference colors that minimizes the associated $P_E(r)$ is computationally very expensive. In particular, the probability of incorrect decoding for all combinations of r reference colors from a large set of colors needs to be evaluated. We have considered a suboptimal greedy technique to reduce the complexity associated with r reference colors selection. Our approach is to insert one reference color at a time to compute the $P_E(r)$ as follows: we select a reference color from the set $\mathcal{R}_1 \subset \mathcal{C}_M$ that minimizes the $P_E(r = 1)$. Then we build a set $\mathcal{R}_2$ of groups of two reference colors of which contain the selected reference color in previous step. Then, we search for the group (of reference colors) that minimizes the $P_E(r = 2)$. We continue this procedure until r reference colors satisfy the desired $P_E(r)$. Basically, for $r > 1$ we build all possible combinations ($\mathcal{R}_r$) of r length groups of reference colors of which contain the reference colors selected in the previous steps.

We considered all possible reference colors that could build sets of reference color groups $\mathcal{R}_r$. We then estimated (via cross-validation over multiple illuminants) the probability that the color i (represented by the vector $\mathbf{e}$) is incorrectly decoded as j. The sum of all these probabilities, divided by the number of colors, gives the probability of incorrect decoding $P_E(r)$ for a given reference color group of length r. For PCA-based approach, we repeated this procedure for subspace dimensions from one to five. For each r length reference colors, we selected the subspace dimension D that minimizes $P_E(r)$ for chosen r reference colors.

Fig. 2 shows the probability of incorrect decoding $P_E(r)$ for the number of reference colors r between one and five and the subspace dimension between one and five. We select the subspace dimensions 3 and 4 for $r = 1, 2$ and $r = 3, 4, 5$ respectively.

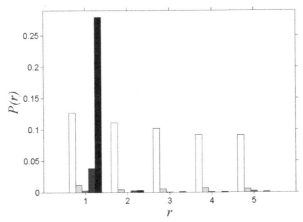

Fig. 2. The probability $P_E(r)$ of incorrect decoding as a function of the number of reference colors r and subspace dimension from 1 (white) to 5 (black)

5   Experiments

For our experiments, we printed a colorchecker with $5 \times 25 = 125$ colors on paper by a regular printer, uniformly sampled in (R, G, B) color space. Images were taken of the printed colors with a Canon EOS 350D camera in raw (CR2) format from zero degree (with respect to the normal to the colorcheckers surface) under 64 different lighting conditions including indoor and outdoor under direct sunlight, diffuse skylight with overcast sky, cloudy sky, or under cast shadow, and various types of artificial light. The color value of each patch was calculated by averaging over a few hundreds color values within the patch to reduce noise.

We then selected $N = 24$ color patches using images under all 64 illuminants. For each illuminant, we used k-means to select 24 colors. Commonly used initialization methods for k-means algorithm is Random Partition. To make sure that the k-means clustering selects 24 distinct colors, we run k-means 10 times with different starting point to select 24 colors with highest occurrences in all runs. Once we have 24 colors for each illuminant, we selected 24 colors with highest occurrences among all illuminants. The color of reference patches were

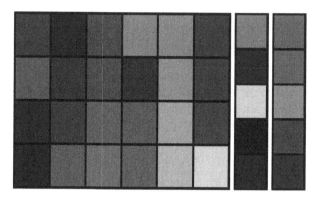

Fig. 3. The 24 color patches, 5 reference color patches selected for PCA-based and diagonal model

selected from $M = 125 - 24$ colors as described in Sec. 4.2. The colors for reference colors are different than the $N = 24$ colors since it is desired to build each vector **e** with distinctive colors rather than allowing color repetition in the vector **e**. Synthetic images of all 24 colors and $r = 1 \ldots 5$ reference color patches were built from the average color values of the images of the color patches seen under the 64 representative illuminants. For PCA-based approach, we compute the probability of incorrect decoding $P_E(r)$ for number of reference colors r ranging between one and five as follows. We ran ten rounds of cross-validation, each time randomly selecting 32 illuminants, learning the subspaces for each vector **e** representing a color and r reference patches considered based on its images under these illuminants, and testing each vector **e** in turn on 32 of the remaining illuminants. We count the number of times any color was incorrectly decoded, and divided the result by the number of test illuminants (32), by the number of cross-validation rounds (10) and by the number of colors (24). We also tested the decoding algorithm based on the diagonal model discussed in Sec. 4.1 In this case, the color subspaces were built from observation of the colors under just one illuminant. We ran ten rounds of cross-validation, each time randomly selecting one illuminant (without repetition), training our model on such illuminant and testing it with vectors **e** seen under 32 illuminants randomly chosen.

We expanded our experiments to more realistic illumination situations. We showed the robustness of our algorithm when a color barcode is observed from different viewing angles under different illuminants. Typically, the colored surfaces produced by a color printer are far from being Lambertian. They may have a strong specular refection component. In the presence of specular refection, a viewpoint-dependent component with the same color as the illuminant adds to the perceived color of the surface from diffuse refection [11]. We took 32 test images from our printed colorchecker under four illuminants from multiple viewpoints ranging from -50 to 50 degrees with respect to the normal to the colorcheckers surface and from a constant distance about 1.5 to 2 meter. We extracted eight images taken under the same illuminant from these 32 test images. Then, similar to the scatter-plot in [2], we showed the scatter-plot of the normalized values $R/(R+G+B)$ vs. $G/(R+G+B)$ of the color of $N = 24$ patches. Under an ideal Lambertian model, the normalized color for a color patch should be constant regardless of the viewpoint under the same illuminant. The scatter-plot in Fig. 4 suggests that normalized colors from most of color patches are scattered. The scattering within each color cluster may be due to the specular component as a portion of illuminant color is captured along with the surface color. In particular, a subset of point clusters are oriented towards the white surface point (the white cross in the scatter-plot), whose color is similar to the color of the illuminant. We also compute the probability of incorrect decoding $P_E(r)$

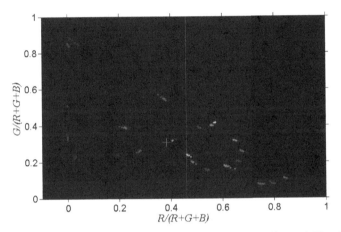

Fig. 4. The scatter-plot of the normalized color values of $N = 24$

for number of reference colors r by running ten rounds of cross-validation, each time randomly selecting 32 illuminants (from 64 training illuminants), learning the subspaces, and testing on the data of these 32 images.

Fig. 5 shows the probability of decoding error $P_E(r)$ and $P_E(K,r)$ (for a $K = 120$ length barcode, computed using Eq. (2)) for number of reference colors r using $N = 24$ colors. We tested the decoding method on the data with zero viewing angle and the data with different viewing points ranging from -50 to 50 degrees. Both types of subspace modeling (via PCA or via the diagonal model) are considered.

These results suggest that it is possible to reach high information rate with a very low probability of decoding error. For example, PCA-based subspace modeling for $r >= 2$, $N = 24$ colors, and a length $K = 120$ barcode results in a probability of zero incorrect decoding of any length of barcode, while allowing one to encode information at a rate of about 4.51 bits per bar if only two reference colors are used. In presence of specular reflection, the information rate is 4.43 bits per bar with a probability of zero incorrect decoding if four reference colors

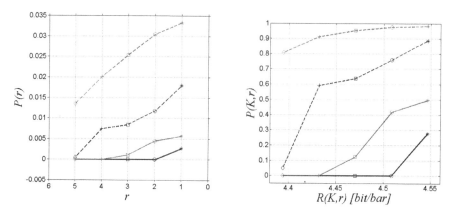

Fig. 5. Left: the probability of incorrect decoding $P_E(r)$ to decode a single color patch as a function of the number of reference colors r. Right: the probability incorrect detection $P_E(K,r)$ for a length $K = 120$ barcode versus the information rate compute using Eq. (1) and (2). '*': $r = 1$; 'o': $r = 2$; '□': $r = 3$; '+': $r = 4$; '◇': $r = 5$. Subspaces learnt via PCA (solid line) over 32 illuminants, and diagonal model (dashed line). Black line: the algorithm tested on data with zero viewing angle. Red line: the algorithm tested on data with different viewing points ranging from −50 to 50 degrees.

are used. Using the diagonal model to build the subspaces leads to less accurate decoding. The probability of decoding error using five reference colors is equal 0.048 at 4.39 bits per bar. The probability of decoding error for smaller barcode such as $K = 60$ bars ($N = 24$ and $r = 5$) reduces to 0.02 with an information rate of 4.2 bits per bar using Eq. (2). The subspace modeling based on diagonal model does not produce promising results in presence of specular reflection.

Decoding each color patch requires finding the nearest subspace in a database of only 24 elements regardless of the number of reference colors chosen. This makes this algorithm suitable for implementation on a low powered mobile device.

6   Conclusions

We introduced a new color barcode decoding approach that requires few reference colors attached to the color barcode. Our experiments have shown that, by carefully selecting a set of reference colors, it is possible to achieve a high information rate at the low probability of decoding error with relatively low computational complexity which is suitable for implementation on low powered mobile device. In the future, we hope to extend our decoding strategies in more realistic situations such as errors due to color mixing from two neighboring patches, to printed color drift and fading, or to color barcodes printed from different printers.

Acknowledgement. This material is based upon work supported by the National Science Foundation under Grant No. IIS - 0835645.

References

1. Bagherinia, H., Manduchi, R.: A theory of color barcodes. In: IEEE Color and Photometry in Computer Vision Workshop (CPCV 2011) (2011)
2. Bagherinia, H., Manduchi, R.: Robust real-time detection of multi-color markers on a cell phone. Journal of Real-Time Image Processing (2011)
3. Brainard, D.H., Freeman, W.T.: Bayesian color constancy. Journal of the Optical Society of America A 14, 1393–1411 (1997)
4. Dixon, E.R.: Spectral distribution of Australian daylight. Journal of the Optical Society of America 68, 437–450 (1978)
5. Finlayson, G.D., Hordley, S.D., Hubel, P.M.: Color by correlation: A simple, unifying framework for color constancy. IEEE Trans. Pattern Anal. Mach. Intell. 23, 1209–1221 (2001)
6. Forsyth, D.A.: A novel algorithm for color constancy. Int. J. Comput. Vision 5, 5–36 (1990)
7. Maloney, L.T., Wandell, B.A.: Color constancy: a method for recovering surface spectral reflectance. In: Fischler, M.A., Firschein, O. (eds.) Readings in Computer Vision: Issues, Problems, Principles, and Paradigms, pp. 293–297. Morgan Kaufmann Publishers Inc., San Francisco (1987)
8. Parikh, D., Jancke, G.: Localization and segmentation of a 2D high capacity color barcode. In: Proceedings of the 2008, IEEE Workshop on Applications of Computer Vision (WACV 2008), pp. 1–6. IEEE Computer Society, Washington, DC (2008)
9. Parkkinen, J.P.S., Hallikanen, J., Jaaskelainen, T.: Characteristic spectra of Munsell Colors. Journal of the Optical Society of America A 6, 318–322 (1989)
10. Sali, E., Lax, D.: Color bar code system. U.S. Patent 7210631 (2006)
11. Shafer, S.A.: Using color to separate reflection components. Color Research and Application 10, 210–218 (1985)
12. Wang, F., Manduchi, R.: Color-constant information embedding. In: Proc. IEEE Workshop on Color and Reflectance in Imaging and Computer Vision (2010)

Uzawa Block Relaxation Methods
for Color Image Restoration

Cédric Loosli[1], Stéphanie Jehan-Besson[2], and Jonas Koko[1]

[1] LIMOS, Université Blaise Pascal – CNRS UMR 6158, Complexe des Cézeaux,
63173 Aubiere
[2] GREYC Laboratory, CNRS UMR 6072, Bd du Maréchal Juin, 14050 Caen, France
cloosli@isima.fr, jehan@ensicaen.fr, koko@sp.isima.fr

Abstract. In this paper we propose to investigate the use of a vectorial total variation model with spatially varying regularization and data terms for color image denoising and restoration. We pay attention to two main minimization problems: the minimization of a weighted vectorial total variation term TV_g, which acts as a regularization term, using the L^2 norm as data term or the minimization of the vectorial total variation with a spatially varying L_g^1 norm. The optimization process takes benefit of convex optimization tools by introducing an augmented Lagrangian formulation. This formulation leads us to simple and efficient algorithms based on Uzawa block relaxation schemes that are also robust towards the choice of the penalty parameter. In this paper, We propose to study more particularly the impact of spatially varying terms (total variation term or data terms) for color image restoration. A new weighted total variation term is proposed for old parchments restoration and we also compare the use of a weighted total variation term with a spatially varying data term for impulse noise removal in color images.

1 Introduction

In this paper, we are interested in addressing the vectorial (color) image restoration problem through the minimization of a unique criterion that takes benefit of a vectorial total variation term acting as a regularization term. Such a criterion proves to be interesting notably to cope with the regularization of correlated vectorial image features and may avoid to find an appropriate color space change when dealing with color image restoration. Let first remind that the importance of total variation for image restoration has been largely proved since the seminal ROF model introduced by Rudin, Osher and Fatemi [1]. In this work, the authors propose to recover the restored image u from a noisy image f by minimizing the following criterion :

$$E(u) = \int_\Omega |\nabla u(x)|\, \mathrm{d}x + \lambda \int_\Omega |f(x) - u(x)|^2\, \mathrm{d}x \qquad (1.1)$$

where Ω is the image domain, $u : \Omega \to R$ is the unknown restored image, f is the observed image and λ a positive scale parameter. The model (1.1) is also called

A. Fusiello et al. (Eds.): ECCV 2012 Ws/Demos, Part II, LNCS 7584, pp. 492–503, 2012.

$TV + L^2$ model. Such a framework has been intensively investigated for denoising [1,2]. It has also been extended by changing the L^2 norm by a L^1 norm ($TV + L^1$ model) for salt and pepper noise removal (see for example [3]), texture extraction or decomposition (e.g. [4]) or shape denoising (e.g. [5]). The minimization issues of such problems are not trivial due to the non differentiability of the total variation regularization term and also of the L^1 norm and have been addressed by many authors. For example, standard calculus of variations and Euler-Lagrange equations can be used to compute the PDE that will drive the functional u towards a minimum of E. This method requires a smooth approximation of the L^1 norm and a small time step must be chosen so as to ensure the convergence. This often leads to a large number of iterations as mentioned in [5]. In [6], a MRF (Markov Random Field) model is proposed which uses the anisotropic separable approximation (i.e. $|\nabla u| = |D_x u| + |D_y u|$ where D_x and D_y are the horizontal and vertical discrete derivative operators). This approximation is also used in [7] where the authors proposed an efficient graph-cut method. In all these approaches, an approximation or a smoothing of the L^1 norm is required. In [5,8], based on the works of [2,9,10,4], a fast minimization algorithm based on a dual formulation is proposed for the minimization of $TV + L^1$. Thanks to such approaches, they do not need any approximation or smoothing of the L^1 norm, they rather take benefit of a convex regularization of the criterion which was first proposed by [4]. More recently, a lot of very efficient numerical methods using convex analysis tools have been proposed. Among them, we can cite the primal-dual method proposed in [2], the split Bregman method [11] or the unified framework proposed by Pock and Chambolle [12]. Such algorithms have become popular due to their low computational cost. In this paper we also take benefit of convex optimization tools by using a simple and efficient algorithm based on Uzawa block relaxation schemes and an augmented Lagrangian formulation [13,14]. This scheme is efficient and have the nice property to be robust towards the choice of the penalty parameter. Moreover, it is here computed and applied in the special case of vectorial (color) image restoration.

When dealing with multi-components images (such as color images), the image f becomes a vector with n components (e.g. $\mathbf{f} = (f_1, f_2, f_3)^T$ and $n = 3$ for color images) which leads to revise the above criterion and to propose a well-adapted definition of the vectorial total variation term. In a first work, Blomgren and Chan [15] propose to restore vector-valued images using a vectorial adaptation of the total variation term. Later, some other color total variation models have been proposed by different authors (see for example [16,17]) for color image restoration. In [16,17] the vectorial total variation term to minimize becomes an integral over a function of the larger and smaller eigenvalues of the structure tensor proposed by di Zenso [18] (see also [19] for a recent review on anisotropic color diffusion PDEs). When the function is chosen to be the identity, their scheme leads to the minimization of the following regularization term $\int_\Omega (||\nabla \mathbf{u}||) \, dx$ where $||\nabla \mathbf{u}(x)|| = \left(\sum_{i=1}^n |\nabla u_i(x)|^2\right)^{1/2}$ is the Frobenius norm of the derivative $\nabla \mathbf{u}$. This vectorial total variation regularization term has then proven to be convenient when dealing with minimization using dual approaches

[20,21,22,23] and leads to good results for color restoration due to its link to the eigenvalues of the structure tensor. However, this regularization term fails in preserving sharp details like edges and texture regions.

In order to circumvent such problems, recent works (see for example [24] for color restoration) propose some spatially varying terms in the functional to minimize. The idea is to weight the data term differently according to the localisation in the image by minimizing a spatially adaptive functional of the form:

$$E(\mathbf{u}) = \int_\Omega ||\nabla\mathbf{u}(x)||\,\mathrm{d}x + \frac{1}{\tau}\int_\Omega \lambda(x)|\mathbf{f}(x) - \mathbf{u}(x)|^\tau \qquad (1.2)$$

with $\tau \in [1,2]$. Here, the function $\lambda(x)$ is similar to the constant λ but is calculated on each point of the image. For example, a recent work [24] establishes a general framework for color image restoration dealing with both the L^2 and L^1 cases. It is solved by Fenchel-duality and semi-smooth Newton techniques. Some other works rather propose to deal with a weighted total variation term as for example in [25] for color image restoration or [5,26,8] for grey level image restoration.

In this work, we then propose to study spatially varying regularization and data terms for color image restoration. We first solve the minimization of the following vectorial $TV_g + L^\tau$ model:

$$E(\mathbf{u}) = \int_\Omega g(x)||\nabla\mathbf{u}(x)||\,\mathrm{d}x + \lambda \int_\Omega |\mathbf{f}(x) - \mathbf{u}(x)|^\tau\,\mathrm{d}x \qquad (1.3)$$

where Ω is the image domain, $\mathbf{u} : \Omega \to \mathbb{R}^3$ is the restored image, $\mathbf{f}$ is the observed image and $g : \Omega \to]0, A]$ $(A > 0)$ is a function chosen according to the application or the noise model. In this paper, for space reasons, we propose the minimization scheme only for $\tau = 2$ but the minimization for the L^1 norm can be performed using the same mathematical framework as proposed in [8]. The constant $\lambda > 0$ is a positive scale parameter. Such a spatially varying regularization term appears to be interesting both for Gaussian [5] using the L^2 norm and salt and pepper denoising [27,8] by using a well adapted function g and the L^1 norm. Here, we propose an adapted function g for the restoration of old parchments. One may ask whether it is more interesting to use a spatially varying data term or a spatially varying regularization term. Indeed, it depends on the application. The spatially varying regularization term seems better adapted for a structural filtering (edges preservation or removing components according to their structure) while the spatially data term seems better adapted for a syntactic filtering and can better preserve the intensity of some pixels. In this paper, we then provide an example which attests the real interest of the TV_g term for old parchments restoration but we also propose an example of impulse noise removal where a well designed spatially varying data term may be more interesting. To this end, we then propose to solve the minimization of the following criterion:

$$E_2(\boldsymbol{u}) = \lambda \int_\Omega \left[|\nabla u_1|^2 + |\nabla u_2|^2 + |\nabla u_3|^2\right]^{1/2}\,\mathrm{d}x + \sum_{i=1}^{3}\int_\Omega g_i(x)|u_i(x) - f_i(x)|\,\mathrm{d}x, \quad (1.4)$$

where $\mathbf{g} = [g_1, g_2, g_3]^T$ is now a vectorial function with different components according to the color channels. Experimental results on simulated noisy images (salt and pepper on each color channel) provide a first example where this spatially varying data term may be advantageously used.

The minimization problem and notations are given in section 2 while the Augmented Lagrangian formulation is detailed in section 3 for $TV_g + L^2$ and section 4 for $TV + L_g^1$. Experimental results are given in section 5.

2   Problem Statement

2.1   Notations and Minimization Problems

Let Ω be a three-dimensional bounded open domain of $\mathbb{R}^d$, $d = 2, 3$. We consider a vector-valued function $\boldsymbol{u}(x) = (u_1(x), u_2(x), u_3(x)) \in \mathbb{R}^3$ defined on Ω. For a color image defined on Ω, the components u_i stand for the three values of each color channel (for example the RGB color space). To simplify, vector valued functions are denoted by bold-face letters (e.g. $\boldsymbol{u} = (u_1, u_2, u_3)$). The Euclidean scalar product is $\boldsymbol{u} \cdot \boldsymbol{v} = \sum_{i=1}^d u_i v_i$, for $\boldsymbol{u}$ and $\boldsymbol{v}$ in $\mathbb{R}^d$. Moreover, for $\boldsymbol{u} \in \boldsymbol{R}^d$, we use the notations: $|\boldsymbol{u}|_2 = (\boldsymbol{u} \cdot \boldsymbol{u})^{1/2}$, $\quad |\boldsymbol{u}|_1 = \sum_{i=1}^d |u_i|$, $\quad |\boldsymbol{u}|_\infty = \max_{i=1,\dots,d} |u_i|$ for the Euclidean norm, the 1-norm and the infinity norm, respectively.

Let $\boldsymbol{f} = (f_1, f_2, f_3)$ be an observed (blurry or noisy) color image. We propose to address the two following minimization problems where $\boldsymbol{u} = (u_1, u_2, u_3)$ is the unknown image to restore and $\boldsymbol{V}$ is a suitable functions space (or a finite dimensional space):

- The $TV_g + L^2$ which is defined as follows :

$$\min_{\boldsymbol{u} \in \boldsymbol{V}} E_1(\boldsymbol{u}) = \int_\Omega g(x) \left[|\nabla u_1|^2 + |\nabla u_2|^2 + |\nabla u_3|^2 \right]^{1/2} \mathrm{d}x + \lambda \int_\Omega |\boldsymbol{u}(x) - \boldsymbol{f}(x)|_2^2 \, \mathrm{d}x, \tag{2.1}$$

  where g is a scalar function.
- The $TV + L_g^1$ model which is defined as follows :

$$\min_{\boldsymbol{u} \in \boldsymbol{V}} E_2(\boldsymbol{u}) = \lambda \int_\Omega \left[|\nabla u_1|^2 + |\nabla u_2|^2 + |\nabla u_3|^2 \right]^{1/2} \mathrm{d}x + \sum_{i=1}^3 \int_\Omega g_i(x) |u_i(x) - f_i(x)| \, \mathrm{d}x, \tag{2.2}$$

  where $\mathbf{g} = [g_1, g_2, g_3]^T$ is a vectorial function.

In the case $TV_g + L^2$, we precise the first term. Let g be a continuous, positive valued and bounded function defined on Ω. Let us introduce the weighted total variation regularization term, denoted by TV_g, derived from [5]

$$J(\boldsymbol{u}) = \int_\Omega g(x) \left[|\nabla u_1|^2 + |\nabla u_2|^2 + |\nabla u_3|^2 \right]^{1/2} \mathrm{d}x = \sup_{\boldsymbol{\phi} \in \Phi_g} (\boldsymbol{u}, \nabla \cdot \boldsymbol{\phi})_{L^2(\Omega; \mathbb{R}^3)}$$

where $\Phi_g = \left\{ \boldsymbol{\phi} \in \mathcal{C}^1(\Omega, \mathbb{R}^3) \ : \ |\boldsymbol{\phi}(x)| \leq g, \text{ for all } x \in \Omega \right\}$.

3   Augmented Lagrangian Methods for the $TV_g + L^2$ Model

In this section we present Uzawa (dual) methods for solving (2.1). To this end, we need to transform the convex minimization problem (2.1) into a suitable saddle-point problem by introducing an auxiliary unknown as for the scalar case [8]. For space reasons, only few elements are given.

3.1   Augmented Lagrangian Formulation

Let us introduce the auxiliary unknown $p = f - u$ and rewrite the functional E_1 as

$$E_1(u,p) = J(u) + \lambda \int_\Omega |p(x)|_2^2 \, dx. \tag{3.1}$$

The minimization problem (3.1) becomes

$$\min_{(u,p)\in K} E_1(u,p), \tag{3.2}$$

where the constraint set K is defined by $K = \{(u,p) \in X \times X \mid u + p - f = 0 \text{ in } \Omega\}$.

It is obvious that problems (3.1) and (3.2) are equivalent. To the constrained minimization problem (3.2) we associate the Lagrangian functional $\mathscr{L}$ defined on $X \times X \times X$ by

$$\mathscr{L}(u,p;s) = E_1(u,p) + (s, u + p - f)_X. \tag{3.3}$$

In (3.3), s is the Lagrange multiplier associated with the constraint in K. Since E_1 is convex and continuous, a saddle point $(u^*, p^*; s^*)$ of $\mathscr{L}$ exists and verifies $\mathscr{L}(u^*, p^*; s) \leq \mathscr{L}(u^*, p^*; s^*) \leq \mathscr{L}(u, p; s^*), \quad \forall (u, p, s) \in X \times X \times X$.

We now introduce the augmented Lagrangian defined, for $r > 0$, by

$$\mathscr{L}_r(u,p;s) = \mathscr{L}(u,p;s) + \frac{r}{2} \| u + p - f \|_{L^2}^2 \tag{3.4}$$

where r is the penalty parameter. It can be proved (easily) that a saddle point of $\mathscr{L}_r$ is a saddle point of $\mathscr{L}$ and conversely. This is due to the fact that the quadratic term in $\mathscr{L}_r$ vanishes when the constraint $u + p - f = 0$ is satisfied. Some efficient numerical schemes can be used to solve this problem like notably the Uzawa Block Relaxation method detailed thereafter. One important feature is that this algorithm is well conditioned against the choice of the penalty parameter r.

3.2   Uzawa Block Relaxation Methods

We apply Uzawa block relaxation methods to the augmented Lagrangian functional (3.4). We can give a symmetric role to the unknowns u and p by updating the multiplier s between Step 1 and Step 3. We obtain the following Uzawa block relaxation algorithm.

Algorithm UBR
Initialization. p^{-1}, s^0 and $r > 0$ given.
Iteration $k \geq 0$. Compute successively u^k, p^k and s^k as follows.
 Step 1. Subproblem 1 : Find $u^k \in X$ s.t. $\mathscr{L}_r(u^k, p^{k-1}; s^k) \leq \mathscr{L}_r(v, p^{k-1}; s^k)$, $\forall v \in X$.
 Step 2. Update the Lagrange multiplier $s^{k+1/2} = s^k + \frac{r}{2}(u^k + p^{k-1} - f)$
 Step 3. Subproblem 2 : Find $p^k \in X$ s.t. $\mathscr{L}_r(u^k, p^k; s^k) \leq \mathscr{L}_r(u^k, q; s^k)$, $\forall q \in X$.
 Step 4. Update the Lagrange multiplier $s^{k+1} = s^{k+1/2} + \frac{r}{2}(u^k + p^k - f)$

3.3   Solution of Subproblem 1

The functional $u \mapsto \mathscr{L}_r(u, p^{k-1}; s^k)$ can be rewritten as

$$\Phi_1(u) := \frac{r}{2} \| u \|_{L^2}^2 + J(u) + (\tilde{p}, u)_X + C,$$

where C is a constant. We first compute v^k using the following semi-implicit scheme derived from [9].

$$v_i^{\ell+1} = \frac{v^\ell + \tau\nabla(\nabla \cdot v_i^\ell - \tilde{p}_i)}{1 + (\tau/g)\left[\sum_{i=1}^3 |\nabla(\nabla \cdot v_i^\ell - \tilde{p}_i)|_2^2\right]^{1/2}}, \quad i = 1, 2, 3, \qquad (3.5)$$

where $\tau > 0$. With v^k computed using (3.5) and the extremality condition we recover the minimizer of Subproblem 1

$$\bar{u}_i^k = \frac{1}{r}(\nabla \cdot v_i^k - \tilde{p}_i), \quad \text{i.e.} \quad u_i^k = f_i - p_i^{k-1} + \frac{1}{r}(\nabla \cdot v_i^k - s_i^k), \quad i = 1, 2, 3.$$

3.4   Solution of Subproblem 2

The functional $p \mapsto \mathscr{L}_r(u^k, p; s^k)$ can be rewritten as

$$\Phi_2(p) = (\lambda + r/2) \| p \|_{L^2}^2 + (s^k + r(u^k - f), p)_X + C,$$

where C is a constant. We deduce the solution of the minimization subproblem in p

$$p^k = -(s^k + r(u^k - f))/(r + 2\lambda).$$

With the results above, we can now present the Uzawa block relaxation algorithms for the $TV_g + L^2$ model.

3.5   Uzawa Block Relaxation Algorithms

Algorithm TVL2/UBR2
Initialization. p^{-1}, s^0 and $r > 0$ given.
Iteration $k \geq 0$. Compute successively u^k, p^k and s^k as follows.

Step 1. Set $\tilde{p} = s^k + r(p^{k-1} - f)$ and compute v^k with (3.5).

Compute u^k

$$u_i^k = f_i - p_i^{k-1} + \frac{1}{r}(\nabla \cdot v_i^k - s_i^k), \quad i = 1, 2, 3.$$

Step 2. Update the Lagrange multiplier

$$s^{k+1/2} = s^k + \frac{r}{2}(u^k + p^{k-1} - f).$$

Step 3. Compute p^k

$$p^k = -(s^k + r(u^k - f))/(r + 2\lambda)$$

Step 4. Update the Lagrange multiplier

$$s^{k+1} = s^{k+1/2} + \frac{r}{2}(u^k + p^k - f).$$

4   Augmented Lagrangian Methods for the $TV + L_g^1$ Model

In this part, we give some elements for the resolution of the $TV + L_g^1$ model where L_g^1 is a vectorial spatially adaptive data term. The function $g(x)$ is then here chosen as a vectorial function $g(x) = (g_1(x), g_2(x), g_3(x))$. The new model $TV + L_g^1$ corresponds to the minimization of the functional (2.2). For this minimization problem, we apply the same kind of minimization procedure as in the previous section and as in [8] but, in the development of the solution of subproblem 1, we have the next change:

$$v_i^{\ell+1} = \frac{v^\ell + \tau\nabla(\nabla \cdot v_i^\ell - \tilde{p}_i)}{1 + (\tau/\lambda)\left[\sum_{i=1}^3 |\nabla(\nabla \cdot v_i^\ell - \tilde{p}_i)|_2^2\right]^{1/2}}, \quad i = 1, 2, 3, \qquad (4.1)$$

where $\tau > 0$.

The algorithm then becomes:

Algorithm TVL1g/UBR2

Initialization. p^{-1}, s^0 and $r > 0$ given.

Iteration $k \geq 0$. Compute successively u^k, p^k and s^k as follows.

Step 1. Set $\tilde{p} = s^k + r(p^{k-1} - f)$ and compute v^k with (4.1).

Compute u^k

$$u_i^k = f_i - p_i^{k-1} + \frac{1}{r}(\nabla \cdot v_i^k - s_i^k), \quad i = 1, 2, 3.$$

Step 2. Update the Lagrange multiplier

$$s^{k+1/2} = s^k + \frac{r}{2}(u^k + p^{k-1} - f).$$

Step 3. Compute p^k

$$p_i^k = \begin{cases} 0 & \text{if } |s_i^k + r(u_i^k - f_i)| \leq g_i, \\ f_i - u_i^k - \frac{1}{r}\left[s^k - g_i \frac{s_i^k + r(u_i^k - f_i)}{|s_i^k + r(u_i^k - f_i)|}\right] & \text{if } |s_i^k + r(u_i^k - f_i)| \geq g_i. \end{cases}$$

Step 4. Update the Lagrange multiplier

$$s^{k+1} = s^{k+1/2} + \frac{r}{2}(u^k + p^k - f).$$

5   Numerical Experiments

In the numerical experiments, for the fixed-point algorithm (3.5), the step size is $\tau = .125$ and the tolerance for the relative error is 1. Numerical experiments not reported here for space reasons prove that the UBR scheme is robust towards the choice of the penalty parameter r. In this paper, we provide two main examples to show the potential of spatially varying regularization and data terms.

5.1   Spatially Varying Regularization Term, the $TV_g + L^2$ Model, for Old Parchments Restoration

In this subsection, we propose to test the impact of the function g within the framework of parchments restoration. In order to restore the background of these images while preserving the text, we propose to define a well-adapted g function in the weighted total variation term. On the basis of several tests, we finally choose to introduce an information on the vectorial gradient through the use of a mask function. In order to do so, we first compute the image corresponding to the norm of the gradient of each channel. We then perform a basic classification of each gradient image by partitioning its histogram into $nb_{classes}$ by minimizing the sum of the class variances. The number of classes was chosen equal to 3 and we pay attention to the minimum class of each gradient image, namely $C_{min}(|\nabla f_i|)$ in order to detect non significant gradients. The proposed mask function is then the following:

$$m(x) = \begin{cases} \alpha_n & \text{if} \quad x \in (C_{min}(|\nabla f_1|) \cap C_{min}(|\nabla f_2|) \cap C_{min}(|\nabla f_3|)) \\ \alpha & \text{elsewhere} \end{cases} \quad (5.1)$$

We choose $\alpha_n = 1$ and $\alpha = 0.001$ in order to uppermost smooth the pixels of smaller gradients. We then take $g(x) = m_\sigma(x)$ where $m_\sigma(x) = G_\sigma * m(x)$ is a slight regularized version of m ($\sigma = 0.05$). As far as the removing of non significant edges is concerned in old parchments, this adjunction of a weighted TV leads to interesting results that can not be obtained using a classical TV regularization term. In Figure 1, we show an example of restoration of an old parchment using $g = 1$ (Figure 1.(b)) and the function $g = m_\sigma(x)$ (Figure 1.(c)). The parameter λ was chosen in order to visually obtain the best results ($\lambda = 3$ when $g = 1$ and $\lambda = 0.2$ when $g = m_\sigma(x)$). When choosing $g = 1$, the parameter λ is difficult to tune. Indeed choosing a small value for this parameter leads to a global smoothing of the image and does not allow a preservation of the characters while choosing a high value does not smooth enough the background. On the contrary, when using the weighted TV term, the impact of the parameter λ is less important. We can then choose a small value in order to smooth the background while preserving the important information.

This first experimental result is here to illustrate the behaviour of the function g in the weighted total variation term. Further experiments are needed in order to validate this term for the specific application of old parchments restoration and analysis. It could also be interesting to test some different space colors than RGB in order to improve these first results.

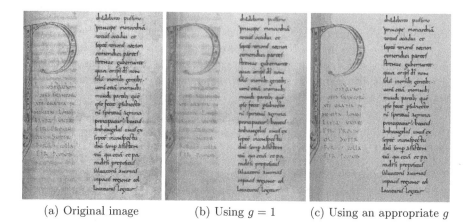

(a) Original image   (b) Using $g = 1$ (c) Using an appropriate g

Fig. 1. Restoration of a parchment (a) using the weighted total variation term with $g = 1$ (b) and the function $g(x) = m_\sigma(x)$ (c)

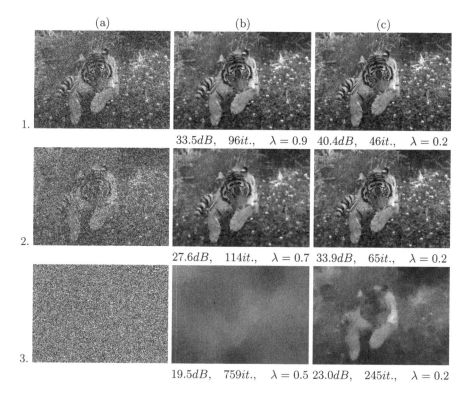

Fig. 2. (a) : noisy image (20%, 70%, 95%); (b) : restored image using $TV_g + L^1$; (c) : restored image using $TV + L_g^1$ (with the associated PSNR, number of iterations and λ)

5.2 Spatially Varying Data Term, the $TV + L_g^1$ Model, for Impulse Noise Removal

In order to test the potential of such a vectorial varying data term, we first propose to test it on simulated noisy images where an impulse noise is added on each color channel. To achieve this, we introduce the vector-valued function $g(x) = (g_1(x), g_2(x), g_3(x))$ defined by

$$g_i(x) = \begin{cases} 0 & \text{if } x \in C_i(f) \\ 1 & \text{if not} \end{cases}$$

where $C_i(f)$ designates the set of corrupted pixels in the channel i. In the experiments, we consider that the corrupted pixels correspond to the minimum or maximum values of the intensity but, in the real case, an adapted noise detector should be used (see [28] for an interesting bibliography on such detectors). Figure 2 shows interestingly that the new model outperforms the $TV_g + L^1$ model where g is the function proposed in [8] for salt and pepper noise removal. The spatially varying data term gives very interesting results even for high levels of noise that are only handled by very few methods [28].

6 Conclusion

This paper deals with color image restoration using a vectorial adaptation of the seminal ROF model. An augmented Lagrangian functional is introduced leading to Uzawa block relaxation algorithms for the minimization of both the $TV_g + L^2$ and the $TV + L_g^1$ functionals. Such algorithms are fast and easy to implement allowing a simple resolution for the minimization of such functionals. They are also robust towards the choice of the penalty parameter r. Once the mathematical framework was settled, we propose to test the behaviour of spatially varying regularization and data terms in the framework of color image restoration. We first propose to test the impact of the weighted total variation term through the definition of a new function g that proves to be valuable for the restoration of old parchments. We use it in order to restore the background of medieval parchments while preserving the text. We obtain very good results that need to be completed by further investigations and tests. One problem that needs to be further studied is the impact of the additional term that appears when computing the PDE of such a problem. This problem was mentioned in [28]. This additional term may introduce some oscillating boundaries if the function g is not smooth enough and must then be further studied and quantified. A post-processing (smoothing in the direction of the tangent of the gradient) can also be used to solve this artifact. Secondly, we also investigate the use of a spatially data varying term where the parameter λ becomes a vectorial local function. This term can also be solved using our mathematical framework with only a slight change and leads to very good results for salt an pepper denoising. We also compare it to an adapted weighted total variation term. In this case, the spatially varying data term gives better results both visually and in terms of

PSNR. These first tests need to be further developed for example regarding with the sensitivity to the parameters and color space. They also demonstrate that the selection of the point-wise weight function is very important and may lead to a real improvement compare to the results obtained using a simple $TV+L^\tau$ model. Our on going research is then directed towards a deeper investigation of such terms notably within the framework of old parchments restoration.

Acknowledgements. We would like to thank the Scriptorial Museum of Avranches (France) in link with the MRSH (Home of the Research of Human Sciences) within the University of Caen for providing us with the Medieval manuscripts of Mont St Michel. We thanks P.Y. Buard from the MRSH to make a bridge between the different scientific domains. We also thank R. Clouard and D. Tschumperlé for their useful tools for image processing (namely *pandore* and *gmic*).

References

1. Rudin, L., Osher, S., Fatemi, E.: Nonlinear total variation based noise removal algorithms. Physica D 60, 259–268 (1992)
2. Chan, T., Golub, G., Mulet, P.: A nonlinear primal-dual method for total variation-based image restoration. SIAM Journal of Scientific Computing 20, 1964–1977 (1999)
3. Nikolova, M.: A variational approach to remove outliers and impulse noise. Journal of Mathematical Imaging and Vision 20, 99–120 (2004)
4. Aujol, J.F., Gilboa, G., Chan, T.F., Osher, S.: Structure-texture image decomposition - modeling, algorithms, and parameter selection. International Journal of Computer Vision 67, 111–136 (2006)
5. Bresson, X., Esedoglu, S., Vandergheynst, P., Thiran, J.P., Osher, S.: Fast global minimization of the active contour/snake model. Journal of Mathematical Imaging and Vision 28, 151–167 (2007)
6. Chambolle, A.: Total Variation Minimization and a Class of Binary MRF Models. In: Rangarajan, A., Vemuri, B.C., Yuille, A.L. (eds.) EMMCVPR 2005. LNCS, vol. 3757, pp. 136–152. Springer, Heidelberg (2005)
7. Darbon, J., Sigelle, M.: Image restoration with discrete constrained total variation part I: Fast and exact optimization. Journal of Mathematical Imaging and Vision 26, 261–271 (2006)
8. Koko, J., Jehan-Besson, S.: An Augmented Lagrangian Method for $TVg+L^1$-norm Minimization. Journal of Mathematical Imaging and Vision 38, 182–196 (2010)
9. Chambolle, A.: An algorithm for total variation minimization and applications. Journal of Mathematical Imaging and Vision 20, 89–97 (2004)
10. Aujol, J.F., Chambolle, A.: Dual norms and image decomposition models. International Journal of Computer Vision 63, 85–104 (2005)
11. Goldstein, T., Osher, S.: The split bregman method for L^1 regularized problems. SIAM J. on Imaging Sciences 2, 323–343 (2009)
12. Pock, T., Cremers, D., Bischof, H., Chambolle, A.: Global solutions of variational models with convex regularization. SIAM J. Imaging Sciences 3, 1122–1145 (2010)
13. Fortin, M., Glowinski, R.: Augmented Lagrangian Methods: Application to the Numerical Solution of Boundary-Value Problems. North-Holland, Amsterdam (1983)

14. Glowinski, R., Tallec, P.L.: Augmented Lagrangian and Operator-splitting Methods in Nonlinear Mechanics. SIAM, Philadelphia (1989)
15. Blomgren, P., Chan, T.F.: Color TV: total variation methods for restoration of vector-valued images. IEEE Transactions on Image Processing 7, 304–309 (1998)
16. Sapiro, G.: Vector-valued active contours. In: International Conference on Computer Vision and Pattern Recognition, pp. 680–685 (1996)
17. Tschumperlé, D., Deriche, R.: Diffusion PDE's on vector-valued images: Local approach and geometric view-point. IEEE Signal Processing Magazine 19, 16–25 (2002)
18. Di Zenzo, S.: A note on the gradient of a multi-image. In: Computer Vision, Graphics, and Image Processing, vol. 33, pp. 116–125 (1986)
19. Tschumperlé, D.: Anisotropic Diffusion PDEs. In: Digital Color Imaging, pp. 75–121. Wiley (2012)
20. Bresson, X., Chan, T.F.: Active contours based on Chambolle's mean curvature motion. In: ICIP (1), pp. 33–36 (2007)
21. Bresson, X., Chan, T.: Fast dual minimization of the vectorial total variation norm and applications to image processing. Inverse Problems and Imaging 2, 455–484 (2008)
22. Duval, V., Aujol, J.-F., Vese, L.: Projected Gradient Based Color Image Decomposition. In: Tai, X.-C., Mørken, K., Lysaker, M., Lie, K.-A. (eds.) SSVM 2009. LNCS, vol. 5567, pp. 295–306. Springer, Heidelberg (2009)
23. Duval, V., Aujol, J.F., Vese, L.: Mathematical modeling of textures: Application to color image decomposition with a projected gradient algorithm. Journal of Mathematical Imaging and Vision 37, 232–248 (2010)
24. Dong, Y., Hintermüller, M., Montserrat Rincon-Camacho, M.: A multi-scale vectorial L^{τ}-TV framework for color image restoration. International Journal of Computer Vision 92, 296–307 (2011)
25. Goldlücke, B., Cremers, D.: An approach to vectorial total variation based on geometric measure theory. In: Int. Conf. on Computer Vision and Pattern Recognition, vol. 106, pp. 327–333 (2010)
26. Grasmair, M.: Locally Adaptive Total Variation Regularization. In: Tai, X.-C., Mørken, K., Lysaker, M., Lie, K.-A. (eds.) SSVM 2009. LNCS, vol. 5567, pp. 331–342. Springer, Heidelberg (2009)
27. Jehan-Besson, S., Koko, J.: Fast dual minimization of weighted TV + L1 norm for salt and pepper noise removal. In: VISAPP, Angers, France (2010)
28. Duval, V.: Variational and non-local methods in image processing: a geometric study. PhD thesis, Ecole Nationale Supérieure des Télécommunications, Telecom Paris Tech. (2011)

Monocular Rear-View Obstacle Detection Using Residual Flow

Jose Molineros[1], Shinko Y. Cheng[1], Yuri Owechko[1],
Dan Levi[2], and Wende Zhang[3]

[1] HRL Laboratories, LLC
3011 Malibu Canyon Road,
Malibu CA 90265
{jmmolineros,sycheng,yowechko}@hrl.com
[2] GM Advanced Technology Center-Israel
[3] GM Research
{dan.levi,wende.zhang}@gm.com

Abstract. We present a system for automatically detecting obstacles from a moving vehicle using a monocular wide angle camera. Our system was developed in the context of finding obstacles and particularly children when backing up. Camera viewpoint is transformed to a virtual bird-eye view. We developed a novel image registration algorithm to obtain ego-motion that in combination with variational dense optical flow outputs a residual motion map with respect to the ground. The residual motion map is used to identify and segment 3D and moving objects. Our main contribution is the feature-based image registration algorithm that is able to separate and obtain ground layer ego-motion accurately even in cases of ground covering only 20% of the image, outperforming RANSAC.

1   Introduction

Many automotive accidents involve cars backing up [1]. Existing backup warning systems based on sonar or radar sensors provide gross localization information, not enough to accurately determine if the vehicle will collide with an obstacle. Ranges go

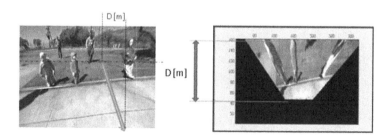

Fig. 1. (Left) An image taken from a camera rigidly mounted on a vehicle. (Right) Result of virtually rotating the camera view to bird-eye view.

A. Fusiello et al. (Eds.): ECCV 2012 Ws/Demos, Part II, LNCS 7584, pp. 504–514, 2012.
© Springer-Verlag Berlin Heidelberg 2012

up to 5m. Reaction times for humans are between .25s and .8s before brakes are even applied [2]. A car backing up at 15mi./h will travel 5m in .75s, which might be too close for comfort.

Cameras offer the capability to extend range and determine the nature of the alarm. Research work in rear obstacle detection using cameras include [3][4][5].

Previous systems for obstacle detection based on cameras sometimes utilize stereo and sometimes monocular input. Many utilize the idea of inverse perspective mapping (IPV) in polar histogram analysis, for example [5] and [6]. The paper in [6] uses stereo, IPV and polar histograms to detect close range obstacles. Work in [5] uses only one camera but coarsely uses polar histogram analysis due to not being able to obtain accurate ego motion. In [3] a system is presented that uses monocular input and ego-motion from odometry sensors. The authors in [4] present a system for backup aid that detects obstacles from three independent methods, fused at the output stage. It assumes road boundaries are always within the video image and has some difficulty with false positives due to shadows not being totally eliminated.

We introduce a method utilizing monocular camera input from a wide angle camera that is a valuable alternative to polar histogram analysis. A novel ground ego-motion recovery algorithm is developed. Obstacle segmentation is based on variational optical flow algorithms. We assume an urban setting with a ground layer that in a short range around the car is parallel to the car longitudinal axis.

The rest of the paper is organized as follows: section II describes our system. Section III describes its use in a child detection application. Section IV is implementation details and section V presents the conclusions.

2   System Overview

Our system termed VOFOD (variational optical flow obstacle detection) uses a combination of methods that to the best of our knowledge is novel. By registering the ground plane in consecutive image frames and exploiting the obtained ego-motion we generate an optical flow map where areas corresponding to the ground layer are set to zero. This map provides a motion saliency mechanism that directs attention to areas in the image containing obstacles.

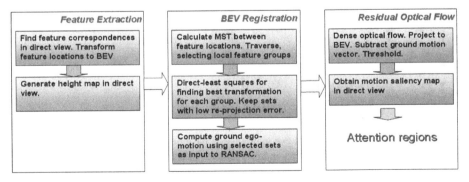

Fig. 2. System block diagram. There are three defined stages: feature correspondences, BEV registration and ground ego-motion estimation, and residual optical flow for obstacle detection.

We change the point-of-view to a virtual camera view looking straight down, termed bird-eye view, or BEV (figure 1). This allows us to run fast, accurate registration based on point features, and ultimately to obtain the ground motion vector.

We obtain optical flow information for each point in the image, and use the knowledge about ground motion to select the flow vectors corresponding to objects not part of the ground plane. We accomplish this by projecting the optical flow vectors to BEV. The obtained ground motion vector is then subtracted from projected dense optical flow, selecting moving areas not belonging to the ground plane.

In BEV, points at a height with respect to the ground plane will have a different difference in deformation than points in the ground plane when looking at consecutive images. Optical flow vectors in BEV are easily classified into ground/non-ground, and by assuming a planar ground, classified into obstacles and non-obstacles.

The algorithm consists of three stages (figure 2):

-*Stage 1*: Finding feature correspondences in consecutive images. Transforming point feature locations to BEV. A map is generated to obtain metric distance from the camera to a particular pixel location.

-*Stage 2:* Classifying feature points into ground/non-ground by means of our registration algorithm. Obtaining three-parameter homography (ground ego-motion).

-*Stage 3*: Estimating an 8-parameter homography transformation between consecutive frames, in original camera viewpoint. Obtaining residual optical flow and segmenting obstacles. Outputting metric distances from vehicle to obstacles.

2.1   Stage 1

Stage 1 is an algorithm to extract image feature points and virtually transform them to a virtual camera viewpoint looking straight down. Figure 1 shows an example image after virtual camera rotation. Changing viewpoint simplifies the problem of estimating ego-motion by reducing the number of unknown parameters from eight to three. This simplification allows us to estimate orthographic transformation parameters directly, with corresponding benefits in terms of registration accuracy and speed (see figure 5).

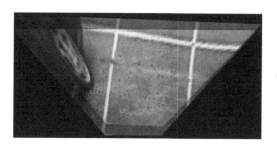

Fig. 3. Result of stage 2. Two bird-eye view images have been registered. (Left) The red dots are features in image 1. Green circles indicate features in image 2 that have been classified as ground. (Right) Simulation to obtain registration error: Ground points are localized in a small area. Red = image 1 points. Green = image 2 points. Blue = transformed image 2 'obstacle' points. Thick blue = transformed 'ground' points.

Suitability to obstacle detection applications of a particular feature detector/descriptor will depend on video quality, feature matching accuracy and computation speed. In our application scenario, images are captured by a fish-eye rear production camera with relatively low video quality. Another important fact is that concrete surfaces tend to have low feature density, making it difficult to extract enough quality features for registration. A BEV camera viewpoint exploits the approximation of vehicle motion as planar motion and offers the advantages of no ambiguity between rotational and translational ego-motion parameters, and reliability in transformation parameter estimation due to the linearity of image motion.

Point feature types found in literature include SIFT, SURF, Harris, KLT, and CenSurE. Perhaps not surprisingly, SIFT[10] produced the best quality registration in terms of average re-projection error. However, unless accelerated by GPU, it might be unsuitable for hard real-time applications. A second best is Center Surround features (CenSurE) [12], a feature type designed in the context of visual odometry in rough outdoor terrain over long periods. We found its reliability to be close to SIFT with speed improvements of four to five times. It produces the best compromise between match quality and speed. In all of our video test sequences, both CenSurE and SIFT have produced enough quality correspondences in production fish-eye cameras currently installed in automobiles. Other detectors we tested, such as SURF and KLT, have not.

2.2   Stage 2

The main novelty of our obstacle detection approach lies in this registration algorithm. It estimates orthographic transformation parameters, minimizing re-projection error and eliminating outliers.

Stage 2 takes as input BEV feature locations and their matched correspondences and calculates ground ego-motion. Ground points are found by first finding image features lying on a plane parallel to the virtual camera plane and refined by eliminating features lying on surfaces 'at height' with respect to the ground.

Methods to determine the ground plane include 2D dominant motion estimation and layer extraction. These methods can be top-down or bottom-up. Top-down

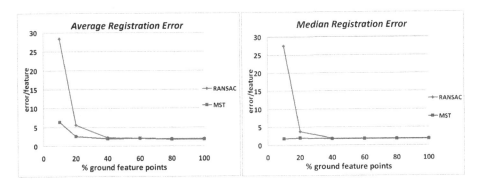

Fig. 4. Euclidean error per feature correspondence (pixels). RANSAC-based BEV registration (blue) vs. MST-based method (red). The X-axis represents the percentage of 'ground points'.

approaches assume the ground plane is dominant in the scene, or alternatively that the scene can be modeled with a few planar layers. In car backing up scenarios the ground plane might not be dominant and the scene is not necessarily well modeled with a few planar layers.

Bottom up approaches divide the image into small patches where a local patch transformation is calculated. These transformation calculations are then grouped together to form layers. In [7] measurements are combined with a robust weighting scheme for global ego-motion determination and ground plane segmentation. A regularization step is later applied to recover small non-planar motions. Our own preliminary implementation of the scheme in [7] yielded performance and speed that convinced us point features are still the way to go.

We developed a point feature-based registration scheme that does not assume a dominant ground layer. Our approach produces good quality registration even in cases of 80% of the image being background clutter and obstacles.

We utilize a two-tiered algorithm to obtain matches between two BEV clusters of points according to an orthographic projection model. The two tiers are a Minimum-Spanning Tree (MST) [17] followed by RANSAC or one of its variants [8][9]. A feature selection strategy outputs a "bag" of candidate ground features, after traversing an MST generated between the point correspondences in the first image. We test each vertex plus its immediate connected neighbors (a local set) against the corresponding local set in the second image. A direct least-squares estimation technique [12] is used to compute the transformation parameters between local sets, as well as to choose sets with low average re-projection error. These sets of features are added to a global "bag" of candidate ground points. Finally, we use RANSAC to obtain the final global orthographic transformation between bag points. Although the MST stage is enough most of the time, local sets of points in surfaces (at height and parallel to the ground) will pass the least-squares re-projection error test. RANSAC is applied to eliminate these outlier sets.

MST allows us to exploit naturally occurring clusters of ground features and produces more accurate registration in the presence of higher number of outliers than RANSAC. It also avoids having to unnaturally segment the image into coarse blocks for analysis that a two-tiered RANSAC scheme would require. Exploiting the fact that ground features tend to cluster together becomes crucial in cases where it is difficult to localize repeatable feature points, such as concrete surfaces in roads and parking lots. Figure 3 shows registration of two BEV frames after obtaining 2-D ground motion parameters.

In order to compare registration quality between MST and RANSAC, we tested both algorithms on simulated data over 100+ trial runs. We generated a number of random points in one set, belonging to ground and non-ground (fig. 3, right). Ground points in a second set correspond to the first set, transformed according to known rotation and translation. Uncertainty in position is added to points in the second set. Ground points have a Gaussian spatial error in pixels of $(\mu=2.5, \sigma=1.45)$ and non-ground points follow a Gaussian distribution with $(\mu=25, \sigma=14.5)$. The proportion of ground points is varied from 10% to 90% and re-projection error for both algorithms is obtained. We added a tendency of ground points to cluster together spatially.

Figure 4 compares registration quality of MST vs. RANSAC [8]. X-axis represents percentage of true ground points in the set. MST efficiently exploits the tendency of points of the same class to cluster together in order to register images with a minority of ground points.

Our registration algorithm provides an improvement over other conventional methods for ground registration [16] (Fig.5).

Description of stage 2 is as follows:

1. Generate an *MST graph* between BEV point locations.
2. Obtain groups of features that are spatially close, by traversing MST.
3. Classify clusters as ground/non-ground according to conformance to an orthographic transformation model. Classification is based on average re-projection error [12].
4. Calculate 2-D ground motion using all selected ground point clusters. Global orthographic transformation is obtained by a RANSAC-style algorithm [9] to eliminate entire clusters that might have low average re-projection error but are non-ground.
5. Classifying original feature points obtained *in direct view*, into ground/non-ground, by their corresponding BEV re-projection error.
6. Obtain ground motion vector.

Once ground has been registered, obstacles can be detected by exploiting misregistration that objects at height or moving objects exhibit. We accomplish segmentation by obtaining a residual dense optical flow map in stage 3.

2.3   Stage 3

Stage 3 produces a residual motion map for non-ground plane objects. With a moving camera detected obstacles can be stationary or moving. If the camera is stationary, only moving objects will be detected.

To find obstacles it is not enough to cluster point features that have been classified as non-ground. More exhaustive image analysis is needed. We utilize dense optical flow for that purpose. Optical flow obtains regions of interest in the image, as well as provides an interest score to a particular pixel locations, according to the magnitude of the flow vector.

Fig. 5. Comparison of ground registration quality. (Left) Using a top-down method from literature to directly estimate 8-parameter homography. (Right) Using stage 2 algorithm, re-projected to normal camera view.

Recently, variational numerical schemes have been used successfully to obtain high accuracy and real-time dense optical flow. We use a bidirectional multi-grid method for accelerated variational optical flow computations (VOF) [13]. This method enables generation of our obstacle likelihood map.

The approach found in [13] can be considered a generalization of the traditional Horn-Schunck algorithm, but allowing for multi-grid schemes with non-dyadic grid hierarchies, as well as fast variational numerical methods for solving systems of equations.

Residual motion maps indicate motion different to ground plane motion. After obtaining optical flow vectors from two consecutive images, we project the vectors to BEV and subtract them from ground motion obtained in stage 2 (figure 6, center). Resulting BEV residual flow is used to obtain flow in direct view without barrel distortion. We use the mapping between BEV coordinates and direct view coordinates to create a binary mask in direct view that in combination with the optical flow map produces residual motion (fig. 6).

As the ground plane has been obtained, the camera has been calibrated, and the relationship between bird-eye views and original views are known, distances (in feet or meters) from the vehicle to the base of obstacles are straightforward to calculate. They vary linearly with height (fig. 1, right).

While varying the point-of-view to estimate ground motion and VOF computation are methods found in literature, their combination and application to obstacle detection is new to the best of our knowledge. Our registration algorithm plus VOF methods provide a powerful, novel alternative (and perhaps complement) to other simpler real-time algorithms in automotive applications.

Calculation of dense optical flow and BEV ground ego-motion estimation are currently implemented as parallel threads. Once the ground motion vector is obtained, we merge the results to produce the residual motion map and obstacle segmentation.

In summary, stage 3 consists of:

- Calculating dense variational optical flow for the image.
- Transforming VOF to bird-eye view (BEV).
- Subtracting BEV-VOF from ground plane motion vector
- Determining VOF of obstacle pixels in direct view.

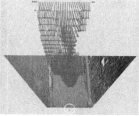

Fig. 6. (Left) Original image. (Center) BEV residual flow. Ground motion is shown as a small green arrow enclosed in the yellow circle. (Right) Residual optical flow map: color represents flow vector direction, intensity represents flow magnitude.

Figure 6 (right) shows the color-coded map obtained from stage 3. Distances from the camera to the corresponding position in the ground plane are known, varying according to Y coordinate in the undistorted image. When looking for obstacles that have an expected height range, this information allows us to estimate the size in pixels such an obstacle would have.

In the optical flow map in figure 6 (right), intensity represents magnitude of the flow vector, whereas color represents vector direction. This image can be used as a saliency map or it can be combined with other static-image saliency algorithms [14] to indicate regions of interest. In our example application, normalized magnitude of the optical flow vector at a pixel represents a likelihood of it belonging to an obstacle.

3   Application: Child Detection

VOFOD is used in combination with a state-of-the-art parts-based person classifier termed FSM (feature synthesis [15]) to detect children in arbitrary poses. Processing times for state-of-the-art parts-based classifiers is still far from real-time unless the number of input windows is drastically reduced. VOFOD is used to reduce the typical number of input windows from >50K to less than 500 after non-maximal suppression (nms).

Figure 7 is the result of exhaustively searching for windows of height approximately expected of children. Boxes were generated with a fixed aspect ratio, and their height is adjusted according to Y-coordinate to fall within an acceptable range. We sum the values of the VOFOD saliency map inside each box and obtain a child detection likelihood. Only boxes with a score above a predefined threshold are colored. Lighter colors represent higher box scores.

Although it is making great strides, state-of-the-art in human arbitrary pose detection still needs to improve. At the same time, in a collision warning application it is important to eliminate false positives as they desensitize the driver to ignore alerts. Under such conditions, it might be desirable to operate under low probability of *child* detection but very low false positives. Meanwhile, moving and close obstacles are still detected. VOFOD excels under such conditions.

Fig. 7. (Left) Using residual flow map for child detection: boxes were generated according to expected child height and scored according to average flow intensity. Only boxes scoring above a threshold are colored (Right) Detections with a parts-based classifier.

Our video sequences include children at all distance ranges. Camera is moving less than 50% of the time. With a moving platform, static children at close and mid ranges can be detected by residual optical flow. However, non-moving children standing far away will not be detected. By using VOFOD in combination with an image-based saliency algorithm, such as frequency-tuned saliency (FTS [18]), we operate in high probability of child detection with approximately 50% window reduction over nms. Figure 8 shows the probability of child detection by FSM parts-based classifier, according to the reduction in number of input windows. We compare VOFOD, VOFOD + FTS, FTS itself, and random scoring. We detail our experiments to determine system performance in [14].

4   Implementation

We feel the VOFOD implementation can be greatly optimized, perhaps up to an order of magnitude. Current execution times, in C++ are 3.3 FPS for stage 1 + 2 (combined, in 640 x 480 resolution) and 2.5 FPS for stage 3 in 320 x 240 resolution. Timings are in an Intel Xeon CPU W3550 @ 3.07 MHz.

Many optimizations are possible in our proof-of-concept code, including avoiding processing in parts of the image and making the code more efficient. The slowest components are point feature extraction and dense optical flow. The complete system runs at video rate by processing only two or three pairs of consecutive images per second of video.

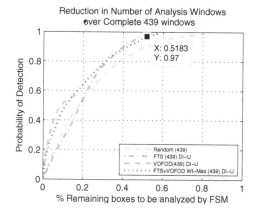

Fig. 8. Probability of child detection by FSM, according to number of input analysis windows. VOFOD+FTS eliminates 49% of all windows over exhaustive approach after nms. 25% more windows over random scoring.

5   Conclusion

We have introduced an obstacle detection system based on BEV registration for estimating ground motion, and variational dense optical flow for detecting obstacles.

Our approach of using an MST for ground point selection resulted in acceptable separation of ground regions in cases with very few ground points, the instances in which RANSAC by itself tends to fail. This in turn allows for better registration and egomotion estimation. Fast variational optical flow allows us to segment obstacles by analysis of a residual motion map. One example application of our algorithm is as an attention mechanism for child detection. Highlighted areas can be later processed with a parts-based classifier to identify children. Utilization of this attention mechanism greatly reduces computation time allowing for real-time performance.

References

[1] http://www.osha.gov/dcsp/success_stories/compliance_assistan ce/motor_vehicle_case_study.html

[2] Sens, M.J., Cheng, P.H., Wiechel, J.F., Guenther, D.A.: Perception/Reaction Tim Values for Accident Reconstruction. SAE 890732, Society of Automotive Engineers, pp. 79–94 (1989)

[3] Vestri, C., et al.: Real-Time Monocular 3D Vision System. In: 16th World Congress on Intelligent Transport Systems, Stockholm (2009)

[4] Ma, G., et al.: A Real-Time Rear View Camera Based Obstacle Detection. In: 12th IEEE International Conference on Intelligent Transportation Systems, pp. 1–6 (September 2009)

[5] Yankun, Z., Chunyang, H., Norman, W.: A Single Camera Based Rear Obstacle Detection System. In: Proc. IEEE Intelligent Vehicles Symposium (2011)

[6] Broggi, A., Medici, P., Porta, P.P.: StereoBox: A Robust and Efficient Solution for Automotive Short-Range Obstacle Detection. EURASIP Journal on Embedded Systems (2007)

[7] Ke, Q., Kanade, T.: Transforming Camera Geometry to a Virtual Downward-Looking Camera: Robust Ego Motion Estimation and Ground-Layer Detection. In: Proceeding of the IEEE Computer Vision and Pattern Recognition, CVPR 2003 (2003)

[8] Fischer, M.A., Bolles, R.C.: Random Sample Consensus: A Paradigm for Model Fitting with Applications to Image Analysis and Automated cartography. Comm. of the ACM 24, 381–396 (1981)

[9] Torr, P.H.S., Zisserman, A.: MLESAC: A New Robust Estimator with Application to Estimating Image Geometry. In: IEEE Conference on Computer Vision and Image Understanding, CVPR 2000 (2000)

[10] Lowe, D.G.: Distinctive Image Features from Scale-Invariant Keypoints. International Journal of Computer Vision 60(2), 91–110 (2004)

[11] Konolige, K., Agrawal, M., Sola, J.: Large Scale Visual Odometry for Rough Terrain. In: Proc. International Symposium on Robotics Research (2007)

[12] Umeyama, S.: Least-squares Estimation of Transformation Parameters Between Two Point Patterns. IEEE Transactions on Pattern Analysis and Machine Intelligence (PAMI) 13(4), 376–380 (1991)

[13] Bruhn, A., et al.: Variational Optical Flow Computation in Real Time. IEEE Trans. on Image Processing 14(5) (May 2005)

[14] Cheng, S., et al.: Parts-based Object Recognition Seeded by Frequency Tuned Saliency for Child Detection in Active Safety. In: Intelligent Transportation Systems Conference-ITSC (2012)

[15] Bar-Hillel, A., Levi, D., Krupka, E., Goldberg, C.: Part-Based Feature Synthesis for Human Detection. In: Daniilidis, K., Maragos, P., Paragios, N. (eds.) ECCV 2010, Part IV. LNCS, vol. 6314, pp. 127–142. Springer, Heidelberg (2010)

[16] Zhou, J., Li, B.: Homography-based Ground Detection for a Mobile Robot Platform Using a Single Camera. In: IEEE Conference on Robotics and Automation, ICRA 2006 (2006)

[17] Chazelle, B.: A Minimum Spanning Tree Algorithm with Inverse-Ackermann Type Complexity. Journal of the Association for Computing Machinery 47(6), 1028–1047 (2000)

[18] Achanta, R., et al.: Frequency-tuned Salient Region Detection. In: IEEE Conference on Computer Vision and Pattern Recognition (CVPR), pp. 1597–1604 (2009)

Subtraction-Based Forward Obstacle Detection Using Illumination Insensitive Feature for Driving-Support

Haruya Kyutoku[1], Daisuke Deguchi[2], Tomokazu Takahashi[3],
Yoshito Mekada[4], Ichiro Ide[1], and Hiroshi Murase[1]

[1] Graduate School of Information Science, Nagoya University,
Furo-cho, Chikusa-ku, Nagoya, Aichi, 464–8601, Japan
[2] Information and Communications Headquarters, Nagoya University,
Furo-cho, Chikusa-ku, Nagoya, Aichi, 464–8601, Japan
[3] Faculty of Economics and Information, Gifu Shotoku Gakuen University,
1–38, Nakauzura, Gifu, Gifu, 500–8288, Japan
[4] School of Information Science and Technology, Chukyo University,
101, Tokodachi, Kaizu-cho, Toyota, Aichi, 470–0393, Japan
kyutoku@murase.m.is.nagoya-u.ac.jp

Abstract. This paper proposes a method for detecting general obstacles on a road by subtracting present and past in-vehicle camera images. The image-subtraction-based object detection approach can be applied to detect any kind of obstacles although the existing learning-based methods detect only specific obstacles. To detect general obstacles, the proposed method first computes a frame-by-frame correspondence between the present and the past in-vehicle camera image sequences, and then registrates road surfaces between the frames. Finally, obstacles are detected by applying image subtraction to the registrated road surface regions with an illumination insensitive feature for robust detection. Experiments were conducted by using several image sequences captured by an actual in-vehicle camera to confirm the effectiveness of the proposed method. The experimental results shows that the proposed method can detect general obstacles accurately at a distance enough to avoid them safely even in situations with different illuminations.

1 Introduction

Nowadays, development of driving support systems has became an active research topic. Forward obstacle detection from in-vehicle camera images is one of the most important techniques in ITS. This technique is essential to realize a collision-warning system that can reduce the number of traffic accidents significantly. Accordingly, a number of techniques to detect forward obstacles have been developed. Still, most of them detect only specific obstacles such as pedestrians or vehicles. These approaches can improve the detection accuracy by learning image features of the obstacles. However, they cannot detect obstacles that are not considered in the learning phase. Thus, detection of general obstacles is a challenging task because various obstacles exist on a road.

A. Fusiello et al. (Eds.): ECCV 2012 Ws/Demos, Part II, LNCS 7584, pp. 515–525, 2012.

Recently, in-vehicle camera image databases such as Google Street View[1] have become a familiar service. Moreover, the development of higher speed wireless telecommunications and rapid growth of data storage capacities are remarkable. This allows us to collect and store large amount of in-vehicle camera images for driving support purposes.

We proposed a method for detecting forward general obstacles, based on image subtraction between an in-vehicle camera image and its past image captured at the same location [1]. However, this method did not consider the difference of illumination conditions between the present and the past images. This would degrade the detection accuracy in practical situations because the illumination conditions are not the same between the different days/times. Therefore, in this paper, we propose a subtraction-based forward obstacle detection method using an illumination insensitive local feature, and try to improve the accuracy of obstacle detection even when the illumination conditions have changed.

This paper is organized as follows: Section 2 describes related work. Section 3 explains details of the proposed method. Experimental results and discussions are described in Section 4. Finally, Section 5 summarizes the paper.

2   Related Work

Various techniques have been proposed to detect forward obstacles, using different kinds of sensors including millimeterwave radar, stereo, monocular, or infrared camera [1][2][3][4]. However, millimeterwave radars cannot be used for detecting small obstacles due to their low spatial resolutions. On the other hand, stereo cameras still have hurdles with their calibration [5]. It may be difficult to obtain accurate point correspondences between the images. Meanwhile, the techniques using infrared cameras are specialized for pedestrian detection to assist a driver's visibility at nighttime.

Obstacle detection methods with a monocular camera has been actively researched. However, most of these methods are learning-based methods, so they detect only specific obstacles such as pedestrians or vehicles [3][4]. Here, one of the most effective approaches to detect general obstacles is the subtraction-based approach [1]. This method detects obstacles by comparing present and past in-vehicle camera images. Assuming that the past sequence does not include any obstacle, the detection can be done by a background subtraction strategy. The advantage of this method over the learning-based methods is that it does not require to learn image features of the obstacles beforehand, so it can handle arbitrary objects. Again, since this method uses simple local features in the subtraction operation, such as brightness value of each pixel, the detection accuracy is strongly affected by the difference of illumination conditions between the present and the past sequences. Unlike the background subtraction using a fixed camera [6], the illumination conditions between the input and the background images are quite different in the case of subtraction between the present

---

[1] Google Street View, http://maps.google.com/

and the past in-vehicle camera images because they are usually taken on different days/times. Therefore, the proposed method introduces an illumination insensitive local feature for the subtraction. As another approach, the optical-flow-based approach can also detect general obstacles, but it has a difficulty when detecting obstacles that are not moving.

The proposed method needs past in-vehicle camera images with no obstacles. There are some techniques [7] for constructing and updating an in-vehicle camera image database. The database contains images corresponding to each road on a street map. We assume that past images could be obtained from such databases. Furthermore, some methods have been developed to remove obstacles from an in-vehicle camera image database [8][9], which could be used to obtain obstacle-free image sequences.

3   Proposed Method

The cruising speed and trajectory of each vehicle may be different between the sequences. To detect obstacles based on subtraction between the present and the past in-vehicle camera image sequences captured along the same road, the proposed method performs the following two processes:

1. **Frame-Level and Pixel-Level Registrations**
   The cruising speed and the trajectory differ between the sequences. Therefore, this process first finds a frame in the past sequence that was taken at the same location as the present frame, and then finds correspondences of pixels in road surface regions between the present and the past frames.
   The proposed method performs this process in the same manner as the method introduced in [1].

2. **Subtraction-Based Obstacle Detection Using an Illumination Insensitive Local Feature**
   This process detects obstacles based on differences between the local features extracted from road surface regions of the present and the past frames. Here, we propose an illumination insensitive local feature.

3.1   Frame-Level and Pixel-Level Registrations

Here, we briefly explain the registration process. Detailed information of the process is described in [1].

Finding Frame Correspondences. To obtain the frame correspondences, a Dynamic Time Warping (DTW) method is applied to the present and the past image sequences by introducing a penalty calculated from the relationship between the two cameras. This penalty is defined as

$$\frac{1}{|e_x| + \alpha}, \tag{1}$$

(a) Present   (b) Past

Fig. 1. Corresponding frames in the present and past image sequences

(a) Direct subtraction   (b) Subtraction after registration

Fig. 2. The subtraction results of corresponding frames in Fig. 1

where e_x is the horizontal position of the epipole between the present and the past frame, and α is a positive constant. Based on the theory of the epipolar geometry analysis, the epipole is calculated from correspondig point-pairs between the frames. The penalty term is robust against the difference in running positions of a vehicle and the occlusions caused by obstacles.

Registration of Road Surfaces. This step performs registration of road surface regions between the corresponding frames. It is difficult to detect obstacles by directly applying an image subtraction operation between the corresponding frames because of the difference in the running positions between the frames. Figure 1 shows an example of corresponding frames obtained by the frame-level registration. The result of the image subtraction is shown in Fig. 2(a), where we can see a spatial gap. To compensate for the gap, this method performs the pixel-level registration of the road surface regions. The subtraction result after the registration is shown in Fig. 2(b). It is assumed that the road surface is flat, and the obstacle detection area is restricted to the road surface region. This step makes correspondences of pixels in the road surface regions between the present and the past images by a projective transformation. The projective transformation matrix is calculated from the epipolar lines and the road boundary lines.

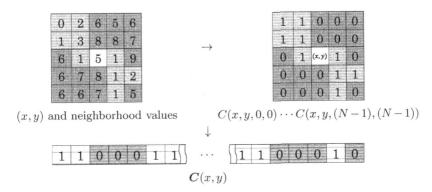

(x, y) and neighborhood values $C(x, y, 0, 0) \cdots C(x, y, (N-1), (N-1))$

$C(x, y)$

Fig. 3. Example of Census Transform $(N = 2)$

3.2 Subtraction-Based Obstacle Detection Using an Illumination Insensitive Feature

The proposed method detects obstacles by the subtraction of road surface regions after the registration process. In this paper, we define an "obstacle" as the image difference compared to a past road surface where obstacles do not exist. For each location in the road surface region, the method calculates the difference of local features between the present and the past images, and then significantly different regions are detected as obstacles. Here, the features for measuring the difference is very important because simple features, such as the brightness, are easily affected by the illumination condition changes. Hence, we propose an illumination insensitive local feature that is robust for different illumination conditions.

Illumination Insensitive Local Feature. Census Transform [10] is a method for extracting local features from an image, which encodes the relationship between a pixel and its neighbors. The method was first proposed to calculate the cost of stereo matching. Similar to Local-Binary-Patterns (LBP) [11], the local feature extracted by the Census Transform is robust against the illumination changes [12]. The Census Transform constructs a vector $C(x, y)$ for each pixel. The LBP uses the pixels only along a ring around the target pixel, although the Census Transform uses all pixels in a $(2N + 1) \times (2N + 1)$ region around the target pixel. Thus, the vector consists of $4N(N + 1)$ elements. Each element is calculated as

$$C(x, y, i, j) = \begin{cases} 1 & I(x, y) > I(x + i, y + j) \\ 0 & \text{otherwise} \end{cases}, \tag{2}$$

where $-N \leq i \leq N$ and $-N \leq j \leq N$ except $i = j = 0$. $I(x, y)$ represents the pixel value at position (x, y). Figure 3 shows an example of the construction of a census transform vector. The difference between the two vectors is calculated based on Hamming distance. However, this representation may be unsuitable for

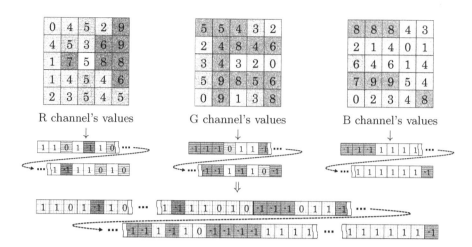

Fig. 4. Example of modified Census Transform ($N = 2$ and $\beta = 0$)

feature extraction from a road surface region, because pixel values are almost equal in most parts of the road surface. Therefore, this paper introduces trinary representation [13] that is used for LBP. Thus, instead of Eq. (2), we use the following representation.

$$C(x, y, i, j) = \begin{cases} 1 & I(x, y) > I(x + i, y + j) + \beta \\ -1 & I(x, y) < I(x + i, y + j) - \beta \\ 0 & \text{otherwise} \end{cases}, \qquad (3)$$

where β is a small positive value that absorbs small changes of pixel values in a road surface region. We also consider that color information would work effectively for obstacle detection. Therefore, the proposed method extracts a vector from each color channel, and concatenates the vectors as shown in Fig. 4. We define the difference between two vectors as the sum of absolute differences of each element pair.

Integration of Results from Multiple-Frames To improve the reliability of the detection results, the proposed method integrates results obtained from successive frames. This reduces false detections caused by noises and registration errors. Here, we employ a simple strategy to integrate multiple-frame information as shown in Fig. 5.

First, the proposed method computes a spatio-temporal subtraction image by using the past successive T subtraction images (Fig. 5(a)), and then detects highly different pixels as obstacle candidates. Next, each candidate is tracked in the temporal direction, and tracking trajectories are obtained (Fig. 5(b)). Assuming that the vehicle and the obstacle move linearly for a very short time in the spatio-temporal subtraction image domain, candidates having straight-line trajectories are extracted as the final results (Fig. 5(d)).

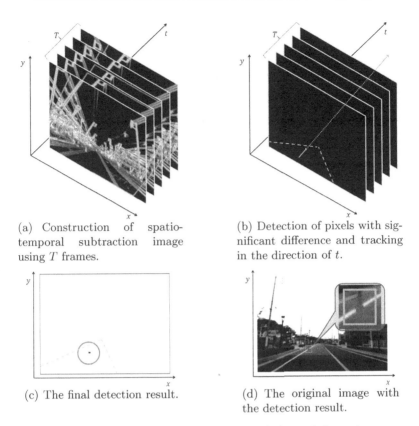

(a) Construction of spatio-temporal subtraction image using T frames.

(b) Detection of pixels with significant difference and tracking in the direction of t.

(c) The final detection result.

(d) The original image with the detection result.

Fig. 5. Overview of integration of multiple-frame information

4 Experiments

To confirm the effectiveness of the proposed method, obstacle detection experiments were conducted by using in-vehicle camera images.

4.1 Experimental Condition

To acquire images used for the experiments, we mounted a web camera "Logicool Qcam® Pro 9000" on the windshield of a vehicle as shown in Fig. 6. The image size was 640 × 480 pixels, and the frame rate was 15 fps. We prepared a total of six sequences by driving along the same 150 meters road six times. Four of them including obstacles were used as the present sequences, and the others which did not include any obstacle were used as the past sequences. The total number of frames in the present sequences was 879, and 329 of these sequences included obstacles in the distances from 12 to 80 m. The obstacles were a pedestrian crossing the road, a street-parking vehicle, a forward running vehicle, a pylon, and a ball. On the other hand, the past sequences were captured under

(a) From outside (b) From inside   (a) Present   (b) Past

Fig. 6. Car-mounted in-vehicle camera

Fig. 7. Example of large illumination change between present and past frames

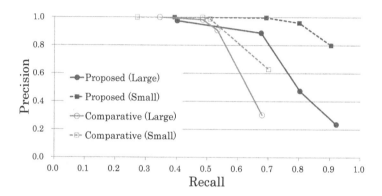

Fig. 8. The precision-recall curves of the obstacle detection

different illumination conditions that had small and large differences from the illumination condition of the present sequences as shown in Fig. 7.

We evaluated the detection accuracy by the following criteria:

$$\text{Precision rate} = \frac{\text{\# of true-positives}}{\text{\# of true-positives} + \text{\# of false-positives}},$$

$$\text{Recall rate} = \frac{\text{\# of true-positives}}{\text{\# of obstacles}},$$

$$\text{F-value} = \frac{2 \cdot \text{Precision} \cdot \text{Recall}}{\text{Precision} + \text{Recall}}$$

Here, 4-connected pixels of the detection result were merged to one region, and used for calculating the above criteria. The true-positives were counted for each obstacle in the image, even if multiple detected regions existed on an obstacle. On the other hand, the false-positives were counted for each detected region. We compared the detection accuracy between the proposed method and the method described in [1]. The comparative method detects obstacles based on simple subtraction of brightness values after the registration of road surface regions. We set the parameters used in the proposed method as $N = 3$ and $\beta = 5$. As for

Table 1. The accuracy comparison when maximum F-values were obtained

Illumination change	Method	F-value	Precision	Recall
Small	Proposed	**0.87**	0.96	0.80
	Comparative	**0.67**	0.99	0.51
Large	Proposed	**0.77**	0.89	0.68
	Comparative	**0.67**	0.91	0.53

(a) Pedestrian	(b) Pylon	(c) Ball

Fig. 9. Examples of detection results for obstacles approximately 50m ahead. The rectangles represent the detected regions. The pair of images in the balloon in each image is the close-ups of the detected region (left) and its original image (right).

the integration parameter T, we used the same value for the proposed method and the comparative one as $T = 5$. We determined these values based on the results of preliminary experiments.

4.2   Results

Figure 8 shows the precision-recall curves of obstacles closer than 80 m. The solid lines show the accuracy when large illumination change occured, while the dashed lines show the accuracy in the case of small illumination change. Table 1 shows the accuracy comparison when the maximum F-values were obtained in Fig. 8. In addition, Fig. 9 shows the detection results of distant obstacles.

4.3   Discussion

From Table 1, we confirmed that the proposed method provided higher F-values than those of the comparative methods in both cases when small and large illumination changes exist between the image sequences. Moreover, as Fig. 8 shows, for example, in case when the recall rate is about 0.7, the proposed method keeps high precision rates over 0.9 even if the sequences had a large illumination difference, while the recall rates of the comparative methods dropped to less than 0.8. These results proved the effectiveness of the proposed method.

Additionally, the proposed method could detect small obstacles such as a ball or a pylon at a distance of more than 44 m, as seen in Fig. 9. It was confirmed that distant obstacles could be detected by the proposed method. Especially,

Fig. 9(c) demonstrates the remarkable ability of the proposed method. The proposed method successfully detected a ball with a diameter of only 20 cm at a distance of 46 m. This means that small obstacles could be detected far enough to avoid safely even when cruising at a speed of 60 km/h.

5   Summary

We proposed the method for detecting general obstacles on a road by subtracting the present and the past in-vehicle camera images with an illumination insensitive local feature. Compared to the existing learning-based approach that detects only specific obstacles, the proposed image-subtraction-based approach can detect any kind of obstacle. To achive this, the proposed method first performed frame-level and pixel-level registrations of the present and the past image sequences, and then detected obstracles based on the subtraction of the road surface regions with an illumination insensitive local feature.

To demonstrate the effectiveness of the proposed method, obstacle detection experiments were carried out by applying the proposed method to several in-vehicle camera image sequences. The experimental results shows that the proposed method can detect general obstacles accurately at a distance far enough to avoid them safely even under large difference of illumination conditions.

Acknowledgement. Parts of this research were supported by JST CREST and MEXT Grant-in-Aid for Scientific Research. This work was developed based on the MIST library (http://mist.murase.m.is.nagoya-u.ac.jp/).

References

1. Kyutoku, H., Deguchi, D., Takahashi, T., Mekada, Y., Ide, I., Murase, H.: On-road obstacle detection by comparing present and past in-vehicle camera images. In: Proc. 12th IAPR Conf. on Machine Vision Applications, pp. 357–360 (2011)
2. Liu, F., Sparbert, J., Stiller, C.: IMMPDA vehicle tracking system using asynchronous sensor fusion of radar and vision. In: Proc. 2008 IEEE Intelligent Vehicles Symposium, pp. 168–173 (2008)
3. Nishida, K., Kurita, T.: Boosting with cross-validation based feature selection for pedestrian detection. In: Proc. 2008 IEEE World Congress on Computational Intelligence, pp. 1251–1257 (2008)
4. Mitsui, T., Fujiyoshi, H.: Object detection by joint features based on two-stage boosting. In: Proc. 9th IEEE Int. Workshop on Visual Surveillance 2009, pp. 1169–1176 (2009)
5. Collado, J.M., Hilario, C., de la Escalera, A., Armingol, J.M.: Self-calibration of an on-board stereo-vision system for driver assistance systems. In: Proc. 2006 IEEE Intelligent Vehicles Symposium, pp. 156–162 (2006)
6. Kawanishi, Y., Mitsugami, I., Mukunoki, M., Minoh, M.: Background image generation by preserving lighting condition of outdoor scenes. Procedia—Social and Behavioral Sciences 2, 129–136 (2010)

7. Sato, J., Takahashi, T., Ide, I., Murase, H.: Change detection in streetscapes from GPS coordinated omni-directional image sequences. In: Proc. 18th IAPR Int. Conf. on Pattern Recognition, vol. 4, pp. 935–938 (2006)

8. Boehm, J.: Multi-image fusion for occlusion-free facade texturing. Int. Archives of Photogrammetry, Remote Sensing and Spatial Information Sciences 35, 867–872 (2004)

9. Uchiyama, H., Deguchi, D., Takahashi, T., Ide, I., Murase, H.: Removal of moving objects from a street-view image by fusing multiple image sequences. In: Proc. 20th IAPR Int. Conf. on Pattern Recognition, pp. 3456–3459 (2010)

10. Zabih, R., Woodfill, J.: Non-parametric Local Transforms for Computing Visual Correspondence. In: Eklundh, J.-O. (ed.) ECCV 1994, Part II. LNCS, vol. 801, pp. 151–158. Springer, Heidelberg (1994)

11. Ojala, T., Pietikainen, M., Harwood, D.: A comparative study of texture measures with classifcation based on featured distributions. Int. Journal on Computer Vision 29, 51–59 (1996)

12. Hirschmuller, H., Scharstein, D.: Evaluation of stereo matching costs on images with radiometric differences. IEEE Trans. on Pattern Analysis and Machine Intelligence 31, 1582–1599 (2009)

13. Tan, X., Triggs, B.: Enhanced local texture feature sets for face recognition under difficult lighting conditions. IEEE Trans. on Image Processing 19, 1635–1650 (2010)

Adaptive Visual Obstacle Detection for Mobile Robots Using Monocular Camera and Ultrasonic Sensor

İbrahim K. İyidir, F. Boray Tek, and Doğan Kırcalı

Robotics and Autonomous Vehicles Laboratory
Department of Computer Engineering,
Işık University, 34980, İstanbul, Turkey
{ibrahim.iyidir,boray,dogan}@isikun.edu.tr
http://ravlab.isikun.edu.tr

Abstract. This paper presents a novel vision based obstacle detection algorithm that is adapted from a powerful background subtraction algorithm: ViBe (VIsual Background Extractor). We describe an adaptive obstacle detection method using monocular color vision and an ultrasonic distance sensor. Our approach assumes an obstacle free region in front of the robot in the initial frame. However, the method dynamically adapts to its environment in the succeeding frames. The adaptation is performed using a model update rule based on using ultrasonic distance sensor reading. Our detailed experiments validate the proposed concept and ultrasonic sensor based model update.

Keywords: Obstacle detection, ViBe, ultrasonic sensor, mobile robot.

1   Introduction

In the last decade the mobile robot technologies have made a significant progress. Beside big budget commercial efforts, we see that small projects which are conducted by individuals or small groups who have limited budgets provide a noticeable addition to its momentum. This work is a part of our efforts where we aim to transform a model car kit into an autonomous navigating robot using a camera, electronic sensors and an onboard PC.

For a ground vehicle, an obstacle may be defined as a protrusion or extrusion of the ground surface, which segments the current planned path. However, in practice it is not simple to construct a generic method to implement obstacle detection due to huge variation in environmental conditions [1].

In line with human sensory organization the most used sensor for obstacle detection is visible light camera. Though analyzing two dimensional images for obstacle detection is challenging, in the last two decades there are significant amount of attempts [1,2]. Several concepts have been investigated using two dimensional images for obstacle avoidance problem such as edge detection [3], optical flow [4] and pixels values [5]. Additional third dimension information

A. Fusiello et al. (Eds.): ECCV 2012 Ws/Demos, Part II, LNCS 7584, pp. 526–535, 2012.

can be obtained using more than one camera which involves a pre-calibration process but it required more computation until recent commercial development of low-cost depth sensors such as MS-Kinect[1].

In addition to a visible light camera various other sensors (e.g. radar, lidar, and sonar) can be used for obstacle detection [6]. One of the earlier works that has done by Borenstein and Koren [7] uses only ultrasonic sensors for obstacle avoidance. Laser based sensors such as 3D-lidar are quite successful in scanning the environment however they are expensive and require significant computing resource.

(a)   (b)

Fig. 1. (a)Model car equipped with camera and sensors (b)Obstacle free region

Ultrasonic distance sensors provide a cheaper way to measure distance in an unstructured environment. Any obstacle surface which is parallel to the sensor and inside the ultrasonic beam region reflects the sound emitted by the sensor. The reflected wave is captured by the sensor and time-of-flight is calculated to measure the distance. However, the measurements can only be localized to a limited precision (i.e. location in the beam pattern). Moreover, ultrasonic sensors may not give reliable results on reflective surfaces. In [7] Borenstein and Koren investigated the limitations of the ultrasonic range finders for obstacle avoidance task.

Our robot is based on a model car, equipped with an RGB color camera, an ultrasonic distance sensor, a compass and a gps sensor (Figure 1(a)). The obstacles that we aim to detect may appear in any shape or color in the scene.

Several other algorithms have assumptions about the operating environment [1,2] and we unavoidably make an assumption about expecting an obstacle free bounded region in front of the car in the first frame. However, the method dynamically adapts to its environment in the consecutive frames. Therefore it can be suitable for both indoor and outdoor environments even in places where there is no structural nature. Our method mainly relies on a monocular camera to model the ground plane and other obstacles in the scene. Since the robot is mobile and also that there are no assumptions about the scene structure, the ground plane model must be updated continuously. This model update is controlled based on the ultrasonic distance sensor reading to avoid ground plane like obstacle regions included in the model. Authors of [3,8] also used combination of

---

[1] http://www.microsoft.com/en-us/kinectforwindows/develop/overview.aspx

a monocular camera and ultrasonic range finder for obstacle avoidance purposes. In contrast to their work, we utilize ultrasonic sensor's data only for the decision of updating the ground plane model.

Our ground plane modelling scheme is inspired from ViBe [9] which is a background subtraction algorithm that is proposed for motion detection. ViBe keeps positive samples for every pixel location and classifies a previously unseen pixel according to its distance from stored samples. In other words, every pixel location has an independent classifier to decide whether a given candidate pixel for that location is from the ground plane or not. Through time, some random samples are updated with some random new pixels collected and classified from the scene. This update mechanism gives ViBe its dynamic adaptive behavior and robustness against local illumination changes, reflections and shadows. ViBe [9] is simple, efficient and faster than its counterparts which suits well to our robot where we cannot operate with high performance computers due to limitations of size and payload.

We also incorporate a methodology of a simple obstacle detection algorithm developed by Ulrich and Nourbakhsh [5] which assumes that the area in front of the mobile robot is the ground plane and can be modeled by hue and intensity histograms. A previously unseen pixel is classified as a ground plane pixel if corresponding index in one of the histograms has accumulated sufficient samples (i.e. above a threshold). Moreover, they propose a post-update rule based on odometry information and successful passing from a region. Thus the method relies on a feedback mechanism which has some trial and error nature which cannot be assumed to be safe under many conditions. In contrast to their method, our ground plane model update rule is based on a pre-update mechanism that uses the ultrasonic distance sensor to control the ground plane model update.

This paper is organized as follows: In Section 2, we present our proposed method. In Section 3, we discuss the parameters of our method and give the results of our experiments. Our conclusions and future work are presented in Section 4.

2   Method

2.1   Initialization

Following the work of [5], our obstacle detection technique is based on the assumption that the square region in front of the mobile robot is free of obstacles at the initialization step of the algorithm (Figure 1(b)). As in [9], we define and maintain a sample set $\mathbf{S}(x,y)$ for each pixel location (x,y) of the image $\mathbf{I}$ of dimensions WxH where W is width and H is height of the image. Each sample set $\mathbf{S}(x,y)$ stores N samples.

$$\mathbf{S}(x,y) = \{p_1, p_2, p_3, ...p_N\} \tag{1}$$

For initialization, in the first frame, random pixels are chosen from the obstacle-free square region (OFR) in front of the robot and their values are added to

$\mathbf{S}(x, y)$ for every (x, y) in $\mathbf{I}$. The set of sample sets $\mathbf{S}$ whose size is $NxWxH$ forms our ground plane model. The size of OFR must be determined based on the width of the car and camera's field of view. If the region that we collect samples from gets larger, the chance of including obstacle pixels in the ground plane model increases whereas a smaller area would mean less variation in the model. Because the ground plane model $\mathbf{S}$ is created using only the first frame, the initialization is very fast.

Fig. 2. Original Image

2.2 Obstacle Detection

After initialization, each new frame is processed to detect ground plane and obstacle pixels. A given pixel value at location (x, y) is classified as an obstacle or not using its $\mathbf{S}(x, y)$. The classification is based on finding similar values to the pixel's own value in its $\mathbf{S}(x, y)$. Finding at least M similar pixels in $\mathbf{S}(x, y)$ is sufficient to mark the pixel in location (x, y) as ground plane pixel.

Let the pixel value at position (x, y) be q, then we can express the number of similar pixels (SPC) as follows:

$$SPC = \|dist(q, p_i) < R)\|, \quad where \; p_i \, \epsilon \, \mathbf{S}(x, y) \, , i = 1, ..., N \qquad (2)$$

$dist$ is the Euclidean distance metric which measures how close two sample are and R is the distance threshold which defines being similar with a limiting distance value.

Our camera produces images in RGB (Red-Green-Blue) color space (Figure 2). We operate our algorithm in normalized RGB color space in order to provide illumination invariance (Figure 4(a) (b)). Figure 3(a) shows an example distance image which is formed by pixel values that indicate the distance between $\mathbf{S}(x, y)$ and corresponding pixel value q at location (x, y). Distance image is obtained by calculating average of N distance values between the values in $\mathbf{S}(x, y)$ and q. Euclidean metric is used when calculating the distances. After classifying each pixel of the input image $\mathbf{I}$, a binary obstacle map is generated (Figure 3(b)).

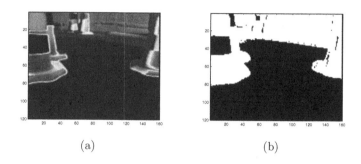

(a)   (b)

Fig. 3. (a)Distance image (b)Binary obstacle map

2.3   Updating Sample Sets

ViBe applies a random update rule to the background model [9]. If the pixel q at position (x, y) is classified as background, its value is used to update a random value in $\mathbf{S}(x, y)$. The update is not carried out at every frame, instead the update decision depends on a term called "subsampling factor". For each found new background pixel the probability of inclusion in the sample set is (1/subsampling factor) and decision is made using a random value. Moreover, one of the neighboring pixel's sample set of q is updated using the same probabilistic approach. Motivation here is that the adjacent pixels often share a similar temporal distribution [10].

This continuous update rule provides a dynamic adaptation to environmental changes in illumination, reflections. However, to adapt the sudden significant changes in the ground plane model, (e.g. from carpet to tiles) we needed another mechanism. We keep histograms of both OFR and sample pixels $\mathbf{S}(x, y)$. We re-initialize $\mathbf{S}(x, y)$ if these histograms differ significantly and also if ultrasonic sensor indicates that OFR is free. Significant difference of one of the histograms (normalized red or normalized green) is sufficient for the model re-initialization. The significant change is detected by a percentage threshold (Figure 4(c)-(d)). Figure 5 shows a situation where both histograms are similar therefore there is no need to re-initialize sample sets.

Effect of Ultrasonic Distance Sensor on Update. In our work, the update mechanism of $\mathbf{S}$ is dependent on the ultrasonic distance sensor data (UD). At each frame, we read ultrasonic distance sensor (UD). The reading gives us the distance to the closest obstacle in front of the robot in terms of centimeters in range (10,300). We let the update of $\mathbf{S}$ if the mobile robot can safely move one step forward afterwards. In other words, we control the update using a "safe-to-move-threshold" value (t).

Thus, this pre-update rule mechanism that is based on the safe distance check prevents our robot to update the model unselectively. If the ultrasonic distance sensor is not used, the ground plane model continues updating from

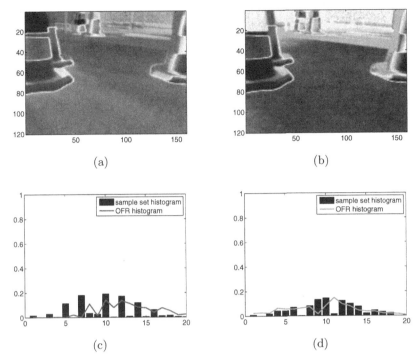

Fig. 4. (a)Normalized red image (b)Normalized green image (c)Normalized red histogram (d)Normalized green histogram

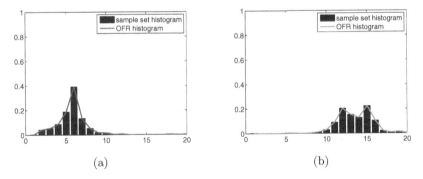

Fig. 5. (a)Normalized red histogram (b)Normalized green histogram. Both histogram pairs (sample set and OFR) are similar.

OFR whether there is an obstacle or not in the front. Moreover, if the appearance of the ground plane changes suddenly (e.g. carpet to tile), the robot cannot move towards to the different appearing ground plane because the robot treats this new appearance as an obstacle. However, when the ultrasonic distance sensor gives a safe-to-move-threshold for the new ground plane, the robot updates its ground plane model effectively. If UD is above t, we replace two samples from $\mathbf{S}(x, y)$ with values one is randomly chosen from OFR and the value of q at the location (x, y). Also one of the adjacent pixel's sample set is updated in the same way. Note that, during the update process, only the sample sets of pixel locations that are classified as ground plane are updated. Figure 6 shows the distribution of $\mathbf{S}$ at two different time lines. Only two samples for each $\mathbf{S}(x, y)$ are drawn on the scatters.

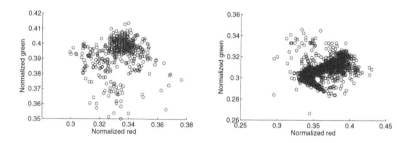

Fig. 6. Distribution of sample sets at different time lines

3   Experiments

During the tests, we run the algorithm in normalized RGB color space. Normalizing red and green channels eliminate problems that occur due to differently illuminated ground plane areas. However, we also performed some preliminary experiments using HSI (Hue-Saturation-Intensity) color space but we observed that using Hue value creates more problems than normalized red-green does in dark or saturated bright regions. We validated our proposed method using three different recorded videos which included manually segmented ground truth data that can be reached through our website[2]. The videos were recorded in our laboratory resting pitch which has illumination reflections, shadows, different colors of floor and it contains many obstacles that have different colors and shapes.

Each RGB frame in the recorded dataset has an image size of 160x120 pixels where the square that we collect samples from (OFR) contains only 20x20 pixels. During the experiments, we set the size of the sample sets (N) as 20 and UD threshold (t) as 100cm. In addition, we set the threshold value for the number of close samples (M) as 2, and we set distance threshold value (R) as 0.05

In addition to first Figures 2, 3(b), Figure 8 shows more input-output-ground truth triplets of our algorithm. We defined the ground plane as the negative class and the obstacles as the positive class. We observed that the method detects obstacles generally successfully. However, false negatives occur when the obstacle is in the same color with the ground plane (see Figures 2-3(b)). We also observed that the algorithm performs not well specifically for gray colored ground plane and gray colored obstacles (e.g walls, doors) with the above parameter settings.

---

[2] http://ravlab.isikun.edu.tr

Table 1. Performance of the algorithm on different data sets

Dataset Name	True Positive	False Positive	Accuracy
Dataset-1	0.8251 ±0.1897	0.1685 ±0.1153	0.8221 ±0.1026
Dataset-2	0.8102 ±0.1949	0.1853 ±0.2826	0.7737 ±0.2268
Dataset-3	0.7269 ±0.2301	0.1471 ±0.1726	0.8119 ±0.1532

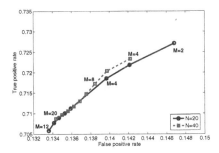

Fig. 7. ROC curve for varying M values

In order to quantify the results, we measured the overall accuracy, true and false positive rates for each frame in the different datasets (Table 1). As it can be seen, we achieved over 70% of true positive rate while false positive rate is under 20% in all datasets. Note that, these are quite challenging sequences and many errors occur during frame transitions from one ground plane character to another.

The distance threshold R value was set to 0.05 for all datasets to provide consistency through processing all the datasets. However, we observed that changing this value could improve performance of different datasets because lower R values perform better for gray colored ground plane and grayish obstacles. This is possibly due to the fact that a constant threshold value is not optimal through normalized red-green color space.

Furthermore, to observe the effect of parameters N and M, we plot a ROC curve for their different values for dataset-3. It can be seen in Figure 7 that choosing larger values of M lowers both false and true positive rates whereas lower values produce opposite condition. From different ROC curves obtained from different $N = 20, 40$ values, we observed that the algorithm is not so sensitive to the sample set size N, so we set it as 20.

In overall, we observed that our combined obstacle detection algorithm performed acceptable while we noted above mentioned points for improvement. Furthermore, most false positive detections were either isolated pixels or very small regions. Hence, they can be removed using morphological operations like erosion. During above experiments, such post-processing was not used to show the reader the exact outputs of our algorithm.

Fig. 8. Input image, obstacle map and ground truth triplets are shown in left, center and rights columns respectively

4   Conclusion

In this paper, we introduced a novel vision based obstacle detection method. Our method relies on images acquired by a monocular color camera and an assisting ultrasonic distance sensor to update its ground plane model over time. The method is adapted from ViBe which is an efficient background subtraction algorithm that is used for motion detection. ViBe model gives robustness against local illumination changes, reflections and shadows. Ultrasonic distance sensor is used to control the update decision of the ground plane model. Additionally, we detect sudden significant changes in the ground plane appearance using histograms and let re-initialization of the ground plane model.

This paper can be seen as an initial step to develop a vision based obstacle detection algorithm which has no assumptions about the scene structure and ground plane. The only assumption we made is an obstacle free region in front of the car in the first frame. However, this assumption is not a strong necessity, instead of "expecting", it is possible to "seek" an obstacle free region. If the car happens to be in front of an obstacle in the first frame (that can be detected by the ultrasonic sensor), it can perform small maneuvers through backwards and search for an obstacle free region.

The only visual feature that was used by the algorithm is the normalized red-green pixel values. It may be possible to extend this work by adding a computationally feasible textural feature. Also, we did not use any supervised learning mechanism nor a history of observed previous ground planes. Addition of such features can lead to more accurate detection of obstacles.

References

1. Desouza, G., Kak, A.: Vision for mobile robot navigation: a survey. IEEE Transactions on Pattern Analysis and Machine Intelligence 24, 237–267 (2002)
2. Bonin-Font, F., Ortiz, A., Oliver, G.: Visual navigation for mobile robots: A survey. J. Intell. Robotics Syst. 53, 263–296 (2008)
3. Ohya, I., Kosaka, A., Kak, A.: Vision-based navigation by a mobile robot with obstacle avoidance using single-camera vision and ultrasonic sensing. IEEE Transactions on Robotics and Automation 14, 969–978 (1998)
4. Ohnishi, N., Imiya, A.: Featureless robot navigation using optical flow. Connection Science 17, 23–46 (2005)
5. Ulrich, I., Nourbakhsh, I.R.: Appearance-based obstacle detection with monocular color vision. In: Proceedings of the Seventeenth National Conference on Artificial Intelligence and Twelfth Conference on Innovative Applications of Artificial Intelligence, pp. 866–871. AAAI Press (2000)
6. Discant, A., Rogozan, A., Rusu, C., Bensrhair, A.: Sensors for obstacle detection - a survey. In: 30th International Spring Seminar on Electronics Technology, pp. 100–105 (2007)
7. Borenstein, J., Koren, Y.: Obstacle avoidance with ultrasonic sensors. IEEE Journal of Robotics and Automation 4, 213–218 (1988)
8. Yu, M., Shu-qin, L.: A method of robot navigation based on the multi-sensor fusion. In: 2010 2nd International Workshop on Intelligent Systems and Applications (ISA), pp. 1–4 (2010)
9. Barnich, O., Van Droogenbroeck, M.: Vibe: A universal background subtraction algorithm for video sequences. IEEE Transactions on Image Processing 20, 1709–1724 (2011)
10. Jodoin, P.M., Mignotte, M., Konrad, J.: Statistical background subtraction using spatial cues. IEEE Transactions on Circuits and Systems for Video Technology 17, 1758–1763 (2007)

Data-Driven Vehicle Identification
by Image Matching

Jose A. Rodriguez-Serrano[1], Harsimrat Sandhawalia[1], Raja Bala[2],
Florent Perronnin[1], and Craig Saunders[1]

[1] Xerox Research Centre Europe, Meylan, France
[2] Xerox Research Center Webster, NY, USA

Abstract. Vehicle identification from images has been predominantly
addressed through automatic license plate recognition (ALPR) techniques which detect and recognize the characters in the plate region of
the image. We move away from traditional ALPR techniques and advocate for a data-driven approach for vehicle identification. Here, given a
plate image region, the idea is to search for a near-duplicate image in an
annotated database; if found, the identity of the near-duplicate is transferred to the input region. Although this approach could be perceived
as impractical, we actually demonstrate that it is feasible with state-of-
the-art image representations, and that it presents some advantages in
terms of speed, and time-to-deploy. To overcome the issue of identifying
previously unseen identities, we propose an image simulation approach
where photo-realistic images of license plates are generated for desired
plate numbers. We demonstrate that there is no perceivable performance
difference between using synthetic and real plates. We also improve the
matching accuracy using similarity learning, which is in the spirit of
domain adaptation.

1   Introduction

This article focuses on vehicle identification from images [1–4], which finds a
variety of applications in the transportation industry. For instance, on-board
cameras in police cars and buses are employed to identify vehicles incurring
traffic violations; fixed cameras are installed as part of the traffic infrastructure
to automate payments in tolls or parkings, and cameras in portable devices and
even mobile phones allow identifying vehicles by parking enforcement staff or for
vehicle social networks[1].

A vast number of off-the-shelf automatic license plate recognition (ALPR)
[3, 4, 1] tools exist which detect and recognize plate characters in vehicle images.
Despite the perception that ALPR is a solved problem, the identification of
vehicles with low-quality cameras (such as from mobile phones), at high speed,
or in countries with a vast number of plate designs (such as the USA) still poses
research challenges. Also, industry experts estimate that the time to deploy an

---

[1] See, for instance, `www.bump.com`

A. Fusiello et al. (Eds.): ECCV 2012 Ws/Demos, Part II, LNCS 7584, pp. 536–545, 2012.

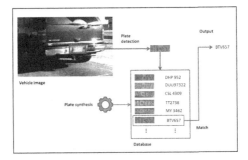

Fig. 1. Overview of the system. *Note: For privacy reasons, license plate images and numbers are fictitious.*

existing ALPR system in a new state or country, including sample acquisition, manual annotation, re-training and fine-tuning can take months.

In this paper, we move away from traditional ALPR techniques and advocate for data-driven approaches for vehicle identification. Here, given a plate image region, the idea is to search for a near-duplicate image in an annotated database; if found, the identity of the near-duplicate is transferred to the input region. Our goal is to show that with state-of-the-art image representations for retrieval, such as Fisher vectors [5, 6], the data-driven approach is feasible in terms of speed and robustness, and presents advantages. First, *a very significant and somewhat counter-intuitive finding of this paper is that a matching approach can actually outperform ALPR in close-world systems* - i.e. when for all the vehicles to identify an annotated instance exists in the database. Secondly, the time-to-deploy is reduced: image matching requires plate-level annotations while ALPR demands character-level segmentations and definition of character sets or language models, which is more costly to obtain. And thirdly, the accuracy of image matching degrades less critically than for ALPR when moving to low-quality cameras.

However, an obvious issue of near-duplicate matching is that a vehicle which has not been previously registered in the database cannot be identified. For example, an authority needs to perform a search for a vehicle with known license plate number but the image database might not contain that plate. To overcome this difficulty, we propose to use a photo-realistic rendering approach [7] to generate a license plate image for "wanted" plates and add them to the database. We demonstrate that using those simulated images does not impact the matching accuracy, and also that this accuracy can be boosted using a better similarity function obtained through *similarity learning*, in the spirit of recent works on domain adaptation [8].

An overview of the method is shown in Fig. 1. The rest of the article is structured as follows. §2 describes the matching approach and image descriptor. §3 elaborates on the image simulation approach. §4 reports the experimental validation. In §5 the conclusions are drawn.

2   Data-Driven Vehicle Identification

So far the predominant technique for image-based vehicle identification has been ALPR. We refer the reader to the survey [3] and the more specific papers [1, 4, 2] for details. However, in recent years there has been an impressive progress in image retrieval, both in terms of discriminative power of features and compression/indexing, and state-of-the-art methods are capable of comparing an image with a database of millions of images in milliseconds [9] with high accuracy and modest computing resources.

Inspired by these recent results, this article proposes a data-driven view for vehicle identification. Here, given an image of an unknown vehicle, captured either from the infrastructure, from an on-board camera or from a mobile device, the approach we propose is to describe the license plate sub-image and match it against a database of annotated license plate images with state-of-the-art retrieval techniques. If a near-duplicate image is found, the annotated license plate number is transferred to the input image. Similar ideas have been used with success to solve the problems of image geo-tagging [10] or image completion [11] , among others, but we are not aware of previous attempts for ALPR (or in general any scene text recognition).

This section discusses the plate image descriptor and matching approaches. We omit the details on plate localization here as this is not the core of the work. For reference, Fig. 4 illustrates the achieved level of plate segmentation.

Plate Features. For the license plate image descriptor we extract Fisher vectors [5] since these have been reported to be state-of-the-art descriptors for image categorization tasks [6] and very large-scale image retrieval [9], and show robustness in the range of photometric and geometric variability present in our application.

In a nutshell, Fisher vectors work by aggregating local patch descriptors into a fixed-length representation. First, SIFT patches are extracted at multiple scales on a regular grid, and their dimensionality is reduced using principal component analysis (PCA). A visual vocabulary is built by estimating a Gaussian mixture model (GMM) with patch descriptors extracted from a held-out set of images. The Fisher vector is computed as the derivative of the log-likelihood with respect to the GMM parameters. For instance, if we consider the means only, it can be shown that the expression is given by

$$f_{id} = \gamma_i(\mathbf{x}_t) \left[\frac{x_{t,d} - m_{i,d}}{(S_{i,d})^2} \right], \tag{1}$$

where $\gamma_i(\mathbf{x}_t)$ is the soft-assignment probability of the tth patch to the ith Gaussian, $x_{t,d}$ is the dth component of the ith patch, and $m_{i,d}$ and $S_{i,d}$ are the dth components of the mean and standard deviations of the ith Gaussian, assuming diagonal covariances. Here, $i = 1 \ldots K$ and $d = 1 \ldots D$. If we only use the derivatives with respect to the mean[2], then the resulting Fisher vector is a

---

[2] We discard derivatives with respect to the weights or the variance since they only bring a small improvement but do impact computation time and signature sizes.

concatenation of the $K \times D$ elements f_{id}. We also apply the square-rooting and ℓ_2-normalization of [5], and make use of spatial pyramids to account for spatial information.

Matching. Since the Fisher vector is an explicit embedding of the Fisher kernel, the corresponding similarity measure between two such image descriptors $\mathbf{x}$ and $\mathbf{y}$ is the dot product $\mathbf{x}^T\mathbf{y}$. A candidate plate is compared against all images in a database and we assign the identity of the closest match, provided the similarity is sufficiently high.

The advantage of matching with respect to ALPR systems is that character segmentation is not necessary, and that it is "agnostic" of the character set, layout and design of the plates; it just assigns an identity by finding a near-duplicate image. This is advantageous e.g. for US plates, which present stacked characters, graphical symbols or complex backgrounds for which character recognition techniques have difficulties dealing with. An illustration of these difficulties is shown in Fig. 2.

Fig. 2. License plate templates showing typical difficulties for ALPR systems: state symbols, stacked characters, complex backgrounds

Also, the time to deploy a matching platform in a new location is much shorter than for an ALPR system since the latter requires manual character-level annotation and learning the character classifiers.

3 License Plate Image Simulation and Matching

A requirement of data-driven identification is that each potential identity needs to be represented at least by one example in the database. This requirement is fulfilled in "close-world" applications such as entry-exit matching, identification of returning vehicles, or access control of pre-registered vehicles. However, in many situations it is also useful to search for or identify unexpected or previously unseen vehicles.

We propose to bypass this limitation by *simulating* images of license plates for previously unseen vehicles, following the approach of [7]. This was used to generate a dataset of realistic license plate images for character classifiers for ALPR in an inexpensive way. Nevertheless, to the best of our knowledge, this method has not been applied before to produce images to populate a dataset for matching[3].

---

[3] In computer vision, data simulation has been used to synthesize training data for pedestrian detectors [12], 3D object recognition [13] or scene text classification [14]. In the document analysis literature we find works which synthesize word images for search [15, 16] but the complexity of these document images is much smaller than for outdoor license plates.

3.1   Image Synthesis and Photo-Realistic Transformation

License plate simulation consists of two main steps: (i) synthesizing an ideal license plate image, and (ii) applying transformations to reproduce the characteristics of real license plate images. Next we summarize the process. We refer the reader to [7] for the details.

Synthesizing an Ideal License Plate Image. Synthesizing an ideal license plate image basically requires defining the background template, the font properties, and the valid character sequences and positions. This information can be obtained from existing specifications. Also, existing resources such as on-line repositories of license plate templates[4], character erasure methods or software tools that produce TrueType fonts from character examples can be exploited to assist this one-off procedure.

Thus, license plate images can be produced by overlaying the desired character sequences with the appropriate font in the template at adequate positions. See first steps of Fig. 3(a) for illustration.

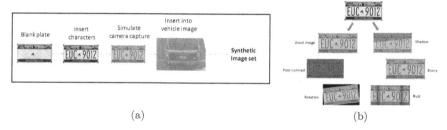

(a)   (b)

Fig. 3. (a) Overview of license plate simulation. (b) Distortions considered.

Photo-Realistic Transformation. A number of transformations and distortions are applied next to produce realistic images which simulate camera capture. Fig. 3(b) illustrates some operations considered.

For instance, in ALPR it is common to use near-infrared cameras since they present better signal-to-noise ratio across different illuminations and day/night variations. Thus, a color-to-infrared transform is needed. Here, a transformation $I_{IR} = \max(w_R R, w_G G, w_B B)$ is applied to (R, G, B) pixel intensities, where w_R, w_G, and w_B are relative material transmittances in the R/G/B channels and are adjusted from RGB-IR value pairs.

Then, image brightness and contrast are adjusted using a simple affine transformation $I_{out} = \alpha I_{IR} + \beta$ to the IR intensities, the parameters also being learned from contrast value pairs of real and synthetic plates.

A number of other transformations are considered: blur (in the form of a resolution conversion which was found to be more effective than spatial filtering), or adding shadows, rust or spurious noise.

---

[4] e.g. www.blankplates.com

Finally, to ensure that we produce tight plate regions in similar conditions as for the real plates (see section 2), simulated license plate images are inserted into a set of full-vehicle images with the four license plate corners manually marked. The corresponding affine transformation between the simulated image plane and the 4 corners is determined. After that, the plate localization algorithm is run to yield the tight plate regions. An example of a real and simulated tight regions as obtained by the detection algorithm is shown in Fig. 4.

Fig. 4. Plate regions of simulated (left) and real license plates (right)

3.2   Similarity Learning

To increase the efficiency of matching synthetic and real plate images, we employ similarity learning. A number of distance and similarity learning methods have been proposed in the machine learning community (see, e.g. [17, 18]) which basically seek a projection of the data more suitable for nearest-neighbor classification or ranking. Interestingly, asymmetric distance learning has been employed in the computer vision literature to match images of two different domains [8], which is close to our problem.

Denote $\mathbf{s}$ the descriptor of a simulated plate image and $\mathbf{r}$ that of a real plate image. We search for a function of the form $k(\mathbf{r}, \mathbf{s}) = \mathbf{r}^T \mathbf{W} \mathbf{s}$. In a default setting where $\mathbf{W}$ equals the $L \times L$ identity matrix, k is the dot product which is the standard measure of similarity between Fisher vectors. However, we aim at finding a more suitable $\mathbf{W}$ inspired by the large-margin supervised semantic indexing [17] approach.

We search for a matrix $\mathbf{W}$ which minimizes the following loss

$$\sum_{(\mathbf{r}, \mathbf{s}^+, \mathbf{s}^-)} \max\{0, 1 - k(\mathbf{r}, \mathbf{s}^+) + k(\mathbf{r}, \mathbf{s}^-)\}. \tag{2}$$

where $\mathbf{s}^+$ is a simulated sample with the same identity as the real sample $\mathbf{r}$, and $\mathbf{s}^-$ has a different identity. Note that minimizing the loss encourages $k(\mathbf{r}, \mathbf{s}^+) > k(\mathbf{r}, \mathbf{s}^-) + 1$, i.e. pairs with the same identity should have a higher similarity than non-matching pairs, which is a desirable property of a similarity function, and the +1 acts as a "safety" margin to promote generalization.

This loss function can be optimized using Stochastic Gradient Descent (SGD) [19]. Following straightforward derivations, it is possible to show that the training procedure consists in repeating the two following steps: (i) sample a triplet $(\mathbf{r}, \mathbf{s}^+, \mathbf{s}^-)$ randomly, and (ii) perform the gradient update

$$W \leftarrow W + \eta \mathbf{r}(\mathbf{s}^+ - \mathbf{s}^-)^T \tag{3}$$

if the loss $\max\{0, 1 - k(\mathbf{r}, \mathbf{s}^+) + k(\mathbf{r}, \mathbf{s}^-)\}$ is positive, where η is a learning rate.

We initialize **W** with the identity matrix so we start from a reasonable solution (dot product).

4   Experiments

The proposed data-driven vehicle identification method is validated using real data collected in open-road tolls in several installations in the USA. Vehicles driving at about 50mph are detected by loop sensors which trigger an image capture of the full vehicle. Images contain a vast variety of vehicle types and times of day and the different locations imply different camera perspectives and from front/back directions with expensive tolling cameras. The images come in resolutions of 768×484 and 1920×512 and contain near-infrared intensity values (as this has a better signal-to-noise ratio for the license plate region across a range of illuminations, which for instance permits capturing license plates even at nighttime). The equipment and configuration is optimized for ALPR. An example image is shown in Fig. 1.

Note that this corresponds to the case where vehicles are identified by the infrastructure but the method is general and could apply to other settings such as on-board cameras and mobile phones (note the resolution and high vehicle speed). We obtain a dataset for our experiments by running a license plate detection algorithm.

Image Matching for Vehicle Identification. We evaluate image matching alone as a vehicle identification method and compare it to two industrial ALPR products representing two off-the-shelf baselines for identification. We will demonstrate not only that image matching is feasible for identification, but also that matching can outperform ALPR in some cases.

To that end, we use a "database" of about 35K images (corresponding to one week of data) and an evaluation set of 11K samples, with license plate number ground-truth. For each query image, we determine the most similar image in the database and output the license plate number of the match and the similarity value as confidence score. This is directly comparable to the ALPR baselines which also output a license plate number associated with a confidence.

Figure 5(a) shows the accuracy-reject curves for the two ALPR systems and the image matching, where we use the dot product between Fisher vectors as the similarity measure. Reject represents the fraction of samples with confidence below a threshold, and accuracy the fraction of samples with confidence above the threshold whose outputs match the ground-truth annotations. We observe that the ALPR systems reach a maximum accuracy in the range 80%-90%, for reject rates of about 40%. The reason why the accuracy never reaches 100% is because some plates contain graphical symbols, stacked characters and other artifacts that the ALPR systems are not able to deal with. In contrast, matching yields a much higher maximum accuracy, close to 100%, since it is agnostic on character dictionary, language, etc. However, this accuracy is only reached at a very high reject rate (about 90%) and quickly drops for smaller reject rates. This is because most of the plates in the query set are not present in the database and are rejected by the system.

However, the situation changes if the query images do have at least one "true" match in the database. If we consider only the set of about 5K queries which have an instance in the database, we obtain the result of Fig. 5(b). Now not only image matching reaches close to 100% at a much smaller reject rates, but it also clearly outperforms the ALPR systems both in accuracy and reject rate.

Thus, *image matching is a good vehicle identification method, actually better than commercial ALPR systems, provided that annotated examples are available.*

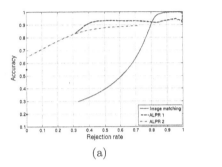
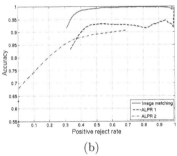

(a)   (b)

Fig. 5. Accuracy of image matching for identification: (a) when not all queries have a matching instance in the database, (b) when all the queries have an instance in the database

Use of Simulated Plates. In this section we evaluate the capability of the system to identify previously unseen vehicle identities through image simulation. We consider a set of 582 plate identities for which we synthesize a random number of plate images with different distortions using the method described in section 3, resulting in a set of 3,476 images. A set of 582 real images of the same identities is selected, to query with those and assess whether they are found in the database. This corresponds to a situation where there is a list of identities to be checked and a system captures images and compares each image with the synthesized images of the wanted identities, using again the dot product as similarity measure (i.e. no metric learning yet; experiments with metric learning are reported in the next paragraph). The error-reject characteristic of this setting is depicted as a solid, blue curve in Fig. 6 .

Then we repeat the experiment by replacing each synthetic image with a real image of the same license plate number (with random selection when there are more real images than synthetic ones). The corresponding curve is displayed in dashed red in Fig. 6. We observe that the curves corresponding to a synthetic and a real database are essentially on par. Therefore, we conclude that using a synthesized license plate has essentially the same effect as the real plate. *Thus, generating license plate images is an effective way to enable the search for previously unseen vehicle identities.*

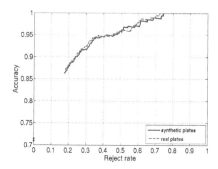

Fig. 6. Comparison between accuracies of real and synthetic plates in a retrieval task

Similarity Learning. We evaluate the similarity learning method of section 3.2 for the task of matching real to synthetic images. We essentially use the same set as for the previous experiment but we divide the query and database into two halves both containing synthetic and real plates for training and evaluation. We report both identification accuracy rates at 0% reject (acc0) and at 20% reject(acc20) and the mean average precision (mAP) to assess whether the learned similarity also performs well in ranking the database images beyond the first-best result. Results are summarized in Table 1.

Table 1. Results with similarity learning

	acc0(%)	acc20(%)	mAP(%)
No learning	78.6	87.8	77.2
Similarity learning	**81.9**	**92.7**	**81.5**

These results are with 100 training epochs and $\eta = 10^{-2}$. Table 1 shows that the metric learning algorithm improves both the accuracy and the mAP.

5   Conclusions

This article demonstrates that a data-driven view of vehicle identification without ALPR is feasible, and actually more accurate than ALPR in some scenarios. We believe that entry/exit control or matching for assisting manual plate verification are two applications that can benefit from the proposed method.

The proposal has been validated on images captured from the infrastructure. Although validation for on-board or mobile device cameras has not been performed, we believe the method is general and also applicable to these scenarios. Actually, in a set of experiments not reported here, it was observed that reducing the resolution of the images does not degrade the image matching accuracy as severely as it did for ALPR.

A line of future work is to go for compressed signatures in applications where the large database size is of concern.

References

1. Arth, C., Limberger, F., Bischof, H.: Real-time license plate recognition on an embedded DSP-platform. In: CVPR (2007)
2. Donoser, M., Arth, C., Bischof, H.: Detecting, Tracking and Recognizing License Plates. In: Yagi, Y., Kang, S.B., Kweon, I.S., Zha, H. (eds.) ACCV 2007, Part II. LNCS, vol. 4844, pp. 447–456. Springer, Heidelberg (2007)
3. Anagnostopoulos, C.N.E., Anagnostopoulos, I.E., Psoroulas, I.D., Loumos, V., Kayafas, E.: License plate recognition from still images and video sequences: A survey. IEEE Trans. on Intelligent Transportation Systems 9 (2008)
4. Chang, S.L., Chen, L.S., Chung, Y.C., Chen, S.W.: Automatic license plate recognition. IEEE Trans. on Intelligent Transportation Systems 5, 42–53 (2004)
5. Perronnin, F., Sánchez, J., Mensink, T.: Improving the Fisher Kernel for Large-Scale Image Classification. In: Daniilidis, K., Maragos, P., Paragios, N. (eds.) ECCV 2010, Part IV. LNCS, vol. 6314, pp. 143–156. Springer, Heidelberg (2010)
6. Chatfield, K., Lempitsky, V., Vedaldi, A., Zisserman, A.: The devil is in the details: an evaluation of recent feature encoding methods. In: BMVC (2011)
7. Bala, R., Zhao, Y., Burry, A., Kozitsky, V., Fillion, C., Saunders, C., Rodriguez-Serrano, J.A.: Image simulation for automatic license plate recognition. In: Proceedings of SPIE, vol. 8305 (2012)
8. Kulis, B., Saenko, K., Darrell, T.: What you saw is not what you get: Domain adaptation using asymmetric kernel transforms. In: CVPR (2011)
9. Jégou, H., Perronnin, F., Douze, M., Sánchez, J., Pérez, P., Schmid, C.: Aggregating local image descriptors into compact codes. IEEE Trans. on PAMI (2011)
10. Hays, J., Efros, A.A.: im2gps: estimating geographic information from a single image. In: CVPR (2008)
11. Hays, J., Efros, A.A.: Scene completion using millions of photographs. ACM Trans. on Graphics 26 (2007)
12. Marin, J., Vazquez, D., Gerenimo, D., Lopez, A.M.: Learning appearance in virtual scenarios for pedestrian detection. In: CVPR (2010)
13. Schels, J., Liebelt, J., Schertler, K., Lienhart, R.: Synthetically trained multi-view object class and viewpoint detection for advanced image retrieval. In: ICMR (2011)
14. Wang, K., Babenko, B., Belongie, S.: End-to-end scene text recognition. In: ICCV (2011)
15. Konidaris, T., Gatos, B., Ntzios, K., Pratikakis, I., Theodoridis, S., Perantonis, S.J.: Keyword-guided word spotting in historical printed documents using synthetic data and user feedback. IJDAR 9, 167–177 (2007)
16. Rodríguez-Serrano, J.A., Perronnin, F.: Synthesizing queries for handwritten word image retrieval. Pattern Recognition 45, 3270–3276 (2012)
17. Bai, B., Weston, J., Grangier, D., Collobert, R., Chapelle, O., Weinberger, K.: Supervised semantic indexing. In: CIKM (2009)
18. Weinberger, K., Saul, L.: Distance metric learning for large margin nearest neighbor classification. JMLR (2009)
19. Bottou, L.: Stochastic Learning. In: Bousquet, O., von Luxburg, U., Rätsch, G. (eds.) Machine Learning 2003. LNCS (LNAI), vol. 3176, pp. 146–168. Springer, Heidelberg (2004)

A Vision-Based Navigation Facility for Planetary Entry Descent Landing

Piergiorgio Lanza[1], Nicoletta Noceti[2], Corrado Maddaleno[1],
Antonio Toma[3], Luca Zini[2], and Francesca Odone[2]

[1] Thales Alenia Space Italy
[2] DIBRIS - Università degli Studi di Genova, Italy
[3] Politecnico di Torino, Italy

Abstract. This paper describes a facility set up as a test bed and a proof of concept to study open issues of future space missions. The final goal of such studies is to increase the on board autonomy, of primary importance for missions covering very high distances. We refer in particular to vision-based modules, in charge of acquiring and processing images during the Entry Descent and Landing (EDL) phases of a Lander, and contributing to a precise localization of the landing region and a safe landing. We will describe the vision-based algorithms already implemented on the facility, and a preliminary experimental analysis which allowed us to validate the approaches and provided very promising results.

1 Introduction

The key factor for the future space robotic missions is the *on board autonomy*, particularly relevant for missions towards planets at high distances from Earth, where a robotic closed loop control in real time is not possible — as an example, the travel time of a radiofrequency signal requires from 4 to 22 minutes covering the distance between the Earth and Mars.

In this general and ambitious goal, Computer Vision algorithms may help obtaining information about the 3D environment of space missions to verify the correct execution of robotic commands. Unfortunately, the difficulty of gathering real data and experimenting on the field is a real limitation for these approaches, and indeed most of the Computer Vision research for space applications is carried out by very few well known premises — such as the NASA JPL. With the exception of some early works (see e.g. [1,2]), DIMES (Descent Image Motion Estimation System) [3], developed by NASA, can be considered as the first historical attempt to exploit Computer Vision to control a spacecraft during the EDL phase. More recently, thanks to the successful application to the Mars Exploration Rovers (MER) landings, NASA invested in the last years in designing and developing vision-based solutions for EDL. The works in [4,5], describe improvements of DIMES technology for what concerns the problems of slope estimation and hazard detection on the planet surface.

This paper reports a work in progress in the design and the development of a facility – the Vision Based Navigational Facility (VBNF) – for the benchmarking

A. Fusiello et al. (Eds.): ECCV 2012 Ws/Demos, Part II, LNCS 7584, pp. 546–555, 2012.

of software modules and sensors to be used during planetary Entry Descent and Landing (EDL). This facility will allow us to generate a realistic environment for testing Computer Vision algorithms against various degrees of complexity, and acquire and distribute such data to the benefit of other research groups.

We will start with a description of the facility layout, with particular emphasis on technical characteristics and operability. Then, we will present the vision-based software modules tested and installed so far, having in mind two main requests: *landing precision* – that is, a small error between actual and expected landing coordinates – and *safety* – that is, an appropriate landing spot in terms of sunlight illumination, absence of rocks and limited surface slope. The remainder of the paper is organized as follows. Sec. 2 discusses the requirements of landing approaches. Sec. 3 is devoted to a detailed description of the facility. The software validation plan and the vision-based algorithms are described in Sec. 4 and 5. Sec. 6 is left to a final discussion.

2   Lander Approach Main Requirements

This section summarizes state of the art and challenges of planetary EDL, with a specific reference to vision-based approaches. Two common requirements for future scientific missions are the exploitation of a *more precise* and *safer* landing.

Over the last decades, within the Viking1 and Viking2 lander missions (1976), Mars Path Finder (1997), Mars Exploration Rover (Spirit and Opportunity) (2004), Phoenix (2008), and Mars Science Laboratory (2009), the landing major axis ellipse has been reduced from 300 km to 20 km [6]. The current aim is to further reduce this dispersion ellipse in order to achieve, within few years, ellipse landing of hundreds of meters. This precision is strictly necessary to reach particular interesting landing zones, as the so called Peaks of Eternal Light (PELs) – zones where the sunlight is almost always guaranteed, found on Mercury and on the Moon. Depending on the distance from the landing surface, a combination of sensors, including video cameras and altimeters, may be adopted.

A second driving criterion, beyond the landing precision, is the definition of safe or unsafe landing zones. The evaluation of the safeness of a zone can be performed by means of image processing algorithms applied to images acquired during the last lander descent phase (lander altitude from 3000 m to 100 m). More specifically, according to the European Space Agency (ESA) recommendations [7], the parameters taken into account are the following:

Level of illumination. There is usually a minimum level of illumination (defined by the producer) for the solar panels to operate.
Slope. Terrains within a 10 deg of maximum slope can be considered as safe for landing.
Rock height. Rocks with height up to 0.5 meter are considered not dangerous for the landing.
Terrain morphology. Unfortunately no objective criteria exist in the definition of safe zones with respect to the morphology. So far, only human judgment with respect to a ground truth has been employed. Sharp cliffs, big

rocks, and high craters rims are considered critical zones. It can be observed that they are characterized by distinctive local textures.

Finally, the use of image processing techniques calls for a further requirement: the capability of acquiring and possibly storing images during the mission approach to the target. The acquired images can be directly sent to the Earth Ground Station in real time, or stored on dedicated mass memory and transferred afterwards.

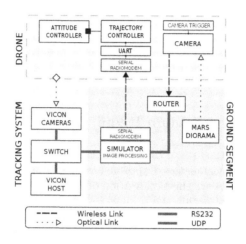

Fig. 1. The functional Layout of the VNF

3   Vision-Based Navigation Facility

The VBNF (Vision-based Navigation Facility) installed at the Thales Alenia Space Italy premises is a platform to be used as a test bed for innovative vision-based technologies and solutions. It is suited to validate them and to analyse their performances in operative situations similar to real ones. In fact, the VBNF simulates EDL operations of a laboratory *lander* represented by a drone equipped with a video camera.

From a functional point of view the facility is composed by three main components (see Fig. 1): (1) the Tracking System, (2) the quadrotor Drone, (3) the Diorama and the Simulator/Image Processing workstation.

The *tracking system* is based on the Vicon Motion Capture System and is composed by 13 Vicon Bonita infrared cameras, connected together in a PoE (Power over Ethernet) network hosted by a dedicated workstation on which runs the proprietary Vicon Tracker software. The infrared cameras are attached on a cube-shaped aluminum structure with 9 meters long sides (Fig. 2, left). They acquire 0.3 Megapixel images up to 240Hz and can track a single marker with a precision of 1 mm. The markers are small spheres covered with an infrared-reflective coating that are fixed on the body to track. The purpose of the tracking

Fig. 2. Left: the Vision-based Navigation Facility. Right: the drone flying (note the camera facing down observing the diorama).

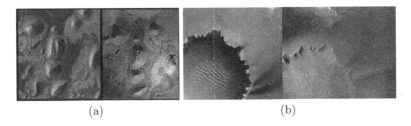

(a)   (b)

Fig. 3. (a) Left: part of Western Arabia Terra. Right: the same portion of Arabia Terra on the diorama. (b) Left: the Victoria Crater. Right: the Victoria Crater on the diorama.

system is to provide to the trajectory controller the position and the attitude angles of the quadrotor while it flies inside the tracked volume.

The *quadrotor drone* is a rotorcraft propelled by 4 rotors (Fig. 2, right). The model used in the VBNF has a lightweight carbon fiber frame and can bring a payload up to 1 Kg heavy with an endurance of about 15 minutes. The payload is constituted by the camera, the trajectory control board and the serial radio modem, for an in-flight weight of the drone of 2.7 Kg. While the flight stability of the quadrotor is guaranteed by a commercial autopilot (Mikrokopter) that accurately balances the roll and pitch angles of the drone in order to keep it hovering in the air, the trajectory controller is implemented on an additional board running 4 parallel PID (Proportional-Integral-Derivative) controllers, one for each of the remaining degrees of freedom (x, y, z and yaw angle). This board receives on a dedicated wireless-serial link the feedback obtained from the UDP (User Datagram Protocol) Vicon data stream and sends the commands to the Mikrokopter board using a second UART (Universal Asynchronous Receiver-Transmitter) port. Finally it also takes care of triggering the camera when a new picture is requested by the Image Processing Workstation. The video camera is a CMOS gray level camera (1Kb x 1Kb, 8 bits per pixel) with a rolling shutter. These characteristics are comparable to the already space qualified camera based on STAR1000 sensor used for space applications.

The 1:300 scale *diorama* (8m × 8m, 1.5m of maximum relief height) accurately reproduces some geographic peculiarity of the Mars surface: the Nili Fossae, the Victoria Crater, the Xanthe Terra, the Arabia Terra, and the Dilly Crater. Fig. 3(a) and Fig. 3(b) show, on the left, images of two real Mars surfaces, and on the right the diorama corresponding portions. As it can be observed, the representation is very accurate.

4   Software Validation Plan

All vision-based algorithms to be installed on the Image Processing Workstation(see Sec. 5) are tested in accordance to a *validation plan*. It can be summarized according to the following pipeline:

Preliminary tests (few tests). They include evaluations of the consistency for each software module on a small set of data. The goal is to verify and validate the algorithm and all its modules.

First tests campaign (100 tests). The objective is twofold: first, optimizing the algorithms and, second, characterizing the method and determining their performances.

Second tests campaign (> 10000 tests). It aims at evaluating the robustness of the selected methods with respect to scenarios with variable clutter, noise, angle of the sunlight, texture.

Full chain tests validation (> 65000 tests). The goal here is to evaluate the precision of the whole algorithmic chains.

Datasets include synthetic data, created with a viewer of 3D terrain models developed by ESA (PANGU [8]). Real data include public data from NASA and NASDA and a dataset of video sequences from the VBNF facility.

5   Vision-Based Algorithms

In the following we describe the main Computer Vision modules currently included in the facility. They all have been thoroughly examined following the validation plan (Sec. 4) with the exception of the slope estimation, which is under characterization (Second Tests Validation Campaign). All feature based methods make use of an optimized implementation of SURF features [9] chosen as a trade-off between efficiency and accuracy, although other features (such as, SIFT and Harris corners) are available.

5.1   Relative and Absolute Pose Estimation

The lander pose estimation, which controls the landing position, is based on two different algorithmic chains (see Fig. 4), that are described in the following.

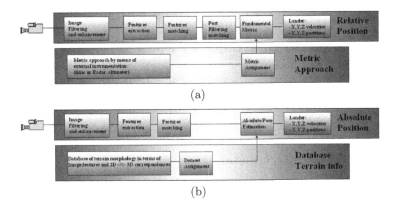

(a)

(b)

Fig. 4. Flowchart of the main steps of Relative and Absolute Pose determination

Relative Pose Estimation. Relative pose estimation is evaluated between two consecutive images of the sequence acquired during the descent phase. At each time instant, we extract SURFs and compute sparse correspondences between adjacent frames [10,11]. Such correspondences are used to estimate the relative geometry between the two views, that is the *fundamental matrix F*. To this purpose we adopt an approach proposed in [12], where the authors exploit a prior knowledge on the observed scene which appears to be quasi-planar from a large distance (see Fig. 3(b)).

In [12] the authors propose an efficient implementation of the *plane + parallax model* originally proposed in [13] and based on the geometrical model $F = [\mathbf{e}']_\times H$.

An external instrument (Lidar or an altimeter in a real space implementation of the algorithm, the tracking system in the VBNF) delivers the altitude information needed to associate a correct metric to the relative pose estimation. The obtained estimate can finally be applied to infer the spacecraft position with respect to an estimated entry point. This approach can advantageously be used when no 3D landing model terrain is available. Tab. 1 reports average relative errors between adjacent frames w.r.t. the ground truth on both synthetic and real data, at the end of the validation pipeline: $RelativeError = \frac{||TrueStep - EstimatedStep||}{||TrueStep||}$.

Absolute Pose Estimation. The absolute pose is determined by Perspective-n-Point (PnP) [14] algorithm which evaluates the matching correspondences between the features extracted from an input image and their equivalent 3D points measured from the 3D terrain model of the landing zone. Thus, this requires such 3D points to be known in advance. For instance, they may correspond to relevant elements of the planet surfaces, as craters or rock structures. Within this context, we adopted a set of labeled correspondences, and obtained very promising results in terms of estimation accuracy, with an error limited to the 3-4 % with respect to the ground truth.

Table 1. Relative pose estimation results on the full chain validation

Sequences type	Trajectory type	Relative error
Synthetic	linear	0.08 ± 0.01
	polynomial	0.3 ± 0.05
Real	linear	0.2 ± 0.18
	polynomial	0.4 ± 0.14

5.2 Hazard Map Determination

In this section we review the main steps performed to derive an hazard map of the surface. The map combines danger levels produced by the various algorithms running in parallel at different resolution levels (patch level for illumination and texture, variable region size level for slope).

Analysis of the Illumination. The algorithm we adopt relies on well known techniques. A simple thresholding is performed on the values of the image pixels. The threshold should correspond to the minimum acceptable level of illuminance required for an exploration mission to operate autonomously.

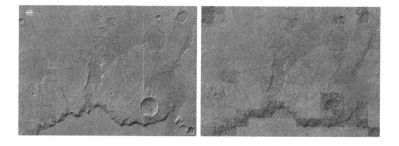

Fig. 5. Left: a real image of a Mars terrain. Right: the output of Hazard Map algorithm. The dangerous areas have been highlighted with colors of increasing intensity depending on the dangerousness.

Texture Analysis. Texture is an important element to human vision and people also tend to relate texture elements of varying size to a plausible 3D surface. The algorithm we adopt is based on the local evaluation of statistical properties of an image, considering local regions of 16x16 pixels. The statistical approach is based on Intensity Standard Deviation (ISD) developed at JPL [4]. The output of the procedure is an evaluation of the danger level (safe, low, medium, high dangerous). Fig. 5 reports a visual representation of such levels of dangerousness, for an example image of variable complexity.

Slope Determination. The slope of the planetary surface can be computed exploiting the relationship between two adjacent images of the planet surface acquired during descent (see the examples in Fig. 6). This relationship is defined by a homography, since the surface is quasi-planar because of the relative distance between the spacecraft and the surface. It is well known, the homography

Fig. 6. Examples of images, acquired by the VBNF, of a terrain of slope $15°$

H encodes information on the lander relative motion between poses (rotation matrix R and translation vector t) and on the slope of the observed landing site [13]. It holds that $H = R - \mathbf{T}\frac{\mathbf{n_0}^\top}{\mathbf{d}}$ where $\mathbf{n_0}$ is the normal of the surface and $\mathbf{d}$ is the distance between the plane and the camera center. This can be seen a special case of Structure from Motion, when the scene is planar.

In our work we start from a set of feature correspondences and estimate the homography H with RANSAC [15]. Since the homography H can be recovered only up to a scale factor, the equation becomes $H \approx R + \mathbf{Tn}^\top$ where $n = -\frac{\mathbf{n_0}^\top}{\mathbf{d}}$. The obtained solution carries a two-fold ambiguity which can be solved by looking at a further view (that is, combining the solutions from another pair of views).

A previous work in the literature disregarded this ambiguity [4] proposing a solution based on Levenberg-Marquardt, which could lead to one of the possible solutions, not necessarily the right one. Instead, we adopt a spectral approach proposed in [16] (see also [17]) and based on computing a SVD of H and extracting the unknowns from the factorization. We obtain 4 possible solutions, 2 of which may be discarded by geometrical constraints. A unique solution may be obtained by estimating the most stable solution from consecutive image pairs.

Finally, the slope λ of the surface is simply computed as the angle between the estimated normal vector $\mathbf{n_s}$ and the reference normal vector of the surface $\mathbf{n_r}$ in the coordinate system of the camera as $\lambda = \arccos \frac{\mathbf{n}_r^t \mathbf{n}_s}{\|\mathbf{n}_r\|\|\mathbf{n}_s\|}$ (see Fig. 7).

The results obtained at the end of the second campaign on real images representing a variable texture, illumination, and an even distribution of the slope in the range $[0, 30]$ degrees, produced a 1.2% average error (estimated slope diverging from the real one of more than 5 degrees). The performances degrade when the quality of images (and image features) degrades. A set of experiments carried out on the previous set of images, after a low-pass filtering with Gaussian

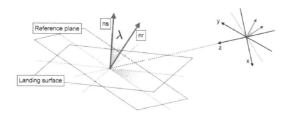

Fig. 7. The slope λ can be recovered computing the angle between ns and nr

filters with standard deviation equal to $\sigma = 3$ and $\sigma = 4$ causes an increasing of the average error to 1.8% and 2.5% respectively.

Preliminary experiments carried out on the full pipeline campaign confirm this analysis. However, they also highlight that a main drawback of real images within the domain of interest is a poor texture and, therefore, a high degree of noise in the estimation of H.

6   Discussion

In this paper we presented a work in progress on the design and the development of the VBNF facility whose main goals are the benchmarking of software modules and sensors to be used during Planetary EDL. We are currently improving both the hardware and the software modules, working on a more stable quadrotor, a more precise camera calibration, and vision-based modules more robust to poorly textured images.

Here we presented very promising results of the vision based algorithms in terms of accuracy with respect to synthetic ground truths. In particular, the error for the Relative and Absolute Pose estimation is within the 3-4 %. By means of the VBNF it will be possible to further verify the algorithm performances against optical deformation introduced by rolling shutter, quadrotor mechanical vibrations and real illumination effects in terms of visible terrain textures and shadows. All these effects are present in a real space mission environment and they shall be taken into account to determine the performances of vision based EDL algorithms.

The facility will also allow us to acquire benchmark datasets, some of which will be shared with the research community.

Acknowledgments. The VBNF facility has been designed and integrated with the support of the STEPS project co-funded by Regione Piemonte (Project co-financed by EC Platform: POR FESR 007/2013).

References

1. Cheng, Y., Johnson, A., Matthies, L., Wolf, A.: Passive imaging based hazard avoidance for spacecraft safe landing. In: Proc. iSAIRAS 2001 (2001)
2. Cheng, Y., Goguen, J., Johnson, A., Leget, C., Matthies, L., Martin, M.S., Willson, R.: The mars exploration rovers descent image motion estimation system. IEEE Intelligent Systems 19, 13–21 (2004)
3. Cheng, Y., Johnson, A., Matthies, L.: Mer-dimes: A planetary landing applications of computer vision. In: IEEE Proc. CVPR (2005)
4. Huertas, A., Cheng, Y., Madison, R.: Passive imaging based multi-cue hazard detection for spacecraft safe landing. In: Aerospace Conf. IEEE (2006)
5. Cheng, Y.: Real time surface slope estimation by homography alignment for spacecraft safe landing. In: ICRA (2010)
6. Braun, R.D., Manning, R.M.: Mars exploration entry, descent and landing challenges. In: IEEE 29th AAS Guidance and Control Conference (2006)
7. ESA: Navigation for planetary approach a general approach and landing (2006)
8. Parkes, S., Martin, I., Dunstan, M.: Planet surface simulation with pangu. In: Int. Conf. on Space Operations (2004)
9. Bay, H., Ess, A., Tuytelaars, T., Van Gool, L.: Surf: Speeded up robust features. CVIU 110, 346–359 (2008)
10. Scott, G.L., Longuet-Higgins, H.C.: An algorithm for associating the features of two images. Proc. of the Royal Society Biological Sciences 244, 21–26 (1991)
11. Delponte, E., Isgrò, F., Odone, F., Verri, A.: Svd-matching using sift features. Graphical Models 68 (2006)
12. Zini, L., Odone, F., Verri, A., Lanza, P., Marcer, A.: Relative Pose Estimation for Planetary Entry Descent Landing. In: Koch, R., Huang, F. (eds.) ACCV 2010 Workshops, Part II. LNCS, vol. 6469, pp. 255–264. Springer, Heidelberg (2011)
13. Hartley, R., Zisserman, A.: Multiple view geometry in computer vision, vol. 2. Cambridge Univ. Press (2000)
14. David, P., Dementhon, D., Duraiswami, R., Samet, H.: Softposit: Simultaneous pose and correspondence determination. Int. J. Comput. Vision 59, 259–284 (2004)
15. Fischler, M., Bolles, R.: Random sample consensus: a paradigm for model fitting with applications to image analysis and automated cartography. Communications of the ACM 24, 381–395 (1981)
16. Faugeras, O.: Three-dimensional computer vision: a geometric viewpoint. The MIT Press (1993)
17. Zhang, Z., Hanson, A.R.: 3d reconstruction based on homography mapping. In: ARPA Image Understanding Workshop, pp. 249–399 (1996)

CYKLS: Detect Pedestrian's Dart Focusing on an Appearance Change

Masahiro Ogawa, Hideo Fukamachi, Ryuji Funayama, and Toshiki Kindo

Future Project div., Toyota Motor Co.
1200, Mishuku, Susono, Shizuoka, Japan
{masahiro@ogawa,fuka@machi,ryuji@funayama,toshiki@kindo}.tec.toyota.co.jp

Abstract. We propose a new method for detecting "pedestrians' dart" to support drivers cognition in real traffic scenario. The main idea is to detect sudden appearance change of pedestrians before their consequent actions happen. Our new algorithm, called "Chronologically Yielded values of Kullback-Leibler divergence between Separate frames" (CYKLS), is a combination of two main procedures: (1) calculation of appearance change by Kullback-Leibler divergence between descriptors in some time interval frames, and (2) detection of non-periodic sequence by a new smoothing method in the field of time series analysis. We can detect pedestrians' dart with 22% Equal Error Rate, using a dataset which includes 144 dart scenes.

1 Introduction

We propose a new method for detecting "pedestrians' dart" to support drivers cognition in real traffic scenario.

The main idea is to detect sudden appearance change of pedestrians before their consequent actions happen.

To confirm that there exist such an appearance change as a premonitory phenomenon of dart, we first checked several drive recorder data. (Unfortunately, we don't allowed to process the drive recorder data. In addition to that, if we were allowed to process the data, the resolution is too coarse.) Those consist of 2099 near-miss scenes involving pedestrians. About 25% of these scenes include sudden acceleration or direction changes of the pedestrians, unrelated to the car motion. Then we investigated whether these scenes include any appearance change of the pedestrian, and we confirm there exist some appearance changes, such as "upper body turning toward traveling direction", "head bending forward", "increasing the length of stride" and "broadening legs". So if we can detect these appearance changes, we could predict pedestrian's dart and it has the potential to reduce car-pedestrian accidents.

Until now, variation detection has not been studied so extensively, especially for car mounted camera. As far as we know, in the field of automatic risk detection involving pedestrians, this is the first study of these types.

A. Fusiello et al. (Eds.): ECCV 2012 Ws/Demos, Part II, LNCS 7584, pp. 556–565, 2012.

Fig. 1. Typical detection result of CYKLS. Red rectangle indicates dart detection result.

1.1 Related Work

Gesture Recognition by Supervised Learning. There have been many works concerning detection of specific postures and gestures. A.Efros et al [1] developed a method to detect low resolution human movement. It tracks humans and gets the local motion using optical flow. The recognition is performed using a nearest neighbor framework. I.Laptev [2] introduces local spatio-temporal image features, which do not need spacial segmentation. Recognition is done by linear discrimination. E.Shechtman et al [3] also propose a method which does not need detection or tracking. It uses space-time patch and detects similar movements in 2 video sequences. L.Yeffet et al [4] introduce LTP feature which extend LBP [5] to time dimension , and recognize actions using linear SVM. M.Andriluka et al [6] introduce a 3D pose estimation method based on 2D inference and dynamical model, and apply it to the real world. All above-mentioned methods need learning/prior data set, which are sometimes hard to create, especially for all dart postures or gestures.

Abnormal Behavior Detection. There also have been many attempts to detect abnormal behavior in scenes [7][8]. In recent years, F.Nater et al [9] proposed a method which can build hierarchical activity model automatically. However in a real traffic scenario, pedestrians can be seen only for a few seconds at most, so there is only about one-third of a second to make a decision. All these methods use static background assumption, so they can not be applied directly to car mounted camera.

Optical Flow Based Method. Daimler researchers develop a 6D-Vision [10][11] to estimate objects 3D position and 3D motion in traffic scene using car mounted camera. It successfully combines a dense variational optical flow with Kalman filters at every single pixel. This method cannot detect premonitory phenomenon of dart. On the other hand, our method use appearance change to catch premonitory phenomenon of dart so that we can detect dart as early as possible.

2 Dart Detection Method

2.1 CYKLS

In this section, we give an explanation of our dart detection method which we named CYKLS (Chronologically Yielded values of Kullback-Leibler divergence between Separate frames).

CYKLS, is a combination of two main processes:

1. Calculation of appearance change by Kullback-Leibler divergence [12] between descriptors in some time interval frames, and
2. Detection of non-periodic sequence using a smoothing method

The second part is a totally new change detection algorithm in the field of time series analysis. The detailed algorithm of CYKLS is described below.

Calculation of Appearance Change. After detecting pedestrians, we catch the pedestrian's shape:

$$\mathbf{v}(t) : \text{some descriptor inside the ROI} \tag{1}$$

using some descriptor of a region of interest (ROI) inside the pedestrian's image window at each frame t , and L1 normalize the descriptor into:

$$\mathbf{p}(t) := \frac{\mathbf{v}(t)}{\|\mathbf{v}(t)\|_{L1}}. \tag{2}$$

We then consider the normalized SIFT feature vector [13] $\mathbf{p}(t)$ as a probabilistic distribution, and compute the difference of the distribution between frame t and t-n using KL divergence as:

$$d(t, n) := D_{KL}(\mathbf{p}(t)\|\mathbf{p}(t - n)). \tag{3}$$

Detection of Non-periodic Sequence. Next, we create a l-dimension vector:

$$\mathbf{u}(t, n, l) := (d(t - l + 1, n), \dots, d(t, n)) \tag{4}$$

from the time series data $d(t, n)$, and sum up backward to get:

$$\mathbf{U}(t, n, l, K) := \sum_{k=0}^{K} \mathbf{u}(t - k, n, l). \tag{5}$$

Then, we compute the cost:

$$\text{cost} := \cos\Theta(t, n, l, K) := \frac{\mathbf{U} \cdot \mathbf{I_1}}{\|\mathbf{U}\|_{L2}\|\mathbf{I_1}\|_{L2}} = \frac{\sum_i U_i}{\sqrt{l}\|\mathbf{U}\|_{L2}} \tag{6}$$

as the cosine of the angle between $\mathbf{U}(t, n, l, K)$ and the constant vector:

$$\mathbf{I}_l := (1, 1, ..., 1) \; ; \; l-\dim. \tag{7}$$

If a pedestrian's movement is cyclic, like walking, and parameter K is constant factor of walking cycle, then the sum, $\mathbf{U}$, become constant factor of $\mathbf{I}_l$. So if we compare $\mathbf{U}$ and $\mathbf{I}_l$ in angle, we can suppress periodic movement. This algorithm is a new smoothing method in the field of time series analysis.

Finally, the cost $\cos\Theta$ is compared to a detection threshold T:

$$\text{cost} < \mathrm{T} \Rightarrow \text{detect dart} \tag{8}$$

The total flow of CYKLS is in Fig.2, and output examples are in Fig.4.

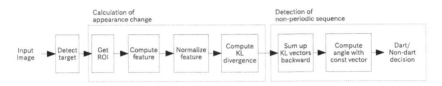

Fig. 2. Flow chart of CYKLS

2.2 Notes

The first part of the process ("Calculation of appearance change") allows to detect sudden direction change, while, in addition to that, the second part ("Detection of non-periodic sequence") deals with sudden acceleration. This is illustrated in the Fig.4c.

3 Evaluation

3.1 Dataset

We created a new dataset to evaluate our method. We depicted the typical 4 dart pattern which cause the danger from the drive recorder data. The dataset includes 6 pedestrians(A-F), 6 environmental settings(a-f) and 4 dart patterns(1-4), so the total is 144 sequences. The image size is XGA, and each sequence is about 10 seconds long with 15 fps and only includes one person and one dart. In order to evaluate only the dart detector, we annotate all pedestrians by hand, and use these annotated windows instead of the output of a pedestrian detector. The composition of our dataset is listed below.

- pedestrians: A:woman, B:man wearing long sleeve shirt, C:man wearing coat, D:man wearing black clothes, E:man wearing short sleeve shorts, F:man wearing similar color clothes to the background (see Fig.3)

– environmental settings:

	a	b	c	d	e	f
Background	plain	plain	natural	natural	natural	plain
Movement before dart	walk	stop	walk	stop	walk	walk
Distance at the dart moment [m]	22	22	22	22	10	10

– dart patterns: 1:change of direction, 2:change of direction followed by running, 3:running, 4:zigzag slightly (see Fig.4)

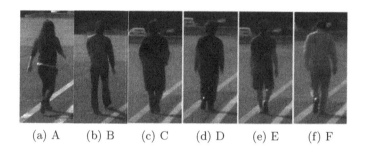

(a) A   (b) B   (c) C   (d) D   (e) E   (f) F

Fig. 3. Pedestrians of our dataset

3.2   Evaluation Scheme

We annotate every pedestrian with dart or non-dart, and evaluate the result by drawing standard DET(False Positive(FP)-False Negative(FN)) curve. Once the parameter set $\{n, l, K, T\}$ is given, we can calculate FP and FN.

3.3   Evaluation Results

Using the dataset mentioned in section 3.1, we compute the FP-FN rates for each 7980 parameter sets($1 \leq n \leq 20, 2 \leq l \leq 20, 0 \leq K \leq 20$). We compare CYKLS with other methods. Dart detection is somewhat new problem, and we cannot find out state-of-the-art method in this field, so we compare CYKLS with below baseline detectors. 3 norm options(KL divergence(same as CYKLS),L1,L2) and 5 smoothing methods(no smoothing, same as CYKLS, moving average with weight vector=const,x,exp(x)), so there are 15 detectors in total for comparison. The result is shown in Fig.5, in which we abbreviate each norm to "KL,L1,L2", and each smoothing method to "no,CY,const,x,exp". As a result, CYKLS get the lowest FP-FN rate (about 22% EER). One of the best parameter set we found is $(n, l, K) = (2, 19, 8)$, and using this parameter, we can detect dart with FP 20%, FN 26%. The percentage is not as bad as it may seems. We want to detect dart as early as we can, so we annotate the pedestrian who has very slight appearance change as dart, for example second from left pedestrian image in Fig.4. This causes large FN.

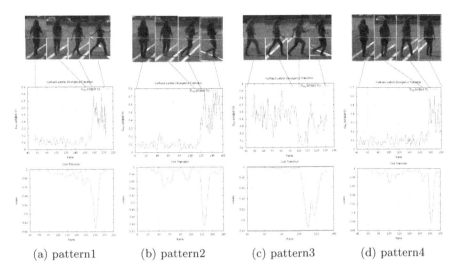

(a) pattern1   (b) pattern2   (c) pattern3   (d) pattern4

Fig. 4. Dataset examples of 4 dart patterns with result graphs. Top row is annotated windows with ROI (yellow rectangle). The second row is the graph of KL divergence transition. The third row is the graph of cost transition. We can see that all 4 dart patterns are detectable in the graph of the third row.

3.4   ROI Test

Actually there is no necessity that the ROI used for dart detection coincides with the window used for detecting pedestrians. We then test several ROIs inside the detected pedestrian's window, for which we compute $\mathbf{v}(t)$ in (1).

We first create 7 ROI as shown in Fig.6. For the latter 4 ROI, we move the ROI inside the detector window such as it minimizes the appearance change using SIFT descriptor and a template model. The template model is computed using the first frame. Finally, the total number of tested ROI is then 11.

We evaluate those 11 ROI by the method mentioned in section 3.2 using the one of the best parameter set which is found in section $3.3((n, l, K) = (2, 19, 8))$. As a result, block0 (whole window) give the lowest EER of the 11 ROI (see Fig.7).

3.5   Effect of Tracking Error

In practice, before detecting dart, we first need pedestrian detection and tracking. The detected pedestrian's window has some motion noise. But as mentioned above, as we want to divide the problem of dart detector and pedestrian tracker, we simulate scale and center position errors as a Gaussian distribution around the hand annotated center. We fix the standard deviation of the center position error to 3 pixels, and of the width error to 3 pixels (aspect ratio is fixed at 1:2).

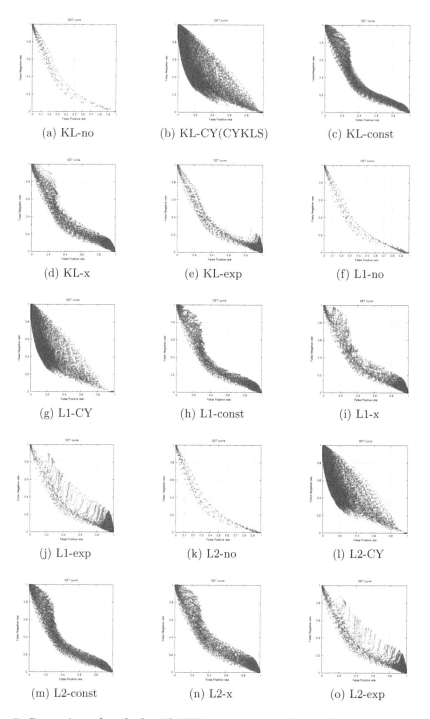

Fig. 5. Comparison of methods with 7980 parameter sets. Every title represents norm-smoothing method. CYKLS gets the minimum Equal Error Rate(EER).

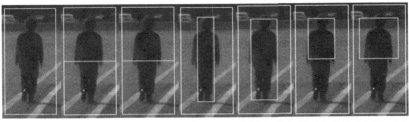

(a) block0 (b) block1 (c) block2 (d) block3 (e) block4 (f) block5 (g) block6

Fig. 6. ROI images. Yellow rectangle suggests the ROI, and white one suggests the hand annotated rectangle.

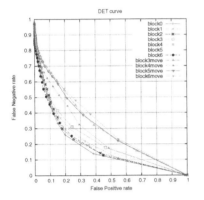

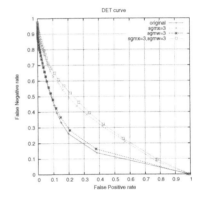

Fig. 7. ROI test results. "block0"(whole window) give the lowest EER.

Fig. 8. Simulation result of tracking error

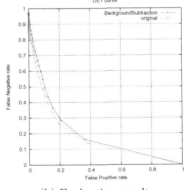

(a) Input image example

(b) Evaluation result

Fig. 9. Evaluation for background subtraction

The result is shown in Fig.8(Again, we use the one of the best parameter set $(n, l, K) = (2, 19, 8)$). As we can see, while width error hardly slow down the performance, position error cause performance degration in some degree.

4   Discussion

4.1   The Relationship with Fourier Transformation

CYKLS contains a new algorithm to detect non-periodic movement, but one might think it can be detected using Fourier Transformation for time series data. To check this, we carry out FFT to the time series data of output from the first part ("Calculation of appearance change") of CYKLS. However, we cannot see walking period peak shifting at dart point because pedestrians walk so short before dart in our dataset.

4.2   Background Subtraction

All of our dataset have white lines in the background of the pedestrian window(see Fig.1), so CYKLS may actually detect the presence of a white line. To check this, we did a background subtraction for our dataset in order to remove the white lines (see Fig.9a). We use median image following erosion and dilation method, because background is almost static. As it turns out, CYKLS can also detect dart without white lines in the background, though performance goes slightly down. This result is shown in Fig.9b (We fix $(n, l, K) = (2, 19, 8)$).

5   Conclusion

We have developed a new algorithm to detect dart by focusing on an appearance change, which we named CYKLS. We compared 15 baseline detectors including CYKLS, and found CYKLS marked the best score. And we also tested 11 ROI to compute CYKLS, and found the whole window marked the best score. As a result, we can detect pedestrians' dart with 22% Equal Error Rate, using a dataset which includes 144 dart scenes.

CYKLS can also be applied to detect other object's non-periodic movement, including cars and bicycles.

Future Work. In this paper we use static images, but we are ready for testing this algorithm on a moving car. In this case, tracking error and background change will become a big issue. To treat such issue, we will search for better features and smoothing methods. Also, dynamically adapting the parameters during the sequence may improve the performance.

References

1. Efros, A.A., Berg, A.C., Berg, E.C., Mori, G., Malik, J.: Recognizing action at a distance. In: ICCV, pp. 726–733 (2003)
2. Laptev, I.: Local Spatio-Temporal Image Features for Motion Interpretation. PhD thesis, Department of Numerical Analysis and Computer Science (NADA), KTH (2004)
3. Shechtman, E., Irani, M.: Space-time behavior based correlation. In: IEEE Conference on Computer Vision and Pattern Recognition (CVPR), vol. 1, pp. 405–412 (June 2005)
4. Yeffet, L., Wolf, L.: Local trinary patterns for human action recognition. In: 2009 IEEE 12th International Conference on Computer Vision, pp. 492–497. IEEE (2009)
5. Ojala, T., Pietikäinen, M., Mäenpää, T.: Multiresolution gray-scale and rotation invariant texture classification with local binary patterns. IEEE Trans. Pattern Anal. Mach. Intell. 24(7), 971–987 (2002)
6. Andriluka, M., Roth, S., Schiele, B.: Monocular 3d pose estimation and tracking by detection. In: The Twenty-Third IEEE Conference on Computer Vision and Pattern Recognition, CVPR 2010, San Francisco, CA, USA, June 13-18, pp. 623–630. IEEE (2010)
7. Adam, A., Rivlin, E., Shimshoni, I., Reinitz, D.: Robust real-time unusual event detection using multiple fixed-location monitors. IEEE Trans. Pattern Anal. Mach. Intell. 30(3), 555–560 (2008)
8. Yin, J., Meng, Y.: Abnormal Behavior Recognition Using Self-Adaptive Hidden Markov Models. In: Kamel, M., Campilho, A. (eds.) ICIAR 2009. LNCS, vol. 5627, pp. 337–346. Springer, Heidelberg (2009)
9. Nater, F., Grabner, H., Van Gool, L.: Temporal relations in videos for unsupervised activity analysis. In: British Machine Vision Conference (2011)
10. Franke, U., Rabe, C., Badino, H., Gehrig, S.K.: 6D-Vision: Fusion of Stereo and Motion for Robust Environment Perception. In: Kropatsch, W.G., Sablatnig, R., Hanbury, A. (eds.) DAGM 2005. LNCS, vol. 3663, pp. 216–223. Springer, Heidelberg (2005)
11. Rabe, C., Müller, T., Wedel, A., Franke, U.: Dense, Robust, and Accurate Motion Field Estimation from Stereo Image Sequences in Real-Time. In: Daniilidis, K., Maragos, P., Paragios, N. (eds.) ECCV 2010, Part IV. LNCS, vol. 6314, pp. 582–595. Springer, Heidelberg (2010)
12. Kullback, S., Leibler, R.A.: On information and sufficiency. Ann. Math. Statist. 22, 79–86 (1951)
13. Lowe, D.: Distinctive image features from scale-invariant keypoints. International Journal of Computer Vision 60(2), 91–110 (2004)

Pose-Invariant Face Recognition in Videos
for Human-Machine Interaction

Bogdan Raducanu[1] and Fadi Dornaika[2,3]

[1] Computer Vision Center, 08193 Bellaterra, Barcelona, Spain
bogdan@cvc.uab.es
[2] University of the Basque Country UPV/EHU, San Sebastian, Spain
[3] IKERBASQUE, Basque Foundation for Science, Bilbao, Spain
fadi_dornaika@ehu.es

Abstract. Human-machine interaction is a hot topic nowadays in the communities of computer vision and robotics. In this context, face recognition algorithms (used as primary cue for a person's identity assessment) work well under controlled conditions but degrade significantly when tested in real-world environments. This is mostly due to the difficulty of simultaneously handling variations in illumination, pose, and occlusions. In this paper, we propose a novel approach for robust pose-invariant face recognition for human-robot interaction based on the real-time fitting of a 3D deformable model to input images taken from video sequences. More concrete, our approach generates a rectified face image irrespective with the actual head-pose orientation. Experimental results performed on Honda video database, using several manifold learning techniques, show a distinct advantage of the proposed method over the standard 2D appearance-based snapshot approach.

1 Introduction

In the field of human-machine interaction, faces play a major role. For instance, socially oriented robots are specifically designed to support richer forms of interactions with humans. Their primary mission is to detect human presence, engage in an interaction and behave in a personalized manner. State-of-the-art face recognition techniques can achieve very high accuracy rates under controlled conditions. However, most of current face recognition systems lack robustness in uncontrolled environments (e.g., outdoor scenarios, homes, offices, etc.), since they are pretty sensitive to pose, lighting, occlusions and other variations (such as the presence of natural or artificial structures: beards, moustaches, glasses, etc.). Hence, the challenge is two-fold: to discriminate between different persons and at the same time to be able to recognize the same person affected by one or several of the aforementioned transformations. In particular, head pose problem has been one of the bottlenecks for most current face recognition techniques, because it changes significantly a person's appearance. In order to generalize the use of robots in the context of human-machine interaction, it is mandatory to increase the robustness of the face recognition approach to correctly identify a person showing an arbitrary head pose.

In the robotics context, the system must continuously deal with an incoming flow of face images and has to guarantee a temporal coherence of a person's identity during the

A. Fusiello et al. (Eds.): ECCV 2012 Ws/Demos, Part II, LNCS 7584, pp. 566–575, 2012.

whole duration of the interaction process. In many cases, the difficulty arises from the fact that there is only a small time frame to capture a face with a high probability that the grabbed images do not contain the required frontal face images. On the other hand, videos very often provide non-frontal faces. To this end two categories of approaches were proposed. The first category uses manifold learning paradigms [1,2] in which the face subspace is constructed using many examples depicting subjects in different poses. The second category generates frontal face from the input image and then apply classic face recognition methods on the reconstructed frontal face image. The second category can be split into two main kinds of approaches: i) 3D morphable models [3], and ii) View-based methods [4]. View-based methods train a set of 2D models, each of which is designed to cope with shape or texture variation within a small range of viewpoints.

In [5], the authors propose a Local Linear regression method for pose invariant face recognition. The proposed method can generate the virtual frontal view from a given non-frontal face image. The whole non-frontal face image is partitioned into multiple local patches and then linear regression is applied to each patch for the prediction of its virtual frontal patch. The method requires the pose of the non-frontal pose as input in order to predict the frontal face. Following the approach of Active Appearance Models, [6] develops a face model and a rotation model which can be used to interpret facial features and synthesize realistic frontal face images when given a single novel face image. In [7], the authors address the non-frontal face recognition using morphable models. The morphable model serves as a preprocessing step by estimating the 3D shape of novel faces from the non-frontal input images, and generating frontal views of the reconstructed faces at a standard illumination using 3D computer graphics. The transformed images are then fed into state of-the-art face recognition systems that are optimized for frontal views. In [8], the authors use view-based active appearance models to fit to a novel face image under a random pose. The model parameters (combined appearance parameters) are adjusted to correct for the pose and used to reconstruct the face under a novel pose. This preprocessing makes face recognition more robust with respect to variations in the pose.

As can be seen, 3D based and view based methods have many limitations. For instance, the 3D morphable models require 3D scans and have high computational load. Although the Active Appearance Models are faster than the 3D morphable models, they require very tedious learning procedure and may generate very low quality images due to the fact the face textures are limited to offline learned statistical face texture models.

In this paper, we propose a strategy that generates virtual view of rectified faces taken from video sequences. We show that this way, we obtain a significant increase in face recognition rate when compared with standard 2D appearance-based snapshot approach. We also show that by adopting rectified faces simple linear manifold learning techniques (e.g., Principal Component Analysis) can provide very good results for face recognition. Our novel scheme is based on fitting a 3D mesh face representation to input images, which efficiently generates rectified facial view from an arbitrary head pose. Thus, our proposed approach is pose- and expression invariant. The proposed technique has the following properties:

- It compensates for all six degrees of freedom of the face pose.
- It compensates for the facial expression and/or facial actions since the rectified face image (geometrically normalized image) corresponds to a neutral face.
- The technique runs in real-time meaning that rectified faces can be provided online from a camera, which is a crucial constraint in human-robot interaction. It uses online appearance models in order to fit a generic 3D model to input images. It is much more practical then 3D morphable models.

The remainder of the paper is structured as follows: in Section 2, we provide the proposed pose and expression compensation based on a deformable 3D face model. The experimental results on face recognition are presented in Section 3. Finally, we provide some concluding remarks and guidelines for future work in Section 4.

2   Generating Rectified Faces in Continuous Videos

In this section, we present the main stages used for generating rectified face textures from videos. Firstly, we describe the 3D deformable model used in the fitting process. Secondly, we describe the process of generating the rectified face assuming that the fitting parameters are correctly estimated. Thirdly, we sketch out the fitting process.

A Deformable 3D Wireframe Model. Building a generic 3D model of a face is a challenging task. Indeed, such a model should account for the differences between specific human faces as well as between different facial expressions. This modelling was explored in the computer graphics, computer vision and model-based image coding communities. In our study, we use the 3D face model *Candide* [9]. This 3D deformable wire-frame model was first developed for the purpose of model-based image coding. The 3D shape of this model is directly recorded in coordinate form, i.e., the 3D coordinates of the vertices. The theoretical 3D face model is given by the 3D coordinates of the vertices $\mathbf{P}_i, i = 1, \ldots, n$ where n is the number of vertices. Thus, the shape up to a global scale can be fully described by the $3n$-vector $\mathbf{g}$ – the concatenation of the 3D coordinates of all vertices $\mathbf{P}_i$. The vector $\mathbf{g}$ can be written as:

$$\mathbf{g} = \overline{\mathbf{g}} + \mathbf{S}\,\tau_\mathbf{s} + \mathbf{A}\,\tau_\mathbf{a} \tag{1}$$

where $\overline{\mathbf{g}}$ is the standard shape of the model, and the columns of $\mathbf{S}$ and $\mathbf{A}$ are the shape and action units, respectively. A shape unit provides a way to deform the 3D wire-frame such as to adapt the eye width, the head width, the eye separation distance, etc. Thus, the term $\mathbf{S}\,\tau_\mathbf{s}$ accounts for shape variability (inter-person variability) while the term $\mathbf{A}\,\tau_\mathbf{a}$ accounts for the facial action (intra-person variability). The shape and action variabilities can be approximated well enough for practical purposes by this linear relation. Also, we assume that the two kinds of variability are independent. In this study, we use 12 modes for the shape unit matrix and six modes for the action units matrix.

In Equation (1), the 3D coordinates are expressed in a local coordinate system. However, one should relate the 3D coordinates to the image coordinate system (the 2D image coordinates). To this end, we adopt the weak perspective projection model [10]. We neglect the perspective effects since the depth variation of the face can be considered as small compared to its absolute depth[1].

For a given person, τ_s is constant. Estimating τ_s can be carried out using either feature-based [11] or featureless approaches [9]. In our recent work, we have shown that some components of the shape control vector can be automatically initialized with a featureless approach [12].

The state of the 3D model is given by the 3D head pose (three rotations and three translations) and the control vector τ_a. This is given by the vector **b**:

$$\mathbf{b} = [\theta_x, \theta_y, \theta_z, t_x, t_y, t_z, \tau_a{}^T]^T \tag{2}$$

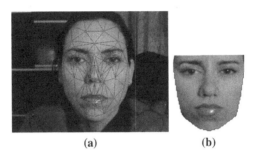

(a)   (b)

Fig. 1. Rectified face image based on model fitting. (a) an input image with correct fitting. **(b)** the corresponding rectified facial image.

Rectified Facial Texture. Our goal is to generate a rectified facial texture, as shown in figure 1.b, which compensates for the 3D head pose (3 rotational degrees of freedom and the 3 translational degrees of freedom) as well as for the facial expression and/or facial actions. In this Section, we briefly describe how this rectified texture is computed from the input image. In the sequel, this rectified texture will be used for face recognition.

The basic idea is to compute a geometrically normalized face image (rectified face) from the input image by fitting a deformable 3D mesh to the input image.

The 2D mesh associated with the rectified texture is obtained by projecting the standard shape $\bar{\mathbf{g}}$ (wire-frame), using a centered frontal 3D pose, onto an image with a given resolution. The texture of the rectified facial image is obtained by texture mapping from the triangular 2D mesh covering the face in the input image (see figure 1.a) using a piece-wise affine transform, $\mathcal{W}$. Similarly to [13], we have taken advantage of the fact that the barycentric coordinates of the pixels within each triangle are invariant under affine transforms. In other words, since the geometry of the 2D mesh in the rectified image is fixed the barycentric coordinates are fixed and can be computed once for all, which considerably reduces the CPU time associated with the texture mapping process - the warping process.

---

[1] The perspective projection is the classical pin-hole camera model. The weak perspective projection can be seen as the zero approximation to the perspective projection.

Once an instance of the 3D model (encoded by the vector **b**) is projected onto the input image, the warping process proceeds as follows. The rectified image bounding the fixed 2D mesh is scanned pixel by pixel. For every scanned pixel in this image, we know its triangle as well as its barycentric coordinates within this triangle. Therefore, the 2D location of the corresponding pixel in the input image can be easily inferred using a linear combination of the coordinates of the triangle vertices where the coefficients are given by the barycentric coordinates. The greylevel of the scanned pixel is then set by blending the greylevels associated with the four closest pixels to the non-integer coordinates of the returned location - the bilinear interpolation.

Mathematically, the warping process applied to an input image **y** is denoted by:

$$\mathbf{x}(\mathbf{b}) = \mathcal{W}(\mathbf{y}, \mathbf{b}) \tag{3}$$

where **x** denotes the rectified facial texture and **b** denotes the geometrical parameters. Without loss of generality, we have used two resolution levels for the rectified textures, encoded by 1310 and 5392 facial pixels bounded by 40×42 and 80×84 rectangular boxes, respectively. Obviously, other levels can be used. Generally speaking as the resolution increases, the fitting accuracy increases. However, by experience we found that the second resolution level is a good trade-off between the accuracy and the computational cost. In the sequel, all results are obtained with this resolution. The fitting and face rectification processes for the 80×84 rectified face image took about 40 ms on a PC equipped with a dual-core Intel processor at 2 Ghz.

Model Fitting: 3D Head Pose and Facial Action Estimation. In the previous section, we have shown that if the 3D deformable model is fitted to the input image, i.e., the geometric parameters **b** are estimated, then generating the rectified face image will be straightforward. In this section, we describe how these parameters are estimated in videos sequences using the temporal tracker developed in [14]. The basic idea is to recover **b** by minimizing a distance between the incoming warped frame and the current appearance of the face. This minimization is carried out using a difference decomposition-like approach [15]. This tracker has two interesting features. First, the statistics of the appearance model are updated online. Second, the empirical gradient matrix is computed for each input frame. This scheme leads to a fast, efficient and robust tracking algorithm. Figure 2 displays the tracking results associated with eight frames of a 750-frame sequence featuring quite large pose variations as well as large facial actions. The sequence is of resolution 720×480 pixels.

Pose Invariant Face Recognition. For every input frame, the above tracker provides the geometrical parameters (3D pose and facial actions) of the 3D model. It also provides the rectified face image associated with the input image. This rectified facial image corresponds to a frontal and neutral face. Thus, unlike existing methods, our proposed method simultaneously compensates for 3D pose and facial expression.

Once non-frontal face images are converted to virtual views, face recognition can be easily achieved by using the virtual generated views instead of all the non-frontal face images. The proposed method can be regarded as a preprocessing procedure independent of the following feature extraction and classifier design. Therefore, the proposed method can be combined with any face recognition technologies.

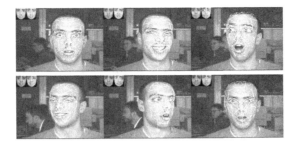

Fig. 2. Face and facial action tracking results using our appearance-based tracker. The snapshots correspond to frames 63, 181, 282, 418, 492, and 683, respectively in a 750-frame video sequence.

Fig. 3. Some samples from the Honda Video database

3 Experimental Results

Data Preparation. Our approach has been tested on the Honda video database (HVDB) [16,17]. HVDB has been acquired for the purpose of face tracking and recognition. It depicts persons sitting in front of a camera in a totally uncontrolled environment and performing unconstrained in-plane and out-of-plane head motion. Some samples are depicted in figure 3. The resolution of the images is 640x480 pixels and the videos were recorded at 15 frames per second. We selected from this database a subset of 22 video clips belonging to 22 different persons[2]. The rectified face texture was extracted according to the approach presented in the section 2. Some examples of rectified faces, under arbitrary head poses, are presented in figure 4. The iconic images that appear in the upper left corner of the image on the left column have the following meaning: the left represents the temporal average of the facial texture (used by the Online Appearance Model) and the right one, the rectified face (a higher resolution version is presented on the right column). In the end, we collected two datasets: one containing the rectified faces and the other, the cropped ones. Each dataset contains 2317 images organized in 22 classes, with an average of 100 images per class. Both rectified and cropped images were resized to 50×50 pixels.

---

[2] To guarantee optimal results from the Candide model, we limited the pan/tilt variation in head pose to the interval $[-45°,45°]$.

Fig. 4. Some samples of rectified face images from the Honda Video database based on model fitting. **Left column:** the input image with correct fitting. **Right column** the corresponding rectified facial image.

Face Recognition Results. For face recognition evaluation, we applied a manifold representation approach. This implies that the original, high-dimension data, are embedded into a low-dimensional subspace, without any relevant loss of information. The projection function could be either linear or non-linear. More concrete, we used the following manifold learning techniques: Principal Component Analysis (PCA), Locally Linear Embedding (LLE) [18], Locality Preserving Projections (LPP) [19] and Laplacian Eigenmaps (LE) [20]. PCA and LPP belong to the category of linear embedding techniques, while LLE and LE are non-linear. The PCA method estimates orthogonal projection directions that maximize the variance of original data. The LPP method searches a linear projection that preserve the locality of the neighboring data. The LLE algorithm seeks the nonlinear embedding in a neighborhood preserving manner by exploiting the local symmetries of linear reconstructions, and seeking the optimal weights for local reconstruction. The embedding is obtained using the estimated local weights. The LE method seeks the nonlinear embedding by preserving locality. It should be noticed that the LPP method is the linearized version of LE.

For classification purposes, we adopted 10 random splits of data. We split the data in several ratios for training and test: $10\% - 90\%, 20\% - 80\%, 30\% - 70\%, 40\% - 60\%$ and $50\% - 50\%$. The reason we decided to start with such a low percentage of training images (10% is motivated by the fact that we have a pretty high number of instances per class. The classification in the embedded space has been carried out using the Nearest Neighbor (NN) approach. The recognition rates for rectified images and cropped ones are reported in the tables 1 and 2, respectively. From these tables, we can observe that: (i) the use of rectified faces has improved the face recognition rate for all manifold learning techniques used and for all train/test ratios; (ii) the PCA technique has provided the best recognition results for both the cropped and rectified faces; (iii) the LLE method has provided the worst results. This is very consistent with the fact that LLE is not very suited for classification task; and (iv) for the rectified face, the LE method provided better results than the LPP method, whereas for the the cropped faces we got in general the reverse.

Table 1. Best average recognition accuracy using rectified faces

Train	10%	20%	30%	40%	50%
PCA	**99.08%**	**99.89%**	**100.00%**	**100.00%**	**100.00%**
LLE	60.64%	75.02%	79.60%	81.95%	85.76%
LPP	85.47%	94.02%	97.04%	98.33%	98.91%
LE	91.35%	97.87%	99.06%	99.45%	99.65%

Table 2. Best average recognition accuracy using cropped faces

Train	10%	20%	30%	40%	50%
PCA	**74.73%**	**85.86%**	**91.67%**	**94.24%**	**95.85%**
LLE	34.18%	42.71%	47.84%	53.99%	64.53%
LPP	67.54%	80.40%	86.36%	89.62%	91.64%
LE	68.82%	77.48%	82.34%	85.52%	87.62%

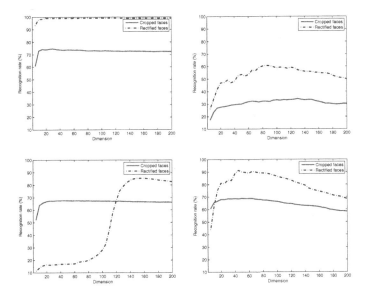

Fig. 5. Comparison of recognition rates between rectified and cropped face images with a 10% ratio of images used for training. The four plots depict the following embedding techniques (left-right and top-bottom order): PCA, LLE, LPP and LE.

In figure 5 we plot a comparison of recognition rates between rectified and cropped face images. The recognition rate is computed for a dimensionality of the embedded space up to 200 (in five-step increments). These plots correspond to the case when 10% of the data is used for training. We can see that the rectified faces have provided better recognition rates than the cropped faces for all dimensions used by PCA, LLE, and LE methods. This holds for LPP method as long as the dimension is above 120. Additionally, we plot in figure 6 a comparison between all the manifold representation

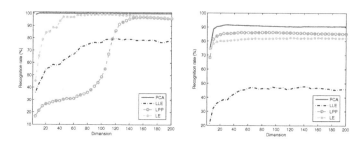

Fig. 6. Comparison of recognition rates between all 4 manifold representation techniques with a 30% ratio of images used for training: rectified faces (top) and cropped faces (bottom)

techniques in the two cases: rectified images and cropped images. This plot corresponds to the case when 30% of the data was used for training. We can observe that PCA-based representation provided the best recognition rates (for both cropped and rectified faces have), even with very few dimensions. This allows us to conclude that simple representation as PCA outperforms more sophisticated manifold representation techniques, which can be seen as an improvement in system's performance.

4   Conclusions and Future Work

In this paper, we proposed a novel approach for robust face recognition in a human-computer interaction scenario. Our method consists in a real time fitting of a 3D deformable model to input images taken from video sequences. More concrete, our approach generates a rectified face image irrespective with the head-pose orientation. This approach is fast and is working in real-time, which is a very important requisite for human-robot interaction. Moreover, experimental results performed on Honda video database, using several manifold learning techniques, show a distinct advantage of the proposed method over the standard 2D appearance-based snapshot approach. Future work will address the problem of video based face recognition using sequences of rectified face images.

Acknowledgements. B. Raducanu is supported by the project TIN2009-14404-C02-00, Ministerio de Educación y Ciencia, Spain.

References

1. Cai, D., He, X., Zhou, K., Han, J., Bao, H.: Locality sensitive discriminant analysis. In: International Joint Conference on Artificial Intelligence, pp. 708–713 (2007)
2. Tenenbaum, J.B., de Silva, V., Langford, J.C.: A global geometric framework for nonlinear dimensionality reduction. Science 290(5500), 2319–2323 (2000)
3. Blanz, V., Vetter, T.: Face recognition based on fitting a 3D morphable model. IEEE Transactions on PAMI 25(9), 1063–1074 (2003)

4. Cootes, T.F., Wheeler, G.V., Walker, K.N., Taylor, C.J.: View-based active appearance models. Image and Vision Computing 20(9-10), 4165–4176 (2002)

5. Chai, X., Shan, S., Chen, X., Gao, W.: Locally linear regression for pose-invariant face recognition. IEEE Trans. on Image Processing 16(7), 1716–1725 (2007)

6. Shan, T., Lovell, B.C., Chen, S.: Face recognition robust to head pose from one sample image. In: IEEE Intl. Conf. on Face and Gesture Recognition, pp. 515–518 (2006)

7. Blanz, V., Grother, P., Phillips, P.J., Vetter, T.: Face recognition based on frontal views generated from non-frontal images. In: IEEE Intl. Conf. on Computer Vision and Pattern Recognition, pp. 454–461 (2005)

8. Huisman, P., Munster, R., Veldhuis, R., Bazen, A.: Making 2d face recognition more robust using AAMs for pose compensation. In: IEEE International Conference on Face and Gesture Recognition, pp. 113–116 (2006)

9. Ahlberg, J.: An active model for facial feature tracking. EURASIP Journal on Applied Signal Processing 2002(6), 566–571 (2002)

10. Faugeras, O.: Three-Dimensional Computer Vision: a Geometric Viewpoint. The MIT Press (1993)

11. Lu, L., Zhang, Z., Shum, H., Liu, Z., Chen, H.: Model- and exemplar-based robust head pose tracking under occlusion and varying expression. In: Proc. IEEE Workshop on Models versus Exemplars in Computer Vision (CVPR 2001), pp. 1–8 (2001)

12. Dornaika, F., Raducanu, B.: Person-specific face shape estimation under varying head pose from single snapshots. In: IEEE Intl. Conf. on Pattern Recognition, pp. 3496–3499 (2010)

13. Ahlberg, J.: Real-time facial feature tracking using an active model with fast image warping. In: International Workshop on Very Low Bitrate Video (VLBV), Athens, Greece, pp. 39–43 (2001)

14. Dornaika, F., Davoine, F.: On appearance based face and facial action tracking. IEEE Transactions on Circuits and Systems for Video Technology 16(9), 1107–1124 (2006)

15. Gleicher, M.: Projective registration with difference decomposition. In: Proc. of Intl. Conf. on Computer Vision and Pattern Recognition, pp. 331–337 (1997)

16. Lee, K.-C., Ho, J., Yang, M.-H., Kriegman, D.: Visual tracking and recognition using probabilistic appearance manifolds. Computer Vision and Image Understanding 99, 303–331 (2005)

17. Lee, K.-C., Kriegman, D.: Online learning of probabilistic appearance manifolds for video-based recognition and tracking. In: Proc. of Intl. Conf. on Computer Vision and Pattern Recognition, pp. 852–859 (2005)

18. Roweis, S., Saul, L.: Nonlinear dimensionality reduction by locally linear embedding. Science 290(5500), 2323–2326 (2000)

19. He, X., Niyogi, P.: Locality preserving projections. In: Conference on Advances in Neural Information Processing Systems (2003)

20. Belkin, M., Niyogi, P.: Laplacian eigenmaps for dimensionality reduction and data representation. Neural Computation 15(6), 1373–1396 (2003)

Hierarchical Properties of Multi-resolution Optical Flow Computation

Yusuke Kameda, Atsushi Imiya, and Tomoya Sakai

Graduate School of Advanced Integration Science, Chiba University
Institute of Media and Information Technology, Chiba University
1-33, Yayoi-cho, Inage-ku, Chiba, 263-8522 Japan
Graduate School of Engineering, Nagasaki University
1-14, Bunkyo-cho, Nagasaki, 852-8521 Japan
yu-kameda@graduate.chiba-u.jp, imiya@faculty.chiba-u.jp,
tsakai@cis.nagasaki-u.ac.jp

Abstract. Most of the methods to compute optical flows are variational-technique-based methods, which assume that image functions have spatiotemporal continuities and appearance motions are small. In the viewpoint of the discrete errors of spatial- and time-differentials, the appropriate resolution for optical flow depends on both the resolution and the frame rate of images since there is a problem with the accuracy of the discrete approximations of derivatives. Therefore, for low frame-rate images, the appropriate resolution for optical flow should be lower than the resolution of the images. However, many traditional methods estimate optical flow with the same resolution as the images. Therefore, if the resolution of images is too high, down-sampling the images is effective for the variational-technique-based methods. In this paper, we analyze the appropriate resolutions for optical flows estimated by variational optical-flow computations from the viewpoint of the error analysis of optical flows. To analyze the appropriate resolutions, we use hierarchical structures constructed from the multi-resolutions of images. Numerical results show that decreasing image resolutions is effective for computing optical flows by variational optical-flow computations in low frame-rate sequences.

1 Introduction

In this paper, we analyze the appropriate resolutions for optical flows estimated by variational optical-flow computations from the viewpoint of the error analysis of optical flows. To analyze the appropriate resolutions, we use hierarchical structures constructed from the multi-resolutions of images. In the error analysis, we measure the average spatiotemporal angle errors (ASAE) between the ground truths of optical flows in each hierarchy of resolutions and estimated optical flows from the corresponding hierarchy of resolutions. Since the spatiotemporal angle error normalizes the norms of flow vectors, the effects of the decreases of the norms by making lower resolutions. Candidates for computation methods

A. Fusiello et al. (Eds.): ECCV 2012 Ws/Demos, Part II, LNCS 7584, pp. 576–585, 2012.

are [1, 2] that both assume that optical flows are small and approximate space derivatives from the previous and next frames.

Optical flows are appearance motions computed from image sequences and contain some feature-quantities such as self-motions of cameras and motions of objects. By computing optical flows from the image sequences taken by car-mounted cameras, we can obtain information about self-motions and obstacles [3, 4]. Furthermore, there are some researches about analyses and classifications of the motion properties of objects by using optical flows [5]. Thus, optical flows are widely applied to motion analyses such as motion detections and recognitions.

Optical flows are estimated under an assumption that the brightness of corresponding points on image sequences does not change temporally. However, optical flows are underspecified only by this assumption since it is an ill-posed problem. To avoid this problem, many researchers have been proposing block-matching based methods and variational-technique based methods [6] since 1980s. These methods adds another assumption that optical flows are locally smoothed.

One of the advantages of variational-technique based methods is that the partial differential equations (PDE) to be solved are analytically derived by defining an energy-minimization problem from some assumptions about optical flows. Thus many researchers have been proposing various assumptions since 1980s [6–9]. Most of these assumptions are expressed by PDE for images and optical flows. Therefore, images and optical flows should have spatiotemporal continuities naturally. Moreover, optical flows in itself are expressed by spatiotemporal derivatives and therefore it is assumed that the flow vectors are very small.

Because the images on computers are discrete, optical flows are also discrete. Then its physical unit is denoted as pixel/frame from the pixel of images and frame of sequences. In the discretization of the PDE above, space- and time-derivatives are approximated by using step sizes of pixels and frames respectively. The frames of optical flows should correspond to the intermediate frames of two successive frames in an image sequence. To synchronize the frames of images and optical flows, the space derivatives of images should be approximated from the previous and next frames of each intermediate frame.

Although image resolutions become higher and higher by the performance upgrades of cameras, frame rates of image sequences do not upgrade so much. This induces the image sequences with high resolutions and low frame-rates in the viewpoint of approximations of spatiotemporal derivatives. The optical flows computed from such image sequences have larger appearance velocities in pixel unit than those computed from images with lower resolutions in the same scenes. Therefore, in this case the assumption that optical flows are small is not satisfied. Furthermore, there is a problem about the accuracy of the approximations of space derivatives since the approximations from the previous and next frames assumes implicitly that images does not change so much around the intermediate frames. Thus in the case of the images that have higher resolutions and lower frame-rates, the optical-flow computations by using PDE have less accuracy. Therefore, from the viewpoint of spatiotemporal derivatives, we should compute optical flows with appropriate resolutions against its frame rates.

2   Mathematical Preliminary

2.1   Optical Flow

For a time dependent image $f(\boldsymbol{x}, t)$ defined in $\mathbb{R}^n \times \mathbb{R}_+$, where n is the dimension of images, the total differentiation for time t is give as

$$\frac{d}{dt}f = \nabla f^\top \boldsymbol{v}(\boldsymbol{x}) + \partial_t f \qquad (1)$$

where $\nabla = (\partial_x, \partial_y)^\top$ and $\boldsymbol{v}(\boldsymbol{x}, t) : \mathbb{R}^n \times \mathbb{R}_+ \to \mathbb{R}^3$ is an image velocity or optical flow function on the image, and in $n = 2$, $\boldsymbol{v}(\boldsymbol{x}) = (u(\boldsymbol{x}), v(\boldsymbol{x}))^\top = (\dot{x}, \dot{y}) = \frac{d\boldsymbol{x}}{dt}$. Optical flow consistency $\frac{d}{dt}f = 0$ implies that the flow vector $\boldsymbol{v}$ of the point $\boldsymbol{x}$ is the solution of the singular equation,

$$F(f, \boldsymbol{v}) = \nabla f^\top \boldsymbol{v} + \partial_t f = 0. \qquad (2)$$

To solve the eq. (2), the additional constraints are required. We generalize the data term such as the square of eq. (2) to $E_1(\boldsymbol{x}, t, \boldsymbol{v}, f)$.

Equation (2) is an ill-posed problem and therefore $\boldsymbol{v}$ is underspecified. Thus $\boldsymbol{v}$ is solved by using the energy minimization problem

$$\min \iint_\Omega E_1(\boldsymbol{x}, t, \boldsymbol{v}, f) + \alpha E_2(\boldsymbol{x}, t, \boldsymbol{v}) d\boldsymbol{x} \qquad (3)$$

in variational method [6, 10]. Here, E_1 is a data term and the positive constant α is the weight coefficient of a prior term E_2, which is a convex function [1] for $\boldsymbol{v}$ and regularizes $\boldsymbol{v}$ under some assumption. Some examples of E_2 are the smoothness regularizer [6]

$$(\partial_x u)^2 + (\partial_y u)^2 + (\partial_x v)^2 + (\partial_y v)^2, \qquad (5)$$

total variation regularizer $|\nabla u| + |\nabla v|$, and deformable-model regularizer $u_{xx}^2 + 2u_{xy}^2 + u_{yy}^2 + v_{xx}^2 + 2v_{xy}^2 + v_{yy}^2$, respectively. In the method [1], $E_1 = (F(f, \boldsymbol{v}))^2$ and E_2 is eq. (5) and then its energy functional is

$$\min \iint_\Omega (F(f, \boldsymbol{v}))^2 + \alpha \left((\partial_x u)^2 + (\partial_y u)^2 + (\partial_x v)^2 + (\partial_y v)^2 \right) d\boldsymbol{x}. \qquad (6)$$

In the conventional methods expressed as eq. (3), α is a given parameter and its appropriate value depends on images. Although, in general, the appropriate value depends on $\boldsymbol{x}$ and t, α is a constant value in eq. (3).

The boundary condition of the optical-flow computation is the free boundary condition

$$\forall \boldsymbol{x} \in \partial\Omega, \forall t, \forall \boldsymbol{n} \quad \frac{\partial \boldsymbol{v}}{\partial \boldsymbol{n}}(\boldsymbol{x}, t) = \boldsymbol{0} \qquad (7)$$

---

[1]   A function g that satisfies

$$\forall \boldsymbol{a}, \boldsymbol{b} \in \mathbb{R}^2, \forall k \in [0, 1] \quad g(k\boldsymbol{a} + (1 - k)\boldsymbol{b}) \le kg(\boldsymbol{a}) + (1 - k)g(\boldsymbol{b}). \qquad (4)$$

that is derived from variational method. Here, n is a unit normal vector for the image boundary $\partial\Omega$. The meaning of this condition is that optical flow continues smoothly beyond the image boundary.

2.2 Pyramid-Based Multiresolution

We define $g(x,y) = R^k f(x,y)$ of image $f(x,y,t)$ for an integer $k \geq 1$, such that

$$R^k f(x,y) = \iint_{\mathbb{R}^2} w_k(i)w_k(j)f(2^k x - i, 2^k y - j)didj, \tag{8}$$

for

$$w_k(i) = \begin{cases} \frac{1}{2}^k(1 - \frac{|i|}{2}^k), & |i| \leq 2^k \\ 0, & |i| > 2^k \end{cases}, \tag{9}$$

and then there is the relation

$$R^{k+1}f = R(R^k f). \tag{10}$$

The dual operation of R^k is defined as

$$E^k g(x,y) = 4^k \iint_{\mathbb{R}^2} w_k(i)w_k(j)g(\frac{x-i}{2^k}, \frac{y-j}{2^k})didj. \tag{11}$$

3 Variational Problem for Adaptive Optimization

We describe about the summary of variational optical-flow computation using the Lagrange Multiplier Method [2]. This method assumes the higher frame-rate of image sequences. However, ordinary image sequences are not so. Therefore we use this method to analyze the effects of resolutions of images in variational optical-flow computation.

To generalize weight coefficient α to the function of x and t and determine it mathematically, they define $(F(f,v))^2$ as a constraint equation and use the energy-minimization problem with the constraint, which is

$$\min_{v(x,t)} \int_\Omega E_2(x,t,v)dx \quad \text{subject to} \quad (F(f,v))^2 = 0. \tag{12}$$

Converting this problem using the Lagrange Multiplier Method, they get the energy-minimization problem without constraint

$$\min_{v(x)} \int_\Omega J(u,f,\lambda)dx, \quad \text{w.r.t.} \quad J(u,f,\lambda) = \lambda(x,t)(F(f,v))^2 + E_2(x,t,v) \tag{13}$$

where $\lambda(x,t) : \Omega \times \mathbb{R}_+ \to \mathbb{R}_+$ is the Lagrange multiplier. In the method, E_2 is eq. (5) and then its Euler-Lagrange equations are

$$(F(f, \boldsymbol{v}))^2 = 0 \tag{14}$$
$$\lambda F(f, \boldsymbol{v})\nabla f - \nabla^2 \boldsymbol{v} = \mathbf{0}, \tag{15}$$

where, $\nabla^2 = \partial_x^2 + \partial_y^2$ is Laplacian and $\nabla^2 \boldsymbol{v} = (\nabla^2 u, \nabla^2 v)^\top$.

Tab. 1. Experimental Methodology. We use two methods that assume both spatiotemporal continuities to compute optical flows by variational method. We analyze the relationship between the number of down-sampling operation R of images and the evaluation of estimated optical flows.

	weight	number of R	initial
Lagrange method [2]	$\lambda(\boldsymbol{x}, t)$	0,1,2,3,4,5	$\{\mathbf{0}\}$
competitive [1]	1 or 0.1, $^\forall\boldsymbol{x}, ^\forall t$	0,1,2,3,4,5	results of previous frame

The numerical computation of the PDE above is defined as

$$\lambda^{(m+1)} = \lambda^{(m)} + \tau_1 \left(F(f, \boldsymbol{v}^{(m)}) \right)^2 \tag{16}$$

$$\boldsymbol{v}^{(m+1)} = \boldsymbol{v}^{(m)}$$
$$- \tau_2 \left(\lambda^{(m+1)} F(f, \boldsymbol{v}^{(m+1)})\nabla f - \nabla^2 \boldsymbol{v}^{(m)} \right), \tag{17}$$

where, $\lambda^{(m)}, \boldsymbol{v}^{(m)}$ is the variables at the iterative number $m \geq 0$ and $\tau_1 > 0, \tau_2 > 0$ are small constants.

4   Experiments

4.1   Evaluations

We analyze the relation of the errors and the resolutions of images, where we use all frames of EISATS set 2 sequence 1 and 2 [11]. Table 1 shows the experimental methodology of it.

Defining i, j as the coordinates of square grid points on discrete images and h as the step size between grid points, we denote $\boldsymbol{v}_{i,j}$ as the value $\boldsymbol{v}(h(i,j)^\top, t)$ at i, j and define

$$(i^*, j^*)^\top = \arg \max_{i,j} |\boldsymbol{v}_{i,j}^{(m+1)} - \boldsymbol{v}_{i,j}^{(m)}|. \tag{18}$$

The iteration ends when the convergence condition

$$\frac{|\boldsymbol{v}_{i^*,j^*}^{(m+1)} - \boldsymbol{v}_{i^*,j^*}^{(m)}|}{\boldsymbol{v}_{i^*,j^*}^{(m+1)}} < 10^{-5} \tag{19}$$

is satisfied or m reaches 10^3.

We choose the large step sizes $\tau_1 = 10^3, \tau_2 = \frac{1}{4}$ of the iteration for the Lagrange method [2]. On the other hand, we choose 10^3 and 10^4 for α, and $\frac{1}{4}$ for the step size corresponding to τ_2 for the method [1]. The initial optical flows of both methods are $\{\mathbf{0}\}$. After second frame for the method [1], we use the estimated optical flows of previous frames as initial flows of next frames.

The evaluation is based on spatiotemporal angle error [12, 13]

$$\arccos\left(\frac{\mathbf{w}_{i,j}^\top \mathbf{v}_{i,j}^{(m)} + 1}{\sqrt{(|\mathbf{w}_{i,j}|^2 + 1)(|\mathbf{v}_{i,j}^{(m)}|^2 + 1)}}\right), \tag{20}$$

where $\mathbf{w}_{i,j}$ is the flow vector at i, j of the ground truth. Spatiotemporal angle error is the angle between $\frac{(\mathbf{w}^\top, 1)^\top}{|(\mathbf{w}^\top, 1)|}$ and $\frac{(\mathbf{v}^{(m)\top}, 1)^\top}{|(\mathbf{v}^{(m)\top}, 1)|}$, and the errors in a region of smooth non-zero motion are penalized less than errors in regions of zero motion. [12]. We compute the average values at each frame. However, we do not include the region in which the ground truth is undefined.

4.2   Results and Discussions

Figure 1 and 2 shows the computed optical flows and the evaluations of it, respectively. From the figure 1, the result of the Lagrange method is better than the competitive method to compute the spatial differences of appearance motions which are induced by the leading and oncoming vehicles. From the result of down-sampling, the errors decreased when the resolutions reduced. Similarly, in Fig. 3, the error analysis of EISATS set 2 sequence 2 shows the same effects.

The errors from the 40th frame to the 50th frame are larger than those of other frames. In these frames shown in Fig. 1 (f), there are much larger appearance motions since the oncoming vehicle falls out to the image boundary. It is hard to express such larger appearance motions even if the image resolution is decreased. Thus there are large errors comparatively.

Figure 4 shows the comparison of the Lagrange and competitive methods. The Lagrange method indicates the performance as much as that of the competitive method in low-resolutions. From the results, if the appearance motions are made small by decreasing the resolution, the Lagrange method satisfies the assumption.

From these resluts, $R4$ and $R5$ have lower errors than higher-resolutions, however, the stability for time-direction is also lower. Therefore, to find an appropriate resolution we have to analyze the stability of time-direction of the errors.

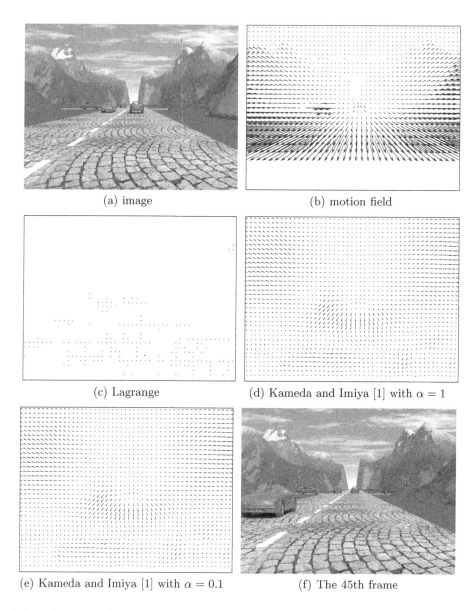

(a) image

(b) motion field

(c) Lagrange

(d) Kameda and Imiya [1] with $\alpha = 1$

(e) Kameda and Imiya [1] with $\alpha = 0.1$

(f) The 45th frame

Fig. 1. The optical flows between the 24th and 25th frames of EISTAS set 2 sequence 1. The Lagrange method is better than the competitive method to compute the spatial differences of appearance motions which are induced by the leading and oncoming vehicles. In (f), since the oncoming vehicle falls out to the image boundary, the appearance motions are larger than the other frames.

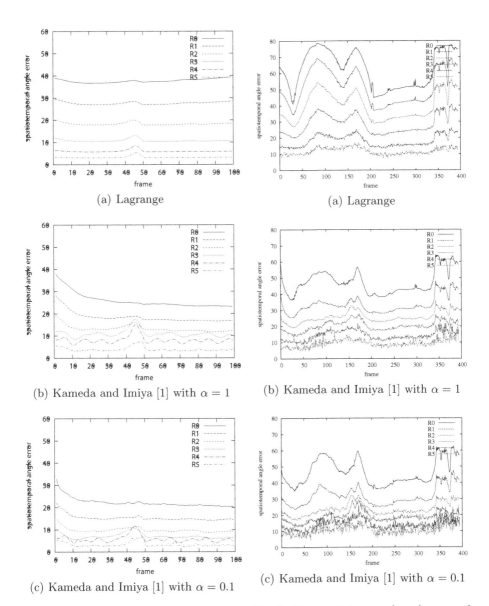

(a) Lagrange

(a) Lagrange

(b) Kameda and Imiya [1] with $\alpha = 1$

(b) Kameda and Imiya [1] with $\alpha = 1$

(c) Kameda and Imiya [1] with $\alpha = 0.1$

(c) Kameda and Imiya [1] with $\alpha = 0.1$

Fig. 2. The spatiotemporal-angle error of all frames of EISATS set 2 sequences 1. R* means the number of down-sampling operator R and the error functions of those are shown in the order corresponding to the numbers of R. Thus the errors decreased when the resolutions reduced.

Fig. 3. The spatiotemporal-angle error of all frames of EISATS set 2 sequence 2. R* means the number of down-sampling operator R and the error functions of those are shown in the order corresponding to the numbers of R. Thus the errors decreased when the resolutions reduced.

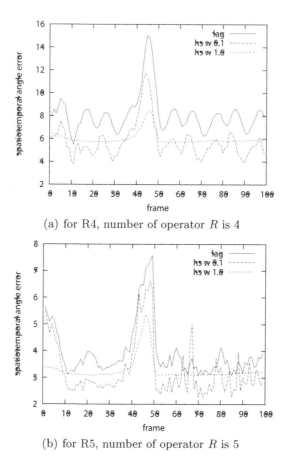

(a) for R4, number of operator R is 4

(b) for R5, number of operator R is 5

Fig. 4. The comparison of the Lagrange and competitive methods in the cases of low resolutions of EISATS set 2 sequence 1.

5   Conclusion

In this paper, we analyzed the appropriate resolutions of optical flows estimated by variational optical-flow computations from the viewpoint of the error analysis of optical flows. To analyze appropriate resolutions, we used hierarchical structures constructed from the multi-resolutions of images. Numerical results show that decreasing image resolutions is effective to compute optical flows by variational optical-flow computations in low frame-rate sequences. From the results, if the appearance motions are made small by decreasing the resolution, the variational optical-flow computations satisfies the assumption of spatiotemporal continuities of images and optical flows.

References

1. Kameda, Y., Imiya, A.: Classification of Optical Flow by Constraints. In: Kropatsch, W.G., Kampel, M., Hanbury, A. (eds.) CAIP 2007. LNCS, vol. 4673, pp. 61–68. Springer, Heidelberg (2007)
2. Kameda, Y., Imiya, A., Sakai, T.: Adaptive estimation of Lagrange Multiplier functions of constraint terms for variational computation of optical flow. The Transactions of the Institute of Electronics, Information and Communication Engineers D J95-D, 1644–1653 (2012) (Japanese)
3. Ohnishi, N., Imiya, A.: Featureless robot navigation using optical flow. Connection Science 17, 23–46 (2005)
4. Klette, R., Kruger, N., Vaudrey, T., Pauwels, K., van Hulle, M., Morales, S., Kandil, F.I., Haeusler, R., Pugeault, N., Rabe, C., Lappe, M.: Performance of Correspondence Algorithms in Vision-Based Driver Assistance Using an Online Image Sequence Database. IEEE Transactions on Vehicular Technology 60, 2012–2026 (2011)
5. Jagadeesh, V., Karthikeyan, S., Manjunath, B.S.: Spatio-temporal optical flow statistics (STOFS) for activity classification. In: Proceedings of the Seventh Indian Conference on Computer Vision, Graphics and Image Processing, ICVGIP 2010, pp. 178–182. ACM, New York (2010)
6. Horn, B.K., Schunck, B.G.: Determining optical flow. Artificial Intelligence 17, 185–203 (1981)
7. Nagel, H.H., Enkelmann, W.: An investigation of smoothness constraints for the estimation of displacement vector fields from image sequences. IEEE Transaction on Pattern Analysis and Machine Intelligence 8, 565–593 (1986)
8. Weickert, J., Schnörr, C.: A theoretical framework for convex regularizers in PDE-based computation of image motion. International Journal of Computer Vision 45, 245–264 (2001)
9. Zimmer, H., Bruhn, A., Weickert, J.: Optic Flow in Harmony. International Journal of Computer Vision 93, 368–388 (2011)
10. Pock, T., Unger, M., Cremers, D., Bischof, H.: Fast and exact solution of Total Variation models on the GPU. In: CVPR Workshop on Visual Computer Vision on GPU's, pp. 1–8 (2008)
11. Vaudrey, T., Rabe, C., Klette, R., Milburn, J.: Differences between stereo and motion behaviour on synthetic and real-world stereo sequences. In: 2008 23rd International Conference Image and Vision Computing, New Zealand, pp. 1–6. IEEE (2008)
12. Baker, S., Scharstien, D., Lewis, J.P., Roth, S., Black, M.J., Szeliski, R., Scharstein, D.: A Database and Evaluation Methodology for Optical Flow. International Journal of Computer Vision 92, 1–31 (2010)
13. Barron, J.L., Fleet, D.J., Beauchemin, S.S., Burkitt, T.A.: Performance of optical flow techniques. International Journal of Computer Vision 12, 43–77 (1994)

Semantic Road Segmentation via Multi-scale Ensembles of Learned Features

Jose M. Alvarez[1,3,*], Yann LeCun[1], Theo Gevers[2,3], and Antonio M. Lopez[3]

[1] Courant Institute of Mathematical Sciences, New York University, New York, NY
[2] Faculty of Science, University of Amsterdam, Amsterdam, The Netherlands
[3] Computer Vision Center, Univ. Autònoma de Barcelona, Barcelona, Spain

Abstract. Semantic segmentation refers to the process of assigning an object label (e.g., building, road, sidewalk, car, pedestrian) to every pixel in an image. Common approaches formulate the task as a random field labeling problem modeling the interactions between labels by combining local and contextual features such as color, depth, edges, SIFT or HoG. These models are trained to maximize the likelihood of the correct classification given a training set. However, these approaches rely on hand–designed features (e.g., texture, SIFT or HoG) and a higher computational time required in the inference process.

Therefore, in this paper, we focus on estimating the unary potentials of a conditional random field via ensembles of learned features. We propose an algorithm based on convolutional neural networks to learn local features from training data at different scales and resolutions. Then, diversification between these features is exploited using a weighted linear combination. Experiments on a publicly available database show the effectiveness of the proposed method to perform semantic road scene segmentation in still images. The algorithm outperforms appearance based methods and its performance is similar compared to state–of–the–art methods using other sources of information such as depth, motion or stereo.

1 Introduction

Road scene understanding from a mobile platform is a central task for vehicle environment perception. This process is the key to success in autonomous driving and driver assistance systems such as vehicle and pedestrian detection. Understanding road scenes involves comprehending the scene structure (e.g., sidewalks, buildings, trees, roads), scene status (i.e., traffic situations) or understanding the motion patterns of other objects present in the scene. A core component of road scene understanding systems is its semantic segmentation [1,2]. Semantic segmentation is the process of partitioning an image into disjoint regions and the interpretation of each region for semantic meanings (Fig. 1). Semantic segmentation provides important information to support higher level scene interpretation tasks. Therefore, in this paper, we focus on the semantic segmentation of road images.

---

* This work was partially supported by Spanish Government under Research Program Consolider Ingenio 2010: MIPRCV (CSD200700018) and MINECO Projects TRA2011-29454-C03-01, TIN2011-25606 and TIN2011-29494-C03-02.

A. Fusiello et al. (Eds.): ECCV 2012 Ws/Demos, Part II, LNCS 7584, pp. 586–595, 2012.

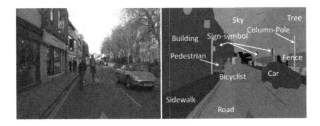

Fig. 1. Semantic scene segmentation aims at assigning every pixel in an image by one of the predefined semantic labels available (i.e., pedestrian, car, building, road, sidewalk, tree, sky). Image taken from [3].

Common semantic scene segmentation approaches formulate the problem as a random field labeling problem and model the dependencies of labels of pairs of variables by combining different types of features such as color, texture, depth, edges among others [4,5]. Then, a model describing these interactions is built and trained to maximize the likelihood of the correct classification. For instance, Gupta *et al.* [6] include the 3D geometry of the scene to improve the segmentation task by discarding physically implausible relations between segments. Floros *et al.* [5] include top–down segmentations from a densely sampled part–based detector. Other approaches include other sources of information such as structure from motion [2] or stereo disparity [4]. However, these conditional random field models have two main limitations. First, their dependency on hand–designed features that may not be appropriated for the specific task. Second, these approaches tend to be costly in terms of inference since inference requires searching over different label configurations.

In this paper, we focus on multi–scale learning features for road detection. Feature learning has received a lot of attention recently. For instance, a multi–scale end to end learning algorithm is proposed in [7]. In that approach, the authors train a Convolutional Neural Network in two steps. First, features are extracted at different scales and their output is concatenated to generate a feature vector. Then, in a second stage these features are trained to learn predictions of different classes. The approach shows promising results in different databases. However, the training stage is complex and also involve large (intermediate) feature vectors. Therefore, we propose a different approach to obtaining pixel potentials to represent the unary potentials of a conditional random field. The core of the algorithm is a Convolutional Neural Network trained to extract local features exploiting the 2D structures present in an image. In addition, the algorithm includes contextual information by extracting features at different visual scales (i.e., the larger scale, the smaller area of the image is occupied by the object being analyzed). Finally, robustness to scale variations is achieved by extracting these features at multiple resolutions. Then, all these features are considered as weak features and combined into a CRF as unary potentials. The ensemble of features is learned using global optimization to exploit inter–feature diversification. Different experiments conducted on a publicly available database show the effectiveness of the proposed method to perform semantic road scene segmentation.

The rest of this paper is organized as follows. First, in Sect. 2, we introduce conditional random fields for image segmentation. Convolutional neural networks for feature extraction are introduced in Sect. 3 and the algorithm to compute ensembles of multi–scale features is detailed in Sect. 3.1. Then, in Sect. 4, experiments are presented and the results are discussed. Finally, conclusions are drawn in Sect. 5.

2   Conditional Random Fields for Image Segmentation

Image segmentation consists of partitioning an image into several disjoint regions that show homogeneity to certain features such as color, texture, edges. This process is usually formulated as a random field labeling problem to aggregate local cues such as color, texture along with contextual cues describing the possible spatial interactions between labels [4,5]. To this end, an image is represented with a graph structure $\mathcal{G} = <\mathcal{V}, \mathcal{E}>$ where $\mathcal{V}$ is a set of N random variables $\mathbf{Y} = Y_1, \ldots, Y_N$ representing the nodes of the graph (i.e., $|\mathcal{V}| = N$) and corresponding to the pixels in the image. Each of these variables is allowed to take values from a discrete domain of labels $\mathcal{L} = l_{1,}, \ldots, l_K$. Furthermore, $\mathcal{E}$ is the set of edges modeling the relationships between neighboring pixels. Then, image segmentation is done by assigning every pixel in the image $x_i \in \mathcal{V}$ a meaningful label $l_i \in \mathcal{L}$. Finally, let $y = \{Y_i \in \mathcal{V}\}$ a label assignment with values in $\mathcal{L}$. Then, we consider a Conditional Random Field (CRF) to model the Gibbs energy as follows:

$$E(y) = \sum_{i \in \mathcal{V}} \psi_i(l_i, x_i) + \sum_{(i,j) \in \mathcal{E}} \psi_{ij}(l_i, l_j), \tag{1}$$

where $\psi_i(l_i, x_i)$ is the unary potential modeling the likelihood of a pixel taking a certain label, and $\psi_{ij}(l_i, l_j)$ is the pairwise potential modeling the coherence of neighboring pixels taking the same label. Then, the most probable label assignment $\hat{y}$ is obtained by minimizing the Gibbs energy on the graph structure: $\hat{y} = \arg\min_y E(y)$.

Conventionally, the unary potential is computed using features in an image such as color, texture, shape or hand–designed features such as SIFT or HoG. Then, the model is build and trained to maximize the likelihood of the correct classification. In the next section, we introduce the use of convolutional neural networks to extract specific features representing each possible label.

3   Feature Learning via Convolutional Neural Networks

In this paper we focus on learning/extracting features from training images using convolutional neural networks (CNN). CNNs are hierarchical architectures widely used for object detection and recognition [8] that alternate different type of layers (e.g., convolution, sub–sampling) to extract and combine visual patterns presents in the input data [9]. An example of this type of architectures is shown in Fig. 2. This architecture can be interpreted as a set of filter banks divided in three different layers and a set of connections to fuse them. The kernels of these filters and the connection weights are learned off–line using training data [9].

Based on this learning architecture we extract features at two different visual scales: fine and coarse. These two scales (levels from now on) consider different amount of

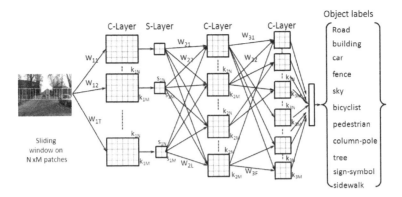

Fig. 2. Convolutional neural networks alternate layers of convolution (C–layers) and sub–sampling layers (S–layers) to learn high–order local features directly from training data. Connection weights are given by w_{ij} (i–th layer, j–th kernel), the size of convolutional kernels is $k_{iN} \times k_{iM}$ and the subsampling size for the S–layer is $s_{iN} \times s_{iM}$.

contextual information by varying the size of the input patch. In particular, we consider patch sizes of 32×32 and 64×64 for the fine and coarse levels respectively. Moreover, robustness to scale variations is improved by extracting features using different kernel sizes. In practice, this is done by resizing input images to 4 different scales: $1, \frac{1}{2}, \frac{1}{4}$ and $\frac{1}{5}$. Hence, this stage takes a *RGB* image of size $X \times Y$ as input and extracts fine and coarse features at multiple resolutions by applying a sliding window on patches of size 32×32 and 64×64 respectively. The output is a $K \times X \times Y$ confidence map relating a set of K (i.e., number of labels available) floating point numbers, ranging from 0 to 1, to each pixel in the image to indicate their per–class potential. The higher the potential is, the more likely the pixel belongs to that class.

3.1 Multi–scale Feature Ensembles as Unary Potentials

Unary potentials (e.g., ψ_i in Eq. (1)) model the likelihood of a pixel taking a certain label. These potentials are usually estimated using common features extracted from incoming data (e.g., color, texture, depth, edges). If more than one feature is available, the unary potentials are estimated as a combination of them either using predefined rules (e.g., sum, product, maximum, minimum [10]) or learned weighted combinations. Using fixed rules does not exploit the fact that different objects (classes) have different needs in terms of context and scale information. Therefore, if training sets are available, a more powerful combining approach consists of a weighted combination of features. In this case, the unary potentials can be estimated as follows:

$$\psi_i(l_i, x | \Theta_i) = \sum_{r=1}^{R} w_r \psi_r(l_i, x | \Theta_r), \tag{2}$$

where $\Theta_1, \ldots, \Theta_R$ is the set of R features and w_r is the weight modeling the relative relevance of that feature for the given label. In this section, unary potentials are computed as a weighted combination of multi–scale learned features. To this end, we consider the output of each CNN (different scales and different levels) as a different feature and fuse them using a weighted linear combination. More precisely, we focus on class–dependent weighted linear combination were each feature (scale and resolution) for each class receives a different weight. These class–dependent weights are learned globally (all weights and all classes at the same time) off–line by minimizing the sum of squared errors between the output of the CNN and the target label.

4 Experiments

Experiments validating the proposed algorithm are conducted on the Cambridge-driving Labeled Video Database (CamVid) [3]. CamVid is a publicly available database of high-quality images acquired using a camera mounted on the windshield of a vehicle driving in an urban scenario at different daytime. Thus, these sequences include challenging situations as crowded scenes, different lighting conditions and different road type. Ground–truth is provided as manual annotations at 1fps. These annotations include 32 different classes [3]. However, for fair comparison with other approaches, we use 11 object categories as in [2,11]. We follow the experimental setup in [2,11] by dividing into 367 training and 233 testing images and providing evaluations by down–scaling the images by a factor of 3. Quantitative evaluations are provided using pixel–wise confusion matrices including global and average accuracy. The former is the number of pixels correctly classified over the number of pixels in the testing set. The latter is the number of pixel correctly classified per class divided by the total number of pixels in that class.

For testing purposes we devise a simple road scene segmentation algorithm based on CNN and CRF. The core of the algorithm is a CNN which takes an $N \times M$ image as input and outputs a $K \times N \times M$ confidence map relating a set of K (i.e., number of labels available) floating point numbers indicating the per–class potential of each pixel in the image. The higher the potential is, the more likely the pixel belongs to that class. Then, a single unary potential per class is computed using Eq. (2). Finally, the most probable label assignment is estimated minimizing the energy function in Eq. (1).

The parameters of the algorithm are empirically fixed as follows. First, the algorithm uses two levels (fine and coarse) and four different scales ($R = 8$): 1x, $\frac{1}{2}$x, $\frac{1}{4}$x and $\frac{1}{5}$x resolution. Further, the input layer (RGB data) at each level is sparsely connected to the first convolutional layer: each color plane is connected to two different kernels and then all three color planes are connected to two more kernels. The first connections enforce learning independent preprocessing kernels for each color while the last ones combine them.

4.1 Training and Data Preparation

The training set consists of 367 high–quality images manually labeled. This results in millions of highly correlated training samples that difficult the training process. Hence, to obtain a reasonable overhead we reduce the number of training samples by considering only a subset of training patches for each image. This subset per image is generated using over–segmentation and selecting a representative number of pixels within each region. In this paper, the over–segmented image is obtained using the turbo–pixel approach in [12]. Then, training samples are selected as the centroid of each superpixel. This sampling technique has two main advantages. First, it improves diversity in the training set by reducing the number of samples (i.e., iterative learning algorithms such as back–propagation can explore more samples in less time). Second, the selection of the centroid improves the intra–class variance since the centroid is the best representation of the superpixel area and maximize the distance between samples from two consecutive superpixels. Based on this sampling technique, two non–overlapping training sets are generated using different dilation masks around the centroid of each superpixel (Fig. 3). The first subset is used to train the CNN and, the second one is used to learn the weights. Thus, the weights of the ensemble are learned globally using the approach in Sect. 3.1 using unseen samples. Both training subsets are resampled to improve the balance between classes.

Fig. 3. The number of training samples is sub–sampled to reduce the computational training overhead. The incoming image is over–segmented using superpixels. Then, patches centered at the centroid of each superpixel and several pixels in its surrounding area are selected as training samples.

The layers of the CNN are trained in supervised mode using the pixel labels in the first training subset. To this end, image patches centered in the training set are extracted. Robustness to scale and noisy acquisition conditions is reinforced using jitter in each patch. More precisely, we consider a random scale per sample between $[0.6, \ldots, 1.4]$, random Gaussian noise $\sigma = [0.3, \ldots, 1.2]$ and random rotations in the range $[-17°, \ldots, 17°]$. Given this resampled training set, CNN at each level is trained (weight learning) independently using classical back–propagation. The parameters of the CNN are corrected due to standard stochastic gradient descent by minimizing the sum of square differences between the output of the CNN and the target label. Training is stopped when the error in consecutive epochs does not decrease more than 0.001. Finally, the CRF is trained using the Conditional Random Field toolbox in [13].

The set of weights obtained is listed in Table 1. The larger the weight, the more important the feature. As shown, different weights are obtained for each class. For instance, high weights are given to the 4th–scale of the coarse level for the bicyclist and sign–symbol classes (i.e., more contextual information is needed to predict these classes) while the road ensemble mainly consists of fine scales.

Table 1. Set of weights obtained for the experiments. Weights are computed globally without bounding their possible values.

Scales	Fine Level				Coarse Level			
	1st	2nd	3rd	4th	1st	2nd	3rd	4th
Byciclist	0.023	0.360	0.120	−0.009	0.008	0.608	0.062	−1.0
Building	0.185	0.658	0.244	0.106	0.188	0.388	0.280	−1.0
Car	0.092	0.296	0.220	0.192	−0.007	0.337	0.189	−1.0
Column-pole	0.022	0.132	0.078	−0.020	0.101	0.251	0.021	−0.536
Fence	−0.145	0.344	0.182	0.027	0.058	0.487	0.181	−1.0
Pedestrian	0.020	0.197	0.100	0.032	0.079	0.320	0.092	−0.746
Road	0.050	0.272	0.074	0.109	0.089	0.478	0.3414	−1.0
Sidewalk	−0.040	0.309	0.174	0.051	−0.023	0.546	0.184	−1.0
Sign–symbol	0.060	0.247	0.191	0.048	0.076	0.314	0.040	−0.823
Sky	0.383	0.375	0.361	−0.008	0.026	0.096	0.062	−0.867
Tree	0.063	0.351	0.380	0.087	0.208	0.301	0.047	−1.0

4.2   Results

Representative qualitative results are shown in Fig. 4 and pixel–wise confusion matrices are shown in Fig. 5. These matrices provide per–class classification rates given by the total number of correctly classified pixels divided by the total number of pixels in the training set. For comparison, we provide confusion matrices for three different configurations. First, using a linear combination only at the finner level. Second, the confusion matrix using both levels and learned weights and finally, the confusion matrix using the CRF framework and CNN to estimate the unary potentials. As shown, the best average per–class accuracy is provided by the fusion of weights without the pairwise potentials Fig. 5b. However, using the pairwise potentials reinforce relation between neighboring pixels and improves the global accuracy of the algorithm. In this case, the accuracy of large classes (e.g., road, sidewalk) is improved at the expense of lowering the accuracy of classes with small presence in the dataset (e.g., sign–symbol). These contingency table suggests that miss–classifications are mainly located in small objects such as column-pole and sign-symbol corresponding with those classes with less examples in the training set. Further, the algorithm exhibits lower performance in classifying bicycles, buildings, fences and trees. The former are usually classified as pedestrian due to their similarity (Fig. 1).

The performance of the proposed CNN–CRF algorithm is also compared to several methods in the state–of–the–art. These approaches include different types of features such as appearance [2], motion cues (SfM) [2], their combination [2] , depth [11], semantic texton and superpixels [11] and their combination [11,4] to improve their performance. We also include approaches including object detectors [5,4] since they provide the highest accuracy within the state–of–the–art. Moreover, for comprehensive evaluation, we include five different instances of our algorithm. First, the complete CNN–CRF using all the scales and features. Then, two different multi–scale instances excluding the CRF: using both levels (MultiScale CNN–no CRF) and using only the fine level (CNN–MR Fine). Finally, an instance where histogram of superpixel labels is used to reinforce the spatial consistency of object labels (CNN–superpixels) is also included. We also include a CNN approach based on a single scale at the finer level (Fine Level). This configuration outputs the maximum response over each class,

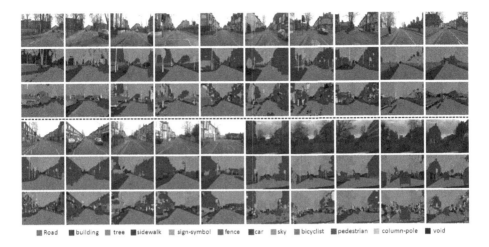

▪ Road ▪ building ▪ tree ▪ sidewalk ▪ sign-symbol ▪ fence ▪ car ▪ sky ▪ bicyclist ▪ pedestrian ▪ column-pole ▪ void

Fig. 4. Qualitative semantic road segmentation results. First and fourth rows: input image. Second and fifth rows: manually annotated labels. Third and sixth rows: results of our algorithm.

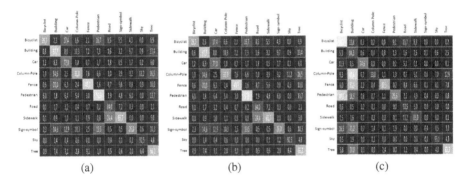

(a)   (b)   (c)

Fig. 5. Confusion matrix over the CamVid test set. a) Using directly the ensemble of learned features (average recognition rate per class is 54.95% ± 23.3). b) Using directly the ensemble of learned features (average recognition rate per class is 58.6% ± 21.7%). b) Using the ensemble of learned features and the CRF (average rate per class is 55.57% ± 33.41).

computes the superpixel histogram of object labels (using the approach in [14]) and finally, assigns the predominant class label to each pixel in the superpixel. The baseline is the appearance based algorithm in [2] since it is based on appearance features extracted in a single image. A summary of per–class accuracy is listed in Table 2. As shown, our approach significantly improves the performance of the maximum fusion method, the baseline and the combination of motion and appearance. Furthermore, the proposed approach provides similar per class average accuracy compared to the rest of methods. However, the proposed algorithm provides a lower global performance. This is mainly due to the lack of accuracy in the road class (89.0% compared to 95%) since this is the class with more pixels in the database. As shown, using depth information provides the highest accuracy for the road class and high global accuracy but lower per class average performance. Hence, we expect a significant improvement in the overall performance by including temporal information to our approach. From these results, we can conclude that using learning ensembles of trained multi–scale features provides promising semantic road image segmentation in a single image.

As shown, compared to state–of–the–art approaches, the proposed algorithm provides the higher accuracy for car, column–pole and bicyclist and it outperforms algorithms combining appearance and structure from motion features. In addition, it provides promising results compared to algorithms using CRF frameworks to combine multiple features from diversified sources of information. For instance, the top per-forming algorithm combines depth, semantic textons, object detection and superpixel features to achieve the higher class average accuracy. Nevertheless, the proposed algo-rithm outputs a per–class confidence map indicating the pixel potential per class that could be combined with the rest of features and integrated into a CRF framework im-proving the global and class average accuracy.

Table 2. Quantitative comparison of our method with state–of–the–art road scene recognition approaches on the CamVid database. These approaches include different cues such as motion, appearance, depth or stereo information. Bold names indicate an instance of the proposed method. Bold values indicate the best performing method.

	Building	Tree	Sky	Car	Sign-Symbol	Road	Pedestrian	Fence	Column-Pole	Sidewalk	Bicyclist	Average	Global
Our approach (CNN–CRF)	84.3	65.3	93.1	74.6	0.4	93.5	25.6	32.3	13.8	**85.0**	54.3	56.6	83.6
MultiScale CNN - noCRF	47.6	68.7	95.6	73.9	32.9	88.9	**59.1**	49.0	**38.9**	65.7	22.5	58.6	72.9
CNN–MR Fine	37.7	66.2	92.5	77.0	26.0	84.0	50.9	43.7	31.0	65.7	29.7	54.9	68.3
CNN–superpixels	3.2	59.7	93.5	6.6	18.1	86.5	1.9	0.8	4.0	66.0	0.0	30.9	54.8
Fine Level	33.2	53.9	87.8	67.1	23.2	83.9	42.7	44.1	31.3	63.0	26.1	50.6	63.5
[11] Unary	61.9	67.3	91.1	71.1	**58.5**	92.9	49.5	37.6	25.8	77.8	24.7	59.8	76.4
Baseline (App. [2])	38.7	60.7	90.1	71.1	51.4	88.6	54.6	40.1	1.1	55.5	23.6	52.3	66.5
[2](SfM)	43.9	46.2	79.5	44.6	19.5	82.5	24.4	**58.8**	0.1	61.8	18.0	43.6	61.8
[2](SfM combined)	46.2	61.9	89.7	68.6	42.9	89.5	53.6	46.6	0.7	60.5	22.5	53.0	69.1
[11] Unary & pairwise	70.7	70.8	94.7	74.4	55.9	94.1	45.7	37.2	13.0	79.3	23.1	59.9	79.8
[11] higher order	84.5	72.6	**97.5**	72.7	33.0	95.3	34.2	45.7	8.1	77.6	28.5	59.2	83.8
[4] (no det.)	79.3	76.0	96.2	74.6	43.2	94.0	40.4	47.0	14.6	81.2	31.1	61.6	83.1
[4] (det.)	81.5	**76.6**	96.2	78.7	40.2	93.9	43.0	47.6	14.3	81.5	33.9	**62.5**	**83.8**
[5] (top down)	80.4	76.1	96.1	**86.7**	20.4	95.1	47.1	47.3	8.3	79.1	19.5	59.6	83.2
[1] depth	**85.3**	57.3	95.4	69.2	46.5	**98.5**	23.8	44.3	22.0	38.1	28.7	55.4	82.1

Finally, the computational cost required to process a single image is analyzed. Currently we have a sub–optimal implementation based on Lua code and Matlab. Our implementation takes approximately 5 seconds to output the features of a 320×240 image and approximately 5 seconds to estimate the optimum labeling. Further, our ap-proach is highly parallelizable and specially suitable for FPGA–based processors [15]. From these results, we can conclude that the proposed CNN–based algorithm provide promising semantic road scene segmentation in a single image.

5 Conclusions

In this paper, we proposed a semantic road image segmentation algorithm based on the fusion of multiple features. The algorithm first extracts learned features at multiple scales and multiple resolutions and then, fuses them at pixel level using a weighed linear combiner. Features and weights are learned off–line directly from training data.

Experiments conducted on a publicly available database demonstrate that a weighted combination outperforms other fusion methods based on fixed rules or single scale methods. Moreover, the algorithm outperforms state–of–the–art appearance based methods and it performs similar in terms of class average performance compared to algorithms using other types of cues such as motion, depth or stereo.

References

1. Zhang, C., Wang, L., Yang, R.: Semantic Segmentation of Urban Scenes Using Dense Depth Maps. In: Daniilidis, K., Maragos, P., Paragios, N. (eds.) ECCV 2010, Part IV. LNCS, vol. 6314, pp. 708–721. Springer, Heidelberg (2010)
2. Brostow, G.J., Shotton, J., Fauqueur, J., Cipolla, R.: Segmentation and Recognition Using Structure from Motion Point Clouds. In: Forsyth, D., Torr, P., Zisserman, A. (eds.) ECCV 2008, Part I. LNCS, vol. 5302, pp. 44–57. Springer, Heidelberg (2008)
3. Brostow, G.J., Fauqueur, J., Cipolla, R.: Semantic object classes in video: A high-definition ground truth database. Pattern Recognition Letters (2008)
4. Ladický, Ľ., Sturgess, P., Alahari, K., Russell, C., Torr, P.H.S.: What, Where and How Many? Combining Object Detectors and CRFs. In: Daniilidis, K., Maragos, P., Paragios, N. (eds.) ECCV 2010, Part IV. LNCS, vol. 6314, pp. 424–437. Springer, Heidelberg (2010)
5. Floros, G., Rematas, K., Leibe, B.: Multi-class image labeling with top-down segmentation and generalized robust p^n potentials. In: BMVC 2011 (2011)
6. Gupta, A., Efros, A.A., Hebert, M.: Blocks World Revisited: Image Understanding Using Qualitative Geometry and Mechanics. In: Daniilidis, K., Maragos, P., Paragios, N. (eds.) ECCV 2010, Part IV. LNCS, vol. 6314, pp. 482–496. Springer, Heidelberg (2010)
7. Farabet, C., Couprie, C., Najman, L., LeCun, Y.: Scene parsing with multiscale feature learning, purity trees, and optimal covers. In: ICML 2012 (2012)
8. Cecotti, H., Graser, A.: Convolutional neural networks for p300 detection with application to brain-computer interfaces. PAMI 33, 433–445 (2011)
9. LeCun, Y., Bengio, Y.: Convolutional networks for images, speech, and time-series. In: Arbib, M.A. (ed.) The Handbook of Brain Theory and Neural Networks. MIT Press (1995)
10. Kuncheva, L.I.: Combining Pattern Classifiers: Methods and Algorithms. Wiley-Interscience (2004)
11. Sturgess, P., Alahari, K., Ladicky, L., Torr, P.H.S.: Combining appearance and structure from motion features for road scene understanding. In: BMVC 2009 (2009)
12. Levinshtein, A., Stere, A., Kutulakos, K., Fleet, D., Dickinson, S., Siddiqi, K.: Turbopixels: Fast superpixels using geometric flows. PAMI 31 (2009)
13. Domke, J.: Graphical models toolbox, http://phd.gccis.rit.edu/justindomke/JGMT/ (accessed July 31, 2012)
14. Felzenszwalb, P.F., Huttenlocher, D.P.: Efficient graph-based image segmentation. IJCV 59, 167–181 (2004)
15. Farabet, C., LeCun, Y., Kavukcuoglu, K., Culurciello, E., Martini, B., Akselrod, P., Talay, S.: Large-scale FPGA-based convolutional networks. In: Scaling up Machine Learning: Parallel and Distributed Approaches. Cambridge University Press (2011)

Monocular Visual Odometry and Dense 3D Reconstruction for On-Road Vehicles

Menglong Zhu[1], Srikumar Ramalingam[2], Yuichi Taguchi[2], and Tyler Garaas[2]

[1] University of Pennsylvania, Philadelphia, PA, USA
[2] Mitsubishi Electric Research Labs (MERL), Cambridge, MA, USA

Abstract. More and more on-road vehicles are equipped with cameras each day. This paper presents a novel method for estimating the relative motion of a vehicle from a sequence of images obtained using a single vehicle-mounted camera. Recently, several researchers in robotics and computer vision have studied the performance of motion estimation algorithms under non-holonomic constraints and planarity. The successful algorithms typically use the smallest number of feature correspondences with respect to the motion model. It has been strongly established that such minimal algorithms are efficient and robust to outliers when used in a hypothesize-and-test framework such as random sample consensus (RANSAC). In this paper, we show that the planar 2-point motion estimation can be solved analytically using a single quadratic equation, without the need of iterative techniques such as Newton-Raphson method used in existing work. Non-iterative methods are more efficient and do not suffer from local minima problems. Although 2-point motion estimation generates visually accurate on-road vehicle trajectory, the motion is not precise enough to perform dense 3D reconstruction due to the non-planarity of roads. Thus we use a 2-point relative motion algorithm for the initial images followed by 3-point 2D-to-3D camera pose estimation for the subsequent images. Using this hybrid approach, we generate accurate motion estimates for a plane-sweeping algorithm that produces dense depth maps for obstacle detection applications.

Keywords: Visual odometry, 2-point motion estimation, pose estimation, plane sweeping.

1 Introduction and Related Work

Accurate ego-motion estimation of a vehicle from video sequences is a challenging and important problem in robotics and computer vision [11]. Existing algorithms can be classified based on the camera model (monocular, stereo) and motion model (planar, non-planar). To compute the relative motion between images, it has been shown that using a minimum number of feature correspondences in a hypothesize-and-test framework such as RANSAC produces accurate and robust results in the presence of outliers.

Several SLAM techniques for general motion sequences exist in the robotics community [9,13]. In this paper, we focus on ego-motion estimation from monocular video sequences [22,24,18] for almost planar road sequences. We present a

A. Fusiello et al. (Eds.): ECCV 2012 Ws/Demos, Part II, LNCS 7584, pp. 596–606, 2012.

novel analytical solution to the planar motion estimation problem using 2 points. Existing approaches solved this problem using an iterative algorithm. Our non-iterative solution is more efficient and does not have local minima problems.

Dense depth estimation from video sequences using a car-mounted camera can be extremely useful for car safety applications such as obstacle detection. In this work, we use the 2-point motion estimation algorithm followed by 3-point 2D-to-3D pose estimation to compute the camera poses, and then reconstruct a dense depth map at each frame. Instead of using just two images and motion-based stereo, we use several images, typically of the order of 20 to 30, to reconstruct depth maps using a plane-sweeping algorithm [4]. Plane sweeping can be implemented on GPUs and it can be performed in real time [16].

Minimal Solutions: Nistér's 5-point algorithm [14] with a RANSAC framework has been established as the standard method for motion estimation in the presence of outliers. In the case of relative motion between two cameras, there are 6 degrees of freedom (DOF) in the motion parameters: 3 DOF for rotation and 3 DOF for translation. For conventional cameras with a single center of projection, only 5 parameters can be estimated, i.e., the translation can only be estimated up to a scale. Accordingly, we need a minimum of 5 feature correspondences to estimate the motion parameters. The feature correspondences can be obtained using, e.g., Harris corners, SIFT, or KLT. Usually, minimal approaches lead to a finite number of solutions for the motion and the correct motion is chosen based on physical realizability or additional point correspondences.

Minimal solutions have been proposed for several calibration and 3D reconstruction problems: the five point relative pose problem [14], the six point generalized camera problem [23], point-to-plane registration using six correspondences [17], pose estimation for stereo setups using either points or lines [2,3]. The last few years have seen the use of minimal problems in various applications [21] and there are even unification efforts to keep track of all the existing solutions[1].

Restricted Motion Models: In real-world scenarios, the relative motion of a camera is usually constrained by the associated application. For example, a camera mounted on a car does not generally have all 6 DOF. If the road is planar, the camera can only undergo 3 DOF (2 DOF of translation and 1 DOF of rotation). Recently, Scaramuzza et al. [19] have shown that there exists a class of vehicles (cars, bicycles, differential-drive robots) whose motion can be parameterized using only one parameter and thus a 1-point algorithm can be developed. The underlying idea is to use the fact that there exists an instantaneous center of rotation (ICR) and the vehicle follows a circular course around this point. When inertial measurement unit (IMU) is available, one can get two measurement angles using the gravity vector. The remaining unknowns are just three parameters (1 DOF of rotation and 2 DOF of translation). Fraundorfer et al. [5] solved this 3-point motion estimation problem using a quartic equation. This motion estimation algorithm can be useful if one uses cell phone cameras to capture images.

---

[1] http://cmp.felk.cvut.cz/minimal/

Several researchers have compared the performance of minimal algorithms such as 1-point, 2-point and 5-point algorithm. As shown in many of the recent results, 2-point is comparable to 1-point and 5-point [18]. However, the existing algorithm used for 2-point is an iterative one. Ortin and Montiel [15] proposed a 2-point motion estimation algorithm for planar motion sequences. This is applicable for indoor robot ego-motion estimation when the camera mounted on the robot moves on a plane. The number of degrees of freedom is 3 (1 DOF of rotation and 2 DOF of translation). However, the relative motion can be recovered only up to a scale. In the RANSAC framework, the number of iterations required is usually smaller when we decrease the number of points required to compute the motion. Given the complexity of the equations, Ortin and Montiel determined the solutions iteratively with the Newton-Raphson method and this iterative approach is still used in several recent results [18]. In this paper, we show that 2-point motion estimation can be solved easily with a simple quadratic equation. Independently, Booij and Zivkovic have developed an analytical solution for 2-point motion estimation using a trignometric approach in their unpublished technical report [1]. Similar to their approach, we also obtain a quadratic polynomial for the 2-point problem. However, our formulation is different and we show an entire pipeline including dense 3D reconstruction for driver assistance in car-navigation.

Organization: In Section 2, we present a minimal 2-point relative motion estimation algorithm. In Section 3, we detail our system pipeline and experimental results, including the calibration procedure, 2-point motion estimation followed by 3-point 2D-to-3D pose estimation, and dense depth reconstruction using plane sweeping for obstacle detection application.

2   2-Point Motion Estimation

In this section, we first describe some background of motion estimation problems and then present our analytical solution to the 2-point motion estimation problem.

2.1   Background

Motion estimation refers to estimating the relative pose between two images. Corresponding feature points $\mathbf{p}$ and $\mathbf{p}'$ in two images are related by the essential matrix E by the relation $\mathbf{p}'^{T}\mathsf{E}\mathbf{p} = 0$. Note that $\mathbf{p}$ and $\mathbf{p}'$ are expressed as unit vectors in spherical image coordinates ($\mathbf{p}$ and $\mathbf{p}'$ are pixels back-projected onto a unit sphere such that $||\mathbf{p}|| = ||\mathbf{p}'|| = 1$). This is always possible when the camera is calibrated. The essential matrix E can be computed using the relationship $\mathsf{E} = [\mathbf{T}]_{\times}\mathsf{R}$, where R is the 3×3 rotation matrix and $[\mathbf{T}]_{\times}$ is the skew symmetric matrix of the 3×1 translation vector $\mathbf{T}$.

Planar Motion: As shown in Figure 1, we assume that the camera moves on a plane. In the case of a camera mounted on a car, we assume that the road

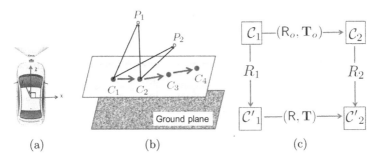

Fig. 1. Two-point motion estimation for planar motion of an on-road vehicle. (a) The motion of the car is assumed to be on the XZ plane. (b) The camera moves on a plane parallel to the ground plane. We show the projection rays for two 3D points P_1 and P_2 from two camera positions C_1 and C_2. (c) The general idea behind our coordinate transformation technique for the 2-point motion estimation algorithm. Our goal is to compute the motion $(\mathbf{R}_o, \mathbf{T}_o)$ between the coordinate frames C_1 and C_2. We transform the coordinate frames C_1 and C_2 to two intermediate coordinate frames C'_1 and C'_2 respectively. We compute the motion $(\mathbf{R}, \mathbf{T})$ between C'_1 and C'_2, which is much simpler than computing $(\mathbf{R}_o, \mathbf{T}_o)$ directly.

is parallel to the XZ plane and the camera moves on the XZ plane, as shown in Figure 1(a). Accordingly, the rotation matrix and the translation vector are given by

$$
\mathsf{R} = \begin{pmatrix} \cos\theta & 0 & \sin\theta \\ 0 & 1 & 0 \\ -\sin\theta & 0 & \cos\theta \end{pmatrix} = \begin{pmatrix} \alpha & 0 & \beta \\ 0 & 1 & 0 \\ -\beta & 0 & \alpha \end{pmatrix}, \quad \mathbf{T} = \begin{pmatrix} T_x \\ 0 \\ 1 \end{pmatrix} \tag{1}
$$

The above rotation matrix represents a rotation around the Y axis by an angle θ. We rewrite the rotation matrix by replacing $\cos\theta$ and $\sin\theta$ with α and β. According to the orthonormality constraint, we have $\alpha^2 + \beta^2 = 1$. Since the camera moves on the XZ plane, the Y coordinate of the translation vector is 0. Since the absolute scale cannot be computed, we choose the scale of the motion by fixing $T_z = 1$. Due to the coordinate transformation we later perform in the algorithm, this assumption will hold true even if the motion is along the X direction. We use the essential matrix to compute the unknown parameters (T_x, α, β). Although there are three variables, the number of independent variables is only 2 since $\alpha^2 + \beta^2 = 1$. By directly solving the essential matrix for two sets of points correspondences, we obtain two quadratic equations in three variables (T_x, α, β). Using the orthonormality constraint on α and β, we may get 8 solutions or less. By using algebraic geometry tools like Groebner basis [10], one can directly get two solutions. On the other hand, below we show that a coordinate transformation approach will lead to a simple quadratic equation for computing the motion.

2.2 Analytical Solution

Our goal is to compute the motion between the first camera coordinate frame C_1 to the second camera coordinate frame C_2. Let the required motion be (R_o, T_o). Instead of directly computing the motion between these two coordinate frames, we pre-rotate both C_1 and C_2 to intermediate reference frames C_1^i and C_2^i respectively. Figure 1(c) shows our transformation approach. We choose these intermediate reference frames such that the motion estimation equations become as simple as possible. Once we compute the motion between these intermediate reference frames (R, T), we can find the motion in the original coordinate frames using a simple post-rotation.

Intermediate Reference Frames: Let the two point correspondences be $(\mathbf{p}_1, \mathbf{p}_1')$ and $(\mathbf{p}_2, \mathbf{p}_2')$. Let us rotate the first camera coordinate system C_1 by a rotation matrix R_1 such that the z coordinate of the first point $\mathbf{p}_1$ becomes 0. Similarly, let us rotate the second camera coordinate system C_2 by a rotation matrix R_2 such that the z coordinate of the second point $\mathbf{p}_2'$ becomes 0. Let the new reference frames be C'_1 and C'_2. Let the new correspondences be $(\mathbf{a}_1, \mathbf{b}_1)$ and $(\mathbf{a}_2, \mathbf{b}_2)$ as $\mathbf{a}_i = R_1 \mathbf{p}_i$, $\mathbf{b}_i = R_2 \mathbf{p}_i'$ where $i = \{1, 2\}$. In the new reference frames, we have

$$\mathbf{a}_1 = \begin{pmatrix} a_{1x} \\ a_{1y} \\ 0 \end{pmatrix}, \quad \mathbf{a}_2 = \begin{pmatrix} a_{2x} \\ a_{2y} \\ a_{2z} \end{pmatrix}, \quad \mathbf{b}_1 = \begin{pmatrix} b_{1x} \\ b_{1y} \\ b_{1z} \end{pmatrix}, \quad \mathbf{b}_2 = \begin{pmatrix} b_{2x} \\ b_{2y} \\ 0 \end{pmatrix}. \tag{2}$$

The rotation matrices R_1 and R_2 can be easily computed as they are just equivalent to rotating the coordinate frames around the Y axis such that the Z coordinate of the point becomes 0:

$$R_i = \begin{pmatrix} \cos\theta_i & 0 & \sin\theta_i \\ 0 & 1 & 0 \\ -\sin\theta_i & 0 & \cos\theta_i \end{pmatrix}. \tag{3}$$

Here $\theta_1 = \tan^{-1}(p_{1z}/p_{1x})$ and $\theta_2 = \tan^{-1}(p_{2z}'/p_{2x}')$.

Solution: Using Equation (1), we obtain the essential matrix

$$E = [T]_\times R = \begin{pmatrix} 0 & -1 & 0 \\ 1 & 0 & -T_x \\ 0 & T_x & 0 \end{pmatrix} \begin{pmatrix} \alpha & 0 & \beta \\ 0 & 1 & 0 \\ -\beta & 0 & \alpha \end{pmatrix} = \begin{pmatrix} 0 & -1 & 0 \\ \alpha + \beta T_x & 0 & \beta - \alpha T_x \\ 0 & T_x & 0 \end{pmatrix}. \tag{4}$$

The equation based on the essential matrix becomes $\mathbf{b}_i^T E \mathbf{a}_i = 0$ for $i = \{1, 2\}$ after the coordinate transformation. When $i = 1$, we have

$$\begin{pmatrix} b_{1x} \\ b_{1y} \\ b_{1z} \end{pmatrix}^T \begin{pmatrix} 0 & -1 & 0 \\ \alpha + \beta T_x & 0 & \beta - \alpha T_x \\ 0 & T_x & 0 \end{pmatrix} \begin{pmatrix} a_{1x} \\ a_{1y} \\ 0 \end{pmatrix} = 0, \tag{5}$$

resulting in

$$g_1 \beta T_x + g_2 T_x + g_1 \alpha + g_3 = 0, \tag{6}$$

where $g_1 = a_{1x}b_{1y}$, $g_2 = a_{1y}b_{1z}$ and $g_3 = -a_{1y}b_{1x}$. When $i = 2$, we have

$$\begin{pmatrix} b_{2x} \\ b_{2y} \\ 0 \end{pmatrix}^T \begin{pmatrix} 0 & -1 & 0 \\ \alpha + \beta T_x & 0 & \beta - \alpha T_x \\ 0 & T_x & 0 \end{pmatrix} \begin{pmatrix} a_{2x} \\ a_{2y} \\ a_{2z} \end{pmatrix} = 0, \tag{7}$$

resulting in

$$f_1 \alpha T_x + f_2 \beta T_x + f_2 \alpha - f_1 \beta + f_3 = 0, \tag{8}$$

where $f_1 = -a_{2z}b_{2y}$, $f_2 = a_{2x}b_{2y}$ and $f_3 = -a_{2y}b_{2x}$. Using Equations (6) and (8), we get the following relation for T_x:

$$T_x = \frac{-g_1\alpha - g_3}{g_1\beta + g_2} = \frac{-f_2\alpha + f_1\beta - f_3}{f_1\alpha + f_2\beta} \tag{9}$$

$$(-g_1\alpha - g_3)(f_1\alpha + f_2\beta) = (g_1\beta + g_2)(-f_2\alpha + f_1\beta - f_3) \tag{10}$$

By simplifying the above equation, we get

$$h_1\alpha + h_2\beta + h_3 = 0, \tag{11}$$

where $h_1 = g_3 f_1 - f_2 g_2$, $h_2 = f_1 g_2 - f_3 g_1 + f_2 g_3$ and $h_3 = f_1 g_1 - f_3 g_2$. Using the orthonormality constraint $\alpha^2 + \beta^2 = 1$ to replace all β's in Equation (11), we obtain the following quadratic equation:

$$(h_1^2 + h_2^2)\alpha^2 + (2h_1 h_3)\alpha + (h_3^2 - h_2^2) = 0. \tag{12}$$

We have two solutions for α by solving the above quadratic equation. Once we compute α, we obtain the corresponding two solutions for β. We can then compute T_x using Equation (9). Note that there will be two solutions for (T_x, α, β) and we can find the correct solution using additional correspondences. Finally we perform the following operations to obtain the motion between the original coordinate frames $R_o = R_1^T R R_2$ and $T_o = R_1^T T$.

2.3 Sensitivity Analysis of Planarity Assumption

We studied the effect to the planarity assumption on the accuracy of our algorithm. In accordance with our algorithm, we assume that the camera moves on the XZ plane. The only rotation the algorithm can compute is the one around the Y axis. In simulations, we considered rotations that had an off-plane rotation along with the rotation around the Y axis. Any rotation around the X or Z axes can not be computed. In Figure 2(a) we show the error in rotation. Since the translation can only be up to a scale, the error shown is with respect to the direction of the motion on the plane. In many car navigation applications and localization problems, the rotation error around the Y axis is more important. We also studied the error in rotation around the Y axis and this is much lower than the overall rotation error. We considered images of size 100×100 pixels with a focal length of 100. The scene size is a cube of dimension 100 units. We added Gaussian noise with standard deviation of 0.2 in the simulations.

(a)   (b)   (c)   (d)

Fig. 2. (a) Simulations to study the sensitivity to out of plane rotation. The red and blue curves show the error in rotation and translation respectively. (b) We show the epipole (white circle) obtained from the intersection of the line segments showing the point correspondences from two consecutive images. For a car moving on a planar road, these epipoles should lie on the horizon. (c) We show the horizon (red line) and a trajectory of epipoles. The green line segments show the trajectory of the epipoles for several consecutive pairs of images. Note that the epipoles do not lie on the horizon. (d) We computed the motion parameters for 3400 images in a video sequence from a GoPro camera mounted on the front of a car. We project the computed trajectory on the Google Earth's aerial image. The entire trajectory is approximately 1 km long.

3   System Pipeline and Experimental Results

3.1   Setup and Calibration

The experiments were conducted with Hero-GoPro cameras, which are extremely small in size and easy to mount on cars. We tested several video sequences by mounting the camera on both front and rear side of a car. We calibrated this camera using the omni-directional toolbox of Scaramuzza et al. [20]. The calibration is used to rectify the video sequence captured from the camera. The original image resolution is 1920×1080 pixels. Using the calibration we constructed rectified images of 1000×500 pixels. All the experiments shown in this paper use these rectified images. Once the camera is calibrated and the images are rectified, the algorithmic components shown in this paper will apply to any central camera. We compute the pose of the ground plane in the camera coordinate frame using a large calibration grid on the ground.

Feature Computation: We compared Harris corners, SIFT features, and KLT features. We observed that KLT produced more evenly distributed features compared to SIFT and Harris, thus used KLT features in our experiments. In this work we performed the feature-matching on the rectified images, but one can also do it directly on the original images [12].

3.2   Motion and Pose Estimation Algorithms

In our real experiments, we found that the planarity assumption holds for a short distance, but is violated for a long distance on most roads. For a camera moving on a plane with one degree of rotation, the epipole should always lie on the horizon. Note that the epipole can be computed by the intersection of line segments joining the point correspondences from two images as shown in Figure 2(b). We computed the epipoles for several image pairs as shown in Figure 2(c) and found that the epipoles do not lie on the horizon line.

In all the video sequences, therefore, we compute the 3 DOF planar motion estimates for the first 20 images using the 2-point motion estimation algorithm, and then estimate the 6 DOF poses for the subsequent images using the standard 3-point camera pose estimation algorithm [7]. The initial camera poses given by our 2-point algorithm are used to triangulate the feature correspondences and obtain a sparse point cloud. As the ground plane is the dominant plane, we use homography to identify points on the ground. The reconstruction is updated to global scale using the knowledge of the ground plane in the camera coordinate system. Using this sparse reconstruction, we compute the 6 DOF poses of the subsequent images [7]. This partial sparse 3D point cloud is updated as new 3D points become available in the subsequent frames. Such a hybrid approach has been used in many real-time 3D reconstruction pipelines for large scale structure-from-motion problems [16]. In Figure 2(d), we show the motion estimated for a sequence of 3400 images.

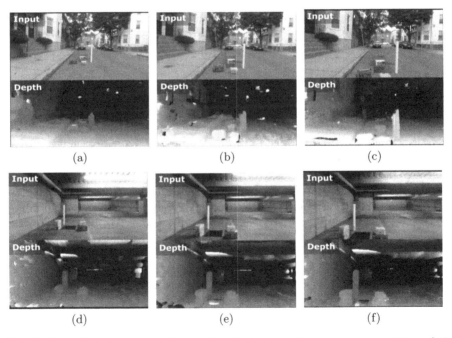

Fig. 3. Dense depth reconstruction results. We tested video sequences consisting of 100 frames and computed a depth map at each frame using the plane-sweeping algorithm with N images and D depth layers. The distances of the objects vary from more than 5 meters to less than 2 meters. (a), (b) and (c) show the snapshots of the depth maps at three different places in the video for an outdoor scene ($N = 20$ and $D = 50$). (d), (e) and (f) show the depth maps for an indoor garage sequence ($N = 30$ and $D = 80$).

3.3   Dense Depth Reconstruction

Given the camera poses, we compute a dense depth map at each frame using a plane-sweeping algorithm [4]. Plane sweeping provides a simple and efficient way to reconstruct a depth map using any number of images and their camera poses as the input. The algorithm is suitable for GPU implementation [25] and has been used for dense 3D reconstruction from vehicle-mounted cameras [6,16].

In our implementation, we define a set of front-parallel planes with depths $d_i(i = 1, \ldots, D)$ in the coordinate system of the current frame. For each depth layer d_i, we project the current image and $N-1$ previous images using projective texture mapping on the GPU [25] and compute a matching cost $C(\mathbf{x}, d_i)$ for each pixel $\mathbf{x}$. As the matching cost, we compute the absolute intensity difference among all combinations of the N images for each pixel and take an average of the smallest 50% values, which makes the cost robust against occlusions [8]. We then smooth the cost in each depth layer with a small local window (11×11 pixels). We finally compute the optimal depth by simply finding the minimum cost for each pixel as $d(\mathbf{x}) = \arg\min_i C(\mathbf{x}, d_i)$.

We tested the plane-sweeping algorithm on several video sequences taken from both indoor and outdoor scenes as shown in Figure 3. We show that it is possible to generate depth maps from monocular video sequences. Such depth maps can be used for car-navigation applications like obstacle detection. Our algorithm is accurate enough to reconstruct small objects (10 cm wide poles and boxes of dimensions 30 cm) at close distances (less than 2 meters).

4   Conclusion

We presented a complete system for relative motion estimation and dense 3D reconstruction of nearby scenes from a monocular video sequence captured by an omni-directional camera mounted on a car. We proposed a simple non-iterative solution for the planar 2-point relative motion estimation algorithm. Using a plane-sweeping algorithm along with the motion estimation, we compute a sequence of dense depth maps of the scene. Most of the code is written in Matlab and unoptimized. It currently takes 0.2 seconds for motion estimation, 0.4 seconds for KLT tracking, and 5 seconds for plane sweeping. We believe that the entire system can easily be made real time by using C++ and GPUs.

Acknowledgments. We would like to thank Jay Thornton, Amit Agrawal, Joseph Katz, Hiroshi Kage, Makito Seki, and Shintaro Watanabe for their valuable feedback, help and support. This work was done at and supported by MERL. Menglong Zhu contributed to the work while he was an intern at MERL.

References

1. Booij, O., Zivkovic, Z.: The planar two point algorithm. IAS Technical Report IAS-UVA-09-05, University of Amsterdam (2009)
2. Chandraker, M., Lim, J., Kriegman, D.: Moving in stereo: Efficient structure and motion using lines. In: ICCV (2009)

3. Clipp, B., Zach, C., Frahm, J.M., Pollefeys, M.: A new minimal solution to the relative pose of a calibrated stereo camera with small field of view overlap. In: ICCV (2009)
4. Collins, R.T.: A space-sweep approach to true multi-image matching. In: CVPR, pp. 358–363 (June 1996)
5. Fraundorfer, F., Tanskanen, P., Pollefeys, M.: A Minimal Case Solution to the Calibrated Relative Pose Problem for the Case of Two Known Orientation Angles. In: Daniilidis, K., Maragos, P., Paragios, N. (eds.) ECCV 2010, Part IV. LNCS, vol. 6314, pp. 269–282. Springer, Heidelberg (2010)
6. Gallup, D., Frahm, J.-M., Mordohai, P., Yang, Q., Pollefeys, M.: Real-time plane-sweeping stereo with multiple sweeping directions. In: CVPR (2007)
7. Haralick, R.M., Lee, C.N., Ottenberg, K., Nolle, M.: Review and analysis of solutions of the three point perspective pose estimation problem. IJCV 13(3), 331–356 (1994)
8. Kang, S.B., Szeliski, R., Chai, J.: Handling occlusions in dense multi-view stereo. In: CVPR, vol. 1, pp. 103–110 (2001)
9. Karlsson, N., Bernardo, E., Ostrowski, J., Goncalves, L., Pirjanian, P., Munich, M.: The vslam algorithm for robust localization and mapping. In: ICRA (2005)
10. Kukelova, Z., Bujnak, M., Pajdla, T.: Automatic Generator of Minimal Problem Solvers. In: Forsyth, D., Torr, P., Zisserman, A. (eds.) ECCV 2008, Part III. LNCS, vol. 5304, pp. 302–315. Springer, Heidelberg (2008)
11. Longuet-Higgins, H.C.: A computer program for reconstructing a scene from two projections. Nature, 133–135 (1981)
12. Lourenco, M., Barreto, J.P., Vasconcelos, F.: srd-sift: Keypoint detection and matching in images with radial distortion. IEEE Trans. on Robotics (2012)
13. Newcombe, R.A., Lovegrove, S., Davison, A.J.: Dtam: Dense tracking and mapping in real-time. In: ICCV (2011)
14. Nistér, D.: An efficient solution to the five-point relative pose problem. In: CVPR, vol. 26, pp. 756–770 (2003)
15. Ortin, D., Montiel, J.: Indoor robot motion based on monocular images. Robotica (2001)
16. Pollefeys, M., Nistér, D., Frahm, J.-M., Akbarzadeh, A., Mordohai, P., Clipp, B., Engels, C., Gallup, D., Kim, S.-J., Merrell, P., Salmi, C., Sinha, S., Talton, B., Wang, L., Yang, Q., Stewénius, H., Yang, R., Welch, G., Towles, H.: Detailed real-time urban 3D reconstruction from video. IJCV 78(2-3), 143–167 (2008)
17. Ramalingam, S., Taguchi, Y., Marks, T.K., Tuzel, O.: $P2\Pi$: A Minimal Solution for Registration of 3D Points to 3D Planes. In: Daniilidis, K., Maragos, P., Paragios, N. (eds.) ECCV 2010, Part V. LNCS, vol. 6315, pp. 436–449. Springer, Heidelberg (2010)
18. Scaramuzza, D.: Performance evaluation of 1-point-ransac visual odometry. Journal of Filed Robotics (2011)
19. Scaramuzza, D., Fraundorfer, F., Siegwart, R.: Real-time monocular visual odometry for on-road vehicles with 1-point RANSAC. In: ICRA, pp. 4293–4299 (May 2009)
20. Scaramuzza, D., Martinelli, A., Siegwart, R.: A toolbox for easy calibrating omni-directional cameras. In: IROS (2006)
21. Snavely, N., Seitz, S., Szcliski, R.: Photo tourism: Exploring image collections in 3D. ACM Trans. Graphics (2006)
22. Stewenius, H., Engels, C., Nister, D.: Recent developments on direct relative orientation. ISPRS J. of Photogrammetry and Remote Sensing (2006)

23. Stewenius, H., Nister, D., Oskarsson, M., Astrom, K.: Solutions to minimal generalized relative pose problems. In: OMNIVIS (2005)
24. Tardif, J.P., Pavlidis, Y., Daniilidis, K.: Monocular visual odometry in urban environments using an omnidirectional camera. In: IROS (2008)
25. Yang, R., Pollefeys, M.: Multi-resolution real-time stereo on commodity graphics hardware. In: CVPR, vol. 1, pp. 211–217 (June 2003)

Author Index